Principles of Politics

Benjamin Constant

Principles of Politics Applicable to All Governments

BENJAMIN CONSTANT

Edited by Etienne Hofmann

Translated from the French by
Dennis O'Keeffe

Introduction by Nicholas Capaldi

LIBERTY FUND
Indianapolis

This book is published by Liberty Fund, Inc., a foundation established to encourage study of the ideal of a society of free and responsible individuals.

The cuneiform inscription that serves as our logo and as the design motif for our endpapers is the earliest-known written appearance of the word "freedom" (*amagi*), or "liberty." It is taken from a clay document written about 2300 B.C. in the Sumerian city-state of Lagash.

English translation of the Etienne Hofmann edition of *Principes de politique* of Benjamin Constant, by permission of Librairie Droz S.A., Geneva.

Originally published as *Principes de politique applicables à tous les gouvernements,* edited by Etienne Hofmann, Librairie Droz S.A., Geneva, 1980.

Printed in the United States of America

07 06 05 04 03 C 5 4 3 2 1
07 06 05 04 03 P 5 4 3 2 1

Library of Congress Cataloging-in-Publication Data
Constant, Benjamin, 1767–1830.
[Principes de politique applicables à tous les gouvernements. English]
Principles of politics applicable to all governments / Benjamin Constant; edited by Etienne Hofmann; translated from the French by Dennis O'Keeffe; introduction by Nicholas Capaldi.
p. cm.
Includes bibliographical references and index.
ISBN 0-86597-395-4 (alk. paper) — ISBN 0-86597-396-2 (pbk.: alk. paper)
1. Liberalism—France. 2. Democracy—France. 3. France—Politics and government—1814–1830. I. Hofmann, Etienne. II. O'Keeffe, Dennis. III. Title.
JN2509.C6613 2003
320'.01—dc21

2003047474

Liberty Fund, Inc.
8335 Allison Pointe Trail, Suite 300
Indianapolis, Indiana 46250-1684

CONTENTS

Translator's Note xi
Acknowledgments xv
Introduction xvii

PRINCIPLES OF POLITICS APPLICABLE TO ALL GOVERNMENTS

BOOK I. *On Received Ideas About the Scope of Political Authority* 1

1. The purpose of this work. 3
2. Rousseau's first principle on the origin of political authority. 6
3. Rousseau's second principle on the scope of political authority. 8
4. Rousseau's arguments for boundless political authority. 15
5. That Rousseau's error comes from his wanting to distinguish the prerogatives of society from those of the government. 17
6. The consequences of Rousseau's theory. 19
7. On Hobbes. 21
8. Hobbes's opinion reproduced. 23
9. On the inconsistency with which Rousseau has been reproached. 24

BOOK II. *On the Principles to Replace Received Ideas on the Extent of Political Authority* 29

1. On the limitation of political authority. 31
2. On the rights of the majority. 32
3. On the organization of government when political power is not limited. 35
4. Objection to the possibility of limiting political authority. 36
5. On the limits of political authority restricted to a minimum. 38
6. On individual rights when political authority is thus restricted. 39
7. On the principle of utility substituted for the idea of individual rights. 39

Book III. *On Arguments and Hypotheses in Favor of the Extension of Political Authority* 45

1. On the extension of political authority beyond its necessary minimum, on the grounds of utility. 47
2. On the hypotheses without which extension of political authority is illegitimate. 49
3. Are governors necessarily less liable to error than the governed? 50
4. Are governmental mistakes less dangerous than those of individuals? 55
5. On the nature of the means political authority can use on the grounds of utility. 57

Book IV. *On the Proliferation of the Laws* 61

1. Natural causes of the proliferation of the laws. 63
2. The idea which usually develops about the effects which the proliferation of the laws has and the falsity of that idea. 63
3. That the principal benefit which supporters of democratic government are looking for in the proliferation of the laws does not exist. 65
4. On the corruption which the proliferation of the laws causes among the agents of the government. 66
5. Another drawback of the proliferation of the laws. 67

Book V. *On Arbitrary Measures* 71

1. On arbitrary measures and why people have always protested less about them than about attacks on property. 73
2. On the grounds for arbitrary measures and the prerogative of preventing crimes. 74
3. Specious argument in support of arbitrary government. 77
4. On the effect of arbitrary measures in terms of moral life, industry, and the duration of governments. 78
5. On the influence of arbitrary rule on the governors themselves. 80

Book VI. *On Coups d'Etat* 83

1. On the admiration for coups d'Etat. 85
2. On coups d'Etat in countries with written constitutions. 89
3. The condition necessary to stop constitutional violations. 93

Book VII. *On Freedom of Thought* 101

1. The object of the following three books. 103
2. On freedom of thought. 103
3. On the expression of thought. 105
4. Continuation of the same subject. 112
5. Continuation of the same subject. 117
6. Some necessary explication. 123
7. Final observations. 124

Book VIII. *On Religious Freedom* 129

1. Why religion was so often attacked by the men of the Enlightenment. 131
2. On civil intolerance. 135
3. On the proliferation of sects. 137
4. On the maintenance of religion by government against the spirit of inquiry. 139
5. On the reestablishment of religion by government. 140
6. On the axiom that the people must have a religion. 141
7. On the utilitarian case for religion. 142
8. Another effect of the axiom that the people must have a religion. 143
9. On tolerance when government gets involved. 144
10. On the persecution of a religious belief. 144

Book IX. *On Legal Safeguards* 149

1. On the independence of the courts. 151
2. On the abridgment of due process. 153
3. On punishments. 157
4. On the prerogative of exercising mercy. 160

Book X. *On the Action of Government with Regard to Property* 163

1. The purpose of this book. 165
2. The natural division of the inhabitants of the same territory into two classes. 165
3. On property. 167
4. On the status property should occupy in political institutions 168
5. On examples drawn from antiquity. 171
6. On the proprietorial spirit. 173

7. That territorial property alone brings together all the advantages of property. 174
8. On property in public funds. 179
9. On the amount of landed property which society has the right to insist upon for the exercise of political rights. 182
10. That owners have no interest in abusing power vis-à-vis nonowners. 183
11. On hereditary privileges compared to property. 185
12. Necessary comment. 186
13. On the best way of giving proprietors a large political influence. 190
14. On the action of government on property. 192
15. On laws which favor the accumulation of property in the same hands. 193
16. On laws which enforce the wider spreading of property. 196

Book XI. *On Taxation* 203

1. The object of this book. 205
2. The first right of the governed with regard to taxation. 205
3. The second right of the governed with regard to taxation. 207
4. On various types of taxes. 207
5. How taxation becomes contrary to individual rights. 212
6. That taxes bearing on capital are contrary to individual rights. 214
7. That the interest of the state in matters of taxation is consistent with individual rights. 215
8. An incontestable axiom. 219
9. The drawback of excessive taxation. 220
10. A further drawback of excessive taxation. 221

Book XII. *On government jurisdiction over economic activity and population* 225

1. Preliminary observation. 227
2. On legitimate political jurisdiction vis-à-vis economic activity. 228
3. That there are two branches of government intervention with regard to economic activity. 228
4. On privileges and prohibitions. 229
5. On the general effect of prohibitions. 247

6. On things which push governments in this mistaken direction. 248
7. On the supports offered by government. 251
8. On the equilibrium of production. 255
9. A final example of the adverse effects of government intervention. 258
10. Conclusions from the above reflections. 259
11. On government measures in relation to population. 260

Book XIII. *On War* 275

1. From what point of view war can be considered as having advantages. 277
2. On the pretexts for war. 279
3. The effect of the politics of war on the domestic condition of nations. 282
4. On safeguards against the war mania of governments. 286
5. On the mode of forming and maintaining armies. 289

Book XIV. *On Government Action on Enlightenment* 295

1. Questions to be dealt with in this book. 297
2. On the value attributed to errors. 298
3. On government in support of truth. 301
4. On government protection of enlightenment. 304
5. On the upholding of morality. 307
6. On the contribution of government to education. 308
7. On government duties vis-à-vis enlightenment. 315

Book XV. *The Outcome of Preceding Discussion Relative to the Action of Government* 319

1. The outcome of the preceding discussion. 321
2. On three pernicious ideas. 322
3. On ideas of uniformity. 322
4. Application of this principle to the composition of representative assemblies. 326
5. Further thoughts on the preceding chapter. 328
6. On ideas of stability. 338
7. On premature ameliorations. 340
8. On a false way of reasoning. 345

Book XVI. *On Political Authority in the Ancient World* 349

1. Why among the ancients political authority could be more extensive than in modern times. 351
2. The first difference between the social State of the ancients and that of modern times. 352
3. The second difference. 353
4. The third difference. 355
5. The fourth difference. 358
6. The fifth difference. 359
7. The result of these differences between the ancients and the moderns. 361
8. Modern imitators of the republics of antiquity. 365

Book XVII. *On the True Principles of Freedom* 381

1. On the inviolability of the true principles of freedom. 383
2. That the circumscription of political authority, within its precise limits, does not tend at all to weaken the necessary action of the government. 385
3. Final thoughts on civil freedom and political freedom. 386
4. Apologia for despotism by Louis XIV. 392

Book XVIII. *On the Duties of Individuals to Political Authority* 395

1. Difficulties with regard to the question of resistance. 397
2. On obedience to the law. 398
3. On revolutions. 405
4. On the duties of enlightened men during revolutions. 407
5. Continuation of the same subject. 413
6. On the duties of enlightened men after violent revolutions. 419

Additions to the Work Entitled *Principles of Politics Applicable to All Governments* 425

Index 535

TRANSLATOR'S NOTE

Principles of Politics Applicable to All Governments (1810) by Benjamin Constant (1767–1830) has never before been translated into English in its entirety. It is hard to judge why it is not better known, why it has been relatively neglected. It is written in graceful and clear prose. It is informed by very wide reading and understanding of philosophy, history, economics, politics, and law. The failure of recent scholarship to pay this enormous work more attention may be attributed to the general demise of liberal thought which began in mid-nineteenth-century France and which itself remains unexplained. Frédéric Bastiat (1801–1850), another significant social scientist, in some ways Constant's heir, has suffered similarly from neglect by posterity. Neither man is included in *The Fontana Dictionary of Modern Thought* (edited by Alan Bullock et al., London, Macmillan, 1988) nor in Roger Scruton's *Dictionary of Politics* (London, Macmillan, 1982). Scruton later came to regard the omission of Constant in this first edition as a serious underestimation of a writer now emerging as a formidable figure in the debate on political and economic modernity. Scruton's 1996 edition (London, Macmillan), therefore, while it still omits Bastiat, has included a pithy summary of the main positions of *Principles of Politics.*

This first complete translation into English of *Principles of Politics* is based solely on Etienne Hofmann's 1980 edition. Constant's book in fact appears as Tome II of this 1980 publication by Librairie Droz of Geneva, Tome I of which is a version of Hofmann's Ph.D. dissertation on Constant. I have translated all eighteen books, together with the lengthy Additions which Constant appended to them. The latter are a series of summaries, extensions, and further thoughts on the eighteen books of the main text. My intention throughout has been to retain as much as possible of the general elegance and subtle rhetoric of Constant's writing while seeking to render it in accurate, graceful, and accessible English. Where meaning and aesthetic effect permit, I have not only kept to an English prose as close as possible to the exact sense of the French original but have also striven where the

French vocabulary has close English counterparts to use those counterparts. The only notable exception is the word "liberté" with its two possible translations in English, "freedom" and "liberty." In most cases I have preferred the word *freedom* as capturing in English a truer representation of *liberté* with its nuanced variations in French.

As far as the English language permits, I have also attempted to retain in translation even the longest of Constant's very long sentences. There is no disadvantage to exposition and meaning in this, since even within these very long sentences there is a shining clarity to be found. Only where the length of sentence hindered intelligibility in English have I broken the construction. Thus for the most part I have kept the original structure.

This translation does not attempt to reproduce Dr. Hofmann's elaborate *apparatus criticus*. Most students or even professional teachers of politics do not need to know, when they are working on Constant in English, in which handwritten folio a particular passage appears in the French original. Nor are slight errors or verbal infelicities in the original text of great interest to those whose first wish is to read an accurate English version of Constant's meaning. Thus, I have kept only those many footnotes which are intended to add to the reader's understanding of Constant's thinking and erudition. I have added a few footnotes of my own by way of clarification and commentary. In those instances in which Hofmann uses the French first-person plural, "nous," I have subsituted the word "Hofmann."

Constant's text has some errors. Sometimes there are references with inaccurate page or tome details. Sometimes there are mechanical slips in the writing. Hofmann often identifies these. I have mostly corrected them in the translation, so that the text reads more comfortably and fluently. Constant was particularly lax in referring to titles of works (and titles of chapters within works) of Jeremy Bentham. He commonly gives these titles in paraphrased or shortened form. In a work originally constructed with none of the benefits of a technology we now take for granted, it did not seem to me to the purpose that the reader in English be informed of every last little slip of administration or error in vocabulary.

There is one kind of inconsistency to which, however, the attention of readers should be drawn. Sometimes in the main text Constant is not consistent with his chapter titles, which are listed at the front of each book and appear again at the head of each chapter. Sometimes the titles vary between the two locations. I have drawn readers' attention to these differences as, potentially at least, of some conceptual importance.

There would be a greater case for noting, as Hofmann's text constantly does, which sentences and paragraphs from *Principles of Politics* also appear verbatim in Constant's earlier or later works. Even these notes, however, seem likely to be of great concern only to those readers who would also be able to consult the French text at will. In the English text they would serve mostly to interrupt the flow of the reading. For this reason I have not included them. I have, however, inserted in the text Hofmann's page numbers in brackets.

The Additions, longer by far than any of the individual eighteen books of the main text, are intended by Constant both to tighten and to extend and elaborate the arguments of the main text. Constant often picks out a phrase or clause from his original text in order to expand on it in his Additions. In the English version of the Additions these key phrases or clauses appear in italics. Where the word order of English translation permits, I have translated the chosen words in the Additions with the same English used to translate the main text. Where the word order of English is different I have merely translated Constant's chosen words in the Additions. Little meaning has been lost; and, indeed, Constant was fairly careless in his own word sequence and self-quotation. His phrases chosen from the main text to be included in the Additions are quite often abbreviated or altered in some ways. For the most part the Additions stand as commentary in their own right.

Constant often emphasized other writers' words and occasionally his own by underlining. In the English text, such underlining is indicated by the use of italics. Where Constant quotes the verbatim words of another writer, those words are shown in the new English text within quotation marks.

The shortcomings of some of the basic vocabulary have simply to be accepted. Constant uses "power," "authority," "government," "the governors," the "governing class," "social authority," and sometimes even "force" more or less synonymously. The important conceptual distinctions which mainstream twentieth-century philosophers and social theorists, guided by Max Weber, have made between the concepts of authority and power are not there in *Principles,* or at least not overtly. The distinction was not new to Weber. It can be found in Machiavelli. Not till Weber, however, does the distinction become important in political writing, and Constant is not privy to it. Modern Western political science tends, under Weber's tutelage, to see authority as a special *kind* of power—legitimated and lawful—above all because it is acceded to by the people over whom it is wielded.

Constant is, however, though not verbally, at least conceptually in tune with the distinction. One might say that his most important adjective is *legitimate.* For him proper government is legitimate government, and illegitimate government is despotism. Even one arbitrary (despotic) act is for Constant a step on the road toward despotism. Constant's most repeated theme throughout the book is the disastrous results which flow from the abandonment of the rule of law.

Much of Constant's political life was shaped by his experience of the French Revolution, and his subsequent thinking and writing were in reaction to what he regarded as a republicanism gone catastrophically astray. Constant is, like Machiavelli, whom he much admired, by preference a republican, but he is perfectly willing to admit that monarchy can be a civilized form of government. *Principles of Politics* deliberately eschews all constitutional questions such as republicanism versus monarchy and the various merits of different arrangements of first and second chambers, modes of election, and so on. Instead, Constant is out to construct, as the full title of his work makes clear, a lawful politics "applicable to all forms of government."

ACKNOWLEDGMENTS

I am greatly indebted to Liberty Fund for their generous provision of financial assistance with this translation. In the early stage of the enterprise this generosity allowed me to be relieved of some 50 percent of my duties at the University of North London over the course of an entire academic year. The work has been a truly remarkable experience, a wonderful exposure to an extraordinarily powerful and endearing mind.

Many scholars have helped the translation on its way. I must especially thank Dr. Simon Green of All Souls College, Oxford, who was first to persuade me of Constant's outstanding intellectual penetration and prescience. Professor David Marsland of Brunel University has been a constant source of encouragement and optimism. I must add that Dr. Sean Gabb has been throughout more than willing to share with me his extraordinary command of the mysteries of information technology whenever I needed advice or when my computer decided to behave eccentrically.

A number of expert French scholars have helped me with occasional queries. I must mention with gratitude my encouraging colleague at the University of North London, Dr. Lucile Desblache. My old friend Mr. Allan Inglis was generous with advice on some of the more archaic language in the text. With regard to the Latin passages, I have been fortunate that my brother, Mr. Patrick O'Keeffe, has a classical erudition which he was always willing to put promptly at my service.

Professor Pierre Garello gave me detailed and invaluable advice on the very complex economics vocabulary in Books X, XI, and XII. I am much obliged to him.

I must express my particular thanks to Mr. Michael Winterburn for his invaluable and unstinting help and advice. We have spent many hours in concentrated discussion of Constant and *Les Principes de politique*.

Last as well as first in my thanks must come my wife, Mary. As in everything else, her support and advice have been indispensable during this translation.

INTRODUCTION

Benjamin Constant was the key thinker in the French classical liberal tradition between Montesquieu and Tocqueville. He was born 25 October 1767 in Lausanne, Switzerland, to Henriette de Chandieu and Juste Constant de Rebecque. His mother, who died shortly after childbirth, was a descendant of a French Huguenot family that had sought refuge in Switzerland from religious persecution. The Protestant—or more specifically, Calvinist—heritage remained an important part of Constant's framework. His father was a professional soldier in a Swiss regiment in the service of the Netherlands. Constant wrote a detailed account of his private life from 1767 to 1787 in *Le Cahier rouge* (not published until 1907); subsequently he maintained a *Journal intime* (published in unexpurgated form in 1952).

The great intellectual event of Constant's life occurred when he was sent to Edinburgh to study between 1783 and 1785. There he learned to speak flawless English; he read William Blackstone, David Hume, Adam Smith, Adam Ferguson, and Dugald Stewart, as well as Edward Gibbon, Edmund Burke, and William Godwin. The Scottish Enlightenment remained the formative influence on his thought. In a manner not unlike Montesquieu's, throughout the rest of his life, Constant sought to introduce the principles of British classical liberalism into French political life.

From 1788 until 1794, Constant served in the court of the duke of Brunswick, and in 1789 married a lady of the court, Wilhelmine von Cramm. In 1793, Constant began a relationship with Charlotte von Hardenburg, to whom he was secretly married fifteen years later. This relationship was depicted in a novel, *Cécile,* which was not discovered and published until 1951. In 1794, he met Mme. Germaine de Staël (1766–1817), divorced his then-wife Wilhelmine, and returned with Mme. de Staël to Paris in 1795.

Thus began the stormy intellectual and political relationship between Constant and Mme. de Staël. Germaine de Staël, daughter of the statesman and financier Jacques Necker, was herself a leading intellectual and later the author of important works of literature as well as works on literary theory, romanticism, and the thought of Rousseau. She was the center of Paris's most brilliant salon and a political activist. Her political model, also influenced by Montesquieu, adhered to British constitutional monarchy, and her political sympathies in France were with the Girondist faction. She has been described as perhaps the most brilliant and influential woman in Europe in her time. Constant, in his novel *Cécile,* described a Mme. de Malbée (i.e., Mme. de Staël) as follows: "Her intellect, the most far-ranging that has ever belonged to any woman, and possibly to any man either, had, in serious discussion, more force than grace, and in what touched the emotional life, a hint of sententiousness and affectation. But in her gaiety there was a certain indefinable charm, a kind of childlike friendliness which captivated the heart and established for the moment a complete intimacy between her and whoever she was talking to." Constant may have fathered her third child, a daughter, Albertine.

Although not originally a French citizen and not present during the dark days of the Revolution, Constant, through his association with Mme. de Staël, became a supporter of the Directory. Within that group, Constant identified not with those who wanted a restored but constitutional monarchy, but instead with those who were working for a republic with citizenship based on the ownership of property. Constant became a French citizen in 1798. Following the coup d'état of 18 brumaire (1799) he was appointed to the new Tribunate, but by 1802 his classical liberal views and association with Mme. de Staël and the classical liberal economist Jean-Baptiste Say had alienated Napoleon. In 1803, he accompanied Mme. de Staël into exile in Germany and Switzerland. During this time they met Goethe, Schiller, and the von Schlegel brothers, and both Constant and Mme. de Staël became imbued with German romanticism. Constant began working on his religious writings, some of which constitute *On Religion Considered in Its Source, Its Forms, and Its Developments* (published in five volumes between 1824 and 1831).

For the next twelve years, until 1815, Constant was an implacable enemy of Napoleon. One result was a classic critique of authoritarianism, *The Spirit of Conquest and Usurpation and Their Relation to European Civilization* (1814). Constant was also an adviser to Jean Baptiste Jules Bernadotte, a former Napoleonic general, then Prince Royal of Sweden, and an aspirant to the French throne. When Napoleon briefly returned to power and seemed on the verge of accepting the British model of constitutional monarchy, he, along with Constant's then-mistress Madame Récamier, a friend of Mme. de Staël and reputed to be the most beautiful woman in Europe, met with and persuaded Constant to become *conseiller d'état.* During this "Hundred

Days" period, Constant even drew up a new constitution known as the "Benjamine." It was under this inspiration that Constant completed and published his longtime work in progress, *Principles of Politics Applicable to All Governments.* This is to be distinguished from the longer 1810 version, edited in 1980 by Etienne Hofmann, on which the 2003 Liberty Fund translation is based. Clearly there is a huge affinity of subject matter, often explicably so. Even so, where the 1815 version is short and pointed, the 1810 is long and discursive. Where the 1815 version focuses repeatedly on constitutional questions and in particular on the civilizational possibilities of constitutional monarchy, the 1810 version explicitly eschews constitutional issues, cleaving instead to a search for the philosophical, economic, and jurisprudential principles which undergird any free society. And in 1810, the bias, if there is one, is slight, but leans all the same towards a republicanism somewhat akin to that of Machiavelli, whom Constant much admired.

On learning of Napoleon's defeat at Waterloo, Constant fled to England and published what many consider to be the first romantic novel, *Adolphe* (1816). He also wrote an apologia that was acceptable to Louis XVIII, paving the way for a return to Paris. During the remainder of his life, Constant was a prolific author and journalist. In 1819, he published the classic essay "The Liberty of the Ancients Compared with That of the Moderns." The core of the argument is prefigured in Book XVI of the 1810 edition of *The Principles,* which deals with the differences between ancient (political) and modern (civil) freedom. He was to repeat this argument in a famous speech, but this book is the locus classicus. As François Furet has argued, every subsequent French thinker, including Constant, is judged by his interpretation of the Revolution. Constant, like Mme. de Staël, sought to explain how Rousseau's notion of the general will had been used by Robespierre and others to transform the French Revolution into the Reign of Terror. Constant argued that it was the attempt to institute ancient liberty in a modern context that led to this perversion. Constant went on to argue that representative government was the system the moderns had devised for preserving liberty. His persistent defense of freedom of the press and vociferous opposition to the slave trade are representative of the stands he took on a number of issues.

Constant subsequently served in the Chamber of Deputies, being elected as a deputy for Paris in 1824 and from the Lower Rhine in 1827. Despite failing health, he supported the July Revolution of Louis-Philippe and served as *conseiller d'état* again until his death on December 8, 1830. Like so many other great French thinkers and authors, he is buried in Père-

Lachaise cemetery in Paris, and also like so many others, he had persistently been denied membership in the Académie Française. At the time of Constant's death, Louis Blanc and others tried unsuccessfully to have him entombed in the Panthéon. One of the things that distinguished Constant from other classical liberals of his time, whether French or British, was his recognition of the importance of the spiritual dimension for the sustenance of liberal culture. This view is reflected in *On Religion* and a massive amount of unpublished religious speculation that accumulated over his lifetime.

Constant's *Principles of Politics* is a microcosm of his whole political philosophy and an expression of his political experience. As far back as the period between 1800 and 1803, Constant had begun a project of both translating and commenting on Godwin's *Enquiry Concerning Political Justice.* This evolved into an 1806 draft commentary on Smith's *Wealth of Nations,* and finally, in 1815, during the Hundred Days, into an essay on the *Acte additional aux constitutions de l'empire*—the "Benjamine." Out of embarrassment over its Napoleonic association, Constant did not include it in his *Cours de politique constitutionelle* of 1818–20. It was included in the 1861 edition of the *Cours* edited by Édouard Laboulaye.

The *Principes de politique* in all its versions reflected the immense impact of the French Revolution on Constant's thinking. The 1810 edition, however, expresses in purest form the ideas which Constant believed universally applicable to all civilized government. Unlike the 1815 edition, it is in no sense a manual of applied politics. It does not focus on constitutional monarchy or the constitutional balancing of powers and the control of ministers. Despite Constant's gently apparent republicanism, it readily accepts that republics can be despotic and monarchies decent.

Constant, like Tocqueville and Mill afterward, was obsessed with the dangers of popular sovereignty. As he pointed out, where there are no limits on the legislature or the representative body, the representatives (e.g., the Convention during the French Revolution) become not the defenders of liberty, but the agents of tyranny. Constant was focused above all on liberty. The Revolution had destroyed the ancien régime and all its constituent intermediary institutions. Without intermediary institutions, a society of atomized individuals faced an all-powerful state. In order to restore and preserve liberty, new intermediary institutions needed to be established. Prime among these was the free press. It was the free press that provided a context not only for public discussion, but for calling attention to governmental (ministerial) abuse.

In the *Principles* Constant reasserts his lifelong commitment to individual and institutional freedom and the absence of arbitrary power. He affirms that even a single arbitrary act sets government on the road to despotism. Constant always saw freedom as an organic phenomenon: to attack it in any particular was to attack it generally. To construct this thesis he explores many subjects: law, sovereignty, and representation; power and accountability; government, property and taxation; wealth and poverty; war, peace and the maintenance of public order; and above all freedom, of the individual, of the press, and of religion. Early in his text he tackles the difficult issue of the general will. Although recognizing its existence in the abstract, Constant immediately asserts the Lockean view that citizens have rights independent of all social and political authority, and he goes on via a comprehensive critique to enumerate the dangers of Rousseau's views. Individual freedoms reflecting individual rights are sacrosanct even in the face of the popular will. Constant returns again and again with arguments against those who assert the prerogatives of society against those of the individual—Rousseau, Hobbes, and Mably—and equally with arguments favourable to individualism, where he relies very heavily on British commentary from Adam Smith, Jeremy Bentham, and others.

Constant's preference throughout *The Principles* is for limited but strong government. He asserts unambiguously that all successful government must secure the two essentials of internal order and external defense of the realm.

In the first half of *The Principles,* Constant focuses on the specific liberties that were so important to him: private property, freedom of the press, religious liberty, individual liberty, and due process. The legal reflection is extensive, both abstract and focusing on individual examples. In Books IV and V, Constant focuses on the rule of law: the need for due process in order to protect individual rights; laws that lay down the neutral rules of the game, so that individuals can pursue their private economic interests with security; the importance of jury trials; the significance of pardon as a check on the system itself; and the need for judicial independence. Much of this part of Constant's thinking is resonant of the *Federalist Papers.*

The discussion of individual rights, limited government, and the sacrosanct nature of property constitute Constant an apostle of economic modernity. The discussion of property in Book X is a masterpiece. Eschewing abstract arguments, Constant appeals to Smith and Say to show the connections between politics and economics: how prosperity is enhanced by privatization and how the national wealth is undermined by debt, irresponsible taxation, and the delusions of grandeur from which public officials who oversee the surplus created by taxation too often suffer. In Book XVIII, Constant both looks back to the Revolution and anticipates events of our own time with his reflections on the dangers of a civil religion or any form of civil intolerance. Citing Holbach's *System of Nature,* Constant is able to see the dangers of an atheistic secularism itself turned into a civic religion.

Both Tocqueville and Guizot were intrigued by Constant's reflection on the concept of sovereignty and the insight that democracy could be a source of despotism, perhaps the greatest threat to liberal culture. If Constant's brand of liberalism (as well as Tocqueville's) did not prevail on the continent of Europe, it was because European thinking remained mired in some consideration of a collective good. Hegel was greatly influenced by Constant's conception of a monarch who reflected the entire "state" (i.e., community) and the concern for reflecting the important specific interests in the legislature. We can foresee John Stuart Mill in, among other things, Constant's comment that there is a part of human existence that remains individual and independent, and which is, by right, outside any social competence. Perhaps the most enduring contribution of all of his work is, as Benedetto Croce said, in his having raised the question of whether liberal culture can survive without a soul.

Nicholas Capaldi

Principles of Politics

BOOK I

On Received Ideas About the Scope of Political Authority

Ch. 1. The purpose of this work. 3

Ch. 2. Rousseau's first principle on the origin of political authority. 6

Ch. 3. Rousseau's second principle on the scope of political authority. 8

Ch. 4. Rousseau's arguments for boundless political authority. 15

Ch. 5. That Rousseau's error comes from his wanting to distinguish the prerogatives of society from those of the government. 17

Ch. 6. The consequences of Rousseau's theory. 19

Ch. 7. On Hobbes. 21

Ch. 8. Hobbes's opinion reproduced. 23

Ch. 9. On the inconsistency with which Rousseau has been reproached. 24

CHAPTER ONE

The Purpose of This Work

Research relating to the constitutional organization of government having been, since *The Social Contract* and *The Spirit of the Laws*, the favorite speculative focus of the most enlightened of our writers in France, is now very decidedly out of favor today. I am not examining here at all whether this disfavor is justified; but it is certainly quite understandable.[1] In a few years we have tried some five or six constitutions[2] and found ourselves the worse for it. No argument can prevail against such an experience.

Moreover, if despite the universal distaste today for all discussions of this type, one wished to give oneself over to reflecting on the nature of governments, and their forms, limits, and prerogatives, one would probably make the opposite mistake to the [20] current one, but one no less gross and deadly. When certain ideas are associated with certain words, one may repeatedly seek in vain to show that the association is false. The reproduction of the words will for ages summon up these same

1. The bibliographical researches of André Monglond, *La France révolutionnaire et impériale. Annales de bibliographies méthodiques et descriptions des livres illustrés,* Grenoble, B. Arthaud; Paris, Impr. nat., 1930 (1789)–1963 (1812), 9 vol., let us confirm Constant's claim. From the time of the Consulate and above all the Empire, constitutional writings do indeed become rarer. The disfavor indicated, however, is much more a question of censorship than of any natural cause. See Henri Welschinger, *La censure sous le Premier Empire,* Paris, Perrin, 1887. We find in the work of Sismondi, *Recherches sur les constitutions des peuples libres,* edited and with an introduction by Marco Minerbi, Geneva, Droz, 1965, p. 82, a similar reflection to Constant's but much earlier. "The French, surrounded with revolutions which have taught them all too well to mistrust political theories, have grown weary with an important branch of inquiry to which their new duties really summon them. Maybe I will strive in vain to persuade them that the subject has not been exhausted by all the writings which have so wearied them, that we have made scarcely any advance on the *maîtres* who wrote before the Revolution, and that lots of important questions still demand debate, lots of findings need verification, and lots of new ideas need an airing. They will find a great number of these new ideas in the book with which I am presenting them, and if they do not accept them, at least they will find rejecting them stimulating. Perhaps, they might even during the course of their criticism, encounter the lessons they do not want to take from me."

2. Since this text dates from 1806, we are citing in effect the constitutions of 1791, 1793, an III, an VIII, an X, and an XII.

ideas.[3] It was in the name of freedom that we got prisons, scaffolds, and endless multiplied persecution. Quite understandably, this name, which signals a thousand odious and tyrannical measures, can be pronounced today only in a mood of distrust or malevolence.

Extremes do not only touch but also follow each other. One exaggeration always produces a contrary one. This applies especially to a nation in which everyone's aim is to show off, and as Voltaire said, everyone is more concerned to hit hard than accurately.[4] The ambition of the writers of the day is at all times to seem more convinced than anyone else of the reigning opinion. They watch which way the crowd is rushing. Then they dash as fast as they can to overtake it. They think thereby to acquire glory for providing an inspiration they actually got from others. They hope we will take them for the inventors of what they imitate and that because they run panting in front of the crowd they have just overtaken, they will seem like the leaders of the band, though the latter do not even suspect they exist.[5]

[21] A man of horrible memory, whose name should not soil any writing, since death has justly settled his personal account, said, on examining the

3. Constant had already enunciated his conception of the power of words on men and ideas in *De la force du gouvernement,* pp. 84–85. See Etienne Hofmann, *Les "Principes de politique" de Benjamin Constant,* Droz, 1980, Tome I, Première Partie, Ch. 2, pp. 119–120. (Hereafter this work is referred to as Hofmann's thesis.)

4. Hofmann failed to track down this quotation from Voltaire. Neither the analytic tables of the subject matter which accompany the *Oeuvres complètes* (the one by Chantreau, Paris, 1801, and the one by Miger, Paris, 1840), though detailed, nor the compilation by Adrien Lefort and Paul Buquet, *Les mots de Voltaire,* Paris, Librairie illustrée (1887), includes it. Hofmann says this witticism may have been handed down only by oral tradition. The saying turns up again in Constant's *De la religion considérée dans sa source, ses formes et ses développements,* Paris, Bossange, 1824, I, 6, p. 112.

5. Alfred de Musset was to say in 1832 in his dedication to A. Tattet of *La coupe et les lèvres* (the cup and the lips):

> C'est un triste métier que de suivre la foule,
> Et de vouloir crier plus fort que les meneurs,
> Pendant qu'on se raccroche au manteau des traineurs.
>
> (It's a sad life following the crowd,
> And wanting to shout louder than the ringleaders,
> When you're clinging on to the stragglers' coattails.)

Alfred de Musset, *Poésies complètes.* Text edited and annotated by Maurice Allem, Paris, Gallimard, 1957, p. 135 (Bibliothèque de la Pléiade).

English constitution: "I see a king there, and recoil in horror. Royalty is against nature."[6] Some anonymous writer, in a recently published essay, likewise declares all republican government unnatural.[7] It really is true that in certain eras you have to go round the whole circle of follies before coming back to reason.

Yet if it is proven that all research on constitutions, properly so called, must, after the upheavals we have suffered, necessarily be for some people a subject to go mad about, while for everyone else it is a matter of indifference, there are nevertheless principles of politics independent of all constitutions, and these seem to me still worth developing. Applicable under all forms of government, no threat to the basis of any social order, compatible with monarchy and republicanism alike, whatever versions either may take, these principles can be discussed frankly and freely. They are especially open to discussion in an Empire whose leader has just proclaimed, in the most unforgettable way, the freedom of the press, and declared independence of thought the first conquest of our century.

Among these principles one seems to me of the greatest importance. It has been overlooked by writers of all parties. Montesquieu was not concerned with it. Rousseau in his *The Social Contract* based his eloquent and absurd theory on subverting it. All the ills of the French Revolution come from this subversion. All the crimes with which our demagogues have appalled the world have been sanctioned by it. This book is about the reestablishment of this principle, and its developments and consequences, as well as [22] its application to all forms of government, whether monarchical or republican.

6. This "man of horrible memory" is Georges Couthon, who, in his *Discours prononcé à la séance des Jacobins du 1er pluviôse an II de la République* (speech delivered at the session of the Jacobins on 20 January 1794) Paris, Impr. des 86 départements, s.d., declares in fact: "I see in this constitution a king. A king! I recoil in horror. A king! It is a *monster* which nature disclaims, a *master* she does not recognise, a *tyrant* she detests" (pp. 3–4; BN, Lb^{40} 777).

7. [Louis-Matthieu Molé], *Essais de morale et de politique,* Paris, H. Nicolle, 1806, VIII-254 p. This work had already appeared in December 1805; Constant speaks about it twice in his correspondence with Hochet. See Hofmann's thesis, Première Partie, Ch. 3, p. 233 and n. 145. The whole second part of Molé's collection of essays seeks to show that monarchical government is natural.

CHAPTER TWO

Rousseau's First Principle on the Origin of Political Authority

Rousseau begins by establishing that any authority which governs a nation must come from the general will.[8] This is not a principle I claim to challenge. In our day people have tried to obfuscate it; and the evils which have been caused and the crimes committed on the pretext that this was to execute the general will, lend seeming support to the arguments of those who would like to locate the authority of government in another source.[9] Nevertheless, all these arguments are powerless against the straightforward definition of the words we use. Short of reviving the doctrine of divine right, we ought to agree that the law must be the expression of the will of everybody or at least of a few people. Now, if it is the latter, what might be the source of the exclusive privilege conceded to this small number? If it is force, force belongs to anyone who can grab it. It does not constitute law, or if you recognize it as legitimate, this will be true whoever has seized it; and everyone will want to win it in turn. If you think that the power of this small group is sanctioned by everyone else, that power then becomes the general will.

This principle holds for all institutions. Theocracy, royalty, and aristocracy, when they command minds, are the general will. When they do not command minds, they cannot be anything else but force. In sum, the world knows only two kinds of power. [23] There is force, the illegitimate kind; and there is the legitimate kind, the general will.

The objections we may raise against this will, bear either on the difficulty of recognizing or expressing it, or on the degree of power granted to the authority emanating from it. One could claim, often justifiably, that what

8. *Du contrat social,* Livre II, Ch. 1: "The first and most important consequence of the principles previously established is that only the general will can direct the power of the State according to the purpose for which it has been set up, which is the common good." Jean-Jacques Rousseau, *Oeuvres complètes,* published under the direction of Bernard Gagnebin and Marcel Reymond, Paris, Gallimard, 1964, t. III, p. 368 (Bibliothèque de la Pléiade).

9. Constant is perhaps thinking of Joseph de Maistre, whose *Considérations sur la France,* written in 1796, was a reply to *De la force du gouvernement;* and to Louis Amboise de Bonald, whose *Théorie de pouvoir politique et religieux* also came out in 1796. Let us note, however, that Constant never quotes them by name either in his formal corpus nor in his letters.

people call the general will is no such thing and that the things subjected to it should not be. In this case, however, it is no longer legitimacy that is being attacked but its rightful powers or the fidelity of its interpreters.

This principle does not deny the legitimacy of any form of government. In some circumstances society may want a monarchy and in others a republic. So these two institutions may therefore be equally legitimate and natural. Those who declare one or the other illegitimate or against nature are either party mouthpieces and do not say what they think, or else they are ideological dupes and do not know what they are saying.

There are only two forms of government, if we may even give them that title at all, which are essentially and eternally illegitimate, because no society could want them: anarchy and despotism. Moreover, I am not sure that the distinction which often favors the latter is not illusory. Despotism and anarchy are more alike than people think. In our era, people gave the name "anarchy,"[10] meaning the absence of government, to a government which was the most despotic that has ever existed on earth: a committee of a few men, who endowed their functionaries with boundless power, with courts tolerating no appeal, with laws based on mere suspicions, with judgments without due process, with numberless incarcerations and a hundred judicial murders a day. This is to abuse terms and confound ideas, however. The Revolutionary government [24] was most certainly not an absence of government.

Government is the use of public force against individuals. When it is used to stop them hurting each other, it is a good government. When it is used to oppress them, it is a frightful government, but in no sense is it anarchic. The Committee of Public Safety was government; so was the Revolutionary Tribunal. The law of suspects embodied government too. This was detestable, but certainly not anarchic. It was not for lack of government that the French people were butchered by executioners. On the contrary, it happened only because executioners were doing the governing. Government was most

10. It is hard to know to whom Constant is referring. Ferdinand Brunot, *Histoire de la langue française des origines à 1900*, t. IX, *La révolution et l'Empire*, Partie 2e: *Les événements, les institutions et la langue*, Paris, A. Colon, 1937, p. 828, gives the example of the *Ami des lois* of 16 brumaire an V (6 November 1796), defining as anarchists those "who see the republic as booty devolving upon them alone, who demand institutions which perpetuate their tyranny and leave them total mastery of government decision making and the framing of the law." F. Brunot shows very effectively how among the Thermidorians the term "anarchy" took on the meaning of "despotism" or "tyranny" in order to designate the Terror as just such a régime.

certainly not absent. Rather, an atrocious and ubiquitous government was always present. This was absolutely not anarchy, but despotism.

Despotism resembles anarchy in that it destroys public safeguards and tramples on due process. It differs from anarchy only in that it then demands for itself the due process it has destroyed and enslaves its victims in order to sacrifice them.

It is not true that despotism protects us against anarchy. We think it does only because for a long time our Europe has not seen a real despotism. But let us turn our gaze on the Roman empire after Constantine. We find that the legions were endlessly in revolt, with generals proclaiming themselves emperors and nineteen pretenders to the crown simultaneously raising the flag of rebellion. Without going back to ancient history, let us look at the sort of spectacle presented by the territories ruled by the sultan.[11]

Anarchy and despotism bring back the savage state into the social state. [25] But while anarchy puts all men there, despotism puts itself there on its own and beats its slaves, pinioned as they are, with the chains it has cast off.

Whatever may remain unexamined in this comparison, one thing is certain: this comparison will not suffice to tip the balance in favor of either of the two things concerned. So mankind cannot want either anarchy or despotism. Any other form of government can be useful, any other can be good, any other can be what a society desires and, as a consequence, can be legitimate.

CHAPTER THREE

Rousseau's Second Principle on the Scope of Political Authority

If Rousseau's first principle is an incontestable truth, this is not so of a second axiom, which he lays down and develops with all the prestigious force of his eloquence. "The clauses of the social contract," he says, "boil down to just one, namely the total surrendering of each member along with all his rights to the community."[12] The implication is that the general will must exercise unlimited authority over individual existence.

11. A reference to Sultan Selim III, who ruled the Ottoman Empire from 1798 to 1807. His reign was marked by disastrous wars against the European powers and internal revolts in the provinces under his jurisdiction.

12. *Du contrat social,* Livre I, Ch. 6, éd. cit., p. 360. Constant's quotes are rarely a model of precision and accuracy, but Hofmann's editing does not restore the original text unless the very meaning of a passage has been falsified by Constant or he has failed to indicate an important omission.

Political writers before and after Jean-Jacques Rousseau have mostly expressed the same view.[13] None has rejected it formally.[14]

"In all government there must be an absolute authority," says the author of *Natural Politics*. "Wherever that authority resides, [26] it must employ as it chooses all the powers of the society" and work out what all the particular political orientations are in order to oblige them to fall in with the overall view. However the sovereign power is distributed, the overall quantum is unlimited.[15]

Mably says it is an axiom accepted everywhere on earth that legislative power, that which declares and realizes the general will, must not be limited by anything.[16]

The supporters of despotism have in this respect come close to Rousseau's theory. "For a society to subsist," says M. Ferrand (*The Spirit of*

13. In the paragraphs which follow, Constant gives examples only of writers contemporary to Rousseau, or later than he: d'Holbach, Mably, Ferrand, and Molé. When he claims that these writers had the same view as Rousseau, he does not refer to the theory of the surrender of individual rights, which he has just quoted, but to the boundless authority of the general will over the individual.

14. See Constant's Note A at the end of Book I.

15. Paul Henri Dietrich, baron d'Holbach, *La politique naturelle ou discours sur les vrais principes du gouvernement,* London, 1773, t. I, p. 72. Constant is abridging radically and the last sentence is more a summary than a proper quote. Here is the beginning of the paragraph which Holbach entitled *On Absolute Authority* (French original *De l'autorité absolue*): "In all government there must be an absolute authority. Wherever that authority resides it must employ as it chooses all the powers of society. To this end it must not only make laws, but also possess power extensive enough to make them effective, or to overcome the resistances which individual passions may put in their way. These aims would not be fulfilled if the public authorities did not also have enough power to make those who belong within the jurisdiction of the state contribute to its flourishing, its preservation and security. It also has to decide what policy directions are most appropriate to securing these. In sum, this central power is constituted to work out what the particular orientations are and be strong enough to force them to fall in with its overall view. If such power had limits, there could be no vitality or vigor in government. The vices of individual citizens would endlessly vitiate, as pointless or dangerous, any association with no object other than the general flourishing of all. This truth has been felt by societies which are most jealous of their liberties. Surrounded by the most cruel factions, they have often found themselves obliged to submit, at least for a limited period, to a boundless authority. Such was the case with the Roman dictatorship."

16. Hofmann searched in vain for this quote from Mably in two of his works referred to elsewhere by Constant: *De la législation ou principes des lois* and the *Entretiens de Phocion sur les rapports de la morale avec la politique.*

History, I, 134), "it is necessary that there exist somewhere a power greater than any obstacle,[17] which directs individual wills and suppresses factionalist passions."[18]

Some writers,[19] of whom Montesquieu is one, [27] have placed certain apparent restrictions on this doctrine. These have always been too vague, however, to serve to define fixed limits to political authority. To say that justice existed before the laws (*The Spirit of the Laws*, Livre I)[20] is indeed to imply that the laws, and therefore the general will, of which the laws are only the expression, must be subordinate to justice. But what a set of developments this truth in turn demands if it is to be applied! In the absence of such developments, what follows from this assertion by Montesquieu? That the holders of power have often set off from the principle that justice precedes the laws in order to subject individuals to retrospective laws or deprive them of the benefits of existing ones, in this way hiding the most revolting iniquities behind a sham respect for justice. How crucial it is in matters of this sort to be wary of undefined axioms!

M. de Montesquieu, moreover, in his definition of liberty, misconstrues all the limits of political authority. Liberty, he says, is the right to do anything the law permits.[21] Doubtless there is no liberty at all when the citizens cannot do everything the law does not forbid. But so many things could be made illegal that there would still be no liberty.

M. de Montesquieu, like most political writers, seems to me to confuse two things: freedom and constitutional security. Freedom consists in

17. See Constant's Note B at the end of Book I.

18. Antoine Ferrand, *L'esprit de l'histoire ou lettres politiques et morales d'un père à son fils, sur la manière d'étudier l'histoire en général et particulièrement l'histoire de France,* Paris, Vve Nyon, 1802, pp. 134–135.

19. One would have expected Constant to cite Locke before Montesquieu. Perhaps he is assumed to number among this group. Constant's silence on the English writer is at the very least strange. On this question, see Hofmann's thesis, Seconde Partie, Ch. 2, pp. 329–332.

20. *De l'esprit des lois,* Livre I, Ch. 1: "Before there were laws, relations touching on justice were possible. To say nothing can be just or unjust unless it is required or forbidden by positive laws, is like saying that before we could draw circles their radii were not equal. We must therefore admit to relationships of justice prior to the positive laws which reestablish them." Montesquieu, *Oeuvres complètes,* presentation and notes by Daniel Oster, Paris, E. du Seuil, 1964, p. 530 (L'Intégrale).

21. *Ibid.*, Livre XI, Ch. 3, *éd. cit.*, p. 586.

individual rights; social rights, on the other hand, provide constitutional security.[22]

[28] The axiom of the people's sovereignty has been thought of as a principle of freedom. It is in fact a principle of constitutional guarantee. It aims to prevent any individual from seizing the authority which belongs only to the political society as a whole. It determines nothing, however, about the nature of this authority itself. It in no way adds to the sum of individual liberties, therefore, and if we do not turn to other principles for determining the extent of this sovereignty, freedom could be lost, despite the principle of the sovereignty of the people, or even because of it.

M. de Montesquieu's maxim, that individuals have the right to do everything the law permits, is similarly a principle of guarantee. It means that no one has the right to stop someone else doing what the law does not forbid. It does not explain, however, what the law is or is not justified in forbidding. Now, it seems to me that this is exactly where freedom resides. It consists only in what individuals have the right to do and society has no right to prevent.

Since the time of M. de Montesquieu some well-known men have protested against Rousseau's maxim. Beccaria, in his treatise *On Offenses and Punishments*,[23] and Condorcet, in *Commentaries on Public Education*,[24] have reasoned from opposite principles. Franklin produced a pamphlet seeking

22. Constant returns to this distinction when he opposes "civil freedom" to "political freedom" in Book XVI, Ch. 7 and in Book XVII, Ch. 3 of this treatise.

23. Cesare Beccaria's little book, *Dei delitti e delle pene* (on offences and punishments), published in 1764, which swiftly became a great success, was in no sense a refutation of Rousseau. The latter had exerted on the contrary a "deep influence" on Beccaria, as Franco Venturi shows in the introduction to the French translation of the work—*Des délits et des peines,* trans. by Maurice Chevallier, Geneva, Droz, 1965, p. xiv. All the same, speaking of the pact at the origin of human society, Beccaria maintains, contrary to Rousseau: "Necessity constrained men to cede part of their freedom. Now, it is clear that each person wants to hand over to the community *only the smallest portion possible* consistent with the commitment of everybody to the collective defence." *Ed. cit.,* p. 10, Hofmann's italics. This is in opposition to the handover of all individual rights as envisaged by the *Contrat social,* and Constant's view, though insufficiently nuanced, is upheld.

24. The *Mémoires sur l'instruction publique* of the marquis de Condorcet had appeared in the *Bibliothèque de l'homme public,* 2e année, t. I, Paris, Buisson, 1791. Constant's references (pp. 53, 316, 317, and 372 of this treatise) are to this edition and not to t. IX of the *Oeuvres complètes,* edited by Garat and Cabanis, Brunswick, Vieweg; Paris, Heinrichs, 1804.

to show that we should have the smallest extent of government possible.[25] Paine defined [29] government authority as a necessary evil.[26] Siéyès, finally, in an opinion delivered in Parliament, declared that political authority was not boundless.[27] It does not seem, however, that the arguments of these writers have made much impression. People still speak endlessly of a power without limits residing in the people or its leaders, as of a thing beyond doubt; and the author of certain essays on morality and politics has recently reproduced, in support of absolute power, all the arguments of Rousseau on sovereignty.[28]

The Constituent Assembly, at the start, seemed to recognize individual rights, independent of society. Such was the origin of the Declaration of Rights. The Assembly, however, soon deviated from this principle. It set the example by pursuing individual existence into its most intimate retreats. It was imitated and surpassed by the governments which replaced it.

The party men, however pure their intentions, are bound to detest the limitation of political authority. They see themselves as its presumptive heirs and tend to look after their future property even when it is in the hands of their enemies. They distrust this or that kind of government, or such and such a class of governing politicians, but just let them organize government

25. Constant is probably referring to two articles which came out in the *Pennsylvania Gazette,* 1 April and 8 April 1736, under the title *On Government* and for a long time attributed to Benjamin Franklin. These texts are reproduced in *The Complete Works of Benjamin Franklin,* compiled and edited by John Bigelow, New York, G. P. Putnam's Sons, 1887, vol. 1, pp. 425–431. In fact, these articles are by John Webbe, as the latter admits in *The Pennsylvania Gazette* of 28 July 1737. See in this regard *The Papers of Benjamin Franklin,* New Haven, Yale University Press, 1960, vol. 2, pp. 145–146. Whoever was their author, these articles certainly condemned excessive government. Thus, right at the start: "Government is aptly compared to architecture; if the superstructure is too heavy for the foundation, the building totters, though assisted by outward props of art."

26. Thomas Paine, *Common Sense,* first edition, Philadelphia, R. Bell, 1776. At the beginning of the first chapter, entitled *On the origin and design of government in general,* Paine declares in fact: "Society in every state is a blessing, but government, even in its best state, is but a necessary; in its worst state an intolerable one." *The Writings of Thomas Paine,* ed. by Moncure Daniel Conway, New York, G. P. Putnam's Sons, 1894, vol. 1, p. 69 (photomech. reprod. New York, AMS Press, 1967).

27. See Constant's Note C at the end of Book I.

28. In Ch. 2 of the Second Part of his *Essais (op. cit.,* p. 134), Molé writes, for example: "It was necessary to give meaning to this moral being [society] whose existence had been recognized. It was urgent that it be given all-seeing eyes and a sword to make itself obeyed." As to whether Constant was right to identify traces of Rousseau's influence in Molé's work, see Hofmann's thesis, Seconde Partie, Ch. 2, Section 2.

in their own way, [30] allow them to entrust it to the representatives they want, and they will not think they can extend it far enough.

So we can regard Rousseau's theory that political power is unlimited as the only one adopted to date. This is the theory which seems to me false and dangerous. In my view, this is the theory we must hold responsible for most of the difficulties the establishment of freedom has encountered among various nations, for most of the abuses which worm their way into all governments of whatever type, and indeed for most of the crimes which civil strife and political upheaval drag in their wake. It was just this theory which inspired our Revolution and those horrors for which liberty for all was at once the pretext and the victim. I do not mean that the countless iniquities we witnessed and suffered were not usually caused in the immediate sense by the factional interests of the men who had seized power. But these men had managed to get the machinery of public enforcement into their guilty hands only by veiling the interests which controlled them, by laying claim to seemingly disinterested principles and opinions which served them as a banner. Now, all their principles and opinions rested on the theory this chapter has related, rested, that is, on the supposition that society may exercise over its members an unlimited authority and that everything the general will ordains, is rendered legitimate by that alone.

It is worth refuting this theory, therefore. It is useful in general to correct opinions, however metaphysical or abstract they seem to us, because vested interests seek their weapons in opinions.

Interests and opinions differ, first of all, in that the former are hidden and the latter displayed, necessarily, since the latter divide while the former unite. Secondly, interests vary for each individual according to his situation, his tastes, or his circumstances, while opinions are the same, or seem so, as between all people who act together. Finally, each individual can direct only himself in the reckoning of his interests. When he wants other people to support him, he has to present them with opinions which mislead them as to his real views. If you expose the falsity of the opinion he advances, you deprive him of his main support. You annihilate his means of influencing those around him, [31] you destroy the flag, and the army vanishes.

I know that today we have given up refuting ideas we want to fight, professing a general aversion for all theories, of whatever sort. People say all metaphysics is unworthy of our attention. But the antimetaphysical stance has always seemed to me unworthy of thinking people. Its declamations are doubly dangerous. They are as forceful against truth as against error. They tend to make reason wither, to hold our intellectual faculties up to ridicule and to discredit what is noblest in us. Secondly, they do not even possess the advantage commonly supposed. Averting ideas you think dangerous by scorning them or suppressing them violently, is to suspend their present consequences only very briefly, and to double their influence to come. We should not be misled by silence nor take it for agreement. For as long as reason is not convinced, error is ready to reappear at the first event which unleashes it. It then takes advantage of the very oppression it has experienced. Our efforts will be in vain. Thought alone can do battle with thought. Reasoning alone can correct mistakes of reasoning. When power repulses reason it does not fail only against the truth; it also fails against error. To disarm error you have to refute it. Anything else is rank charlatanism, renewed century after century, to the profit of a few, and the misfortune and shame of the rest.

Indeed, if contempt for the intellectual life had been able to preserve men from its dangerous deviations, they would long ago have reaped the benefits of this much-praised protection. There is nothing new about contempt for the mind. It is not novel always to appeal to force against thought, nor to set up a small number of privileged persons to the detriment of all other people, the latter's mental activity being treated as superfluous, and their reflection considered idle and dangerous. From the time of the Goths till today we have seen this mental outlook reproduce itself. From their day till this people have denounced metaphysics and theorizing; yet the theories have always made their reappearance. Before us, people said equality was only a chimera, a vain abstraction, a [32] meaningless theory. Men who wanted to define equality properly in order to separate it from the exaggerations which disfigured it, were treated as dreamers and troublemakers, and an ill-defined equality has never stopped returning to the attack. The Jacquerie, the Levelers, and the revolutionaries of our time have abused this theory, precisely because it had been forbidden rather than put right: incontestable proof of the inadequacy of the measures, taken by the opponents of abstract ideas, first to ward off their attacks, and secondly, so they said, to keep such ideas away from the blind and stupid species they so condescendingly governed. The effect of such measures is never more than temporary. When false theories have misled people, they are ready to listen to commonplaces against theory in general, some through exhaustion, others out of vested interest, but most by way of imitation. But when they have recovered from their weariness or been freed from their fears, they remember that theory is not a bad thing in itself, that everything has its theoretical side, that theory is no more than practice systematized into rules according to experience, and practice only theory applied. They feel that nature did not give them reason just so it could be mute or sterile. They blush at having abdicated the very core of their dignity as human beings. They adopt theories again. If these have not been corrected, if they have been mere objects of disdain, they take them up anew with all their vices intact and are once again entrapped by them in all the errors which led them to reject them before. To hold that because false theories bring grave dangers we must renounce all theories, is to take from men the surest remedy for precisely such dangers. It is to hold that because error has dire consequences, we should refuse ever to search for truth.

So I have tried to fight faulty arguments with ones which seem just to me. I have tried to oppose false metaphysics with metaphysics which I believe to be true. If I have succeeded, I will flatter myself that I have been more helpful than those who demand silence. Their legacy to the future is a set of unresolved issues. In their narrow-minded and suspicious caution they compound the ill effects of wrong ideas by the very fact that they do not allow such ideas to be examined. [33]

CHAPTER FOUR

Rousseau's Arguments for Boundless Political Authority

Rousseau defines the social contract as involving *the unconditional surrender of each individual, along with all his rights, to society as a whole* (Constant's emphasis).[29] To reassure us as to the consequences of this total handing over of every aspect of our lives to the advantage of an abstract entity, he says that the sovereign, that is, the social body as a whole, cannot harm either the collectivity of all its members, or any one of those members individually; that every person makes a total surrender, so that the condition is the same for all members and none has an interest in making it onerous for others; that each person, giving himself to everyone else, gives himself to no one; that everyone acquires over all other members the same rights

29. Constant is quoting from memory. The exact text is: "the total surrender of each member with all his rights to the whole community." *Du contrat social,* Livre I, Ch. 6, *éd. cit.,* p. 360.

he cedes to them, and gains the equivalent of all he loses, along with more strength to protect what is his own.[30] But he forgets that all the life-preserving properties which he confers on the abstract being he calls sovereignty, are born in the fact that this being is made up of all the separate individuals without exception. Now, as soon as the sovereign body has to use the force it possesses, that is to say, as soon as it is necessary to establish political authority, since the sovereign body cannot exercise this itself, it delegates and all its properties disappear. The action carried out in the name of all, being necessarily willy-nilly in the hands of one individual or a few people, it follows that in handing yourself over to everyone else, it is certainly not true that you are giving yourself to no one. On the contrary, it is to surrender yourself to those who act in the name [34] of all. It follows that in handing yourself over entirely, you do not enter a universally equal condition, since some people profit exclusively from the sacrifice of the rest. It is not true that no one has an interest in making things hard for other people, since some members are not in the common situation. It is not true that all members acquire the same rights they give up. They do not all regain the equivalent of what they lose, and the outcome of what they sacrifice is or may be the setting up of a power which takes away from them what they do have.

How is it that these obvious considerations did not convince Rousseau of the error and dangers of his theory? It is because he let himself be misled by an oversubtle distinction. A double hazard is to be feared when we examine important questions. Men go wrong, sometimes because they misconstrue the distinctions between two ideas and sometimes because they base on a simple idea distinctions which do not apply.

30. Here is the complete passage to which the author is referring: "For first of all, each person giving himself entirely, the condition is the same for everyone, and this being so, no one has an interest in making it burdensome to others. Moreover, the alienation taking place unreservedly, the association is as perfect as could be and no member has any longer anything to demand: For, if certain individuals retained some rights, since there would be no superior common authority which could judge between them and the public, each person being in some respect his own judge, would soon claim to be so in everything, the state of nature would continue and the society would necessarily become tyrannical or futile. Thus, each person giving himself to everyone, in fact gives himself to no one, and since there is no fellow member over whom one does not gain only the same rights one also cedes to him over oneself, one acquires the equivalent of everything one has lost with additional force for preserving what one has." *Ibid.*, pp. 360–361.

CHAPTER FIVE

That Rousseau's Error Comes from His Wanting to Distinguish the Prerogatives of Society from Those of the Government

Rousseau distinguished the prerogatives of society from those of government.[31] This distinction is admissible only when the word "government" is understood in a very restricted sense. Rousseau, however, took it in its widest sense, as the bringing together, not only of all properly constituted powers but of all the constitutional ways individuals have for contributing among themselves, in expressing their individual wills, to the formation of the general will.[32] According to these stipulations, any citizen [35] who, in England, elects his representatives, or any Frenchman who, under the Republic, voted in a primary assembly, should be regarded as involved in government. Once the word "government" is taken in this way, any distinction between its prerogatives and those of society itself is rendered illusory and can become in practice an incalculable danger. Society cannot itself exercise the prerogatives bestowed on it by its members. Therefore it delegates them. It sets up what we call a government. From then on any distinction between society's prerogatives and those of government is an abstraction, a chimera. For on the one hand, if society had a legitimate authority greater than the one it delegated, the part it did not delegate would, by reason of its not being exercisable, be effectively void. A right one cannot exercise oneself, nor delegate to others, is a right which does not exist. On the other hand, the recognition of such rights would inevitably entail the disadvantage that those in whom the delegated part had been invested would inexorably contrive to have the rest delegated to them too. An example will clarify my point. I assume that we recognize—it has often been done—that society has a right to expel a

31. This criticism could be leveled also at Thomas Paine, who, in *Common Sense,* says: "Some writers have so confounded society with government as to leave no distinction between them." *Ed. cit.,* p. 69.

32. It is hard to see to which passage Constant is referring, since in *Du contrat social,* Livre III, Ch. 1 (*éd. cit.,* p. 396), Rousseau defines government as: "an intermediate body established between the subjects and the sovereign for their mutual dealings, charged with the execution of the laws, with the maintenance of liberty, both civil and political [. . .] I therefore call the legitimate exercise of executive power *Government* or supreme administration and the man or body charged with carrying out that administration the Prince or magistrate." See Hoffman's thesis, Seconde Partie, Ch. 2, pp. 322–323 and n. 53.

minority part of itself which has given it deep offense. No one attributes this terrible prerogative to the government, but when the latter wants to grab it, what does it do? It identifies the unfortunate minority, at once outlawed and feared, with all life's difficulties and dangers. It then appeals to the nation. It is not as its prerogative that it seeks to persecute, on mere suspicion, wholly innocent individuals. But it quotes the imprescribable prerogative of the whole society, of the all-powerful majority, of the sovereign nation whose well-being is the highest law. The government can do nothing, it says, but the nation can do everything. And soon the nation speaks. By this I mean that a few men, either low types or madmen, or hirelings, or men consumed with remorse, or terror-struck, set themselves up as its instruments at the same time as they silence it, and proclaim its omnipotence at the same time as they menace it. In this way, by an easy and swift maneuver, the government seizes the real and terrible power previously regarded as the abstract right of the whole society.

There really is a prerogative—when we are speaking abstractly—that the society does possess and does not delegate to the government, namely the right to change the organization of the government itself. To delegate this right would set up a vicious circle, since the government could use it [36] to transform itself into a tyranny. But this very exception confirms the rule. If society does not delegate this prerogative, neither does it exercise it itself. Just as it would be absurd to delegate it, so it is impossible to exercise it and dangerous to proclaim it.

The people, Rousseau observes, are sovereign in one respect and subject in another.[33] In practice, however, the two cases are confused. It is easy for powerful men to oppress the people as their subjects, to force them to manifest in their sovereign role the will which these powerful men are dictating. To achieve this, all that is needed is that the individual members of society be terror-struck and then that a hypocritical homage be rendered to the society en masse.

Thus one can recognize as society's only those rights which the government can exercise without their becoming dangerous. Sovereignty being an abstract thing and the real thing, the exercise of sovereignty, that is to say, the government, being necessarily delegated to beings of a quite different

33. ". . . each individual, contracting, so to speak, with himself, finds himself involved in a double relationship; namely as a member of the sovereign in relation to private individuals, and as a member of the society in relation to the sovereign." *Du contrat social,* Livre I, Ch. 7, *éd. cit.,* p. 362.

nature from the sovereign, since they are not abstract beings, we need to take precautionary measures against the sovereign power, because of the nature of those who exercise it, as we would take them in the case of an excessively powerful weapon which might fall into unreliable hands.

CHAPTER SIX

The Consequences of Rousseau's Theory

When you have affirmed on principle the view that the prerogatives of society always become, finally, those of government, you understand immediately how necessary it is that political power be limited. If it is not, individual existence is on the one hand subjected without qualification to the general will, while on the other, the general will finds itself represented without appeal by the will of the governors. These representatives of the general will have [37] powers all the more formidable in that they call themselves mere pliant instruments of this alleged will and possess the means of enforcement or enticement necessary to ensure that it is manifested in ways which suit them. What no tyrant would dare to do in his own name, the latter legitimate by the unlimited extension of boundless political authority. They seek the enlargement of the powers they need, from the very owner of political authority, that is, the people, whose omnipotence is there only to justify their encroachments. The most unjust laws and oppressive institutions are obligatory, as the expression of the general will. For individuals, says Rousseau, having alienated their all to the benefit of the collectivity, can have no will other than that general will. Obeying this, they obey only themselves, and are all the freer the more implicitly they obey.[34]

Such are the consequences of this theoretical system as we see them appear in all eras of history. Their most frightening scope, however, was the one they developed during our Revolution, when revered principles were made into wounds, perhaps incurably. The more popular the government it was intended to give France, the worse were these wounds. When no limit to political authority is acknowledged, the people's leaders, in a popular government, are not defenders of freedom, but aspiring tyrants, aiming not to

34. It seems Constant has condensed two passages: first: "The constant will of all members of the State is the general will; it is through this that they are citizens and free," *Du contrat social,* Livre IV, Ch. 2, *éd. cit.,* p. 440, and second: "So long as the citizens are subjected only to such conventions, they obey no one else but only their own will," ibid., Livre II, Ch. 4, *éd. cit.,* p. 375.

break, but rather to assume the boundless power which presses on the citizens. When it has a representative constitution, a nation is free only when its delegates are held in check. It would be easy to show, by means of countless examples, that the grossest sophisms of the most ardent apostles of the Terror, in the most revolting circumstances, were only perfectly consistent [38] consequences of Rousseau's principles.[35] The omnipotent nation is as dangerous as a tyrant, indeed more dangerous. Tyranny is not constituted by there being few governors. Nor does a large number of governors guarantee freedom. The degree of political power alone, in whatever hands it is placed, makes a constitution free or a government oppressive; and once tyranny subsists, it is all the more frightful if the tyrannical group is large.

Doubtless, the overextension of political power does not always have equally dire consequences. The nature of things and people's dispositions may sometimes soften the excesses; but such a political system always has serious drawbacks nevertheless. This doctrine creates and then carelessly casts into our human arrangements a degree of power which is too great to be manageable and one which is an evil whatever hands you place it in. Entrust it to one person, to several, to all, you will still find it an evil. You lay the blame on the power-holders and depending on the circumstances, you will have to indict in turn monarchy, aristocracy, democracy, mixed constitutions, and representative government. And you will be wrong. The condemnation must be of the extent of the power and not of those in whom it is vested. It is against the weapon and not the person wielding it we need to rail. There are things too heavy for human hands.

[39] Look at the fruitless efforts of different peoples to remedy the evils of the unlimited power with which they think society invested. They do not know to whom to entrust it. The Carthaginians created in succession the Suffetes to rein in the aristocracy of the Senate, the Tribunal of the Hundred to suppress the Suffetes, the Tribunal of the Five to control the Hundred. Condillac says they wanted to put a brake on one authority, and they established a counterforce which was equally in need of restraining, thus always leaving the abuses to which they thought they brought a remedy to carry on.[36]

35. See Constant's Note D at the end of Book I.

36. Etienne Bonnot de Condillac, *Histoire ancienne,* Livre VII, Ch. 7. In the edition published under the title: *Cours d'étude pour l'instruction du prince de Parme,* Geneva, Du Villard et Nouffer, 1780, t. V, pp. 473–474, we find: "They wanted to put a brake on one authority and doing this established another, which needed containing. They therefore left the abuses they thought they were remedying to continue."

The mistake of Rousseau and of writers who are the greatest friends of freedom, when they grant society a boundless power, comes from the way their ideas on politics were formed. They have seen in history a small number of men, or even one alone, in possession of immense power, which did a lot of harm. But their wrath has been directed against the wielders of power and not the power itself. Instead of destroying it, they have dreamed only of relocating it. It was a plague; but they took it as something to be conquered; and they endowed the whole society with it. Inevitably it moved from there to the majority and from the majority into a few hands. It has done just as much harm as before, and hostility to all political institutions has accumulated in the form of examples, objections, arguments, and evidence.

CHAPTER SEVEN

On Hobbes

The man who reduced despotism to a theoretical system most cleverly, Hobbes, was quick to support unlimited political power, in order to declare thereby in favor of the legitimacy of absolute government by a single person. The sovereign, he says (and by this word he understands the general will), is irreprehensible in his actions. All individuals [40] must obey, and they cannot call upon him to account for his measures. Sovereignty is absolute, a truth which has always been recognized, even by those who have stirred up rebellions, or instigated civil wars. Their motive was not the annihilation of sovereignty; but rather to move its exercise elsewhere. Democracy is an absolute sovereignty placed in the hands of everyone; aristocracy is absolute sovereignty in the hands of a few; and monarchy is absolute sovereignty in the hands of one person. The people were able to give up this absolute sovereignty in favor of a monarch, who then became its legitimate possessor.[37]

We can clearly see that the absolute character with which Hobbes endows political authority is the basis of his entire system. This word "absolute" changes the very nature of the question and involves us in a novel chain of consequences. This is the point where the writer leaves the road of truth in order to stride off by way of sophism to the conclusion he set for himself from the start. He shows that men's conventions being

37. Constant is not quoting Hobbes, but summarizing his thought as one finds it in *Leviathan,* Ch. XVII and following.

insufficient to secure obedience, there has to be a coercive force to compel this, that given that a society must defend itself against foreign aggression, there has to be a common force to arm for the common defense; that the existence of conflicting claims among men means there must be laws to establish their rights. He concludes from the first point that the sovereign has an absolute right to punish, from the second that he has an absolute right to wage war, and from the third that he is absolute in legislative power. Nothing could be more false than these conclusions. The sovereign does have the right to punish, but only for culpable actions. He does have the right to wage war, but only when society is attacked. He does have the right [41] to make laws, but only when they are necessary and insofar as they are just. There is, therefore, nothing "absolute," nothing arbitrary in these prerogatives. Democracy is power in the hands of all, but power only in such measure as is needed for the security of the society. Aristocracy is this same authority entrusted to a few; and monarchy is the same thing brought together in one person. The people can divest themselves of this authority in favor of a single man or of a small number, but their power remains limited, like that of the people who vested it in them. With this cutting out of a single word, one Hobbes had inserted gratuitously into the construction of a sentence, his whole frightful system collapses. On the contrary, with the word "absolute," neither liberty, nor, as we will see subsequently, peace, nor happiness, is possible under any institutional arrangements. Popular government is only a convulsive tyranny; monarchical government only a more morose and taciturn despotism.

When we see a distinguished author arrive by way of specious arguments at manifestly absurd results, it will prove instructive in itself and aid greatly in the refutation of error if, by way of research, we retrace the line of this writer's thoughts, so to speak, to try and pinpoint where he started to deviate from the truth. Almost all writers start off from some true principle. Once this principle has been posited, however, all it takes to vitiate their whole theory is an invalid distinction, or an ill-defined term, or a superfluous word. In Helvétius, for example, it is an ill-defined term. His starting point is incontestable: all our ideas reach us through our senses. He concludes from this that sensation is everything. To think is to feel, he says, and therefore to feel is to think.[38] This is where he goes wrong. The error stems from an ill-defined term, in this case "to feel" or "sensation." To think

38. Claude-Adrien Helvétius, *De l'esprit,* Paris, Durand, 1758, Premier Discours, Ch. 1, pp. 18–31. Helvétius is more precise in his definition. "To judge [not to think] is to feel."

is to feel; but to feel is not to think. In Rousseau, as we saw, the mistake came from an invalid distinction. He sets out from a truth, namely that the general will must make the law; but he distinguishes the prerogatives of society from those of government. He believes that society must possess boundless political power, and from there he goes astray. It is clear that in Hobbes a superfluous word is the cause of the trouble. He too has a correct starting point, namely that we need a coercive force in order [42] to govern human societies. But he slips into his sentence a single unnecessary epithet, the word "absolute," and his whole argument becomes a tissue of errors.

CHAPTER EIGHT

Hobbes's Opinion Reproduced

A contemporary writer, the author of *Essays on Morality and Politics,* has revived Hobbes's system, only with much less profundity and much weaker inspiration and logic. Like Hobbes, he sets off from the principle of unlimited sovereignty. He has assumed political authority to be absolute and transferred from society to a man he defines as the species personified, the individualized collectivity. Just as Rousseau had said that the social body cannot hurt either the collectivity of members nor any individual member,[39] this writer says that the depository of power, the man become society itself, cannot harm society, because all the ill he could do to it, he would experience precisely himself, insofar as he is society itself.[40] Just as Rousseau

39. "As soon as the multitude is brought together thus in a single body, any offense to a member is an offense to the whole. Still less could one offend the whole body without its membership feeling the effects. Thus duty and interest alike compel the two contracting parties to support each other, and the same men must seek to bring together under this double relationship all the benefits which depend on it. Now, the sovereign power, being formed only by the individuals who compose it, neither has nor can have any interest contrary to theirs. It follows that the sovereign power has no need to issue guarantees to its subjects, because it is impossible that the body should wish to harm all its parts, and we will later see that it cannot harm any individual one of them." *Du contrat social,* Livre I, Ch. 7, *éd. cit.,* p. 363.

40. In Ch. 3 of his *Essais* (*op. cit.,* p. 140), Molé declares in effect: "The government could not be arbitrary; men were afraid to depend on the fancy or the whims of him who exercised it. So man was not told to do what he thought right for the well-being of society. Rather, given that he was endowed with the force of society itself, he was mandated to conserve the conditions which constituted his existence. He punished outrages, he proceeded with the reparation of civil wrongs, and in all these ways he consecrated this first moral fact, that we should do nothing to others we would not wish done to ourselves."

says that the individual cannot resist society because he has handed over all his rights to it, without reserve,[41] this man claims that the authority of the [43] depository of power is absolute, because no member of the collectivity can struggle against the collectivity as a whole. He also claims that there can be no responsibility on the part of the depository of power, since no individual can be in dispute with the body of which he is a part, and that the latter can respond only by making him return to the order he should never have left. He then adds, so that we should in no way be fearful of tyranny: now, here is the reason his authority (that of the depository of power) was not arbitrary. "This was no longer a man. This was a people."[42] What a marvelous guarantee this switch in reasoning provides!

CHAPTER NINE

On the Inconsistency with Which Rousseau Has Been Reproached

Because he had not felt that political power had to be limited, Rousseau was drawn into a quandary he was able to escape only by undoing with one hand what he had built with the other. He declared that sovereignty could be neither given away,[43] nor delegated, nor represented, which was to declare, less roundly, that it could not be exercised. This destroyed in fact the principle he had just proclaimed. Those seeking to explain his [44] theory

41. "In order, therefore, that the social contract is no worthless formulary, it tacitly includes the only undertaking which can give force to other people, namely that whoever refuses to obey the general will, will be constrained thereto by the whole society. This means nothing else than that he will be forced to be free." *Du contrat social,* Livre 1, Ch. 7, *éd. cit.,* p. 364. Cf. also Livre II, Ch. 4, pp. 372–375.

42. Constant summarizes here the longer passages of the original, whose corresponding text is as follows: "The authority therefore had to be absolute. An individual in danger runs away without consultation or permission. Often he owes his safe delivery only to secrecy and promptness. The authority, moreover, could not be counterbalanced without someone resisting it, and such resistance was absurd. It could never be legitimate. How could some parts of the association have struggled against it? There could exist no responsibility on the part of the depository of power. Under what right could a member enter into dispute with the being of which he is a part? The latter could not respond to him save by making him return to the order he should never have left" (*op. cit.,* pp. 139–140). And later, Molé says again: "But understand his position and why his power is not arbitrary. This was no longer a man but a people" (*op. cit.,* p. 141).

43. *Du contrat social,* Livre II, Ch. 1, *éd. cit.,* pp. 368–369.

have accused him of inconsistency.[44] On the contrary, his reasoning was very consistent. Terror-struck at the spectacle of the immense political power he had just created, he had no idea in whose hands to place so monstrous a power and had thought of no defense against the danger inseparable from sovereignty as he had conceived it, save an expedient which made the exercise of that sovereignty impossible. It was only those who adopted his principle, separating it from what made it less disastrous, who were bad reasoners and guilty politicians. It is the principle which needs rejecting, since so long as it does not produce despotism, it is only an inapplicable theory, since it leads to despotism as soon as people do try to apply it.

So it is not inconsistency of which Rousseau must be accused. The reproach he deserves is that he set off from an invalid hypothesis and went astray in superfluous subtleties.

I do not side at all with his detractors. A rabble of inferior minds, who see their brief success as consisting in calling into doubt every redoubtable truth, is excitedly anxious to take away his greatness. This is just one more reason to render him our homage. He was the first writer to popularize the sense of our rights. His was a voice to stir generous hearts and independent spirits. But what he felt so powerfully, he did not know how to define precisely. Several chapters of *The Social Contract* are worthy of the scholastic writers of the sixteenth century. What is meant by rights which one enjoys all the more for having given them away completely? Just what is a freedom in virtue of which one is all the more free the more unquestioningly one does what runs counter to one's own wishes?[45] These are

44. It is hard to know to whom Constant is referring, given that Rousseau's critics are so numerous (see, for example: Robert Dérathé, "Les réfutations du *Contrat social* au XVIIIe siècle," *Annales de la Société Jean-Jacques Rousseau,* t. XXXII, 1950–1952, pp. 7–54). We do, however, find in Cornelius de Pauw, *Recherches philosophiques sur les Grecs,* Berlin, G.-J. Decker, 1788, t. II, p. 167, this reflection: "Rousseau, the most inconsistent writer ever to appear." Now, Constant had read this work and even borrowed some passages from it. He could also therefore have made a note of this criticism.

45. Constant is undoubtedly referring to the paradoxes of Rousseau Hofmann has cited already: the first: "whoever refuses to obey the general will will be made to by the whole social body: this means only that he will be forced to be free," *Du contrat social,* Livre I, Ch. 7, *éd. cit.,* p. 364; the second: "So when the view opposite to mine carries the day, this proves only that I was wrong, and that what I thought was the general will, was not. If my individual opinion had carried the day, I would have done something other than I had wished. This is when I would not have been free," *ibid.,* Livre IV, Ch. 2, *éd. cit.,* p. 441.

deadly [45] theological sophisms such as give weapons to all tyrannies, to the tyranny of one man, to that of a few people, to the legally constituted kind, and to the kind dominated by popular fury! Jean-Jacques's errors have seduced many friends of freedom, because they were established to counter other, more degrading mistakes. Even so, we cannot refute them strongly enough, because they put insuperable obstacles in the way of any free or moderate constitution, and they supply a banal pretext for all manner of political outrages.

CONSTANT'S NOTES

A. [Refers to page 9.]

Condorcet is an exception. He has very precisely established the limits of political power. See his *Notes on Public Education.* Nor is it in general true that the idea is new. It occurs in Franklin, Payne, Beccaria, and others. No one, however, has drawn out all the consequences flowing from it.

B. [Refers to page 10.]

Even those contrary to morality, such as for example a power which can condemn the innocent? Is this what M. Ferrand means?

C. [Refers to page 12.]

"Unlimited powers are a political monster and a great error on the part of the French nation. It will not make the same mistake again in the future. You will be spelling out again to the people this great truth, all too misunderstood in this country. Namely that the nation does not itself have these powers, these unlimited prerogatives which its flatterers have attributed to it. When a political association forms, one does not communalize all the rights every individual has in society, the whole power of the entire mass of individuals. In political life one communalizes in the name of public power, as little as possible and only what is necessary for maintaining each person in his rights and duties. Power on this scale is far short of the exaggerated ideas with which people have [46] blithely invested what they call sovereignty. Notice that I am speaking of the sovereignty of the people, because if there is such a thing as sovereignty, that is where it is. This word is so vastly inflated in the popular understanding, only because the French mind, still full of royal superstitions, has thought itself bound to endow it with the whole historical baggage of solemn pomposity and absolute powers which have glamorized unlawful sovereignty. We have even seen public feeling, in its vast magnanimity, enraged again for not giving it more. People seemed to be saying to themselves with a sort of patriotic pride, that if the sovereignty of great kings is so powerful, so terrible, the sovereignty of a great nation should be something more remarkable still. What I say is that to the extent that we enlighten ourselves, and distance ourselves from the days when we thought we knew what was what, and were really doing no more than idle wishing, the power of sovereignty will be brought back within its proper limits. Once again let it be said: the power of the people is not unlimited." Siéyès, Opinion dans le Moniteur.[46]

46. *Moniteur universel,* 7–8 thermidor an III (25–26 July 1795), pp. 1236–1239, reproducing the speech Siéyès delivered on 2 thermidor an III (20 July 1795) in the Conven-

D. [Refers to page 20.]

When people wanted to condemn the King to death, they said that the will of the people made the law, that insurrection, demonstrating the will of the people, was a living law, and that Louis XVI was condemned by that law.

---

tion. The text is republished by Paul Bastid, *Les discours de Siéyès dans les débats constitutionnels de l'an III (2 et 18 thermidor)*. This is a critical edition with an introduction and notes. Paris, Hachette, 1939, pp. 13–30. The passage quoted by Constant is on pp. 17–18.

BOOK II

On the Principles to Replace Received Ideas on the Extent of Political Authority

Ch. 1. On the limitation of political authority. 31

Ch. 2. On the rights of the majority. 32

Ch. 3. On the insignificance of the way government is organized when political power is not limited. 35

Ch. 4. Objection to the possibility of limiting political authority. 36

Ch. 5. On the limits of political authority restricted to a minimum. 38

Ch. 6. On individual rights when political authority is thus restricted. 39

Ch. 7. On the principle of utility substituted for the idea of individual rights. 39

Constant's title for Ch. 3 is slightly different inside his text from what appears on this page.

CHAPTER ONE

On the Limitation of Political Authority

A careful distinction must be made between Rousseau's two principles. The first has to be accepted. All authority which does not issue from the general will is undoubtedly illegitimate. The second must be rejected. The authority which issues from the general will is not legitimate merely by virtue of this, whatever its extent may be and whatever objects it is exercised over. The first of these principles is the most salutary truth, the second the most dangerous of errors. The former is the basis of all freedom, the latter the justification of all despotism.

In a society whose members have equal rights, it is certain that no member can on his own make obligatory laws for the others. It is wrong, however, to say that society as a whole enjoys this faculty without restriction. The body of all citizens is sovereign. This is to say that no individual, no group, no faction, can assume sovereignty except by delegation from that body. It does not follow, however, that the citizen body or those in whom it has vested the exercise of its sovereignty, can use it to dispose sovereignly of individual lives. On the contrary, there is a part of human existence which necessarily remains individual and independent, and by right beyond all political jurisdiction. Sovereignty exists only in a limited and relative way. The jurisdiction of this sovereignty stops where independent, individual existence begins. If society crosses this boundary, it becomes as guilty of tyranny as the despot whose only claim to office is the murderous sword. The legitimacy of government [50] depends on its purpose as well as upon its source. When that government is extended to purposes outside its competence, it becomes illegitimate. Political society cannot exceed its jurisdiction without being usurpative, nor can the majority without becoming factious. The assent of the majority is not enough in all circumstances to render its actions lawful. There are acts which nothing can endow with that character. When a government of any sort puts a threatening hand on that part of individual life beyond its proper scope, it matters little on what such authority claims to be based, whether it calls itself individual or nation. Even if it were the whole nation, except for the man it is harassing, it would be no more legitimate for that. If anyone thinks these maxims dangerous, let him think about the other, contrary dispensation which authorized the horrors of Robespierre and the oppressions of Caligula alike.

CHAPTER TWO

On the Rights of the Majority

No doubt individuals should submit to the majority. It is not that majority decisions have to be seen as infallible. Any collective decision, that is to say, any decision taken by a group of men, is exposed to two kinds of drawback. When it is dictated by passionate feelings, it is clear these can lead to mistakes. Even when the decisions of the majority are taken in a spirit of calm, however, they are exposed to dangers of another kind. They are formed by negotiation between divergent opinions. Now, if one of the opinions was right, it is clear that the transaction can have been achieved only to the detriment of truth. It may have corrected wrong opinions in some respects, but it has misrepresented the correct opinion or made it less accurate.

It has been shown by mathematical calculations that, when an assembly is held to choose between a certain number of candidates, usually the victor is not the object of the most [51] complete agreement, but of the least repugnance.[1] The same thing happens to majority opinions as happens to such candidates in an assembly. This is an inevitable ill, however. If we were to conclude, on the grounds of the possible errors of the majority, that we should subordinate our wills to the will of the minority, we would find ourselves with violent or mendacious institutions.

The prerogative of the majority is that of the strongest. It is unjust. It would be still more unjust, however, if the will of the weakest were to prevail. If society has to make a decision, the strongest or the weakest, the most or the least numerous, must triumph. If the right of the majority, that is, the strongest, were not recognized, the right of the minority would be. This is to say that injustice would weigh down on a greater number of people. The *liberum veto* (the free veto) of Poland, which intended that the laws should have force only *nemine contradicente* (no one being opposed), did not make all the citizens free, but rather subjected them all to one person. It is in order to conserve the freedom of the greatest number that the most just lawmakers have found themselves obliged to undermine the freedom

1. A probable reference to the *Essai sur l'application de l'analyse à la probabilité des décisions rendues à la pluralité des voix* by the marquis de Condorcet (Paris, Impr. royale, 1785), in which pp. lix–lxx of the *Discours préliminaire* deal precisely with the choice between several candidates taken in an assembly.

of all.[2] We have to resign ourselves to disadvantages inherent in the nature of things and which the nature of things puts right. There is a restorative force in nature. Everything natural carries its remedy with it. That which is artificial, on the contrary, has disadvantages at least as great, and nature furnishes us with no remedy. But what she does do to counter the errors of the majority, is to circumscribe its rights within precise limits. If you say its power is boundless, you abandon all defenses against the consequences of its errors.

The majority can make the law only on issues on which the law must pronounce. On those on which the law must not pronounce, the wish of the majority is no more legitimate than that of the smallest of minorities.

I ask pardon for perhaps overextending this subject—it is so important—and for having recourse to an example in order to make these [52] truths more tangible. Let us suppose some men get together for a commercial undertaking. They pool part of their wealth. This is the common wealth. What is left to each man is his private wealth. As a majority, members can direct the use of common funds. If, however, that majority claimed the right to extend its jurisdiction to the rest of the wealth of other members, no law court would uphold this claim.

It is the same with political authority. If the comparison is inexact, this is in respect of one point only, and this inexactitude works in favor of our argument. In the case of our private hypothetical association, there exists outside that association a constraint preventing the majority from oppressing the minority. A small group of men cannot take over the name of the majority in order to tyrannize the association. After all, this association may have entered contractual arrangements for which it is jointly liable, with an outside party. In politics, however, none of these conditions obtains. The political community is not responsible to any outside party. There are only two fractions: the majority and the minority. The majority is the judge when it acts within its competence, and becomes a faction when it exceeds this role. No outside force prevents the majority from sacrificing the minority, or a small band of men from calling themselves the majority in order to control everyone. It is therefore vital to make up for this missing external force, by fixed principles from which the majority never deviates.

2. The example of Poland comes, as is indicated in a note by Sismondi, in his *Recherches sur les constitutions des peuples libres (éd. cit.,* p. 89), from Leszek Leczinski, *La voix libre du citoyen, ou observations sur le gouvernement de Pologne,* s.l., 1749. Constant had had this manuscript by Sismondi from October 1800 until the start of 1801.

Political authority is like government credit. Governments, being always more powerful than their creditors, are by this very fact forced into more stringent scrupulousness. For if they deviate from this a single time, no coercive force being exercisable against them, confidence is frightened away and no longer to be reassured. Just so, the majority always having the power to trespass upon individual or minority rights, if it does not most scrupulously abstain from such, all security vanishes, for there is no guarantee either against the repetition of such offenses or ever-increasing excesses.

A frequent source of error about the proper scope of political authority is the constant confusion of the common interest with the interests of all. The common interest concerns only society as a whole. The interests of all are simply the sum of individual interests. Apart from fractional interests which concern only an individual or fraction of society and hence fall outside all political jurisdiction, there are further things which concern all the members of society and which [53] nevertheless must not be subject to the force of the general will. These things interest each person as an individual and not as a member of the collectivity. Religion is a case in point, for example. Political authority must always act upon the common interest, but it must act on the interests of all only when the common interest is also at stake. The comparison I have previously used will explain what I mean. That part of their wealth individuals hold in common is their common wealth. You could call the sum of what each member retains privately the wealth of all, but if members have not pooled it, it is precisely the wealth of all rather than the common wealth. It is not one undifferentiated thing. It is the sum of all individual fortunes, independent one from another. These are not all of a piece, nor do they merge together. The polity can legitimately make use of the common fund but not of the private wealth of all. It is an error to conclude from the fact that an issue touches on all members of a society that it must be an issue of the common interest. It may be something which touches people only as individuals. Religion, for example, is a case in point. Before we concede the right of government to get involved in this issue, we need to see if it includes any point of common interest, that is to say, if the interests of individuals are of such a nature that they collide and cause mutual offense. It is only then that political involvement is called for, and even then only to prevent friction. If, on the contrary, these interests live side by side without troubling each other, they are not under political jurisdiction. It is de jure that they are not, and we will show that they must not be de facto, since such jurisdiction would merely harass them pointlessly. They should retain their independence and their complete individuality.

Most political writers, above all those who wrote according to the most popular principles, fell into a bizarre error when they spoke about majority rights. They represented the majority as a real person whose existence is protracted and which always comprises the same parts. In fact, however, it happens all the time that a section of the population which was in the majority yesterday forms today's minority. To defend the rights of minorities is therefore to defend the rights of all. Everyone in turn finds himself in the minority. The whole society is divided into a host of minorities which are oppressed in succession. Each one, isolated to be made a victim, becomes again, by a strange metamorphosis, a part of what is called the exalted whole, which serves as a pretext for the sacrifice of some other [54] minority. To grant the majority unlimited power is to offer to the people en masse the slaughter of the people piecemeal. Injustice and misfortune make their way round the whole society, becoming ever more oppressive of individuals in isolation in the name of all. At the end of this dreadful rotation, all people find they have lost more, irretrievably, as individuals, than they had transiently gained as members of society.

CHAPTER THREE

On the Organization of Government When Political Authority Is Not Limited

When political authority is not limited, the organization of government becomes a very secondary question. The mutual supervision of the diverse sections of the government is useful only in preventing one of them from aggrandizing itself at the expense of the others. But if the total sum of their powers is unbounded, if when they band together these government sections are permitted to invade everything, who is to stop them forming coalitions to engage in oppression at will?

What matters to me is not that my personal rights shall not be violated by one such power-group, without the approval of another such, but that this violation be forbidden to all sections of government. It is not enough that the executive's agents have to invoke the authorization of the legislature. Rather, it is that the legislature shall not authorize their actions except in a specified jurisdiction. It is not worth much that the executive power has no right to act without the assent of a law, if no limits are placed on this assent, if no one declares that there are things about which the legislature has no right to make laws, or, in other words, that there are areas of individual existence in relation to which society is not entitled to have any will.

If political authority is not limited, the division of powers,[3] ordinarily the guarantee of freedom, becomes a danger and a scourge. The division of powers is excellent in that it draws together, as far as possible, the interests of the governing and the governed. Men in whom executive power is vested have a thousand ways of evading the workings of the law. It is therefore to be feared that if they make the [55] laws, such laws will be worse for having been made by men who do not fear that they will ever fall on them. If you separate the making of laws from their execution, you achieve this end, that those who make the laws, and are thus governors in principle, are yet governed in application; whilst those who execute the laws, though they are governors in application, are yet among the governed in principle. If, however, in dividing power, you do not put limits on the competence of the law, it can happen that one set of men make the laws, without troubling themselves about the evils occasioned thereby, while another set execute them, in the belief that they are innocent of any harm arising from such laws, because they say they had no hand in their making. Justice and humanity find themselves between these two sets, without being able to speak to either. It would be a thousand times better, then, if the authority which carried out the laws were also charged with making them. At least it would appreciate the difficulties and pains of carrying them out.

CHAPTER FOUR

Objection to the Possibility of Limiting Political Authority

There is one obvious objection to the limitation of political authority. Is it possible to limit it? Is there any force strong enough to prevent its breaking through the barriers we have prescribed for it? Some might say we can use various ingenious combinations to limit power by dividing it. We can put its different parts in opposition and in equilibrium. But how can we ensure that its total sum is not unlimited? How can power be limited other than by power itself?

The limitation of political authority in the abstract would probably be a sterile quest, if one did not then back it up with the guarantees it needs in

3. Constant will return to this question of the separation of powers and the interests of the governing and the governed, in Book XVII, Ch. 3.

the organization of government. The investigation of these guarantees is not within the purview of this book. Let me merely suggest that it seems possible to me that we might discover political institutions whose foundations are such as to combine the interests of the various power-holders in such a way that their most obvious advantage, as well as the longest term and securest one, would be for them all to stay within their respective spheres and thereby be mutually [56] contained. Even so, the first question is still the limitation of overall authority. For before organizing anything, one needs to have determined its nature and extent.

Without wanting, as philosophers too often have, to exaggerate the influence truth has on men, I will say next that it can be affirmed that when certain principles are fully and clearly demonstrated, they work in some sense as a guarantee of themselves. The most forceful interests have a kind of sense of decency which stops them from relying on errors which have been too obviously refuted. At the exact moment when the strife of the French Revolution was again stirring up into a ferment all the prejudices still existing, some errors of the same type did not dare to reappear, for the simple reason that they had been proved to be wrong. The defenders of feudal privilege did not dream of reviving the slavery which Plato in his ideal Republic and Aristotle in his Politics thought indispensable.[4]

There forms around all the truths people manage to environ with incontestable proof a universal agreement which soon prevails. If it is widely recognized that political authority is not boundless, that such limitless power exists nowhere on earth, no one will ever again dare to demand such power. Experience itself shows this already. Even though political authority has not yet been limited in theory, it is nevertheless in fact more confined today than before. For example, people no longer attribute powers of life and death without trial even to society as a whole. Nor does any modern government claim such a right. If the tyrants of the ancient republics seem to us far more unbridled than the governments of modern history, this must partly be attributed to this. The most monstrous outrages by despotisms based on one man were often due to the doctrine of

4. This last sentence is very close to a passage by Madame de Staël, *Des circonstances actuelles qui peuvent terminer la révolution et des principes qui doivent fonder la république en France,* critical edition by Lucia Omacini, Paris-Geneva, Droz, 1979, p. 26: "In the struggle of the French Revolution, the most inveterate aristocrats did not dream of proposing the reestablishment of slavery, while Plato in his ideal Republic does not suppose we can do without it."

the boundless power of all. So political power can be curtailed. It will be guaranteed first of all by the same force which upholds all recognized truths, [57] that is, by public opinion. Afterward we can get busy with guaranteeing this in a more fixed way, via the specific organization of political powers. But having obtained and consolidated the first guarantee will always be a great good.

CHAPTER FIVE

On the Limits of Political Authority Restricted to a Minimum

Two things are indispensable for a society to exist and exist happily. First it must be protected against internal disorder and secondly sheltered from foreign invasion. Political authority must therefore be specifically entrusted with repressing this disorder and repulsing this invasion. To this end it must be invested with the right to impose penal laws against crimes, with the right to organize armed force against external enemies, and finally, with the right to demand from individuals the sacrifice of a portion of their individual wealth in order to meet the expenses of these two purposes. The vital jurisdiction of political authority therefore comprises two branches: the punishment of offenses and resistance to aggression.

We must even distinguish two kinds of offenses, those intrinsically harmful and those which offend only as violations of contracted undertakings. Society's jurisdiction over the first kind is absolute. With regard to the second kind it is only relative. It depends on the nature of the undertaking and on the claim of the injured party. Even when the victim of an assassination or theft would like to pardon the guilty person, society should still punish him, because the offense committed is intrinsically harmful. When, however, the breaking of an agreement is agreed to by all the contracting or involved parties, society has no right to enforce prolonged compliance, just as it has no right to dissolve the agreement on the say-so of one party alone.

It is clear that society's jurisdiction cannot stop short of these limits, but it can remain within them. We can scarcely imagine a nation in which individual crimes [58] remained unpunished and which had prepared no means of resisting the attacks foreign nations might launch against it. But we could imagine one in which the government had no mission other than overseeing these two aims. Individual life and national security would be perfectly assured. The necessary minimum would be done.

CHAPTER SIX

On Individual Rights When Political Authority Is Thus Restricted

Individual rights are composed of everything independent of political authority. In the hypothetical case we have just presented in the last chapter, individual rights would consist in the option to do anything which does not hurt others, or in freedom of action, in the right not to be obliged to profess any belief of which one is not convinced, even though it be the majority view, or in religious freedom, in the right to make public one's thought, using all the means of publicity, provided that that publicity does not harm any individual or provoke any wrong act, finally in the certainty of not being arbitrarily treated, as if one had exceeded the limits of individual rights, that is to say, in being guaranteed not to be arrested, detained, or judged other than according to law and with all due process.

The rights of society cannot be meaningfully distinguished from those of government, because it is impossible to indicate a way in which society can exercise its rights without the government getting involved. The rights of individuals can be usefully distinguished from those of government and society, however, because it is possible, as we see, to indicate the things government and society must refrain from pronouncing on and to leave individuals perfectly free.

CHAPTER SEVEN

On the Principle of Utility Substituted for the Idea of Individual Rights

A writer much to be recommended for the depth, precision, and originality of his thinking, Jeremy Bentham, has recently protested[5] [59] against the idea of rights and above all of natural, inalienable, and imprescriptible rights. He has claimed that this idea is liable only to mislead us, and that in its place should be put the idea of utility, which he sees as simpler and more

5. Jeremy Bentham, *Traités de législation civile et pénale, précédés de principes généraux de législation,* published in French by Etienne Dumont, Paris, Bossange, Masson et Besson, an X, 1802, 3 vol. The criticisms which Constant leveled at Bentham were probably drafted in the summer of 1802, hence the use of the adverb "recently," and this chapter was to form part of a grand political treatise written at that time.

intelligible. Since this preferred route of his has led him to conclusions just the same as mine, I would rather not dispute his terminology. I must take issue with it, however, because the principle of utility, in the way Bentham presents it to us, seems to me to have the drawbacks common to all vague locutions, and moreover to have its own special dangers.

No doubt by defining the word "utility" appropriately, one can contrive to base on this notion exactly the same rules as those which flow from the idea of natural right and justice. A careful examination of all the questions which seem to put what is useful in opposition to what is just, leads one always to the finding that what is not just is never useful. It is nonetheless true, however, that the word "utility," in its common meaning, summons up a different notion from that conveyed by justice or right. Now, when usage and common reason attach a fixed meaning to a word, it is dangerous to change that meaning. In vain you go on to explain what you meant. The word stays what it was and your explanation is forgotten.

"One cannot," says Bentham,[6] "reason with fanatics armed with a natural right each one understands as he sees fit, and applies as it suits him." But by his own admission, the utility principle is quite as susceptible to multiple interpretations and contradictory applications. Utility, he says,[7] has often been misapplied. Taken in a narrow sense, it has lent its name to crimes. "But we must not cast back on the principle faults which are contrary to it and which it alone can put right." Why should this apologia be relevant to utility and not to natural right?

The principle of utility has this further danger natural right does not, that it awakens in the human heart the hope of advantage rather than the feeling of duty. Now, the evaluation of an advantage is arbitrary: it is the imagination which settles it. But neither its errors nor its whims can change the idea of duty.

[60] Actions cannot be more or less just; but they can be more or less useful. In hurting my fellow men, I violate their rights. This is an incontestable truth. But if I judge this violation only by its utility, I can get the calculation wrong, and find utility in the violation. The principle of utility is thus much vaguer than the principle of natural rights.

Far from adopting Bentham's terminology, I should like as far as is possible to separate the idea of right from the notion of utility. This may be only a difference of wording; but it is more important than one might think.

6. See Constant's Note A at the end of Book II.

7. See Constant's Note B at the end of Book II.

Right is a principle; utility is only a result. Right is a cause; utility is only an effect.

To wish to make right subject to utility is like making the eternal laws of arithmetic subject to our everyday interests.

It is no doubt useful for the general transactions of men between themselves that numbers involve unalterable relationships. If we claimed, however, that these relationships exist only because it is useful that this should be so, there would be lots of opportunities for proving that it would be infinitely more useful if these relationships were manipulable. We would forget that their constant utility comes from their invariant character, and ceasing to be unalterable, they would cease to be useful. Thus utility, by having been too favorably treated on superficial grounds, and turned into a cause, rather than being left properly as an effect, would soon vanish totally.

Morality and right are like that too. You destroy utility simply by placing it in the first rank. It is only when the rule has been demonstrated that it is good to bring out its utility.

I ask of the very author I am refuting. Do not the expressions he wants to forbid to us refer to better grounded and more precise ideas than those he claims should replace them? Say to a man: you have the right not to be put to death or arbitrarily plundered. You will give him quite another feeling of security and protection than you will by telling him: it is not useful for you to be put to death or arbitrarily plundered. One can show, as I have already acknowledged, that that is indeed never useful. But in speaking of right, you present an idea independent of any calculation. In speaking of utility, you seem to invite that the whole question be put in doubt, by subjecting it to a new verification.

What could be more absurd, cries Bentham's ingenious and learned collaborator,[8] [61] than inalienable rights which have always been alienated, or imprescriptible rights which have been taken away or abandoned? But to say that such rights are inalienable or imprescriptible is only to say that they should not be alienated or taken away or abandoned. One is talking of what ought to be the case, not of what is the case.

By reducing everything to the principle of utility, Bentham condemned himself to an artificial evaluation of the results of all human actions, an evaluation which goes against the simplest and most customary ideas. When he speaks of fraud, theft, etc., he has to admit that if there is loss on one side, there is gain on the other. Then his principle, in order to reject the

8. See Constant's Note C at the end of Book II.

charge of identical actions, has to be that the benefit of the gain is not equivalent to the ill of the loss.[9] The benefit and the ill being separate, however, the man who commits the theft will find that his gain matters more to him than another's loss. Any idea of justice being now out of the question, he will henceforth calculate only his gain. He will say: for me my gain is more than equivalent to the loss by other people. He will thus be held back by nothing except fear of discovery. This theory wipes out all moral motivation.

In repudiating Bentham's first principle, I am far from belittling that writer's merits. His work is full of original ideas and profound perspectives. All the consequences he derives from his principle are precious truths in themselves. It is not that the principle is false; it is only the terminology which is wrong. Once he manages to detach himself from his terminology, he brings together in a most admirable structure the soundest notions on political economy, on the caution with which governments should intervene in people's lives, on population, on religion, on commerce, on the penal laws, on the appropriateness of punishments to crimes. He happened, however, like many estimable writers, to mistake a rewording for a discovery, a rewording to which he then sacrificed everything.

9. Jeremy Bentham, *Traités de législation . . . , éd. cit.*, t. I, pp. 94–95: "As to the motive of cupidity, in comparing the pleasure of acquiring by usurpation with the pain of losing, the one would not be equivalent to the other."

CONSTANT'S NOTES

A. [Refers to page 40.]
Principes de législation, Ch. 13.[10]

B. [Refers to page 40.]
Ibid., Ch. 5.[11]

C. [Refers to page 41.]
M. Dumont of Geneva.[12]

10. *Ed. cit.,* t. I, p. 136. Here is the complete sentence: "One can no longer reason with fanatics armed with *natural right,* which everyone understands as he likes, applies as suits him, in which he does not have to concede a thing, or take anything back, which is at once inflexible and unintelligible, which is venerated in his eyes like a dogma and from which one cannot deviate without committing a crime."

11. *Ed. cit.,* t. I, p. 27: "One can do harm thinking one is following the *principle of utility.* A weak and limited mind makes mistakes, by not taking into consideration more than a small number of the goods and bads. A passionate man goes wrong by attaching too much importance to a good which blinds him to all the disadvantages. What typifies the bad man is indulging in pleasures hurtful to others. And that itself supposes the absence of some kinds of pleasures. But one does not shift onto the *Principle* the blame for faults which are contrary to it and which it alone can rectify."

12. Hofmann failed to find this quotation in Dumont's *Discours préliminaire* on Bentham's *Traités de législation (éd. cit.,* t. I, pp. v–xxxvi). Might not Constant have transcribed once more a remark Dumont might have made orally, in discussions he had with Mme. de Staël and her friends? Dumont stayed at Coppet in 1802, and Constant could have made a note of one of his reflections. On this subject see Norman King, "'The airy form of things forgotten': Madame de Staël, l'utilitarisme et l'impulsion libérale," *Cahier Staëliens,* No. 11, Dec. 1970, pp. 5–26.

BOOK III

On Arguments and Hypotheses in Favor of the Extension of Political Authority

Ch. 1. On the extension of political authority beyond its necessary minimum, on the grounds of utility. 47

Ch. 2. On the hypotheses without which extension of political authority is illegitimate. 49

Ch. 3. Are governors necessarily less liable to error than the governed? 50

Ch. 4. Are governmental mistakes less dangerous than those of individuals? 55

Ch. 5. On the nature of the means political authority can use on the grounds of utility. 57

CHAPTER ONE

On the Extension of Political Authority beyond Its Necessary Minimum, on the Grounds of Utility

In no nation have individuals enjoyed individual rights in all their fullness. No government has confined the exercise of political authority to strictly necessary limits. All have gone far beyond this, and philosophers in all ages, and writers of all persuasions, have endorsed the extension with the whole weight of their approval.

Among this number I do not count merely ordinary and second-rate minds, but the most distinguished authors of the last two centuries: Fénelon,[1] Rousseau, Mably,[2] and even in some respects Montesquieu.

M. Necker is not free from the errors with which I reproach those who favor an increase in political authority. He calls the sovereign power the tutor of public happiness[3] and, when he deals with commercial prohibitions, he constantly assumes that individuals let themselves be dominated by short-term considerations, and that the sovereign power understands their long-term interests better than they themselves.[4] What [66] in M. Necker's case makes this error more excusable and touching, is that he is always so passionately concerned with improving things, and that he sees in government only a more extensive means of benevolence and good works.

Man, such writers say, is a product of law. In the beginning men make institutions, and subsequently institutions make men. Government must seize us from our first moments and surround us with virtue, both by example and precept. It must direct, improve, and enlighten that numerous

1. Fénelon, *Essai sur le gouvernement civil.* In Ch. 5, *De la nécessité d'une authorité souveraine,* Fénelon declares: "All government necessarily therefore has to be absolute" (p. 29 of the third edition, London, 1722); the author makes it equally clear, however, that he does not mean by this an arbitrary power.

2. Constant criticizes Mably at greater length in Book XVI, Ch. 8, pp.367–368.

3. Hofmann did not find the passage where Necker uses this expression, but the spirit of it figures in Necker's book *Sur la législation et le commerce des grains,* Paris, Pissot, 1776, Partie I, Ch. 2–6. Elsewhere, in *De l'administration des finances de la France,* s.l., 1784, t. III, p. 162, he defines government as the "interpreter and trustee of social harmony." Cf. Henri Grange, *Les idées de Necker* (Necker's ideas), Paris, Klincksieck, 1974, p. 163.

4. See for example *Sur la législation . . . , op. cit.,* p. 136: "All [the ideas] which can minister to the common good, belong to the sovereign; and pondering them is an important part of the august functions entrusted to him."

and ignorant class of people who, lacking time for reflection, are forced to receive the verities themselves on others' say-so and in the form of prejudices. Any time the law abandons us is a time it gives to the passions to tempt, seduce, and control us. Law must excite in us the love of work, engrave in the spirit of youth respect for morality, enthuse the imagination with subtly combined institutions, and dig deep into our hearts and uproot guilty thoughts there, rather than limiting itself to repressing harmful actions. Law should prevent crimes instead of punishing them. Law should regulate our least movements, preside over the spread of enlightenment, over industrial development, over the perfecting of the arts. It must lead, as by the hand, the benighted crowd it must instruct, or the corrupted one it must correct.

In support of this doctrine, these illustrious protagonists cite the most memorable examples of the nations of antiquity, in which all the jobs men pursued, all the actions of their lives, were covered by laws, their least words were dictated, and even their pleasures were legally regulated.[5]

Imbued with such principles, the leaders of the French Revolution thought themselves so many Lycurguses, Solons, Numas, or Charlemagnes. At this very time, despite the sorry results of their efforts, one is still more inclined to blame the blundering of the entrepreneurs than the nature of the enterprise.

A general observation is necessary before we examine in detail the theory aiming to legitimate the extension of political authority.

This extension is not absolutely necessary, as we believe we have shown. It is driven solely by the hope that it will be useful. The argument for utility once allowed, [67] however, we are brought back, despite all our efforts, to the disadvantages which flow from the blind, colossal force which seemed to us so terrible when we called it unlimited sovereignty. Utility does not lend itself to precise demonstration. It is a matter of individual opinion and consequently of interminable discussion. You can find utilitarian reasons for all orders and prohibitions. Forbidding citizens to leave their houses would prevent all the crimes which are committed on the highways. To have them appear every morning in front of their town hall would stop vagabonds, thieves, and dangerous men from hiding in the big cities on the lookout for criminal opportunities. This is the kind of thinking which in our day turned

5. The theme of the imitation of the ancients, insofar as it concerns the extension of law, will be developed in Book XVI, Ch. 8: *Des imitateurs modernes des républiques de l'antiquité*.

France into one vast prison. Nothing in nature is immaterial in the rigorous sense of the word. Everything has its cause and its effects. Everything has results, real or possible; everything can be useful or dangerous. In a system in which political authority is sole judge of all these possibilities, it is clear that such authority has absolutely no limits nor could have. If it must be limited, however, everything in its jurisdiction must be so too. What cannot be limited does not belong to such jurisdiction. Now, we have shown jurisdiction must be limited. Therefore, before understanding any system at all in terms of its various prerogatives, we have to see if we can draw a line marking where the exercise of that prerogative must stop. If there is no way of drawing such a line, the prerogative itself must be nonexistent. Authority has been taken beyond its competence. For it is of the essence of that competence that it must not be without limits. Set it up without limits and you fall once again into the bottomless abyss of arbitrary rule. Set it up without limits for a single purpose and there will no longer be any security in the social order. For if the security of a single part of the social order is absent, the security of the rest vanishes. If it is not destroyed de facto it is destroyed de jure. Now, the fact is only an accident. Law alone provides a guarantee. [68]

CHAPTER TWO

On the Hypotheses without Which the Extension of Political Authority Is Illegitimate

The imagination can come up with some singularly useful activity for indefinitely extended political authority, always on the assumption that it will be exercised on the side of reason and in the interests of all and of justice, that the means it chooses are always honorable and bound to succeed, that it will manage to govern human faculties without degrading them, that it will act, in a word, in the way the religiously minded understand providence, as a thing linking the force of command with the deepest heartfelt conviction. To adopt these brilliant suppositions, however, one must accept three hypotheses. First, the government must be imagined to be, if not infallible, at least indubitably more enlightened than the governed. This is because to intervene in people's interpersonal relations with more wisdom than they could show themselves, to steer the development of their faculties and the use of their own resources better than their own judgment could, you must have the assured gift of distinguishing better than they what is advantageous from what is harmful. Without this, what gains do you bring to happiness, social order, or morality by enlarging the powers of governments? You create a blind force whose dispositions are abandoned to chance. You draw lots between good and evil, error and truth, and chance decides which will be empowered. Any extension of authority, vested in the governors, taking place always at the expense of the freedom of the governed, furthermore requires, before we can assent to this sacrifice, that it seems probable that the former will make a better use of their extended power than the latter would of their freedom. In the second place, we must suppose that if, in spite of its superior enlightenment, the government gets it wrong, its errors will be less disastrous than those of individuals. Finally, we have to reassure ourselves that the means in the hands of governments will not produce an evil greater than the good they are supposed to achieve.

We are going to look at these three hypotheses in turn. [69]

CHAPTER THREE

Are Governors Necessarily Less Liable to Error Than the Governed?

It is easy to affirm that light has to come from elevated places and that an enlightened government must lead the masses. Writing these words, one is conceiving government as an abstract being, made up of all that is finest, most learned, and wisest in a nation. But this idea of government which people devise for themselves contains a confused sense of historical period and a petitio principii. Historical eras are confused in that such people do not distinguish barbarous nations from civilized ones. No doubt when some clan possessing only the crudest notions indispensable to physical survival comes, by way of conquest or any other means, under a government which acquaints it with the first elements of civilization, then the members of that government are more educated than those they govern. Thus we can hold Cecrops, if he existed, more enlightened than the Athenians, Numa than the Romans, Mahomet than the Arabs. But to apply this thinking to a civilized society seems to me a great error. In such a society, there are many who become enlightened, it is true, only with the greatest difficulty, working, as they do in the nature of things, in mechanical occupations. The governors are incontestably superior to them. There is also an educated class, however, of which the governors are a part, and only a very small part. The comparison must not be made between the uneducated classes and the governing group, but between the governors and the educated class. The latter must instruct and direct the rest of the nation. But we must distinguish its influence as enlightened from that of a fraction of itself as the government. When the question is posed in this way, it involves a petitio principii to attribute to governments the superiority of enlightenment. It jumps over without examining a prime difficulty which occurs in the formation of governments. Governments can be formed in three ways: by heredity, by election, and by force. We say nothing of this last way. In practice it is not likely to be attacked, because it has the advantage of being able to impose silence. Neither, however, would one take it into one's head to justify it in principle.

[70] When hereditary monarchy rested on divine right, the very mystery which sanctioned this theocratic institution was able to invest the monarch with superior enlightenment, like some gift from heaven. We find just this attitude in the memoirs written by Louis XIV.[6] Nowadays, however, when governments rest on purely human bases, this religious justification is not admissible. Heredity presents us only with a succession of governors brought up to power, and our experience of what results from the two

6. *Mémoires de Louis XIV écrits par lui-même, composés pour le Grand Dauphin, son fils et adressés a ce Prince . . .*, edited and published by J. L. M. de Gain-Montagnac, Paris, Garnery et H. Nicolle, 1806, 2 vol. Constant comes back to these *Mémoires* later on (especially pp. 391–393). They had appeared in February 1806 (as is shown by an order by Napoleon to Cambacérès on 24 February 1806, *Correspondance de Napoléon Ier . . .*, Paris, 1862, t. XII, p. 117). On 27 March Constant writes to Claude Hochet: "This morning I began the *Mémoires* of Louis XIV. I find it very hard to believe that it can all be his. There are sentences of the man of letters type. Although I am still on the thirtieth page only, I have already noticed several, among others one on the finer points of the love of glory, where there is an *if I may be so bold as to say* and an affectation which absolutely smack of the writer, not of the king. I do not call into question the authenticity of the *Mémoires* but their organization and modern editing. The theory of despotism expounded in them rather well, rests as always on the petitio principii these gentlemen always use. They assume the only alternative is between the despotism of a single man and that of several and they conclude that the former is better. No doubt, but we could have neither the one nor the other." Benjamin Constant and Madame de Staël, *Lettres à un ami. Cent onze lettres inédites à Claude Hochet,* published and with an introduction and notes by Jean Mistler, Neuchâtel, La Baconnière (1949), pp. 116–117. Constant's *Journal intime* records the reading of the *Mémoires* of Louis XIV on 28 March 1806 (and not the 27th, as the letter to Hochet suggests). Contrary to what Alfred Roulin thought (Benjamin Constant, *Oeuvres,* Paris, Gallimard, 1957, p. 1531, n. 2 of p. 568), Benjamin had indeed read the text of these *Mémoires* and not just the extracts which appeared in the *Mercure de France.*

elements of chance and flattery is almost too abundant. Election gives governments the sanction of popular opinion. Is this sanction, however, a guarantee of an enlightenment exclusive to those invested with power? The writers who claim so describe a most singular circle. When someone allows himself some doubt on the excellence of the governing group, the people's choice seems to them an unanswerable reply to these insulting doubts. In this part of their intellectual schema the people are therefore infallible. Let anyone demand, however, the same people's right to look after their own interests and opinions, and such writers will say this control belongs to the government. This second part of the schema declares the people incapable of proceeding on their own, without falling into error after error. Thus by some prodigy or other [71] an ignoble, ridiculous, degraded, and stupid rabble, which cannot behave itself, and which needs endless guidance, suddenly becomes enlightened for a unique and unrepeatable moment, in which it can appoint or accept its leaders, before immediately falling back into blindness and ignorance. The people, as first Machiavelli and later Montesquieu show, almost always make good choices as to specific officeholders. But the very arguments of these writers demonstrate that if we are to make sure that the people's choice is a good one, the duties they confer have to be very definitely circumscribed, confined within precise limits. "The people," says Montesquieu,[7] "are admirable when it comes to choosing those on whom they have to confer some part of their authority. They know very well that a man has often been to the wars, with such and such a success. They are thus very capable of electing a general. They know that a judge is assiduous, that many people leave his courtroom very pleased with him and that he has not been convicted of corruption. They are well able to elect a senior magistrate therefore. Say they have been struck by the opulence and wealth of a certain citizen. That equips them to make him a town councillor. They have only to make their mind up for reasons they cannot be ignorant of and with regard to self-evident facts." It will be seen that all the examples M. de Montesquieu rests on, apply only to the functions of political authority kept to a strict minimum. It is the same with what Machiavelli says.[8] Men, he observes, although liable to get things generally wrong, do not get them wrong in their particulars. But to ask the people to appoint the government, if its members do anything more than punish crimes and repel invasions, if, that is, such governors

7. See Constant's Note A at the end of Book III.
8. See Constant's Note B at the end of Book III.

arrogate to themselves jurisdiction over public opinion, over enlightenment, over unimportant actions, over property, over industry, in a word, over everything, then the people are no longer being asked to pronounce on the particular but on the general. The people's choice, when it is a free one and the times are untroubled, speaks in favor of the particular talent of the man to whom it entrusts a specific task. The people appreciate a judge by his judgments, a general by his victories. When, however, it comes to indefinite power, bearing on things which are vague, or arbitrary, or without clear limits, the people's choice proves nothing. In such a situation they do not have anterior facts or self-evident facts on the basis of which to make up their mind. The people's choice naturally destines [72] men of the educated class to political office. But there is no chance that these representatives of the people will be intellectually superior to the rest of their class. Their opinions will be at the level of ideas in the widest circulation. For this very reason they will be excellent at maintaining the society, at negative protection. They will be useless at leadership. For upholding and conserving purposes, the general level suffices. Leadership demands something higher. If you suppose, says Condorcet in the first of his *Five Commentaries on Public Education* (page 55), that the government is more enlightened than the mass, you must also suppose it less enlightened than lots of individuals.[9] We will add that the qualities which lend authority to a government founded on popular choice are always more or less mutually exclusive of those other qualities particularly relevant to the spread of enlightenment. To gain the confidence of the great mass of the people calls for tenacious ideas, a one-sidedness in opinion, a positive way of seeing things and acting, more force than finesse, and greater quickness in

9. Constant is interpreting rather than quoting Condorcet's thought here. Here is the text he is referring to, *Bibliothèque de l'homme public,* 2e année, t. I, Paris, Boisson, 1791, p. 55: "There is all the more reason government must not give its opinions as the basis of instruction, in that it cannot be regarded as attaining the level of the best minds of the century in which it operates. The holders of power will always be at a more or less great distance from the point arrived at by those intelligences destined to raise the body of enlightenment. Even were some men of genius to be numbered among those who exercise power, they could never attain, at all times, a preponderance which would permit them to apply in practice the results of their meditations. This trust in a deep thought whose direction one cannot discern, this willing submission to talent, this homage to fame, all cost too much in terms of self-esteem to become, at least for long, lasting sentiments, rather than a sort of forced obedience due to pressure of circumstances and reserved for times of danger and strife."

grasping the whole picture than subtlety in discerning the details. These things are excellent for purposes of repression and surveillance, for everything in the functions of government which is set, established, or precise. But carried over to the world of intelligence, opinion, enlightenment, or morality, they have about them something primitive, inflexible, and coarse, which goes against the aim of improvement or the perfecting of things one has in view. There is one other thought which must not escape us. There is something about power which more or less warps judgment. Force is far more liable to error than [73] weakness is. Force finds resources in itself. Weakness needs thought. All things equal, it is always likely that the governors will have views which are less just, less sound, and less impartial than those of the governed. Suppose there are two equally enlightened men, one in power, the other a plain citizen. Do you not feel that the first, endlessly called upon to act, more or less compromised in his actions, in a more exposed position, will have less time to reflect, more reason to persist, and thus more chance of mistakes than the second, who can reflect at leisure, is not pledged to any line, has no reason to defend a wrong idea, has compromised neither his power, nor safety, nor self-esteem, and who finally, if he does embrace that wrong idea passionately, has no way of making it prevail? The chances of mistakes by government ministers are not a reason for putting in doubt the need for the functions of government, in matters of security, internal or external. These functions being a proven necessity, an authority must at all cost be set up to exercise them and run the risk of its mistakes. These are anyway not very dangerous. There is nothing simpler than the questions on which these functions of government call it to pronounce. To preserve the State from enemy invasions, the law must decree that responsible agents will keep an eye on the movements of foreigners and that a body of men will be ready to move at a given signal. To maintain good internal order the law must lay down that particular crimes will be followed by particular punishments. To defray the costs of these two objectives, the law must decree that each citizen will supply the public funds with a given proportion of his wealth. These functions demand from government only the common intelligence and enlightenment vouchsafed by the upbringing of most of the educated class. It is not the same with the numberless, unlimited functions which the government must assume when it exceeds these limits. It is at once less necessary that these new functions should be fulfilled, more difficult to do them well, and more dangerous if they are done badly. They do not have the same [74] sanction as the necessary functions. Utility is their only claim. Now, this utility rests only on the supposed superior qualities of the governors over the governed. When the only thing we have shown is that this superiority is doubtful, this constitutes for me an irrefutable objection to these functions. Terminology has been behind most false ideas. Impersonal verbs have misled political writers. They thought they were saying something when they said there has to be direction of men's opinions. One must not abandon men to their erratic minds. There has to be an impact on thought. There are opinions men can usefully take advantage of in order to deceive others. But these words—*there has to be, one must, one must not*—do not these refer to men too? You would think the talk were about another species. All the sentences which deceive us here, however, come down to saying: men must control the views of men. Men must not leave other men to their erratic thoughts. Men can usefully exploit opinions in order to deceive men. Impersonal verbs seem to have persuaded our philosophers that there is something else besides men in governing groups.

We can reply to those who want to subject the intelligence of the many to that of the few what a famous Roman said to his son when the latter proposed to take a town, with the sacrifice of three hundred soldiers. Would you care to be one of this three hundred? And it should also be added that it is not certain that the town will be taken.[10]

CHAPTER FOUR

Are Governmental Mistakes Less Dangerous Than Those of Individuals?

Governments being like individuals subject to mistakes, we must now explore whether governmental mistakes are less serious than those of individuals. For one might confine oneself to saying that mistakes being inevitable, it is better that governments make them, and people obey. This would be in some sense to confer on government full powers to get things wrong in our stead. But government mistakes are a serious nuisance in three ways. First of all, they [75] create positive ill just by their wrongness in principle. In the second place, however, men, being forced to resign themselves to them, adjust their interests and behavior to them too. Then, when the error is recognized, it is almost as dangerous to destroy it as to

10. Hofmann failed to find the source of this anecdote.

let it continue. Government, sometimes struck with the danger of continuing with defective arrangements, sometimes with the danger of repudiating them, follows an uncertain and wavering course and ends up doubly offensive. Finally, when the erroneous policy collapses, new troubles result from the upset to people's calculations and the slighting of their practices. Doubtless individuals can make mistakes too; but several basic differences make theirs far less fatal than those of government. If individuals go astray, the laws are there to check them. When government goes wrong, however, its mistakes are fortified with all the weight of the law. Thus the errors of government are generalized, and condemn individuals to obedience. The mistakes of individual interest are singular. One person's mistake has absolutely no influence on the conduct of another. When government remains neutral, any mistake is detrimental to him who commits it. Nature has given every man two guides: his interest and experience. If he mistakes his interest, he will soon be enlightened by his personal losses, and what reason will he have for persisting? He need consult no one save himself. Without anyone's noticing it or forcing it on him, he can withdraw, advance, or change direction, in a word, freely set himself straight. The government's situation is the exact opposite. Further away from the consequences of its measures and not experiencing their effects in so immediate a way, it discovers its mistake later. When it does discover it, it finds itself in the presence of hostile observers. Quite correctly it is afraid of being discredited by the process of rectification. Between the moment when government strays from the path of virtue and the moment when it notices, lots of time slips by; but even more between the latter point and the moment it starts to retrace its steps, and the very action of retracing is dangerous too. Therefore whenever it is not necessary, that is, whenever there is no question of the punishment of crimes or resistance to foreign invasions, it is better to run the natural risk of individual mistakes than [76] the risk of equally likely government ones. The right I guard most jealously, said some philosopher or other, is to be wrong. He spoke truly. If men let governments take this right away, they will no longer have any individual freedom, and this sacrifice will not protect them from mistakes, since government will merely substitute its own for those of individuals.[11]

11. [Hofmann suggests that the philosopher in question is none other than Constant himself, resorting to a stylistic device. Translator's note]

CHAPTER FIVE

On the Nature of the Means Political Authority Can Use on the Grounds of Utility

We come to the third question. Do not the means which governments possess, when they are used on the vague pretext that they are useful, produce harm greater than the good which governments intend to attain?

All human faculties can be abused. But when we fix our gaze on the abuses of these faculties and persuade ourselves in a facile fashion that it is good to restrain them, or when we think that government must constrain man to make the best use possible of these faculties, we are envisaging the question from a very incomplete perspective. One should never lose sight of what the restrictions on these faculties lead to.

The theory of government comprises two comparative terms: the usefulness of the end and the nature of the means. It is a mistake to think just of the first of these, since this leaves out of the reckoning the pressure these means exert, the obstacles they encounter, and therefore the danger and misfortune [77] of clashes. One can then make a great show of the advantages one is proposing to obtain. As long as one describes these advantages, one will see the purpose as marvelous and the arrangements beyond reproach. There is no despotism in the world, however inept its plans and oppressive its measures, which does not know how to plead some abstract purpose of a plausible and desirable kind. If this is unattainable, however, or achievable only via means whose resultant ill exceeds the good aspired to, a great deal of eloquence will have been squandered in vain, and we will have been gratuitously subjected to a lot of vexations.

This consideration will guide us in this work. We will apply ourselves mostly to pinning down the results of the means which political authority can use, exercising the powers it assumes, when the pretext for its acts is their utility. We will finish by examining how far the examples the nations of antiquity have left us are applicable to modern peoples, to the practices and customs—in a word, the moral nature—of contemporary societies.

Governments can use two sorts of means—prohibitive or coercive laws, and the acts we call measures for securing public order in ordinary circumstances or "coups d'Etat" in extraordinary ones. Several authors say government has means of a third type. They speak constantly of action on public opinion of a gentle or adroit or indirect kind. To create public opinion, to revive public opinion, to enlighten public opinion—these are words we find attributed to the powers of government on every page of all the pamphlets and books, in all the political projects and, during the French Revolution, we found it in all the acts of government. There has always seemed to me, however, to be a troubling side to this thesis. I have always observed that all government measures which seek to influence in this way, result in punishments for those who evade them. Apart from proclamations, which in consequence are seen as mere formalities, government, when it begins with advice, finishes with menaces. Indeed, as Mirabeau put it very well, everything which depends on thought, or opinion, is individual.[12] It is [78] never as a government that a government persuades. In this capacity a government can only command or punish. Therefore I do not count among the real means of authority these double-faced endeavors which for government are only dissimulation, which it will soon drop as useless or inconvenient. I will return to this subject in a special chapter at the end of this book.[13] Here I confine myself to the two means which really are at the disposal of the government.

Republics, when they are at peace, produce endless prohibitive and coercive laws. In troubled times, they are equally liable to coups d'Etat. This form of government has the danger that the men who get to the top do not have the habit of government and do not know how to get around the difficulties. Each time they meet one, they think violence is necessary. They suspend the laws, overturn due process, and bleat stupidly that they have saved the fatherland. But a country made secure each day on such a basis is soon a lost country.

Monarchies, unless they are very stupidly organized, normally restrict themselves to measures for securing public order, though they resort to them widely.

We can say that the multiplicity of laws is a sickness of States which claim to be free, because in these States people demand that the government do everything by means of laws. We have seen our demagogues, having trampled underfoot all ideas of justice and all natural and civil laws, calmly set out again to set up what they called laws.

12. Hofmann was not able to unearth this reference, which could refer equally to Honoré-Gabriel Riqueti, comte de Mirabeau, deputy to the Estates General and member of the Constituent Assembly of 1789, or to his father Victor, marquis de Mirabeau, the physiocrat known for his book called *L'ami des hommes,* which Constant also quotes.

13. See, for example, Book XII, Ch. 7, *Des encouragements.* Constant's remark shows that at this stage of the writing, he had not yet decided on the definitive plan of his book.

One can say that the absence of laws, plus measures for public order and arbitrary acts, are the sickness of governments which make no pretense of being free, because in these governments authority does everything by using men.

This is why in general there is less personal independence in republics, but less personal security in monarchies. I am speaking of these two types of State when they are properly conducted. In republics dominated by factions or monarchies inadequately constituted and established, the two disadvantages go together.

We are going to examine in the first place the effects of the [79] multiplicity of laws on the happiness and moral life of individuals. We may find that this rash proliferation, which in some eras has thrown disfavor onto everything which is most noble in the world, such as freedom, has made men seek refuge in the most wretched, lowest of things, namely slavery. Then we will deal also with the effects arbitrary measures have on the morality and happiness of citizens.

The reader will then be able to compare the means political authority uses when it exceeds its indispensable limits, with the purpose it ought to have in mind, to see if the government attains this purpose and to judge finally whether this purpose, supposing it to be attained, is a sufficient compensation for the effect on moral life of the means used to achieve it.

A. [Refers to page 52.]
Esprit des lois, II, 2.[14]

B. [Refers to page 52.]
Discours sur Tite-Live, I, 47.[15]

14. *Ed. cit.,* p. 533. The last sentence quoted by Constant has been displaced. In the original it comes immediately after the first sentence: "The people . . . a part of their authority." Moreover, he has replaced the word "things" in the last sentence by "reasons" (French "motifs").

15. Machiavelli, *Discours sur la première décade de Tite-Live.* Constant in fact quotes the actual title of Ch. 47: *Que les hommes, quoique sujets à se tromper dans les affaires générales, ne se trompent pas dans les particulières.* Machiavelli, *Oeuvres complètes,* text presented and annotated by Edmond Barincou, Paris, Gallimard, 1952, p. 480 (Bibliothèque de la Pléiade).

BOOK IV

On the Proliferation of the Laws

CH. 1. Natural causes of the proliferation of the laws. 63
CH. 2. The idea which usually develops about the effects which the proliferation of the laws has and the falsity of that idea. 63
CH. 3. That the principal benefit which supporters of democratic government are looking for in the proliferation of the laws does not exist. 65
CH. 4. On the corruption which the proliferation of the laws causes among the agents of the government. 66
CH. 5. Another drawback of the proliferation of the laws. 67

CHAPTER ONE

Natural Causes of the Proliferation of the Laws

The proliferation of the laws flatters the lawmaker in relation to two natural human inclinations: the need for him to act and the pleasure he gets from believing himself necessary. Anytime you give a man a special job to do, he does more rather than less. Those who are ordered to arrest vagabonds on the main roads are tempted to look for quarrels with all travelers. When spies have not found out anything, they invent. It has been remarked that all one needed to do in a country for talk of conspiracies to be heard constantly was to create a ministry to maintain surveillance on conspirators. Those in government always want to be governing; and when, because of the division of powers, a group of them are told to make laws, they cannot imagine they could possibly make too many.

Lawmakers parcel out human existence, by right of conquest, like Alexander's generals sharing the world.

CHAPTER TWO

The Idea Which Usually Develops about the Effects Which the Proliferation of the Laws Has and the Falsity of That Idea

People normally think that when the government allows itself to multiply prohibitive and coercive laws at will, provided that the intention of the legislator is clearly expressed, provided that the laws are not in any way retroactive, provided that citizens are told in time of the rule of behavior they must follow, the [84] proliferation of laws has no drawback other than cramping individual freedoms a little. This is not the case. The proliferation of laws, even in the most ordinary of circumstances, has the bad effect of falsifying individual morality. The actions which fall within the competence of government, according to its primary purpose, are of two kinds: those intrinsically harmful which government must punish; and arrangements contracted between individuals which government must uphold. As long as government stays within these limits, it does not establish any contradiction, any difference, between legislative morality and natural morality. But when it prohibits actions which are not criminal or demands the completion of those which have not become obligatory owing to prior contract and which consequently are based only on its will, there are brought into society two kinds of crimes and two kinds of duties: those which are intrinsically such and those government says are such. Whether individuals make their judgment subservient to government or maintain it in its original independence, this produces equally disastrous effects. In the first hypothetical case, moral behavior becomes hesitant and fickle. Acts are no longer good or bad by reason of their good or bad outcomes, but according to whether law commands or forbids them, much as theology used to represent them as good because they pleased God, rather than as pleasing to God because they were good. The rule of the just and the unjust is no longer in the consciousness of man but in the will of the legislator. Morality and inner feeling undergo an unfathomable degradation through this dependence on an alien thing, a mere accessory—artificial, unstable, and liable to error and perversion. In the contrary case, in which a man—by supposition—opposes the law, the result is first of all many individual troubles for him and those whose fates depend on his. But in the second place, will he bother for very long disputing the law's competence in matters he considers outside it? If he violates prohibitions and orders which seem to him arbitrary, he runs the same dangers as he would infringing the rules of eternal morality. Will not this unjust equality of consequences bring about a confusion in all his ideas? Will not his doubts, without distinction, touch on all the actions the law forbids or requires, and in the heat of his dangerous struggle with the institutions menacing him, do we not have to fear that he will soon not be able to tell good from bad any longer, nor law from the state of nature?[1]

[85] Most men are kept from crime by the feeling of never having crossed the line of innocence. The more restrictedly that line is drawn, the more are men put at risk of transgressing it, however light the infraction. Just by overcoming their first scruples, they have lost their most reliable safeguard. To get around restrictions which seem to them pointless, they use means which they could use against the most sanctified of laws. They acquire thereby the habit of disobedience, and even when they want some end which is still innocent, they go astray because of the means they are forced to follow to achieve it. Forcing men to refrain from things which are not forbidden morally or imposing on them duties which morality does not require of them, is therefore not only to make them suffer, but to deprave them.

1. See Constant's Note A at the end of Book IV.

CHAPTER THREE

That the Principal Benefit Which Supporters of Democratic Government Are Looking for in the Proliferation of the Laws Does Not Exist

We said that proliferation of the laws was the sickness of states claiming to be free. The friends of democratic government have recourse to a specious argument to justify them. It is better, they say, to obey laws than men. The law must command in order that men shall not. This is no doubt true, when it is a question of obeying, and when commanding is called for. On countless matters, however, men and law alike should keep quiet, since one should not obey either.

Moreover, it is a mistake to hope the proliferation of laws will save us from the tyranny of men. In multiplying laws you necessarily create more government agents. Consequently you give a larger number of men power over their fellows and thus double the likelihood of its arbitrary misuse. This is because however precise these laws, there is always the possibility of arbitrariness, if only in the more or less severe exactness with which they are carried out.

[86] Furthermore, all written law is liable to evasion. The legislator tries in vain to provide for this with minatory precautions and detailed formalities. His expectations are always disappointed. Out of the challenge which each individual puts to the laws comes an infinite diversification of actions. A fatal struggle begins between legislator and citizen. Individual wills are irritated to find everywhere a general will which claims the right to repress them. The law subdivides, becomes more complex, multiplies: all in vain. People's actions always manage to slip away from its proceedings. The legislator wants to defend his work just as the citizen defends his freedom. A law disobeyed calls for a tougher one. This in turn, if it is not carried out, calls for a harsher one still. The progression is endless. Finally, the legislator, tired of so many futile efforts, stops making precise laws, because experience has convinced him they are too easy to evade, however strict they may be. He makes vague laws and in this way the tyranny of men is in the final analysis the result of the proliferation of laws. It was in this way in our country that those claiming to be republicans began with hundreds of decrees—puerile, barbarous,

and never carried out—against the clergy. They ended by giving five men the right to deport priests without trial.[2]

CHAPTER FOUR

On the Corruption Which the Proliferation of the Laws Causes among the Agents of the Government

Another drawback of the proliferation of the laws is that it inevitably corrupts the agents charged with making sure that [87] they are not broken or evaded. The law does not need to pay informers to make sure crimes are tracked down and punished. The individuals they hurt naturally take it upon themselves to demand reparation for them. But when laws proliferate, this is a sign that government is no longer keeping to its natural sphere; and then its activities run up against new obstacles. When, on the pretext that this is useful, the laws are aimed at things which are by their very nature not criminal, no one has any interest in denouncing transgressions which do him no harm. Government has to create an interest group; only corruption can create this. In this way, by acting outside its proper sphere, government corrupts, not only in a general way, as we saw above, those on whom it acts; it also corrupts in particular those through whom it acts. Hired ruffians, spies, and informers are men too. When the government buys them to push them to the extremities of perversity and infamy, it is dedicating a portion of the citizen-body to baseness and crime and aiming a blow at the morality of the rest, by offering everyone the example of crime rewarded.

Those in power wrongly imagine that they alone profit from the corruption of their agents. The men who sell themselves to the government by betraying others, sell themselves in the same way to others by betraying government. Such depravity is communicated to all classes of people.

2. This is a reference first of all to the law of 20 fructidor an III (6 September 1795), then to that of 3 brumaire an IV (25 October 1795), which arranged for measures against refractory priests, and that of 7 vendémaire an IV (29 September 1795), which required priests to recognize the people's sovereignty; and next to the law of 19 fructidor an V (5 September 1797), which effectively authorized the Directory to deport priests who would not comply. The issue is summarized in the book by Denis Woronoff, *La république bourgeoise de Thermidor à Brumaire, 1794–1799,* Paris, Ed. du Seuil, 1972, pp. 139–146 (Nouvelle histoire de la France contemporaine, 3). For more details, see Jean Boussoulade, *L'Eglise de Paris du 9 Thermidor au Concordat,* Paris, Procure générale du Clergé, 1950.

Prohibitive and coercive laws are always instruments of a dangerous sort, and the danger increases as their number and complexity grow. Laws even when directed against crime are not without drawbacks, but they are legitimated by their urgent necessity. In face of the certain prospect of the whole of society falling apart, the outcome which the impunity of crimes would produce, any drawbacks in the detail must count for nothing. When, however, it is a question of usefulness only, that is, of an imprecise and shifting calculus, what could be more absurd than sacrificing to this calculus known advantages: calm, happiness, and the good morals of the governed?

These observations hold equally strongly under all forms of government. They apply especially, however, to governments affecting to be free. Some so-called lovers of freedom have for too long cherished the idea of controlling all human actions and destroying in the human heart anything going against their deliberations or resisting their theories. The laws of liberty, says Rousseau, are a thousand times [88] more austere than the tyrant's harsh yoke.[3] It is no wonder these ardent and bungling apostles have made the doctrine they preached in this way so detested. One can repeat in vain: the most indispensable condition for getting men to adopt the principles of liberty will always be, whatever one does, the possession of liberty.

CHAPTER FIVE

Another Drawback of the Proliferation of the Laws

Laws proliferate against the intentions and even without the knowledge of the successive generations of legislators. They pile up in various branches, fall into disuse, and are forgotten by the governed. They hover above them, even so, hidden in a cloud. "One of the worst aspects of the tyranny of Tiberias," says Montesquieu,[4] "was his abuse of old laws."

Tiberias had inherited all the laws produced by the civil strife in Rome. Now, civil strife produces violent and harsh laws and on top of these countless detailed regulations which are destructive of all individual freedom. These things survive the storms which created them. The government which inherits this pernicious armory finds every injustice authorized in advance by the laws. For purposes of large-scale persecution, there is an arsenal of unknown laws, legitimating every iniquity. For everyday purposes there is a repertoire of controls, less odious but more routinely vexatious.

3. Hofmann has not located this sentence anywhere in Rousseau's work.

4. See Constant's Note B at the end of Book IV.

In this situation, everything favors the government and [89] imperils the citizens. The government takes it upon itself not to execute defective laws or barbarous ones. This can hardly be seen as a crime. In this way, however, it gets used to infringing its duties and soon comes to subject the whole corpus of law to its adjudication. All its actions end up being arbitrary. Nor is this all. The government does not repeal these oppressive laws, the nonenforcement of which wins public gratitude. They lie as if in ambush, ready to reappear at the first signal and fall on the citizens unawares.

I think it would be a useful safeguard in all countries if there were an obligatory periodic revision of all the laws at fixed intervals. Among those nations which have bestowed legislative powers on representative assemblies, these bodies would naturally be given this function. After all, it would be absurd if the body which votes the laws did not have the right to rescind them and if its work were to go on in uncorrected error, in spite of that body's own judgment, and in spite of its regrets and remorse. This organization would then be like our former and detestable statutes concerning those accused of trying to emigrate. The government had the power to put people on the list but not to remove them,[5] an admirable arrangement for making injustice irreparable.

In those countries with all power concentrated in the same hands, it would still be salutary to require government to let it be known periodically which laws it wants to keep. All the branches of the law contain some which governments make use of, because they find them ready-made. But they would often be ashamed to take upon themselves the public responsibility of a new approbation.

5. On this jurisprudence, see Marc Bouloiseau, *Etude de l'émigration et de la vente des biens des émigrés (1792–1830),* Paris, Impr. nat., 1963, Deuxième Partie, *Les étapes de la législation,* Ch. 1, pp. 76–91.

CONSTANT'S NOTES

A. [Refers to page 64.]

Esprit des lois, XXIV, 14, "The laws which make what is unimportant be seen as necessary have as a disadvantage that they make what is necessary seem unimportant."

B. [Refers to page 67.]

Esprit de lois, VII, 13.

BOOK V

On Arbitrary Measures

CH. 1. On arbitrary measures and why people have always protested less about them than about attacks on property. 73
CH. 2. On the grounds for arbitrary measures and the prerogative of preventing crimes. 74
CH. 3. Specious argument in support of arbitrary government. 77
CH. 4. On the effect of arbitrary measures in terms of moral life, industry, and the duration of governments. 78
CH. 5. On the influence of arbitrary rule on the governors themselves. 80

CHAPTER ONE

On Arbitrary Measures and Why People Have Always Protested Less About Them Than about Attacks on Property

Governments which make no claim to be free escape some of the disadvantages of the proliferation of laws, by recourse to arbitrary measures. One by one these measures press only on isolated individuals, and though they threaten all citizens, the majority of those so threatened delude themselves about the danger that hangs over their heads unnoticed. Hence it happens that under governments which make only a moderate use of arbitrary measures, life seems at first more pleasant than in republics which harass their citizens with proliferating and irritating laws. Moreover it takes a degree of reflection, it takes accurate understanding and farsighted reason, such as develops only out of habituation to freedom itself, to perceive, right from the start, and in a single arbitrary act, all the consequences of this terrible expedient.

One of the characteristics of our nation is that it has never attached enough importance to individual security. To imprison a citizen arbitrarily, to hold him indefinitely in jail, to separate him from his wife and children, to shatter his social life, to upset his economic plans: all this has always seemed to us quite a simple set of measures, at the least excusable. When these measures hurt us or things dear to us, we complain, but about the mistake rather than the injustice. Indeed, rather few men in the long history of our various oppressions have earned for themselves the easily gained credit of protesting on behalf of those in different situations from themselves.

It has been pointed out that M. de Montesquieu, who vigorously defends the rights of individual property even against the State's own interests, is much cooler in his treatment of individual freedoms,[1] as if people were less sacred than [94] goods. There is a straightforward reason in the case of a preoccupied and egotistical people for the fact that the rights of individual

1. A reference to Livre XXVI, Ch. 15 of *De l'esprit des lois,* in which Montesquieu says: "It is false reasoning to say that the individual good must yield to the public good: that holds only when what is at issue is the authority of the state, that is to say, the liberty of the citizen. This is not what happens in those cases when the issue is the ownership of goods, because the public good is always that everyone shall invariably keep possession of the property which the civil laws allow." *Ed. cit.,* p. 716.

freedom are less well protected than those of property. The man whose liberty is removed is disarmed by this very fact, while the man who is stripped of his property retains his freedom to demand it back. Thus freedom is never defended except by the friends of an oppressed person, while property is defended by the oppressed person himself. One can see that the intensity of the claims is likely to differ as between the two cases.

CHAPTER TWO

On the Grounds for Arbitrary Measures and the Prerogative of Preventing Crimes

Arbitrary measures are often justified in terms of their alleged utility. They aim to preserve order and prevent crime. It has been said countless times that it is better to prevent crimes than to punish them, and since this vague proposition is consistent with a number of interpretations, no one has so far taken into his head to put the question in doubt.

If we mean by the prerogative of crime prevention the right to distribute a mounted constabulary around the highways or break up gatherings before they have caused disorder, government has this right, and it is more appropriately called one of its duties. The right to stop crimes, however, is all too often the freedom to treat innocent people harshly for fear they might become criminal. Are certain individuals thought likely to conspire? They are arrested and kept apart, not because they are criminal but to prevent them from becoming so. Is a particular group considered criminally disposed? It is marked off in a humiliating way from other citizens and subjected to legal formalities and precautionary measures from which other people are exempt.

We will long remember the various innovations signaling what we call the Reign of Terror, the law of suspects, the banishment of the nobles, and the proscription [95] of priests.[2] The interests of these groups, it was asserted, being contrary to public order, it had to be feared they might upset it, and one would rather prevent their crimes than punish them—proof of what we observed above, that a republic dominated by a faction, adds to the disorders of anarchy all the harassment of despotism. On the other hand, some tyrant or other of a small Italian principality arrogated to

2. On these numerous revolutionary laws, see Jacques Godechot, *Les institutions de la France sous la Révolution et l'Empire,* Paris, PUF, 1951, Ch. V, *La justice révolutionnaire,* pp. 316–328.

himself the right to deport people at will, on the pretext that it was part of his clemency to prevent men inclined to crime from giving in to this fatal tendency.[3] Proof again of what we have said: the improperly constituted or ratified government of a single man adds to constant and unspoken abuses, the noisy and scandalous practices of factions.

The pretext of crime prevention has the most immense and incalculable consequences. Potential criminality inheres in everybody's freedom, in the lives of all classes, in the growth of all human faculties. Those in authority endlessly affecting to fear that a crime may be committed, may weave a vast web that envelops all the innocent. The imprisonment of suspects, the endless confinement of those whom due process would acquit, but who instead may find themselves subjected to the indignity of prolonged detention, the arbitrary exile of those believed dangerous, though there is nothing they can be reproached with, the enslavement of thought, and then that vast silence so pleasing to the ear of government: this pretext explains all these. Every event offers a justification. If the crime the government claimed it feared does not occur, the credit goes to its watchfulness. If one or two unjustified actions provoke opposition, this resistance to which injustice alone led is itself quoted in support of such injustice. Nothing is simpler than passing off the effect for the cause. The more a government measure offends against freedom and reason, the more it drags in its wake disorder and violence. Then government attributes the need for the measure to the disorder and violence themselves. Thus we have seen the agents [96] of the Terror among us forcing priests to resistance by refusing them any security when they submit and then justifying clerical persecution by their resistance.[4] Similarly the Romans saw Tiberius, when his victims disappeared in silence, glorying in the peace he was maintaining in the empire, and then when complaints made themselves heard, finding justification for tyranny in what his flatterers called attempted sedition.

The pretext that crime is being prevented can be shifted from domestic politics to foreign affairs. This results in the same abuses just as the same sophisms justify it. Are those in power provoking our most peaceful neighbors and faithful allies? All they are doing, they say, is punishing hostile intentions and forestalling attacks now being considered. How can we show

3. Constant's information, which Hofmann has not been able to trace, probably came from Sismondi, who was a specialist in the history of the Italian republics.

4. On refractory priests and their persecution, see Jacques Godechot, *Les institutions . . . , op. cit., passim,* using the index references.

the nonexistence of these intentions, the impossibility of these attacks? If the unfortunate nation they calumniate is easily intimidated, our governing group has forestalled it, since it is submitting. If it has time to resist these hypocritical aggressors, it wanted war because it is defending itself. To show that this picture is in no way exaggerated, one need only recall the war in Switzerland.[5]

"What?" someone will say, "when the government knows a conspiracy is being hatched in the shadows, or that thieves are plotting to murder a citizen and plunder his home, it will have resources to punish the guilty persons only once the crime has happened!" Two very different things are confounded here: crimes actually begun, and the alleged will to commit crimes. The government has the duty and therefore the right to keep an eye on trends which look dangerous to it. When it has evidence of the conspiracy being hatched or the murder being pondered, it can make sure of the men this evidence points to. In this case, however, this is not an arbitrary measure but a legal action. This is precisely when these men must be brought before independent courts. This is the very time when the detention of the accused must not be prolonged if proof is not forthcoming. As long as government has only [97] suspicions about people's intentions, it must keep guard passively, and the object of its worries must not feel their effect. It would be an intolerable condition for men to be constantly at the mercy of government suspicions.

To render the prerogative of prevention admissible, we must distinguish again between the jurisdiction of authority over actions and its jurisdiction over individuals. Our safeguard against arbitrary government lies in this distinction. The government sometimes has the right to direct its powers against harmless or innocent actions, when they seem to it to lead on to dangerous results. It never has the right, however, to make this same power weigh on individuals who are not clearly guilty, even when their intentions are suspect to it, and their resources seem such as to be feared. If, for example, a country were infested with armed gatherings, it would not be unjust for a brief period to put obstacles in the way of all meetings,

5. On 28 January 1789, General Ménard occupied the Pays de Vaud, which had just emancipated itself from the control of Berne four days earlier. At the beginning of February 1798, Generals Brune and Schauenbourg began military operations against Berne. See Johannès Dierauer, *Histoire de la Confédération suisse,* Lausanne, Payot, 1929, t. IV, Ch. IV and V, pp. 465–573. Constant and Mme. de Staël had tried to oppose the policy of the Directory and of Napoleon against the Swiss. See Hofmann's thesis, Première Partie, Ch. 2, p. 167, n. 215.

obstacles which would hurt innocent and guilty alike. If, as happened in parts of Germany, arson was becoming widespread, one could attach a punishment to the mere transport or mere possession of certain combustible materials. If there were a high murder rate as in Italy, the bearing of arms could be forbidden to all individuals, without distinction. The exemplary nuances here are infinite. The most innocent of actions in intention may in certain contexts cause as much harm as the most criminal ones. Of course this principle must be applied with great caution, since the prohibition of any noncriminal act is always harmful to the moral life as well as the freedom of the governed. Nevertheless, government cannot be denied this latitude. Interdictions of the kind we have been considering have to be regarded as legitimate, as long as they are general. But these same interdictions, were they to be directed exclusively against certain individuals or classes, as happened so often during our Revolution, would become unjust. They would be nothing else than punishments which had got ahead of the crime. For it is a punishment that there should be an unseemly distinction between equally innocent men. The unwarranted deprivation of freedom which others enjoy is a punishment. Now, all punishment which does not stem from legally proven crime is itself a governmental crime. [98]

CHAPTER THREE

Specious Argument in Support of Arbitrary Government

The actions of government, we are told, bear down only on imprudent souls who provoke them. The man who resigns himself and keeps silent is always safe. Reassured by this worthless and specious argument, we do not protest against the oppressors. Instead we find fault with the victims. Nobody knows how to be brave even prudentially. Everyone stays silent, keeping his head low in the self-deceiving hope of disarming the powers that be by his silence. People give despotism free access, flattering themselves they will be treated with consideration. Eyes to the ground, each person walks in silence the narrow path leading him safely to the tomb. But when arbitrary government is tolerated, bit by bit it spreads out between so many participants that the least known of citizens may find his enemy in a position of power. Whatever cowardly hearts may hope for, fortunately for the morality of humankind, our safety calls for more than mere standing to one side and letting the blows fall on others. A thousand links bind us to our peers and even the most frantic egoism cannot break all of them. You think you are safe in your deliberate obscurity and your shameful apathy. But you have a son and youth gets the better of him, a brother less cautious than you permits himself a murmur, an old enemy you once wounded who has got himself a bit of power, and in his fantasies some corrupt military leader is coveting your house in Alba. What will you do then? Having bitterly condemned all struggles against the powers that be, will you struggle in your turn? You are condemned in advance both by your own conscience and by that degraded public opinion you yourself helped to create. Will you give in without resistance? But will they let you give in? Will they not exile or persecute this annoying case, this monument to injustice? Innocent people disappeared. You saw them as guilty. You prepared the road you now walk along in your turn. [99]

CHAPTER FOUR

On the Effect of Arbitrary Measures in Terms of Moral Life, Industry, and the Duration of Governments

If we look at the effects of arbitrary measures in terms of moral life, industry, or even the duration of governments, we will find them equally disastrous.

When a government ruthlessly strikes out against men it suspects, it is not just an individual it persecutes; rather it is the whole nation it slights and degrades. People always try to shake off their sorrow. When what they love is threatened, they either detach themselves from it or defend it. When there is no security, there is no moral life. There are no gentle affections unless we know that the objects of such affection are safe, their innocence a safeguard in itself. Habits become corrupted suddenly in towns attacked by the plague. The dying steal from each other.[6] Arbitrary government is to moral life what plague is to the body. It reduces citizens to the choice between forgetting all finer feelings and hatred of the government. When a people coldly contemplates a succession of tyrannical acts, when, without a word of protest, it watches the prisons fill up and banishments multiply, when every man keeps silent and isolated, and, fearful for himself, tries to disarm the government by dissimulation or by the even worse device of

6. Cornelius de Pauw, *Recherches philosophiques sur les Grecs, op. cit.*, t. I, pp. 174–175, speaks of a plague at Athens under Pericles, but does not speak of the moral consequences of this illness.

assent, can anyone believe, with this despicable example on all sides, that a few banal sentences will suffice to reinvigorate feelings of honesty and generosity? People speak of the need for paternal authority. But the first duty of a son is to defend his father from ill-treatment; and when a father is taken away from his children and the latter are forced to maintain a cowardly silence, what then is the effect of your maxims and codes, your declarations and your laws? People pay homage to the sanctity of marriage; but on the basis of a shadowy denunciation, on a mere suspicion, [100] by measures called precaution, security, and law and order, a man is separated from his wife or a wife from her husband! Do they think conjugal love is by turns born again and vanishes at the government's pleasure? Family ties are much praised. But what upholds these ties is individual freedom, the hope founded on living together, living free in the shelter which justice guarantees the citizen. If family ties persisted, would fathers, children, husbands, wives, and friends—all those close to the people despotism oppresses—submit themselves to such despotism? They talk of credit, commerce, and industry; but the man they arrest has creditors, whose fortunes depend on his, and business partners. The result of his detention is not only the short-term loss of his freedom, but the interruption of his business, perhaps his ruin. This ruin embraces all who share his business activities. It goes further; it strikes against all thought and all personal safety is shaken. When an individual suffers without having been proven in any way guilty, anyone not deprived of intelligence rightly feels menaced by this destruction of constitutionality. People shut up because they are frightened; but all human exchange is affected. The very earth shakes and people walk fearfully.[7] Everything in our complex and extensive social life becomes static. The injustices thought of as individual are unfailingly sources of public ill too. It is not within our powers to restrict them to some fixed category.

Despotism aims at the very core of morality in order to degrade it. The brief respite it brings is precarious and gloomy, the precursor of terrible storms. We must make no mistake about this. However degraded a nation may seem from the outside, generous sentiments will always find shelter in a few solitary hearts, where, scandalized, they will seethe in silence. Parliamentary debating chambers may ring with furious ranting, and palaces echo with expressions of contempt for the human race. The flatterers of the people may stir us against pity itself; the flatterers of kings denounce

7. See Constant's Note A at the end of Book V.

courage to them. But no era will ever be so abandoned by providence that it will deliver up the whole human race in the shape despotism requires. [101] Hatred of oppression, whether in the name of one man or the name of all, has been handed down from age to age, under all forms of despotism. The future will not betray this most just of causes. There will always be men for whom justice is a passion and the defense of the weak something they must do. Nature has willed it so. No one has ever been able to stop it, nor ever will be able to. These men will always give way to this magnanimous instinct. Many will suffer, many perhaps will perish, but the earth with which their ashes will mingle will be stirred thereby and sooner or later will reawaken.

CHAPTER FIVE

On the Influence of Arbitrary Rule on the Governors Themselves

Once they have employed arbitrary measures, those in government find them so swift, so simple, so convenient, that they no longer want to use any other kind. In this way, introduced at first as a last resort in extraordinarily rare circumstances, despotic rule becomes the solution to all problems and an everyday practice. This treacherous mode of governance, however, a torment to those over whom it is exercised, also bears very heavily on the hand which uses it. A gnawing anxiety seizes governments once they enter this pathway. Their uncertainty is a sort of sense of responsibility mingled with remorse which weighs heavily on them. Since they no longer have proper procedure, they move forward and then back, and they get into a most anxious state, never knowing whether they are doing enough or too much. The rule of law would bring them peace of mind.

CONSTANT'S NOTES

A. [Refers to page 79.]

The banks, says Montesquieu, are incompatible with [102] pure monarchy.[8] This is another way of saying that credit is incompatible with despotism.

8. Constant is probably interpreting this passage from *De l'esprit des lois,* Livre XX, Ch. 10 (*éd. cit.,* p. 653): "In the States with commercial economies, banks have fortunately been established, which by means of credit have created new indices of value. But it would be a mistake to set them up in States which have only luxury commerce. To put them in countries governed by single individuals is to suppose money on the one hand and power on the other; that is, on the one hand the option to have everything without power, and on the other power and no option to have anything. Under such governments only the ruler has ever had or ever could have had accumulated wealth. Everywhere there is any such, once it becomes sizeable, it becomes first of all the prince's wealth." Constant has come back to this thought about Montesquieu and the banks in the Additions, p. 532, lines 10–11. See Annexe III in Hofmann, *Les "Principes de politique" de Benjamin Constant,* Droz, 1980, Tome II. [Hereafter referred to as *Principes de politique* (Hofmann's edition).]

BOOK VI

On Coups d'Etat

Ch. 1. On the admiration for coups d'Etat. 85

Ch. 2. On coups d'Etat in countries with written constitutions. 89

Ch. 3. The condition necessary to stop constitutional violations. 93

CHAPTER ONE

On the Admiration for Coups d'Etat

Across the centuries people have been agreed in their admiration for certain examples of expeditious illegality and political outrage. To admire these at one's leisure, one considers them in isolation, as if the facts which followed them did not form part of their consequences. The Gracchi,[1] so it is said, were endangering the Roman Republic. All established legal forms were impotent. Twice the Senate had recourse to the terrible law of necessity and the Republic was saved. The Republic was saved, that is to say that its loss must be dated from this period. All rights were ignored; all constitutionality overturned. The people, in terror one minute, soon resumed their claims, now fortified by vengeance. They had demanded no more than equal privileges; they now vowed that the murderers of their champions should be punished. The ferocious Marius came to preside over this vengeance. Catilina's accomplices were in irons. It was feared that other sympathizers might release them. Cicero[2] had them put to death without trial; and people constantly praise him for his prudence. To be sure, the fruits of his prudence and swift and illegal measures were at least short-lived. Caesar gathered Catilina's supporters around him and Rome's freedom died even before Cicero.[3] But if he had struck Caesar, Anthony was there; and behind Anthony [106] were yet others. The ambitions of the Guises much disturbed the reign of Henry III. It seemed impossible to bring them to trial. Henry had one of them murdered. Did his reign thereby become more peaceful? He was murdered himself. Twenty years of civil wars tore the French realm apart. For perhaps forty years afterward the admirable Henry IV bore the burden of the crime of the last Valois. In crises of this kind the guilty souls who are killed are never more than few in number. Others keep quiet, hide, and wait. They take advantage of the indignation which violence has repressed in people's minds, and of the consternation which seeming injustice spreads among law-abiding souls. In casting off the law, the government has lost both its legal character and its greatest asset; and when it is attacked by factions with weapons similar to its own, the mass of citizens may be divided, for it seems to them they have

1. See Constant's Note A at the end of Book VI.
2. See Constant's Note B at the end of Book VI.
3. See Constant's Note C at the end of Book VI.

only a choice between two factions. The interests of the State, the dangers of delay, public well-being: if you accept these lofty excuses, these specious words, every government or party will see the interests of the State in the destruction of its enemies, the dangers of delay in an hour spent pondering, and public safety in a condemnation without trial or proof.

When the presumed leaders of a conspiracy cannot be tried without fear that the people will release them, then the disposition of this people is such that punishing the leaders of this conspiracy is pointless. In this frame of mind the people will not be lacking in leaders. People speak casually of the effectiveness of coups d'Etat and of that expeditiousness which, by not giving factions time to get their bearings, reaffirms the authority of governments and the constitution of sovereign realms; yet history affords us not a single example of illegal stringencies producing a lasting salutary effect.

Doubtless political societies face moments of danger any degree of human prudence will find hard to avert. Such dangers, however, simply cannot be averted by violence and injustice, by bringing back the chaos of the state of savagery into the social state. On the contrary, this requires our adhering more scrupulously than ever to the established laws and to the tutelary observances and legal guarantees which protect us. Two advantages result from this courageous persistence in what is just and legal. Governments leave to their enemies all the odium [107] of impropriety and the violation of the most sacred laws. They also win, by the calm and security to which they bear witness, the trust of that timorous mass, who would remain at least undecided if extraordinary and arbitrary measures by the authorities showed that they felt there was a pressing danger. Finally, it must be said, it is sometimes decreed by destiny, that is to say by the inexorable chain of causes and effects, that a government must die, when its institutions form too great a contrast with the mores, habits, and outlooks of those it governs. There are, however, certain actions which the love of life cannot legitimize in individuals. It is the same with governments, and perhaps we will cease calling this simple moral rule simple-minded if we stop to reflect that it is fortified by an experience confirmed in the history of all nations. When a government has no other means than illegal measures to prolong its stay, these measures delay its fall only for a little while, and the overthrow it thought to prevent operates then with all the more misfortune and shame. My advice to those in power will always be: above all act justly, for if the existence of your power is not compatible with justice, then your power is not worth the trouble of conserving. Be just, for if you cannot live with justice, however hard you try with injustice, you will not last long.

I agree that this applies only to governments, whether republican or monarchist, claiming to rest on reasonable principles and affecting a show of moderation. A despotism like that of Constantinople can benefit from violating constitutional proprieties. Its very existence violates them permanently. It has perpetually to rain down blows on innocent and guilty alike. It condemns itself to live in fear of the accomplices it enlists, flatters, and enriches. It subsists by coups d'Etat until a coup d'Etat brings its own death at the hands of its henchmen. Any [108] moderate government, however, any wishing to rest on a system of proper order and justice, loses its way by any suspension of justice or any deviation from proper order. As it is in its nature to grow milder sooner or later, its enemies wait for just such a time to take advantage of memories which will do it damage. Violence seemed to save it for a moment. In fact it made its end the more inevitable, because in delivering it from certain adversaries it extended to everyone the hatred these adversaries bore it.

Many men see the causes of the day's events only in the acts of the day before. Thus, when violence, having produced a momentary stupor, is followed by a reaction which destroys the effect of this stupor, these men attribute this reaction to ending the violent measures, to insufficient proscriptions, and to the government's relaxing its grip. It seems to them that even more injustice would have prolonged the government's life.[4] This is like the reasoning of those bandits who are sorry they did not kill the travelers who denounce them, not stopping to think that murderers too are sooner or later discovered. It is in the nature of iniquitous decrees, however, to fall into disuse. Justice alone is stable. It is the nature of government to soften naturally, even without knowing it. Precautionary measures which have become odious are weakened and neglected. Public opinion counts despite its silence; power bends. But because it bends out of weakness rather than moderating itself for just reasons, it does not reconcile hearts to itself. Conspiracies begin anew and hatreds accumulate. The innocent victims of despotism reemerge stronger. The guilty condemned without trial seem innocent. The evil which was held back a few hours returns worse still, aggravated by the evil which has been done.

No, there is no excuse for means which serve all intentions and purposes alike, means which, invoked by good men against brigands, are found again in the words of brigands bearing the authority of good men, with the same apologia: necessity; and the same pretext: public well-being.

4. See Constant's Note D at the end of Book VI.

[109] The law of Valerius Publicola, which permitted the summary killing of anyone aspiring to tyrannical rule, on condition that the necessary evidence for the accusation would then be submitted, was a tool in turn of aristocratic and popular fury and brought down the Roman Republic.[5]

To permit society, that is, those in whom political power is invested, to violate legal proprieties is to sacrifice the very end one has in view to the means one uses. Why do we want the government to repress those who would attack our property, our freedom, or our lives? So that our lives, freedom, and wealth are secure. But if our wealth can be destroyed, our freedom threatened, our lives harassed by despotism, what assured good are we deriving from government protection? Why do we want government to punish would-be conspirators against the constitution of the State? Because we fear these conspirators will substitute an oppressive State for a lawful and moderate one. But if the government itself exercises this oppressive power, in what way is it better than the guilty people it punishes? Perhaps there is de facto superiority for a while, since the arbitrary measures of an established government will be less extensive than those of factions which have to establish their power; but this very advantage is lost progressively if governments act arbitrarily. Not only does the number of their enemies multiply in line with the number of their victims; but suspicion grows out of all proportion to the number of their enemies. One blow against individual freedom calls forth others. Once the government enters this fatal road, it finishes soon by being in no way preferable to a faction.

Almost all men have a mania for parading themselves as something more than they are. The mania writers have is for showing themselves to be statesmen. The result is that coups d'Etat, far from being reproved all around as they deserve, have generally been reported with respect and described obligingly. The author, seated peacefully at his desk, casts despotic advice in all directions. He tries to insert into his style the briskness he is recommending [110] in policy. He fancies himself for a moment cloaked in power because he is preaching its abuses, warming up his speculation with all the soaring force and potency which adorn his sentences. He thus gives himself something of the pleasure of government,

5. This probably refers to the law of Valerius Poplicola, Consul in 509 B.C., to whom Livy refers, *Histoire Romaine,* II.8.2: "Among others the law which permits an appeal to the public against a magistrate and that which places anathemas on the person and goods of anyone who aspires to the throne. . . ." Livy, *Histoire romaine,* Livre II, text edited by Jean Bayet and translated by Gaston Baillet, Paris, Les Belles Lettres, 1954, p. 13.

repeating at the top of his voice all the grand words about the well-being of the people, the higher law, and the public interest. He admires his own profundity and marvels at his own energy. Poor fool! He is talking to men who ask nothing better than to listen to him and one day make him the first victim of his own theory!

This vanity, which has perverted the judgment of so many writers, has caused more difficulties than one might think during our civil upheavals. All the mediocre minds which the flood of events put fleetingly at the head of affairs, filled as they were with all these maxims, all the more agreeable to stupidity in that they served it in cutting through the knots that it could not untie, dreamed only of measures for the public well-being, grand measures and coups d'Etat. They reckoned themselves amazing geniuses, because with each step they diverged from ordinary means. They proclaimed the vastness of their intellects, because justice seemed to them a narrow thing. Is there any need to say where all that has led us?

CHAPTER TWO

On Coups d'Etat in Countries with Written Constitutions

Coups d'Etat are at their most fatal in countries not governed by traditions, or public remembrance, or habit, whose institutions are determined by a positive charter, a written constitution.

During the whole course of our Revolution our governments claimed they had the right to violate the constitution in order to save it. The safekeeping of the constitution having been entrusted to them, they said, their duty was to prevent all the attacks people might dare to make on it; and since the pretext of prevention permits anything one may do or try to do, our governments, with their safeguarding foresight, have always discerned secret plots and treacherous intentions among those who offended them, and generously taken it upon themselves to commit real sins in order to prevent doubtful ones.

[111] Nothing serves to falsify ideas better than comparisons. People have said that you could step outside the constitution in order to defend it, much as the garrison of a beleaguered place might make a sortie against a force blockading it. This reasoning recalls that of the shepherd in the lawyer Patelin.[6] Since, however, it has at times covered France with gallows and

6. [This is a reference to a fifteenth-century farce of unknown authorship, *Le Maistre Pierre Patelin.* Translator's note]

ruins, and at others served as the pretext for the most oppressive despotism, I think it necessary to reply seriously to it.

A government which exists by a constitution ceases to exist as soon as the constitution which created it no longer exists, and a constitution ceases to exist the second it is violated.

Doubtless one can ask what the government ought to do when a party evidently wishes to overthrow the constitution. But this objection, pushed to a certain point, reaches deadlock. One can easily hypothesize a factual situation such as to defy all earlier precautions. One cannot organize moral counterweights to attempts using physical force. What is needed are institutions such as to deter parties from engaging in such attempts and from finding any advantage in them, and from having the means for doing so, institutions which ensure that if some maniac manages all this, the physical resources of the overwhelming majority are ready to resist the physical force he uses. This is what one calls public spirit. This is quite different, however, from the constitutional violations to which we have given the term "coups d'Etat" and which governments think about at their leisure and cause to break out when it suits them, with alleged necessity as their pretext.

It is probably inane to say in praise of a constitution that it would work well if everybody were willing to observe it. It is not inane to say, however, that if your basic objections include the hypothesis that nobody will want to respect the constitution and everyone will take pleasure in violating it without reason, then you will easily be able to show that no constitution can subsist. The physical possibility of an overthrow is always there. The whole point is to oppose moral barriers to this possibility.

[112] Any time people adopt or justify means which can be judged only after the event and are not accompanied by precise due process and legal safeguards, they are turning tyranny into a political system, because once the thing is done, the victims are no longer there to protest, and the only resources their friends have to avoid sharing their fate are acquiescence or silence. What is more, silence takes courage.

What is left after a constitution has been violated? No more security nor public trust. Among those who govern there is a feeling of usurpation, among the governed of being at the mercy of an arbitrary power. All protestation of respect for constitution by the former seems a mockery, and all appeals to that constitution by the latter seem like hostility. Even assuming the purest of intentions, all efforts will be fruitless. The governing group know they have prepared a sword which waits only for an arm strong enough to direct it against them.

Maybe the people might forget that the government is illegitimate and based on violation of the laws. The government cannot. It thinks about it, both because it sees as precarious an authority whose source it knows to be tainted, and because it has always at the back of its mind the worry of a possible coup d'Etat like the first one. It moves with difficulty and by way of shocks from day to day. On the other hand, not only the group attacked, but all those holding offices in the state whose powers are solely constitutional, feel that truth, eloquence, and all moral means are futile against a government which has become purely despotic. So they renounce all intellectual vigor. Slavishly they cringe and hate.

Everywhere the constitution has been violated it is provenly a bad constitution, for one of three things must be true: either it was impossible for the constituted powers to govern on its basis, or all those powers did not possess sufficient vested interest to maintain it, or lastly, [113] the powers opposed to the usurping tyranny did not have the means to defend it. But even supposing, *per impossibile,* that this constitution had been good, its power over men's minds has been destroyed. It loses everything which makes it respectable, or forms its mystique, as soon as its legality is assailed. Nothing is more common than for a State to be seen to live tolerably without a constitution. But the specter of a constitution outraged hurts liberty far more than the total absence of any constitutional act.

There are, I know, meretricious means of clothing constitutional violations with an apparent legitimacy. The people can be encouraged to make their judgment by way of joint petitions; they can be made to sanction the proposed changes.

Recourse was made to this expedient from the first days of our Revolution, though the Constituent Assembly, by allowing into its presence the delegates of the common herd, had done from the start what was needed to render the expedient ridiculous. But we have been wrong in thinking ridicule all-powerful in France. With us, ridicule attacks everything but destroys nothing, since vanity is quite content to have laughed at what happens, and each person, flattered by the superiority he has shown, then tolerates what he laughed at. The people's sanction can never be more than an idle formality. Alongside the acts submitted to this so-called sanction, there is always either the force of the existing government, provisional or fully established, which wants the acts accepted, or, on the unlikely supposition of its complete neutrality, the prospect, if there should be a refusal, of wars and civil dissensions. The people's sanction, and mass petitions, were born in the minds of those men who, finding no support, either in morality or reason, look for it in a simulated approbation which they obtain from ignorance or extract by terror.[7] The [114] legislators who make the worst laws are those who attach the most importance to law's being obeyed, just because it is the law, and without examination. Just so, the men who adopt the measures most contradictory to the common good, being unable to find reasons for them in the public interest, make good the lack by giving them the appearance of the people's will. This device cuts all objections short. Are there complaints that the people are being oppressed? They declared that they wanted to be.

Mass petitions should be banned by all nations having some idea of liberty. They can never be considered as the expression of true feelings. "The term 'people'," says Bentham, "is a forged signature to justify their leaders." Fear comes constantly, borrowing the language of action, to bow down before power, to congratulate itself for its servitude, and to encourage conquerors avid for vengeance to sacrifice the vanquished. Great adulation always follows great injustice. Rome prostrated itself not before Marcus Aurelius but rather before Tiberius and Caracalla. If I saw a nation being consulted in a country where public opinion was choked, freedom of the press annihilated, popular election destroyed, I would think I was watching tyranny asking its enemies for a list so that it could recognize them and strike them at its leisure.

For whom is it claimed that mass petitions are necessary? For the authors of a measure already taken? But they have acted. What belated scruple has suddenly seized them? How comes it that where they were once bold, now they are suddenly timid? For the people? But if the latter found fault with their conduct, would they retrace their steps? Used they not to say that critical petitions are the work of a rebel faction? Would they not have contrary petitions produced?

[115] Mass petitions are a purely illusory ceremony. Now, all illusory ceremony is worse than useless. There is something in this formality which wounds and degrades a people's spirit. All the appearances of freedom are forced on them in order that they vote in a direction prescribed

7. On the subject of mass petitions Constant said in his speech to the Tribunat of 12 pluviôse an VIII (1 February 1800): "There have been too many abuses of these during the course of our Revolution. Each one of our crises has been followed by a deluge of such petitions which never proved anything but the profound terror of the weak and the despotism of the strong." *Archives parlementaires. Recueil complet des débats législatifs et politiques des Chambres françaises de 1800 à 1860,* Paris, P. Dupont, t. I, p. 133.

in advance. This persiflage debases them in their own eyes and makes freedom ridiculous.

Mass petitions corrupt the people. They get them used to bowing before government; this is always a bad thing, even when the government is right.

CHAPTER THREE

The Condition Necessary to Stop Constitutional Violations

Although we have forbidden ourselves in this work any reflection on constitutions as such, what we have just established on the necessity of not violating them under any pretext, where they exist, forces us to speak about a condition which is indispensable for preventing these violations.

The happiness of societies and individual security rest on certain positive and fixed principles. These principles are true in all climates and latitudes. They cannot vary, whatever the extent of the country, its degree of civilization, its customs, religion, and usages. It is as incontestable in a hamlet of a hundred and twenty huts as in a nation of forty million men, that no one can be arrested arbitrarily, punished without having been tried, tried other than according to law and due process, prevented from manifesting his opinion or putting his industry to work or managing his options in an innocent and peaceful way.

A constitution is the guarantee of these principles. Consequently everything which stems from these principles is constitutional, and consequently also, nothing is constitutional which does not. There are great ground rules which all properly constituted powers [116] must be unable to touch. These powers together, however, must be able to do everything not contrary to these rules.

To stretch a constitution to cover everything is to make everything a danger to it. It is to create reefs to surround it. You cannot sufficiently predict the effect of incomplete arrangements to give up any leeway for changing them. A line, a word, in a constitution, can produce results of which you have not the least idea. If the constitution goes into a multitude of details, it will inevitably be violated: in little things, because the hindrances the government meets in its necessary business falling always on the governed, the latter themselves will call for this violation. But this constitution will also be violated in important things, because the government will move on from its violation of little ones in order to arrogate to itself the same freedom in important matters. A rather specious sophism will furnish it with an excuse. If considerations of slight utility permit us to deviate from the constitutional charter, it will say, there is much greater reason when it is a matter of saving the State.

The severe confinement of a constitution within its limits is a thousand times preferable to the superstitious veneration with which in some countries people have wanted to surround the successive constitutions they have been given, as if attachment and enthusiasm were transferable properties, always belonging by right of conquest to the constitution of the day.

This inevitably and manifestly hypocritical mass veneration has a number of drawbacks, like everything lacking in precision and truth.

The people either believe in it or they do not.

If they believe it, they regard the constitution as an indivisible whole, and when the frictions caused by the defects of this constitution hurt them, they break away from it totally. Instead of directing their discontent against certain bits whose improvement they could hope for, they direct it against the whole thing, which they see as incorrigible.

[117] On the other hand, if the people do not believe in the veneration professed, they become accustomed to suspecting the holders of power of hypocrisy and duplicity. They call into question everything the government says. They see lying honored; and it has to be feared that in their private lives they may resort to the same behavior their leaders exemplify publicly.

One can exist tolerably under a vicious government, when there is no constitution, because then the government is a variable thing which depends on men, which changes as they change, and which experience corrects or palliates. A vicious constitution, however, when it is unchangeable, is much more dire, because its defects are permanent, reproduce themselves endlessly, and cannot be imperceptibly or tacitly corrected by experience. To make the disadvantages of an imperfect government disappear for a while, one has only to displace or enlighten a few men. To battle against those of a bad constitution, one has to violate that constitution, that is to say, perform an ill much greater in its consequences to come than the present good one wants to attain.

People always imagine the modifications made to the constitution of a sovereign authority to be accompanied by terrible convulsions and great calamities. If they studied history they would see that these calamities most often take place only because nations form for themselves an exaggerated idea of their constitution and do not reserve for themselves any way of improving it imperceptibly. We noted earlier that man showed a singular facility for failing in his most real duties, once he freed himself from one duty, even an imaginary one. This truth applies to constitutions. When a nation has not kept in reserve in its political organization any way of correcting the latter's defects, the slightest modification [118] becomes as dangerous an act for that nation, and as unsettling, as the most total upheaval. If, however, envisaging its constitution only as a way of arriving at the highest possible degree of good fortune and freedom, the nation had set up within its organization itself, with all due precautions and periods of reflection, a means of bringing to bear on its constitution appropriate improvements, then, since it would not at all, in using this means, feel it was failing in a duty or subjecting society to a universal shake-up, the required or desired modification would be effected peacefully.

Any time it is necessary, to attain an end, that law and due process be violated, one has to fear that this effort in itself oversteps the purpose. When, on the contrary, the course is actually set by the constitution, movement becomes orderly. Men, having decided where they want to get, do not rush forward haphazardly and do not, slaves to the very movement they have chosen themselves, overstep the mark.

For stability itself, the possibility of a gradual improvement is a thousand times preferable to the inflexibility of an unchangeable constitution. The more secure the prospect of improvement, the less will malcontents have any purchase. One can defend a constitution as a whole to far better advantage by demonstrating to the people the appropriateness of postponing a change than by turning their having to persist with something they think an abuse into a kind of mystical duty and by opposing their belief with superstitious scruples which forbid scrutiny or render it pointless. At a certain level of social civilization all superstition, running counter to all other ideas, morals, and habits, has only a fleeting influence. Nothing is durable for a nation as soon as it has started to reason, unless it is explained by reasoning and demonstrated by experience.

The axiom of the English barons: we do not wish to change the laws of England, was much more reasonable than if they had said: we cannot. The refusal to change the laws, because one does not wish to change them, is explained either by the excellence of these laws or by the disadvantages of an immediate change. When such a refusal [119] is motivated by impotence, however, it becomes unintelligible. What is the cause of this impotence? What is the reality of the barrier put in our way? Whenever reason is excluded from the question, the question is falsified and one is working against one's purpose.

There are constitutional principles deriving from the rights of the human race, individual freedom, freedom of opinion, of the laws and the courts.

None of the authorities can be deemed competent to change the things which constitute the purpose of any association. Everything else is a matter of legislation. The longest mainstay of British liberty is that the three powers combined have a very extensive authority even over constitutional law.

I know nothing so ridiculous as what we have seen constantly replayed during our Revolution. A constitution is drawn up, we discuss it, enact it, put it to work. A thousand lacunae are noticed, a thousand superfluities perceived, a thousand doubts arise. The constitution is commented on, interpreted like some ancient manuscript one might newly have unearthed. The constitution is not explicit, people say, the constitution says nothing, parts of the constitution are shadowy. Oh, unhappy people! Do you really think a nation can be governed by enigmas and that what was yesterday the object of severe public criticism can transform itself suddenly into an object of silent veneration and foolish adoration?

Organize your various powers well. Give all their being, all their morality, all their private economic decision making, all their honorable hopes an interest in the conservation of your public establishment, and if the various branches involved wish collectively to benefit from experience in order to make, to their reciprocal relations, changes which in no way weigh down the citizens, nor threaten personal security, nor free thought, nor the independence of the [120] judiciary, nor the principles of equality, then leave them their full freedom in this regard.

"We have to learn to perfect the constitution," said the former Bishop of Autun, in his report on public education, on 10 September 1791. "In swearing to defend it, we have not been able to give up the right to improve it nor the hope thereof."[8]

If your combined authorities abuse the liberty you accord them, your constitution is corrupt, for a good constitution would have given them an interest in not abusing it.[9]

But, it will be said, constitutions are not the product of men's wills. Time makes them. They are brought in gradually and imperceptibly. They are not composed, as has been thought, of new elements, for the combining of which no cement would be solid enough. They are composed of old elements, more or less modified. All deliberately constructed constitutions

8. Charles-Maurice de Talleyrand-Périgord, *Rapport sur l'instruction publique fait au nom du Comité de constitution à l'Assemblée nationale les 10, 11 et 19 septembre 1791*, Paris, Baudoin et Du Pont, 1791, pp. 11–12.

9. See Constant's Note E at the end of Book VI.

have collapsed. All constitutions which have existed, or exist still, were not constructed. Why then seek principles for the construction of constitutions?

Without examining the idea supporting this objection, one which we believe in general true enough, we will say that the principle we have established does not apply solely to constitutions to be made, but to all constitutions which have been made. It demonstrates the necessity of freeing them from superfluous details, which prevent their being easily carried out. It proves they must contain within themselves peaceful means of improvement. For the more inflexible they are, the less they are respected.

As to remaining matters, our positive determination not to treat in this work any questions connected with the forms of government forces us to leave several lacunae unfilled and many objections unanswered. There are certain institutions which we consider incompatible with [121] freedom in certain given situations. It is clear that the various constituted authorities in a country cannot legitimately establish these institutions. But to assign this limit to the jurisdiction of the authorities, it would have been necessary to discuss the institutions they must be forbidden to adopt, and this is what we have resolved not to do.

CONSTANT'S NOTES

A. [Refers to page 85.]

N.B.: "The Gracchi wanted a revolution," says M. Ferrand, Esprit de l'histoire, Tome I, p. 262, "which no one has a right to want, which in a lawfully constituted state carries a sentence of death. Theirs was therefore pronounced by law, by the commonweal, by public order. It was not carried out by legal means, because they themselves had rendered these means impossible, because by disturbing society they had put themselves in a state of war. You will find some writers who have upbraided the Senate for the death of the Gracchi, just as they have upbraided Cicero for the death of Catalina's conspirators, and Henri III for the death of the Guises. In the circumstances in which these events took place, they derived from the right to security, which, belonging to every individual, is all the more the right of every society. A sovereign State, any State whatever, is doubtless at fault when it lets itself be reduced to this necessity as a result of developments it might have been able to stop; but it is guilty of a much greater one if, in turn applying the principles of society to what is subverting them, it did not carry out the condemnation pronounced by the first of these laws, salus populi [the safety of the people]. . . . When there is only one way of saving the State, the first law of all is to use it."[10]

I ask: what answer would there have been to the Committee of Public Safety, if these arguments were accepted? Note that when it is a question of a people, rather than a constituted government, it is quite another matter. Then M. Ferrand claims that the laws of proscription called *salus populi* have never saved the people;[11] that "any man living in a society has acquired three rights no one can take away from him and that he cannot lose other than by his own fault or will; these rights are his personal liberty, his property, his life"[12] (ibid., pp. 307, 310, 319). Now, therefore, [122] we will say to M. Ferrand, if you condemn him without due process or trial, how do you know his fault is such that he has merited losing these benefits? M. Ferrand continues: "It is not by dint of injustice that one can reorganize a

10. *Ed. cit,* pp. 261–263.

11. *Ibid.,* p. 319: "This is why the laws of proscription, of confiscation, which are called: *Salus populi,* have never saved the people."

12. *Ibid.,* p. 307, as Constant's first reference indicates; here is Ferrand's precise text: "Any man living in a society, and who [122] has explicitly or implicitly sworn to obey the laws, has acquired three rights which no one can take from him and which he cannot lose save by his own fault or choosing: the right to liberty, the right to safety, and the right to property."

state."[13] But is there not injustice legally, when you violate due process; and how do you know there is not also substantive injustice?

Wretched supporters of despotism who never see it except as a weapon you want to seize for yourselves![14]

B. [Refers to page 85.]

Here give homage to the character and intentions of Cicero.

C. [Refers to page 85.]

"L. Flaccus, interrex, de Sylla legem tulit, ut omnia, quaecumque ille fecerit, essent rata . . .—nihilo credo magis, illa justa est ut dictator, quem vellet civium, indicta causa, impune possit occidere." Cicero. [Lucius Flaccus, chief magistrate of the interregnum, passed a law in respect of Sulla, that everything he did was valid . . .—I believe nothing more strongly than that it is just that a dictator should be able to kill whomsoever he wishes of the citizens, with impunity, cause having been given (*indicta causa*).] And were not Catilina's accomplices put to death *indicta causa?*[15]

13. *Ibid.*, p. 310. Here is the complete citation of this sentence: "Indeed it is not by dint of injustices that one can reorganize a State, which is only a justly constituted society."

14. In *De la force du gouvernment,* Constant had written in the same way: "As long as you think of arbitrary government as only a tool to be snatched from your enemy for you to use, your enemy will strive to snatch it from you." Ch. 8, p. 104 of the 1796 edition.

15. This Latin quotation has been recopied from Ferrand's work, *op. cit.,* t. I. 2e éd. 1803, p. 418, n. 1, which gives the following reference: "Cic. Hist. pp. 170–171." The first part of the quotation, up to the ellipsis, comes from *De lege agraria,* III, 5; here is the complete text and the translation: "Omnium legum iniquissimam dissimillimamque legis esse arbitror eam quam L. Flaccus interrex de Sulla tulit, ut omnia quaecumque ille fecisset essent rata."—"Of all the laws, I judge to be the most iniquitous and least like a law that which the interrex Lucius Flaccus passed in respect of Sulla, to legalize all the acts of the dictator." Cicero, *Discours,* t. IX, *Sur la loi agraire . . . ,* text edited and translated by André Boulanger, Paris, Les Belles Lettres, 1932, p. 109. The second part of the quotation comes from *De Legibus,* I, 42, whose exact text is "Nihilo credo magis illa [lex] quam interrex noster tulit, ut dictator quem vellet civium nominatem aut indicta causa inpune posset occidere."—I believe in no right more strongly than that law which an interrex passed in our case that a dictator may kill which people he may nominate, with impunity, cause having been given. Cicero, *Traité des lois,* text edited and translated by George de Plinval, Paris, Les Belles Lettres, 1959, p. 24. [The French translation (pp. 122–123 of the Hofmann edition) is very free and seems to be rendering *indicta causa* as "without a trial" (*sans proces*). One of the three classicists consulted by the translator thought that *indicta causa* might be best rendered by "the case made public" or "the case having been made public." Translator's note]

[123] D. [Refers to page 87.]

Following the insurrection in the Cévennes occasioned by the persecution of the Calvinists, the party which had solicited this persecution claimed that the revolt of the camisards was caused only by the relaxation of repressive measures. If the oppression had continued, this party said, there would have been no uprising. If the oppression had not begun, said those who were opposed to the violence, there would not have been any malcontents. Rulhière, Eclaircissements sur la Révocation de l'Edit de Nantes, II, 278.[16]

E. [Refers to page 96.]

Note. What is the guarantee of a lasting government? It is when the different classes of the State like it as it is and do not want to change it. Aristotle. Politics, Book II, Chapter 7.[17]

16. Claude Carloman de Rulhière, *Eclaircissements historiques sur les causes de la Révocation de l'Edit de Nantes et sur l'etat des protestants en France,* s.l., 1788, t. II, pp. 278–279. "At the first report of these movements (the insurrection in the Cévennes), each of the two parties mutually accused each other of having caused them. If the oppression had continued, said one, there would have been no uprising. If the oppression had not started, said the other, if the policy had remained that of conversions by enlightened instruction and gentleness, there would have been no malcontents."

17. This is probably not a quotation. Furthermore, nothing in Book II, Ch. 7 of *Politics* is related to the words indicated by Constant. On the other hand, Aristotle debates at length these questions of the causes of revolutions and of the guarantees against the changing of constitutions, in Book V of this same work. See Aristotle, *La politique,* a new translation with an introduction, notes, and index by J. Tricot, Paris, J. Vrin, 1962, t. II, pp. 337–425.

BOOK VII

On Freedom of Thought

CH. 1. The object of the following three books. 103
CH. 2. On freedom of thought. 103
CH. 3. On the expression of thought. 105
CH. 4. Continuation of the same subject. 112
CH. 5. Continuation of the same subject. 117
CH. 6. Some necessary explication. 123
CH. 7. Final observations. 124

CHAPTER ONE

The Object of the Following Three Books

In the following three books we are going to deal with freedom of thought and of the press and with legal safeguards.

Political freedom would be a thing of no value if the rights of individuals were not sheltered from all violation. Any country where these rights are not respected is a country subjected to despotism, whatever the nominal organization of government may otherwise be.

Till a few years ago these truths were universally recognized. Lasting errors and a long oppression, under wholly contrary pretexts and quite opposite banners, have thrown all ideas into confusion. Questions one would think worked to death if one judged the case in terms of eighteenth-century writers, will seem never to have been the object of human meditation judging by most of the writers of today.

CHAPTER TWO

On Freedom of Thought

"The laws," says Montesquieu, "have responsibility for the punishment of external actions only."[1] The demonstration of this truth might seem unnecessary. Government has nevertheless often failed to recognize it.

It has sometimes wanted to dominate thought itself. Louis XIV's dragonnades,[2] the insane laws of Charles II's implacable Parliament, the fury of our revolutionaries: these had no other purpose.

At other times the government, renouncing this ridiculous ambition, [128] dresses up its renunciation as a voluntary concession and a praiseworthy tolerance. An amusing merit, this granting what you cannot refuse and this tolerating what you do not know about.

As to the absurdity of any attempt by society to control the inner opinions of its members—a few words on the possibility of the idea and on the means available are enough.

There is no such possibility. Nature has given man's thought an impregnable shelter. She has created for it a sanctuary no power can penetrate.

1. See Constant's Note A at the end of Book VII.
2. [The persecution of the Protestants by the dragoons. Translator's note]

The means employed are always the same, so much so that in recounting what happened two hundred years ago, we will seem to be saying what happened not long ago under our eyes. And these unchanging means always work against their purpose.

One can deploy against mute public opinion all the resources of an inquisitorial nosiness. One can scrutinize consciences, impose oath after solemn oath,[3] in the hope that he whose conscience was not revolted by an initial act, will be so by a second or a third. One can strike at people's consciences with boundless severity, surrounding obedience the while with relentless distrust. One can persecute proud and honest men, reluctantly letting off only those of flexible and obliging spirit. One can show oneself equally incapable of respecting resistance and believing in submission.[4] One can set traps for the citizens, invent far-fetched formulae to declare a whole nation refractory,[5] place it outside the protection of the laws when it has done nothing, punish it when it has committed no crimes, deprive it of the very right to silence,[6] and finally pursue men into the sorrows of their final agony and the solemn hour of death.[7]

What happens? Honest men are indignant and feeble ones degraded. Everyone suffers and no one is won back. Enforced oaths are an invitation to hypocrisy. They affect only what it is criminal to affect: frankness and integrity. To demand assent is to make it wither. To prop up an opinion with threats invites the courageous to contest it. To offer seductive motives for obedience is to condemn impartiality to resist.

[129] Twenty-eight years after all the abuses of power devised by the Stuarts as a safeguard, they were driven out. A century after the outrages against the Protestants under Louis XVI, the Protestants took part in the overthrow of his family. Scarcely ten years separate us from revolutionary governments which called themselves republican, and by a fatal but natural confusion the very name they profaned cannot be spoken save with horror.

3. See Constant's Note B at the end of Book VII.
4. See Constant's Note C at the end of Book VII.
5. See Constant's Note D at the end of Book VII.
6. See Constant's Note E at the end of Book VII.
7. See Constant's Note F at the end of Book VII.

CHAPTER THREE

On the Expression of Thought

Men have two ways of showing what their thinking is: speech and writing.

There was a time when speech seemed worthy of the total surveillance efforts of government. Indeed, if we consider that speech is the indispensable instrument of all plots, the necessary precursor of almost all crimes, the means of communication for all criminal intentions, we can agree that it would be desirable if we could circumscribe its use, in such a fashion as to make its disadvantages disappear while it retained its usefulness.

Why, then, have all efforts to achieve this very desirable goal been renounced? It is because experience has shown that the measures necessary to achieve this produced ills worse than those one was wishful to remedy. Espionage, corruption, informing, calumnies, abuse of confidence, treason, suspicion between relatives, dissensions between friends, hostility between unconcerned parties, a commerce in domestic infidelities, venality, lying, perjury, despotism: such were the elements constituting government interference with speech. It was felt that this was to pay too dearly for the advantage afforded by surveillance. In addition, we learned that it was to attach importance to what should have none. Keeping a record of imprudence turned it into hostility. Stopping fugitive words in flight was to lead to their being followed by bold actions, and it was better, while coming down hard on the deeds which speech might perhaps have led to, to let that which had no results at all just evaporate. Consequently, except in some very rare circumstances—some obviously disastrous eras or very touchy governments which do not disguise [130] their tyranny at all—society has introduced a distinction which renders its jurisdiction over the word softer and more legitimate. The declaration of an opinion can in a special case produce an effect so infallible that such an opinion must be regarded as an action. Then, if the action is culpable, the utterance must be punished. But it is the same with writings. Writings, like speech, like the most simple movements, can be part of an action. They must be judged as part of that action if it is criminal. But if they do not constitute part of any action, they must, like speech, enjoy complete freedom.

This answers both those men who in our times singled out certain wise heads and prescribed the need to cut them off, justifying themselves by saying that, after all, they were only expressing their opinions; and those others who want to take advantage of this delirium in order to subject all expressions of opinion to the jurisdiction of government.

If you once grant the need to repress the expression of opinion, either the State will have to act judicially or the government will have to arrogate to itself police powers which free it from recourse to judicial means. In the first case the laws will be eluded. Nothing is easier than presenting an opinion in such variegated guises that a precisely defined law cannot touch it. In the second case, by authorizing the government to deal ruthlessly with whatever opinions there may be, you are giving it the right to interpret thought, to make inductions, in a nutshell to reason and to put its reasoning in the place of the facts which ought to be the sole basis for government counteraction. This is to establish despotism with a free hand. Which opinion cannot draw down a punishment on its author? You give the government a free hand for evildoing, provided that it is careful to engage in evil thinking. You will never escape from this circle. The men to whom you entrust the right to judge opinions are quite as susceptible as others to being misled or corrupted, and the arbitrary power which you will have invested in them can be used against the most necessary truths as well as the most fatal errors.

When one considers only one side of moral and political questions, [131] it is easy to draw a terrible picture of the abuse of our rights. But when one looks at these questions from an overall point of view, the picture of the ills which government power occasions by limiting these rights seems to me no less frightening.

What, indeed, is the outcome of all attacks made on freedom of the pen? They embitter against the government all those writers possessed of that spirit of independence inseparable from talent, who are forced to have recourse to indirect and perfidious allusions. They necessitate the circulation of clandestine and therefore all the more dangerous texts. They feed the public greed for anecdotes, personal remarks, and seditious principles. They give calumny the appearance, always an interesting one, of courage. In sum, they attach far too much importance to the works about to be proscribed.

In the absence of government intervention, published sedition, immorality, and calumny would scarcely make more impact at the end of a given period of complete freedom than spoken or handwritten calumny, immorality, or sedition.

One reflection has always occurred to me. Let us suppose a society before the invention of language, making up for this swift and easy means of communication with other less easy and slower ones. The discovery of language would have produced in this society a sudden explosion. Gigantic importance would surely have been attached to sounds which were still new and lots of cautious and wise minds might well have mourned the era of peaceful and total silence. This importance, however, would gradually have faded. Speech would have become a medium limited in its effects. A salutary suspiciousness, born of experience, would have preserved listeners from unthinking enthusiasm. Finally everything would be back in order, with this difference: now social communication and consequently the perfectioning of all the arts and the correcting of all ideas would have gained an extra medium.

It will be the same with the press wherever just and moderate government does not set about struggling with it. The English government was not at all unnerved by the famous letters of Junius.[8] It [132] knew how to resist the double force of eloquence and talent. In Prussia, during the most brilliant reign, to add luster to that monarchy, press freedom was unlimited. Frederick II in forty-six years never once directed his authority against any writer or writing. This in no way upset the peace of his reign, though it was shaken by terrible wars and he was embattled with the whole of Europe. Freedom spreads calm in the souls and reason in the minds of the men who enjoy this inestimable good, free from anxiety. What proves this is that when Frederick II's successor adopted the opposite course, a general unrest made itself felt. Writers got into conflict with the government, which also found itself abandoned by the courts. If the clouds which rose all around this horizon, formerly so peaceful, did not culminate in a storm, this is because the very restrictions that Frederick William tried to impose on the expression of thought were influenced by the wisdom of the great Frederick. The new king was held in check by the memory of his uncle, whose magnanimous shadow seemed still to watch over Prussia. His edicts were drafted more in a style of apology

8. "The Letters of Junius" appeared anonymously on 21 January 1769 in Woodfall's newspaper, *Public Advertiser.* He published them in complete form in 1772, but other incomplete editions had already come out. The purpose of these letters was to discredit the policies of the duke of Grafton and Lord North. The anonymity of their author has never been definitively unmasked. The names of Gibbon, Burke, and Paine have been mentioned, but various clues permit us to believe it more likely that Sir Philip Francis was the author. These letters are still famous for their style, which constitutes them as a masterpiece of the pamphlet form. See the entry in the *Encyclopaedia Britannica,* vol. 13 (1973), s.v. Junius.

than menace. He gave homage to freedom of thought in the preamble to the very edicts aiming to repress it,[9] and measures which were in principle abuses of power were softened in execution by a tacit moderation and by the tradition of freedom.

Anyway, government has the same means of defending itself as its enemies have for attacking it. It can enlighten public opinion or even seduce it, and there is no reason to fear that it will ever lack adroit and skillful men who will devote their zeal and talent to it. The government's supporters ask nothing better than to make themselves out to be courageous and to represent [133] government apologias as difficult and dangerous. In support of their claims they choose the example of the French government, overthrown, they say, in 1789, because of freedom of the press.[10] In fact it was not freedom of the press which overthrew the French monarchy. Press freedom did not create the financial disorder which was the real cause of the Revolution. On the contrary, if there had been freedom of the press under Louis XIV and Louis XV, the insane wars of the first and the costly corruption of the second would not have drained the State dry. The glare of

9. Constant was probably familiar with the work of Louis-Philippe Ségur, *Histoire des principaux événements du règne de F. Guillaume II, roi de Prusse,* Paris, F. Buisson, an IX (1800), which gives the text of this Edict of Censorship (t. I, pp. 400–405) and gives a commentary (*ibid.,* pp. 62–64). Frederick William II declares indeed at the beginning of this text: "Although we are perfectly convinced of the great and diverse advantages of a moderate and well-regulated freedom of the press in terms of expanding the sciences and all useful knowledge [. . .] experience has shown us, however, the troublesome consequences of complete freedom in this regard."

10. Without being able to be categorical on this point, since he has not found the text to which reference is made here, Hofmann thinks, nevertheless, that Constant is referring to the editors of the *Journal de l'Empire* or of the *Mercure de France,* men completely devoted to Napoleon. See the study by André Cabanis, "Le courant contre-révolutionnaire sous le Consulat et l'Empire" (in the *Journal des Débats* and the *Mercure de France*), *Revue des sciences politiques,* No. 24, 1971, pp. 33–40. Among these editors, there were Fiévée and Geoffroy, whose target was often the ideology of the Enlightenment and 1789 and who advocated all-powerful monarchy. One finds, in particular, in an article in the *Mercure de France* (No. 257, 21 June 1806, pp. 533–554) signed by De Bonald, this reflection which must have struck Constant: "Freedom of thought was only therefore freedom to act; and how could one demand from government an absolute freedom of action, without rendering pointless all the pains taken by the administration to maintain peace and good order, or rather, without turning society upside down?" (*ibid.,* p. 551). And the same author a little further on identifies "diversity of religious and political opinion" as "the main cause of the French Revolution" (*ibid.,* p. 552).

publicity would have restrained the first of these kings in his ventures, the second in his vices. They would not have left the unfortunate Louis XVI with a realm which it was impossible to save. It was not press freedom which inflamed popular indignation against illegal detentions and lettres de cachet.[11] It was on the contrary popular indignation which, to counter governmental oppression, grasped not press freedom but the dangerous resort to satire, something which all the precautionary measures of the police never manage to take away from the enslaved people. If there had been freedom of the press, on the one hand there would have been fewer illegal detentions, and on the other, people would not have been able to exaggerate them. The imagination would not have been struck by suppositions whose plausibility was heightened by the very mystery surrounding them. Finally, it was not press freedom which brought about all the infamies and lunacy of a revolution all of whose ills I acknowledge. It was the long deprivation of press freedom which had made the common people of France credulous, anxious, and ignorant and thereby often savage. It is because for centuries we had not dared to demand the rights of the people that the people did not know what meaning to attach to these words suddenly pronounced in the middle of the storm. In [134] everything people see as freedom's excesses I recognize only the instruction servitude gives.

Governments do not know the harm they do themselves in reserving to themselves the exclusive privilege of speaking and writing on their own acts. People believe nothing affirmed by a government which does not permit one to reply to it and everything said against a government which does not tolerate scrutiny.

It is these detailed and tyrannical measures against writings, as though they were hostile phalanxes, these measures which, attributing to them an imaginary influence, enlarge their real influence. When men see whole codes of prohibitive law along with hosts of interrogators, they must think attacks repulsed in this way very formidable. Since so much trouble is being taken to keep certain writings away from us, they must say to themselves, the impression they would have on us must probably be a very profound one. They probably contain compelling facts.

The dangers of freedom of the press are certainly not prevented by government means. The government does not succeed in its ostensible aim. The end it does achieve is to curb the thinking of all timid or scrupulous

11. [Lettres de cachet. Letters bearing the king's seal, containing orders for imprisonment of individuals or their banishment without trial. Translator's note]

citizens, to deny all access to the complaints of the oppressed, to let abuses become deep-rooted, without any representation being made, to surround itself with ignorance and darkness, to sanctify despotism in its lowest agents, against whom people dare publish nothing, to drive back into men's inner thoughts bitterness, vengeance, resentment, to impose silence on reason, justice, and truth, without its being able to require the same silence from the audacity and exaggeration which defy its laws.

These truths would be incontestable even in the event that we agreed about all the disadvantages attributed to press freedom. How will matters stand if a deeper analysis leads us to deny these drawbacks and if it is shown that the calamities with which freedom of the press is reproached have for the most part been the result only of its enslavement?

Ordinarily, at the very moment when a dominant faction exercises the most scandalous despotism over the press, it directs this instrument against its opponents and, when by its own excesses this faction has brought about its fall, the inheritors of its power [135] argue against press freedom, citing the ills occasioned by mercenary writers and authorized spies. This leads me to a consideration which seems to me to weigh very heavily in the question.

In a country still vigorously contested by various groups, when one of these manages to restrain press freedom, it has much more unlimited and formidable power than ordinary despotisms. Despotic governments do not allow freedom of the press; everybody, however, governors and governed, keeps equally quiet. Public opinion is silent; but it remains what it is. Nothing leads it astray or causes it to deviate. But in a country where the reigning faction has seized the press, its writers argue, invent, and calumniate in one direction the way one could do it in all if there were freedom to write. They discuss as though it were a question of convincing. They lose their temper as if there were an opposition. They insult people as if there were a right of reply. Their absurd calumnies precede barbarous persecutions. Their ferocious jests are a prelude to illegal condemnations. The public, far removed, takes this parody of freedom for freedom itself. It draws its opinions from their mendacious, scurrilous satires. It is persuaded by their show of attack that the victims are resisting, just as from afar the war dances of savages might make one believe they are fighting against the unfortunates they are about to devour.

In the large-scale polities of modern times, freedom of the press, being the sole means of publicity, is by that very fact, whatever the type of government, the unique safeguard of our rights. Collatinus could expose

Lucretia's body in the public square in Rome and everybody was apprised of the outrage done to him.[12] The plebeian debtor could show his indignant fellow citizens the wounds inflicted on him by the greedy patrician, his usurious creditor. In our era, however, the vastness of states is an obstacle to this kind of protest. Limited injustices always remain unknown to almost all the inhabitants in our huge countries. If the ephemeral governments which have tyrannized France have drawn on themselves public detestation, this is less because of what they have done than because of what they have owned up to. They bragged about their injustices. They publicized them in their [136] newspapers. More prudent governments would act silently, and the public outlook, which would be disturbed only by dull rumors, intermittent and unconfirmed, would remain uncertain, undecided, and fluctuating. No doubt, as we have already remarked, the repercussive explosion would be only the more terrible, but this would be one ill replacing another.

All defenses—civil, political, or judicial—become illusory without freedom of the press. The independence of the courts can be violated in scornful mockery of the best-drafted constitution. If open publication is not guaranteed, this violation will not be checked, since it will remain covered by a veil. The courts themselves can prevaricate in their judgments and overthrow due process. The only safeguard of due process is, once again, open publication. Innocence can be put in irons. If open publication does not warn the citizens of the danger hovering over all their heads, the dungeons, abetted by the universal silence, will retain their victims indefinitely. Persecution can be for opinions, beliefs, or doubts, and when no one has the right to call public attention to himself, the protection promised by the laws is only a chimera, another danger. In countries where there are representative assemblies, national representation can be enslaved, mutilated, and calumniated. If printing is only an instrument in the hands of the government, the whole country will resound with its calumnies, without truth finding a single voice raised in its favor. In sum, press freedom, even if it were accompanied by no legal consequence, would still have an advantage in a number of cases, such as when senior members of government are ignorant of the outrages being committed, or in others when they may find it convenient to feign such ignorance. Press freedom meets these two difficulties. It enlightens government and prevents it deliberately closing its eyes. Forced to learn of the facts which happen unbeknown to it and to

12. Titus Livy, *Histoire romaine*, I, 59, 3, éd. cit., t. I, p. 95.

admit it knows of them, it will less often dare to legitimate the abuses it finds convenient to permit, seemingly in ignorance of them.

All the thoughts just presented to the reader apply only to the relations of government to the publicizing of opinion. Individuals whom this publicity offends, either in their interests or their honor, always retain the right to demand reparation. Every man has the right [137] to invoke the law in order to repulse the ill done to him, whatever weapons it employs. Individual campaigns against calumny have none of the disadvantages of government intervention. No one has an interest in claiming he has been attacked nor in having recourse to strained interpretations in order to aggravate the charges directed against him. Trial by jury would moreover be a guarantee against these abuses in interpretation.

CHAPTER FOUR

Continuation of the Same Subject

In the previous chapter we dealt with press freedom only in a rather administrative way. More important considerations, however, in connection with politics and morality, demand our attention.

Today, to restrain the freedom of the press is to restrain the human race's intellectual freedom. The press is an instrument such freedom can no longer do without. Printing has been made the sole means of publicizing things, the only mode of communication between nations as much as between individuals, by the nature and extent of our modern societies and by the abolition of all the popular and disorderly ways of doing this. The question of press freedom is therefore the general one about the development of the human mind. It is from this point of view that it must be envisaged.

In countries where the populace does not participate in government in an active way, that is, everywhere there is no national representation, freely elected and invested with significant prerogatives, freedom of the press in some degree replaces political rights. The educated part of the nation interests itself in the administration of affairs, when it can express its opinion, if not directly on each particular issue, at least on the general principles of government. When, however, a country has neither press freedom nor political rights, the people turn away from public affairs. All communication between governors and governed is broken. For a while, the government and its supporters can regard that as an advantage. The government does not encounter obstacles. Nothing impedes it. It acts freely, but this is simply because it is the only living thing and the nation is dead.

Public opinion is the very life of States. When public opinion is not renewed, [138] States waste away and fall into dissolution. There were institutions in the past in all the countries of Europe, which, though involved in many abuses, nevertheless, by giving certain classes privileges to defend and rights to exercise, fostered in them a level of activity which saved them from discouragement or apathy. It is to this cause that we must attribute the energy certain individuals possessed until the sixteenth century, an energy of which we no longer find any trace. These institutions have been destroyed everywhere or been modified to such an extent that they have lost their influence almost entirely. But around the very same time they collapsed, the discovery of printing furnished men with a new means of discussion, a new motor of intellectual movement. This discovery and the freedom of thought which resulted from it have over the last three centuries been favored by certain governments, tolerated by others, while yet others have smothered them. Now, we are not afraid to say that the nations in which this intellectual activity has been encouraged or allowed are the only ones which have conserved force and life, and those whose leaderships have imposed silence on all free opinion have gradually lost all character and energy. The French under the monarchy were not completely deprived of political rights until after Richelieu. I have already said that defective institutions which nevertheless endow the powerful classes with certain privileges they are ceaselessly busy in defending have, in their favor, amid their many disadvantages, the fact that they do not leave the whole nation to degradation and debasement. The beginning of the reign of Louis XIV was still disrupted by the war of the Fronde, a puerile war in truth, but one which was the residuum of a spirit of resistance, habituated to action and continuing to act almost without purpose. Despotism grew greatly toward the end of this reign. The opposition still maintained itself, however, taking refuge in religious quarrels, sometimes Calvinists against Catholicism, sometimes between Catholics themselves. The death of Louis XIV was the period when government was relaxed. Freedom of opinion gained ground each day. I do not at all want to say that this freedom was exercised in the most decent and useful way. I mean only that it was exercised and that in this sense one could not put the French, in any period up until the overthrow of the monarchy, among those peoples condemned to complete servitude and moral lethargy.

[139] This march of the human spirit finished, I agree, with a terrible revolution. I am more willing than anyone to deplore the evils of this revolution. I think I have shown elsewhere that it had many other causes than

the independence and the airing of thought. Without coming back to this matter here, however, I will say that those who in their bitterness blame freedom of the press have probably not thought of the effects the complete destruction of that freedom would have produced. People can see very well in every instance the evils which took place, and they believe they can see the immediate causes of these evils. They do not notice as clearly, however, what would have resulted from a different chain of circumstances. If Louis XIV's successor had been a tetchy prince, despotic and skillful enough to oppress the people without making them rebel, France would have fallen into the same apathy as neighboring monarchies, formerly no less formidable and populous. But the French have always maintained an interest in public affairs, because they have always had, if not the legal, at least the practical right to be interested in them. In recent years the temporary humbling of France during the Seven Years War and during the years just prior to the Revolution has been much exaggerated.[13] But it would be easy to show that this decline, for which the philosophers are stupidly blamed, resulted from bad government, from bad appointments made, to my mind, not by philosophers but by mistresses and courtiers. This decline did not stem from a lack of energy in the nation. France proved this when she had Europe to battle with.

Spain, four hundred years ago, was more powerful and populous than France. This realm, before the abolition of the Cortes, had thirty million inhabitants. Today it has nine. Its ships plied all the oceans and commanded all the colonies. Its fleet is now weaker than those of the English, the French, and the Dutch. Yet the Spanish character is energetic, brave, and enterprising. Whence comes then the striking difference between the fortunes of Spain and France? From the fact that when political liberty had vanished in Spain, nothing came to offer the intellectual and moral activity of its inhabitants a new lease of life. Probably people will say Spain's decadence is due to the faults of its government, to the Inquisition which controls it, and to a thousand other immediate causes. All these causes, however, [140] relate to the same root. If thought had been free in Spain, the government would have been better, because it would have been enlightened by the intelligence of various individuals. As for the Inquisition, everywhere you have freedom of the press, the Inquisition cannot happen, and everywhere there is no press freedom, there will always be creeping around, in one shape or another, something very like the Inquisition.

13. This reference has not been pinned down by Hofmann.

Germany furnishes us with a very similar and even more striking comparison, in view of the disproportion between the two objects compared. One of the two great monarchies which share that country was formerly a colossus of power. She grows weaker each day. Her finances are deteriorating and her military strength leaking away. Her internal activities are powerless against the decay which undermines her. Her foreign activities are ill-coordinated and her setbacks inexplicable. For all that, her cabinet has often been presented by the political writers as a model of ongoing prudence and secrecy. There is in that realm, however, neither political freedom nor intellectual independence. Not only is the press there subjected to severe restrictions, but the introduction of any foreign book is strictly prohibited. The nation, separated from the government as by a thick night, takes only a feeble part in its proceedings. It is not within the government's power to have the people slumber or bestir itself according to government convenience or passing fantasy. Life is not something you can by turns take away and give back.

It is so true that we must attribute the misfortunes of the monarchy I am talking about to this defect in its domestic life, that the region which has always furnished the best troops and most zealous defenders is a country which, formerly free, has retained its sense of loss, its memories, and a certain show of freedom. The heredity of the throne was not recognized in Hungary until the Assembly of 1687, amid the most bloody executions. The energy of the Hungarians has been sustained under the Austrian government only because that government has not borne down on them for more than a century and a bit. Note that this country is at the same time the most malcontent part of the monarchy. Malcontent subjects are still worth more to their masters than subjects lacking zeal because they lack interests.[14]

Prussia, on the contrary, where public opinion has never been completely smothered and where this opinion has enjoyed the greatest freedom since Frederick II, has successfully struggled against many disadvantages, all the less easy to surmount because they were inherent [141] in her situation and local circumstances. Until about the beginning of the last century, the era of her elevation to the status of monarchy, Prussia showed the effects of the upheaval that the Reformation wrought in all German thinking. The Electors of Brandenburg had always stood out among the chiefs of the league formed to support freedom of religion, and their subjects had joined them in word and deed in that great and noble enterprise. The warlike reign of Frederick

14. See Constant's Note G at the end of Book VII.

William had not weakened that outlook when Frederick II replaced him. He left thought the widest possible latitude, permitting the examination of all political and religious questions. His very dislike of German literature, of which he knew little, was itself very favorable to the complete freedom of German writers. The greatest service government can do to knowledge is not to bother with it. *Laisser faire* is all you need to bring commerce to the highest point of prosperity; letting people write is all you need for the human mind to achieve the highest degree of activity, cogency, and accuracy. Frederick's conduct here was such that his subjects identified themselves with him in all his undertakings. Although there was in Prussia no political liberty, no cast-iron safeguards, a public spirit took shape, and it was with this spirit, as much as with his troops, that Frederick repulsed the European coalition against him. During the Seven Years War he experienced frequent reverses. His capital was taken and his armies dispersed; but there was some kind of moral elasticity which communicated itself from him to his people and from his people to him. The Prussians had something to lose by the death of their king, for they would have forfeited their freedom of thought and of the press and that indefinable but real share that the exercise of these two faculties gave them in his undertakings and administration. They lent him their best wishes; they had a good reaction on his army; they gave him the support of a kind of climate of opinion, a public-spiritedness, which sustained him and doubled his strength. I do not in writing these lines seek to conceal the fact that there is a class of men who will see in them only a cause for derision and mockery. Whatever the cost, these men want there to be nothing moral or intellectual in the government of the human race. They set such faculties as they have to proving the futility and impotence of these faculties. I will ask them, however, to reply to the examples I have [142] cited and tell us why, of the four remaining monarchies, the two strongest formerly, having smothered all intellectual activity and development in their subjects, have gradually fallen into an ever growing weakness and lethargy, and why the other two, of which the first has tolerated, mostly despite itself, the existence and force of public opinion and the second favored it, have raised themselves to a high degree of prosperity and power. I repeat that arguments based on the faults and inconsistencies of the governments in these two first monarchies would not be admissible. This is because they would have committed fewer faults if freedom had surrounded them with more enlightenment, or if, even when they had committed these faults, their nations had conserved some energy just by exercising disapproval, however impotent. Then their nations, like the French nation, would have been ready to revive at the first signal.

I did not want to base my case on the English example, though it would have been much more favorable to it. However one judges England, it will, I think, be agreed that she has a stronger and more active national spirit than any other people in Europe. But one could rightly have attributed England's energy to her political constitution, and I wanted to show the advantages of press freedom independently of any constitution.

Had I wished to multiply the evidence, I could have spoken again about China. The government of that country has contrived to dominate thought and transform it wholly into a tool. Sciences there are cultivated only by its orders, under its management and authority. No one dares to cut out a new path for himself nor to deviate in any way from prescribed opinion. The result is that China has been persistently conquered by strangers less numerous than the Chinese. To arrest the development of people's minds it has been necessary to break in them the energy which would have served them in standing up for themselves and their government.

"The leaders of ignorant peoples have always finished," says Bentham, "by being victims of their narrow and cowardly policies. Those nations grown old in infancy under tutors who prolong their imbecility in order to govern them the more easily, have always offered the first aggressor an easy prey."[15] [143]

CHAPTER FIVE
Continuation of the Same Subject

If you apply this experience of the last three centuries of history to the present state of human intellection, you will readily be convinced that the annihilation of press freedom, that is to say, of intellectual progress, would have results today even more fatal than those we have recounted. The monarchies whose progressive withering and retrograde movement we have described, deprived of the free use of printing from its inception, felt this deprivation only in a dull, slow, imperceptible way. A people deprived of freedom of the press after having enjoyed it, would experience the initial

15. Constant cut the citation in two; after *pusillanime* [cowardly], Bentham had written: "A nation kept in a constant inferiority by institutions who oppose any kind of progress became [*sic*] the prey of the people who had acquired a relative superiority." Constant modified the original text at the end of the citation as well. Bentham said: "These nations . . . always offered an easy conquest and once captivated [or enthralled] they managed only to change the color of their chains." *Ed. cit.*, t. III, p. 21. [Constant was working—excessively freely—from a French translation. His referencing cannot be deemed reliable on this occasion. Translator's note]

pain of this loss more sharply, followed by a more rapid degradation. The thing which debases men is not lacking a right but having to give it up. Condillac says there are two sorts of barbarism, the one which goes before enlightened centuries and the one which succeeds them.[16] In the same way one can say there are two kinds of servitude, the one preceding liberty and the one replacing it. The first is a desirable state of affairs compared to the second. But the choice of these is not left to governments, because they cannot annihilate the past.

Imagine an enlightened nation, enriched by the works of a number of studious generations, possessing masterpieces of all types, having made immense scientific and artistic progress, and having got to this point by the only way that can lead there, the enjoyment, assured or precarious, of freedom of publication. If the government of that nation put such constraints on that freedom that it became every day harder to elude them, if it did not allow the exercise of thought except in a predetermined direction, the nation could survive for a while on [144] its former capital, so to speak, on its acquired intelligence, on habits of thinking and doing picked up earlier; but nothing in the world of thought would renew itself. The reproductive principle would have dried up. For some years vanity might stand in for the love of learning. Sophists, remembering what glamour and esteem literary works used once to bestow, would give themselves over to works of ostensibly the same genre. Their writings would combat any good effects which other writings might have had, and as long as there remained any trace of liberal principles, there would be in such a people's literature some kind of movement, a sort of struggle against these ideas and principles. This very movement, however, this struggle, would be an inheritance of a now-destroyed liberty. To the extent that the last vestiges, the last traditions, could be dispelled, there would be less acclaim and less advantage in continuing these more and more superfluous attacks. When all had been dispelled, the battle would finish, because the combatants would no longer perceive even the shadow of their foes. Conquerors and conquered would alike keep silence. Who knows if the government might not reckon it worth imposing this? It would not want anyone to reawaken extinguished memories, or stir up abandoned ideas. It would come down hard on overzealous acolytes as it used to on its enemies. It would forbid even

16. Etienne Bonnot de Condillac, *Cours d'étude . . . , op. cit.,* t. IV, p. 2: "There are therefore two sorts of barbarism, the one which follows enlightened centuries and the one which precedes them; and they are not like each other."

writings taking its own line, on the interests of humanity, as some pious government once forbade talk of God, for good or ill. Thus a career in real thinking would be definitively closed to the human spirit. The educated generation would gradually disappear. The next generation, seeing no advantage in intellectual occupations, or indeed dangers therein, would break off from them for good. You will say, in vain, that the human spirit could still occupy itself with lighter literature, that it could enter the service of the exact or natural sciences, or devote itself to the arts. When nature created man, she did not consult government. Her design was that all our faculties should be in intimate liaison and that none should be subject to limitation without the others feeling the effect. Independent thinking is as vital, even to lighter literature, science, and the arts, as air is to physical life. One could as well make men work under a pneumatic pump, saying that they do not have to breathe, but must move their arms and legs, as hold intellectual activity to a given object, preventing it from preoccupying itself with important subjects which give it its energy because they remind it of its dignity. Writers strangled in this way start off with panegyrics; but they become bit by bit incapable even of praise and literature finishes [145] up losing itself in anagrams and acrostics. Scholars are no more than the trustees of ancient discoveries which deteriorate and degrade in manacled hands. The source of talent dries up among artists along with the hope of glory which is sustained only by freedom. By a mysterious but incontestable relationship between things from which one thought oneself capable of isolating oneself,[17] they no longer have the ability to represent the human figure nobly when the human spirit is degraded.[18]

Nor would this be the end of the story. Soon commerce, the professions, and the most vital crafts would feel the effects of the death of thought. It should not be thought that commerce on its own is a sufficient motive for activity. People often exaggerate the influence of personal interest. Personal interest itself needs the existence of public opinion in order to act. The man whose opinion languishes, stifled, is not for long excited even by his interests. A sort of stupor seizes him; and just as paralysis extends itself from one part of the body to another, so it extends itself from one faculty to another.

17. [Hofmann has had difficulty deciphering the folio French here, so the English is uncertain too by definition. Translator's note]

18. In writing these pages, Constant is indicating without naming the leading French newspapers, led by the *Mercure de France*, whose content was more and more limited to panegyrics, anagrams, and acrostics.

Interest cut off from reflection is limited in its needs and easy to content in its pleasures, working just as much as is needed for the moment, preparing nothing for the future. Look at Spain, whose example we cited above. Thus it is that governments which wish to kill men's opinions and believe they are encouraging interests find to their great regret that this clumsy twin policy has killed them both. No doubt there is an interest which is not snuffed out under despotism; but it is not one which leads man to work. It is the one leading him to beg and plunder, to enrich himself by the favors of power and the spoils drawn from weakness. This interest has nothing in common with the motive necessary for the working classes. It makes the whereabouts of despots a very busy place; but it cannot serve as a spur either to the efforts of industry nor the speculations of commerce. We have shown by the example of Frederick II how intellectual independence influenced even military success. One does not notice at first glance the link between a nation's public spirit and the discipline or valor of an army which fights away from home and often comprises foreign elements. This link, however, is constant and necessary. [146] People like to think of soldiers today as docile instruments, whom it suffices to know how to handle skillfully. This is all too true in certain respects. It is also necessary, however, that soldiers are aware of a certain public opinion behind them. It moves them almost without their knowing. It is like that music to whose sound these same soldiers advance on the enemy. None pays it a consistent attention, and yet all are moved, encouraged, and carried along by it. If it stopped making itself heard, they would all slacken off imperceptibly. Only barbarian hordes can march ardently into battle unsustained by the public opinion of a nation of their compatriots, whose cause they defend and who share in their success. But this is because the barbarian hordes are driven by the hope of plunder and the desire to make new settlements in the country they are seizing. This hope and desire take the place for them of public opinion, or rather they constitute a real opinion.

"The conquest of the Gauls," remarks Filangieri, "cost Caesar ten years of exhaustion, victories, and negotiations, and Clovis, so to speak, only a day."[19] Yet the Gauls who resisted Caesar were surely less disciplined than

19. Gaëtano Filangieri, *La science de la législation*, Paris, Cuchet, 1786, t. II, p. 105, n. 1. Here is the complete quotation from which Constant also borrows other expressions. "The conquest of the Gauls cost Caesar ten years of exhaustion, victories, and negotiations. It cost Clovis at the head of a handful of Franks, so to speak, a day. Was the fifteen- or sixteen-year-old Clovis a better general than Caesar? Were the Franks more valiant than the Romans? No. Caesar had to fight a people who had always been free or happy. Clovis found the Gauls oppressed and enslaved for more than five centuries. This is the difference in a nutshell."

those who fought against Clovis and had been trained in Roman military tactics. Clovis, at fifteen or sixteen, was certainly not a greater general than Caesar. But Caesar had to subdue a people who took a great part in the administration of their domestic affairs, Clovis one which had been enslaved for five centuries. We have already said, at the start of this chapter, that among modern nations, freedom of the press takes the place in some respects of direct participation in the administration of affairs.

There are two circumstances, I agree, which can briefly stand in for public opinion among civilized nations in the matter of military success. The [147] first is when a great general inspires his soldiers with a personal enthusiasm. The second is when public opinion having been strong for a long time, the army has retained the momentum that opinion once gave it. In this case it is public opinion which has fled the nation and found refuge in the army. It is very easy to grasp that this spirit, which lives only in action and the attachment of interests, should grow dim first in the peaceful and inactive part of the nation, when the government takes away all its nourishment, and that it should flourish longer in the active and warlike part. Of these two circumstances, however, one is accidental and the other ephemeral, and both are artificial substitutes for the only real and durable cause. All man's faculties go together. Industry and the military arts are perfected by scientific discovery. The sciences gain in their turn from the perfectioning of the military arts and industry. Learning has applications to everything. It spurs on progress in industry, all the arts and sciences, and then, in analyzing all this progress, it extends its own horizon. Finally, morality is purified and corrected by such learning. If the government undermines free expression of thought, morality will be the less sound for it,[20] factual knowledge less accurate, the sciences less active in their development, the art of war less advanced, and industry less enriched by discoveries.

Human existence, attacked in its noblest parts, soon feels the poison extending to its most distant ones. You think you have limited it only in respect of some superfluous liberty or denied it only some worthless ceremony. In fact your poisoned weapon has struck it to the heart.

The process we are recounting here is not theory: it is history. It is the history of the Greek empire, that empire which was the heir to that of Rome, invested with much of its strength and all its intellectual achievement, that empire where despotism took root, with all the advantages most

20. See Constant's Note H at the end of Book VII.

favorable to its power and perpetuation, and which perished and fell solely for the reason that all despotic empires must perish and fall.

People often tell us, I know, of an alleged circle which the human spirit describes and which, they say, brings back—by an inevitable [148] determinism—ignorance after enlightenment, barbarism after civilization.[21] Unfortunately for this thesis, however, despotism has always slipped in between these stages in a way making it difficult not to define it as itself counting for something in the cycle. The real cause of these alternations in the history of nations is that man's intelligence cannot stand still. If you do not stop it, it advances. If you stop it, it retreats, because it cannot stay at the same point. Thought is the basis of everything. If you discourage it from self-examination, it will not exercise itself on any other object, except apathetically. One could say that, indignant at seeing itself driven from its proper sphere, it wants to take vengeance, in the form of a noble suicide, for the humiliation which has been inflicted on it. All the efforts of government will not restore it to life. The false, intermittent movement it receives resembles only the convulsions which an art—more frightening than effective—stimulates in corpses, without reanimating them. And if the government wished to make up for the natural activity of muzzled public opinion with its own actions, just as in besieged places they make the horses they keep locked up there paw the ground between the columns, it would be taking on a difficult task. To begin with, a wholly artificial bustle is costly to maintain, indeed can be maintained only by extraordinary things. When each person is free, he interests or amuses himself with what he is doing, saying, or writing. But when most of the nation is reduced to the role of forcibly silenced spectators, to make these dumb spectators applaud, or even just watch, the managers of the show have constantly to reawaken their curiosity with theatrical spectacles or changes of scene. Now, it is probably an advantage for a government to be adept at laying on grand events when the general good demands it. But it is an incalculable nuisance to the governed that the government simply has to put on so-called grand events when the general good does not demand this. Moreover, this artificial activity does not fulfill its [149] purpose for very long. The governed soon stop listening to a long monologue they are never allowed to interrupt. The nation gets tired of a pointless display whose costs and risks are all it supports, but whose purposes and management are alien to it. The interest

21. Constant indicates here all the opponents of the doctrine of human perfectibility, such as Fontanes, Fiévée, de Feletz.

in public affairs is concentrated on the government and its creatures. A moral barrier stands between the bustling of government and the lasting inaction of the people. The former tries in vain to communicate to the latter its concern, and the most dazzling undertakings and the most solemn celebrations of these are only so many funeral ceremonies, with dances on the tombs. All positions are occupied by ciphers, and consent is deprived of all spontaneity. Things keep going, but by command and threat. Everything is more expensive because men insist on payment for being reduced to the level of mere machines. Money has to take over the functions of opinion, imitation, and honor. Everything is harder, because nothing is voluntary. The government is obeyed rather than supported. At the least interruption all the cogs stop operating. It is like a game of chess. The hand of power controls it. No pieces resist. But if the hand were to stop for an instant, all the pieces would remain immobile. Finally, movement weakens in government itself. A nation's lethargy, where there is no public opinion, communicates itself to its government, whatever the latter does. Having been unable to keep the nation awake, the government finishes by falling asleep with it. Thus everything falls silent, subsides, degenerates, and is degraded in a nation which no longer has the right to make public its thoughts, and sooner or later, such a realm presents the spectacle of those plains of Egypt, where we see an immense pyramid pressing down on the arid dust, reigning over the silent wastes. It was a beautiful conceit of nature to place man's recompense outside himself, to have lighted in his heart this indefinable flame of glory, which, nourishing itself on noble hopes, the source of all great actions, [150] our protection against all the vices, the link between all the generations and between man and the universe, repulses gross pleasures and disdains sordid desires. Bad luck to him who extinguishes that sacred flame. He plays the part in this world of the principle of evil, his iron hand bends our brow to the earth, when heaven made us to walk head held high and to contemplate the stars.

CHAPTER SIX

Some Necessary Explication

In saying that freedom of the press in some degree replaces political rights, I did not mean it replaces them perfectly. As it is never other than precarious, where these rights do not exist, it does not do all the good it could do, and the good it does do is mingled with many ills. This is what happened in France at the end of the eighteenth century. But in this as in all such cases, it is not liberty we should blame but the absence of judicial guarantee. It is not necessary to remove the former but to ensure the latter. Freedom of the press can be appropriately restricted only where political freedom exists. Elsewhere, men of enlightenment have to pit themselves against all limits, because despotism cannot put limits on anything appropriately.

CHAPTER SEVEN

Final Observations

To stop people declaring their thoughts is to close to talent its finest career. But nature will not be stopped from giving birth to men of talent and their active side will, indeed, have to be exercised. What will happen? They will split into two classes. Some, true to the purpose they were born for, will attack your government. Others will run headlong into egotism and devote their superior talents to accumulating all the means of pleasure, the sole compensation left to them. Thus [151] the government, in its marvelous goings-on, will have divided men of talent into two parts, one seditious and the other rascally. It will probably punish them, but for its own crime. If their legitimate ambition had found the field free for their hopes and honorable efforts, the former would still be peaceful and the latter still virtuous. They did not seek out a reprehensible route until they had been driven back from the natural ones, which they had a right to follow. I say they had a right to do this because celebrity, renown, and glory are the human race's patrimony. It does not belong to a few men to rob their equals of them. It is not permitted to them to make life wither by depriving it of what gives it its brilliance.

A. [Refers to page 103.]
Esprit des lois, XII, 11.

B. [Refers to page 104.]
Under Charles II perpetual banishment was pronounced on all the ministers who would not swear the oath of supremacy. Burnet, Mémoires de son temps, I, 209.[22]

C. [Refers to page 104.]
In 1688, three years after the Protestants were forced to abjure their faith by means of a persecution which brought ten thousand men death on the wheel or by burning, all the newly converted were disarmed and their exclusion from all municipal offices was announced. Eclaircissements sur la Révocation de l'Edit de Nantes, I, 379.[23]

D. [Refers to page 104.]
Charles II's Parliament declared that the king could demand from the Scottish nation as a whole a bond in earnest of its future submission and act against it, as refractory, if the bond were inadequate. Hume, XI, 286, 287.[24]

[152] E. [Refers to page 104.]
Under Charles II, suspects in Scotland were asked three questions. Silence or hesitation were punished by death. On this pretext some women were hanged and others drowned. Among the latter were a girl of eighteen and one of thirteen. Hume, XII, 15, 17, 18.[25]

22. Gilbert Burnet, *Mémoires pour servir à l'histoire de la Grande-Bretagne sous les règnes de Charles II et de Jacques II* . . . , translated from Gilbert Burnet's English, London, Th. Ward, 1725, 3 vol.

23. Claude Carloman de Rulhière, *op. cit.,* t. I, pp. 378–379: "It was thought necessary to exclude from even the lowest municipal offices, after their abjuration, those who in the same century had given Sully to the Kingdom." There is no question in this passage of torture on the rack!

24. David Hume, *The History of England from the Invasion of Julius Caesar to the Revolution in 1688,* Basil, J.-J. Tourneisen, 1789, t. XI, pp. 272–289, in an article entitled *[The] State of Affairs in Scotland* and describing the effects of the despotism of Charles II on the Scots. The pages given by Constant do not correspond precisely to the text of his note.

25. *Ibid.,* t. XII, p. 17: "And when the poor deluded creatures refused to answer, capital punishments were inflicted on them. Even women were brought to the gibbet for

F. [Refers to page 104.]

The Revocation of the Edict of Nantes was followed by a law laying down that people who were ill and refused the sacraments would after their deaths be dragged through the mire and their goods confiscated. Enraged priests were often to be seen, viaticum in hand, escorted by a judge and his bailiffs and assistants, going to the homes of the dying, urging elderly people at death's door to sacrilege. They exposed them to the crowds drawn to the spectacle by curiosity, who shook with joy at the sight of the heretic humiliated. When the unfortunate person died, this fanatical populace made a sport out of insulting his remains and of executing the law in all its horror. Eclaircissements, Vol. I, 351–355, II, 177.[26]

[153] G. [Refers to page 115.]

It would be curious to calculate what the House of Austria has lost as a result of its management of its subject peoples, from the Peace of Cateau Cambresis to that of Pressburg (Bratislava). Vervins began the restitutions. Westphalia cost her Holland and Alsace. The Treaty of the Pyrenees entailed other sacrifices. Before the end of the same century she gave up Franche-Comté and in the following century in less than fifty years she lost Spain, the New World,

---

the pretended crime." And p. 18: "They all refused and were condemned to a capital punishment by drowning. One of them was an elderly women; the other two were young; one eighteen years of age, the other only thirteen."

26. Constant's references to Rulhière are accurate. It is interesting, however, to compare his note with the original texts in order to appreciate the art with which he mingled with his own prose the language of the author he was quoting. Thus in t. I, p. 351: "This was the occasion of a terrible law: Those who, when they are ill, refuse the sacraments, will, after their deaths, be dragged through the mire, and their goods confiscated. If they recover, they will be condemned to make amends, the men by going to the galleys forever, the women by imprisonment, both having their possessions confiscated." T. I, p. 355: "But in most of our towns we had only too often this dreadful spectacle, corpses dragged through the mire, and too often also we saw enraged priests, viaticum in hand, escorted by a judge and his bailiffs, going to the houses of the dying, and soon afterward the fanatical populace, making cruel sport of carrying out the law themselves in all its horror." T. II, pp. 177–178: ". . . I would say here that one saw at the bedside of the sick, a priest, surrounded by bailiffs and their assistants, carrying in the most solemn pomp the blessed sacrament, the most awesome of mysteries, urging a dying man to commit sacrilege, and making a mock of him to the crowd drawn there by curiosity, some of them trembling at the profanity, some shaking with joy at the sight of the humiliated heretic, reduced to a scandalous hypocrisy in order to keep his substance intact for his family and some worthless adornments for his grave."

Parma, Sicily, Naples, and Silesia. Next add what she has lost from then till the present.[27]

[154] H. [Refers to page 121.]

John Barrow's voyage to China can serve to show what a nation whose government has coerced it into immobility becomes like, morally and in every way.[28]

27. Constant, in this compressed survey of international politics from the sixteenth century to 1805, naturally understands by the House of Austria the Hapsburg dynasty, whose possessions, from Charles V to the War of the Spanish Succession, extended among others to Spain. A series of treaties to which Constant makes reference were signed between France and Spain, the latter understood as an Austrian dominion. Thus, after the Treaty of Cateau-Cambrésis (1559) France takes from the Holy Roman Empire the three bishoprics, Mets, Toul, and Verdun. At the Treaty of Vervins (1598) Spain loses Vermand, Picardy, Calais, etc. In 1648 following the Treaty of Westphalia, Spain loses sovereignty over the United Provinces, and France gains Alsace from the Empire. Eleven years later, following the Treaty of the Pyrenees (1659), France occupies ten Imperial towns in Alsace. By the Treaty of Nijmegen in 1678, France obtains the Franche-Comté. In 1714, by the Treaty of Rastatt, which brings an end to the wars of the Spanish succession, the kingdom of Spain no longer belongs to the Hapsburgs, and as Constant calculates it in the forty-nine years leading up to the Treaty of Hubertsburg (1763), Austria loses in succession Naples and Sicily (1738), Parma (1748), and Silesia (1763). Finally, Austria abandons also some territories after the Treaties of Campoformio (1797), Lunéville (1801), and Bratislava (1805), this last constraining the Austro-Hapsburg Empire to abandon Venice, Dalmatia, the Tyrol, and Vorarlberg. Constant's view is very French. One could object that though Austria lost many possessions to the benefit of France, she obtained significant territorial compensations in the East at the expense of Poland and Turkey (in the eighteenth century). Moreover, Constant's argument is not very convincing. He starts from the principle that the dwindling of the Hapsburg realms stems from the lack of liberty extended to enlightened thought. In fact, what Austria lost was to the advantage of equally despotic princes, such as Louis XIV.

28. John Barrow, *Voyage en Chine, formant le complément du voyage de Lord Macartney*, translated from the English, with notes, by J. Castéra, Paris, F. Buisson, an XIII (1805), 3 vol. Constant must have read at least the two accounts in the *Mercure de France*, 2 frimaire an XIV (23 November 1805), pp. 393–402, and 22 March 1806, pp. 537–542.

BOOK VIII

On Religious Freedom

Ch. 1. Why religion was so often attacked by the men of the Enlightenment. 131

Ch. 2. On civil intolerance. 135

Ch. 3. On the proliferation of sects. 137

Ch. 4. On the maintenance of religion by government against the spirit of inquiry. 139

Ch. 5. On the reestablishment of religion by government. 140

Ch. 6. On the axiom that the people must have a religion. 141

Ch. 7. On the utilitarian case for religion. 142

Ch. 8. Another effect of the axiom that the people must have a religion. 143

Ch. 9. On tolerance when government gets involved. 144

Ch. 10. On the persecution of a religious belief. 144

CHAPTER ONE

Why Religion Was So Often Attacked by the Men of the Enlightenment

In examining the proper role of the government with regard to religion, we are not at all questioning the benefits deriving from religious ideas. The more one loves freedom, the more one cherishes moral ideas, the more high-mindedness, courage, and independence are needed, the more it is necessary to have some respite from men, to take refuge in belief in a God.

If religion had always been perfectly free, it would never, in my view, have been other than an object of respect and love. One could hardly conceive the bizarre fanaticism rendering religion in itself an object of hatred or animosity. This recourse of an unhappy being to a just one, of a weak to a good one, should excite, it seems to me, even among those who consider it chimerical, only interest and sympathy. He who regards all religious hopes as erroneous ought to be more profoundly moved than anyone else by this universal chorus of suffering humanity, these requests of the grieving, cast from all corners of the earth at a stony heaven, to wait unanswered, or by the soothing illusion which takes for an answer the confused sound of so many repeated prayers far away on the wind.

The causes of our pains are numerous. Government can [158] banish us and lies calumniate us. We can be wounded by the bonds of a totally false society. A merciless nature punishes us in what we most cherish. The somber and solemn period of old age moves toward us, when things grow dark and seem to retreat, and a kind of coldness and lifelessness spreads on everything around us.

Faced with so much sorrow, we search everywhere for consolations and all our lasting ones are religious. When the world abandons us, we form some kind of alliance beyond it. When men persecute us, we create for ourselves some refuge beyond them. When we see our most cherished chimeras—justice, freedom, and native land—vanish, we flatter ourselves that there exists somewhere a being who will be grateful that we were true, despite our times, to justice, freedom, and fatherland. When we grieve something we love, we throw a bridge across the abyss, and in our thoughts we cross it. Finally, when life escapes us, we wing our way toward another one. Thus, it is the very essence of religion to be a faithful companion, the ingenious and tireless friend of unhappy souls.

Nor is this all. The consoler of those in misfortune, religion is at the same time the most natural of all our emotions. All our physical sensations, all our moral feelings, make it live again in our hearts, without our knowing. Everything which seems boundless to us, which produces in us the idea of immensity, the sight of the sky, the silence of the night, the vast stretches of ocean, everything which leads us to pity or enthusiasm, awareness of a virtuous action, a generous sacrifice, a danger bravely faced, the grief of another given succor and relief, everything which raises in the depths of our souls the primal elements of our nature, the contempt for vice, the hatred of tyranny, nourishes our religious sentiment.

This feeling relates closely to all noble, delicate, and profound passions. Like all of them it has something mysterious about it. For common reasoning cannot explain any of these passions in a satisfactory manner. Love, that exclusive preference for an object we had been able to manage without for a long time and which so many others resemble, the need for glory, that thirst for a fame which must outlast us, the enjoyment [159] we find in devotion, an enjoyment contrary to the habitual instinct of our egotism, melancholy, that sadness without cause, in the depths of which there is a pleasure we could not begin to analyze, a thousand other sensations we cannot describe, which fill us with vague impressions and confused emotions: these are inexplicable in terms of rigorous reasoning. They all have some affinity with religious feeling. All these things aid the development of morality. They make man break out of the narrow circle of his interests, they give the soul that flexibility, that delicacy, that exaltation smothered by habituation to life in the community and the calculations it necessitates.

Love is the most mixed of these intense emotions, because its purpose is a specific pleasure, this purpose being close to us, and ending up in egoism. Religious feeling, for the opposite reason, is the purest of all emotions. It does not flee with youth. It strengthens sometimes in old age, as if heaven had given it to us to console us in the most deprived period of our lives.

A man of genius said that the sight of the Apollo Belvedere or a picture by Raphael uplifted him.[1] Indeed, there is in the contemplation of beauty of all kinds something which detaches us from ourselves by making us feel that perfection is of greater worth than we, and which by means of this belief, inspiring in us a brief selflessness, awakens within us the power of

1. Hofmann has not identified this man of genius. The passage is repeated in Constant's account of Mme. de Staël's *Corinne* in the *Publiciste* of 12 May 1807. Ephraïm Harpaz in his edition of Constant suggests Fauriel or Charles de Villers. Benjamin Constant, *Recueils d'articles, 1795–1871*, with introduction, notes, and commentaries by Ephraïm Harpaz, Geneva, Droz, 1978, p. 88, n. 6 bis.

sacrifice, which power is the mother of all virtue. Whatever the cause of the emotion, it bears within it something which quickens the blood, arouses a kind of well-being, and heightens in us the sense of our existence and strengths. We become open to a generosity, a courage, and a sympathy above our everyday disposition. Even the corrupted man is better, when he is moved and as long as he stays moved.

I do not at all wish to say that absence of religious feeling proves that any individual lacks morals. There are men [160] in whom the mind is the dominant thing and can give way only to something absolutely clear. These men are routinely given to deep meditation and preserved from most corrupting temptations by the enjoyment of study and the habit of thought. As a result they are capable of scrupulous moral behavior. In the mass of common folk, however, the absence of religious feeling, not deriving from such causes, most commonly indicates, I believe, aridity and frivolity of outlook, a mind absorbed in petty and ignoble interests, a marked sterility in imagination. I make an exception of the case in which these men have been plagued by persecution, which has the effect of causing revolt against its commands. Then it can happen that sensitive but proud men, indignant against a religion imposed on them, blindly reject everything connected to religion. This circumstantial objection, however, in no way affects the general thesis.

I would not have a poor opinion of an educated man, if he were presented to me as a stranger to religious feeling, but a whole people incapable of this feeling would seem to me deprived of a precious faculty and disinherited by nature.

If I were accused here of not defining religious sentiment in a sufficiently precise way, I would ask how one defines with precision that vague and profound part of our moral sensations which by its very nature defies all the efforts of language. How will you define the impression of a deep night, of an ancient forest, of the wind which moans across ruins or above tombs, of the sea which stretches away out of sight? How will you define the emotion caused in you by the songs of Ossian, the church of Saint Peter, the meditation of death, the harmony of sounds or forms? How will you define dreaming, that inner quivering of the soul, where all the powers of the senses and of thought come to gather as though to lose themselves in a mysterious confusion? There is religion at the bottom of all these things. Everything fine, intimate, and profound is religious.

Idea of God, the common center where, above the action of time and the reach of wickedness, there come together all the ideas of justice, love, freedom, and pity which in this brief world [161] constitute the dignity of the human race, permanent seat of everything beautiful, great, and good across the degradation and iniquity of the ages, eternal voice which replies to virtue in its own tongue, when the language of everything around it is low and criminal, call from the present to the future, from earth to heaven, solemn recourse of all the oppressed in all situations, last hope of weakness trampled underfoot, of innocence slain, thought both consoling and noble, no, whatever is done, the human race can never manage without you.

But how does it happen, therefore, that religion, this constant ally, this necessary support, this unique glimmer amid the shadows which surround us, has in all ages been exposed to frequent and bitter attacks? How comes it that the class which has declared itself its enemy has almost always been the most enlightened, the most independent, and the most educated? It is because religion has been distorted. Man has been pursued into this last refuge, this intimate sanctuary of his existence. In the hands of government, religion has been transformed into a menacing institution. Having created most—and the most harrowing—of our sorrows, government has laid claim to the control of man even in his means of consolation. Dogmatic religion, an aggressive and persecuting force, has wished to submit to its yoke both the imagination in its conjecturing and the heart in its needs. It has become a scourge more terrible than those it was intended to enable us to forget.

Hence, in all those eras when men have demanded their moral independence, there is this resistance to religion, seemingly directed against the sweetest of the feelings, and really against only the most oppressive of tyrannies. Intolerance, in putting force on the side of faith, put courage alongside doubt. The fury of the believers has heightened the vanity of the skeptics, and man has in this way managed to turn for himself into a merit what, left to himself, he would have regarded as a misfortune. Persecution provokes resistance. The government, menacing a point of view, whatever it may be, excites all minds of any worth to declare for it. There is in man that which revolts on principle against all intellectual constraint. This spirit [162] is even capable at times of being infuriated. It can cause many crimes. But it springs from everything noble deep in our being.

I have often felt myself struck with sadness and astonishment when reading the famous *System of Nature.*[2] This long-lasting, desperate eagerness by an old man to close off any future lying before him, this inexplicable thirst for destruction, this blind, almost ferocious hatred of an idea so gentle and

2. Paul Henri Dietrich, baron d'Holbach, *Système de la nature ou des lois du monde physique et du monde moral,* M. Mirabaud, London, 1770.

consoling, seemed to me a strange delirium. I understood it nevertheless when I remembered the perils with which the government surrounded that writer. In all ages atheists have been harassed in their thinking. They have never had the time or freedom to consider their own opinions at their leisure. For them freedom has always been a property that people wanted to rob them of. They have dreamed less about deepening it than justifying or protecting it. But just leave them in peace. They will soon cast a sad glance on the world they have stripped of its gods. They will themselves be astonished at their victory. The heat of the struggle, the thirst to regain the right to free enquiry, all these reasons for exaltation will no longer sustain them. Their imagination, so recently preoccupied with success, now having nothing to do, as it were deserted, will come back on itself. They will see man alone on an earth which must engulf him. The world is lifeless. Ephemeral generations appear there, to suffer and die, isolated creatures of chance. Certain ambitious men quarrel and fight over them, hurt and destroy them. They do not even have the consolation of hoping that one day these monsters will be judged, that they will finally see the day of reparation and vengeance shine. No tie exists between these generations whose portion here is servitude, with nothingness beyond. All communication is broken between the past, [163] the present, and the future. No voice from the races which are gone lives on among the living ones, and their voice too must one day fall away into the depths of the same eternal silence. All this simply makes one feel that if atheism had not been met with intolerance, the aspects of the belief which put people off would have constrained the outlook of its disciples in such a way as to keep them in apathy and silence, in a state of indifference to everything.

I repeat. As long as government leaves religion perfectly independent, no one will have an interest in attacking it. The very idea will not arise. But if government affects to defend it, if it wishes above all to make it an ally, free thinking will not hesitate to attack it.

CHAPTER TWO

On Civil Intolerance

Today, when intellectual progress is opposed to religious intolerance properly so called, that is to say, to that kind whose purpose is to enforce opinions, a number of governments take refuge behind the need for a certain civil intolerance. Rousseau, who cherished all the ideas of liberty and furnished pretexts for all the claims of tyranny, is still cited in favor of this way of thinking.

"There is," he says, "a purely civil profession of faith, whose articles it belongs to the sovereign power to fix, not precisely, like religious dogma, but in terms of the feeling of sociability. Without being able to enforce any belief in these dogmas, it can banish from the state anyone who does not believe them, not for being impious but for being unsociable."[3] What is this business of the state deciding which feelings one should adopt? What does it matter to me that the sovereign power does not force me to believe such and such, if it punishes me for what I do not believe? What does it matter that it does not attack me for impiety, if it attacks me as unsociable? What do I care that government eschews theological niceties if it loses its way [164] in a hypothetical morality, no less nice and no less foreign to natural justice?

I know of no system of servitude which has sanctified more fatal errors than the eternal metaphysics of the Social Contract.

Civil intolerance is just as dangerous, more absurd, and above all more unjust than religious intolerance. It is just as dangerous, since it has the same results under a different pretext. It is more absurd, since it is not motivated by conviction. It is more unjust, since the evil it causes is not from duty but a mere calculation.

Civil intolerance borrows a thousand forms and takes refuge behind one administrative pretext after another as it hides away from reason. Defeated on the principle, it disputes the application. We have seen men persecuted for close to thirty centuries, telling the government which released them from their long proscription that if it were necessary for there to be several religions accepted in a State, it was no less necessary for the tolerated sects to be prevented from producing new ones, by way of subdivision.[4] But is not each tolerated sect itself a subdivision of some former one? On what grounds can it refuse future generations the same rights claimed by itself from past generations?

It has been proposed, in a country which prides itself on freedom of religion, that none of the recognized churches be able to change its dogmas without government permission. If by chance, however, these dogmas came to be rejected by most of the religious community, could government enforce that majority to profess them? Now, in matters of opinion, the rights of the majority and minority are the same.

3. See Constant's Note A at the end of Book VIII.

4. See Constant's Note B at the end of Book VIII.

One understands intolerance when it imposes on everybody one and the same profession of faith. It is at least consistent. Maybe it thinks it holds men in the sanctuary of truth. But when just two opinions are allowed, since one of the two must necessarily be false, to authorize government to force individuals in one or the other to stay attached to the opinions of their sect, or the sects never to change their opinions, is to authorize government, formally, to lend assistance to error. [165]

CHAPTER THREE

On the Proliferation of Sects[5]

This proliferation of sects, which causes such panic, is the most salutary thing for religion. It ensures that religion does not lose its sensibility, to become a mere form, an almost mechanical habit, which combines with all the vices and sometimes with all the crimes.

When religion degenerates thus, it loses all its influence on morality. It makes its abode, so to speak, in a recess of the human mind, where it remains isolated from the rest of existence. In Italy we see mass happen before murder, confession follow it, penance absolve it, and the man, thus freed from guilt, meditating on new murders.

Nothing is simpler. To stop sects subdividing, man must be prevented from reflecting on religion. It is necessary then to prevent his taking any interest in it. It must be reduced to repeated symbols and practices observed. Everything becomes outer show, done unreflectingly, and soon, as a result, without interest or care. In all moral things reflection is the source of life; and freedom is the first and indispensable condition of all reflection.

Some Mongol peoples, whose religion enjoins frequent prayers, persuaded themselves that what pleased the gods in these prayers was that the air struck by the movement of the lips proved to them continuously that man was concerned with them. Consequently these people have invented little prayer wheels which, moving the air in a certain way, endlessly maintain the desired movement, and, while these wheels turn, each person, convinced the gods are satisfied, attends to his business or his pleasures

5. Some of the advantages Constant observes in relation to the proliferation of sects had already been spotted by Adam Smith, *Recherches sur la nature et les causes de la richesse des nations,* new translation with notes and observations by Germain Garnier, Paris, H. Agasse, 1802, t. IV, pp. 203–212.

without concern.[6] Religion, in more than one European country, has often reminded me of the little wheels of the Mongol peoples.

[166] The proliferation of sects is advantageous to morality in a way which seems not to have been noted yet. All new sects tend to mark themselves off from those they are breaking with by a more scrupulous morality. Often, too, the sect which sees a new breakaway developing within itself, moved to praiseworthy imitation, does not wish to be stuck in this way behind the innovators. The advent of Protestantism undeniably reformed the morals of the Catholic clergy. If the government did not meddle with religion, the sects would proliferate forever. Each new congregation would seek to prove the goodness of its doctrines by the purity of its morals. Each abandoned one would want to defend itself with the same weapons. A blessed struggle would result in which success would be judged by a more austere morality. Morals would improve effortlessly out of a natural impulsion and honorable rivalry. This can be seen in America or even in Scotland, where tolerance is far from complete but where, nevertheless, Presbyterianism has split into numerous branches. Up until now, no doubt, the springing up of sects, far from being accompanied by these salutary effects, has mostly been marked by strife and misfortune. This is because government has got involved. Nature, like Ormuzd, had infused all things with the principle of good. Government, like Ahriman, came to place the principle of evil alongside.[7]

[167] In opposing the proliferation of sects, governments fail to recognize their own interests. When sects are very numerous in a country, they put

6. Hofmann was not able to find out where Constant got his information on the prayer wheels, but his explanation is certainly wrong. M. Jean Eracle, curator of the Geneva Museum of Ethnography, has kindly furnished some information on the subject: "What is known in the West as a 'prayer wheel' and takes different forms and sizes belongs to Tantrist Buddhism, both in its Tibeto-Mongol and Sino-Japanese forms. The proper name of this object is 'Wheel of the Law.' Whoever makes it turn participates in the teaching of the Buddha who, according to the venerated expression, 'set in motion the wheel of the law.' The prayer wheel then has symbolic significance and is not a way of 'praying without effort.' Moreover, whoever works it generally recites sacred invocations at the same time. Thus one often sees pilgrims telling beads with one hand and making the wheel turn with the other. The wheel is thus like a thought condenser. Moreover, it links the body to the words of the invocations and to the devout thoughts of the person praying." Extract from a letter from M. Jean Eracle to the editor.

7. [For a compendious discussion of these Persian (specifically Zoroastrian) deities, see David J. Levy, "'The Good Religion': Reflections on the History and Fate of Zoroastrianism," in his *The Measure of Man,* Claridge, 1993, pp. 170–190. Translator's note]

mutual checks upon one another and free the government from having to bargain with any one of them in order to contain them. When there is a single dominant sect, the government needs to take countless steps in order to have nothing to fear from it. When there are only two or three, each large enough to threaten the others, there has to be surveillance, nonstop repression. A singular policy indeed! You say you want to keep the peace! So to that effect you prevent opinions from dividing in such a way as to split these fellows up into weak little groups, hardly noticeable, and you set up three or four large, hostile bodies face to face which, thanks to the care you take to keep them large and powerful, are ready to go on the attack at the first signal.

CHAPTER FOUR

On the Maintenance of Religion by Government against the Spirit of Inquiry

However government intervenes in matters pertaining to religion, it does harm.

It does harm when it wants to shore up religion against the spirit of inquiry. For government cannot act on conviction; it does so only on the basis of interest. In granting its favors only to men with the approved opinions, what does it gain? It alienates those who own up to what they think, and are therefore at least frank. The others know how to use facile lies to elude its restrictions, which strike at the scrupulous and are powerless against those who are or become corrupt.

In any case, let me ask the people in government, [168] since this is always the problem requiring resolution when all is said and done: what are your ways of favoring an opinion? Do you entrust the important functions of the State solely to those holding it? If you do, those rebuffed will be angry about the favoritism. Will you have people write and speak for the opinion you are protecting? Others will write or speak in an opposite vein. Will you restrain freedom of writing, speech, eloquence, reason, even irony, or ranting? That will see you involved in new activities, no longer a matter of favoring or convincing, but of stifling and punishing. Do you think your laws can grasp all the nuances and adjust themselves proportionately? Will your repressive measures be light? People will defy them. They will merely embitter without intimidating people. Will they be severe? You will be seen as persecutors. Once you are on that fast and slippery slope, you will seek to stop in vain.

But what successes do you hope for from your persecutions themselves? No king, I think, was surrounded with more prestige than Louis XIV.

Honor, vanity, fashion, that all-powerful thing, had assumed positions of obedience under his reign. He lent religion the support of his throne as well as of his example. He had dignity of manner and propriety of speech. His will, constant rather than brusque, steady rather than violent, and never appearing capricious, seemed to honor whatever was in his protection. He believed his soul's salvation required the maintenance of religion in its most rigid practices, and he had persuaded his courtiers that the salvation of the king's soul was of especial importance. Despite ever growing solicitude, however, plus the austerity of a long-established court and the recollection of fifty years of glory, even before his death, doubt slipped into people's minds. We see among the records of the period intercepted letters, written by assiduous flatterers of Louis XIV, which according to Mme. de Maintenon were offensive both to God and the King. The King died. The philosophic current then swept away all the dikes. Intellectual activity made up for the constraint it had impatiently borne, and the result of long suppression was lack of belief pushed to excess. [169]

CHAPTER FIVE

On the Reestablishment of Religion by Government

Government does no less harm and is no less impotent when, in the context of a skeptical age, it wants to reestablish religion. Religion must be restored on its own according to man's need for it. When you disturb him with alien considerations, you prevent him from feeling the full force of this need. You may say, and rightly, that religion is part of nature: so do not cover up its voice with your own.

Government intervention in defense of religion, when public opinion is unfavorable, has this particular drawback: that religion is then defended by those who do not believe in it. Those who govern, like the governed themselves, are subject to the march of human ideas. When skepticism has penetrated the educated part of a nation, it will come out in the government too. Now, in all eras opinion or vanity is stronger than interests. Those in government can tell themselves in vain that it is to their advantage to favor religion. They can deploy their power on behalf of religion; but they can never bring themselves to show a regard for it. It pleases them to take the public into their confidence as to their mental reservations. They would be scared to seem convinced, lest they be taken for fools. If their first words sanctify the order for belief, their next ones are aimed at winning back for themselves the honors of skepticism. Bad missionaries these, who want to put themselves above their own profession of faith.

CHAPTER SIX

On the Axiom That the People Must Have a Religion

Thus is established this axiom that the people must have a religion, an axiom which flatters the vanity of those who repeat it, because in repeating it, they separate themselves from this people for whom a religion is necessary.

[170] This axiom is false in itself, insofar as it implies that religion is more necessary for the working-class part of society than for the leisured and opulent classes. If religion is necessary, it is equally so for all men and for all levels of education. The crimes of the poor and uneducated are of a more violent and terrible character, but at the same time they are easier to detect and curb. The law encompasses them, recognizes them, and represses them, easily, because these crimes offend it in a direct way. The corruption of the upper classes is more nuanced and diversified. It slips away from positive laws, mocking their spirit as it eludes their letter, opposing them moreover with wealth, influence, and power. What bizarre reasoning! The poor man can do nothing. He is surrounded by obstacles, tied down by all manner of bonds. He has neither protectors nor supports. He can commit an isolated crime, but everything takes up arms against him as soon as he is in the wrong. He does not find in his judges, drawn always from a hostile class, any consideration for him, nor any chance of impunity in his connections, which are as powerless as he. His conduct never influences the general lot of the society he belongs to. And you want the mysterious protection of religion against him alone. The rich man, on the contrary, is judged by his peers and allies. The punishments they inflict on him always more or less rebound on them. Society lavishes support on him. All material and moral opportunities are his solely as a result of wealth. He can influence things far off. He can overthrow or corrupt. And this is the powerful and fortunate being you want to set free from the yoke which it seems to you indispensable to bring to bear heavily on a weak and helpless one.

I say all this within the standard hypothesis that religion is valuable above all in its reinforcing the penal laws. This is not my opinion, however. I place religion higher. I do not see it at all as a supplement to the gallows or the wheel. There is a common morality, based on calculation, interest, and security, which can, I think, at a pinch do without religion. It can do without it in the case of the rich man because he thinks, and in the case of the poor man because the law terrifies him, and besides, all his activities being laid out in advance, the habit of constant work produces the same result as reflection in his life. But woe betide the people who have only this common morality! It is for the creation of a more elevated [171] morality that religion seems desirable to me. I do not invoke it to repress gross crimes but to ennoble all the virtues.

CHAPTER SEVEN

On the Utilitarian Case for Religion

The defenders of religion often believe they can work wonders representing it as above all useful. What would they say if it were demonstrated to them that they are rendering religion the worst service?

Just as in seeking in all nature's beauties a positive purpose, an immediate use and application to everyday life, one causes all the charm of this magnificent whole to fade, so in constantly endowing religion with a vulgar utility, one makes it dependent on that utility. It now has only a secondary status, now seeming only a means, and it is consequently degraded.

The word "utilize" [*utiliser*] has rightly been banned from the French language.[8] I do not know if I am wrong, but it seems to me that in everything relating to the soul's affections and to noble ideas, one should reject the thing, just as in language the word has been rejected.

Moreover, this need for utility both close to hand and, so to speak, material is perhaps the inherent vice of the French character. We could apply to the moral character of our nation what is recounted about the physical laziness of the Turks. It is said that the secretary of a French ambassador to Constantinople took a stroll for a while every evening in a garden. The Turkish neighbors of the ambassador begged him to pardon his secretary and no longer impose on him such a severe punishment. They [172] could not conceive that one could walk for nothing. We apparently cannot conceive that one might believe for nothing. So we are of all the nations the one whose writers have almost always envisaged religion in the most imperfect and narrowest way.[9]

8. Jacques Necker, *Du pouvoir executif dans les grands Etats*, s.l., 1792, t. II, p. 205. Here the economist makes himself a grammarian and criticizes the use of certain neologisms.

9. See Constant's Note C at the end of Book VIII.

CHAPTER EIGHT

Another Effect of the Axiom That the People Must Have a Religion

The axiom that the people must have a religion is furthermore of all things the one most calculated to destroy all religion. The people are alerted by a rather sure instinct as to what is going on over their heads. The cause of this instinct is the same one which gives children, servants, and all the dependent classes their insight. Their interest enlightens them as to the secret thoughts of those in charge of their destiny. It is counting too much on the people's good will to hope they will believe for long what their leaders refuse to believe. I know that atheistic governors with superstitious subjects seem to some statesmen the ideal model today. This sweet chimera cannot be realized, however. The sole result of their endeavor is that the people, seeing them to be unbelievers, break off from their religion without knowing why. What these men gain by prohibiting discussion is to stop people from being enlightened, but not from being impious. This they become by imitation. They treat religion as a foolish thing, as trickery, and each person hands it down to his social inferiors, who in their turn hasten to push it down even further. Thus it declines, more degraded, every day. It was less threatened, and above all less debased, when it was attacked from all sides. It could take refuge in the depths of sensitive souls. Vanity did not fear to seem foolish nor to be demeaning itself by respecting religion.

[173] This is still not all. When a government lends its lofty assistance to a fallen religion in this way, the recognition it demands completes the abasement. Religion is no longer that divine power, coming down from heaven to amaze and reform the world. It is a timid slave and humble dependent which prostrates itself before government, watches its gestures, asks for its orders, flatters the thing which despises it, and teaches the peoples eternal truths only at the government's pleasure. Its priests, trembling at the foot of their servile altars, stammer in censored words. They do not dare to make the old truths ring out in the accents of courage and conscience. And far from speaking, like Bossuet, to the great of this world, in the name of a God who judges kings, in their terror, under the eye of a disdainful master, they try to work out how they should speak of their God.

CHAPTER NINE

On Tolerance When Government Gets Involved

Who would believe it? Government acts adversely, even when it wants to submit the principle of tolerance to its jurisdiction. It imposes on tolerance positive and fixed forms, which are contrary to its nature. Tolerance is nothing else than the freedom of all present and future religions. The Emperor Joseph II wished to establish tolerance. Liberal in his views, he began by ordering a vast inventory of all the religious opinions held by his subjects. Some number or other were registered for admission to the benefit of his protection. What happened? A religion which had been forgotten suddenly came to declare itself, and Joseph II, that tolerant prince, told it that it had come too late. The deists of Bohemia were persecuted in view of their lateness, and the philosopher monarch put himself at the same time at loggerheads with Brabant, which demanded the exclusive domination of Catholicism, and with the unfortunate Bohemians who were asking for freedom of opinion. This limited tolerance [174] embodies a singular error. Only the imagination can satisfy the needs of the imagination. When, in a given polity, you had aimed at tolerating twenty religions, you would still have done nothing for the believers of the twenty-first. Governments which think they are leaving a proper latitude to the governed by allowing them to choose between a fixed number of religious beliefs, are like that Frenchman who, arriving in a village in Germany whose inhabitants wanted to learn Italian, taught them Basque and low Breton.

CHAPTER TEN

On the Persecution of a Religious Belief

Finally, the government acts harmfully when it proscribes a religion because it thinks it dangerous, and the harm will not be any the less when the government's judgment is right. When it punishes the culpable acts a religion causes to be committed, not as religious acts but as culpable ones, it will easily succeed in repressing them. If it attacked them as religious, it would turn them into duties for the fanatical, and if it wanted to reach right back to the thinking which is their source, it would become involved in a labyrinth of endless persecutions, harassments, and iniquities. The only way to weaken an opinion is to establish free discussion. Now, anyone who speaks of free enquiry speaks of distance from government of any type, the absence of any collective intervention. Such enquiry is essentially individual.

In order for persecution, which naturally revolts sensibilities and binds them to the persecuted belief, on the contrary to succeed in destroying this belief, minds must be debased, and not only must the religion one wishes to destroy be subjected to attack, but so must all moral and virtuous sentiments. To persuade a man to despise or abandon one of his fellow creatures whose misfortune is due to an opinion, that is to say, unjustly, to set him today to abandon the doctrine he professed yesterday, because it is suddenly threatened, you have to stifle all the justice and [175] pride in him. To restrict the harsh measures taken against a religion to its ministers, as has been done among us, is to trace an illusory limit. These measures soon attack all those who share the same doctrine, and next they attack all those who pity the misfortune of the oppressed. "Let no one tell me," said M. de Clermont-Tonnerre in 1791, and events have doubly justified his prediction, "let no one tell me that in pursuing to the bitter end priests said to be refractory, we will extinguish all opposition. I hope the opposite precisely because of my regard for the French nation. For any nation which gives way to force in questions of conscience is a nation so vile, so corrupted, that nothing can be hoped from it, either by way of reason or freedom."[10]

Superstition is deadly only when it is protected or threatened. Do not provoke it with injustices; simply take away from it any means of doing harm by its actions. First it will become an innocent obsession, and soon it will extinguish itself, for lack of the ability to appeal by way of its sufferings or command by virtue of its alliance with government. To refuse its mercy and support to persecuted men because they are persecuted thus for what seems to us an error, is to give oneself over to sentiments of inexcusable presumption and fanaticism. These men are defending their rights. Error or truth, the thought of man is his most sacred property. Error or truth, the tyrants are equally guilty when they attack it. He who proscribes superstitious speculation in the name of philosophy and he who proscribes independent thought in the name of God, are equally deserving of the execration of men of good will. [176] Allow me to finish with another quotation from M. de Clermont-Tonnerre. He will not be accused of exaggerated principles. Although he was a friend of freedom, or perhaps because he was a friend of freedom, he was almost always rebuffed by both parties in the Constituent Assembly. He died a victim of his moderation. His opinion, I think, will carry some weight. "Religion and the state," he said,

10. Stanislas-Marie de Clermont-Tonnerre, *Réflexions sur le fanatisme,* in *Recueil des opinions de Stanislas-Marie de Clermont-Tonnerre,* Paris, Migneret, 1791, t. IV, pp. 98–99.

"are two quite distinct and separate things, whose bringing together can only distort both one and the other.[11] Man has a relationship with his creator. He constructs for himself or is given various ideas about this relationship. This system of ideas is called religion. Each person's religion is therefore his opinion of his relationship to God. Each man's opinion being free, he may take up or not take up such religion.[12] The opinion of the minority cannot be subordinated to that of the majority. No opinion can therefore be commanded by social consensus. What is true of religion is also true of cults. The cult is what each person professes in conjunction with those of like religious opinion. The forms of the cult are the agreed rite among those who profess the same religion. The acts of the cult are the stern duty of the man holding the religious opinions which prescribe them. Thus the cult and its acts share in the nature and the freedom of opinion of which they are the necessary consequence. Thus what is true of opinion is also true of the cult and its acts.[13] Religion touches all times, all places, all governments. Its sanctuary is the consciousness of man, and consciousness is the sole faculty which man can never sacrifice to a social convention.[14] Religion will not lend itself to any association, any relation of supremacy or submission with political [177] government. . . .[15] The political body must not have dominion over any religion. It must not reject any of them unless the cult in question is a threat to social order."[16]

11. Stanislas-Marie de Clermont-Tonnerre, *Opinion sur la propriété des biens du clergé, novembre 1789*, in *Recueil des opinions . . . , op. cit.*, t. II, p. 71.

12. *Ibid.*, pp. 74–75. Constant has not given us the following passage: "he can keep it or leave it. If opinions are free, no one can bind the opinions of others. No one can bind even his own, for being free, he reserves the right to abandon it if he judges it wrong."

13. Stanislas-Marie de Clermont-Tonnerre, *Opinion sur la propriété . . . , op. cit*, pp. 75–76.

14. *Ibid.*, p. 73.

15. *Ibid.*, pp. 73–74. The actual text has: "If religion precludes any association, any relationship of supremacy or subjection with political government, the social pact admits for its part no religious clause."

16. *Ibid.*, p. 72. The original text is: "I maintain that the social body is by its nature a stranger to religion, such that it cannot profess any religion, and that it cannot reject any unless this religion is a menace to public order. . . ."

A. [Refers to page 136.]

Rousseau. Contrat Social. Livre IV. Ch. 8.[17] He adds: "Only if someone, after having recognized publicly these same dogmas, behaves as if he does not believe them, let him be punished by death. He has committed the worst of crimes: he has lied before the law."[18] But he who has the misfortune of not believing these dogmas, cannot admit his doubts without giving himself up to banishment. And if his affections hold him back, if he has a family, a wife, children, friends he hesitates about leaving to throw himself into exile, is it not you, you alone, who are forcing him to what you call the worst of crimes, lying before the law? I will say, moreover, that in these circumstances, this lie seems to me far from being a crime. When so-called laws demand the truth from us only to banish us, we do not owe them the truth.[19]

B. [Refers to page 136.]

Address by the Jews to the French government in 1808.[20]

C. [Refers to page 142.]

Justice demands that I except Bossuet, Fénelon, M. Necker,[21] and M. de Chateaubriand. Even so, the latter thought it necessary in order to uphold Christianity to paint it as particularly useful to poetry.[22] This urge to see religion as useful has led its defenders among us to endless childish arguments. Lent has been justified as good for the navy. What a wretched point of view! Moreover, how could this justification apply to landlocked countries which cannot have a navy?

17. The reference is correct.

18. *Ibid.*

19. This obviously recalls the controversy Constant raised against Kant in *Des réactions politiques*. See Hofmann's thesis, Première Partie, Ch. 2, p. 143.

20. The date is wrong. Constant is referring to the *Réponse d'Abraham Furtado, Président de l'Assemblée des Juifs, au discours des commissaires de S.M.I. et R. le 18 septembre 1806*, published in the *Moniteur* of 22 September 1806, pp. 1171–1172, and published as a pamphlet (BN, 4° Ld 184 225).

21. For example, in *De l'importance des opinions religieuses*, London, 1788, and in the *Cours de morale religieuse*, Geneva, 1800.

22. François-René de Chateaubriand, *Génie du christianisme*. Deuxième Partie: *Poétique du christianisme*. The first edition of this work appeared in 1802.

BOOK IX

On Legal Safeguards

CH. 1. On the independence of the courts. 151
CH. 2. On the abridgment of due process. 153
CH. 3. On punishments. 157
CH. 4. On the prerogative of exercising mercy. 160

CHAPTER ONE

On the Independence of the Courts

We have placed among individual rights the certainty that one will not be treated arbitrarily, as though one had exceeded the limits of these rights, that is to say, the guarantee that one will not be arrested, nor detained, nor tried, except according to law and following due process. We are obliged consequently to speak here of judicial power. So far from such discussion going beyond the limits of this work, we believe, on the contrary, that the indispensable conditions for making judicial power the safeguard of citizens are the same under all forms of government.

The first condition is that the judiciary must be independent. This assertion does not need proof. A people whose government can affect the judgments and direct or force the opinion of judges; employ against those it wishes to destroy the appearances of justice; hide behind the veil of the laws to strike its victims with their own sword: such a country is in a situation more unhappy, more contrary to the purpose and principles of the social State, than the savage horde on the banks of the Ohio or the Arab of the desert. There is only one way to make the judiciary independent: its members must be irremovable. Periodic election by the people, appointment for a time by the executive power, the possibility of removal without process, equally undermine the independence of the judiciary.

People protested strongly against the sale of offices. This was an abuse; but this abuse had an advantage which the legal dispensation which existed during the Revolution has often made us regret: the independence and irremovability of the judges.

[182] For sixteen years nothing was free, not the courts, nor the judges, nor the judgments. The various groups seized in their turn the instruments and the processes of law. The courage of the most intrepid warriors would scarcely have sufficed for our magistrates to pronounce their judgments according to their consciences, and such is the frightful weight of civil harassment that the courage which faces death in battle is easier than the public profession of a free opinion, in the midst of menacing factionists. A removable or revocable judge is much more dangerous than one who has bought his job. To have bought one's place is a much less corrupting thing than having always to be scared of losing it.

It is a mistake to be scared of esprit de corps in the judiciary. It is to be dreaded only when the jury system does not exist and when laws which have proliferated, and some by that very fact have necessarily fallen into disuse, supply the judges with means for circumscribing and proscribing all the citizens.

In all other cases, esprit de corps is one of the best safeguards against judges allowing themselves to be dominated by the other powers of the State.

The old Parlements of France have bequeathed us, I agree, some unfortunate memories. The fault lay much less in their organization, however, than in a host of causes which no longer exist. The Parlements deserved far less public hatred for prevaricating in their functions than as the organs of execrable laws.

The eternally infamous sentences on the Calas, Sirven, and La Barre families were a product of the spirit of intolerance with which our laws and our whole political organization were impregnated. If there had been no dominant religion at all, cruel judges would not have sacrificed Calas, nor banished Sirven; and the unfortunate La Barre would not have perished [183] on the wheel, aged seventeen, for insulting the symbols of the privileged religion.[1]

The Parlements [high judicial courts] persecuted courageous writers because oppressive laws hugely increased the number of death sentences on the exercise of our most legitimate rights. Until the end of the eighteenth century, there were edicts (passed in 1767) which condemned to death *authors of writings calculated to stir up people's minds*[2] [Constant's emphasis]. If there had been no vague law violating press freedom, our Parlements would not have been able to pursue men who could not have been open to accusation.

1. A reference to the causes célèbres of religious intolerance against which Voltaire protested in publishing notably his *Treaty on Tolerance* and in interceding each time with the Parlements to have the victims and their families rehabilitated. Jean Calas was broken alive on the wheel in 1762. Jean-François Lefebvre, knight of La Barre, was decapitated (and not executed on the wheel) in 1766 at nineteen (not seventeen). He is the only one of the three whose rehabilitation Voltaire was not able to obtain. Finally, Pierre-Paul Sirven managed to escape death by fleeing to Switzerland. Calas and Sirven were accused of murder, the first of his son and the second of his daughter, La Barre of having committed sacrilegious acts in relation to religion and its symbols.

2. Constant is referring to the "Declaration of 16 April 1757 [not 1767], punishing with death all those convicted of having composed, printed, sold or smuggled writings tending to attack religion, to stir up emotions, to attack royal authority, to upset public order and public peace." Quoted from Marcel Marion, *Dictionnaire des institutions de la France aux XVIIe et XVIIIe siècles,* Paris, A. Picard, 1923, s.v. Censure.

With all their vices, by the single fact of their irremovability, the Parlements were constantly led to struggle against the government, to protest against the increase in taxation and against illegal arrests and lettres de cachet.

I presuppose, moreover, the existence of severe procedures against judges who exceed their powers or deviate from the laws. I presuppose that no judgment is without appeal, because man must always have assured recourse against injustice and error.

Once these precautions have wisely been taken, though, then let judicial independence be complete. The executive power should exert no influence on it, even indirectly. It should never in its acts nor its public proclamations allow itself a [184] murmur against the very basis of political society, the citizens' safeguard, the freedom of the courts. Nothing is more calculated to deprave public opinion than these perpetual declamations, repeated among us on all sides and in all periods, against men who deserved respect if they judged according to their consciences, and punishment if they prevaricated in their judgments.

I have assumed, moreover, the ongoing presence of the institution of the jury system. I know no judicial safeguard without this. Woe to the nation which lets itself be deceived by cunning objections. Juries, people say, enjoy absolving the guilty. But they have an interest as citizens and owners in punishing criminals. They are scared of becoming victims of their severity. The fault then lies with the government, with the lack of order, with the agents charged with pursuing the enemies of public security. If you once agree that despotism is a convenient tool for arresting the rise in heinous crimes, you give the government an interest in heinous crimes increasing. It will be careless in its surveillance in order to force you to give it unlimited powers.

CHAPTER TWO

On the Abridgment of Due Process

This leads me to examine a line of argument used as a pretext for most of the undermining of due process, argument all the more dangerous in that in the eyes of superficial men it clothes this undermining with a semblance of proper order and the appearances of legitimacy.

When crimes multiply or perils menace the State, people tell us we should abridge due process, the slowness of whose details compromises public security. Procedures are abolished and judgments accelerated, special courts are established, and judicial safeguards are totally or partly cut back.[3]

[185] This way of proceeding has always struck me as resting on a singular petitio principii. It is to declare men convicted in advance when so far they are only accused. Due process is a safeguard. Its abridgment is the diminution or loss of that safeguard. It is therefore a penalty. To submit an accused person to that penalty is to punish him before his trial. And if you punish him, it follows that his crime is proved in advance. If his crime is proved, what good is a court, of whatever kind, to decide his fate? If his crime is not proved, by what right do you place this accused in a special proscribed class and deprive him, on mere suspicion, of the benefit common to all members of civil society? This absurdity is not the only one. Due process is either necessary or useless in regard to conviction, conviction being, as I see it, the sole purpose of legal proceedings. If due process is useless, why do we retain it for ordinary trials? If it is necessary, why do we cut it out in the most important ones? What, when it comes to a slight offense, when neither the accused's life nor his honor is in danger, the case is investigated with the greatest solemnity! All due process shall be observed. Safeguards are built up to make sure of the facts and to prevent innocence being punished! But when the question concerns some frightful crime and consequently total disgrace and death, in a single move, all the tutelary safeguards are to be suppressed, the legal code is closed, and formalities are cut short! It is as if one thought that the more serious the charge, the more superfluous its examination.

You will say that it is only from brigands, murderers, and conspirators that you are taking away the benefit of due process. But before we identify them as such, the facts must be determined. Now, what [186] is due process but the best means of determining the facts? If better, swifter means exist, let them be used, but for all cases. For why should there be one class of them in regard to which the unnecessary delays are observed and, on the other hand,

3. Constant in his notes indicated the following reference: "Montesquieu. VI. 2." The second chapter of Livre VI of *De l'esprit des lois* is entitled indeed *De la simplicité des lois criminelles dans divers gouvernements* (On the simplicity of the criminal laws in divers governments). Among other things, Montesquieu says here: "One hears it said constantly that justice should be rendered everywhere as it is in Turkey. Will it therefore be only the most ignorant of all the nations which will have seen clearly into the thing in the world it matters most that men should know? [. . .] you will see that the penalties, the expenses, the delays, the very dangers of justice are the price each citizen pays for his freedom." *Ed. cit.,* p. 557.

another dealt with in dangerous haste? The dilemma is clear: if haste is not dangerous, delays are superfluous; if delays are not superfluous, haste is dangerous. Some would say, would they not, that we can distinguish by means of external and infallible signs, before the judgment or the inquiry, the innocent from the guilty, those who must enjoy the prerogative of due process and those who must be deprived of it? But in this case judicial authority, whatever type it might be, would be pointless. It is because there are no such signs that due process is necessary;[4] it is because due process has seemed the sole means of distinguishing the innocent from the guilty that all the free and humane peoples have demanded its institutionalization. However imperfect due process, it has a protective faculty which cannot be removed without destroying it. It is the natural enemy and the unyielding foe of tyranny, whether popular or otherwise. As long as due process subsists, courts will put in despotism's path a resistance, more or less generous, but which always serves to contain it. Under Charles I, the English courts acquitted several friends of liberty, despite threats from the Court. Under Cromwell, although dominated by the Protector, they often set free citizens accused of royalism. Under James II, Jefferies was obliged to trample on due process and to violate the independence even of judges he had himself appointed, to be sure of obtaining the numerous executions of victims of his fury.[5] In Prussia we saw the courts defending the tradition of intellectual and religious freedom against the suspicions of Frederick II's successor.[6] There is in due process something lofty and unambiguous which forces judges to act respectably [187] and follow a just and orderly course. The dreadful law which under Robespierre declared proofs redundant and abolished defense counsels is an homage made to due process.[7] It shows that a modified due process, mutilated and perverted in every way by the spirit of faction, still put a brake on men carefully chosen from the whole of France as those most devoid of scruples of conscience or any respect for public opinion.

4. Constant had addressed Parliament a few years before on this subject. The law he had opposed in Parliament wanted to abbreviate due process in order to be able to struggle more effectively against banditry raging at the start of the Consulate, which made the roads unsafe. This explains the reference to brigands and murderers. See his oration to the Tribunat of 5 pluviôse an IX (25 January 1801).

5. Hofmann was not able to pin down Constant's references nor to find the sources he used.

6. Hofmann has not uncovered the facts to which Constant is referring here.

7. This is about the law of 22 prairial an II (10 June 1794). On this subject see Jacques Godechot, *Les institutions . . . , op. cit.*, p. 323.

These last observations apply with double force to those jurisdictions whose very names have become odious and terrible, to those Councils or Military Commissions which—a strange thing—during the whole course of a revolution undertaken for freedom, made all the citizens tremble.[8] But the storms of this revolution had thrown all ideas upside down. A long and bitter war had driven the military outlook deep into our political institutions and our legal sanctuaries alike. Our leaders were rather inclined to believe that for freedom just as for victory, nothing was more appropriate than passive obedience and swiftly taken decisions. They looked on opinions as so many army corps to be enrolled or battled against, on representative assemblies as agencies of government and their opposition as acts of indiscipline, on courts as camps and judges as warriors, on accused persons as enemies and on trials as battles.

Hence this substitution of military force for the peaceful and tutelary safeguards of justice. Our descendants, if they have any sense of freedom, will not believe there was a time in which men reared under canvas and ignorant of civil life interrogated accused persons they were incapable of understanding and condemned [188] without appeal citizens they had no right to judge. Our descendants will not believe, if they are not the most degraded of peoples, that legislators, writers, and those accused of political crimes could be made to appear before military courts. Thus—in ferocious derision—opinion and thought were given as their judge unenlightened courage and uncritical obedience. They will not believe that warriors, returning from victory, covered with laurels that nothing had been able to wilt, should have had imposed on them the horrible duty of turning themselves into myrmidons[9] to pursue, seize, and shoot fellow citizens, people who were perhaps guilty, but whose names, like their crimes, were as yet unknown to them. No, it was never thus, they will exclaim, the reward for valor, the triumphal ceremony. No, this is not how the liberators of France made their reappearance in their fatherland and saluted their native soil.

The pretext for this subversion of justice is that the nature of the court is determined by the nature of the crime. Thus crimping, spying, provocation to indiscipline, shelter or help given to desertion, and by a natural extension

8. These military commissions, established by the decree of 9 October 1792 to judge emigrés found with arms, comprised only three or five military judges and a public prosecutor. They pronounced one sentence only: death, which was effected immediately. These commissions were an even more terrible instrument than the revolutionary courts. See Godechot, *op. cit.*, pp. 324–325.

9. [Hirelings. Translator's note]

the conspiracies one presumes to have some collusion with or support in the army, are often regarded as coming under military jurisdiction. This pretext is absurd, however, as we have said, because, once again, it misrepresents accusation as crime, treats the accused as condemned, assumes conviction before the hearing, and imposes a punishment before the sentence.

CHAPTER THREE

On Punishments

The guilty do not lose all their rights. Society is not invested with unlimited authority even over them. Its obligation to them involves inflicting punishments on them only proportionately to their misdeeds. It must not make them undergo sufferings other than those [189] which have been laid down by prior laws. It has yet a further duty, namely to institute against the guilty only such chastisement as cannot stir up or corrupt the innocents who witness it.

This last duty rules out all experimentation with torture. Toward the end of the last century people seemed to have sensed this truth. Human skill no longer sought how to extend as far as possible, in the presence of several thousands of witnesses, the convulsive agony of one of their fellow creatures. We no longer savored premeditated cruelty. It had been discovered that this barbarity, ineffectual as regards the victim, perverted the witnesses of his torment and that to punish a single criminal a whole nation was being depraved.

A few years ago it was suddenly proposed by men of no authority that we revert to these frightful usages. All the sound section of the public shuddered with horror. The government balked at this ferocious blandishment; and if no one deigned to reply to these men, they owed it just to the contempt they inspired that they were repulsed only by silence.

The death penalty, even reduced to the simple deprivation of life, has been the target of objections by several estimable philosophers.[10] Their reasonings have not at all convinced me that this punishment is never just, and I did not need their reasonings to be convinced that it should be extended only to a very small number of crimes.

10. In the proceedings of the National Assembly between 30 May and 1 June 1791, the deputies decided to keep the death penalty. Their speeches made reference to Montesquieu and Beccaria, among other philosophers. Among the speakers, Robespierre was against the death penalty, Brillat-Savarin in favor.

The death penalty has the great advantage that few men devote themselves to odious and degrading functions. It is better that these deplorable agents of harsh necessity, rejected with horror by society, should devote themselves to the horrible work of executing [190] some criminals, than that a mob should condemn itself to looking after the culprits and to turning itself into the perpetual instrument of their prolonged misfortune. Cold-bloodedly to cause the suffering of one's fellows is always a corrupting action, however rightly that punishment may be imposed by the laws.

This consideration leads me to reject life sentences. These corrupt jailers as much as prisoners. They get the former used to a capricious savagery. They are inseparable from a great deal of arbitrariness. They can veil a host of cruelties.

Condemnation to public works, so promoted by most of our modern politicians, has always seemed to me to entail drawbacks of all kinds.

In the first place, it is by no means proven to me that society has any other right over those who trouble public order than that of removing them from any possibility of doing harm. Death is part of this right, but work not at all. A man may merit losing the use or possession of his faculties, but he can alienate them only voluntarily. If you allow that he can be forced to alienate them, you fall again wholly into the system of slavery.

Moreover, to impose work as a punishment is a form of dangerous example. In modern societies the great majority of the human race is obliged to do excessive work. What could be more imprudent, impolitic, and insulting than to present work to it as the punishment for crime?

If convicts' work is indeed a punishment, if it is different from that to which the innocent laboring classes of society are subjected, if, in a word, it is above ordinary human exertions, it becomes a death penalty more extended and painful than any other. Between the Austrian prisoner who, half-naked and his body half in the water, drags ships on the Danube, and the wretch who perishes on the scaffold, I see only a difference of time which favors the latter. Joseph II and Catherine II[11] spoke always of the abolition of the death penalty in the name of humanity, while they inflicted punishments no less fatal and rather longer and harsher.

[191] If, on the contrary, condemnation to public works is not a refined form of death, it is the cause of revolting and contagious depravity. In some countries of Germany, people condemned to this punishment, treated gently, get used to their fate, take pleasure in their opprobrium and, not

11. [Also called Catherine the Great in the Anglophone world. Translator's Note]

working in their servitude any more than they would in freedom, they offer the onlooker a picture of gaiety in degradation, happiness in debasement, security in shame. This must produce in the mind of the poor man, whose innocence serves only to impose on him an existence no less laborious and more precarious, notions which by way of comparison make him despondent or lead him astray.

In sum, the sound of chains, these galley slave clothes, all these insignia of crime and chastisement constantly and publicly exposed to our sight, are, for men bearing within them any feeling for human dignity, a punishment longer lasting and more painful than for the guilty. Society does not have the right to surround us with an eternal commemoration of perversity and ignominy.

The setting up of colonies, where criminals are transported, is perhaps of all harsh measures the closest to justice as well as to the interests of society and those of individuals society finds itself obliged to place at a distance.

Most of our faults are occasioned by a kind of clash between us and social institutions. We reach youth often before knowing and almost always before understanding these complicated institutions. They surround us with barriers we sometimes cross without our noticing them. Then there is established between us and our surroundings an opposition which grows larger because of the very impression it produces. This opposition makes itself felt among almost all social classes. In the upper classes from the self-isolating misanthropist to the man of ambition and the conqueror, in the lower classes from the man who addles himself with drink to the one who commits outrages: all these are men in opposition to social institutions. This opposition develops with most violence where the least enlightenment is found. It weakens proportionately with old age, as the force of the passions collapses, [192] as one reckons life only for what it is worth, and as the need for independence becomes less commanding than the need for peace of mind. But when, before reaching this period of resignation, one has committed some irreparable fault, the memory of this fault, the regret and remorse, the sense that one has been judged too harshly, and that this judgment is nevertheless final—all these impressions keep whomever they are pursuing in anxious irritation, a source of new and even more irreparable mistakes.

If the men in this fatal situation, under pressure from transgressed institutions, and slighted by social relationships they have forever vitiated, were now suddenly snatched out of it, if nothing remained with them from their earlier life other than the memory of what they suffered and the experience they acquired, how many would not follow an opposite road? How readily, being returned suddenly, as by a miracle, to safety, harmony, and to the possession of order and morality, they would prefer these joys to the fleeting temptations which had led them astray! Experience has proved what I say. Men deported to Botany Bay for criminal actions have started their social life again, and, believing themselves no longer at war with society, have become peaceful and estimable members of it.[12]

If it is just and useful, however, to separate culprits thus from environments which can only hurt and corrupt them, we render the establishment of colonies of this nature absurd and barbarous when we pursue men who ought no longer to exist for us, with implacable hate, in another hemisphere, prolonging their punishments and shame, keeping them still in a regime of ill will and ignominy, seeming to demand a metropolitan right to surround them in their far-off refuge with things which will cause them suffering, degradation, and corruption.

Is it necessary to add that nothing that the reader has just read applies to deportation to the colonies except as a punishment? Any arbitrary deportation is the overturning of all principles and a violation of all rights.

[193] The question of extradition is much of a piece with the question of punishment. This question would be easy to resolve if there were no unjust governments. Only culpable actions would be forbidden. Punishments would be pronounced only against real offenses. Nothing then would be more natural than a coalition between all men against that which threatened them all. But as long as there exist artificial offenses, above all as long as opinions are regarded as crimes, extradition will be the weapon of tyrants along with proscription of anyone who dares to resist them. Such are the shortcomings of vicious institutions, then, that they force us to give refuge to crime in order to take away from it the power to pursue virtue. It is a misfortune that we offer the guilty the chance of impunity, but it is not nearly as bad as delivering the good man to the vengeance of the oppressor.

CHAPTER FOUR

On the Prerogative of Exercising Mercy

All legislation which does not admit the right to show mercy or to commute sentences deprives the accused and even the guilty of a right which legitimately belongs to them.

12. By the name Botany Bay, Constant means the colonial penitentiary at Sydney, in Australia.

An inseparable drawback of general laws is that these laws cannot apply with equal justice to several actions of diverse type.

The more general a law, the further it is from the particular actions on which it is nevertheless intended to pronounce. A law can be perfectly just only for one circumstance. As soon as it is applied to two circumstances only minutely different, it is more or less unjust in one of the two.

Facts are infinitely nuanced. The laws cannot follow them in their modifications. The right to exercise mercy or to soften [194] a punishment is necessary to make up for the inflexibility of the law. This right is in reality nothing other than the right to take into consideration an action's circumstances in order to decide if the law is applicable to it.

The prerogative of mercy has been opposed by one of these decisive dilemmas which seem to simplify questions by misrepresenting them. If the law is just, it is said, nothing should have the power to prevent its execution. If it is unjust, it should be changed.[13] Only one condition would be necessary for this reasoning not to be absurd. This would be that there was one law for each fact.

The question of intention replaces in part the prerogative of mercy. But it makes up for it only imperfectly. Moreover, when you call on a jury to pronounce on anything save the facts, you are distorting its function. When you ask judges to do anything other than read the written text of the law, you are distorting their function.

The Court of Cassation[14] in our country indirectly exercises the prerogative of mercy. When a law chances to be literally but too harshly applied to a guilty party, this court searches the procedures for some formal error which allows it to overthrow the judgment. But a good born of a wrong is always bad in other respects. Moreover, if the procedures are perfectly [195] regular, the court finds itself forced to deliver the condemned man

13. Constant summarizes here the critique made particularly by William Godwin. He had translated some of Godwin's work. See Benjamin Constant, *De la justice politique* (unpublished translation of a work by William Godwin), edited by Burton R. Polin, Quebec, les Presses de l'Université Laval, 1972 (Droit, science politique 5), Livre VI, Ch. 7, pp. 307–309. One also finds the same critique of the prerogative of mercy in Jeremy Bentham, in his *Principes du code pénal,* Troisième Partie, Ch. 9, *op. cit.,* t. II, pp. 432–434.

14. The Court of Cassation, according to the terms of the laws of 27 November and 2 December 1790, had the attributions of: "annulling all procedures in which due process had been violated and invalidating any judgment which expressly contravenes the text of the law." Cf. Edmond Seligman, *La justice en France pendant la Révolution (1789–1792),* Paris, Plon-Nourrit, pp. 321 and following.

over to a punishment he does not deserve morally, one it would have been just to mitigate. In truth this case is rare, given the complications of the prescribed formalities; but this too is one more shortcoming.

A single difficulty stands out in relation to the prerogative of mercy. If you entrust this right to the holders of executive power, they will consider this attribution accidental and secondary. They will discharge it negligently. They will not have time to devote themselves to an examination of all the circumstances which ought to motivate their decision. Punishments then not being inflicted according to any precise rule, the principal advantage of positive laws disappears. All the guilty will live in the hope of being favored by luck or caprice. The system will become a lottery of death, in which a thousand unforeseeable incidents will arbitrarily confound all chances of salvation or destruction.

We can prevent this difficulty by attaching this law to a specific authority. The men in whom it is invested would then exercise it with the thoughtfulness and gravity it demands.

But another difficulty would arise. A specific authority or any section whatever of judicial power, invested with the prerogative of mercy, would naturally make rules for itself in order to exercise it. The exercise of the prerogative would therefore become by this very consideration a judgment. We would no longer find in it the kind of vagueness and moral latitude which essentially constitute its justice and usefulness.

It is not part of our researches to decide to which one of these drawbacks to resign ourselves. It is a question which must perhaps be resolved differently according to the circumstances of each country. What is certain is that neither one nor the other of these difficulties is great enough to prevail over the necessity of entrusting to some authority or other the prerogative of mercy.

BOOK X

On the Action of Government with Regard to Property

Ch. 1. The purpose of this book. 165

Ch. 2. The natural division of the inhabitants of the same territory into two classes. 165

Ch. 3. On property. 167

Ch. 4. On the status property should occupy in political institutions. 168

Ch. 5. On examples drawn from antiquity. 171

Ch. 6. On the proprietorial spirit. 173

Ch. 7. That territorial property alone brings together all the advantages of property. 174

Ch. 8. On property in public funds. 179

Ch. 9. On the amount of landed property which society has the right to insist upon for the exercise of political rights. 182

Ch. 10. That owners have no interest in abusing power vis-à-vis nonowners. 183

Ch. 11. On hereditary privileges compared to property. 185

Ch. 12. Necessary comment. 186

Ch. 13. On the best way of giving proprietors a large political influence. 190

Ch. 14. On the action of government on property. 192

Ch. 15. On laws which favor the accumulation of property in the same hands. 193

Ch. 16. On laws which enforce the wider spreading of property. 196

CHAPTER ONE

The Purpose of This Book

We have ruled out in this work any research into the constitution of States and the organization of their political powers. Nevertheless, we cannot absolve ourselves from dealing with the place that property should have in government concerns since we have to determine what the relations between government and property ought to be. We are therefore obliged to put forward some ideas which derive from the first principles of human association. Since these ideas relate equally, however, to all forms of institution, they will not draw us at all into the discussions we want to avoid.

People may be astonished that we should refute in some detail opinions which today seem generally abandoned. Our purpose, however, is not to write simply on opinions which may enjoy favor today, but rather to attack false opinions to the extent that we find them on our way.

Moreover, we know how quickly men go from one view to another, especially in France. Such error as one [200] does not deign to reply to at such a time, because one thinks it without supporters, can at the first emergency show up, resting on arguments one had regarded as forever rebuffed.

In addition, there are among us a rather large number of writers always at the service of the dominant system. We have already seen them go from unbridled demagogy to the opposite exaggeration. Nothing would be less astonishing on their part than a new apostasy. These are real lansquenets,[1] but without the courage. Disavowals cost them nothing. Absurdities do not check them, because for them opinions are only calculation. They search everywhere for a power whose wishes they can reduce to principles. Their zeal is all the more active and tireless in that it dispenses with their conviction.

CHAPTER TWO

The Natural Division of the Inhabitants of the Same Territory into Two Classes

No nation has regarded all the individuals living in its territory, in whatever way this might be, as members of the political association. This is not a question of arbitrary distinctions, such as among the ancients separated free

1. [The lansquenets were German mercenary footsoldiers of the fifteenth and sixteenth centuries. Constant explicitly says the writers in question are cowards and implicitly that they are low-born and mercenary. Translator's note]

men from slaves, or in modern times nobles from the lowborn. The most full democracy still establishes two categories: to the one are relegated foreigners and those below the age decreed by the law for the exercise of citizenship rights. The other consists of men having reached that age and born in the country. Only the latter are members of the political association. There is therefore a principle following which, of those individuals brought together in a given territory, some are citizens and some not.

Obviously, this principle is that to be a member of the political association requires a certain degree of informed outlook and common interests with the other members. Men below the legal age lack this degree of informed outlook. Foreigners are not capable of being guided by that common interest. The proof of this is that the former, on reaching the age [201] the law requires, become members of the political association, while the latter do this by way of residence, ownership, or their social relationships. We take it that these things give enlightenment to the former and the required interest to the latter.

This principle, however, needs further extension. In our present societies, birth in the country and the age of majority are not enough to confer on men the qualities proper to the exercise of citizenship rights. Those whom poverty holds in endless dependence and condemns from childhood to laboring work, are neither more informed than children as to public affairs, nor have a greater stake than foreigners in a national prosperity, with whose elements they are not familiar and whose benefits they share only indirectly.

I do not wish to wrong the working class. It is no less patriotic than other classes. It is often ready for the most heroic sacrifices, and its devotion is all the more admirable in that it is neither rewarded financially nor with honor. As I see it, however, the patriotism which gives one the courage to die for one's country is one thing, while that which makes one capable of understanding one's interests is another. Therefore a condition beyond having been born in the country and the prescribed age is required, namely the leisure needed for developing an informed outlook and soundness of judgment. Only property secures this leisure. Only property can render men capable of exercising political rights. Only owners can be citizens. To counter this with natural equality is to be reasoning within a hypothesis inapplicable to the present state of societies. If from this idea of men's having equal rights we go on to claim that owners must not have more extensive ones than nonowners, we will have to conclude either that all must be owners or none. For most assuredly the right to property establishes between those who have it and those bereft of it a far greater inequality than all political rights. Now, if we come to terms with so decisive an inequality, we must also accept all the further agreements indispensable to the consolidation of this first one. Only the principle is subject to doubt. Once it is admitted, its consequences are entailed. Is property necessary to the well-being and improvement of the social condition? If we adopt the affirmative, people cannot be astonished at seeing us admitting its obvious results. [202]

CHAPTER THREE

On Property

A number of those who have defended property by way of abstract reason seem to me to have fallen into grave error. They have represented property as something mysterious, anterior to society and independent of it.[2] Property is served by the rejection of these hypotheses. Mystery is harmful in everything which does not spring from superstition. Property is not anterior to society. Without political association, which gives it its guarantee, it would be only the right of the first possessor, the right of force, that is to say, a right which is no such thing. It is absolutely not independent of society, since some kind of social condition, admittedly a very wretched one, could be conceived without it, while property without society is unimaginable. Property exists by virtue of society. Society found that the best way to get its members to enjoy goods common to all or disputed by all before its institution, was to concede some of them to each person or to maintain each person in that part of them he happened to possess, guaranteeing to him enjoyment of this, plus such changes as this enjoyment might undergo either by the countless changes of chance or by inequality in the degrees of effort. Property is only a social convention. Our recognizing it as such, however, does not mean we envisage it as less sacred, less inviolable, less necessary than do writers using a different philosophical approach. Some philosophers have considered its establishment an evil and its abolition possible.[3] They have had recourse, however, to found their [203]

2. See on this subject the old but still useful article by Pierre Larousse in the *Grand dictionnaire universel du XIXe siècle*, s.v. Propriété, Section II: *Légitimité du droit de propriété*. This article has the merit of bringing out Constant's originality and locating him both among those who, like him, see property as a social institution (Pascal, Domat, Bossuet, Montesquieu, Mirabeau, Tronchet, Robespierre) and specifically against those who represent property as "anterior to society," such as Mercier de la Rivière, Destutt de Tracy, and Cousin. Locke's name should be added to the latter list.

3. Constant is thinking in the first place of Godwin, in the last book of whose *Enquiry Concerning Political Justice* defects in the system of property are analyzed. One can also number among philosophers hostile to property in the eighteenth century Morelly and his *Code de la nature*, then Linguet, and in some respects Mably.

theories, to a host of suppositions of which some are quite unrealizable and of which the least chimerical are relegated to a future it is not even permissible for us to predict. Not only is their fundamental assumption a growth in enlightenment at which man may perhaps one day arrive but on which it would be absurd to found our present institutions, but they have assumed as proven a diminution in the work required today for the subsistence of the human race of an order which surpasses all invention even suspected. Certainly each one of our discoveries in mechanical science which replaces human force by instruments and machines is a victory for thought; and by the laws of nature, these victories becoming easier as they multiply, they must follow one another at an increasing rate. But what we have done under this heading, and even what we can imagine, fall far short of our total exemption from manual labor. Nevertheless, this exemption would be indispensable for the abolition of property, short of our wishing, as some writers propose, to divide this work equally among all members of the society. Such a division, however, even if it were not an absurd dream, would work against its own purpose, would take away from thought the leisure necessary to make it strong and profound, from ingenuity the perseverance which brings it to perfection, from all classes the advantages of habit, continuity, unity of purpose, and centralization of productive forces. Without property the human race would be in stasis, in the most brutish and savage state of its existence. Each person, responsible for providing on his own for all his needs, would split his energies to meet them and, bent beneath the weight of these multiplied cares, would never advance an inch. The abolition of property would destroy the division of labor, the basis of the perfecting of all the arts and sciences. The progressive faculty, the favorite hope of the writers I am opposing, would die for lack of time and independence. The crass and forced equality they recommend to us would be an invincible obstacle to the gradual setting up of true equality, that of happiness and enlightenment. [204]

CHAPTER FOUR

On the Status Property Should Occupy in Political Institutions

The question being thus resolved, property being necessary, then, to the perfecting and prosperity of the social condition, it follows that it must be surrounded by all the safeguards; and power is the only sufficient safeguard. Property must not be made into an eternal cause of struggles and crimes. Better destroy it, as certain extravagant thinkers want, than tolerate it as an abuse by treating it with disfavor. These thinkers at least present a theoretical system which they believe compatible with the social State, such as they conceive it. What shall we say, however, of these hidden enemies of property who, allowing it without giving it influence, seem to set it up only to deliver it over, helpless, to the vehement hostility it provokes? What shall we think of Mably, who depicts it as a scourge and then urges us to respect it?[4] This is to bequeath to society indestructible seeds of discord. Property must be in charge or annihilated. If you put power on one side and property on the other, the latter will soon be at odds with legislation. Careful reflection and government become separate. Opinion wages war with the latter.

One might say that the present state of society, mixing and mingling owners and nonowners in a thousand ways, gives to some of the latter the same interests and means as the former, that the man who works, no less than the man who owns, needs peace and security; that owners are in law and fact only distributors of the common wealth between all individuals and that it is to the advantage of all that order and peace should favor the development of all abilities and all individual resources.

The fault in these arguments is their proving too much. If they were conclusive, there would be no reason for denying foreigners political rights. Europe's commercial relations are such that it is in the interests of the great majority of Europeans that peace [205] and contentment prevail in all countries. The overthrow of a country of any sort is as fatal for foreigners whose financial speculations have linked their fortune to that country as this overthrow could be to its own inhabitants, with the exception of its propertied class. The facts prove it. During the most savage wars, a country's businessmen make endless appeals and sometimes efforts for the hostile country not to be destroyed. Nevertheless, a consideration so vague will not seem sufficient, in my view, to justify political rights for foreigners.

Doubtless, if you suppose that nonproprietors will always calmly examine all sides of the question, their considered interest will be to respect property and become proprietors; but if you admit the more likely hypothesis that they will often be led by their most obvious and immediate interest, this latter interest will lead them, if not to destroy property, at least to diminish its influence.

4. Honoré-Gabriel Bonnot de Mably, *De la législation ou principes des lois,* Livre I, Ch. 3 *De l'établissement de la propriété,* where Mably preaches a certain egalitarianism, and Ch. 4 *Des obstacles insurmontables qui s'opposent au rétablissement de l'égalité détruite,* where he gives up the idea of imposing social equality. The references are to the *Oeuvres complètes de l'Abbé de Mably,* Lyon, J.-B. Delamollière, 1792, t. IX.

Furthermore, admitting the most favorable hypothesis, that the first concern of nonproprietors is to become proprietors, if the organization of property puts some obstacle in the way of their succeeding, or they merely imagine this to be so, their natural inclination will be to change that organization. Now, the organization of property is something you cannot disturb without harming its nature and upsetting society as a whole. We will see later how many vexatious effects the idea of a forced dissemination of property can give rise to. In short, these arguments bear only on a very small group of nonproprietors. The vast majority will always be deprived of leisure, the indispensable condition of enlightenment. Civil safeguards, individual freedom, free opinion, in a word, social protection, are owed to nonproprietors, because any political association owes them even to the foreigner it receives into its bosom; but political rights are not a protection; they bestow power. The political association must give this only to its members. To grant it to nonproprietors is not to give them a shield, but an offensive weapon.

The necessary purpose of the propertyless is to manage to become propertied. All the resources you give them they will use for this purpose. If you add to the freedom for their talents and efforts, which you [206] do owe them, political rights, which you do not, these rights, in the hands of the vast majority of them, will infallibly be used to encroach on property. They will march on it by that irregular and meretricious route, rather than following the natural route, work. This will be a source of corruption for them, and for the State, of disorder. It has been very properly observed that when the propertyless have political rights one of three things happens. Either their only motivation springs from themselves and then they destroy the society; or they are motivated by the man or men in power and they become the instruments of tyranny, which is what happens in unexceptional times; or they are motivated by those aspiring to power and become the instruments of factions. This is what happens during great political crises.

There are always two classes in a country, those who want to conserve and those who want to make gains.[5] The first need only security; the second, before they need security, need force. Freedom and justice are the sole means of well-being for the former. By means of justice they conserve what they possess; and by way of freedom they enjoy it. For the latter, however, injustice and tyranny may often be the means to success. Their encroachments are by way of injus-

5. The same idea is seen in Madame de Staël, *Des circonstances actuelles, éd. cit.*, p. 173: "Now, there are two elemental interests, so to speak, which split the world: the need to acquire and the need to conserve."

tice and defended by tyranny. Machiavelli establishes that it is better to entrust the defense of freedom to those who want to make gains than to those who wish to conserve.[6] But he is not talking about property. He is talking about power, and oppressive power to boot, like that of the Roman patricians or the Venetian nobles. This is no more than saying that the defense of freedom should be entrusted to those who suffer from tyranny rather than those who enjoy it.

[207] In the countries with representative or republican arrangements, it is important above all that their assemblies should comprise proprietors, whatever their further organization may be in other respects. An individual may capture the crowd through outstanding merit. The ruling body, however, to win public confidence, need material interests manifestly appropriate to their duties. A nation will always presume that people who are united are led by common interest. It will take it for granted that love of order, justice, and conservation will be the prevailing concern among proprietors. The latter are thus useful not only in terms of their inherent qualities but also of those attributed to them, as well as of the interests they are assumed to have, and of the salutary prejudices they inspire. Put the unpropertied class in charge of the State, however well intentioned they may be, and the anxiety of the propertied will hem in all their measures. The wisest laws will be suspected and hence disobeyed. The opposite sort of organization, by contrast, will reconcile popular assent, even to a government which is defective in some regards.

During the French Revolution, owners competed with nonowners in the making of absurd and spoliatory laws. This is because they feared the latter now that they had power. The owners wanted to be forgiven for being owners. The fear of losing what one has renders one every bit as cowardly or enraged as the hope of acquiring that which one has not. These faults and crimes on the part of property holders, however, were a consequence of the influence of the propertyless class.

CHAPTER FIVE

On Examples Drawn from Antiquity

We should separate from this subject all the examples drawn from antiquity. We will devote another book in this work to developing the numberless differences which mark us off from the ancients.[7] Let us merely

6. Machiavelli, *Discours sur la première décade de Tite-Live,* Ch. V, *Oeuvres complètes, op. cit.,* pp. 392–394.

7. Book XVI, *On Political Power in the Ancient World.*

say here that in the small States of antiquity property was far from being the same thing it is with us. [208] The sharing out of conquered territories made or could make proprietors of all individuals. In our times conquests aggrandize States but do not give new lands at all to the citizens. All the laboring work, which takes away all leisure from those committed to it, was done by slaves. Slavery is abolished. The rich appeased the poor in feeding them out of largesse. Our financial system no longer permits handouts of money and corn. The public square contained the whole nation, which was governed by eloquence, a power which in our huge societies no longer exists. The discussions gave the whole nation general ideas on politics, even when they directed it badly on such and such particular occasions. Thus, freed from manual work by the slaves, often fed for nothing by the rich, or by the State, which came to the same thing, given understanding of government by orators, nonowners were able to give almost all their time to public affairs. They acquired the habit of so preoccupying themselves, and this habit made them less unfit for it.

Today private matters, the cares imposed on each person for his subsistance, take at least most of the poor man's time, if not all of it. Public matters are only an accessory. Printing has replaced popular discussion. The lower classes, however, have little time to read. What they read without choice, they take up without examining. No opinion gets debated in their presence. Theirs therefore forms by chance.

Nonowners could consequently exercise political rights in the republics of antiquity with less inconvenience than they could in our modern States; and yet, if we examine the thing closely, we will become convinced that their influence was fatal to these same republics. Athens suffered greatly from not having based its government on property. Its lawmakers had always to battle with the ascendancy of the propertyless. Most of its writers, its philosophers, even its poets have a marked preference [209] for oligarchy.[8] This is because they were seeking in the power of the few the security that they should have reposed in property alone. The Lacedaemonian [Spartan] institutions were not based on property; but these bizarre institutions had distorted property as they had annihilated personal freedom and imposed silence on all the affections. They rested moreover on the most horrible servitude. The helots and the Messenians were the true propertyless class of Laconia, and for them the loss of

8. See Constant's Note A at the end of Book X.

political rights was subsumed in that of natural rights.[9] The opponents of property stress the poverty of some of the illustrious citizens of ancient Rome. These illustrious citizens were, however, despite their poverty, propertied. Cincinnatus owned the land he ploughed. If the propertyless in Rome had what looked like political rights, they paid for that sterile honor, dying of poverty, thrown into prisons, their creditors the patricians legally entitled to defame them.

Such will always be the fate of this class while it has rights it cannot exercise without putting the public good at risk. In their alarm owners will have recourse to the most violent means in order to break the threatening weapon now in the hands of their enemies, entrusted to them by an imprudent constitution. Of all the political passions, fear is the most aggressive. Proprietors will always be oppressive to avoid being oppressed. Property will never be powerless. If it is refused legal influence, it will soon seize upon the arbitrary and corrupting kind.

CHAPTER SIX

On the Proprietorial Spirit

One observation is crucial to prevent a confusion of ideas. To put power into property is not the same as to put property in power. Wealth has influence and commands consideration only insofar as it is not suddenly acquired. More than once, during the Revolution, our governors, constantly hearing government of the propertied nostalgically praised, were tempted to become proprietors to make themselves more worthy of being governors. But even when they had bestowed on themselves, from one day to another, considerable properties [210] by calling their wishes the law, the people were liable to think that what the law had conferred, the law could retract; and so property, instead of protecting the institution, needed continually to be protected by it. New owners, squatting on their spoils, remain conquerors at heart. You do not learn the proprietary spirit as readily as you grab property. During the war of the peasants of Swabia against their lords,[10] the former sometimes donned the armor of their defeated masters. What did this lead to? That one could see under this knightly armor no less insolence and more vulgarity.

9. [The helots were prisoners of war of Sparta, subsequently enslaved. The city of Mycenae, like Sparta situated in Laconia, was conquered by the Spartans and its inhabitants enslaved. Translator's note]

10. A reference to the great peasant war which in 1524 and 1525 ravaged not only Swabia but the whole of what is now southern Germany, including even Alsace.

If the wealthy class inspires more confidence, it is because its members' point of departure is more advantageous, their outlook freer, their intelligence more schooled to enlightenment, their education more cultivated. But enriching men suddenly in midcareer, you do not give them any of these advantages. Their sudden wealth does not work retrospectively.

It is the same with the sizeable salaries attached to particular jobs. These just do not replace property. When they are disproportionate to the previous wealth of those who receive them, they do not serve to form a new rich class. They give individuals new needs and habits which corrupt them. Far from making them independent and assured, they make them dependent and agitated. In wealth as in other things, nothing can stand in for experience.

CHAPTER SEVEN

That Territorial Property Alone Brings Together All the Advantages of Property

Several writers who recognize the need to entrust political rights exclusively to proprietors do not consider [211] landed property the only true property. The economists, as is known, M. Turgot included, had a quite opposite theoretical view. According to them the main element constituting a society is the territory under its jurisdiction. The only positive and legal distinction between men emanates from ownership or nonownership of the national territory. The nonowners of territory, not being able to reside in a country without the consent of the owners, who grant them, in exchange for their work or capital, a refuge which they could deny them, are not members of a political association in which their residence is not by right. This reasoning, however rigorous it may appear, seems to me too slight a foundation for a practical institution. I dislike reasoning from a hypothesis which rejects reality, and nothing seems to me less capable of reconciling those without land to the necessary sacrifice of citizen rights, than their being represented as homeless vagabonds, who can be expelled on the whim of a man who has no preeminence over them save having seized the land first. Besides, I think it worthless to have recourse to such forced suppositions. Arguments of another kind, more applicable and less abstract, will lead us to the same end.

Two types of property different from territorial property have been distinguished. The first is business property. The other has been called intellectual and moral property.

Let us speak first of all of business property.

This lacks several of the advantages of landed property, and these advantages are precisely those in which the safeguarding spirit necessary for political association consists.

Landed property has an influence on the character and lot of man by the very nature of the cares it demands. The cultivator gives himself over to constant and ongoing occupations. Thus he contracts regularity of habit. Chance, which is a great source of immorality because it overturns all calculations and therefore those of morality, has absolutely no part in the life of the cultivator. All interruption harms him. Any imprudence means certain loss to him. His successes come slowly. He can achieve them only by work. He cannot speed them up nor make them grow by lighthearted daring. He depends upon nature and is independent of men. All these things give him a calm disposition, a sense of security, and a feeling for order which [212] attach him to the vocation to which he owes his peace of mind as much as his living.

Business property influences man only by the positive gain it procures him or promises him. It puts in his life less order, more artificiality, and less fixity than landed property. The operations of the businessman are often made up of fortuitous transactions. His successes are more rapid, but chance plays a greater part therein. Business property does not have that necessary element of slow and sure progression which gives man the habit and soon the need for uniformity. Business property does not make him independent of other men. On the contrary, it makes him dependent on them. Vanity, that fertile seed of political agitation, is constantly wounded in him. It almost never is in agriculture.[11] The latter case calculates in peace the order of the seasons, the nature of the soil, the character of the climate. The elements of the calculations of the businessman are whims, passions, pride, the luxury of his fellows. A farm is a native land in miniature. One is born there, raised there, grows up with the trees which surround it. Business property excludes these sources of sweet sensation. The objects of speculation pile up on one another; but everything within them is static. Nothing carries the impress of natural development. Nothing speaks to the imagination nor to memory, nothing to the moral part of man. People say my ancestors' fields, my parents' cabin. People never say my parents' workshop or shop counter. The improvements of landed property cannot be separated from the soil which receives them and of which they become part. Business property is not susceptible to improvement but to growth, and that growth can be moved around freely. The landowner rarely gains, except in

11. See Constant's Note B at the end of Book X.

an indirect way, from what his competitors lose. It is never in his power to contribute to their loss. The tillage farmer cannot by his speculations threaten his neighbor's harvest. The businessman gains directly from what others lose. Often it lies with him to add to their losses, and in many circumstances this is his most adroit speculation, his most assured advantage. In terms of intellectual faculties, the cultivator is greatly superior to the artisan. Agriculture demands a sequence of observations, of experiences which form and develop judgment.[12] From this peasants [213] derive that just and accurate sense which astonishes us. Industrial jobs are, for the most part, limited by the division of labor to mechanical operations. Landed property binds man to the country he lives in, puts obstacles in the way of displacement of people, creates patriotism through interests. Business makes all countries much the same, facilitates displacements, separates interests from patriotism.[13] This advantage of landed property, this drawback of business property, in political terms increases as the value of the property diminishes. An artisan loses almost nothing in being displaced. A small landowner is ruined when he has to move. Now it is above all by the class of smaller proprietors that one must judge the effects of different types of property, since these classes are the most numerous.

Independently of this moral preeminence of landed property, it is favorable to public order by the very situation in which it puts those who possess it. Workmen concentrated in the towns are at the mercy of factions. Cultivators, spread around the country districts, are almost impossible to unite and therefore to be led to rebel. Business proprietors, it has been said, must be much more attached to order, stability, and public peace than landed proprietors, because they lose much more during upheavals. Burn the harvest of a cultivator and he still has the field. He loses only a year's income. Pillage a merchant's shop and his assets are destroyed. But the loss is not made up solely of the instantaneous damage the proprietor experiences. We have to consider the degradation which happens to the property. Now, a pillaged shop can be full again of the kind of wealth that was stolen within twenty-four hours. But a farm burnt down, a soil impoverished for lack of cultivation, can be reestablished only by a long sequence of work and care. This becomes more striking still, when it is a question of poor proprietors. Seditionaries could in a single day compensate all the workers in a town, even if this was only in leaving them to plunder the rich.

12. See Constant's Note C at the end of Book X.
13. See Constant's Note D at the end of Book X.

But nature alone can compensate, with her accustomed slowness, the cultivators of a district. These truths were felt by Aristotle. He contrived to bring out, very forcefully, the distinctive characters of the agricultural and mercantile classes, and he decided without hesitation in favor of the former.[14] Doubtless, business property has its advantages. [214] Industry and commerce have created a new means of defense for liberty, namely credit. Landed property guarantees the stability of institutions; business property assures the independence of individuals. Therefore the refusal of political rights to these capitalists and business people, whose activity and opulence double the prosperity of the countries they live in, this refusal, if it were absolute, in my view would be an injustice and moreover an imprudence. It would be to do that of which we have already shown the danger above. It would put wealth in opposition to power.

If one reflects, however, one will easily perceive that the exclusion will not hit in any way those businessmen it would be a pity to exclude. What could be easier for them than to acquire a property in the country which would make them citizens? If they refused, I would not reckon much for their attachment to their country, or rather to their government. For it always is the fault of governments when men do not love their native soil. Such business proprietors as will not be able to buy landed property will be men whom a necessity which your institutions will never circumvent commits to mechanical work. These are therefore men lacking all means of educating themselves, likely with the purest intentions to make the State carry the cost of their inevitable errors. These men must be protected, respected, guaranteed against any harassment by the rich. We must brush aside any obstacles impeding their work and make their laborious lives as smooth as possible. They must not be transferred, however, to a new situation for which their calling does not equip them, where their participation would be pointless, or where their strong feelings would be threatening, or where their very presence would become fearfully disturbing for the other social groups, a cause for suspicion and for this very reason of hostile defensive measures and of flagrant injustices.

The property which has been entitled intellectual has been defended [215] in a rather ingenious way. A distinguished professional man, it has been said, a legal expert, for example, is no less strongly attached to the country he lives in than the landed proprietor. It is easier for this latter to

14. Aristotle, *La politique,* VI, 4, a new translation with an introduction, notes, and index by J. Tricot, Paris, J. Vrin, 1962, t. II, pp. 441–442.

alienate his patrimony than it would for the former to move his reputation. His fortune is the confidence he inspires. This derives from a number of years of work, from intelligence, skill, the services he has rendered, the habit people have acquired of consulting him in difficult circumstances, and the local understanding his long experience has formed. Expatriation would deprive him of these advantages. He would be ruined by the single fact of having to present himself as an unknown in a foreign land.

This property called intellectual, however, resides only in public opinion. If all are allowed to attribute it to themselves, doubtless all will demand it. For political rights will become not only a social advantage but a proof of talent, and to refuse them to oneself would be a rare act at once of disinterestedness and of modesty. If it is the opinion of others which has to confer this intellectual property, that opinion is made plain only by the success and wealth which are the necessary result. Thus there will be distinguished men in the professions, like opulent capitalists. Nothing will be easier for them than acquiring the landed property required.

There are, however, considerations of higher significance to be weighed. The professions require more than any other job perhaps, if their influence in political discussion is not to be fatal, to be joined with landed property. The professions, so praiseworthy in so many ways, do not always number among their good qualities the putting into ideas of that practical accuracy necessary for pronouncing on men's positive interests. We saw during our Revolution writers, mathematicians, and chemists lending themselves to the most exaggerated opinions, not because in other respects they were not enlightened and estimable, but because they had lived apart from men. Some had been accustomed to indulging their imagination, others to taking into account only rigorous evidence, a third lot [216] to seeing nature in its reproduction of human beings, paving the way to destruction. They had arrived by different routes at the same result, namely disdaining considerations drawn from facts, scorning the real sensible world, and reasoning like visionaries on the social condition, like geometers on our passions and like doctors on our human sorrows.

If these mistakes have been the portion of superior men, what will the errors of inferior candidates and defective applicants be? How very necessary it is to put a brake on wounded amour propre, on sour vanity, on all the causes of bitterness, agitation, and dissatisfaction, against a society in which people find themselves displaced, of hatred against men who seem unjust in their evaluations! All intellectual works are no doubt honorable. All must be respected. Our first attribute, our distinctive faculty, is thought. Whoever makes use of it has the right to our esteem, even independently of success. Whoever outrages or rebuffs it abdicates the name human and puts himself outside the human race. Every science, however, gives to the mind of him who cultivates it an exclusive slant, which becomes dangerous in matters political, unless it is counterbalanced. Now, the counterweight can be found only in landed property. This alone establishes uniform ties between men. It puts them on guard against the imprudent sacrifice of the happiness and peace of others by enveloping within this sacrifice their own well-being, by obliging them to reckon on their own account. It makes them come down from lofty, chimerical theories and inapplicable exaggerations by establishing between them and other members of the society numerous complicated relations and common interests.

Let it not be thought, though, that this safeguard is useful only for maintaining order. It is no less so for maintaining freedom. By a bizarre coming together, the sciences which, during political upheavals, sometimes incline men to impossible ideas of freedom, render them at other times indifferent and servile under despotism. Scholars proper are rarely bothered by power, even unjust power. It is only reflective thought such power hates. It likes the sciences well enough as tools for the governors and the fine arts as distractions for the governed. Thus the road followed by men whose studies have no connection with the active interests of human life protects them from the harassments of a government which never sees them as rivals. They often display too little anger at abuses of power which weigh only on other groups. [217]

CHAPTER EIGHT

On Property in Public Funds

The present situation of the great states of Europe has created in our times a new kind of property, that of public funds. This property does not at all tie its possessor to the soil, as does landed property. It demands neither assiduous work nor difficult speculations, like business property. It does not suppose distinguished talents, like the property we have termed intellectual.

The state's creditor is interested in the wealth of his country only as any creditor is in the wealth of his debtor. Provided the latter pays him, he is satisfied, and the dealings whose purpose is to assure his payment always seem fair enough, however costly they may be. The right he has all the time to sell his holding makes him indifferent to the probable but distant chance of national ruin. There is not a corner of land, not a manufacture, not a source of production whose impoverishment he does not contemplate with insouciance, as long as there are other resources which defray the payment of his income and which sustain the market value of his capital in the public mind.[15]

Some writers have considered the establishment of the public debt as a cause of prosperity. Among the sophisms with which they have propped up this bizarre opinion, they have got across a consideration well tuned to seduce governments, namely that a State's creditors are the natural supports of government. Associated with its fortunes, they have to defend it with all their might, as the sole guarantee of the capital due to them. What seems true to me is that in all circumstances, a lasting force, equally favorable to the worst and best of institutions, has at the very least as many drawbacks as advantages. It has to be added, however, that a body of men which depends [218] on government only out of a desire to see its assets secured is always ready to break off the instant anxiety affects its hopes. Now, is it a good thing for a realm that there should be a group of individuals who consider government only in purely pecuniary terms, sustaining it despite its abuses when it pays them and declaring themselves its bitter enemies the second it stops paying them?

Doubtless the bad faith of the administration and its slackness in the fulfillment of its promises imply a neglect of justice which must extend to many other things. Free governments have always been distinguished by their scrupulous reliability.[16] England has never put the creditors of its immense debt through the least worry or delay. America, since the consolidation of its independence, has scrupulously observed the same principles of trustworthiness. Holland has deserved the same praise for as long as it has existed. It is not thus with states subject to despotic governments. The fact is, only free governments can in no circumstances separate their interests from their duties. In this respect, the creditors of national debts must desire like all other citizens that freedom be established and maintained.

I confess to preferring that they be animated by nobler motives. It might happen that a despotic government, aware of the danger of annoying its creditors, came to put all its efforts into pleasing them, and succeeded for a more or less long period in weighing the nation down with excessive taxes. In this case the holders of the national debt, cut off from the rest of the nation, would remain faithful to a government treating only them justly.

15. See Constant's Note E at the end of Book X.
16. See Constant's Note F at the end of Book X.

Property in public funds is of an essentially egotistical and solitary nature, one easily becoming aggressive, because it exists only at others' expense. By a remarkable effect of the complex organization of modern societies, while the natural interest of any nation is that taxation be lowered to the least possible, the creation of a national debt gives one part of each nation an interest in increasing it.[17]

We could muster many other arguments, furthermore, [219] against a theory which, in reality, like many other theories, is only an excuse, disguised as a precept. In thinking of the existence of a public debt as morally and politically unfortunate, however, I do envisage it at the same time, in the present situation of society, as an inevitable evil for the large States. Those which habitually make subventions to national expenditure out of taxation are almost always forced to anticipate, and their anticipations constitute debt. Moreover, at the first out-of-the-way happening they are all obliged to borrow. As for those which have adopted the loan system, in preference to the tax system, establishing taxes only to service their loans (today this is virtually the English system), a public debt is inseparable from their existence. Thus to recommend modern States to relinquish the resources that credit offers them would be a pointless exercise. But precisely because public debt creates a new kind of property, whose effects are very different from those of other kinds of property and above all from those of landed property, landed property must be given all the more importance to counterbalance the bad effects of this new kind.

This is what the English constitution has done effortlessly. The owners of a debt of fifteen billion have less political influence than the proprietors of land whose total income would not pay the interest on that debt.[18] This explains why it has not corrupted British public-spiritedness. National representation, founded in large part on landed property, has maintained the integrity of that public spirit—an admirable result of well-managed freedom! The outlooks brought about by state rentiers in France conspired to overthrow the French monarchy, because under that monarchy there was no other center of legal and lasting public opinion. The State's creditors in England identify with national feeling, because political organization, there taking as its base landed property, as its means of action the people's rights,[19] and for its limits the most important individual rights,[20] has been able

17. See Constant's Note G at the end of Book X.
18. See Constant's Note H at the end of Book X.
19. See Constant's Note I at the end of Book X.
20. See Constant's Note J at the end of Book X.

thereby to render salutary [220] the very features of the case whose natural tendencies seem most dangerous.

CHAPTER NINE

On the Amount of Landed Property Which Society Has the Right to Insist upon for the Exercise of Political Rights

Despite my wish to steer clear of details, I must add a few words on the amount of property which should be required.

A property can be so confined that he who owns it is a proprietor only in appearance. According to the writer I have cited above,[21] anyone whose income from land is not sufficient to see him through the year, without having to work for other people, is not fully a proprietor. In terms of the proportion of property he is lacking, he is back among the wage-earning class. Proprietors are masters of his life, for they can refuse him work. Therefore only he who has the necessary income to exist independently of any other party's will, can exercise political rights. A lesser property condition is illusory, a higher one unjust. Given the necessary minimum, independence is entirely relative, a matter of character and impartiality. The advantages of landed property come more from its nature than its magnitude.

The economists have had the idea of linking land to political rights in such a way that landowners would have more or fewer votes according to the extent of their holdings. This idea would distort property. It would soon turn it into an oligarchy, which would become narrower every day, because the tendency of large properties is to swallow small ones. Once the minimum land holding carrying citizenship rights is fixed, the big proprietors must not have any legal superiority over the others. The division of powers applies in a way to the government of property owners, as to all forms of government; and just as in all free constitutions an attempt is made to endow the subordinate powers [221] with the ability to resist the encroachments of the superior, and an interest in so doing, so small owners must be given an interest in opposing the aristocracy of the large and the ability so to do. This happens naturally if all proprietors enjoying true independence have equal rights.

21. Hofmann was able to find neither author nor definition.

CHAPTER TEN

That Owners Have No Interest in Abusing Power vis-à-vis Nonowners

Is there a fear that proprietors, as sole holders of political powers, may make these weigh heavily on the deprived class? The nature of property is enough to dispel this fear. Since the birth of commerce,[22] proprietors have no longer formed a distinct class, separated from the rest of men by lasting prerogatives. The membership of this class renews itself constantly. Some people leave, others enter it. If property were immobile and always stayed in the same hands, it would be a most improper institution. It would split the human race in two. One part would be everything, the other nothing. Such is not the essence of property, however. In defiance of those who possess it, it tends to a continual changing of hands. The eventuality to be studiously avoided, as I will say presently, is anything which could stop this salutary changing of hands.

If the law favors the accumulation of property, rendering it inalienable in certain families or classes, the government of proprietors becomes tyrannical. It is the circulation of property which guarantees the justice of the institution. This circulation is in the nature of things. It suffices not to hinder it.

Moreover, in the present state of civilization, the interest of proprietors is not separate from that of the industrial or wage-earning classes. A very great number of proprietors belong to one or the other of these classes. What hurts them falls on the proprietors themselves.

For these two reasons proprietors always eschew vexatious laws. If these laws were directed solely at nonproprietors, they would doubly menace [222] their own authors.

Among certain ancient peoples, in Rome for example, proprietorial government involved abuse of power. This was due to circumstances which have not been remarked upon. Among the ancients the poor were always indebted to the rich, because the latter used only their slaves for work. In modern times it is normally the rich who are indebted to the poor. In the former case the rich demanded from the poor what the latter lacked completely, that is to say, money. That demand, needing violence to be satisfied, and, despite the violence, being mostly unsatisfied, there was a source of hatred and continual opposition between these two classes. In modern societies the rich demand from the poor what the latter can always supply in plenty, their labor, and from this there results much better agreement.

22. See Constant's Note K at the end of Book X.

Even were someone to prove to me that today there are still abuses in proprietorial government, I should not abandon my view. I would undertake to show that these abuses, vestiges of less enlightened centuries, do more harm every day to the proprietors themselves. I include an example in a note.[23] I would hope for the rectification of these abuses simply through progress by way of education and experience, and I would see far fewer drawbacks in putting up with them temporarily than in giving nonproprietors political rights, that is to say, power. Once one is convinced that property is indispensable to the prosperity of the social State, one must, as has already been said,[24] guarantee it come what may, and its only sufficient means of guarantee is the power of the owners. [223] One has to will the institutions one establishes, and any institution which supports property is on a suicide course when it gives power to nonproprietors.

It would be a mistake for merchants and manufacturers to fear the government of landowners. It is not the latter who have passed laws disastrous for commerce and industry. Such laws have been caused either by universal ignorance of the first principles of political economy, an ignorance common once to all classes, or by the ferocious violence of the propertyless, or by the private calculations and passing interests of traders. These last above all have been deadly. Monopolies, prohibitions, and privileges, by supplying some particular industry with disproportionate means and destroying the competition, are fatal to production in general. These contrivances are mercantile. Commerce is the child of freedom, yet the trader can enrich himself by the constraints with which he surrounds his competitors. Used as he is to speculating on everything, he is often given to speculating on the laws themselves. Unchecked, he will make laws to favor his business, instead of being content to make sure that his business enjoys the safeguard of the law.

Adam Smith's wise commentator has said: "as much as the influence of manufacturers, merchants, and capitalists on legislation expresses itself in narrow outlooks, complicated rules, and oppressive constraints, so the proprietorial dispensation is to be recognized in fair intentions, simple arrangements, and the free and easy flow of all types of circulation."[25]

Precisely in the interest of commerce, it is therefore useful that legislative power be entrusted to landowners, whose activity is less restless and whose calculations are less volatile.

23. See Constant's Note L at the end of Book X.
24. In Ch. 3 and 4 of this same Book X.
25. See Constant's Note M at the end of Book X.

In all this our hypothesis assumes a society without privileged castes. Castes of this type, being means for conserving and moreover for acquiring property, corrupt it. If owners possess improper powers, they will be enemies of freedom and justice, not as owners, but as privileged persons. If they are not privileged, they will be their most faithful supports. [224]

CHAPTER ELEVEN

On Hereditary Privileges Compared to Property

Hereditary privileges have been compared to property. Property's enemies have adopted this comparison with alacrity. Privileges having become an odious thing, they have wanted this disfavor to fall on property. The friends of privilege have taken up this comparison for a contrary motive. Property being indispensable, they wanted to justify privileges as provenly necessary. This comparison would be right only if property did not change hands. Only then would it resemble privilege. Then it would also be, however, the most oppressive usurpation, as we said earlier. If property is the constant interest of the majority across the generations, this is because anyone can aspire to it and be assured of getting it through work. Hereditary privileges, however, are only, and can never be other than, the interest of the few. They exclude all who do not belong to the favored caste. They bear not only on the present but on the future and deprive generations unborn. Property stirs emulation; privilege rebuffs and discourages it. Property puts a value on all social relations, all social conditions. Privileges hold themselves aloof. Property communicates and thus improves itself. Privileges surround themselves with defenses and in communication lose their advantages. The more proprietors there are in a country, the more property is respected and the more people are affluent. The more privileged people there are, the more privileges are depreciated and the more people are for all that oppressed. For it is on them that the immunities of the privileged bear down. It is hard, even when we extend our conjectural sphere as far as possible, to imagine a tolerable social condition without property. America shows us a wise and peaceful government without privileged institutions.[26] Privileges and society are always at war. The latter wants a rule; the former want exceptions. If property has its drawbacks sometimes, they come from privileges, which, as a result of their diverse combinations, make the acquisition of property often impossible and always difficult for the nonprivileged class. Entails, primogeniture, and all

26. [It had one huge such institution: slavery. Translator's note]

the regulations which make property immobile and troublesome are in the nature of privileges, in fact their emanations.

[225] In our era a number of men, having abolished hereditary privileges, went on to undermine property. We should not conclude that these things are intimately linked. In all questions there is a point where the mad and the sane split. The latter stop after the overthrow of prejudices which it was important to destroy. The former want to extend the destruction to things worth keeping.[27]

When it is suggested that property is a convention of the same kind as hereditary privileges, we need to separate these two ideas again, in the countries where these privileges have been discredited. Nothing harms useful things more than their resting on improper things. The two collapse together. The relationship between privileges and property is like that between superstition and morality. Superstition can give morality a meretricious succor. If superstition loses its force, however, morality itself is undermined.

Privileges and proscriptions are social errors of the same kind. They likewise take citizens away from the law, either by abitrary punishments or arbitrary favor.

Montesquieu is often quoted in favor of privileges. But he examines rather than judges the laws. He explains the reasons for them, assigning causes without justifying institutions. He wrote, moreover, under a government mild in practice, though arbitrary by nature. Now, under such a government, privileges can be useful.[28] Where rights have disappeared, privileges can be a defense. For all their drawbacks, they are better than the absence of any intermediary power. To do without privileges, a constitution has to be excellent. Under despotism equality becomes a scourge. [226]

CHAPTER TWELVE

Necessary Comment

What has happened to the privileged castes in our times in France obliges me to enter here some explanation of my opinion on the matter. I would not wish to be confused with men who sought in the abolition

27. A very similar argument is found in Mme. de Staël (*éd. cit.*, p. 46): "There is a point in all debate where the foolish and the wise separate. It is when destructive action is over and the matter in hand is to form a link which reunites what the emptiness of some prejudice or other has disunited." Constant will return to this theme in Ch. 4 and 5 of Book XVIII, in relation to revolutions.

28. See Constant's Note N at the end of Book X.

of improprieties only a means of satisfying their hatred and long-wounded vanity.

The destruction of hereditary privileges in France was an inevitable consequence of the progress of civilization. From the time the nobility had ceased being feudal, it had become a brilliant ornament but without a definite purpose, agreeable to its possessors, humiliating to those who did not possess it, but without real means and above all without power. Its advantages consisted more in exclusions for the lower orders than in prerogatives for the preferred class. The nobles obtained improper favors but were not invested with any legal power. They did not constitute an intermediary body which kept the people in order and the government in check. They formed an almost imaginary corporation, which for everything which was not just recollection or prejudice, depended on the government. Heredity in England does not confer on its members a contested power, arbitrary and vexatious, but a specified authority and constitutional functions. Its prerogatives, being legal in nature and created for a definite purpose, are less wounding for those who do not enjoy them and give more power to those who do. Therefore, this heredity is less exposed to attack at the same time as it is more readily defended. The nobility in France, however, invited attack from every vain and worthless thing and armed almost no interest to defend itself. It had no base, no fixed position in the community. There was nothing to guarantee its survival. Quite the contrary: everything conspired to its ruin, even the education and individual superiority of its own members. This is why it was destroyed almost without commotion. It vanished like a shadow, being only an indefinable memento of a half-destroyed system. Therefore its abolition cannot be the object of justified censure. Everything the [227] leaders of our Revolution have added to this measure, however, has been unjust and insane.

One cause which has not been sufficiently noted contributed, if I am not mistaken, to the mingling of wise principles with odious and unreasonable means. We can count the origins of hereditary privileges among the differences between us and the ancients.

Among the peoples of antiquity, civilized by colonies without being conquered by them, inequalities in rank had their origin solely in superiority, either physical or moral. You will be conscious that I am not speaking of slaves, who have to be counted for nothing in the social system of the ancients. Among them, the privileged were a class of compatriots, come to wealth or esteem because their ancestors had acquired merit in the youthful society, teaching it either the first principles of government, or the ceremonies of religion, or discoveries necessary to life's needs and the elements of civilization. Among the moderns, by contrast, inequalities of rank have their basis in conquest. The civilized peoples of the Roman empire were shared out like cheap cattle among ferocious aggressors. European institutions have for centuries borne the imprint of military force. Overcome by the sword, the conquered have also been kept in servitude by it. Their masters did not deign to disguise the origin of their power by ingenious fables or make it respectable by well or badly founded claims to superior wisdom. The two races reproduced themselves, for a long time with no other relationship than bondage on the one hand and oppression on the other. Everything from the fourth to the fifteenth century served to remind a Europe civilized but overrun, of the scourge it had received from the north. The superiority of the ancient peoples derives from this cause. They walked free from all domination, on land that no proud foot of a conqueror had ever trampled on. The moderns, a race debased and dispossessed, went wrong following a single conquest.

From this difference between the ancients and us has resulted a striking difference in the intellectual systems of the friends of liberty in the two eras. Despite the drawbacks of hereditary privilege, even among the ancients, almost all the publicists of antiquity [228] want power concentrated in the hands of the upper classes. Aristotle makes this an essential part of a well-constituted democracy.[29] By contrast, since the Renaissance of learning, the supporters of political freedom have never believed its establishment possible without the destruction of the predominant castes. Those whom Aristotle sees as our guides, Machiavelli sees as victims who must be sacrificed.[30] From the fifteenth century until our times, those who have taken a position in the matter have written in favor of equality, and acted or spoken on behalf of the descendants of the oppressed and against the descendants of the oppressors. In proscribing not only hereditary privileges but also their possessors, they have themselves without knowing been dominated by hereditary prejudices. At the foundation of the Republic in France, the aim was more, as in the Italian republics, the rebuffing of conquerors than the giving of equal rights to citizens. Scanning the laws against the nobles in Italy, especially Florence,

29. Above all, Aristotle attributes a great importance to the middle class. On this subject see Raymond Weil, *Politique d'Aristote,* Paris, A. Colin, 1966, pp. 94–97, *Le citoyen et l'homme de bien,* and pp. 159–173.

30. See Constant's Note O at the end of Book X.

you would think yourself reading the laws of the Convention.[31] These eighteenth-century nobles have been depicted like fifteenth-century barons. Hateful men have skillfully blended all the centuries to rekindle and maintain hatred. Just as we once went back to the Franks and Goths when we wanted to be oppressors, they now revisited the Franks and Goths in the search of pretexts for the opposite oppression. Puerile vanity once searched for noble titles in archives and chronicles. A harsher and more vindictive vanity now drew on them for the wherewithal of accusations. A little reflection, however, must convince us that privileges of a naturally improper kind can be a means of leisure, of improvement and enlightenment, for their possessors. Great independent wealth is usually a guarantee against several kinds of baseness and vice. Knowing one is respected saves one from that thin-skinned and restless vanity which sees insult and imagines scorn everywhere, those violent, implacable feelings which take revenge in the ill they do, on the sorrows they undergo. Being given to gentle ways [229] and accustomed to very refined nuances gives the outlook a delicate susceptibility, and the mind a ready flexibility.

These precious qualities had to be put to good advantage. The spirit of chivalry had to be circled with barriers it could not transgress, without its being excluded from the careers open to everyone. Thus would be formed that class of men which the ancient lawmakers regarded as destined by nature for government. It would be formed by the enlightened section of the commoners and the enlightened section of the nobility.

Woe betide the men who have prevented this amalgam, as easy as it is necessary. They did not want to take account of the centuries, nor to distinguish between nuances, nor to reassure apprehensions, nor to pardon fugitive vanities, nor to let pointless complaints subside and foolish menaces evaporate. They have recorded the doings of wounded pride. In treating all nobles as enemies of freedom, they made countless enemies for freedom. Nobility was restored by a new distinction, persecution, and strong in this privilege, fought the better against the so-called free institutions, in whose names it was being oppressed. It found in its proscription legitimate reasons for resistance and infallible means of attracting interest to its cause. To accompany the abolition of improprieties with injustices, is not to put obstacles to their returning, but to offer them the hope of coming back along with justice.

31. A reference to the National Convention, 1792–1795. See Constant's Note P at the end of Book X.

CHAPTER THIRTEEN

On the Best Way of Giving Proprietors a Large Political Influence

The surest and easiest way of giving proprietors great political influence has already been indicated by Aristotle: "To combine your laws and institutions in such a way," he says, "that the high positions cannot be the object of a calculated interest. Without that, the masses, which, it must be said, are affected little by exclusion from honors, [230] because they like to get on with their own business, will envy honors and profit. All the safeguards are fine, if the magistracy is not a temptation to greed. The poor will prefer lucrative occupations to difficult and unpaid ones. The rich will fill the magistracy, because they will not need payment."[32]

These principles are probably not applicable to all the jobs in the modern State apparatus, because there are some which require wealth beyond any individual holding. Nothing stops their being applied, however, to legislative positions, which increase only slightly the routine expenditures of those in whom they are invested.

Thus it was in Carthage. All the magistratures appointed by the people discharged their functions without payment. Other jobs were salaried. It is the same in England. I think myself on strong ground when I take as my proof that home of liberty. In this country people often denounce the corruption of the House of Commons. Just compare what this corruption, even in difficult circumstances, has done for the crown with what elsewhere other assemblies, largely paid, have done for a thousand successive tyrants.

In a free constitution, where nonproprietors have no political rights, it is outrageously contradictory to keep the people out of representation, as if only the rich ought to represent them, and then to make them pay their representatives, as if the latter were poor.

I do not like strong property requirements. I have given my reason elsewhere.[33] Independence is entirely relative. As soon as a man has the necessary minimum, he need only elevate his soul to do without superfluities. It is desirable, however, that legislative positions be in general filled by wealthy men. [231] Now, on declaring them unpaid, we place power in the hands of the leisured class, without refusing a fair chance to all the legitimate exceptions.

When sizeable payments are attached to legislative positions, these payments become the main objective. Mediocrity, ineptitude, and baseness

32. Aristotle, *La politique,* V, 8, *éd. cit.,* t. II, p. 382.

33. In Ch. 9 of this same Book X.

perceive in these august duties only a miserable speculation of chance, whose success is guaranteed them by silence and servility. The corruption which is the product of ambitious designs is far less deadly than that which results from ignoble calculations. Ambition is compatible with a thousand generous qualities: probity, courage, impartiality, and independence. Avarice is compatible with none of these. If we cannot keep ambitious men out of public positions, at least let us keep the greedy out. This way we will diminish the number of competitors considerably, and those we drive away will be precisely the least worthy.

Paying the people's representatives is not to give them an interest in fulfilling their functions well, but in exercising them a long time.

Two conditions are necessary for representative duties to be unpaid. The first is that they be important. No one would want to take on, unpaid, jobs rendered puerile by their insignificance, or which would be shameful if they ceased being puerile. But, it must be added, under such a constitution, it would be better were there no legislative positions at all.

The second condition is that reelection be possible indefinitely.[34] The impossibility of reelection under a representative government is in all respects a great mistake. [232] Only the chance of uninterrupted reelection offers merit a fitting reward and lodges in the public mind a body of imposing and respected names. Far from any free people should be both those shameful prejudices which demand distinctions of birth giving access to positions and their exclusive exercise, and also those prohibitive laws which prevent the people reelecting those who have not lost its trust. The influence of individuals is not destroyed by jealous institutions. In every era such influence of this sort as exists freely is always indispensable. The influence of individuals diminishes of its own accord with the spread of enlightenment. Let us not meddle therein with envious laws. Individuals naturally lose their supremacy when a larger number are educated to the same level. Let us not dispossess talent by arbitrary exclusions. There are in the assemblies weak men, who cannot be reelected, men who want either the goodwill of government, in order to obtain some compensation, or to make as few enemies as possible, in order to live in peaceful retirement. If you put obstacles in the way of indefinite reelection, you deprive talent and courage of their due and prepare a comfortable and secure shelter for cowardice and ineptitude. You put on the same level the man who has faced every danger and him who has bent his degraded head under

34. We can compare Constant's arguments on the advantages of reelection with Madame de Staël's in *Des circonstances actuelles, éd. cit.*, pp. 187–190.

tyranny. Reelection favors righteous calculation. Such calculations alone have lasting success, but to obtain it, they need time. Upright and brave men versed in public affairs are not so numerous that one can reject those who have already merited public esteem. New talents will appear too. The people tend to welcome them. Do not impose any constraint on them in this matter. Do not force them at each reelection to choose newcomers, ones still with their fortunes to make in matters of self-esteem and hell-bent on fame. Nothing costs a nation more dearly than the creation of reputations. Look at America. The people's votes have never stopped supporting the founders of liberty. Look at England. There famous names have become a sort of popular property, in an unbroken series of reelections. [233] Happy those nations which offer like examples and know how to trust durably!

CHAPTER FOURTEEN

On the Action of Government on Property

The reader will have been able to spot that among the considerations we have advanced for upholding the high place property must have in our political life, none has been drawn from the metaphysical nature of property itself. We have treated it only as a social convention.

We have seen, however, that this viewpoint does not stop us seeing property as a thing society must surround with every protection. Our axiom is always that it would be better not to set up property than to make it a subject of struggle and bitterness, and that this danger can be avoided only by giving it inviolability on the one hand and power on the other.

Like considerations will guide us in our efforts to determine the limits of political jurisdiction over property.

Property, to the extent it is a social convention, falls within the scope of political jurisdiction. Society has rights over property it definitely does not have over the freedom, lives, and opinions of its members.

Property, however, has intimate links with other aspects of human existence, some of which are not subject at all to collective jurisdiction while the remaining ones are so only in a limited way. Society must therefore restrain its jurisdiction over property, because it could not be exercised to its full extent without menacing things which are not subject to it. Political authority must never, as part of its action over property, offend inviolable rights. Society must also restrict its jurisdiction over property so as not to give individuals an interest in eluding the law. Such an interest is morally adverse, firstly in that [234] it entails the habit of hypocrisy and fraud, and secondly in that it requires the encouragement of informing. We dealt with this earlier.[35] Since this observation applies, however, to almost all the things government wants to take action on, necessarily it recurs often in our theorizing.

CHAPTER FIFTEEN

On Laws Which Favor the Accumulation of Property in the Same Hands

The property laws can be of two kinds. They can be intended to favor its accumulation and perpetuate it in the same hands, the same families or individual classes. Such is the origin of lands declared inalienable, of the exempting of certain classes from taxation, of entailments, of primogeniture—in sum, of all the feudal or noble customs.

This legal system, taken in all its extent and the severity it had in the past throughout Europe, takes away from property its true character and greatest advantage. It makes it a privilege. It disinherits the class finding itself without property. It transforms passing chance, which the next moment would have put right, into a permanent injustice. If the country is commercial and industrious, this system of property undermines it, because it forces individuals in commerce or industry to seek refuge or property in a more hospitable country. If the country is purely agricultural, this system brings in the most oppressive despotism. A terrible oligarchy forms. The peasants are reduced to the condition of serfs. The landowners themselves are corrupted by the improprieties which benefit them. They develop a ferocious, almost savage mentality. They need for their perpetuation to banish all enlightenment, to repel all improvement in the poor man's lot, to oppose the formation of that intermediary class which, bringing together the advantages of education and the absence of prejudices which the privileged condition entails, is among all peoples [235] the depository of just ideas, of useful knowledge, of impartial opinion and the hopes of humanity.

Today there are few countries where this system continues in its entirety; but almost everywhere we find vestiges of it, not without drawbacks. Such laws, when they are only partial, have, indeed, a new disadvantage. The group forbidden to acquire certain properties is angry at this exclusion, which is anyway always accompanied by other humiliating distinctions, since one abuse never stands alone. The excluded group takes advantage of what it possesses to demand the rights it is denied. It encourages discontent

35. In Book IV, Ch. 2, *The idea which usually develops about the effects which the proliferation of the laws has and the falsity of that idea.*

and exaggerated opinions in all nonproprietors. It prepares troubles, struggles, and revolutions to which everybody afterwards falls victim.

In the countries where these oppressive laws continue in undiminished rigor, it has been claimed, as always in such cases, that the classes they oppress recognize the advantages therein. It has been said that serfdom, a natural consequence of this system of property, was felicitous for the peasants and examples were given. Nobles one could suspect of hypocrisy and who should at least be accused of lack of foresight, have offered their vassals freedom. This is to say that they proposed to men brutalized by ignorance, without energy or capability or ideas, that they leave their fields and cabins, to go freely with their infirm parents and children of tender years, in search of a subsistence they had no means of procuring. These vassals preferred their chains, from which it was concluded that serfdom was agreeable. What, however, does such experience show? What we knew, that for men to be given freedom, they must not have been degraded to a subhuman condition by slavery. Then, freedom is doubtless only an illusory and deadly gift, just as the daylight becomes sorrowful for him whose view is enfeebled by the shadows of a dungeon. This truth holds for all types of servitude. Men who have never known freedom's advantages may well enthusiastically submit to the yoke: [236] reject their sheepish and deceptive witness. They have no right to make depositions in so holy a cause. As to freedom, listen to those ennobled by its blessings. Only they should be heard, only they consulted.[36]

I would add that all governments today are working, commendably, to eliminate the last traces of this barbarous legislation. Alexander I is one prince in particular who seems to have brought to the throne the love of humanity and justice and who puts his renown not to driving his people back into barbarism but to preparing them by instruction for freedom, encouraging on his vast lands the freeing of the serfs and the dissemination of landownership.[37]

36. For once, Constant agrees with Rousseau, who declared in his *Discours sur l'origine et les fondements de l'inégalité parmi les hommes:* "It is not, therefore, by the degradation of enslaved peoples that the natural disposition of man for or against servitude should be judged, but by the huge efforts made by all free peoples to guarantee themselves against oppression . . . I feel that it is not for slaves to reason on freedom." *Oeuvres complètes, éd. cit.,* t. III, pp. 181–182.

37. On the reform projects of Alexander I, see the letter from F.-C. de La Harpe to the Emperor on 16 October 1801, in *Correspondance de Frédéric-César de La Harpe et Alexandre Ier,* published by Jean-Charles Biaudet and Françoise Nicod, t. I, 1785–1802, Neuchâtel, La Baconnière, 1978, pp. 316–330.

The thing about the inalienability of goods is something common to everything human. Its intention was reasonable in the era which gave it birth; but the institution has outlived its usefulness. When there was no public justice and force was the sole guarantee against robbery, this force being found only in sizeable properties, which provided numerous vassals ready to defend their master, the inalienability of property was a means of security. Today, when social conditions are quite different, this inalienability is an evil for agriculture and pointless to boot. The owner of very large properties inevitably neglects a large proportion of his property. As Smith says in *The Wealth of Nations,* Book III, Ch. 2, to convince oneself of this, one need only compare big estates which have stayed in the same family continuously since the days of feudal anarchy, with the small holdings surrounding them. What is true of States is true of properties. Excessive smallness deprives them of the most efficient means of improvement. Excessive size [237] makes them liable to careless management, haste, and negligence.[38]

He who wants to sell proves he lacks the means or motivation for improvement. He who wants to buy proves he has will and means. Entailments and all types of inalienability force the former to keep that which is a burden on him and prevent the latter acquiring what would be advantageous to him. To society this is a double loss, since amelioration of property constitutes national wealth.

We must observe, in finishing this section, that the order of ideas has forced us to invert the facts. It was not at all by way of laws forbidding the wider distribution of property that the feudal oligarchy was established, but by conquest. It was then that this oligarchy, to perpetuate itself, had recourse to these prohibitive laws. Thus it would be wrong to fear a like result from proprietorial government. This government, when it rests on the principles established above,[39] will stay true to them because proprietors have no interest in replacing the legitimate enjoyment they are assured of by property they know they can guard, if they so choose, by impediments which would add nothing to their enjoyment and offend their wishes. Proprietorial government has nowhere produced a feudal one; rather, feudal government has corrupted proprietorial government.

38. Adam Smith, *op. cit.,* t. II, p. 421. "There are still today, in each of the United Kingdoms, these great estates which have remained, without interruption, in the same family, since the time of feudal anarchy. One only has to compare the present state of these domains with the possessions of neighboring small proprietors, to judge, without other argument, how little such extensive holdings are favorable to progressive cultivation."

39. In Ch. 14 of this same Book X, *On the Action of Government on Property.*

CHAPTER SIXTEEN

On Laws Which Enforce the Wider Spreading of Property

The laws can have an opposite tendency. They can purpose the widest possible spread of ownership. Such is the avowed motive of the agrarian laws, of the dividing up of lands, of the ban on [238] wills, and of that host of regulations aimed at preventing people managing to make light of these laws.

This activity of government, above all that which bears on the right to make wills—for the agrarian laws are sufficiently discredited—seems at first more legitimate and in keeping with egalitarian principles than the contrary action. In fact, it is superfluous. It wants to force what would happen naturally. Property tends to split up. If the government leaves it to itself, it will no sooner be acquired than you will see it dispersed. The proof of this is the proliferating laws necessary under all aristocratic governments to keep it in the same families. The accumulation of property is always a consequence of institutions.

It follows that the simplest and surest means of encouraging the widening ownership of property would be to abolish all the laws which oppose it.

Since governments, however, never content themselves with negative actions, they have usually gone further. They have not only abrogated vicious institutions, but combated the effects of the habits, recollections, and prejudices which might have survived these institutions with positive regulations.

What has happened is what naturally must happen when government arbitrarily restrains men's freedom. The laws on this matter have been evaded. Further laws were needed to curb these infractions. From this followed innumerable obstacles to the transfer, disposal, and transmission of property.

These restrictions having entailed further inconveniences, people accused each other of having violated them. Greed armed itself with what was intended to check it.

During our Revolution a host of circumstantial safeguards were built up into eternal principles. Legislators who imagined they had the deepest outlooks and widest perspectives have always fixed their gaze on the possibility of a small refractory minority. To get at this they have borne down on all the French. Blind legislators, to make laws not for their fellow citizens but against their enemies! Insane legislators, under whose rule the law was no longer the shelter of all but an offensive arm against the few!

Freedom is constantly attacked by reasoning applicable only to constraint. Thus in our time the free transmission of property has been attacked with arguments which were valid only against the restrictions put on such transmission [239] by the laws of old. The right to make wills and primogeniture have been confused, when the latter is on the contrary an encroachment on and the destruction of the right to make wills.

On this question, I will not stop to refute other sophisms drawn from an obscure and abstract metaphysics. People have argued that death entails annihilation, holding it absurd to let a man dispose of goods which were no longer his and to lend a fictitious existence to his will when he no longer existed. These arguments are fundamentally unsound. They could be applied to all men's transactions; for if their intentions must cease to have effect once their lives are ended, long-term debts, leases, and all operations which have to be completed only by some fixed, far-off date would end by law with their deaths.

The question of wills, it seems to me, furnishes a striking example of the good which the absence of government intervention in a matter could sometimes do, without pain or effort, whenever this good is obtained only in an imperfect and artificial way, one hampered by two contradictory laws.

Legislators in several free societies, on the one hand seeing the dispersal of property as favorable to freedom and on the other paternal power as necessary to morality, have consequently made laws to impede the accumulation of property and have tried out a thousand institutions in support of paternal power. Now, these laws and institutions have been at loggerheads and their twin purposes have failed. Properties have not undergone the dispersal the law intended because fathers, jealous of their disputed rights, have used every deception which might promote either their own individual interests or that tendency, natural to man, to elude the regulations which hurt him. This has not in the least stopped paternal power weakening. The sons, jealously guarding the equal rights the law gave them, regarded the fathers' attempts to strip them of part of the enjoyment of these as wicked contrivances.

If the legislator had abstained from all such commands in this matter, paternal power would have found a solid basis in the right to make wills. Fatherly fair play, which, whatever is said about it, is overwhelmingly the norm, would have given the dispersal of property a far more secure guarantee than is to be found in all the precautionary measures of positive law. Governments, however, [240] when they think both that it is their duty and that it serves their renown to have a useful purpose in view for all things, make partial laws at cross-purposes, which cancel each other out and create only harassment.

Restrictions on the free disposition of properties after their owners' deaths have the drawback we have called attention to in so many other laws, that of inviting fraud, of existing only to be eluded, of entailing inquisition, suspicion, and informing. They have the further drawback, however, that the vices they lead to reach right into families. It is not solely the citizens but the parents who are at war with one another. Not just social relations but nature itself is poisoned. Parents are made no less unjust but are also in bad faith. Children whose ingratitude is authorized think themselves likewise authorized to a sort of inspection of their parents' actions. The domestic sanctuary, which ought to be a refuge of calm and of peaceful affections, becomes the shameful site of domestic struggle between a legally supported filial independence and the resentment of fathers, who punish this surveillance as they strive to elude the laws.

The legitimate jurisdiction of government over the transmission of property is extremely limited. It should guarantee the latter and leave it alone, establishing some procedures for determining owners' real wishes, without placing restrictions or impediments on those wishes.

Tolerate partial injustices, which are inevitable among men, but much less frequent than you like to believe in order to give yourself pretexts for perpetual interference. If you want to remedy them, you will be throwing yourself into an endless course of action, upsetting yourself pointlessly over it; and without managing to block individual injustices, you will succeed only in becoming an unjust creature yourself.

Every time that an abuse exists, the rest of the social institutions encourage it. Unable to destroy it, they make room for it and set themselves up, so to speak, around it. Formerly, the right to make wills felt the effects of hereditary privileges, but only because it was sacrificed to these.

When institutions have done harm, and this goes on after the institutions are destroyed, it is better to put up with the inconvenience caused by the traces of these defective institutions, than to hasten to remedy this with further institutions which might also have unforeseen drawbacks.

The same considerations which inspired the restrictions on [241] the free transmission of property have led governments to progressive taxation, compulsory borrowings, and taxes directed solely against the wealthy. These measures have been so fully rebuked by experience, however, that it is almost superfluous to demonstrate their futility and danger. They are in direct opposition to the present trends in society. They condemn wealth to lying. They put it at loggerheads with our institutions. Now, what could be more pernicious and absurd than stirring up war between governmental power and wealth, the most instantly disposable power, the one most serving of every interest, and therefore much more real and genuinely obeyed! Government is a threat, wealth a reward. You get away from government by deceiving it. To gain wealth's blessings, you have to serve it. The latter must prevail.

Furthermore, it is a mistake to imagine that the poor gain what is taken thus from the rich. He who has not will always depend, whatever we do, on him who has. If you upset the rich man, he will concentrate more on his pleasures, his speculation, his fantasies. As far as possible he will withdraw his capital from circulation, and the poor man will feel the effects of this.

CONSTANT'S NOTES

A. [Refers to page 172.] See above all Xenophon and Aristophanes' comedies.

B. [Refers to page 175.] Cato the Elder, on agriculture: "Pius questus stabilissimus, minimeque invidiosus, minimeque male cogitantes qui in eo studio occupanti sunt."[40]

[242] C. [Refers to page 176.] See Smith, Richesse des nations, Livre I, Ch. 10.[41]

D. [Refers to page 176.] Montesquieu remarks in Esprit des lois, XX, 2, that "if commerce unites nations, it does not similarly unite individuals"; hence it happens that nations, being united, are confused, that is to say that there is no more patriotism, and that individuals, not being united, there is no longer anything but traders, that is to say, there are no longer any fellow citizens.

E. [Refers to page 180.]
Smith, Livre V, Ch. 3.[42]

40. This quotation from Cato the Elder has clearly been borrowed from Adam Smith, *op. cit.,* t. III, p. 73, and not from the original, which says: "Ut ex agricolis et viri fortissimi et milites strenuissimi gignuntur, maximeque pius questus stabilissimusque consequitur minimeque invidiosus, minimeque male coginantes sunt qui in eo studio occupati sunt."—"But it is the peasants who produce the strongest men and the bravest soldiers. It is to them the most just gains accrue, as well as the most reliable and least subject to envy. Those absorbed by these concerns are the least evil minded." Cato, *De l'agriculture,* edited, confirmed, and translated by Raoul Goujard, Paris, Les Belles Lettres, 1975, p. 9. [Constant here takes from Adam Smith, unacknowledged, a supposed quotation from Cato the Elder. Hofmann corrects the Latin quotation wrongly reproduced by Smith. Translator's note]

41. Constant quotes from *The Wealth of Nations,* Book I, Ch. 10 (French translation from the English, *op. cit.,* t. I, p. 262). Smith here opines that apart from fine arts and the high professions, no activities require such a range of knowledge and experience as agriculture.

42. Adam Smith, *op. cit.,* t. IV, pp. 509–510. It may be useful to relate the English author's argument here: "A creditor of the state has unquestionably a general interest in the prosperity of a country's agriculture, manufacturing, and commerce, and therefore in the various lands being well maintained and the capital advantageously managed. If one of these things were lacking or were to fail generally, the product of the various taxes would no longer be sufficient to pay him the annuity or the return which is owed him. But a state creditor, considered simply as such, has no interest in such and such a piece of land being in good shape or such and such a piece of capital being well run. As a state creditor he is not familiar with any piece of land or capital; he has none under inspection, none he can busy himself with. There is not one particular one that cannot be totally wiped out without for the most part his even suspecting or at least without his being directly affected."

F. [Refers to page 180.]

I am speaking here of modern states only. The Roman Republic more than once broke away from the rules of justice with respect to its creditors.[43] The ancients, however, did not have the same ideas as we either on income or public credit.

G. [Refers to page 181.]

Administration des finances, Tome II, pp. 378–379.[44]

[243] H. [Refers to page 181.]

See A brief examination into the increase of the revenue, commerce and navigation of Great Britain by M. Beeke.[45]

I. [Refers to page 181.]

Popular election.

J. [Refers to page 181.]

Freedom of the press, habeas corpus, juries, freedom of conscience.

K. [Refers to page 183.]

Smith, Wealth of Nations, III.4.[46]

L. [Refers to page 184.]

The laws of England forbade any individual without property to move from one parish to another, without the latter's consent, from fear that this individual, having no means of support, might become a charge on his new fellow citizens. These laws seem to the advantage of owners, against the nonowner seeking refuge. They are a clear attack, however, on individual freedom. He who cannot earn his living

43. Constant had left a blank in which to indicate the precise place in *De l'esprit des lois* where Montesquieu explains how the Romans swindled the financiers by devaluing the currency during the Second Punic War. [Livre XXII, Ch. 11. Translator's note]

44. Jacques Necker, *De l'administration des finances de la France,* s.l., 1784, t. II, pp. 378–379: "The growth of public debt in like manner has distorted the social outlook, by multiplying in some countries the number of people with an interest contrary to the general interest. Rentiers desire, above all else, the wealth of the royal treasury; and since the extension of taxation is the most fertile source of this, the contributors (and above all the people, who are the biggest element in this, and have no money to lend) find today within the very bosom of the State, an adversarial faction whose credit and influence grow from day to day."

45. Constant is in error here. The book he means, *A brief examination into the increase of the revenue, commerce, and navigation of Great Britain, from 1792–1799,* Dublin, Graisberry and Campbell, 1799, is not by Beeke but by George Rose.

46. Adam Smith, *op. cit.,* t. II, pp. 439–489; Ch. 4 of Book III is called *How the commerce of the towns contributed to the improvement of the country.*

by the kind of work for which he is fitted, in the parish where he lives, is kept out of the one where his work could feed him easily. What is the result of this injustice? [244] Often a parish is oversupplied with labor while another is short of it. Then the daily rate in the latter goes up excessively. The owner who has driven away the hardworking man, whose upkeep he feared might one day be charged to him, therefore now pays in a dearer price for his iniquitous calculation. It is thus that all such abuses fall on those they seem to favor.

M. [Refers to page 184.]
Garnier. Notes on translating Smith.[47]

N. [Refers to page 186.]
This is truly the point of view from which Montesquieu considered privileges. "Since despotism," he says, "causes frightful evils to the natural order, the very evil which limits it is a good." Esprit des lois, Livre II, Ch. 4.

O. [Refers to page 188.]
For Titus Livy see Décades.[48] See also Condillac, or rather Mably writing under his name, in Cours d'étude,[49] Siéyès, Essai sur les priviléges.[50]

P. [Refers to page 189.]
See *gli ordinamenti della justizia*, laws which subjected the nobles of Florence to special legal arrangements, excluded them from citizenship, authorized their condemnation without other proof than public rumor. These laws were carried by the people around 1294, at the instigation of Gianno della Bella (noble), who placed himself at its head.[51]

47. Germain Garnier, *Notes du traducteur*, in Adam Smith, *op. cit.*, t. V, p. 309. Note XXXII, called *Des pouvoirs législatifs et judiciaires, et de leur rapport avec la propriété.*

48. In particular Ch. 5 of *Discours sur la première décade de Tite-Live* in Machiavelli, *Oeuvres complètes, éd. cit.*, pp. 392–394. This chapter is entitled, more precisely, *To whom more confidently to entrust the care of liberty, to the great or the people, and which of the two more often cause difficulty, he who wishes to acquire or he who wishes to conserve.*

49. Etienne Bonnot de Condillac, *Histoire moderne*, Livre X, Ch. 4 *Considérations sur l'Europe au moment du seizième siècle et par occasion sur les effets du commerce*, in *Cours d'étude . . . , op. cit.*, t. IX, pp. 456–471.

50. Emmanuel Siéyès, *Essai sur les privilèges*, s.l.n.d. [1788], 48 p.

51. Constant was mostly inspired for this note by Jean-Charles-Léonard Sismondi, *Recherches sur les constitutions des peuples libres, éd. cit.*, pp. 114–115, n. 9.

BOOK XI

On Taxation

Ch. 1. The object of this book. 205

Ch. 2. The first right of the governed with regard to taxation. 205

Ch. 3. The second right of the governed with regard to taxation. 207

Ch. 4. On various types of taxes. 207

Ch. 5. How taxation becomes contrary to individual rights. 212

Ch. 6. That taxes bearing on capital are contrary to individual rights. 214

Ch. 7. That the interest of the state in matters of taxation is consistent with individual rights. 215

Ch. 8. An incontestable axiom. 219

Ch. 9. The drawback of excessive taxation. 220

Ch. 10. A further drawback of excessive taxation. 221

CHAPTER ONE

The Object of This Book

The nature of this work does not allow profound research into the theory of taxation, nor into the best type of taxes one might set up. Such research would involve us in details which belong only in treatises devoted solely to this question. Our only aim must be to determine the respective rights of governors and governed in this matter.

CHAPTER TWO

The First Right of the Governed with Regard to Taxation

The government, having to provide for the internal defense and external security of the State, has the right to ask individuals to sacrifice a portion of their substance to defray the expenses which the accomplishment of these duties necessitates.

The governed have the right for their part to demand of the government that the sum of all taxes does not exceed what is necessary for the purpose it must attain. This condition can be fulfilled only by political arrangements which put limits on the demands and thereby on the prodigality and greed of the governors. Traces of such arrangements can be found in the institutions of the most untrammeled monarchies, such as most of the German principalities or the hereditary States of the House of Austria; and the principle is solemnly recognized by the French constitution.[1]

[250] The details of these arrangements are not within our purview, yet I think one observation must not be omitted.

The right to say yea or nay to taxes can be considered from two viewpoints, as a limit on government or as a tool of financial economy. It has been said a thousand times that a government being unable to wage war, or even survive domestically, without its necessary expenses being defrayed, the ability to refuse taxes puts into the people's hands or into

1. In Proclamation VII of the Constitution of an XII, Article 53 we find: "The oath of the Emperor is understood as follows: 'I swear never to levy any taxation, never any tax, save in observance of the law.'"

those of their representatives, a most efficacious weapon, which, used bravely, empowers them to make the government not just keep the peace with its neighbors but also respect the freedom of the governed. Those reasoning thus forget that what seems at first glance compelling at the theoretical level is often impossible practically. When a government has begun a war, even an unjust one, to deny it the resources to sustain it is not to punish only the government but also the nation, innocent of its faults. It is the same with refusing taxation on the grounds of domestic malpractices or harassment. The government indulges in despotic acts. The legislative body thinks it can be disarmed if no monies are voted. Even supposing, however, which is difficult, that in this extreme crisis everything happens constitutionally, on whom will this struggle rebound? The influence of the executive will secure it temporary wherewithal, in funds already put at its disposal, in loans from those who, profiting from its favors or even its injustices, will not wish it reversed, and from yet further people who, believing it will win, will be speculating in its present requirements. The first victims will be lower-grade workers, entrepreneurs of all types, the State's creditors, and as a side effect the creditors of all these groups. Before the government succumbs or gives way, all private wealth will have been badly hit. The result will be universal hatred of Parliament, which the government will accuse of all the personal privations of citizens. The latter will not examine the reason for Parliament's resistance and without giving their attention, amid their hardship, to questions of law or political theory, they will blame it for their indigence and misfortune.

The right to reject taxation is not, then, on its own, a sufficient [251] guarantee for the curbing of excessive executive power. We can consider this right as an administrative means of ameliorating the nature of the taxes or as an economizing device for diminishing their volume. For Parliaments to be able to protect liberty, however, there have to be many other prerogatives. A nation can have so-called representatives endowed with this illusory right and yet be groaning the while in the most complete slavery. If the body charged with this function does not enjoy great prestige and independence, it will become the agent of the executive power, and its assent will be only a vain and illusory formula. For the freedom to vote on taxation to be other than a frivolous ceremony, political freedom must exist in its entirety, just as in the case of the human body, all the parts must be healthy and well constituted if the functions of a given one are to take place regularly and fully.

CHAPTER THREE

The Second Right of the Governed with Regard to Taxation

A second right of the governed with regard to taxes is that their nature and mode of collection should cause as little hardship as possible for the taxpayers, tending neither to harass nor to corrupt them and not giving rise, by way of pointless expenditures, to further taxation.

From this right it follows that the governed may also demand that taxes fall equally on all, proportionately to their wealth, that they leave nothing uncertain nor arbitrary as to their incidence or mode of collection, that they do not render any property or industry unproductive, that they are wholly cost-efficient, and finally that their basis is reasonably stable.

Setting up a new tax always causes a perturbation which spreads from taxed activities to untaxed ones too. Much labor and capital flow into the latter to escape the impositions hitting the former. Profits fall in the former because of the tax and in the latter because of the competition. Equilibrium is restored only slowly. Whatever change takes place is therefore irksome for a given period.

[252] It is by applying these rules to diverse forms of taxation that one can judge which are and which are not admissible.

It is not within our brief to examine all of them. We will choose only certain examples to convey a sense of the mode of reasoning which seems to us the best.

CHAPTER FOUR

On Various Types of Taxes

Some enlightened men in the last century recommended taxes on land as the most natural, simplest, and fairest. They even wanted to make them the sole form of taxation. Taxing the land is indeed a very seductive idea, one which speaks for itself and seems to rest on an incontestable truth. Land is the most obvious and durable source of wealth. Why pursue indirect, contrived, and complicated measures instead of going straight to this source?

If this doctrine has not been practiced, this has a lot less to do with people thinking they saw evils in land tax than with their feeling that even in raising it to the highest level, they could not draw from it the sums they wished to extract from the people. Other taxes have been combined with it; but in most of the countries of Europe, it has continued to be the most important one of all and in some sense the basis of the financial system.

This approach has meant that rejecting the principle has certainly not entailed, as it ought to have done, rejecting all its consequences. To reconcile the contradictions in this procedure, some people have had recourse to a theory whose outcomes are almost the same as those of the partisans of taxes on land. The latter claimed that in the last analysis all taxes bore on the land, while some of their opponents claimed that in the final analysis they were all paid by the consumer. While the former, arguing that taxes, so to speak, passed by way of the consumer before getting to the land, concluded from this that from the start taxes should be spared this detour and be imposed straight on the land, the latter, imagining that an opposite movement took taxes settled on the land back up to the consumer, thought it pointless to free the land of a burden which in reality it was not carrying.

[253] If we apply the rules we have established to the land tax, we will be led to very different conclusions.

On the one hand it is not true that all taxes on consumption fall on the land. Taxes on postal services do not fall on landowners *qua* owners. A landowner who takes neither tea nor tobacco pays no part of the taxes on these commodities at the points of their dispatch, their transportation, or sale. The taxes on consumption in no way fall on those groups which neither produce nor consume the items taxed.[2]

It is likewise false that the land tax has an effect on the price of the commodity, one borne by the purchaser. What determines the price of a commodity is not always what it costs to produce, but the demand for it. When demand exceeds supply, the price of the commodity rises. It falls when supply exceeds demand. Now land taxes, when they diminish production, ruin the producer, and when they do not diminish it, in no way increase demand. Here is the proof.

When a tax bears on the land, one of two things happens. Either it removes the whole of net product; that is, the production costs of the commodity exceed its sales revenue, and cultivation is necessarily abandoned, with the producer who abandons cultivation getting no advantage from the imbalance this may create between overall demand and the amount of the commodity he is no longer producing. Or the tax does not remove the whole net product; that is to say that the sales revenue of the commodity still exceeds costs, and the proprietor continues to cultivate. In this case, however, supply being the same after the tax as it was before, the balance between supply and demand remains the same and price cannot rise.

2. See Constant's Note A at the end of Book XI.

A tax on land therefore bears and—whatever may have been said—continues to bear, on the landed proprietor. The consumer pays no part of it, unless because of the gradual impoverishment of the farmer, the products of the land diminish so far as to occasion famine. This calamity, however, cannot be an element in the calculations of a tax system.

The land tax, such as it exists in many countries, is therefore [254] not consistent with the first rule we have enunciated. It does not bear equally on all, but falls especially on one group.

Secondly, this tax, whatever its amount, always blights part of the farmland in any country.

There are lands which by reason of the soil or the situation yield nothing and are therefore left fallow. There are those which produce only the tiniest bit more than nothing. This progression mounts until you have lands which yield the most remarkable output possible. Imagine it as a series of numbers running from 1 to 100. Imagine 1 represents a level of output so small it is indivisible. The tax on land removes part of the output of each of these holdings. Even if it is the smallest conceivable, it will not be less than 1. Therefore, all the holdings which yielded only 1, and would have been cultivated in the absence of the tax, are put among the nonproductive holdings by the tax, and join the class of uncultivated ones. If the tax goes up to 2, all the holdings yielding only 2 suffer the same fate and so on. Thus, if the tax rose to 50, all holdings up to 50 would remain idle. It is therefore clear that when the tax goes up, it removes from cultivation a portion of the holdings proportionate to the increase, and when it falls, it restores a portion proportionate to the fall. If the counterargument is that the land tax is not fixed but proportional, this will not resolve my objection. The proportional tax bears on gross production. Now, costs constituting a more or less great part of gross production, it always follows that if you fix the tax at an eighth of gross output, lands which cost 9 to cultivate in order to yield 10 will be rendered idle by the tax. If the tax is fixed at a quarter, those which cost 8 to yield 10 will suffer the same fate and so on.

That the tax has this effect is proved precisely by the actual precautionary measures taken by governments. The more enlightened, like the English and Dutch, have exempted all rented land below a certain rent value from all taxation.[3] The most brutal have declared all lands their proprietors have left uncultivated, confiscated. What owner would leave his holding unworked, however, if he stood to gain from working it? None, since the rich man himself would either lease [255] it or give it to the poor

3. See Constant's Note B at the end of Book XI.

man. Lands are left idle only for the reasons developed above or because they are incapable of yielding output or because taxation takes away the output they could produce. Thus governments punish individuals for ills they themselves have done to them. This law of confiscation is as odious as it is unjust, as absurd as it is pointless. The fact is, in whatever hands the government places confiscated lands, if the costs of working them exceed the revenue therefrom, someone may well try and cultivate them; but assuredly he will not continue thus. In this second case, the land tax strays again from one of the conditions necessary if a contribution is to be justifiable, in that it makes individuals' property unproductive.

Thirdly, the tax on landed property rests on the foresight of the cultivator, who, in order to be in a condition to pay it, has to put aside in advance some largish sums. The working class just do not have this foresight; and they cannot struggle constantly against the temptations of the moment. Many a one who will pay off his taxes daily, in detail, almost without knowing, if they are intertwined with his habitual purchases, will never accumulate in a given period the sum needed to pay things off en masse. The gathering of the land tax, though elementary, is therefore by no means easy. The coercive measures required make it very expensive. From this last point of view, the land tax is vicious, in that it incurs collection costs which another mode of taxation might avoid.

I do not conclude from this that the land tax should be done away with. As there are taxes on consumption which landowners can avoid, they should properly carry some share of public taxation, in their capacity as property holders. Since, however, the other groups in society do not pay any land taxes, the amount landowners pay should not exceed their proper due proportion. There is no justice therefore in making the land tax the sole or even the main tax.

[256] We have just said that the land tax taken beyond a certain point blights the property of its owners. A tax on patents makes industry unproductive. By removing freedom to work it establishes a rather ridiculous vicious circle. The man who is not working cannot pay anything, yet if people have previously not paid, the government forbids them the work they are suited for. The tax on patents is therefore an attack on the rights of individuals. It does not take away from them only a portion of their profits. It also dries up the source of their livelihood, unless they possess prior means of maintaining this, a quite unjustified supposition.

This tax may nevertheless be bearable if it is restricted to jobs which by their nature imply a certain prior affluence. This is then an advance the individual makes to the government, one he compensates himself for out of the returns to his own efforts. This is like the merchant who pays duties on the commodity he trades in, includes them then in the price of the commodity and gets the consumer to pay them. Aimed at trades marked by poverty, however, the tax on patents is revoltingly iniquitous.

Indirect taxes, bearing on consumer goods, get mixed up with that consumption. The consumer who pays them when he buys what he needs or likes does not experience, amid the feeling of satisfaction he is procuring himself, the repugnance the paying of direct taxation inspires. He pays them at his convenience. These taxes adapt themselves to times and circumstances, to various options, to individual tastes. They divide into imperceptible fractions.[4] The same weight we bear easily when it is shared across the whole body would become intolerable bearing on a single part. Just so the weight of the air spread across the whole body of a man exceeds thirty thousand liters. He can take it without noticing, while a much lighter weight trained on a single part of the [257] body would be unendurable.[5] The incidence of indirect taxation organizes itself, so to speak, by way of consumption, which is voluntary. Considered in this light, indirect taxes in no way offend the rules we have established. They do have three grave drawbacks, however. First, they are liable to be multiplied indefinitely, in an almost imperceptible way. Second, their collection is difficult, vexatious, and often corrupting in several respects. Thirdly, they create an artificial crime, smuggling.

The first drawback can be remedied by the authority which votes the taxes. If you suppose the authority independent, it will be able to block the growth of pointless taxes. If it is not independent, whatever the nature of the tax, do not hope to limit the sacrifices which will be demanded of the people. It will be defenseless in this respect, and in all others.

The second drawback is more difficult to prevent. Even so, I find in the first one itself some proof that the second can be prevented. For if one of the vices of indirect taxes is their ability to grow almost imperceptibly, then their collection must be organized in such a way that they are not insupportable. As to the third, I am more disposed than anyone to lessen it. I have said more than once that artificial duties tended to drive men to abandon real ones. Those who break the laws against smuggling soon break those against theft and murder. They run no more danger and their conscience gets used to the revolt against the social order.

If we think about it carefully, however, we will see that the real cause of smuggling is less in indirect taxes than in prohibitions. Governments sometimes disguise their prohibitions as taxes. They hit goods whose entry they

4. See Constant's Note C at the end of Book XI.

5. See Constant's Note D at the end of Book XI.

wish to prevent with duties disproportionate to their value. If all prohibitive systems were abolished, this disproportion would never occur. Then smuggling, that apprenticeship in crime, that school of lies and intrepidity, all the more dire in that it gains a certain nobility from its likeness to soldiering and from the credit which skill and courage give rise to, would not find encouragement and irresistible temptation in the huge profits this [258] disproportion leads it to expect.

CHAPTER FIVE

How Taxation Becomes Contrary to Individual Rights

Taxes become contrary to individual rights when by definition they authorize the harassment of citizens. One example is Spain's Alcavala, which enforces its duties on the sale of all things, transferable or fixed, each time they change hands.

Taxes also become contrary to individual rights when they bear on objects which are easy to hide from the knowledge of the authority charged with their collection. In aiming the tax against objects which are easily purloined, you make visits and inquisitions necessary. You are led to demand from the citizens spying and reciprocal denunciations. You reward these shameful actions and your tax falls into the category of those which are inadmissible because their collection is morally harmful.

It is the same with taxes so high they invite fraud. The ease, more or less great, with which an object can be kept from the knowledge of the authorities, is constituted by material facility, which can derive from the nature of the object, and by the interest people have in such concealment. When profits are considerable they can be divided among more hands and the cooperation in the fraud of a greater number of agents makes up for any physical difficulty the collecting agent would have been able to count on. When the object the tax bears on does not permit this kind of evasion, the tax sooner or later annihilates the branch of business or the type of transaction on which it presses. It must, then, be rejected as contrary to the rights of property or industry.

It is obvious that individuals have the right to limit their consumption according to their means and wills and to forgo objects they do not want to consume or cannot do so. [259] Consequently, indirect taxes become unjust when instead of resting on voluntary consumption, they are based on enforced consumption. What was odious about the gabelle, which was so absurdly intended to blend in with the salt tax, was its ordering citizens to consume a given quantity of this commodity. This harassment excited in them a just and natural indignation against a government which prescribed their lives even to the extent of needs they ought to have.

To establish a tax on a commodity, one should never forbid industry or an individual establishment[6] to produce that commodity, as formerly happened in some parts of France, in relation to salt, and as happens in several European countries today in relation to tobacco. This is a manifest violation of property and an unjust harassment of industry. To secure compliance with these interdictions severe penalties are required, and these penalties prove repulsive both for their severity and their iniquity.

Indirect taxes must bear as little as possible on commodities which are basic necessities, otherwise all their advantages disappear. The consumption of these commodities is not voluntary. It does not fit itself to the situation or proportion itself to the wealth of the consumer.

It is not true, as has too often been said, that taxes on basic necessities, by making them dearer, increase the price of labor. On the contrary, the more expensive commodities needed for subsistence are, the more the need to work grows. The competition of those whose labor is on offer exceeds the demand from employers and the price of labor falls, at the very moment it should be better paid so that workers can live. Taxes on basic necessities produce the same effect as years of sterility and dearth.[7]

There are taxes which are easy to collect and yet have to be rejected because they tend directly to the corruption and perversion of men. No tax, for example, is so pleasurably paid as the lottery. Government needs no coercive force to guarantee the collection of this revenue. But lotteries, offering a way to wealth which does not derive from industry, work, and prudence, throw into people's calculations the most dangerous sort of disorder. The many opportunities delude people over the improbability [260] of winning. The cheapness of the betting encourages repeated attempts. Trouble, financial embarrassment, ruin, and crime are the results. The lower orders of society, victims of the seductive dreams with which they are intoxicated, commit crimes against the property within their reach, deluding themselves that a favorable outcome will permit them to hide their baseness by correcting it. No fiscal logic can justify institutions which entail such consequences.

From the fact that individuals have the right to demand that the way taxes are collected be the least onerous possible for those who pay them, it

6. [Constant says *propriété* (property), where English would expect *proprietor* (*propriétaire*). Translator's note]

7. See Constant's Note E at the end of Book XI.

follows that governments must not adopt an essentially oppressive and tyrannical mode of administration in this matter. I want to speak about the practice of contracting out collection. This puts the governed at the mercy of certain individuals who do not have even as much interest as the government in treating them considerately. It is to create a class of men who, sanctioned by the force of law and supported by government, whose cause they seem to uphold, daily invent new harassments and call for the most sanguinary measures. Tax farmers in all countries are, so to speak, the natural representatives of injustice and oppression.[8]

CHAPTER SIX

That Taxes Bearing on Capital Are Contrary to Individual Rights

Whatever the kinds of taxes a country adopts, they must bear on income and never encroach upon capital. This is to say that they must never confiscate more than part of annual production and never touch previously accumulated assets. These assets are the sole means of reinvestment, of feeding the workers, of generating abundance.[9]

Though governments and many writers fail to recognize it, this proposition can be proved evidentially.

If taxes are trained on capital rather than on income alone, the result will be capital diminished each year by a sum equal to what the tax extracts. By this very fact annual reinvestment is diminished proportionately to the diminution of assets. This diminution [261] in reinvestment, diminishing incomes and the tax remaining the same, every year a larger sum of assets will be confiscated and therefore every year a smaller sum of incomes will be reinvested. This double progression is exponential.

Imagine a landowner who makes his property worthwhile. He needs three things: his land, his personal industry, and his capital. If he had no land, his capital and his industry would be pointless.[10] Without his industry, his land and capital would be unproductive. If he had no capital, his industry would be pointless and his land sterile, since he would not be able to supply the funding indispensable to his production; he would not have the wherewithal for farming, fertilizing, sowing, or livestock. These are all the things which constitute his capital. Therefore whichever of these three

8. See Constant's Note F at the end of Book XI.
9. See Constant's Note G at the end of Book XI.
10. See Constant's Note H at the end of Book XI.

things you attack, you impoverish the taxpayer equally. If, instead of taking away from him each year some of his capital, you take away some of his land, equivalent to some given sum, what will happen? In the next year, in taking away from him the same amount of land, you will deprive him of a relatively larger part of his property and so on and on, until he finds himself utterly dispossessed. The same happens when you tax his capital. The effect is less obvious but no less inevitable.

For any individual, whatever work he does, his capital is to him what a plough is to the farmer. Now, if you take from the farmer a sack of wheat he has just gathered, he goes back to work and produces another the following year. If you take his plough, however, he cannot produce more wheat.

Let it not be thought that the economizing of individuals can remedy this setback, creating capital stocks afresh. If you tax capital, you diminish individual incomes by taking away the means of replenishing these incomes. On just what are they then supposed to economize?

Let it not be said either that capital reproduces itself. Capital is only accumulated assets, gradually taken out of income. The more you encroach on capital, the more income declines, the less asset accumulation can happen, and the less capital can reproduce itself.

The State which taxes capital therefore prepares the ruin of individuals. It gradually takes away their property. Now, the security of that property being one of the State's obligations, it is apparent [262] that individuals have the right to reassert that obligation against a system of taxation with results contrary to that end.

CHAPTER SEVEN

That the Interest of the State in Matters of Taxation Is Consistent with Individual Rights

Let us now show that the interest of the State in matters of taxation is consistent with individual rights. For unfortunately it is not enough to show what is just. One has also to convince government that what is just is no less functional.

We have shown the iniquity of the land tax when it exceeds the level necessary to make landowners contribute their due part in the payment of taxes. The same tax is hurtful to government both by being expensive to collect and by its effects on agriculture. It keeps the majority of the working class in poverty. It keeps a crowd of workers employed only to collect it in barren activity. It soaks up assets which, not being reinvested, are removed from individual wealth and lost to public wealth. Our costs of enforcement, our innumerable deputy bailiffs, the armed force spread over the countryside to effect the gathering of overdue taxes should have convinced us of these truths. It has been shown that the raising of 250 million via this mode of taxation entailed 50 million just in enforcement costs. As a result the nation most famous for its adroit financial management, so far from making the land tax the basis of its revenue, does not take it any further than to a twelfth of total taxation.[11]

We have condemned taxes on patents as assaults on the sacred rights of work, assaults aimed at the occupations the poor man can engage in. By reason of its organization, this tax is one of the least easy to collect and involves the most unproductive efforts, that is to say the most losses to the exchequer.

We have said[12] that taxes became contrary to individual rights when they authorized persecutory investigations. We [263] cited the Alcavala in Spain, a tax which subjected every sale of any article, whether transferable assets or real estate, to a charge. Don Ustariz considers it the cause of the decay of Spanish finances.[13]

We have rejected taxes which encourage fraud. Is there any need to show how deadly this struggle between government and citizens is? And can one not see at a glance that it is ruinous even in financial terms? We added that when excessive taxes wiped out a branch of commerce, this was an attack on industry. Spain was punished for just such an attack. Several of her mines in Peru remain undeveloped because the tax due to the King absorbs the whole output of their proprietors. This hurts both the treasury and individual people.[14]

We condemned lotteries, though their revenue is easily collected, because they have the effect of corrupting men. Governments themselves, however, pay the penalty for that corruption. First of all, the harm lotteries do to production diminishes reinvestment and therefore national wealth. Secondly, the crime they cause among the working class is, when we put all moral questions to one side and think of it only in fiscal terms, a public expense. Thirdly, minor officials let themselves be seduced by the spell of lotteries, and the costs fall on governments. There were under the Directory in a single year twelve million francs' worth of bankruptcies among tax collectors, and it was shown

11. See Constant's Note I at the end of Book XI.

12. In Ch. 5 of this same Book XI, *How Taxation Becomes Contrary to Individual Rights.*

13. See Constant's Note J at the end of Book XI.

14. See Constant's Note K at the end of Book XI.

that about two-thirds of these collectors had been ruined by the lottery. Finally, the gathering of a tax of this sort, though easy, is nonetheless expensive. To make lotteries pay, you must multiply the temptations, and to multiply the temptations you must also multiply the offices. Hence the high collection costs. In M. Necker's day, income from the lotteries stood at 11,500,000. Collection cost 2,400,000 or close to 21 percent, such that the most immoral tax was at the same time the most costly to the state.[15]

[264] We showed lastly that taxes should never bear on anything save incomes. When they cut into capital, first of all they ruin individuals and then the government. The reason is simple.

All men with some idea of political economy know that expenditures fall into two types: the productive and unproductive. The first are those which create wealth, and the second those which create nothing. A forest which is cut down to build ships or a town is used up as much as one consumed by a fire. In the first case, however, the fleet or city which has been built more than replaces the forest which has disappeared; in the second only ashes remain.

Unproductive expenditures can be necessary. Each person commits part of his income to food. This expenditure is unproductive but indispensable. A state of war with neighboring countries consumes a part of public resources for the subsistence of the armed forces and so that they may be supplied with the war munitions needed for attacking and defending. This is not wasted expenditure though it is an unproductive one. Even so, if unproductive expenditures are often necessary to secure the lives or security of individuals and nations, it is only productive expenditures which can augment the wealth of either. That which is consumed unproductively is always an excusable and legitimate loss when the need requires it, but crazy and inexcusable when it does not.

The money called into play between all productions as a medium of exchange has served to spread a certain obscurity on this question. Since money is used without destroying itself, it has been believed that however it was used, it came to the same thing. It ought to have been thought that money could be used for reinvestment or it could be used without producing anything. If a government spends ten million making an army march in different directions or on giving magnificent parties, spectacles, illuminations, dances, firework displays, the ten million thus consumed is not destroyed. The nation is not made poorer by ten million. Yet this ten million

15. The example and figures come from Jacques Necker, *De l'administration des finances, op. cit.,* t. I, pp. 84–88.

has produced nothing. The society retains only the ten million it originally possessed. If, on the contrary, [265] this ten million has been used to build factories or buildings suitable for any kind of manufacturing or industry, to improve land, in brief, to reinvest in some commodity, the nation would have had on the one hand the ten million consumed in this way and on the other the assets this ten million would have produced.

I would like to expand somewhat on this important subject, since there is a disastrous viewpoint which holds that all the uses of capital are the same. This opinion is popularized by all those who benefit from government squandering and by those who repeat on trust maxims they do not understand. Doubtless money, the sign of wealth, does no more in all cases than pass from one hand to another. But when it is used in reinvestment expenditures, then its value is twofold; when the expenditure is nonproductive, there is only one value. Since in order to be dissipated in unproductive expenditures, money is snatched away from the class which would have used it productively, the nation, if not made poorer in money terms, is deprived of all the production which has not taken place. The nation keeps the sign but loses the reality. The Spanish example is sufficient instruction to us that the sign of money is anything but real wealth.

It is therefore certain that the only means of prosperity for a nation is the use of capital in productive expenditures.

Now, even the wisest governments cannot use funds taken from individuals except in unproductive expenditures. The costs of the salaries of public functionaries of all sorts, the maintenance of order, of the law courts, of war finance, of all branches of the civil service, are expenditures of this type. When the State uses only a part of income for these expenditures, the assets remaining in the hands of individuals secure the necessary reinvestment. If the State deflects assets from their intended purpose, however, reinvestment shrinks, and since it becomes necessary then every year, as we have shown above, to confiscate proportionately more assets, reinvestment will finish by ceasing completely and State and individuals alike will be ruined.

"Just as the wastrel who consumes beyond his income," says Ganilh in his history of public revenue,[16] "diminishes his property by the whole amount by which he has exceeded his income and soon sees income and property disappear, [266] the State which taxes property[17] and consumes its product like income, is marching to certain and fast-approaching decadence."

16. See Constant's Note L at the end of Book XI.
17. See Constant's Note M at the end of Book XI.

So then, in matters of taxation as in all things, the laws of equity are the best ones to follow, even were one to think of them only in terms of their utility. The government which violates justice in the hope of some wretched gain pays dearly for this violation; and the rights of individuals should be respected by governments even when these have only their own interests in mind.

CHAPTER EIGHT
An Incontestable Axiom

In indicating, as we have done in this section, necessarily in a very abbreviated way, some of the rules regarding taxation, our intention was to suggest to the reader ideas he could enlarge on, rather than develop any of them. This task would have taken us well beyond the confines we have set ourselves. One incontestable axiom no sophism can obfuscate is that any tax, of any sort, always has a more or less unfortunate influence.[18] If the use of the tax sometimes produces a benefit, its levying always produces an ill.[19] The ill may be necessary. Like all such ills, however, it must be rendered as small as possible. The more resources are left at the disposal of individual activity, the more a State prospers. A tax, just because it takes some portion or other of these resources away from those efforts, is inevitably harmful. The more money is taken away from the various nations, says M. de Vauban in *The Royal Tithe,*[20] the more it is taken away from commerce. The best-employed money in the realm is that which stays in the hands of individuals, where it is never pointless nor idle.

[267] Rousseau, who was uninformed in things financial, followed many others in saying that in monarchies the excessive surplus of the subjects must be consumed in the opulence of the prince, because it was better that this surplus be absorbed by government than dissipated by individuals.[21] This doctrine reveals an absurd mix of monarchical prejudices and

18. See Constant's Note N at the end of Book XI.

19. See Constant's Note O at the end of Book XI.

20. Hofmann was unable to locate the passage indicated by Constant. On the other hand, in Ch. 11 of *La dîme royale* (the royal tithe), Vauban does express himself analogously. "I even dare say that of all the temptations against which princes must most guard themselves, those are they which drive them to extract everything they can from their subjects, since being able to do anything to the peoples entirely subject to them, they are quite likely to ruin them without noticing." Sébastian Le Prestre de Vauban, *La dîme royale,* ed. Georges Michel, Paris, Guillaumin, s.d. [1887], p. 192.

21. See Constant's Note P at the end of Book XI.

republican opinions. The prince's opulence, far from discouraging that of individuals, gives it encouragement and example. It must not be thought that in despoiling them he is reforming them. He can plunge them into poverty; but he cannot bring them back to innocence. All that happens is that the poverty of some occurs in combination with the opulence of others, the most deplorable of all combinations.

Equally inconsequent arguments have concluded that because the most heavily taxed countries, such as England and Holland, are also the richest, they are richest because most heavily taxed. They take the effect for the cause. "People are not rich because they contribute. They contribute because they are rich."[22]

"Everything which goes beyond real needs," says a writer of incontestable authority on this subject,[23] "loses its legitimacy. The only difference between personal violations and those of the sovereign, is that the injustice of the former results from straightforward ideas which everybody can easily distinguish, while the latter are linked to mixed causes as vast as they are complicated, such that no one can judge them other than conjecturally."

CHAPTER NINE

The Drawback of Excessive Taxation

Everywhere that the constitution of the State does not block [268] the arbitrary proliferation of taxes, everywhere the government is not held up by insurmountable barriers to its ever growing demands, as when no one ever contests them, neither justice, nor morality, nor individual freedom can be respected. Neither the government which takes away from the laboring classes their hard-won subsistence, nor these oppressed classes who see that subsistence snatched away to enrich greedy masters, can stay faithful to the laws of equity in this scandalous struggle of weakness against violence, of poverty against greed, of want against theft. Any pointless tax is a theft which the force accompanying it renders no more legitimate than any other outrage of this nature. It is a theft all the more odious in being carried out with all the solemnity of the law. It is a theft all the more culpable in that it is the rich who carry it out against the poor. It is a theft all the more cowardly in that it is committed by an armed government against the unarmed individual. Government itself will not have to wait long to be punished for it.

22. See Constant's Note Q at the end of Book XI.
23. See Constant's Note R at the end of Book XI.

The people in the Roman provinces, says Hume,[24] were so oppressed by the tax gatherers, that they threw themselves joyfully into the arms of the barbarians, happy that these coarse, plain masters offered them a domination less greedy and rapacious than the Romans.

CHAPTER TEN

A Further Drawback of Excessive Taxation

It would be yet a further mistake to suppose that the disadvantages of excessive taxation are limited to the poverty and privation of the people. A greater evil results, one which it seems to me has till now not been sufficiently remarked on.

The possession of great wealth inspires in individuals immoderate desires, whims, and fantasies which they would not have felt in more modest and restrained circumstances. It is [269] the same with governments. Excessive opulence intoxicates them, as does excessive power, because opulence is a kind of power, indeed the most real kind. From this flow your unreal public squares, your immoderate ambitions, your gigantic projects, which a government with only basic resources would never think of. Thus the people are not poor only in that they are taxed beyond their means, but poorer still from the use their government makes of their taxes. Their sacrifices turn against them. They no longer pay taxes to have peace assured by a good system of defense. They pay them to have war, because the government, proud of its huge wealth, invents a thousand pretexts for spending this in ways it calls glorious. The people pay, not so that good domestic order will be maintained, but on the contrary so that an insolent government,[25] enriched with its spoils, can with impunity disturb public order with its harassments. In this way a nation which has no safeguard against the proliferation of taxes, purchases by its privations misfortune, trouble, and danger. The father pays for his son to be snatched out of his arms and sent to die far from his country. The farmer pays so that his fields will be devastated by a mob fed on the money he has contributed. In this situation the government is corrupted by its wealth and the people by its poverty.

24. See Constant's Note S at the end of Book XI.

25. [Constant uses the word *cour*, which suggests that he typically has *royal* government in mind for this fault. Translator's note]

A. [Refers to page 208.]
Say, Economie politique, Livre V, Ch. 13.[26]

B. (Refers to page 209.)
In Holland £30, and in England £20 sterling.

C. (Refers to page 211.)
The land tax in England raises only £2,037,627. It causes a lot of repeated complaint. The tax on barley on its own, in its various forms, raises £3,000,000. [270] It is barely noticed. Sinclair, On the public revenue of England.[27]

D. (Refers to page 211.)
See Encylopédie. Article: Atmosphère.[28]

E. (Refers to page 213.)
Smith, Livre IV, Ch. 2.[29]

F. (Refers to page 214.)
Smith, Livre V, Ch. 2. Ganilh, Tome II, p. 449.[30]

26. Jean-Baptiste Say, *Traité d'économie politique ou simple exposition de la manière dont se forment, se distribuent et se consomment les richesses,* Paris, Impr. de Crapelet, an XI, 1803, t. II, pp. 480–494.

27. This example has been made available by Charles Ganilh, *Essai politique sur le revenu public des peuples de l'antiquité, du moyen-age, des siècles modernes et spécialement de la France et de l'Angleterre, depuis le milieu du XVe siècle jusqu'au XIXe,* Paris, Giguet et Michaud, 1806, t. II, p. 350: "In England the land tax which at four shillings in the pound produces £2,037,627, about 47,000,000 francs, occasions lots of grumbling, while the barley tax in its various forms yields £3,000,000, about 69,000,000 francs, and is barely felt."

28. In the article "Atmosphère" in the *Encyclopédie,* signed by d'Alembert, it is said that a man carries a weight of 33,600 pounds.

29. Adam Smith, *op.cit.,* t. III, p. 81.

30. Adam Smith, *op. cit.,* t. IV, pp. 450–451. Smith here asserts that it is never advantageous to subcontract taxation. Charles Ganilh, *op. cit.,* t. II, p. 449: "It seems to me that if one wished to harmonize the interests of public revenue with the security of taxpayers, then only the lower tax officials should be concerned with the volume of revenue, while the superiors should be accorded only salaries sufficient to purchase talent and even satisfy ambitions."

G. (Refers to page 214.)

On the operation of capital and its indispensable part in all forms of production, see Sismondi, De la richesse commerciale, Livre I, Ch. 1, and Ganilh, Du revenu public, Volume II, pp. 281–306. The nature of my work does not permit me to enter into further detail.[31]

[271] H. (Refers to page 214.)

I assume for the sake of argument that he cannot employ his capital or effort elsewhere. If he can, the comparison will be based on the first use he puts his capital and effort to.

I. (Refers to page 216.)

The public revenue in England was in 1799 close to £27,000,000 and the land tax only £2,000,000.[32]

J. (Refers to page 216.)

Théorie pratique du commerce d'Espagne.[33]

K. (Refers to page 216.)

See de Ulloa.[34]

L. (Refers to page 218.)

Tome II, p. 289.

M. (Refers to page 218.)

Capital.

31. Jean-Charles-Léonard Sismondi, *De la richesse commerciale ou principes d'économie politique appliqués à la législation de commerce,* Geneva, J.-J. Paschoud, an XI (1803), t. I, pp. 19–38. This first chapter, to which Constant refers, is entitled *The Origin of National Wealth.* In the pages indicated the author shows how any contribution must be based on income.

32. These figures and this example come from Ganilh, *op. cit.*, t. II, pp. 350–351, himself drawing on George Rose, *A brief examination . . . , op. cit.*

33. Don Geronimo de Ustariz, *Théorie et practique de commerce et de la marine,* Paris, Vve Estienne et Fils, 1753, Seconde Partie, Ch. XCVI and XCVII; especially p. 107: "I do not doubt for a moment that such is the cause of the destruction of our manufactures." This example of the Alcavala and the reference to Ustariz are taken from Charles Ganilh, *op. cit.,* t. II, pp. 306–307. Adam Smith speaks of it too, *op. cit.,* t. IV, pp. 444–445.

34. Antonio de Ulloa, *Voyage historique de l'Amérique méridionale fait par ordre du roi . . . ,* Paris, C.-A. Jombert, 1752, 2 vol. This reference too comes from Adam Smith, *op. cit.,* t. I, p. 34.

[272] N. (Refers to page 219.)
Smith, Book V, for the application of this general truth to each tax in particular.[35]

O. (Refers to page 219.)
Say, Livre V, Ch. 8.[36]

P. (Refers to page 219.)
Contrat social III, Ch. 8.[37]

Q. (Refers to page 220.)
Say, V, Ch. 11.[38]

R. (Refers to page 220.)
Administration des finances, Livre I, Ch. 2.[39]

S. (Refers to page 221.)
Essai politique, 8.[40]

35. Adam Smith, *op. cit.,* t. IV, pp. 257–554.

36. Jean-Baptiste Say, *op. cit.,* t. II, pp. 408–448.

37. Jean-Jacques Rousseau, *ed. cit.,* p. 416.

38. Jean-Baptiste Say, *op. cit.,* t. II, pp. 465–466, Ch. 11.

39. Jacques Necker, *op. cit.,* t. I, p. 43. Constant has changed the text slightly. The original says simply: "That which exceeds this measure."

40. Constant got this reference to Hume from Charles Ganilh, *op. cit.,* t. II, p. 404 (note).

BOOK XII

On Government Jurisdiction over Economic Activity and Population

CH. 1. Preliminary observation. 227

CH. 2. On legitimate political jurisdiction vis-à-vis economic activity. 228

CH. 3. That there are two branches of government intervention with regard to economic activity. 228

CH. 4. On privileges and prohibitions. 229

CH. 5. On the general effect of prohibitions. 247

CH. 6. On things which push governments in this mistaken direction. 248

CH. 7. On the supports offered by government. 251

CH. 8. On the equilibrium of production. 255

CH. 9. A final example of the adverse effects of government intervention. 258

CH. 10. Conclusions from the above reflections. 259

CH. 11. On government measures in relation to population. 260

CHAPTER ONE

Preliminary Observation

In the enumeration of inalienable individual rights at the beginning of this work,[1] I did not include the freedom of economic activity. The most enlightened philosophers of the last century, however, have shown the whole evidential case against the injustice of the restrictions experienced by this freedom in almost all countries. They likewise showed, just as clearly in my view, that these restrictions were as pointless and misconceived as they were unfair.

This last point nevertheless still seems doubtful to many people. One would need volumes to clarify the case in a way that would seem satisfactory to them. The principles of economic freedom rest on a multitude of facts, and each fact which seems contrary to it demands, in order to give way to its correct perspective, a long and detailed discussion.[2] Freedom of commerce is useful only when it is scrupulously observed. A single violation, spreading uncertainty through the whole system, destroys all its benefits, and governments then turn their very faults to advantage in order to justify their intervention. They argue from the imperfect, sometimes dire results of precarious and restricted freedom, against the invariably salutary results of full and well-established freedom. Consequently, I did not wish, although all questions of this kind are interlinked, to put commercial freedom and civil freedom at the same level, for fear that the men who would disagree about [276] the former might be just as likely to dispute the important principles on which the felicity of civil society and the security of citizens are based. Nevertheless, certain moral considerations struck me which return to the subject of this work and which in moral terms decide the issue in favor of freedom, as well as yet further observations and facts which also decide in the same way in the case of economic activity. I thought I ought not to hold these back. But I beg the reader not to forget, though, that this section is not a treatise in commercial economy and contains just some general reflections which I expressly separate from the rest of my research, so that my mistakes, if I have made any, or the disagreement my opinions in this matter might encounter, will not bear on the other questions I have

1. In Book II, Ch. 6 *On Individual Rights When Political Authority Is Thus Restricted.*
2. See Constant's Note A at the end of Book XII.

discussed. I could be wrong in my claims about freedom of production and trade without my principles of religious, intellectual, and personal freedom being weakened by this.

CHAPTER TWO

On Legitimate Political Jurisdiction vis-à-vis Economic Activity

Society having no political prerogatives over individuals except when these prevent them harming each other, likewise economic activity, unless taken to be injurious, is subject to no such jurisdiction. But one man's economic activity cannot hurt his peers, as long as he does not invoke in favor of his own activity and against theirs, help of another sort. It is in the nature of business to struggle against rivals, by way of perfectly free competition and efforts to attain an intrinsic superiority. All other types of means it might try to use constitute not economic activity but oppression or fraud. Society would be in the right, indeed, even obliged, to stop this. From this right which society possesses, however, it follows not at all that it has the right to use against the economic activity of one person, in favor of another's, means which it must forbid equally to all.

All the objections brought together in Book X against the obstacles put in the way of property's being possessed or [277] transferred acquire a double force when they are applied to production. These objections are based for the most part on the ease with which prohibitive laws are eluded and on the corruption entailed by the opportunities men get to disobey the laws. Now, the nature of economic activity offers far more openings to secret and unpunished transgressions than the nature of landed property.

CHAPTER THREE

That There Are Two Branches of Government Intervention with Regard to Economic Activity

Government intervention with regard to economic activity can be divided into two branches: prohibitions and supports. Privileges must not be separated from prohibitions, because necessarily they imply them.

Since we want to give examples here rather than examine all parts of the economic system, we will take at random some of the prohibitions most used by most governments, ones which consequently at least have in their favor the support of the governing class. We will not say anything about those whose absurdity, long denied, is now generally recognized.

CHAPTER FOUR
On Privileges and Prohibitions

What is a business privilege? It is the use of the power of political authority to pass to some men advantages which it is the aim of society to guarantee to everyone. England did this when before the union of Ireland with that kingdom, she banned the Irish from almost all forms of foreign trade. This is what she does today when she forbids all English people to set up in the Indies any trade [278] independent of the company which has seized that vast monopoly. This is what the Zurich bourgeoisie did, before the Swiss revolution, by forcing those in the surrounding countryside to sell, only to them, almost all their commodities and all their manufactures.

This is manifestly injustice in principle. Is there any value in the practice? If the privilege is extended only to a few, doubtless some value accrues to these few. It is value of the kind, however, which goes with all spoliation. This is not what we intend or not at least admit to intending. Does it have any value for the nation? Undoubtedly not, since in the first place the vast majority of the nation is excluded from the benefit. There is therefore uncompensated loss for this majority. In the second place, the branch of industry or trade which receives the privilege is being taken care of more negligently and less economically by those whose gains are secured by the simple effect of the monopoly than would be the case if competition obliged all the rivals to outdo each other in their application and skill. Thus the national wealth does not derive from this economic activity the whole benefit it could. Therefore there is relative loss for the whole nation. Finally, the means which government must use to keep the privilege going and forcibly keep people not privy to it from competing are inevitably oppressive and vexatious. Once again, therefore, the entire nation suffers a loss of freedom. Thus we have three real losses which this type of prohibition entails, and compensation for these losses is reserved for a mere handful of privileged people.

The trite excuse made for privileges is the inadequacy of individual resources and the value of encouraging combinations to make up for this. People make too much of this inadequacy, however, just as they do of this need.[3] If individual resources are insufficient, perhaps some individuals will be ruined, but a small number of examples will enlighten all the citizens, and a few private misfortunes are much better than the incalculable mass

3. See Constant's Note B at the end of Book XII.

of misfortune and public corruption which privileges bring in. If the State wished to oversee individuals in all the operations through which they might potentially harm each other, this would amount to restricting almost all freedom of action. Once [279] having set itself up as the citizens' guardian, it would soon become their tyrant. If combinations are necessary for a vital branch of production or long-distance commerce, combinations will form and individuals will not struggle against them, but try to join them in order to share their advantages. If existing combinations refuse this, we will soon see new combinations forming, and the ensuing rival competition will be more active. Let government intervene only to maintain both combinations and individuals in their respective rights and within the limits of justice; freedom will see to the rest, and successfully at that.

It is a mistake, moreover, to look on commercial companies as beneficial by their very nature. Any powerful company, says an author well versed in this matter,[4] even when it trades only in competition with individual enterprises, ruins them first of all by lowering the prices of merchandise; then, when they are ruined, this company, now the only one in business or almost such, ruins the country by raising prices. Afterward, its excessive profits leading its employees into negligence, it ruins itself. We see in Smith, Book V, ch. 1,[5] through numerous incontestable examples, that the more English companies were exclusive and granted large privileges and the more they were rich and powerful, the more drawbacks marked their histories and the more they ended badly. By contrast, the only ones which succeeded or sustained themselves were companies limited to a modest capital, made up of a small group of individuals, employing only a few workers, that is to say, in their administration and resources coming as close as can be to small firms. The Abbé Morellet in 1780 counted fifty-five companies set up since 1600, invested with exclusive privileges in different European countries, which had all finished up bankrupt.[6] Companies which are [280] too powerful are like all forces which are too strong, as with States which are too strong. They begin by devouring their neighbors and then their subjects, and then destroy themselves.

4. We do not know whom Constant means—perhaps the Abbé Morellet, who appears a bit later.

5. Adam Smith, *op. cit.*, t. IV, Ch. 1.

6. This example is taken from Adam Smith, *op. cit.*, t. IV, p. 143. Smith says the distiguished French economist, the Abbé Morellet, had listed fifty-five joint-stock companies in various parts of Europe which had failed since 1600 despite the exclusive privileges they enjoyed, because their administration was poor.

The only circumstance which justifies the establishment of a company is when individuals come together to set up, at their own peril and risk, a new branch of trade with distant and barbarous peoples. The State may then grant them, as compensation for the dangers they face, a few years of monopoly. Once the term expires, however, the monopoly must be abolished and free trade be reestablished.[7]

One can cite isolated facts in favor of privileges, and these facts seem all the more conclusive in that we never see what would have happened if these privileges had never existed. I affirm in the first place, however, that if we bring time into the reckoning—something which we seek vainly to dispense with—and do not give way to puerile impatience, freedom always ends up producing, uncontaminated by any evil, the same good we might strain to force into place by way of privileges bought at very harmful cost. Secondly, I declare that if there existed a branch of industry which could not be developed except by our bringing in privileges, then its drawbacks are such for the morals and freedom of the nation that no advantage would compensate for them.[8]

Too many writers before me have denounced wardenships, guild masters, and apprenticeships for me to enter into long detail on the subject. These institutions are privileges of the most iniquitous and absurd type, most iniquitous because the individual is permitted the work which keeps him from crime only at the good [281] pleasure of another; most absurd because under the pretext of the perfecting of crafts, obstacles are put in the way of competition, the surest spur to such perfecting. The interest of buyers is a much safer guarantee of the quality of production than arbitrary regulations, which, coming from a government which inevitably confuses everything, does not distinguish clearly between the various trades and prescribes apprenticeships as long for the easiest as for the most difficult. It is bizarre to imagine the public a bad judge of the workers it employs and to think that government, with so much else to do, will be better informed as to what dispositions must be made in order to appraise their merits. It has no choice save to rely on men who, forming an organized group within the State, have a different interest from the mass of the people and who, working on the one hand to reduce the number of producers and on the other to raise the price of the goods, render them at once more faulty and more expensive. Experience has everywhere pronounced against the

7. See Constant's Note C at the end of Book XII.
8. See Constant's Note D at the end of Book XII.

alleged value of this mania for regulation. The English towns where trade is most active, which have experienced in a very short time the greatest growth and where production has been carried to the highest degree of perfection, are those which have no charters[9] and where there exist no corporations.[10]

Even more outrageous and vexatious, because it is more [282] direct and undisguised, is the rigging[11] of daily wages. Smith says this rigging is the sacrifice of the greater to the smaller party. I will add that it is the sacrifice of the poor to the rich party, of the hardworking party to the idle, at least comparatively, of the party which already suffers from society's harsh laws, to the party which chance and social institutions have favored. One could not without pity take stock of this struggle of poverty against greed, where the poor man, already burdened with his needs and those of his family, having no hope save in his work, and unable to wait for an instant without his very life and the lives of his loved ones being threatened, meets the rich man, not only strong in his wealth and in his power to constrain his adversary by refusing him that work which is his only resource, but reinforced still further by oppressive laws, which fix earnings without regard to the circumstances, the skill or the zeal of the workman. And let no one think this rigging necessary to put down exorbitant claims and the rise in labor costs. Poverty has humble demands. Does not the workman have hunger pressing at his back, leaving him scarcely an instant to discuss his rights and disposing him all too readily to sell his time and effort below their worth? Does not competition settle the price of labor at the lowest level compatible with physical subsistence? In Athens, just as in France today, the journeyman's wage was equivalent to four people's food. Why impose regulations when the nature of things settles the case, without oppression or violence?

The rigging of the price of labor, so fatal to the individual, absolutely does not work to the public advantage. Between the public and the workman there stands a pitiless class, the masters. They pay as little and demand as much as possible and thereby profit uniquely at once from the needs of the workers and of the leisured class. What a strange complication in social

9. See Constant's Note E at the end of Book XII.

10. See Constant's Note F at the end of Book XII. [Constant here, and in the previous note, is referring to premodern economic and legal forms, the charters and corporations of medieval origin. Translator's note]

11. [The French noun "fixation" could be translated by the more neutral "determination" or "setting." Translator's note]

institutions! There exists an abiding source of equilibrium between the price and the value of labor, one which acts without force, in such a way that all calculations are reasonable, and all interests happy. This source is competition. But it is thrust aside. Obstacles are put in competition's way by unjust regulations. Then people want to restore equilibrium by equally unjust regulations, [283] ones which have to be maintained by punishments and harsh controls.

Governments resemble Molière's doctors in almost everything they do. When they are told of what has been established and organized by nature, they endlessly reply: *we have changed all that.*[12]

The laws against products of foreign manufacture are designed to get or constrain the inhabitants of a country to make themselves what they would otherwise buy abroad. These laws are necessary therefore, in the actual understanding of the government which imposes them, only when such products could be acquired more cheaply abroad than they can be produced. For in the case of the opposite supposition, personal interest on its own suffices to ensure that individuals will manufacture themselves what would cost them more if they bought it ready-made. Even when prices are equal, a country's own products have a great advantage. "Sale," says an author of repute,[13] "is a kind of prize for winning the race, and foreign goods start from further off."

Is it an advantage, however, for a nation to set up manufactures on its own territory which, in order to furnish it with a certain money income and quantity of production, absorb more funds than the purchase of these products would have required? We can reply in the affirmative only in supposing that if these funds were not thus employed, they would not be employed at all. Now, this supposition is clearly absurd. If these funds were not employed in this way, they would be employed in some other way and more advantageously. This is to say that with a portion of these resources one would buy products which the whole lot of them is now used in producing, while the remainder would be redirected to some other branch of production [284] which it would vitalize. Governments, in forcing their subjects to manufacture themselves things they would not voluntarily have manufactured, force them to employ their resources inefficiently. They diminish the output of their capital and their labor. They therefore diminish their wealth and thereby the national wealth.

12. Reply by Sganarelle to Géronte in *Le médecin malgré lui,* Acte II, Scene IV.

13. See Constant's Note G at the end of Book XII.

Adam Smith's ingenious comparison in this regard has often been cited.[14] I cite it again, because the evidence with which he has enveloped this truth seems scarcely to have convinced those in charge of States. In Scotland, one could, he says, by using hothouses, forcing beds, and glass frames, make very good grapes grow, from which one could also make extremely good wine, thirty times dearer than one can buy from abroad. If that seems absurd, it is equally so to require the manufacture in a country of something that manufactured thus would cost twice as much again, as much again, or even half as much again, as the same thing coming from abroad. The absurdity seems stronger because the sum strikes us more; but the principle is equally insane.[15]

Is it feared that free importation of foreign merchandise may encourage a nation into laziness by relieving it from the necessity to work to procure what it needs? But what it does not procure for itself by direct work, it must obtain by an outlay of funds, and to acquire funds it must work. Only full freedom will permit it to choose the most profitable types of production and perfect itself therein, in dedicating itself to them more exclusively. For the division of labor has the same result for the products of nations as for those of individuals. The prohibition of foreign goods tends to deprive a people of the advantages of the division of labor. This people then resembles an individual who, far from devoting himself solely to a job which would make him rich, wishes on his own, and through his own work, to make his tools, fashion his clothes, prepare his food, build his house. Splitting himself thus between various jobs, in order to take away from the workers in each one of them the benefit they deserved, he would stay wretched and poor in the midst of his fruitless, interrupted efforts.

Among a people still in the infancy of civilization, [285] frequent recourse to manufactures from outside can retard the establishment of home manufactures. But since it is very probable that the government of such a people will itself be extremely ignorant, there is little to hope for from its efforts in support of business. One should resign oneself and wait. There is no case of a nation which was not industrious having been made forcibly so by government. There is a very good reason for this. The government which forces men toward any end whatsoever is an arbitrary and vicious government and can do nothing well.

As for industrious nations, it suffices to leave each individual perfectly free in the deployment of his capital and his labor. He will discern better

14. In particular by Jean-Baptiste Say, *op. cit.*, t. I, p. 163.
15. See Constant's Note H at the end of Book XII.

than any government the best use he can make of them. If such economic activity is advantageous, he will not let foreigners reap its profits. If he does abandon some other comparable economic activity to them, this is because he has found a third which is more profitable.

Barriers against the importation of foreign goods are ill-advised for yet another reason. If you stop foreigners from selling to your subjects, with what do you expect them to buy from them? The richer a people are, the more the nation maintaining commercial relations with them gains by these relations. But to stop a people selling their products is to do all one can to impoverish them. It is therefore to do all one can to diminish the profits one could extract from trading with this people.

But when foreigners refuse to take our country's products, must we, someone will say, allow the free importation of theirs? When a people close their territory to your goods, this is either to make them themselves, or to favor some other nation. In the first case, one of two things happens. Either they manufacture these goods more cheaply than they would buy them from you, and then the prohibition is without effect since your products would always be at a disadvantage, or they will manufacture them more expensively and pay more for goods of lower quality. Yours, better and cheaper, will be smuggled in. The nation which wanted to keep them out impoverishes itself because it diverts funds from profitable uses into manufacturing objects it would be better to buy elsewhere. It imposes on itself constraints which hurt it in a thousand ways. The State struggles vainly against a smuggling which frustrates all its efforts. Individuals suffer from the obstacles they encounter at almost every step. The vices of such a system soon make themselves felt; and if you have kept to one based on complete freedom, [286] beyond all doubt the nation which had deviated from this will find it in its interest to come back.

If this nation rejects your goods in favor of merchandise from another country, the question is once again almost the same. Either the products of the favored nation are better than yours, with the same outcome as would obtain without the prohibitions, or these productions are inferior and yours will prevail sooner or later.

The drawback to reciprocal action is that it engages people's pride and in this way prolongs the stresses and the uneasiness. It no longer suffices that he who was first in error sees this and corrects himself. It calls for a coming together of two wills not able to agree in the swift succession of events. Injustice leads on to injustice; reciprocal prohibitions perpetuate prohibitions.

There are few questions on which governments talk as much nonsense as they do on reciprocity. The argument here constantly serves them in the maintaining of laws whose fatal consequences they cannot dispute. The law of aubaine[16] is proof of this. Because neighboring countries have made a law preventing our fellow citizens from settling among them, we quickly make a law stopping our neighbors from settling among us.[17] A marvelous vengeance this! If on the contrary we had not stupidly followed their example, we would gain from their bad law, since our fellow citizens, driven from their place, would stay with us, wealth and all. And we would profit even more from not having made a similar law, because our neighbors, welcomed by us, would freely bring us their business and their assets.

Be just with the just. You owe it them. But be just even to those who are unjust. It is the best way to get them to bear the pain of their injustice, while leaving them free to repair it.

[287] The same motives which have led governments to put barriers to the importation of foreign products have led them to ban the export of gold or silver specie. Just as a number of philosophers have taken words, the signs of ideas, for ideas themselves, administrators have mostly taken money, the sign of wealth, for wealth itself.

It would nevertheless be easy to show that specie is exported from a country only when this is advantageous to it. In fact, it is exported only when it provides a means of acquiring externally, by exchange, a greater value than the same volume of specie would purchase internally. Now, it is clear that by this operation one enriches the country into which this greater value is made to enter.[18]

When there is too little specie in a country, it is useless to prohibit its exportation. For the specie being worth more in this country than in any other, individuals have an interest in not having it exported. When, on the contrary, there is in a country more specie than the needs of commerce and

16. [The right of aubaine enabled French monarchs to claim the property of nonnaturalized persons dying in France. It was finally abolished in 1819. Translator's note]

17. This reference seems aimed at exposing the motives presented to the Conseil d'Etat on 3 March 1803, by Jean-Baptiste Treilhard with regard to the Civil Code. This is where Treilhard justifies the partial reestablishment of the right of aubaine, abolished in 1789. *Procès-verbaux du Conseil d'Etat contenant la discussion du projet du Code civil,* t. II, Paris, 1803, pp. 444–447. [The key idea was that a foreigner who died in France would have his goods confiscated unless a Frenchman living in that foreigner's country had the right to leave his wealth to his heirs. Translator's note]

18. See Constant's Note I at the end of Book XII.

circulation demand, it is fatal to forbid its exportation. What results from this is that all goods and activities cost proportionately more in this country than everywhere else. Then this State can only buy and never sell.[19] It can buy because in buying it can tolerate the loss occasioned by the low value of its money. But it cannot sell, because it cannot find purchasers willing to resign themselves to tolerating that loss. In that way the enforced superabundance of the specie is fundamentally harmful to economic progress.

If we consider specie in the most usual way, that is, as a medium of exchange, its exportation must remain free. It will not be exported unprofitably, and if it is exported to advantage, the total of public wealth increasing by [288] the amount the individual gains, the whole nation will benefit. We can also, however, think of specie as a manufacture, and as such, as something whose exportation is worth encouraging.

Among almost all peoples, the manufacture of money not being costless, its exportation is as advantageous to the State which mints it as that of any other manufactured good. How singularly illogical are our statesmen-financiers! The trade in jewelry is regarded as lucrative, although it dispatches gold and silver abroad, and the exportation of money, whose production brings a return of the same kind, and which, therefore, is nothing other than a national manufacture, is envisaged as a calamity. It has to be said that governments, until now, have not had the first idea about the questions on which they have piled up law after law.

It must readily be acknowledged, however, that some governments find it convenient rigorously to prohibit the exportation of specie. These are governments so unjust, so arbitrary, that each man works secretly to escape their yoke. Then, no doubt, specie is exported without any advantage coming back to the country thus governed. It is exported at any price, even at loss, because everyone acts as if in a fire, randomly hurling the furniture he wants to save, far from the blaze, without troubling himself over the damage it will suffer from its fall, certain that he will conserve only what he has been able to get away from the devastating element. In this case, no doubt, frontiers must be watched, so individuals can be stripped of their sad and last possession. The exit of specie must be stopped, as must the exit of persons. Just so must the privacy of letters be violated, and in a word all the faculties, all the rights, all the freedoms of man be interfered with. All these faculties, freedoms, and rights are, unwittingly, in permanent conflict with oppression. And as everything in

19. See Constant's Note J at the end of Book XII.

nature tends to free itself from despotism, despotism cannot permit anything, cannot leave anything free in nature.

[289] Governments have made two kinds of laws prohibiting commerce in grain. The first kind express their wish that the trade in this commodity be made directly between producer and consumer, without a group able to intervene between them, buying from the former and reselling to the latter. Hence the regulations against speculators. The second kind express the wish that no exportation of food products shall happen. Hence the severe penalties in some countries attaching to the export of grain.

The pretext for the first kind of laws was probably that a middleman class between consumer and producer, having to find a profit in the trade it was undertaking, tended to raise the price of the commodity, and being able easily to take advantage of circumstantial difficulties, had the dangerous ability to push prices disastrously high.

The reason for the second kind of laws was fear that undue exportation might entail famine.

In both cases the intentions of governments were praiseworthy; but in both cases they took wrong means and failed in their purposes.

All the advantages of the division of labor are found in the establishment of a middleman class, placed between the grain producer and the consumer. These middlemen have more funds than the producer and more resources for setting up warehouses. Dealing solely with this trade, they can study better the needs they undertake to meet. They free the farmer from having to get involved in speculations which absorb his time, divert his resources, and drive him into the middle of towns, where he loses his morals and dissipates his savings, a quadruple loss for agriculture. No doubt the middlemen have to be paid for their trouble. But the farmer himself has to be paid for this same trouble, which he takes less effectively and skillfully, since it is not his main activity, and at greater cost consequently. This extra expense comes back to the consumer, whom people thought they were helping. The middlemen who are proscribed as the cause of famine and high prices are precisely those who put obstacles in the [290] way of high prices becoming excessive. They buy corn in the years of overabundance and thereby prevent its falling too low in price, or its being squandered or frittered away.[20] They withdraw it from the market when its oversupply, occasioning a disastrous price fall for the farmer, would discourage the latter and lead him to neglect or imprudently limit production the following year. When the need makes itself felt, they put back what they have amassed into

20. See Constant's Note K at the end of Book XII.

the market. In this way they come to the help, at one time of the producer, in sustaining his commodity at a reasonable price, at another of the consumer, by reestablishing plentiful supply of this commodity at the point where its market price exceeds certain limits.[21]

They produce, in a word, the effect one hopes for from state-instituted warehouses, with the difference that warehouses managed and watched over by individuals, whose sole business they are, are sources neither of abuses nor waste, unlike everything which is publicly managed. They perform all this good out of personal interest, no doubt, but the fact is that under freedom's dispensation, personal interest is the most enlightened, constant, and useful ally of the general interest.

The talk is of hoarding, of machinations, of coalitions between hoarders. Who cannot see, however, that freedom alone supplies the remedy to these ills? The remedy is competition. There would be no more hoarding if everyone had the right to hoard. Those who held back their commodities to get an excessive price for them would be victims of their calculation, as absurd as it is wicked, since others would reestablish a state of plenty, contenting themselves with a modest return. The laws remedy nothing, because they are eluded. Competition remedies everything, because personal interest cannot stop competition when the government allows it. But as laws lead to their authors being talked about, people always want them, and as competition is a thing which speaks for itself and no one sings its praises to governments, governments despise and misunderstand its advantages.

If there have been hoarding and monopolies, this is because the commerce in grain has always been hit with regulations and surrounded by fears. Therefore it has never been other than a suspect commerce, mostly a clandestine one. Now, in things commercial, everything which is suspect, everything clandestine, [291] becomes vicious; everything authorized, everything public, becomes honest again.

To be sure, one has scarcely grounds for astonishment that an economic activity proscribed by government, stigmatized by an erroneous and violent public opinion, menaced by severe, unjust legal punishments, and yet further menaced by the rifling and pillaging of a mistaken populace has to this day been an activity undertaken only by stealth, by greedy and vile men, who, seeing society in arms against them, have made it pay, whenever they could, in times of crisis, for the ignominies and dangers with which it surrounded them. Access to a natural and vital activity has been closed to all

21. See Constant's Note L at the end of Book XII.

merchants who care about their safety and honor. How could so mistaken a policy not have issued in a premium for adventurers and rogues? At the first sign of dearth, on the first suspicions of government, the warehouses were broken into, the grain was carried off and sold below market price, with confiscation and fines and with the death penalty pronounced against proprietors.[22] Did not proprietors have to indemnify themselves against these obstacles, by pushing to excess all the profits they could extract by fraud, in the midst of the perpetual hostility exercised against them? With nothing assured in their legitimate profit, they had to turn to illegitimate kinds, by way of indemnity. Society had to pay the penalty for its folly and rage.[23]

The question of grain exports is even more delicate to deal with than that of the warehouses. Nothing is easier than painting a touching picture of the misfortune of the poor and the hardness of the rich, with a whole nation dying of hunger, while greedy speculators export grain, the fruit of their labor and sweat. There is a slight drawback to this way of considering things, namely that everything sayable about the danger of free exportation, which is only one of the functions of property, can be said with no less force and just as much foundation, against property itself. True, nonowners are in all respects at the mercy of owners. If one wants to assume that the latter have a strong interest in crushing, oppressing, and starving the former, an abundance of the most pathetic pictures will result from that supposition.

That is so true, that the opponents of freedom of exports have always been forced to offer some insults in passing to the [292] proprietors. Linguet called them monsters[24] whose prey must be snatched from them, without our being upset by their howling; and the most enlightened, the most virtuous, and the most respectable of defenders of the prohibitive system ended by comparing proprietors and those who spoke in their favor to crocodiles.[25]

22. See Constant's Note M at the end of Book XII.

23. See Constant's Note N at the end of Book XII.

24. The only place Hofmann has identified where Linguet calls owners *monsters* is in the conclusion of his *Théorie des lois civiles;* having accused philosophy of bringing no remedies to the pains of the human condition, but only consolations, Linguet exclaims: "How much wiser would be the terrible but sincere voice willing to tell me: 'Suffer and die in chains; such is your lot. . . . Be content with your portion, since you can hope for no other. And even when the monster whose fodder you must be devours you, submit to your fate with resignation, since you cannot change it.'" Simon Nicholas Henri Linguet, *Théorie des lois civiles ou principes fondamentaux de la société,* London, 1767, t. II, p. 519.

25. See Constant's Note O at the end of Book XII.

I would wish to envisage this matter from a point of view such as to push to one side all the ranting and thereby move forward on a principle all interests might adopt. Now, the principle is this, if I am not mistaken.

For wheat to be plentiful, there must be as much of it as possible. For there to be as much as possible, we must encourage production. Everything which encourages production of wheat favors abundance. Everything which discourages this production calls directly or indirectly to famine.

Now, if you wished to encourage production of a manufacture, what would you do? Would you reduce the number of buyers? Certainly not. You would increase them. The maker, sure of his sales, would increase his production, insofar as this increase were in his power. If, on the contrary, you diminish the number of buyers, the maker would cut his production. He would not wish it to exceed the amount he could get rid of. He would calculate, therefore, with scrupulous exactness, and as it would be much more annoying to him to have too few buyers than too many, he would cut his production in such a way that it fell short of rather than beyond the strict minimum.

Which is the country where most watches are made? I think it is the one where the watchmakers export the most. If you forbade the exportation of watches, do you think more would stay in the country? No; but there would be fewer made.

The case with grain, as to production, is the same as with other things. The mistake made by apologists for prohibitions [293] is to have considered grain as an object only of consumption, not production. They have said: the less is consumed, the more is left. False reasoning, in that grain is not a preexisting commodity. They ought to have seen that the more limited consumption is, the more production will be restrained, and that in consequence the latter will soon become insufficient for the former.

For grain production differs from that of ordinary manufactures in that it depends not solely on the manufacturer but also on the seasons. The producer, however, forced to limit his production, can calculate only on an average year basis. The result of his limiting his output to the strict minimum is that if the harvest falsifies his calculations, his output, thus limited, is inadequate. The majority of farmers, no doubt, do not limit their production deliberately. But these very people are put off by the idea that their work, should it be favored by nature, may not be profitable, that their commodity may not find buyers and therefore be a liability to them. Though they do not form any plan according to such considerations, they are more negligent in their cultivation. Earning less accordingly, they have fewer funds to put into their cultivation, and so production falls.

In preventing the export of wheat, therefore, you do not ensure that the surplus wheat necessary to the provisioning of a country stays in it, you ensure that it does not get produced. Now, since it can happen through the inclemency of nature that this surplus becomes necessary, you are ensuring that the minimum is missing.

To forbid exporting is to forbid selling, at least above a certain measure, since, once the home market is provided for, there are no buyers for the surplus. Now, to forbid selling is to forbid producing, since it takes away from the producer his reason for acting. Forbidding exports is therefore in other words forbidding production. Who could believe that this is the chosen way to keep production ever abundant?

I cannot leave this subject. Obstacles to exporting are an attack on property. Everybody agrees. Now, is it not clear that if property is less well respected, when it is associated with grain, than with any other commodity, then for purposes of sale people will prefer to hold a surplus of any other commodity rather than of grain?

If by turns you allow and forbid exportation as you please, [294] then your permission, never bearing except on existing production and always subject to your revocation, will never constitute a sufficient encouragement to future production.

I wish to reply to an objection. I said elsewhere[26] that the high price of indispensable primary commodities seemed to me fatal to the people, because daily earnings did not rise proportionately. Will not the export of wheat, someone will say, bring about an increase in the price of the commodity? It will probably prevent the price falling very low. If, on the other hand, however, the prohibition of exports stops the grain from being produced, may not the price increase perhaps be more inevitable and excessive?

Do you think you can enforce the production of grain? I should like to see you try. You will prevent owners from taking their land out of wheat production. Straightaway this is another surveillance. But will you oversee how they cultivate too? Will you oblige them to arrange the funding, dress the soil, get hold of the requisite manures, and all to produce a commodity, which if it is abundant will be impossible for them to sell and costly even to keep? When a government wants its own way to be done in a single thing, it soon finds itself reduced to doing everything.

I have not put forward other reasons for free exportation because they have been developed a thousand times. If wheat is dear, people will not

26. A little earlier in this same Book XII.

export it, since at the same price, it is better to sell it on the spot than to export it. People will export it, therefore, only when it is good to do so. You can suppose universal dearth, with famine in your own country or in neighboring ones. Then you will need singular laws for a singular disaster. An earthquake which threw all farm holdings into confusion would demand special legal arrangements for a new sharing out of real estate. One takes special measures for distributing subsistence food in a beseiged town. But to make habitual legislation for a calamity which has not taken place naturally once in two centuries is to turn legislation into a habitual calamity.

Nature is not reckless with her hardships. If we compared the number of dearths which have been caused by truly bad years with those caused by regulations, we would be pleased at how little ill comes to us from nature, and we would tremble at the ill which comes to us from men.

[295] I would have liked to take a middle course on this question. There is a certain credit for a moderation which it is pleasant to attribute to oneself and which it is not hard to acquire, provided one is not very sincere. One testifies in this way in one's own favor for having properly looked at both sides of questions, turning one's hesitation into a discovery. Instead of being right against a single view, one appears to be in the right against two. So I would have preferred to find as a result of my investigations that the government can be left the right to allow or forbid exportation. In trying to determine the rules according to which it should act, however, I felt I was plunging again into the chaos of prohibitions. How will the government judge, for each province, at a huge distance, and remote from others, circumstances which can change before knowledge of them gets to it? How will it stop fraud by its agents? How will it guard itself against the danger of taking a momentary blockage for a real dearth, or a local difficulty for a universal disaster? Lasting general arrangements based on brief and partial difficulties produce the ill we want to prevent.[27] The men most lively in recommending this versatile legislation do not know how to go about it when it comes to the means of carrying it out.[28]

If there are drawbacks in everything, leave things be. At least the people's suspicions and the injustices of government will not be joined with nature's calamities. Out of three scourges you will have two less, and you will have moreover this advantage—that you will get men used to not regarding

27. See Constant's Note P at the end of Book XII.
28. See Constant's Note Q at the end of Book XII.

violation of property as a resource.[29] Then they will seek and find other ones. If on the contrary they notice the former, they will always come back to it because it is the swiftest and the most convenient.

If you justify, as being in the public interest, the obligation imposed on owners to sell in a particular place, that is to say, to sell at a loss, given that they could sell better elsewhere, you will end up fixing the prices of their commodities. The one will be no more unjust than the other and will easily be represented as equally necessary.

Therefore I admit only very few exceptions to the complete freedom of [296] commerce in grain, as in any other commodity; and these exceptions are purely circumstantial.

The first is the situation of a small country, without territory, obliged to maintain its independence against powerful neighbors. This little country could establish warehouses so that others did not seek to subjugate it by starving it, and since the administration of such a country is like that of a family, the abuses of these warehouses would be largely avoided.

The second exception is a sudden and general famine, the effect of some unforeseen cause, natural or political. I have already spoken of this above.

The third is at once the most important and the most difficult to resign oneself to. Its necessity results from popular prejudices nourished and sacralized by the rooted habit of error. It is certain that in a country where the commerce in grain has never been free, sudden freedom produces a fatal disturbance. Opinion revolts, and its blind and violent action creates the ills which it fears. Therefore we need, I admit, to exercise great care to bring the people around on this subject to the principles closest to justice and truth. The shocks are painful, on the right road as well as the wrong; but the government which does this decent thing often only with regret does not devote much zeal to the prevention of these shocks, and educated men, when they succeed in dominating it by force of enlightenment, too often believe they are engaging it more by dragging it into precipitate measures. They are not aware that this is to furnish it with specious pretexts for retrogressing. This is what happened in France around the middle of the last century.

The question of the rate of interest is perhaps the one which for some time had been best argued. In our times, some men, probably tired of seeing people agreeing on this question, have begun considering it again from a

29. See Constant's Note R at the end of Book XII.

theological viewpoint.[30] I hardly feel inclined to see it in [297] this light. I will say, though, that even religiously the prohibition of all interest is an absurd precept, because it is an unjust and moreover inoperable one. Religion does not at all fault the owner of land for living on the income it yields. How can it forbid the owner of capital to live off its income? This would be ordering him to die of hunger.

If you then turn the precept into advice, this change will have only one advantage, that people will no longer think themselves so guilty for disobeying it. Lending without interest might be an act of charity, like almsgiving; but this can never be other than an individual act, and you cannot make it a habitual rule of human conduct. It is useful for society that funds be employed. It is therefore useful that those who do not use them themselves lend them to others to use them. But if funds do not yield any income when they are lent, people would rather bury them than lend them, since they avoid the dangers of the loan.

Government has only three things it can do in this regard. It must stop fraud, that is, prevent abuse of youth, inexperience, or ignorance, stop people lending to children, minors, and any whom the law regards as incapable of watching over their own interests. For this purpose it suffices that government does not recognize any contracts such persons may enter into.

Secondly, it must guarantee legitimate compacts and ensure their carrying out. The easier and more assured this is, the more the rate of interest will come down. For lenders always get themselves paid for the risks they incur.

Finally, government must determine a legal rate of interest just for the case where the debtor, depositary, holder of a sum does not make it good by the time and on the conditions agreed. This legal interest rate must be as high as possible, for if it were less than the ordinary rate of interest, the fraudulent debtor would find himself enjoying resources retained against all justice, more advantageously than the honest debtor who had borrowed it with its owner's consent.[31]

All further intervention in this matter by government is iniquitous and off target. Restricting the charging of interest promotes usury. Capitalists need, on top of the natural rate of profit for the funds they lend, a "risk premium" against the laws they infringe. This rule of nature [298] has made itself respected in all eras, in spite of all regulations. Popular power

30. Hofmann has not been able to identify these men.

31. See Constant's Note S at the end of Book XII.

in Rome, religious power among Christians and Moslems have equally failed against it.[32]

I find two errors on this subject in the work of two equally famous and estimable writers, Adam Smith and M. Necker.

The former says that the legal rate of interest[33] must not be raised too high, or the bulk of the money lent will go to spendthrifts, only they being willing to pay so dear. In this way the country's resources will be taken out of hardworking hands and passed over to men unable to do other than dissipate and destroy them.

This author forgets, however, that spendthrifts who dissipate the funds they borrow are rarely in shape to pay them back after they have dissipated them. Consequently the vast majority of lenders will always prefer to high but precarious returns, lower, safer ones. They will entrust their funds, therefore, to the hardworking, thrifty class who, borrowing only to engage in profitable speculation, can meet obligations by the due date.

M. Necker too[34] approves of government fixing the legal rate of interest. "Lenders are in general," he says, "only inactive proprietors. Borrowers, on the contrary, have a purpose, an activity from which society benefits in some way. So when there are conflicts over the rate of interest, the government ought to want the advantage to belong to them." But if the advantage belongs to borrowers, when the rate of interest is disputed, lenders will have themselves compensated for the disadvantage to their side. The borrowers we believed we were helping will carry the burden. This is inevitable and will work against the purpose M. Necker wishes the government to have in mind. He feels this himself, since he adds: "since the relationships which determine the interest rate are more powerful than government, sovereigns can never hope to control it by way of imperious laws."[35] But how else other than by laws will government intervene in the contestations between lenders and borrowers? "The profits of agriculture," he continues, "and those of all enterprises which [299] are not unique and privileged, cannot bear the expense of an interest rate above ordinary usages, and it is absolutely no help to production to favor the position of the lenders."[36] Is it not clear, however, that those who borrow for farming or industrial enterprises will not be

32. See Constant's Note T at the end of Book XII.
33. See Constant's Note U at the end of Book XII.
34. See Constant's Note V at the end of Book XII.
35. Jacques Necker, *De l'administration . . . , op. cit.*, t. III, p. 239.
36. *Ibid.*, p. 240.

tempted to pay an interest rate greater than their profits? And will those who borrow for dissipation be checked by laws which are easy to elude? Regulations are superfluous for the former, illusory for the latter.

When interest is banned, it takes all sorts of forms. It disguises itself as capital. What else is selling dearer on credit than having oneself paid the interest on one's money?

Except in the circumstance we spoke of above, that of capital illegally retained by a debtor, the rate of interest must not be fixed. The rate, like the price of all goods, should be regulated by demand. To fix the rate of interest is to fix the maximum price of capital, and a maximum price of capital has the same effect as one for commodities. It causes the flight of what can be placed elsewhere and makes what is sold in contravention of the law more expensive.

Without doubt there is a moral element in this question. But opinion alone can pronounce on this moral element, and it always does so wisely. Solon[37] did not want to fix the interest rate in Athens. Those who demanded unreasonable rates of interest there, however, were regarded as infamous.

You fear the excesses of clandestine usury. Yet it is your prohibitions which bring it to this level. Let all transactions be out in the open. Public scrutiny will moderate them.

CHAPTER FIVE

On the General Effect of Prohibitions

Prohibitions in the matter of industry and commerce, like all other prohibitions and more than all the others, put individuals at odds with the government. They form one nursery [300] for men preparing for every kind of crime by accustoming themselves to violate the laws, and another for men familiarizing themselves with wickedness, by living off the misfortune of their fellows.[38] Not only do commercial prohibitions create artificial crimes, but they encourage the committing of these crimes by the profit which they attach to the fraud which is successful in deceiving them. This is a drawback on top of those which other prohibitive laws have.[39] They tend to be traps for the poor, that class already surrounded by irresistible temptations, of which it has rightly been said that all its actions are hasty,[40]

37. See Constant's Note W at the end of Book XII.
38. See Constant's Note X at the end of Book XII.
39. See Constant's Note Y at the end of Book XII.
40. See Constant's Note Z at the end of Book XII.

because want presses on it, its poverty robs it of any enlightenment, and obscurity frees it from the force of opinion.

I said at the start of Book XII that I did not place the same importance on freedom of production as on other types of freedom. Nevertheless, the restrictions obtaining here involve laws so cruel that all others feel their effects. Look at the riots in Portugal occasioned first by the privileged position of the Company of Wines, riots requiring barbarous punishments, whose spectacle discouraged commerce, riots leading finally to a succession of constraints and cruelties which brought a host of proprietors to tear up their vines themselves, destroying in their despair the source of their riches, so that these would no longer furnish a pretext for all kinds of harassment.[41] Look at the severity in England, the violence and the despotic acts which the exclusive privileges of the East India Company[42] entail to keep themselves going. Open up the statutes of this otherwise humane and liberal nation. There you will see the death penalty multiply for actions impossible to consider criminal.[43] When we examine the history of English settlements in North America, we see, so to speak, every special privilege followed by the emigration of the nonprivileged. The colonists fled in the face of [301] commercial restrictions, leaving lands they had scarcely finished clearing, to regain their freedom in the forest, asking from a savage nature a refuge from the persecutions of society.[44]

If the system of prohibitions has not destroyed all the enterprise of the nations it harasses and torments, this is, as Smith remarks,[45] because each individual's natural effort to improve his lot is a repairing principle, which in many respects remedies the bad effects of administrative regulation, just as the life force struggles, often successfully, in the physical organization of man, against the illnesses which flow from his passions, intemperance, or laziness.

CHAPTER SIX

On Things Which Push Governments in This Mistaken Direction

It is all the more important that these truths make some breakthrough in the outlooks of government, in that each category of proprietors, makers, and manufacturers endlessly begs the intervention of government against

41. See Constant's Note AA at the end of Book XII.
42. See Constant's Note BB at the end of Book XII.
43. See Constant's Note CC at the end of Book XII.
44. See Constant's Note DD at the end of Book XII.
45. See Constant's Note EE at the end of Book XII.

everything which diminishes its immediate profit, whether by useful discoveries or some kind of new production; and it has to be feared that the governors may take the interests of these groups to be those of society. These two sets of interest are, for all that, almost always mutually opposed.[46]

The demands addressed to government by those in trade, to prevent competition, the installation of equipment, improvement in communications, and proliferation of commodities, could be translated thus: allow us alone to buy or sell such and such an object, so that we can sell it to you dearer. [302] Is it not odd that such demands have been welcomed so often?

When profits fall, business people are inclined to complain of the decline of trade. The diminution in profits is, however, the natural effect of progressive prosperity. Business profits fall: 1. Because of competition. 2. Because earnings rise, as a result of competition which increases labor prices. 3. By the increased flow of capital into commerce, which lowers the rate of interest. Now, these three causes of the diminution in profits are three signs of prosperity. This, however, is when business people complain and appeal about it to government, for special intervention,[47] such that in the event, business people call for the intervention of government against commercial prosperity.

When the commercial mind mingles with the administrative one and dominates it, a thousand errors and ills ensue. Nothing is more dangerous than the habit and means used by individual interest to attain its purposes [303] transported into the administration of public affairs. Doubtless, the general interest is only the joining of all private ones. It is the joining of all these interests, however, by the cutting off of that part of each one which hurts the others. Now, it is precisely this part to which each private interest attaches the most value, because this is what in each circumstance is the most profitable to it. It follows from this that the private interest, which is very enlightened when it reasons on what matters to it and on what it must do, is a very bad guide when people want to generalize its reasonings and make them the basis of an administrative system. We see an individual enriching himself through a monopoly, and without reflecting on the fact that this is at the nation's expense, we establish monopolies precisely as a means of wealth for the nation in question, when the reality is that they impoverish and despoil it. This is because governments are ordinarily

46. See Constant's Note FF at the end of Book XII.
47. See Constant's Note GG at the end of Book XII.

steered toward these stances by men imbued with mercantile prejudices; and by a singular contradiction, but one they do not notice, by basing their prohibitive measures on the blindness or harmful tendency of special interests, they constantly institutionalize the calculations of special interest, as rules of their public conduct.

What we say about the business outlook does not apply solely to the group which is called "business" to distinguish it from other groups. This outlook becomes common to all people in society who harvest, produce, or accumulate in order to sell. Thus farmers contract the business outlook when it comes to selling grain, and we see them drawn into the same errors as men involved in purely mercantile speculation. Did not the owners of vineyards in France ask the King's Council in about 1731 to forbid the plantation of new vineyards?[48] Did not landowners in counties near London petition the House of Commons, for no large roads to be opened to the more distant [304] areas, for fear that the wheat from these areas, arriving more easily in the capital, might lower the price of theirs?[49] If rentiers dared, they would speak about falling interest rates the way business people do of falling profits. A rentier, having for long lent his money at ten percent and now finding he can place it only at five percent, would ask nothing better than to say that the country he lived in was going to ruin because he was finding himself less well off there. He would most readily solicit the government for measures to stop interest rates falling. It is nevertheless incontestable that a fall in interest rates proves the prosperity of a country and a rise proves its bad financial situation.

In industry, prohibitions are the type of arbitrary measure which some men can use against others; and just as in civil disagreements they seek to seize arbitrary power instead of destroying it, in the cause of trade they seek to seize control of arbitrary regulations. They almost never protest against prohibitions in general, but strive to have them put to their advantage. Following the introduction of silk manufacture, under Henry IV, the cloth manufacturers demanded these manufactures be banned.[50] Following the introduction of cotton stuffs, the silk manufacturers called for a prohibitive law against them. Following the invention of prints, cotton manufacturers represented them as a frightful calamity.[51] If all this pleading had been

48. Constant found the example of this decree of 1731 in Adam Smith, *op. cit.*, t. I, p. 332.

49. See Constant's Note HH at the end of Book XII.

50. See Constant's Note II at the end of Book XII.

51. See Constant's Note JJ at the end of Book XII.

listened to, France would have neither silks, nor cottons, nor prints. Each manufacture, like each newborn religion, claims freedom. Each manufacture, like each established religion, preaches persecution.

What is most fatal in regulations is that motivated by necessity which does not exist, they sometimes create it. Men arrange their calculations and their habits according to regulations, which then become as dangerous to revoke as they are troublesome to maintain.[52]

M. de Montesquieu, as a judicious writer observes,[53] had only very superficial ideas about political [305] economy. We must avoid taking him for a guide in this matter. Everything he explained as regards institutions he believed he justified; the discovery of the motive made him indulgent of the institution, because it made him pleased with himself. Speaking of the system of prohibitions in England, he said, "they obstruct the trader, but this is in favor of the trade";[54] he would have been more correct to say: they obstruct the trade in favor of some traders.[55]

CHAPTER SEVEN

On the Supports Offered by Government

A regime of subsidies and various supports has fewer disadvantages than one based on monopolies. It seems to me dangerous, though, in several respects.

First, one must fear that government, once it has arrogated to itself the right to intervene in the affairs of business, if only through supports, may soon be pushed, if the incentives are not enough, to have recourse to measures of constraint and harshness. Government rarely resigns itself to not taking revenge for failed policies. It runs after its money like some gambler. While the latter appeals to luck here, however, government often appeals to force.

Secondly, there is also the worry that government, by its unwonted incentives, may deflect funds from their natural usage, which is always the most profitable one. Funds move of their own accord to their most profitable employment. To attract them there, there is no need for supports. For those which would stand to lose, supports would be fatal. Any industry

52. See Constant's Note KK at the end of Book XII.
53. See Constant's Note LL at the end of Book XII.
54. See Constant's Note MM at the end of Book XII.
55. See Constant's Note NN at the end of Book XII.

which cannot stand independently of government help finishes up second-rate.[56] The government then pays individuals to work at a loss, and thus seems to be indemnifying them. Since the indemnity cannot be drawn other than from taxation, however, it is, in a word, private individuals who [306] bear the burden. Finally, government supports seriously attack the morality of the working classes. Morality is constructed from the natural sequence of causes and effects. To upset that sequence is to damage morality. Anything which brings chance among men corrupts them. Anything which is not the direct, necessary, and habitual effect of a cause, pertains more or less to hazard. What makes work the most efficacious cause of morality is the independence of other men in which the working man finds himself, and the way he depends on his own conduct, on the order, continuity, and regularity he puts in his life. Such is the real cause of the morality of those groups busy with routine work, and of the immorality so common among beggars and gamblers. These last are of all men the most immoral, since of all men they count the most on chance.

Supports and help for business by government are a kind of game. It is impossible to suppose that government never grants its help and its supports to men who do not deserve them nor never grants more of these than the objects of this favor deserve. A single mistake of this kind turns supports into a lottery. A single eventuality is enough to bring hazard into all calculations and therefore to destabilize them. The probability of the chance does not matter, since imagination trumps the calculation. Even the distant, uncertain hope of government help casts into the life and reckoning of the hardworking man an element quite different from the rest of his existence. His situation changes, his interests become complicated. His condition becomes open to a sort of speculation. This is not your peaceful merchant or manufacturer, who made his prosperity depend on the wisdom of his speculations, on the quality of his products and the approval of his fellow citizens, accorded for the regularity of his conduct and in recognition of his sobriety. This is a man whose immediate interest and pressing desire is to attract government attention to himself. The nature of things, for the good of the human race, once put an almost insurmountable barrier between the great mass of peoples and those who held power. Only a small number of men were condemned to run hither and thither in the political sphere, to speculate in favor, to grow rich on corruption. The rest followed their road peacefully, asking government only to guarantee their peace, and the

56. See Constant's Note OO at the end of Book XII.

exercise of their faculties. If government, however, discontented with this salutary function and committed through generosity or promises made in the presence of all, provokes hopes and creates passions which did not exist before, then everything is [307] turned upside down. Without doubt this will spread a new activism among the business class. This is a vicious activism, though, one more concerned with the external effect it produces than with the solid basis of its own work, which pursues publicity rather than success, because success is seen as possible even from a meretricious publicity, an activism which in short turns the whole nation reckless, restless, greedy, rather than thrifty and hardworking as it would have been.

And do not imagine that in substituting for financial incentives, motives drawn from vanity, you will be acting less harmfully. Only too often governments number charlatanism among their means. It is easy for them to believe that their mere presence, like that of the sun, vivifies the whole of nature. So they display themselves, they talk and smile, and in their view their performance should be honored for centuries. This is once again, however, to take those who must work for their livelihood away from their natural employment. It is to give them the need for credit. It is to inspire in them the desire to exchange their commercial relationships for supple ones, those of a clientele. They will learn courtly vices without at the same time the elegance which at least veils them.

The two hypothetical situations most favorable to a regime of government incentives or supports are, without question, on the one hand when one is establishing a branch of production as yet unknown in a country, one demanding large prior investments, on the other the help which has to be given to certain business or farming classes, when unforeseen calamities have considerably diminished their resources.

I am not sure, however, whether even in these two cases, except perhaps for some very rare circumstances, for which it is impossible to establish fixed rules, government intervention is not more harmful than advantageous.

In the first case, the new branch of production, protected thus, will undoubtedly establish itself sooner and more widely; but resting more on the help of government than on calculated management by individuals, its foundations will be weaker. The individuals involved, indemnified in advance for potential losses, will not bring the same zeal and care as if they had been left to their own devices and could not expect any success save what they deserved. They will rightly flatter themselves that the government, in a way committed by the first sacrifices it has agreed to, will come to their help once more, if they fail, so as not to lose the fruits of its sacrifices; and this [308] lurking thought, different in nature from that which must act as a spur to business, will always more or less damage their activity and efforts in a perceptible way.

Moreover, in countries used to the meretricious help of government, it is assumed much too readily that such and such an enterprise exceeds individual means. This is a second cause of the slackening off of the particular industry. It waits for the government to supply the stimulus, because it is used to the government's making the first move.

In England scarcely does a discovery become known before numerous subscriptions provide the inventors with all the means of development and application. The whole point is that these subscribers examine the promised advantages much more carefully than a government could, since the interest of all those in business on their own account is not to let themselves be deceived, while that of most of those who bank speculatively on government help is to deceive the government. Work and success are the only means open to the former. Exaggeration or patronage are for the latter a much more certain and above all swifter way. Systematic reliance on supports is immoral in principle in this respect too.

True, individual effort, deprived of all outside help, sometimes comes to a halt in the face of obstacles. But first it will turn to other projects and secondly it will assuredly regroup its resources to return to the attack, sooner or later, and overcome the difficulty. Now, my assertion is that this partial and short-lived difficulty will be nothing like as disadvantageous as the general disorder and discontinuity which any artificial aid brings into ideas and calculations.

Almost identical reasoning applies in the case of the second hypothesis, which at first glance seems even more legitimate and favorable. In coming to the help of the business or farming classes, their resources depleted by unforeseen and inevitable calamities, the government first of all weakens in them the feeling which gives most energy and morality to man: that of total obligation to oneself and of putting hope only in one's own resources. Secondly, the hope of such help encourages classes in distress to exaggerate their losses and conceal their resources, in this way giving them an interest in lying. I agree that this help may be distributed prudently and parsimoniously. But what may not hold for its effect on people's affluence may hold for the effect on their morals. The government [309] will nonetheless have taught them to rely on others instead of on themselves alone. It will go on to disappoint their hopes; but their work will still have slackened as a result of all this, and their veracity will still have suffered a change. If they do not get government help, this will be because they have not learned a sufficiently skillful deception. Finally, government runs the risk of finding itself deceived by unreliable agents. It cannot follow in detail the carrying out of its orders, and cunning is always more skillful than surveillance. Frederick the Great and Catherine II used a system of supports for agriculture and industry. They frequently visited in person the provinces they thought they had helped. Well-dressed, well-fed men were put along their route, in apparent proof of the affluence resulting from their generosity, but assembled to this effect by the distributors of their grace, while the true inhabitants of these regions were groaning in the depths of their huts, in their age-old poverty, ignorant even of the intentions of the monarchs who thought themselves their benefactors.

In countries with free constitutions, the question of a regime of incentives and supports can moreover be considered from another point of view. Is it salutary that the government should attach to itself certain groups of those it governs by handouts which even were they wisely distributed are intrinsically arbitrary? Is it not to be feared that these groups, seduced by immediate and positive advantage, might become indifferent to violations of individual freedom or justice? One would then be right to think of them as suborned by government.

CHAPTER EIGHT

On the Equilibrium of Production

To read a number of writers, you would be tempted to think that nothing could be more stupid, less enlightened, or more careless than individual interest. They gravely inform us sometimes that if the government does not promote agriculture then all labor will turn [310] toward manufacturing and the fields will lie fallow, sometimes that if the government does not promote manufactures, then all labor will stay in the countryside, that the product of the land will be far more than is needed, and that the country will languish without trade or industry.[57] As if it were not clear on the one hand that agriculture will always take account of a people's needs, since artisans and manufacturers must always have the means of feeding themselves, while on the other that manufactures will always increase as soon as agricultural products are sufficiently plentiful, since individual interest will push people into applying themselves to something more lucrative than

57. See Constant's Note PP at the end of Book XII.

increasing commodity production, where quantity will reduce price. Governments can change nothing with respect to men's physical needs. The output and prices of products, of whatever sort, always comply with the demands arising from these needs. It is absurd to believe that when those who take up a line of work find it useful, this will not itself suffice to increase the scale of production. If there is more labor than is needed to release the fertility of the soil, the people will naturally turn their labor to other branches of production. They will feel, without the government warning them about it, that beyond a certain point competition destroys the advantages of the job. Individual interest will by its very nature be sufficiently stirred, without government support, to seek out some more profitable job. If the nature of the terrain requires a large number of cultivators, artisans and manufacturers will not become more numerous, because a people's first need is to subsist. A people never neglects its subsistence. Moreover, the farming sector being more crucial, it will for that very reason be more lucrative than any other. When there is no improper privilege such as may invert the natural order, the value of a line of work always comprises its absolute usefulness and its relative scarcity. The real stimulus for all types of work is how much they are needed. Freedom in itself suffices to keep them all in a salutary and accurate balance.

Outputs always tend to move to the level of needs, without government getting involved.[58] When one kind of product is scarce, its price rises. With price rising, production, being better paid, attracts to itself activity and funds. The [311] result is that supply becomes more plentiful. With supply increasing, price falls. With price falling, some activity and some funds go elsewhere. Then with production shrinking, price rises again and activity returns, until output and price have attained a perfect equilibrium.

What misleads many writers is their being struck by the listlessness or malaise which the nation's working classes experience under despotic governments. They do not go back to the cause of the evil, but delude themselves that it could be remedied by a direct action by the government in favor of the afflicted classes. Thus in the case of farming, for example, when unjust and oppressive institutions expose farmers to harassment by the privileged classes, country areas are soon fallow because they are depopulated. The farming classes flock as fast as they can to the towns to escape from their servitude and humiliation. Then idiotic theorizers recommend positive and preferential supports for farmers. They do not see that everything

58. See Constant's Note QQ at the end of Book XII.

is interconnected in human societies. Rural depopulation results from bad political organization. Neither help to a few individuals, nor any other artificial and fleeting palliative, will cure it. Our only resource is in freedom and justice. Why do we always delay seizing it as long as possible?

Sometimes it is said that we should ennoble agriculture, lift it up again, render it honorable as the source of the prosperity of nations. Rather enlightened men have developed this idea. One of the most penetrating but most bizarre minds of the last century, the marquis de Mirabeau, repeated it endlessly. Others have said as much for manufacturing. But ennobling is done only by way of distinctions, if indeed ennobling happens at all, by way of distinctions thus deliberately contrived. Now, if work is useful, since it will be profitable, many will pursue it. What distinction do you want to accord to something commonplace? Moreover, the necessary work is always simple. Now, it does not lie within government discretion to influence opinion such that it will attach special merit to what everyone can do equally well.

The only truly imposing distinctions are those which indicate power, because they are real, and the power they embellish can act for good or ill. Distinctions based [312] on merit are always contested by opinion, because opinion always reserves to itself alone the right to decide what merit is. Power it must recognize, like it or not. Merit, however, it can deny. This is why the *cordon bleu* commanded respect.[59] It established that whoever bore it was a great lord, government being very well able to judge that this or that man is a great lord. The *cordon noir* on the contrary was ridiculous. It declared the man decorated with it a man of letters, a distinguished artist.[60] Now, governments cannot pronounce on writers and artists.

Honorary distinctions for farmers, artisans, and manufacturers are even more illusory. These groups want to reach affluence or wealth through work and peace of mind by the rule of law. They want none of your artificial distinctions, or if they do aspire to them, it is because you have perverted their intelligence by filling their heads with meretricious ideas. Leave them to enjoy in peace the fruits of their labors, the equality of rights, and the freedom of action which belong to them. You will serve them much better by not showering them either with favors or injustices, than in harassing them on the one hand or seeking on the other to honor them.

59. Decoration of the Order of the Holy Spirit, created in 1578 by Henry III and abolished under the Revolution.

60. Decoration of the Order of St. Michael, created in 1469 by Louis XI and abolished under the Revolution.

CHAPTER NINE

A Final Example of the Adverse Effects of Government Intervention

I want to finish by showing that government intervention in questions of production is equally harmful whether it orders something or forbids the same thing. The example I use is the division of labor.

The division of labor has immense advantages. It facilitates increased output of all products, it economizes greatly on time and labor, it leads man to a perfection he cannot attain without it. It gives the businessman's speculations a clarity, a precision and accuracy which simplify his operations and make his calculations more confident. It is therefore [313] certain that government does harm when it opposes the division of labor with prohibitive laws. This is what it did, as we explained earlier,[61] with the commerce in grains, in forbidding the farmer to sell his wheat in bulk to those who wanted to hold it in warehouses. This resulted in countless difficulties for this trade, difficulties which often led to real famines or false alarms as troublesome as real famines.

If you conclude from this, however, that government, far from putting obstacles or limits to the division of labor, must actually prescribe it, what will happen? Along with its advantages, the division of labor has great drawbacks. It circumscribes and thereby narrows the intellectual faculties. It reduces man to the level of a simple machine. He can resign himself to this when his interest dictates this voluntarily. He would be hurt, however, by government action which, seeming to him against his interest, would appear gratuitously offensive and degrading. Nothing could be more unjust than preventing a skillful workman who can successfully combine two jobs from doing both or passing freely between them. It is clear, therefore, that the government does wrong to drive the division of labor by its regulations. This is what it did with the system of guild leaders and master craftsmen,[62] which condemns the individuals in this or that job to follow no other.

61. Earlier in this same Book XII.

62. [We would speak more easily today of the guild system. "*Jurandes*" (guild leaders) is a fifteenth-century term; "*maîtrises*" (master craftsmen) is thirteenth century, and the phrase "*jurandes et maîtrises*," which Constant uses here, is itself fifteenth century. Translator's note]

Everywhere we have seen these institutions harm the economy, encourage fraud, and even retard the progress of jobs whose perfecting they proposed to promote.

What must government do then? Stay out of it. The division of labor must limit and maintain itself spontaneously. When any division of labor is advantageous, it establishes itself naturally. When men in specialized jobs revert to combining two types of work, it is because this combination suits them better.

This example shows that government can do harm not only by acting in a certain way but also by acting in the opposite way. There are numerous circumstances when it can do good only by not acting at all. [314]

CHAPTER TEN

Conclusions from the Above Reflections

As I said at the start of the foregoing reflections, I am absolutely not presenting a complete case for the very least interference by government in economic activity. A thousand arguments and facts crowd around me, all tending to supply ever stronger evidence for this principle. I am putting them aside, because I feel it is impossible to expound them on a satisfactory scale. Each fact in isolation may furnish an exception and it would require verification, that is, giving oneself over to local investigations, historical, geographical, and even political, to show either that the exception is not upheld or that it does not weaken the principle. In this treatise I cannot take on this workload. I think I have said enough, nevertheless, to show that the effect of government intervention in matters of production, though sometimes necessary perhaps, is never positively advantageous. We can resign ourselves to it as an inevitable ill; but we should always strive to limit this ill as closely as possible.

My views will probably encounter many opponents. This will not make me think them any less correct. In a country where the government hands out assistance and compensation, many hopes are awakened. Until such time as they have been disappointed, men are bound to be unhappy with a system which replaces favoritism only by freedom. Freedom creates, so to speak, a negative good, although a gradual and general one. Favoritism brings positive, immediate, personal advantages. Selfishness and short-term views will always be against freedom and for favoritism.

CHAPTER ELEVEN

On Government Measures in Relation to Population

If governments have wanted to influence economic activity, they have similarly wanted to influence population and—who would believe it?—they have passed [315] coercive laws to force man to satisfy the sweetest penchant of his nature.

They thought they had an obvious interest in interfering with population. It constitutes their most concrete force. They did not know that their very bringing their power to bear on it could only harm it.

They were not short of a pretext. Domestic affections are the best guarantee of morality.

Celibacy favors disorder and selfishness. Marriage inspires in man more need for stability. What good reasons for coming down hard on celibacy and encouraging marriage!

It is a pity that a number of governments, in proscribing celibacy by law, reduce marriage to sterility by way of harassment and poverty.

Two kinds of causes can impede the population's growth and make it smaller. Some influence population directly. These include epidemics, floods, earthquakes, emigrations, and lastly war, considered, not in its political aspect, but in terms of its immediate effect of devastating part of a country's population. Others exert a mediate influence, institutional vices and government harassment being examples. The former destroy living people. The latter prevent the birth of those who would be born.

The marquis de Mirabeau, one of the most original minds of the last century, who in a singular mixture brought together very philanthropic ideas with a very despotic character, and a very sincere love of freedom with all the prejudices of the nobility and even of feudalism, showed very clearly in *The Friend of Men* that direct causes have a brief effect only, on population. "They say," he says, with astonishment, "that after a time of trouble or calamity, a state is just as populous as it was before, while the buildings and roads, in a word, everything which indicates apparent prosperity, shrinks visibly because of the interruption to order and justice."[63] Indirect causes, seemingly less harmful, have much more extensive and lasting effects. This is because [316] they attack the population at its very root, that

63. Victor Riqueti, marquis de Mirabeau, *L'Ami des hommes ou traité de la population*, Hambourg, Chrétien Hérold, 3e éd., 1758, t. I, p. 28.

is to say, its means of subsistence. The peasant labors, builds, and gets married on fields turned topsy-turvy by earthquakes, after an epidemic or in the wake of an army which has ransacked his property, because he hopes the earthquake will not return, he sees that the epidemic has ceased, and because peace having been made, he thinks he is sure the ravaging army has moved away forever. But he works, builds, or marries only with anxiety under an oppressive government, which snatches from him the means of subsistence necessary to feed and raise his family.

Man very quickly gets over calamities which seem temporary to him. The dead leave the living better off and put more means of subsistence at their disposal. The latter multiply on account of the vacant places and the resources they find for living. Nature has placed the remedy alongside all the ills which come from her. She has endowed man with a faculty which seems like carelessness or improvidence but in reality is rational. He senses that natural misfortunes recur only at periods very distant from each other, while those born of the whims of fellow men weigh on him at every moment.

The vices of government prolong some causes of depopulation which, absent these vices, would be only short-lived. These causes should therefore be considered under two aspects, as harming the population directly and then harming them again insofar as they are multiplied by government errors. For example, the expulsion of the Jews and the Moors contributed to the depopulation of Spain only because that expulsion resulted from an oppressive and persecutory administrative system. For the same reason, the settlers who left that country for the New World have never been replaced, while a free nation can send numerous settlers abroad without its depopulating. In a free nation, everything which brings about a social vacuum, at the same time encourages all those who remain to fill it. The direct ill which causes war is soon corrected. When a government, however, can restart or prolong the war at will, this supposes a despotic will in this government, one which is a quite separate scourge from the war itself, one which, bearing down on the means of subsistence, prevents the population from growing and from filling the gaps which the war has occasioned.

[317] It is the same with celibacy. If some individuals do not marry and reproduce, there are others who will. But when celibacy results either from poverty or the absurdity of institutions, the evil is irreparable in a totally different sense. I will cite the marquis de Mirabeau again. He shows clearly that clerical celibacy in itself is in no way harmful to

population.[64] On the contrary, whenever a certain number of individuals manage by coming together to live from the product of a smaller section of land than would be needed for the subsistence of the same number of individuals in isolation, this coming together is favorable to the numerical growth of the species. The individuals who come together draw closer voluntarily and leave more space to others. It is never the population which is lacking, but space, that is, land, and above all the means of subsistence. Priestly celibacy, however, implies a more superstitious state of things, and therefore worse government. Such influences spread to everything. It is not because priests do not marry that the country becomes depopulated but because a government which consecrates priestly celibacy is an ignorant government. Now, ignorant government is always oppressive. It harasses men who marry, takes away their means of subsistence, pushes them into despondency, thereby prevents them from multiplying or, if they do multiply, causes their children to die from destitution or want.

The more populous and flourishing condition of the Protestant countries is attributed to the suppression of the celibate orders. It should have been attributed to the diminution of prejudices and the growth of civil freedom which the Reformation introduced into these countries.

It is not because a certain number of individuals have married that a population has increased, but rather that there have been a few more possibilities for scrutiny and a bit more enlightenment, first on one question and then, since all ideas are linked, on all the others. There follows a more just regime, less oppression, less poverty, and better subsistence. This leads me to regard as truly wretched the calculation by some governments which, not content with declaring the celibacy of priests purely voluntary, have sought to force into marriage men who thought themselves bound by conscience and the holiest of oaths to abstain from it. As if the marriage of a few religious would have been a truly efficacious means of population growth, and as if the birth [318] of a few more children were preferable to the refinements of honor and the virtues of scruple, which, whether rightly or wrongly founded, is still a virtue, in a word, as if man were an ignoble and pliant creature, cast on this earth only to obey and propagate.

When men have the wherewithal for subsistence, for them and their children, population increases. When they do not, either they do not marry

64. Constant in fact merely refers to rather than quotes the marquis de Mirabeau's book, *L'Ami des hommes, op. cit.*, t. I, pp. 31–33.

or they have fewer children, or if they have children, most of these die young. The population always reaches the level of subsistence. In America the population doubles in twenty or twenty-five years. This is because work is so well paid that a large family, instead of being a burden, is a source of opulence and prosperity. "A young widow with four or five children" would hardly find a second husband in Europe "in the middle or lower classes." In America, "this is a person sought after like a kind of treasure." Smith, Book I, ch. 8.[65] Writers have long talked the most bizarre nonsense about population. They have noticed isolated truths which they have not known how to reconcile nor to define clearly, and on the basis of a single inaccurate observation, they have aimed at constructing a set of laws. Governments which cannot have other than superficial ideas on anything, because they do not have time to check it out for themselves, have adopted now this set of laws, now that one, always on trust, which is a sure way of deriving no advantage, even from the truth.

It has been recognized that in a certain way poverty favored population growth. Beggars have many children. But the distinction between two kinds of poverty, that of the beggars and that of the laboring classes, has not been made. Vagabonds with absolutely nothing have many children, says Montesquieu. "It costs the father nothing to teach his art to his children, who are even, in being born, instruments of that art."[66] The people who are poor, however, only because they live under a harsh government, have few children. They do not have enough food for themselves. How could they dream of sharing it? If they live on little, this is not because they need little, but because they do not have what they need. Just as the little bit they need favors population growth among the beggars, so the little which the working classes possess goes against [319] growth in their numbers. Writers and governments have seen on the backs of beggar women, or round their huts, a crowd of wretched children. They have not lifted their gaze a year beyond, a time before which three-quarters of that unhappy generation were cut off by hunger. They have thus envisaged only half the question, and yet on the question considered in this way, the most inhuman system has been based.

The poorer people are, it has been said, the larger families are. A sophism, exclaims Montesquieu, "which has always ruined kingdoms and always

65. Adam Smith, *op. cit.*, t. I, p. 142. [The sections within quotation marks are from the 1802 French translation by Garnier, here translated back into English. Translator's note]

66. Montesquieu, *De l'esprit des lois*, Livre XXIII, Ch. 11.

will."[67] Population growth born of poverty has an evident limit, namely the death of that population because of this selfsame poverty which seemed at first to favor it. From another viewpoint it was clear that affluence favored population growth. It was thought that the luxury of the rich classes was a cause of affluence for the poor classes. There were two errors in this way of reasoning, however. First, the affluence which luxury produces is very uncertain and artificial. Luxury doubles consumption expenditures, soon rendering them disproportionate with the population. Neither the rich nor the poor multiply: the rich because they fear the privations a large family entails; the poor because of the suffering they undergo. Secondly, even true affluence favors population growth only to a certain degree. On the one hand, it makes numbers grow more, on the other it makes consumption expenditures grow. Now, the more consumption expenditures a country has, the less it can feed its inhabitants. To get the sums right, one would have to be able simultaneously to add to the means of subsistence and prevent the people from consuming more of them: an impossible task. An author who in recent years has been ridiculously mistaken about the principles of population is Sir Francis d'Ivernois in his *Historical and Political Survey of the Losses Sustained by the French Nation.* He has put the loss of life caused by the revolution at two million souls.[68] And since according to Buffon's calculations,[69] [320] a marriage must produce six children to get two of them to the normal age of a man in replacement of father and mother, you therefore have, according to him, twelve million people less for the next generation. It is a pity, as Garnier observes,[70] that he stopped after such a good start and did not push this

67. The whole passage reads: "It is condescending talk and feeble analysis which have led to its being said that the poorer people were, the larger the families would be, while the more burdened with taxes we are, the more we will equip ourselves to pay them: two sophisms which have always ruined kingdoms and always will." *Ed. cit.*, p. 689.

68. Sir Francis d'Ivernois, *Tableau historique et politique des pertes que la Révolution et la guerre ont causées au peuple français, dans sa population, son agriculture, ses colonies, ses manufactures et son commerce,* London, Impr. de Baylis, 1799, t. I, p. 18: "All I have managed to put together from witness and conjecture leads me to conclude that the scythe of Revolution and war killed between two and three million French people. It is true that I lack the documents and official papers to lend this figure evidential proof."

69. George Louis Leclerc, comte de Buffon, *Histoire naturelle générale et particulière,* t. XI, *Histoire naturelle des animaux et de l'homme,* t. II, nouvelle éd., Lausanne, J.-P. Heubach; Berne, Nouvelle Societé typographique, 1785, pp. 207–208.

70. Germain Garnier, *Notes du traducteur,* in Adam Smith, *op. cit.*, t. V, pp. 284–286, Note XXX *De ce que la guerre dernière a coûté à la population de la France.* What Constant presents as an observation by Garnier does not in any case figure in this note. Garnier is

learned reckoning one or two generations further. If he had, he would have found, from the second generation, a loss for France of seventy-two million inhabitants. Governments have no direct measure to take in relation to population. They must respect the natural course of things. Let people be happy, that is, let everyone be free to seek his own happiness, without hurting other people's, and the population will be adequate.

All detailed legislation, the prohibition on celibacy, the stigmatizing, the penalties, the rewards for getting married—none of these artificial means ever achieves the purpose envisaged, and insofar as such means interfere with freedom, they are far removed from it. The laws enforcing marriage cannot enforce population growth. Since the law of Papia Poppaea[71] forbade those who were not married to receive anything from strangers, either by the institution of inheritance or bequest, and those who being married had no children to receive more than half a legacy or bequest, the Romans contrived to repudiate their wives or make them abort after having a single child. Let us add that most of the governments which make laws against celibacy are like the Chinese scholars and mandarins who make long sermons [321] exhorting people to engage in farming, but who let their nails grow to preserve them from the very suspicion of being farmers.

What misleads superficial observers is that we sometimes see a flourishing of population in certain countries and simultaneously positive laws which encouraged the unmarried to wed. It was certainly not because of these positive laws, however, that the population flourished, but on account of other circumstances, all of which can be expressed in one word: freedom. What proves this is that in the same countries, these circumstances having changed, the population fell, although the laws remained the same or became even more severe. Consider the time of Augustus and the vain efforts of that emperor. When the vices of government do not put obstacles in the way of population, laws are superfluous. When they do, laws are bootless. The basis of population growth is growth in the means of subsistence. The basis of growth in the means of subsistence is security and calm. The basis of security and calm is justice and freedom.

---

actually quarrelling with Buffon's calculations but not in the terms Constant cites and not in the same figures.

71. This law is discussed at length by Montesquieu in *De l'esprit des lois,* Livre XXIII, Ch. 21, and by Gaëtano Filangieri, *La science de la législation, éd. cit.,* t. II, pp. 26–27.

CONSTANT'S NOTES

A. [Refers to page 227.]

The judicious Say observes that "a particular fact is not enough to destroy a general one, since we cannot be sure that some unknown circumstance has not produced the difference we see between the results of the one or the other. . . . How few particular facts are completely established! How few are observed in all their circumstances." Economie politique. Preface.[72]

B. [Refers to page 229.]

People have endlessly said that the trade with India could not be done without a company. For more than a century, however, the Portuguese undertook this commerce without a company, with more success than any other nation.[73]

[322] C. [Refers to page 231.]

Smith, V, 1.[74]

D. [Refers to page 231.]

I think it necessary to add, to prevent a finicky objection, but one which would appear justified, that I certainly do not include the technical patents we use among the set of privileges. These patents are contracts with society and accordingly legitimate. Moreover, the task of watching over the execution of these contracts falls only on the interested parties and does not therefore require any immoral or vexatious inquisition on the part of the government.

E. [Refers to page 232.]

For Birmingham and Manchester see Baert-Duholant.[75]

72. Jean-Baptiste Say, *op. cit.*, t. I, *Discours préliminaire,* pp. viii–ix.

73. Say, *op. cit.,* t. I, p. 193: "It should not be carelessly assumed that a certain commerce can absolutely not be done other than with a company. This has very often been said of the trade with India, and yet for more than a century the Portuguese did it without a company, better than any other nation."

74. Adam Smith, *op. cit.,* t. IV, pp. 130–131: "When a society of merchants undertakes, at its own expense and risk, to establish some new branch of commerce with distant and uncivilized people, it may be reasonable to incorporate it as a joint-stock bank, and to grant it if successful, the monopoly of this trade for a certain number of years."

75. Alexandre-Balthazar de Paule, baron de Baert-Duholant, *Tableau de la Grande-Bretagne, de l'Irlande et des possessions anglaises dans les quatre parties du monde,* Paris, Maradan, an X, 1802, t. I, pp. 90–93 on Birmingham and pp. 105–108 on Manchester.

F. [Refers to page 232.]

"The most sacred and most inviolable of properties is that of one's own industry, because it is the original source of all other property. The poor man's patrimony is in the strength and skill of his hands, and to prevent his using that strength and skill in the way he reckons most appropriate, as long as he hurts no one, is a manifest violation of that elemental property. It is a flagrant encroachment on legitimate freedom, as much of the workman as of those disposed to give him work. At a stroke it prevents one party from working at what he thinks opportune and the other from employing whoever seems good to him. One can quite safely trust in the good sense of him who employs a workman, to judge whether this workman deserves the job, since his interest is involved. That solicitude which the lawmaker affects, [323] for stopping one from employing incapable people, is obviously as absurd as it is oppressive."[76] See also Bentham, Principes du code civil, Partie III, Ch. 1.[77]

G. [Refers to page 233.]

Say, Economie politique, Livre I, Ch. 35.[78]

H. [Refers to page 234.]

Smith, Richesse des nations, Livre IV, Ch. 2.[79]

I. [Refers to page 236.]

Smith, Livre IV, Ch. 1.[80]

J. [Refers to page 237.]

Sismondi, Richesse commerciale, pp. 139–151.[81]

K. [Refers to page 238.]

"A tillage farmer who cannot sell his corn profitably, seeks to have it consumed to avoid the costs and losses he will undergo by keeping it. All the more grain is given to the fowls and animals if its value is down. Now, this is what is lost to human sustenance. It is not in the place where or the year when this wastefulness occurs that the consumers have to regret it. But this grain [324] would have filled a gap in some famine-stricken provinces or in a year of dearth. It would have saved the lives of whole families and prevented excessively high prices, if free trade by presenting it with an ever open outlet, had given the owner in former times a great interest in

76. Adam Smith, *op. cit.*, t. I, pp. 252–253.

77. Jeremy Bentham, *op. cit.*, t. II, pp. 176–178.

78. Jean-Baptiste Say, *op. cit.*, Livre I, Ch. 35, p. 290.

79. Adam Smith, *op. cit.*, Livre IV, Ch. 2, t. III, pp. 64–65. Constant is inspired by Smith's text rather than reproducing it faithfully.

80. *Ibid.*, t. III, pp. 3–52.

81. Jean-Charles-Léonard Sismondi, *op. cit.*, t. I, pp. 119–157.

conserving it and in not prostituting it in usages for which one could employ less valuable grains." Septième lettre de M. Turgot à l'abbé Terray, pp. 62–63.[82]

L. [Refers to page 239.]

Smith has admirably shown that the interests of the merchant who works in the inland corn trade and those of the mass of the people, seemingly at odds, are precisely the same in the years when prices are highest. Smith, Livre IV, Ch. 5.[83]

M. [Refers to page 240.]

Decree of the High Judicial Court of Paris, 2 December 1626.[84]

N. [Refers to page 240.]

See for further developments Smith, Livre IV, Ch. 5.[85] Morellet, Représentations aux magistrats, 1769.[86]

[325] O. [Refers to page 240.]

Sur la législation et le commerce des grains, p. 180.[87]

P. [Refers to page 243.]

One can find all these difficulties fully developed by the Abbé Galiani, in his Dialogues sur le commerce des blés, London, 1770.[88] I like to refer the reader to this author, though he has written in too light a tone for so serious a matter. But since he is the first and one of the most redoubtable foes of the dispensation based on

82. Anne-Robert-Jacques Turgot, *Lettres sur les grains, écrites à M. l'abbé Terray, contrôleur général, par M. Turgot, intendant de Limoges,* s.l.n.d. [1788].

83. Adam Smith, *op. cit.,* t. III, p. 207.

84. This decree forbade all persons, on pain of death, to engage in the exportation of wheat, grains, and vegetables or to construct warehouses for these commodities.

85. Adam Smith, *op. cit.,* t. III, p. 216: "However, the popular hatred to which this occupation is exposed in famine years, the only years when it can be lucrative, puts off all the people with wealth and position in the society."

86. There is a confusion over the author here: the work quoted is by Pierre-Joseph-André Roubaud, *Représentations aux magistrats contenant l'exposition raisonnée des faits relatifs à la liberté du commerce des grains et les résultats respectifs des règlements de la liberté,* s.l., 1769. The Abbé Morellet was also an expert on the grain trade, since he had written a *Réfutation de l'ouvrage qui a pour titre: Dialogue sur le commerce des blés* [of the Abbé Ferdinando Galiani], London, 1770; and an *Analyse de l'ouvrage intitulé: De la législation et du commerce des grains* [by Jacques Necker], Paris, Pissot, 1775.

87. Jacques Necker, *Sur la législation et le commerce des grains,* Paris, Pissot, 1776, p. 180: "This is an evil practice, this making compassion for the people serve to fortify proprietors' rights; it is almost to imitate the art of those terrible animals who, on the banks of the rivers of Asia, take on the voices of children in order to eat grown-ups."

88. Ferdinando Galiani, *Dialogues sur le commerce des blés,* London, 1770.

freedom, his avowals of the drawbacks of political intervention in this respect must carry great weight.

Q. [Refers to page 243.]

See the work of M. Necker, Sur la législation et le commerce des grains. He has examined in a remarkably sagacious way all the restrictions, rules, and measures which make up what is known as the policy for grains, and although his purpose was to show that constant action by the government was necessary, he has been forced to condemn all the measures which have been tried.

R. [Refers to page 244.]

See Lettres de M. Turgot to l'abbé Terray.

S. [Refers to page 245.]

See Garnier, Notes on Smith, Note XXII.[89] An estimable author [326] bases a completely opposite teaching on this point, but one which seems quite inadmissible to me. "It is appropriate," he says, "that the law should fix an interest rate for all those cases where it is due, in the absence of prior agreement, as when a judgment orders the restitution of a sum with the interest outstanding. This rate must be fixed at the lowest level of interest rates paid in the society, because the lowest rate is the one for the least risky uses. Now, the law may well want the borrower of capital to return it and even with interest. In order for him to return it, however, the law must assume he still has it. This can be assumed only insofar as he has made it profitable in the least hazardous way, earning therefore the lowest possible returns." Say, Economie politique, Livre IV, Ch. 15.[90]

1. Fixing at the lowest level the rate of interest on a wrongfully unrepaid loan rewards the borrower. An honest man, who will wish to borrow only by mutual agreement, will pay a higher rate of interest, and he who has borrowed, so to speak, coercively, that is, stolen the use of what does not belong to him, will pay a lower one. 2. It is not because society supposes a borrower in a condition to repay that it constrains him to do this, but because it is right that he repay. 3. Society's supposition cannot change the facts. If the debtor is not in a position to repay, however low the interest rate he is condemned to, he will not repay. 4. A withholder deserves a punishment. A high rate of interest is the most natural one and repairs in some degree the harm he has done. 5. In sum, according to this teaching, it would be an excellent move to seize in one way or another all the funds one could get control of short of a criminal prosecution, and lend them to others. As a withholder one would pay the lowest possible interest. As a lender one would get a higher rate.

89. Germain Garnier, *Notes du traducteur,* in Adam Smith, *op. cit.,* t. V, pp. 204–208 *Du taux de l'intérêt de l'argent.*

90. Jean-Baptiste Say, *op. cit.,* t. II, pp. 366–367.

T. [Refers to page 246.]
See Say, Economie Politique IV, Ch. 14 and Ch. 15.[91] Montesquieu, Esprit des lois, XXII, Ch. 19, Ch. 20, Ch. 21, Ch. 22.

U. [Refers to page 246.]
Richesse des nations, II, 4.[92]

[327] V. [Refers to page 246.]
Jacques Necker, De l'administration des finances, III, pp. 239–240.

W. [Refers to page 247.]
Lysias against Theomnestes; Demosthenes against Lacrites.[93]

X. [Refers to page 247.]
The numbers of smugglers arrested in France under the Monarchy was in an ordinary year some 10,700 individuals, of whom 2,300 were men, 1,800 women, and 6,600 children. [Necker] Administration des finances, II, 57. The detachment of men charged with their pursuit was more than 2,300 men and the expense between eight and nine million. *Ibid.,* 82.

Y. [Refers to page 247.]
Smith, Tome V, Garnier's translation.[94]

Z. [Refers to page 247.]
Administration des finances, II, 98.

AA. [Refers to page 248.]
The memoires of the marquis de Pombal. The Portuguese government stationed soldiers to prevent the owners from pulling up their vines. This is nothing other than a dispensation forcing government to uphold property in the face of its owners' despair.[95]

91. *Ibid.,* pp. 275–303; Ch. 14 is on lending at interest and Ch. 15 on the legal rate of interest.

92. Adam Smith, *op. cit.,* t. II, pp. 366–367: "It has to be said that if the legal rate of interest must be something above the current market rate, it still must not be too much above it. If, for example, in England the legal rate were fixed at eight or ten percent, the greater part of the money would go to spendthrifts or schemers, the only group of people willing to pay so dearly for money."

93. The references to the two Greek orators were furnished to Constant by Cornelius de Pauw, *Recherches philosophiques sur les Grecs, op. cit.,* t. I, p. 372.

94. Germain Garnier, *Notes du traducteur,* in Adam Smith, *op. cit.,* t. V, pp. 214–233.

95. Sebastien-Joseph de Carvalho e Melo, marquis de Pombal, *Mémoires,* s.l., 1784, t. I, pp. 118–124.

[328] BB. [Refers to page 248.]
Baert-Duholant.[96]

CC. [Refers to page 248.]
"By the statute of the eighth year of the reign of Elizabeth, Ch. 3, anyone who exported ewes, lambs, or rams had to undergo on the first offense confiscation in perpetuity of all his possessions and a year in prison, after which time on a market day in a town his left hand was cut off and left nailed up. Acts of the thirteenth and fourteenth years of the reign of Charles II declared the export of wool a capital offense." Smith, Livre IV, Ch. 8.[97]

DD. [Refers to page 248.]
Mémoires sur les Etats-Unis.[98]

EE. [Refers to page 248.]
Richesse des Nations, Livre IV, Ch. 9.[99]

FF. [Refers to page 249.]
See Smith, Livre I, Ch. 11.[100]

[329] GG. [Refers to page 249.]
Smith, Livre I.[101]

HH. [Refers to page 250.]
Some details of the obstacles placed in the way of work in England by the laws on domicile in the parishes.[102]

96. Alexandre-Balthazar de Paule, baron de Baert-Duholant, *Tableau de la Grande-Bretagne . . . , op. cit.*, t. IV, pp. 91–120.

97. Adam Smith, *op. cit.*, t. III, p. 473. Hofmann says Constant takes liberties with the text, but retains the meaning. [Critics of modernity rarely draw attention to the sheer savagery of economic regulation in premodern times. Translator's note]

98. Probably a reference to Charles Pictet de Rochemont, *Tableau de la situation actuelle des Etats-Unis d'Amérique*, Paris, Du Pont, 1795.

99. Adam Smith, *op. cit.*, t. III, p. 529: "If a nation could not prosper without the enjoyment of perfect freedom and justice, there is no nation in the world which would ever have been able to prosper. Fortunately, nature in her wisdom has placed in the body politic many protections proper to remedying most of the bad effects of human folly and injustice, just as she has put them in the human body to remedy those of intemperance and sloth."

100. Adam Smith, *op. cit.*, Livre I, Ch. 11, t. II, pp. 164–165: "However, the particular interest of those who follow a particular branch of commerce or manufacturing is always in some respects different and even contrary to that of the public."

101. *Ibid.*, t. I, pp. 179–201, in Ch. 9 *Des profits des capitaux.*

102. These details are brought together at the beginning of A Few Additional Points, p. 529.

II. [Refers to page 250.]
Sully's Mémoires.[103]

JJ. [Refers to page 250.]
Say, Livre I, Ch. 30.[104]

KK. [Refers to page 251.]
Smith, Livre IV, Ch. 7.[105] Say, I, Ch. 36.[106]

LL. [Refers to page 251.]
Garnier, Notes on Smith.[107]

MM. [Refers to page 251.]
Esprit des lois, XX, 12.

[330] NN. [Refers to page 251.]
When one allows oneself to censure one of M. Montesquieu's opinions, one is in duty bound to give good reasons. The one I will cite will show that this great man, so superior writing on political questions, sometimes did not apply himself to commercial questions. "Whaling," he says, Esprit des lois, XX, 6, "almost never recoups its costs; but those who have been employed in building the vessel, those who have supplied the gear, the tackle, the provisions, are also those who take the greatest interest in this whaling. If they lose on the whaling, they have earned on the supplying."[108] But if they are at once in the business of fishing [*sic*] and supplying, from whom do they earn on the supplying what they lose on the fishing? To listen

103. This reference to Sully's *Mémoires* comes from Charles Ganilh, *op. cit.*, t. I, pp. 315–316, n. 1, the text being as follows: "Sully, who did not see the benefits of manufacturing and trade, opposed the edict favoring navigation, and constantly found fault with Henry IV's provisions for establishing the manufacture of Flemish-style tapestries in France and Dutch-style linens, as well as for setting up colonies in Canada, and trading establishments in the Indies." See on this point *Mémoires de Maximilien de Béthune, duc de Sully,* Liège, F.-J. Desoer, 1788, t. V, pp. 63–72 (Livre XVI, 1603).

104. Jean-Baptiste Say, *op. cit.,* t. I, p. 247.

105. Rather than Ch. 7 it is Ch. 5, *Digression sur le commerce des blés et sur les lois y relatives,* to which Constant seems to be referring; Adam Smith, *op. cit.,* t. II, pp. 206–249. The precise idea that the regulations create an imaginary necessity is not, however, explicit in this chapter.

106. Jean-Baptiste Say, *op. cit.,* t. I, pp. 293–311; Ch. 36 is called *Du commerce des grains* and, just as in Smith, it does not feature the idea put forward by Constant.

107. Germain Garnier, *Notes du traducteur,* in: Adam Smith, *op. cit.,* t. V, pp. 202–204, Note XXI *Des erreurs de Montesquieu en économie politique.*

108. This critique of Montesquieu comes directly from Say, *op. cit.,* Livre I, Ch. 23.

to M. de Montesquieu, one would think that they indemnified themselves against their own losses. A strange kind of profit!

OO. [Refers to page 252.]
Smith, Livre IV, Ch. 9.[109]

PP. [Refers to page 255.]
See Filangieri and many others.[110]

QQ. [Refers to page 256.]
See Smith, Livre I, Ch. 7[111] and Say, Economie politique.[112]

109. Adam Smith, *op. cit.,* t. III, pp. 525–526. Constant summarizes rather than quotes here.

110. Gaëtano Filangieri, *La science de la législation,* Livre II, Ch. 15 and 16, *éd. cit.,* t. II, pp. 186–215. By "many others" Constant certainly means the physiocrats, Quesnay, Gournet, Le Mercier de la Rivière, etc.

111. Adam Smith, *op. cit.,* t. I, pp. 110–128; we read, for example: "The quantity of each product brought to market naturally adjusts itself to the effective demand."

112. Jean-Baptiste Say, *op. cit.,* t. I, pp. 241–251, Livre I, Ch. 30 *Si le gouvernement doit prescrire la nature des productions,* p. 241. Here one reads: "Truth to say, no government action has any influence on production."

BOOK XIII

On War

CH. 1. From what point of view war can be considered as having advantages. 277
CH. 2. On the pretexts for war. 279
CH. 3. The effect of the politics of war on the domestic condition of nations. 282
CH. 4. On safeguards against the war mania of governments. 286
CH. 5. On the mode of forming and maintaining armies. 289

CHAPTER ONE

From What Point of View War Can Be Considered As Having Advantages

We will not repeat here the endless denunciations of war. A number of philosophers, inspired by a love of humanity, in praiseworthy exaggeration, have seen it only from its adverse perspectives. I am happy to acknowledge its advantages.

War itself is not an evil. It is in man's nature. It favors the development of his finest and greatest faculties. It opens up to him a store of exquisite pleasures. He is indebted to it as the protector of cherished objects of his affections. He cheerfully places himself between these and danger. He acquires largeness of spirit, skill, coolness, courage, scorn for death—without which he cannot be sure he will not commit all the dastardliness demanded of him. War teaches him heroic devotion. It makes him form sublime friendships. It joins him in the tightest of bonds with his companions in arms. It renders his fatherland real so that he will defend it. It brings in turn elevated endeavor and elevated leisure. Overlong periods of peace degrade nations and make them ready for servitude.

All these advantages of war, however, are subject to an indispensable condition, namely that it results naturally from the situation and character of nations. When war results only from the ambition of governments, from their greed, their policies and calculations, then war can bring only ill.

[334] Nations of warlike character are usually free nations, because the same qualities which inspire love of war fill them with a love of freedom. Governments which are warlike against the national grain, however, are never anything but oppressive ones.

War is like all things human. They are all, in their day, good and useful. Outside it, they are all fatal. Likewise, when it is desired to uphold religion against the spirit of the age, it becomes a kind of mixture of mockery and hypocrisy. When, ignoring the peaceful character of peoples, one wishes to perpetuate war, it will consist only in oppression and massacre.

The Roman Republic, lacking commerce, letters, or art, its only domestic occupation farming, its only territory too confined for its population, surrounded by barbarian peoples, always menaced or menacing, followed its destiny in committing itself to nonstop military undertakings. A modern government which let itself be carried away by a rage for conquest, by an unquenchable thirst for domination, by endless projects of aggrandizement, and which believed it could imitate the Roman Republic, would face precisely this difference, that going against the tide of its nation and its era, it would be forced to resort to such extreme means, to such oppressive measures, to such scandalous lies, to such a multiplication of injustices, that the conquerors of its empire would be as wretched as the conquered. A people thus governed would be the Roman people, but without the freedom and the national commitment which make all sacrifices easy, without the hope every individual had of a share in the land, in short, without all the circumstances which in Roman eyes embellished this hazardous and stormy way of life.

The situation today prevents nations from being warlike in character. "The risks and fortunes of war," says an estimable writer,[1] "will never be able to offer a prospect comparable to that which today presents itself to the working man, in all countries, where work is paid the wages due to it." The new mode of combat, the changes in weaponry, artillery: these have deprived military life of what used to be most attractive about it. There is no longer a struggle against danger; there is fatality. Courage today is no longer a passion; it is indifference. One [335] no longer tastes therein that joy in will and vitality, in the development of physical strength and the moral faculties, which made hand-to-hand combat so beloved of the heroes of antiquity and the knights of the Middle Ages. War has lost its greatest charms. Thus the time it could be loved has passed. We must not let ourselves be deceived by our memories, but envisage it in a new light, the only true one in our day, as a necessity to be endured.

Considered in this way, modern war is now only a scourge. In the case of commercial, industrious, and civilized nations, with lands sufficiently extensive for their needs, with links whose interruption becomes a disaster, with no prosperity or increase in affluence to be expected from conquest, war unsettles, without compensation, every kind of social guarantee. The domestic controls it seems to authorize put individual freedom at risk. It brings a destructive acceleration to legal processes both in terms of their sanctity and their purpose. It tends to represent all the adversaries of government, all those it regards with ill will, as accomplices of the foreign enemy. Finally, troubling the security of all, war also presses on the general wealth, through the pecuniary sacrifices to which all citizens are condemned. War's very successes throw conquering nations into exhaustion. They lead only to the creation of States without bounds, whose governance

1. See Constant's Note A at the end of Book XIII.

demands limitless power and which, after having been during their span of life a cause of tyranny, are brought to collapse in the midst of crime, by countless disasters.

CHAPTER TWO
On the Pretexts for War

Governments themselves have been forced to recognize these truths for some time, at least in theory. They no longer claim that the nations are there to establish, at the price of their blood and their poverty, the disastrous fame of some of their leaders. [336] However despotic a modern leader, I think he would scarcely dare to present his subjects with his personal glory as compensation for their peace and their lives. Only Charles XII misconstrued his century thus.[2] But since that revolution in ideas, governments have invented so many pretexts for war that the peace of nations and the rights of individuals are still far from guaranteed.

We will examine only very much in passing these various pretexts. National independence, national honor, the need to make our influence respected abroad, the rounding off of our frontiers, commercial interests. What else can I say? The fact is that this vocabulary of hypocrisy and injustice is inexhaustible.

What would one say of an individual who held his honor and independence compromised as long as other individuals possessed some honor and independence, and thought himself safe only when surrounded by slaves and trembling victims? Aside from the insolence and immorality of such a reckoning, this individual would be headed for destruction, precisely and solely because hatred would unite against him those whom his skill and daring had momentarily surprised and subdued. It is the same with a State. The independence of peoples rests on equity as much as force. The kind of force necessary to hold all the other peoples in subjugation is a situation against nature. A nation which places the guarantee of its independence, or to put it more accurately, its despotism, in such force, is in greater danger than the feeblest of nations, for all public opinion, all wishes, all hatred menace it. Sooner or later this hatred, this public opinion, these wishes, will break out and envelop it. Doubtless there is something unjust about these sentiments. A people is never guilty of the excesses its government

2. King of Sweden (1682–1718), whose famous military genius Voltaire related in his *Histoire de Charles XII* (1731).

makes it commit. It is the government which leads it astray, or more often dominates it without leading it astray. But the nations which are victims of its deplorable obedience cannot take into account the hidden sentiments to which its behavior gives the lie. They blame the instruments for the excesses of the hand which directs them. The whole of France suffered from Louis XIV's ambition and detested it; [337] but Europe accused France of that ambition, and Sweden paid the penalty for the madness of Charles XII.

As for influence abroad, without our examining whether the excessive extent of that influence is not frequently a misfortune for a nation rather than an advantage, we have to consider the instability of all headstrong and disordered influence. Even when acceding to its momentary ascendancy, the world does not believe in its lasting character. Everyone in such a period, at such a given moment, will perhaps obey the dominant government. But nobody identifies its reckonings with his own. It is seen as a transient calamity. People wait until the torrent ceases to roll its waves along, sure it will perish one day in the arid sand and that they will sooner or later trample dry-footed on the earth its course has furrowed.

If the talk is of rounding off our frontiers, we will reply that guided by this pretext, the human species could never enjoy an instant of peace. No monarch to my knowledge has ever sacrificed a portion of his territory to give his lands a greater geometric regularity. So it is always outside that peoples wish to do their rounding off. This, then, is a dispensation whose basis moves to destruction of its own accord. It is one whose elements are at war and whose operation can rest only on the spoliation of the weakest, one which inexorably renders illegitimate the possessions of the strongest. International law could thereby be nothing more than a code of expropriation and barbarism. All the ideas of justice which the enlightened scholars of several centuries have brought into international relations, as into those between individuals, would be repelled and banished anew by this dispensation. The human race would step back toward those times of devastation and invasion which used to seem to us the opprobrium of history. The only difference now would be the hypocrisy, a hypocrisy all the more scandalous and corrupting in that no one would believe it. All words would lose their sense. That of moderation would presage violence, that of justice would announce iniquity. There is a theory of rounding off of frontiers which resembles, save for the good faith of those who profess it, ideal theories of the perfection of constitutions. This perfection is never attained, [338] but every day it serves to motivate some new upheaval.

Were someone to put forward the interests of commerce, I would ask whether people believed in good faith that we serve commerce by depopulating a country of its most thriving young men, uprooting the labor most necessary to agriculture, manufacturing, and other production, by raising between other peoples and oneself barriers sprinkled with blood? "War costs more than its expenses," a wise writer has said; "it costs everything it stops from being earned."[3] Commerce rests on a good understanding of nations between themselves. It is sustained only by justice. It rests on equality. It prospers in peace. Yet it is for the sake of commerce that a nation is to be kept in nonstop wars, that universal hatred is to be heaped on its head, that the march is to be from one injustice to another, that every day credit is to be disrupted by violence, and that equals are absolutely not to be tolerated.

During the French Revolution a pretext for war hitherto unknown was invented, that of delivering nations from the yoke of their governments, which we took to be illegitimate and tyrannical. Under this pretext death and devastation were brought into places where men either lived peacefully under faulty institutions, ones nevertheless softened by time and habit, or had enjoyed for several centuries all the benefits of freedom. A period forever shameful, in which we saw a perfidious government inscribe sacred words on its guilty standards, to trouble the peace, violate the independence, destroy the prosperity of its innocent neighbors, adding to the scandal of Europe by lying protestations of respect for the rights of man and of zeal for humanity. The worst conquest is the hypocritical type, says Machiavelli, as if he had predicted our history. *Discourses on the First Ten Books of Titus Livy*.[4]

To give a people freedom in spite of itself is only to give it slavery. Conquered nations can contract neither free spirits nor habits. Every society must repossess for itself rights which have been invaded, if it is worthy of owning them. Masters cannot impose freedom. For nations [339] which enjoy political freedom, conquests have furthermore, beyond anything else we might hypothesize, this most clearly insane feature, that if these nations stay faithful to their principles, their triumphs cannot help but lead to their depriving themselves of a portion of their rights in order to communicate them to the conquered.

When a nation of ten million people governed by its representatives adds to its territory a province in which a million more live, what it gains is the

3. See Constant's Note B at the end of Book XIII.

4. Hofmann failed to find this quotation from Machiavelli.

loss of a tenth of its representation, since it transfers this tenth to its new fellow citizens.

One is forced to believe that the absurdity of the politics of conquest in conjunction with a representative constitution, somehow eluded the republican government of France. Ancient habits have so great an empire over men, however, that they act in virtue of these habits, even when they have solemnly abjured them. Under the Directory, by dint of victories and territorial mergers, France came close to being represented in the main by foreigners. Every new success was for the French one less French representative.

CHAPTER THREE

The Effect of the Politics of War on the Domestic Condition of Nations

After our examination of the most specious pretexts of war on the part of modern governments, let us dwell on one of their effects, one in my view insufficiently remarked on hitherto. This politics of war casts into society a mass of men whose outlook is different from that of the nation and whose habits form a dangerous contrast with the patterns of civil life, with the institutions of justice, with respect for the rights of all, with those principles of peaceful and ordered freedom which must be equally inviolable under all forms of government.

Over the last sixteen years there has been much talk about armies composed of citizens. To be sure, we do not wish to visit insults on those who so gloriously defended our national independence, on those who by so many immortal exploits founded the French Republic. When enemies dare to attack a people on its territory, the citizens become soldiers to repulse them. They were citizens, [340] they were the leading citizens, those who freed our soil from the profaning foreigner. In dealing with a general question, however, we must set aside remembrance of glory, which surrounds and dazzles us, seductive and captivating feelings of gratitude. In the present state of European societies the words "citizen" and "soldier" imply a contradiction. A citizen army is possible only when a people is virtually confined to a single city-state. Then the soldiers of that nation can rationally justify obedience. When they are in the bosom of their native land, between governors and governed whom they know, their understanding can count for something in their submission. A very large country, however, whether monarchy or republic, renders that supposition absolutely chimerical.

A very large country requires from soldiers a mechanistic subordination and makes them passive, unreflective, and docile agents. As soon as they are displaced, they lose all the prior information capable of illuminating their judgment. The size of the country permitting those in charge of the armed forces to dispatch the natives of one province to another distant one, these men, subject to a discipline which isolates them from the local natives, are only strangers to the latter, although they are nominally their compatriots. They see only their commanders, know only them, obey their orders alone. Citizens in their birthplace, everywhere else they are soldiers. Once an army is among strangers, however it is organized, it is only a physical force, a pure instrument. The experience of the Revolution demonstrated only too well the truth of what I am affirming. We were told it was important for soldiers to be citizens, so they would never turn their arms against the people, and yet we have seen the unfortunate conscripts taken away from their ploughs, not only to contribute to the seige of Lyon, which could not be other than an act of civil war, but also to make themselves instruments of torture of the Lyonnais, disarmed prisoners, which was an act of implicit obedience and discipline, of [341] precisely that discipline and that obedience from which we had believed that the citizen soldiers would always be able to protect themselves.

A large army, whatever its basic elements, contracts, involuntarily, an esprit de corps. Such a spirit always seizes hold of organizations assembled for a single purpose, sooner or later. The only lasting thing men have in common is their interest. In all countries, in all centuries, a confederation of priests has formed, within the State, a State apart. In all centuries and countries, men associated together in the army for long periods have separated themselves from the nation. The very soldiers of freedom, in fighting for such, conceive a kind of respect for the use of force, regardless of its purpose. Without knowing it they contract thereby morals, ideas, and habits which are subversive of the cause they defend. The measures which ensure the triumph of war prepare the collapse of the law. The military spirit is haughty, swift, swaggering. Law must be calm, often slow, and always protective. The military spirit detests the thinking faculties as incipient indiscipline. All legitimate government rests on enlightenment and conviction. So in the annals of nations we often see armed force driving enemies from the territory; but we also see it no less often handing the fatherland over to its chiefs. It carries the glory of nations to the highest level; but it also adds their rights to the tally of their conquests, to be ceremoniously deposited at the feet of the Triumpher. We see the Roman legions, composed at least in part of citizens of a Republic illustrious from six centuries of victories, men born under freedom, surrounded by monuments raised by twenty generations of heroes to that tutelary deity, trample underfoot the ashes of Cincinnatus and the Camilli and march to the orders of a usurper, to profane the tombs of their ancestors and enslave the eternal city.[5] We see the English legions who, with their own hands, had broken the throne of kings and shed their blood for twenty years to establish a republic spring into action with Cromwell against that nascent republic and impose on the people a tyranny more shameful than the chains from which their valor had delivered it.

[342] The idea of citizen soldiers is singularly dangerous. When armed men are directed against unarmed governments or peaceful individuals, it is said that citizens are being opposed to citizens. The Directory had the soldiers deliberate beneath their banners, and when it ordered a political opinion from them as if it were a drill, it said that citizen soldiers, far from having less right than the others, had more, since they had fought for the fatherland. Thus did the military spirit emerge in the Republic. It was claimed that for freedom as for victory, nothing was more appropriate than swift movements. Opinions were seen as like troops, to enroll or to fight, representative assemblies as agencies of command, opposition to them as acts of indiscipline, law courts as camps, judges as warriors, the accused as enemies, trials as battles. So it is not immaterial that there be created in a country, systematically, by way of war prolonged or constantly renewed under various pretexts, a mass of men imbued exclusively with the military spirit. The severest despotism becomes inevitable, if only to contain these men. And this is itself a great evil, that there should be a large minority of people containable only by the severest discipline. But these men, against whom despotism is called for, are at the same time despotism's instruments against the rest of the nation. It is hard for soldiers, whose first duty is obedience to the slightest signal, not to persuade themselves effortlessly that all citizens are subject to this duty.

Detailed safeguards against this danger, the most terrible which can menace a nation, are not enough. Rome had taken strong ones. No army could come near the capital. No soldier under arms could exercise citizen rights. It is always easy, however, for a government to evade these precautions. In vain we may give the legislative power the right to move the troops away, to fix their numbers, to block those of their movements whose hostile intentions seem apparent—and finally power to disband them. These

5. See Constant's Note C at the end of Book XIII.

means are at once extreme and impotent. Executive power must have de jure, and [343] always has de facto, control of the armed forces. Charged with watching over public security, it can make trouble break out to justify the arrival of a group of regiments. It can make them come in secret, and when they are gathered it can extract from the legislative power the appearance of agreement. All the safeguards which require the legislature to deliberate subsequently on the danger which threatens it turn in a vicious circle. The legislature has power to act only at the moment when the peril is displayed, that is to say, when the harm is done, and when the harm is done the legislative power can no longer act.

The military spirit, however, wherever it exists, is stronger than the written laws. It is this spirit which must be restrained. Only a national spirit focused on another purpose can do this. The national spirit communicates itself from the nation to the army, whatever the composition of the latter. When this national spirit does not exist, the soldiers, though formerly citizens, adopt the military spirit nonetheless. When this national spirit exists, the military spirit, even among soldiers who are not citizens, is checked by this, and tyranny itself is softened. "Those who corrupted the Greek republics," says Montesquieu,[6] "did not always become tyrants. That is because they were more attached to eloquence than the art of war."

Under whatever point of view we consider this terrible question of war, we have to be convinced that any enterprise of this kind which does not have a defensive purpose is the worst outrage a government can commit, because it brings together the disastrous effects of all the outrages of government. It endangers all kinds of freedom, harms every interest, tramples underfoot all rights, combines and authorizes all the forms of domestic and foreign tyranny, depraves the rising generations, divides the nation into two parts, of which one scorns the other and passes readily from scorn to injustice, prepares future destructions by way of past ones, and purchases with the misfortunes of the present those of the future.

These truths are not new, and I do not offer them as such, but truths which seem recognized often need repetition.[7] For [344] government, while

6. See Constant's Note D at the end of Book XIII.

7. This reflection can be compared with what Constant says in his *Journal intime,* 10 June 1804: "The new ideas one has should be announced as new only as little as possible. On the contrary, they should be given as far as may be [344] the appearance of received wisdom, so that they may be accepted less painfully. And if one is obliged to agree on the novelty of one of one's ideas, it should be surrounded with a whole cortege of ideas to which the public is already more accustomed."

calling them commonplaces, in its haughty disdain constantly treats them like paradoxes. It is, furthermore, a rather remarkable thing, that while our government, in all its public speeches, in all its communication with the people, professes the love of peace and a desire to give the world tranquillity, men who claim to be devoted to that government write daily that the French nation being essentially warlike, military glory is the only kind worthy of her and that France must win renown by her military brilliance. These men ought to tell us how military glory can be acquired other than through war and how the purpose they are proposing to the French people alone fits in with the peace of the whole world. I might well add that these authors themselves may never have thought about it. Happy to speak in flowery language, sometimes on one subject, sometimes on another, following the fashion of the moment, they rely, rightly, on forgetfulness to cover up their inconsistency.[8] I have sometimes thought that this doctrine, wherever it dared to present itself, deserved rebuffing, and that it was worthwhile discomfitting writers who, when they deal with future government, recommend despotism, because they hope never to be other than its agents and, when dealing with international relations, see nothing so glorious as war, as if from the depths of their obscure study, they were the distributors of all the scourges which can weigh on the human race.

CHAPTER FOUR

On Safeguards against the War Mania of Governments

We ought now to indicate some safeguards against the unjust or pointless wars which governments may undertake, [345] since, in the present state of society, those undertakings which are great evils in themselves also lead to all the other ills. But general maxims would be inadequate and reflections on constitutional limits which can be assigned to government would take us beyond the boundaries of this work.

Nothing is easier to judge in the light of reason than the measures of government in relation to war. Public opinion is always accurate enough in this matter because the interest of one and all speaks out loud and clear on this question. Everyone thinks war is a fatal thing. Everyone also feels that cowardly patience when foreigners hurt or insult us, inviting them to

8. On these writers who preach war thus, see Constant's letter of 13 messidor an X (2 July 1803) to Fauriel, in: Victor Glachant, *Benjamin Constant sous l'oeil du guet,* Paris, Plon, 1906, pp. 50–51.

become doubly vainglorious and unfair, sooner or later brings the war we wanted to avoid, and that once hostilities have begun, arms cannot be put down until we have acquired solid safeguards for the future, since a shameful peace is only a cause of new wars with less favorable prospects. But just as public opinion is infallible on this question, so it is impossible to prescribe or determine anything in advance.

To say we must confine ourselves to defensive wars is to say nothing. It is easy for governments to insult or menace their neighbors to such an extent that they feel bound to attack, and in this case the guilty party is not the aggressor, but the one who, joining treachery to violence, forced the other to aggression. Thus defense can sometimes be only adroit hypocrisy while attack may become a legitimate defensive precaution. One can affirm that any war which national feeling disapproves of is unjust; but no means exist for ascertaining this national feeling. Governments alone have the floor. They can seize the press exclusively, and their creatures and writers, speaking in the name of a silent, repressed people, form a concert of artificial agreement which prevents real public opinion from making itself heard.

As for the nations which enjoy political freedom, we would probably find in the public discussions of political assemblies, in the consent to taxes or their refusal, in ministerial responsibility, means of checking abuses relating to war, in a way which, if not satisfactory, is at least generally useful and such as to prevent the worst excesses. Furthermore, we would find, [346] on close inspection, that these guarantees are too often illusory, that it is always easy for the executive power to start a war, that the legislative power is then forced to support it against foreigners the executive has provoked, that if, in propping up that executive, the legislature engages in censure, the enemy will be encouraged by this disagreement between the branches of government, that the armed forces will be less ardent in a war disapproved of by the nation's representatives, that the people will cooperate less by way of pecuniary sacrifices, that the government, feeling itself accused, will bring to its operations less decisiveness, less certainty, less speed, that the hostile claims will get larger, that peace will become more difficult to conclude, simply because the war will have fallen under public disapprobation. I do not mean that there is no remedy for these drawbacks. On the contrary, I think it would be possible to indicate one, the seed of which is present in several nations, though it does not yet exist completely in any single one. We could not examine this issue here, however, without distorting this book totally. We have kept separate from it everything concerning political freedom, and we would find ourselves drawn by it into all the discussions about constitutions. For all questions of this sort hold tightly together. For a constitution to work in one respect, it has to do so for all the others.

You may believe that a representative assembly can stop the executive power in its military undertakings. For a representative assembly to impose its will on the executive power, however, it must derive its commission from a legitimate source, it must be armed with prerogatives and encircled with guarantees which put its independence beyond all danger. If it is armed with extensive prerogatives, it must also at the same time be contained in its acts and checked in its excesses, since an unrestrained assembly is more dangerous than the most absolute despot. Thus from whatever part of the circle you start, you will be forced to go around it entirely before arriving at a satisfactory result.

I will make one reflection only on political constitutions, because I am not aware that any such reflection has ever been made. Some modern writers claim that the institutions which limit and separate the powers are only misleading formalities which governments skillfully elude. Even if this were true, these formalities would still be useful. Governments obliged to elude them have less time to devote to foreign undertakings. They are [347] too busy at home to be looking outside for some meretricious occupation. Despots keep their subjects in far-off wars to distract them from domestic matters. People who want to enjoy some peace must give government something to do at home, so as not to be precipitated by its idleness and ambition into the calamities of war.

I will add that I am far from agreeing that the institutions protecting freedom are only worthless formalities. They give citizens a great feeling of their importance, a great enjoyment of this feeling, and a lively interest in the prosperity of the State. In this way, independently of their direct advantages, they are advantageous in creating and maintaining public spirit. This public spirit is the only effective guarantee. It is based in public opinion; it penetrates the offices of ministers; it modifies or stops their projects without their knowing. But take good note that this public spirit comes much more from the organization of government than from its actions. An absolute government under a virtuous despot can be very gentle without creating any public spirit. A limited government may, under a bad prince, be very vexatious despite its limits, yet for all that the public spirit will not be destroyed. But, I repeat: all these things are foreign to our topic.

CHAPTER FIVE

On the Mode of Forming and Maintaining Armies

The aversion of modern nations to the hazards of war, which have ceased to be pleasures, makes the question of recruitment very difficult. When the spirit of the human race was warlike, men ran to combat. Today they have to be dragged to it.

The rights of government in regard to recruitment very much need to be fixed. If it is invested in this respect with boundless power, it is as if it had unlimited sway over everything. What does it matter if it cannot arrest citizens at home and keep them indefinitely in dungeons, if it can send them, them or their children, to die on faraway shores, if it can have this threat hover above the heads of loved ones and bring [348] despair into every home at will, by the exercise of bogus right?

There are two modes of recruitment, which subdivide again, but to one or the other of which one can relate all the different ways adopted in all countries.

The first consists in imposing on all citizens of a given age the duty of bearing arms for a certain number of years; the other is free and voluntary recruitment.

The drawbacks of the first mode are incontestable.

In certain periods of human life, interruptions to the exercise of intellectual or working faculties are never made good. The dangerous, careless, and coarse ways of soldiering, the sudden rupture of all family dealings, mechanical thralldom to minute duties when the enemy is not around, complete independence of moral ties at the age when the passions are most actively in ferment, these are not immaterial things in terms of morality and education. Condemning to a life in camps and barracks the younger sons of the affluent classes, in which reside, in short, education, refinement, and right thinking, as well as that tradition of gentleness, nobility, and elegance which alone distinguishes us from barbarians, this is to do the whole nation an ill uncompensated either by worthless success or the profitless terror she inspires. To commit to the soldier's life the merchant's son, or the artist's, the magistrate's, the young man devoted to letters, to science, to the exercise of some difficult and complicated activity, is to rob him of the fruit of all his previous education. This education itself will be affected in advance by the prospect of an inevitable interruption. Parental zeal will be discouraged. The young man's imagination will be struck for good or ill by what lies in store. However his imagination may react to all this, his application can only be the worse. If he is intoxicated by brilliant dreams of military glory, he will scorn peaceful study, sedentary occupations, work of application contrary to his fancies, and the changeableness of his nascent faculties. If he thinks of himself sorrowfully as being dragged away from home, if he works out how much the sacrifice of several years will retard his progress, he will despair of himself. He will not want to exhaust himself in efforts whose fruits an iron hand will steal from him. He will tell himself that since his country contends with him for the time necessary to acquire [349] his learning, perfect the art he cultivates or the work he has embraced, it is pointless to struggle against power; he will resign himself, lazily, to what lies in store.

If, transforming in some way the obligation to bear arms into a tax on the rich, you restrict it in reality to the working-class poor, although this inequality seems to have something more revolting about it, then probably it will be less dire in its results than so-called equality, which weighs on all classes. An unskilled laborer or a day laborer suffers less from the interruption of his routine job than men committed to jobs demanding experience, assiduity, watchfulness, and thought. Plucking a farmer's son away from his plough, you do not render him incapable of resuming his first job on his return. Other drawbacks are apparent, however, ones of no less importance. You will see parents punished for the faults of their children, with children's interests separated from those of their fathers as a result, with families reduced either to uniting to resist the law, or to division so that one part can constrain the other to obedience, fatherly love treated like a crime, the filial tenderness which does not wish to abandon a father to old age and isolation turned into revolt and struck down harshly, spying and informing, those eternal resources of government once it has created bogus crimes, encouraged and rewarded, odious duties imposed on lesser magistrates, with men unleashed like ferocious mastiffs, in town and country, to pursue and lock up fugitives, innocent in the light of morality and nature. And perhaps all these vexations take place, not for legitimate defense but in order to facilitate the invasion and devastation of faraway regions whose possession adds nothing to the national prosperity, unless one calls the worthless renown of a few men and their fatal celebrity, national prosperity.[9]

9. See Constant's Note E at the end of Book XIII.

The arguments pleaded in favor of institutions which force all citizens to bear arms resemble in some respects those of the enemies of property, which, under the pretext of a primitive equality, wish to divide manual labor without distinction between all men, not reflecting that the [350] work split thus will not only be less useful, since it will be badly done, but that moreover it would block all continuity, all specialized work, all the good effects of habit and concentration of effort, and thereby all progress, all perfectioning. Similarly, military life, seizing all the generations in turn during their youth, would infallibly cast a nation into brutishness and ignorance.

The only drawback of the second mode, I mean free and voluntary recruitment, is possible insufficiency.

I think this insufficiency is much exaggerated. The obstacles to recruitment the government finds always pertain to the futility of the war. Once a just war is involved, these obstacles diminish. Public opinion speaks, everyone's interest makes itself heard. Everybody is drawn by this interest and this opinion. Each soul comes to life. Each offers himself to march to battle, aware of the cause. National movement exists, which the government has no need to create by orders and threats. It has only to direct it.

One can affirm this fearlessly. If governments undertook only just wars, if at home too they took justice as their standard, they would find very few obstacles to the composition of armies. In the present condition of Europe we do not at all dispute their right to maintain a standing military force even in time of peace, and to impose on citizens certain duties for the formation and maintenance of this force. But on the assumption that the government would undertake only legitimate wars, that is, motivated by the need for defense, although circumstances might render them offensive, how much less numerous on this assumption, we repeat, would the indispensable military force be, and how much simpler would it be for the citizens to fulfill these duties! Do not be distrustful then of their zeal. They are not slow to run to take up arms for their fatherland, when they have one. They spring to the maintenance of their independence abroad when they possess security at home. When they remain motionless and have to be constrained, it is because they have nothing to lose, and whose fault is that?

It might be objected perhaps that this unanimous movement cannot take place in a very large polity, that men run to the defense of their frontiers only when those frontiers are [351] near their homes and that a war occasioned by entry of an enemy in a faraway province will not produce in the center or at the opposite end of the country either indignation or zeal to repel it. First of all, this assertion is much more contestable than one might think. Suppose a great free people, happy in its freedom, attached by the feeling of good fortune to its government. It will contract wider and more generous ideas than those people who base their power on the degradation of the human race like to believe. Just as men used to freedom see in the oppression of a single citizen, however unknown he may be to them, a punishable assault against the whole of civil society, so also a nation which has a fatherland sees in the invasion of a part of its territory an insult made to the whole of that fatherland. The enjoyment of freedom creates a feeling of national pride so refined and easily offended that government has more often to restrain than arouse it. Doubtless this truth has limits. What follows from it, though, is simply that large countries must have it too. When a country is so extensive that no national link can exist between its different provinces, I can scarcely conceive the argument for this excessive extent.

A nation refuses to defend itself against an enemy which menaces it or to contribute in sufficient proportion to the establishment necessary for the security of the country it inhabits, only when its government by its injustices has detached it from its interests, or when this government's frenzied ambition, wishing to set up everywhere at the expense of its subjects a tyrannical domination, demands efforts and sacrifices which neither the security nor the prosperity of this nation requires. This government is then reduced to dragging its slaves to war in irons.

Nevertheless, that voluntary recruitment be supposed insufficient suffices to oblige us to indicate the remedy for this insufficiency. It has been said that if a government were not good enough to inspire in its subjects the desire to defend it, then it must bear the penalty for its vices. This is true. But no government will resign itself to that. It is pointless proposing principles whose nature is such that they will not be observed.

When voluntary recruitment is insufficient, the government must indeed be given the right to resort to conscription. When it is not accorded this right, it will take it. To combine this prerogative, however, with a degree of freedom and individual security, we have to revert to political freedom, for as we said at the start, if the right to conscription is not strictly limited, there are no longer any limits to despotism. Everything [352] leads us back therefore, in spite of ourselves and by every route, to political freedom.

The representatives of the nation must determine how, in what numbers, in what conditions, and for what end the citizens must be obliged to march to the defense of their country. This determination by the nation's representatives must not be permanent, but it must happen each time circumstances demand it, and it must cease, by law, when the circumstances have changed. And this forces us to repeat what we said above, about all the prerogatives to be granted to the representative assemblies in order for them to attain their goal.[10] For if they are weak and dependent, they will vote for everything the executive power wishes.

10. On pp. 287–288, but the reference is not clear.

CONSTANT'S NOTES

A. [Refers to page 278.]
Ganilh, I, 237.

B. [Refers to page 281.]
Say, V, Ch. 8.[11]

C. [Refers to page 284.]
"Nec civis meus est, in quem tua classica Caesar,
Audiero. . . .
His aries actus disperget saxa lacertis
Illa licet penitus tolli quam jusseris urbem
Roma sit. . . ." Pharsale.[12]
[Nor is he my fellow citizen, against whom I shall have heard your trumpet signals, Caesar. . . . The ram driven by these shoulders shall scatter the stones, even if that city which you have ordered to be utterly destroyed be Rome.][13]

D. [Refers to page 285.]
Esprit des lois, VIII.[14]

E. [Refers to page 290.]
There were under the monarchy 60,000 militiamen in France; the period of service was six years. Thus fate fell every year on 10,000 men. Administration des finances, I, 30. M. Necker called the militia a frightful lottery. What would he have said about conscription?

11. Jean-Baptiste Say, *op. cit.*, t. II, p. 426.

12. Lucain, *La guerre civile (La pharsale)*, Livre I, vv. 373–374 and 384–386. See the edition by A. Bourgery, Paris, Les Belles Lettres, 1926, t. I, pp. 17–18. "It is no longer my fellow citizen, against whom I will have heard the call of your trumpets, Caesar [. . .] our arms will push the battering ram which will sunder the foundation walls of the city whose annihilation you command, even were it Rome."

13. [The French translator thinks the "arms" are "ours." The Latin has "these shoulders." Translator's note]

14. In Ch. 2 *De la corruption du principe de la démocratie.*

BOOK XIV

On Government Action on Enlightenment

Ch. 1. Questions to be dealt with in this book. 297

Ch. 2. On the value attributed to errors. 298

Ch. 3. On government in support of truth. 301

Ch. 4. On government protection of enlightenment 304

Ch. 5. On the upholding of morality. 307

Ch. 6. On the contribution of government to education. 308

Ch. 7. On government duties vis-à-vis enlightenment. 315

CHAPTER ONE

Questions to Be Dealt with in This Book

The relations between government and enlightenment are of a kind even more difficult and delicate to determine than those concerning only external and material things: actions, property, or production. Man's orientation is to independence in the exercise of all his faculties, but he feels the need for it above all in the exercise of thought. The more he reflects, the more aware he becomes that all his thoughts form a whole, an indissoluble chain from which it is impossible to break off or remove arbitrarily a single link. Religion can dominate thought because it can become thought itself. Government cannot. These two things have between them no real point of contact.

The materialists often repeated against the doctrine of pure spirit an objection which lost its force only when a less daring philosophy made us recognize the impotence we suffer with respect to understanding anything regarding what we call matter or what we entitle spirit. Pure spirit cannot act on matter, they said. One could say, with greater reason and without losing oneself in subtle metaphysics, that where government is concerned, matter cannot act on spirit. Now government, *qua* government, never has anything but matter at its disposal. Government changes in nature when it wishes to employ reasoning, and rather than dominating the reflective mode, subjects its own reasoning to the latter. Seeking to win the argument, government recognizes the criteria of reflection. Consequently, we always find that after a few tries of this kind government realizes it is now out of its element, deprived of its habitual weapons; and when it wishes to reassume them, its struggle with thought begins anew.

To confer the management of enlightenment on government, one must [358] suppose either that men cannot from their own resources arrive at truths the knowledge of which is salutary to them, or that there are certain truths whose discovery would be dangerous and that consequently there are certain errors which it is useful to maintain. On the first supposition we charge government with the destruction of error, on the second with its protection.

This leads us back to a subject we have dealt with earlier.[1] The means government has for the maintenance of error consist in large measure of restrictions imposed on the manifestation of thought. We will not come

1. In Book VIII.

back to this issue, which I think has been sufficiently clarified. But the principle itself of the usefulness of errors seems worthy of some exploration. This often troubled issue has not yet in my view been considered as it ought to be. A few words will suffice to resolve it if it is considered properly, and we will show in these few words that the supporters of this policy have not gone deeply into their own opinion.

CHAPTER TWO

On the Value Attributed to Errors

There is no doubt that the apparent consequence of an error can be very useful; that is, the effect which seems bound to result from it naturally can appear very advantageous. The real difficulty, however, is that nothing guarantees that the moral effect of an error will be such as one supposes or wishes. The supporters of useful errors fall into a misapprehension which we have pointed out elsewhere.[2] They bring into their calculations only the purpose and do not consider the effect of the means used to secure it. They consider such error only as something established in isolation, forgetting the danger of giving man the habit of error. Reason is a faculty which improves or deteriorates. Imposing error on man causes the faculty to deteriorate. You break the connectedness of his thought. Who can guarantee it will not break again when it comes to the application of the error you [359] have inculcated in him? If it were given to man to invert, just once, the order of the seasons, whatever advantage he might derive from this privilege in a particular circumstance, he would nonetheless experience as a result an incalculable disadvantage, in that subsequently he would no longer be able to rely on the uniform sequence and unvarying regularity which serve as a base for his working activities. Moral nature is like physical nature. Any error distorts the mind, since to penetrate it, error must stop it moving according to its purpose, from principle to consequence. Whose assurance have you that this operation will not constantly repeat itself? Who can trace the path a mind which has abandoned reason's path must follow? An error is an impetus, its direction incalculable. In creating that impetus and by the very operation you had to perform to create it, you have placed yourself outside the ability to control it. Therefore you must fear the thing seeming least likely to result from it. It is by a petitio principii that you say: such and such an error is favorable to morality. Not so, since in order for that error

2. In Book III, Ch. 5.

truly to be favorable to morality it would be necessary for the man who had falsely reasoned in adopting that error, to reason rightly in departing from that given point, and nothing is less certain. A mind you have got used to reasoning falsely on such and such an occasion, when the imperfection of his logic seemed convenient to you and fitted in with your views, will reason falsely on another such occasion and then the viciousness of his reasoning will run counter to your intentions. A particular man may adopt absurd ideas on the nature of a supreme being. He imagines Him incomprehensible, vindictive, jealous, capricious, and so on. If he nevertheless went on to reason well henceforth on the basis of these givens, despite their absurdity they could still regulate his behavior usefully. He would say to himself: "this all-powerful being, often bizarre, sometimes cruel, nevertheless wills the maintenance of human societies, and in our uncertainty as to his particular wishes, the surest way of pleasing him is justice, which satisfies his general will." But instead of this kind of reasoning, this mind, sufficiently misled to have adopted an absurd initial premise, will probably go from supposition to supposition, from mystery to mystery, from absurdity to absurdity, until he has forged himself a morality utterly contrary to the kind we believed we had entrusted to the safekeeping of religion. Therefore it is not advantageous to deceive men, even when a momentary advantage can be gained from this expedient. The general who tells his troops that the thunderbolt's roar presages victory, [360] risks seeing his soldiers take to flight if some more cunning deceiver persuades them that this terrible noise signifies the anger of the gods. Similarly, those enormous animals which barbarous peoples put in the vanguard of their armies to drive them onto their enemies would suddenly recoil, terror-struck or overcome with fury, and failing to recognize their masters' voice, crush or scatter the very battalions which were expecting their salvation and triumph to come from them. But here is quite another difficulty. The errors you call useful necessitate a series of ideas different from the sequence for which nature intended us. Should chance uncover some truth for us, that false series is broken. What will you do then? Reestablish it by force? There you will be, carried back to prohibitive laws, whose impotence and danger we have demonstrated elsewhere.[3]

Moreover, this would be a great inconsistency on your part. Having asserted on principle that man is not up to being governed by truth and that error, by subjugating the mind, absolves us from forcible means,

3. In Book XII, Ch. 4.

straightaway you are going to use them to uphold the very same error whose advantage ought to be that it makes them superfluous. To maintain public order you have recourse to what you call illusions, and you are lost in admiration of this expedient, so much gentler according to you, and no less efficacious, than penal laws. Doubt is cast, however, on your tutelary illusions. You cannot defend them by ideas of like nature: the sanction itself is attacked. Will you call the law to your aid? That severity which in the name of public peace you recently boasted of not employing, will you now invoke it in support of the errors you believe necessary to that peace? You might as well have saved yourself this long detour, it seems to me, and merely been harsh on the crime, which would have spared you the odium of persecuting thought. Your task would have been easier, for thought will escape you a thousand times more readily than actions would have. Finally, one objection to the usefulness of errors presents itself, one we have already given an account of in this book[4] and will for that reason make do with a sketch of. The discredit which attaches to proven error also comes back, by way of blind fanaticism and clumsy reasoning, on the [361] truth associated with that error. "Men of good will," says Bentham,[5] "think one should never remove from morality any one of its props, even when it is out of true. . . . But when a man of depraved mind has triumphed by means of a false argument, he always thinks he has triumphed over morality itself." Errors are always fatal, both because of the effect they produce on the mind itself and because of the means indispensable, to put it succinctly, to secure their durability. The errors which seem most salutary to you are only scourges in disguise. You want a government maintained. You thrust aside the truths opposed to the principles on which this government rests. You encourage the errors contrary to these truths. But a government can be overthrown by a thousand unpredictable causes. Then, the more the errors you have encouraged have put down deep roots, the more the truths you have rebuffed will be unknown. The less men are prepared for what will have to be put in place of that which no longer exists, the more violence, misfortune, and disorder there will be in the overthrow and its consequences.

It can be affirmed with confidence that whenever people believe they have observed an abuse attributable to enlightenment, in fact enlightenment

4. In Book I, Ch. 3: "For as long as reason is not convinced, error is ready to reappear at the first event which unleashes it."

5. See Constant's Note A at the end of Book XIV.

has been in short supply. Always when truth is accused of wrongdoing, this evil has been the effect not of truth but of error. Providence has numbered among men's needs the search for truth. To say truth can be dangerous is to proffer a terrible accusation against providence. This hypothesis sees providence as having marked out for the human race a route it is condemned to follow by irresistible impulsion, a route which finishes in an abyss.

Moreover, truth is unitary and errors countless.[6] What are your means for choosing among the host of errors? Error is to truth as Machiavellianism is to morality. If you abandon truth in order to plunge into the cunning schemes of Machiavellianism, you are never sure of having chosen the best among these schemes. If you renounce the search for truth, you are never certain of having chosen the most useful error.

[362] Truth is not just good to know; it is good to search for. Even when we go wrong in that search, we are happier than in renouncing it. The idea of truth is peace for the spirit, as the idea of morality is for the heart.

CHAPTER THREE

On Government in Support of Truth

Very well, someone will say, since error is always fatal, government must keep men from it and lead them to truth. But what means has government for finding it? We demonstrated at the start of this work that those who govern are as prone to error as the governed.[7] Moreover, the objections we have leveled against so-called useful errors, apply almost equally to the truths the government might wish to inculcate and have brought in on its authority. Government support, even for truth, turns into a source of error. Truth's natural support is obvious rightness. The natural road to truth is via reasoning, comparison, analysis. To persuade man that the obviousness, or what seems such to him, is not the only reason which must determine his opinions, that reasoning is not the only road he must follow, is to pervert his intellectual faculties. It is to establish a false relationship between the opinion he is presented with and the instrument with which he must judge it. It is no longer according to the intrinsic worth of the opinion he must decide, but according to alien considerations, which pervert his intelligence as soon

6. See *De la force du gouvernement,* Ch. 7, p. 94, note: "Truth is one, but error is multiform."

7. In Book III, Ch. 3.

as it follows in that direction. Let us suppose the government infallible in arrogating to itself the right to say what truth is. In this matter it will still use diverse means, it will still disfigure both the truth it proclaims and the intelligence whose own abnegation it ordains. M. de Montesquieu rightly says[8] that a man condemned to death by laws he has consented to is politically freer than he who lives peacefully under [363] laws instituted without the agreement of his will. It would be equally right to say that the adoption of an error on our own accord, because it seems true to us, is an operation more favorable to the perfectioning of the mind than the adoption of a truth on the say-so of any government whatever. In the former case, analysis is formative. If this analysis in the particular circumstance does not lead us to happy results, we are on the right track even so. Persevering in our scrupulous, independent investigation, we will get there sooner or later. Under the latter supposition we are reduced to a plaything of the government before which we have humbled our own judgment. Not only will this result in our adopting errors if the dominating government gets things wrong or finds it useful to deceive us, but we will not even know how to derive from such truths as this government has given us the consequences which must flow from them. The abnegation of our intelligence will have rendered us wretchedly passive creatures. Our mental resilience will be broken. Such vigor as we have left will serve only to mislead us. A writer gifted with remarkable insight[9] observes on this subject that a miracle enacted to demonstrate a truth would entirely fail to convince the spectators. It would instead spoil their judgment, since between a truth and a miracle there is no natural link. A miracle is not proof of an assertion. A miracle is proof of power. To ask someone to accept an opinion on account of a miracle is to demand that people accord to power what should be accorded only to facts; it is to reverse the order of ideas and want an effect to be produced by something which could not be its cause.

We have pointed out elsewhere[10] that morality is only a linked sequence of causes and effects. In the same way, knowledge of the truth is composed only of a linked sequence of principles and consequences. Anytime you interrupt this sequence, you destroy either morality or truth.

Everything imposed on opinion by government turns out to be not only useless but harmful, truth as much as error. In this case truth is not

8. See Constant's Note B at the end of Book XIV.

9. See Constant's Note C at the end of Book XIV.

10. For example, Book XII, Ch. 7.

[364] harmful *qua* truth, but harmful for not having penetrated human intelligence by the natural route.

There is a class, however, whose opinions can be only prejudices, a class which, lacking time for reflection, can learn only what it is taught, a class which has to believe what it is told, a class which, lastly, not being able to devote itself to analysis, has no interest in intellectual independence. Perhaps people will want the government, leaving the educated part of the society completely free, to oversee the views of the ignorant part. But a government which arrogates itself this exclusive prerogative will necessarily demand it be upheld. It will not want any individuals, whoever they may be, acting in a sense different from its own. I agree that initially it will hide this will with sweet and tolerant formalities. From then on, however, some restrictions will appear. They will always keep on growing. A religion professed by government entails the persecution, more or less disguised, of all others. It is the same with opinions of any kind. From preferential treatment of an opinion to disfavor for the contrary opinion, there is a gap which it is impossible not to cross.

This first disadvantage is the cause of a second. Educated men do not delay in separating themselves from a government which hurts them. This is in the nature of the human spirit, above all when it is strengthened by meditation and cultivated by study. Government action, even the best intended, is in some ways rude and gross and ruffles a thousand delicate sensibilities which suffer and rebel.

It is to be feared therefore that if government is endowed with the prerogative of managing the opinion of the uneducated, even if this were toward truth, separating that management from any action taken with regard to the educated class, this latter class, which regards opinion as belonging to its domain, will put itself at odds with the government. A thousand ills then result. Hatred for a government which intervenes in what is not its province can grow so much that when it acts in favor of enlightenment, the friends of enlightenment line up on the side of prejudice. We saw this bizarre spectacle at several periods of our Revolution. A government founded on the clearest principles and professing the sanest opinions, but which, by the nature of the means it uses, alienates the educated class, becomes, infallibly, either the most degraded or the most oppressive of governments. Often it actually combines these two seemingly exlusive things.

[365] The French Revolution was directed against errors of any kind, that is to say that its purpose was to remove the support of government from

these errors. The revolutionary leaders wanted to go further. They wanted to employ government itself in the destruction of these errors. Straightaway national movement came to a halt. Opinion was astonished at the weird impulsion some people desired to impress on it, and it recoiled before its new allies. A subtle and swift instinct warned it that the cause had changed although the banner was the same, and it abandoned the banner. What had they actually wanted, this mass of educated men, of honest mind, who during the last half of the eighteenth century had supported the philosophers against the court and the clergy? Independence of opinion, freedom of thought. As soon as the government put itself on the philosophers' side, however, and exerted itself in supporting it, opinion was no longer independent, thought no longer free.

We must distinguish the influence of the enlightened class, insofar as it is enlightened, from that of a section of the enlightened class, insofar as it is vested in government. No one wants the influence of enlightenment more than I. But precisely because I want it, because I prefer it to any means of another kind, and because I do not want it distorted. It is to conserve in all its force the domain of the enlightened class that I feel repugnance at its subordination to a tiny fraction of itself, necessarily less impartial and probably less enlightened than the rest. The free, gradual, and peaceful action of all would be retarded and often even arrested by this privilege accorded to a few.

CHAPTER FOUR

On Government Protection of Enlightenment

Do you restrict yourself to demanding that government favor with all its might the indefinite growth of enlightenment? In charging government with this function, however, are you quite sure you are not imposing on it a duty directly opposed to its interest? We need to distinguish between the sciences proper and enlightenment in the widest sense of that word. We have said, and [366] we think we have shown,[11] that the sciences always gained from the progress of enlightenment and lost from its decay. But the material of science is nevertheless liable to become isolated in many respects from the interests most dear to the happiness and dignity of the human race. Mathematics or physics in the hands of d'Alembert, Condorcet, Biot, or Cabanis are means for the perfectioning of intelligence

11. In Book VII, Ch. 5.

and rationality and thereby of morality. These sciences can also become separated, however, from the wider purpose of thought; they become then a form of work of a kind more difficult and of more extensive utility than the work of the majority of men, but no less foreign to what we understand specifically by philosophy. All governments have an interest in encouraging sciences thus circumscribed and consequently almost all encourage them. They make a bargain with them whereby the sciences agree not to step outside the agreed sphere. A famous author ingeniously observed that government sought to divide man's faculties, as it divides citizens among themselves, in order to keep them the more easily in slavery.[12] It is not thus, however, with enlightened activities. Such a bargain is contrary to their nature. The personal interest of those in power is therefore by no means to protect them frankly and to the utmost.

The interest of the governors as such is for the governed to be sufficiently enlightened to be skillful economically, with no loss of their docility and without their in any way harming or worrying the government. Government, of any kind, however legitimate or moderate you suppose it, is keen on surveillance. Now, the more enlightened nations are, the more redoubtable surveillance is. The growth of the intellectual powers of the governed is the creation of a rival power to that of the governors. The consciousness of each individual of the cultivated class constitutes an inflexible tribunal, which judges the acts of government. The governors, therefore, as governors, have an interest not in an indefinite progress of enlightenment, but in a relative and limited one.

As individuals, it is more obvious still that their immediate interest in relation to enlightenment is not the same as that of the governed. It would be too simpleminded of us to stop here and show that it is [367] more agreeable for the holders of power, however well-intentioned they may be, for ministers, however pure they want to be, to be surrounded by men less educated than they and from whom they can easily command admiration and obedience, the implication being that even when the ostensible purpose of the government is to encourage enlightenment, its secret desire is still to keep it dependent and therefore to limit it. This desire would not exist in the holders of power, however, if the objects of their protection were not inclined to take it for granted. From this derives some kind of constraint, some eternal obstacle to all free movement, all strict logic, all precise research, all impartial reasoning. Government protection hurts enlightenment even when the

12. Hofmann does not know who this author is.

government, sincere and disinterested in all its views, repudiates all ulterior motive and all idea of domination. Compare the respective progress of French literature and German literature in Berlin under Frederick II. No sovereign was in better faith than Frederick in his zeal for the development of the human spirit. He invited his academy to prove that error could never be useful.[13] His country's literature seeming to him still in its infancy, he showered his favors on all the French men of letters who gathered around him. He overwhelmed them with distinctions and wealth. He allowed them that familiarity with the great which is said to throw almost all men into such a sweet intoxication. The French writings published at his court, however, were never more than inferior and superficial productions. Frederick's genius could not efface the autonomous character of government. It is true that his protégés repeated philosophical ideas, because these ideas were the watchword; but truths themselves are sterile when they are produced to order. They wrote audacious things, only with a trembling hand, uncertain about the conclusions it was prudent to come to therein and endlessly and anxiously returning to consult officialdom. Voltaire made a short appearance in this literary circle, warmed by royal protection; but since Voltaire was not one of protection's creatures and was himself a power, the two potentates could not live together, and Voltaire soon left the monarch to protect his humble *littérateurs* at his leisure.

The German writers scorned by Frederick had no [368] portion of his encouragement or favor. They worked only for the public and themselves. It is to their writings, however, that Germany owes the high degree of enlightenment she has reached; and their writings owe their merit to the government's neglect. If one had to choose between persecution and protection, persecution is the more valuable to intellectual life.[14]

There is among the resources nature has given man a resilience which reacts in the hand which oppresses it, but relaxes or bends when that hand, become more adroit, has managed to seize hold. It was in terror of being accused of sorcery by the government that Roger Bacon outstripped his century. Galileo was to discover the movement of the earth under the

13. Hofmann was unable to verify this.

14. In an article in the *Moniteur* of 9 fructidor an IV (26 August 1796), *De la restitution des droits politiques aux descendants des religionnaires fugitifs,* Constant had already said: "The late king of Prussia, by his blind contempt for everything which appeared in German, has rendered the progress of enlightenment the only service which government could, that of leaving it alone." From the text published in Béatrice Jasinski, *L'engagement de Benjamin Constant. Amour et politique* (1794–1796), Paris, Minard, 1971, p. 255.

Inquisition's yoke. It was far from his country, whence tyranny had banished him, that Locke analyzed man's faculties. It is too often concluded, since a cause has produced an effect, that differently employed it would produce an opposite effect. Governments can sometimes succeed in stopping the march of human intelligence for a while. One would be wrong to infer, however, that they succeed in encouraging it. Ignorance can at their behest prolong itself on earth. Enlightenment shines only at the behest of freedom.

CHAPTER FIVE

On the Upholding of Morality

There are the same drawbacks in the upholding of morality by government as in the protection it affords enlightenment. There is even a further danger. These supports have the effect of adding a motive of material interest to the natural motives which bring man to virtue. Some philosophers, following this basic idea, have feared even the intervention of divine omnipotence by way of punishment or reward, as threatening impartiality. Each man bringing together in [369] the idea of God all the perfections, however, he is at least sure that the decisions of eternally infallible providence will never be in opposition to the justice which must direct men's actions. It is not the same with governments, though, since they are exposed to error, liable to bias, and capable of injustice. You are not subordinating the morality of man only to a more powerful being, itself already a drawback, but to beings like himself, and perhaps ones less worthwhile than he. You thereby familiarize him with the idea of making what seems to him his duty, bend the knee before their power, from no calculation save interest. Even were the protection of the government never granted save to virtue, I would still hold that virtue would be better off independent. The protection of government being grantable, however, to the vice which deceives or serves it, it seems to me we should reject an intervention which in principle harms the purity of our sensibilities and in application often lacks the special advantage attributed to it.

It is, moreover, far less necessary than people think that government, in a legal way, should encourage men to be moral, kindly, and generous. Provided society prevents its members from hurting each other, they will find enough reasons for mutual service. A positive personal interest engages men in rendering one another reciprocal services, in order to receive them in their turn, while only negative interest gets them to abstain from harmful actions. Their activity, which is one of their natural penchants, brings them to do good to one another; but this same activity can also bring them to do ill. Each man has only two ways of getting his fellows to collaborate with what he wishes: force and persuasion. He must either constrain them or lead them to his purpose by gaining their goodwill. If the law cuts off the first way, individuals will invariably take the second. If they lose all hope of success through violence, they will wish to achieve such success by deserving recognition and affection. Government has nothing to do save to see that men do not hurt each other. If they do not hurt, they will serve each other. [370]

CHAPTER SIX

On the Contribution of Government to Education

Education can be considered under two headings. We can see it in the first place as a means of transmitting to the nascent generation the knowledge of all kinds gained by previous generations. In this respect it is entirely within the jurisdiction of government. The conservation and growth of all knowledge is a positive good. The government must guarantee us the enjoyment of these.

We can also see education, however, as the means of seizing men's opinions, in order to shape them to the adoption of a certain number of ideas, whether religious, moral, philosophical, or political; and it is above all as leading to this end that writers in all centuries heap their eulogies on it.

We might first of all, without calling into question the facts which serve as the basis of this theory, deny that these facts could apply to modern societies. The domain of education, in the all-powerful sense attributed to it, and if one admitted that all-powerful sense as demonstrated in antiquity, might with us even be thought a reminiscence rather than an existing fact. People fail to recognize times, nations, and epochs and apply to modern societies what was practicable only in a different era of the human spirit.

Among peoples who, as Condorcet[15] says, had no notion of personal freedom and where men were only machines, whose springs the law regulated and whose movements it directed, government action could have a more efficacious effect on education because nothing resisted that constant

15. See Constant's Note D at the end of Book XIV.

and uniform action. But today the whole society would revolt against government pressure; and individual independence, which men have regained, would react forcefully in the case of children's education. That second education, worldly and circumstantial, would very soon undo the work of the first.[16]

It might be the case, moreover, that we mistake for historical facts the romancing of some philosophers imbued with the same prejudices as those who in our time have adopted their principles. Then instead of formerly at least having been a practical truth, this conceit would be only a perennial error.

[371] Where in effect do we see this marvelous power of education? Is it in Athens? But there the public education sanctioned by government was confined to subaltern schools restricted to simple instruction. Furthermore, there was complete freedom of teaching. Is it in Sparta? The uniform and monkish spirit of the Spartans depended on a whole group of institutions of which education was only one part, and in my view the ensemble would be neither easy nor desirable for us to set up anew. Is it in Crete? But the Cretans were the most ferocious, troubled, and corrupted people in Greece. The institutions are separated from their effects and they are admired on the basis of what they were intended to produce, without consideration of what in reality they did produce.

People cite the Persians and Egyptians. We know them very imperfectly, however. Greek writers made Persia and Egypt the theater of their speculations the way Tacitus did with the Germans. They put into action among these far-off people what they would have liked to see established in their fatherland. Their dissertations on Egyptian and Persian institutions are sometimes proven false by the simple, manifest impossibility of the facts they contain and almost always rendered doubtful by irreconcilable contradictions. What we know beyond question is that the Persians and Egyptians were despotically governed and that cowardice, corruption, and degradation, those eternal consequences of despotism, were the portion of these wretched peoples. Our philosophers acknowledge this in the very pages where they propose them as exemplary, for example in matters educational. A bizarre weakness of the human mind, which, noticing only objects in detail, lets itself be so dominated by a cherished idea that the most decisive effects do not enlighten it as to the impotence of causes, whose power it is disposed to proclaim. Most historical proofs resemble those

16. See Constant's Note E at the end of Book XIV.

which M. de Montesquieu advances in support of gymnastics. The practice of wrestling enabled the Thebans to win the battle of Leuctra. But against whom did they win this battle? Against the Spartans, who had practiced gymnastics for four hundred years.[17]

[372] The argument which entrusts education to government rests on two or three cases of petitio principii.

The first supposition is that the government will be a desirable one. People think of it as always an ally, without reflecting that it can often become an enemy. They are unaware that sacrifices imposed on individuals may not result in advantage to such institutions as they believe to be perfect but to that of any institution whatsoever.

This consideration applies with equal force to the holders of all viewpoints. You regard absolute government as the supreme good, for the order it maintains, the peace you see it as demonstrating. If government claims the right to control education, however, it will not claim it only in the calm of despotism, but in the midst of factional violence and rage. Then the result will be quite different from what you expect. Surrendered to government, education will no longer inspire in nascent generations those peaceful habits, those principles of obedience, that respect for religion, that submission to visible and invisible powers you regard as the basis of happiness and social tranquillity. Once education is their instrument, factions will make it serve to spread in the minds of the young exaggerated views, wild maxims, pitiless axioms, contempt for religious ideas which will seem to them like hostile doctrines, bloodlust, hatred of pity. Is this not what the Revolutionary government would have done if it had lasted longer, and was not the Revolutionary government a government too?

This reasoning would be just as forceful if we put it to the friends of wise and moderate freedom. You wish, we will say to them, for government to control education in a republic, in order to school the children at the youngest possible age in the knowledge and maintenance of their rights, to teach them to defy despotism, to resist unjust government, to defend innocence against oppression. But despotism will use education to put its docile slaves under the yoke, to break every noble and courageous senti-

17. Constant has drawn the example of this so-called error of Montesquieu from Cornelius de Pauw, *op. cit.,* t. I, pp. 150–151: "M. de Montesquieu says that the practice of wrestling caused the Thebans to win the battle of Leuctra; but he has forgotten that this battle was joined in the 102d olympiad; such that it was then four hundred years that the Spartans had also practiced wrestling, which did not, however, save them from a total defeat." De Pauw gives no reference, and it seems probable that Montesquieu never alluded to this anecdote.

ment in our hearts, to overturn every notion of [373] justice, to mantle with obscurity the most obvious truths, to push into the darkness or sully with ridicule everything which connects with the most sacred and inviolable rights of the human race. Is this not what they would do today, if they had power, these ardent enemies of all light, these calumniators of any noble idea, who, finding the career of crime cleaned out, compensate for this, at least amply, with careers in baseness?

One could think the Directory was intended to give us some memorable lessons on all objects of this nature. We saw it for four years, seeking to direct education, harassing the teachers, reprimanding them, displacing them, degrading them in their pupils' eyes, submitting them to the inquisition of its most inferior agents and men of the least enlightenment, hindering individual teaching, and worrying state education with endless and puerile actions. Was not the Directory a government? I would like to know the mysterious guarantee people have received, that the future will never be like the past.

In all these hypothetical cases, what people want the government to do for the better, it may do for the worse. Thus hopes can be disappointed and the government which has been indefinitely extended on the basis of unfounded suppositions can march in the opposite direction from the purpose for which it was created.

Education supplied by the government ought to be limited to simple instruction. Government can multiply the channels and resources of instruction, but it must not manage it. Let it ensure that the citizens have equal means, let it make sure that the various occupations get taught real knowledge which facilitates their practices, let it clear the way for individuals freely to get access to all proven factual truths[18] and to reach the point where their intelligence can spontaneously dash forward to new discoveries, let it bring together for the use of all inquiring minds, the major works of all opinions, all the [374] inventions of all the centuries, the discoveries of all methods, let it, finally, organize instruction in such a way that each person can devote to it the time appropriate to his interest or desire and perfect himself in the occupation, the art or science to which his tastes or his lot call him. Let it not appoint teachers; let it only pay them a salary which, assuring them the necessaries of life, nevertheless makes it desirable for them to have lots of pupils, let it provide for their needs when age or illness has put an end to their active careers, let it never

18. See Constant's Note F at the end of Book XIV.

sack them without grave cause and without the agreement of men independent of it.[19]

Teachers subject to the government will be at once negligent and servile. Their servility will serve to excuse their negligence. Subject only to public opinion, they would be both active and independent.[20]

In managing education, government is claiming the right and assuming the duty to maintain a body of doctrine. The word itself tells you the means of which it is obliged to make use. If we allow that it might choose the gentlest ones at first, it is still at least certain that it will not permit the teaching in its schools of any save its preferred opinions.[21] There will therefore be rivalry between state education and private education. State education will be salaried; there will therefore be opinions invested with privilege. But if this privilege is not enough to secure dominance for the favored opinions, do you believe that government, jealous by nature, will not resort to other means? Do you not see as the final outcome persecution, more or less disguised, but the constant companion of all unnecessary activity by government?

We see governments, which seem not to trouble individual education in anything, nevertheless favoring always the establishments they have founded, by demanding of all candidates for appointments in the state schools, a kind of apprenticeship in these establishments. Thus the talent which has followed the independent route, and which by solitary work has perhaps assembled as much knowledge and probably more originality than it would have done under classroom routine, finds its natural career, the one in which it can communicate and reproduce itself, suddenly closed before it.[22]

[375] It is not that, all things being equal, I do not prefer public education to private education. The former makes the rising generation undergo a novitiate of human life, more useful than all the lessons of pure theory, which never replace reality and experience save imperfectly. Public education is salutary above all in free societies. Men brought together at any age and above all in their youth, naturally contract from their reciprocal dealings a sense of justice and habits of equality, which prepare them to become courageous citizens and enemies of despotism. We saw, even under

19. See Constant's Note G at the end of Book XIV.
20. See Constant's Note H at the end of Book XIV.
21. See Constant's Note I at the end of Book XIV.
22. See Constant's Note J at the end of Book XIV.

the despotism, schools dependent on the government, reproducing in spite of it seeds of freedom which it strove vainly to stifle.

I think, however, that this advantage can be obtained without constraint. The good never needs privileges, and privileges always disfigure the good. It is important, furthermore, that if the educational system the government favors is vicious, or seems so to some people, they can seek refuge in private study or in schools with no government connections. Society must respect individual rights, including parents' rights over their children.[23] If its actions harm them, a resistance will grow which will render government tyrannical and corrupt individuals by obliging them to elude it. There may be objections perhaps to this respect we demand from government for parents' rights, that the lower classes, reduced by their poverty into making use of their children, once the latter are capable of helping them in their labors, will not have them instructed in the most basic knowledge, even if the instruction were free, if the government is not authorized to constrain them to this. This objection rests, however, on the hypothesis of such poverty among the people that no good can exist alongside it. What is needed is for this poverty not to exist. Once the people enjoy the affluence due to them, far from retaining their children in ignorance, they will hasten to get them schooled. Their vanity will play a part. They will sense the interest in it. The most natural inclination of parents is to raise their children to a higher status. We see this in England, and it is what we saw in France during the Revolution. During that period, though it was disturbed and the people had to suffer a lot from their government, nevertheless simply because there was more affluence, education made astonishing progress [376] among that class. Everywhere the education of the people is proportionate to its affluence.

We said at the beginning of this chapter that the Athenians subjected only workaday schools to official inspection. Schools of philosophy remained always absolutely independent, and this enlightened nation has left us a memorable example on this subject. Sophocles the demagogue having proposed the subordination of philosophy teaching to the authority of the Senate, all these men, who, despite their numerous mistakes, ought to serve forever as models, both for love of truth and for respect for tolerance, resigned their positions. The whole nation solemnly declared them exempt from inspections and condemned their absurd opponent to a fine of five talents.[24]

23. See Constant's Note K at the end of Book XIV.
24. See Constant's Note L at the end of Book XIV.

You will answer, however, that if there were set up an educational establishment resting on immoral principles, you would fight for the right of the government to check that abuse. This is to forget that for such an establishment to form and survive, it needs students, and parents who place them there, and putting aside, which is not at all reasonable, actually, the parents' morality, it will never be in their interests to leave those with whom they have the most important and intimate relationships of their whole lives, to be misled in judgment and perverted in their hearts. The practice of injustice and perversity may be useful fleetingly, in a particular situation, but the principle can never have any prerogative. The principle will never be professed save by fools whom a hostile general opinion will repudiate, without government getting involved. There will never be a need to suppress educational establishments where lessons in vice and crime are given, because there will never be such establishments, and if there were, they would hardly be dangerous, because the teachers would remain on their own. For lack of plausible objections, however, people lean on absurd suppositions, and the calculation is not without guile, since there is a danger of leaving suppositions unanswered, and it appears in a sense foolish to refute them.

I hope for much more, for the perfecting of the human race, [377] from private educational establishments, than from the best-organized public instruction by government.

Who can limit the development of the passion for enlightenment in a free country? You attribute governments with a love of learning. Without examining here the extent to which this tendency is in their interest, I would simply ask you why you assume a lesser love in cultivated individuals, in clear minds and generous spirits. Everywhere government does not weigh on men, everywhere it does not corrupt wealth, conspiring with it against justice, then letters, study, science, the growth and exercise of the intellect will be the favorite pastimes of the opulent classes in society. Look how they carry on in England, forming coalitions, rushing eagerly from all sides. Think of those museums and libraries, those independent learned societies devoted solely to the pursuit of truth, those travelers braving every danger to take human knowledge a step further.

In education as elsewhere, government should be watchful and protective, but always neutral. Let it remove obstacles and make smooth the roads. We can leave it to individuals to walk them successfully.

CHAPTER SEVEN

On Government Duties vis-à-vis Enlightenment

The duties of government vis-à-vis enlightenment are simple and easy. They are of quite another nature, however, from the direction they too often claim. Each generation adds to the resources, physical or moral, of the human race. Sometimes new methods are discovered, at other times machines invented, sometimes communication is perfected, at others facts are clarified. All these things are in some degree the acquisition of new faculties. They are worth preserving independently of the incidental purpose for which they can be used. Doubtless all man's faculties, from those nature [378] has given him to those which time reveals to him or his efforts invent, have drawbacks as well as advantages. But the drawbacks of any faculty are not in the faculty itself but in the use made of it. Consequently, as long as government applies itself only to conserving the resources, the discoveries, the new abilities man has won, without giving them an aim or directing their use, it fulfills a salutary function, its action neither equivocal nor complicated. It does only unequivocal and harmless good.

A. [Refers to page 300.]
Principes de législation publiés par Dumont, Tome II, p. 211.

B. [Refers to page 302.]
Esprit des lois, XII, 2.[25]

C. [Refers to page 302.]
Godwin.[26]

D. [Refers to page 308.]
Mémoires sur l'instruction publique.[27]

[379] E. [Refers to page 309.]
Helvétius, De l'homme.[28]

F. [Refers to page 311.]
One can teach the facts parrot fashion, but never the arguments.

G. [Refers to page 312.]
For the details of the organization of state education which are not within the scope of this work, I refer the reader to the Mémoires of Condorcet, where all the

25. It is in Ch. 2 of Book XII that Montesquieu writes: "A man who was tried and was to be hanged the next morning, would be freer than a Pasha is in Turkey." *Ed. cit.,* p. 509.

26. William Godwin, *Enquiry Concerning Political Justice and Its Influence on General Virtue and Happiness,* London, 1793, vol. 1, p. 124. Constant translated this work. See Benjamin Constant, *De la justice politique,* unpublished translation of the work of William Godwin, edited by Burton R. Pollin, Quebec, University of Laval Press, 1972.

27. In the *Bibliothèque de l'homme public, op. cit.,* p. 47: "The ancients had no notion of this kind of liberty; they seemed indeed to have no purpose in their institutions save to annihilate it. They would have liked to allow men only ideas and feelings found in the legislator's provision. For them nature had created only machines, whose springs law alone must regulate, whose actions law alone direct."

28. Claude-Adrien Helvétius, *De l'homme, de ses facultés intellectuelles et de son education,* London, 1776. Constant refers the reader above all to the first section of the work, entitled: *Que l'éducation nécessairement différente des différents hommes est peut-être la cause de l'inégalité des esprits, jusqu'à présent attribuée à l'inégale perfection de leurs organes.*

questions relating to this matter are examined and resolved and to whose views I doubt whether anything could be added.[29]

H. [Refers to page 312.]
Smith, Richesse des nations.[30]

I. [Refers to page 312.]
Condorcet, 1er Mémoire, p. 55.[31]

J. [Refers to page 312.]
"Everything which obliges or engages a certain number of students to remain at a college or university, independently of the merit or reputation of the masters, such as on the one hand the necessity of [380] taking certain degrees which can be conferred only in certain places and on the other hand the scholarships and grants given to poor scholars, has the effect of slowing down the zeal and rendering less necessary the knowledge of the masters privileged thus under any system at all."[32]

K. [Refers to page 313.]
Condorcet, 1er Mémoire, p. 44.[33]

L. [Refers to page 313.]
Diogenes Laertius, Vie de Theophraste.[34]

29. Constant is evidently referring to *Mémoires sur l'instruction publique* in *Bibliothèque de l'homme public,* t. I, Paris, Buisson, 1791.

30. Adam Smith, *op. cit.,* Book V, Ch. 1, t. IV, pp. 143–145.

31. Condorcet, *op. cit.* Condorcet says here: "It is much more important that the government does not dictate the common doctrine of the moment as eternal truth, lest it make of education a tool for consecrating prejudices it finds useful, and an instrument of power out of that which should be the most certain barrier against all unjust power."

32. Adam Smith, *op. cit.,* t. IV, p. 146.

33. Condorcet, *op. cit.,* p. 44.

34. The anecdote of the demagogue Sophocles and the reference to Diogenes Laertius are in Cornelius de Pauw, *Recherches philosophiques sur les Grecs, op. cit.,* t. I, pp. 232–233.

BOOK XV

The Outcome of Preceding Discussion Relative to the Action of Government

CH. 1. The outcome of the preceding discussion. 321
CH. 2. On three pernicious ideas. 322
CH. 3. On ideas of uniformity. 322
CH. 4. Application of this principle to the composition of representative assemblies. 326
CH. 5. Further thoughts on the preceding chapter. 328
CH. 6. On ideas of stability. 338
CH. 7. On premature ameliorations. 340
CH. 8. On a false way of reasoning. 345

CHAPTER ONE

The Outcome of the Preceding Discussion

We have surveyed almost all the matters on which government, exceeding the limits of strict necessity, can take action on grounds of alleged utility. We found that in all these, had people been left to themselves, less bad and more good would have resulted. "When the controls of empires are rooted in good principles," says Mirabeau,[1] "there will be only two concerns, that of maintaining external peace by a good system of defenses, and that of conserving domestic order by the exact, impartial, and inflexible administration of justice. Everything else will be left to individual effort, whose irresistible influence effecting a larger total of satisfactions for each citizen, will infallibly produce a larger amount of public happiness. A sovereign or minister cannot know the affairs even of a thousand men, while each individual in general knows his own very well."

The governing class create duties for themselves to extend their prerogatives. Overobliging agents of the nation, they constantly assault its freedom, that is to say, the means of happiness nature has given it, and they do this in the name of rendering it happy. They want to control enlightenment, when only experience can guide it. They want to stop crimes, when only the spectacle of punishment stops them surely and without despotism. They want to encourage production, when only individual interest gives it life. They want to establish institutions; habit alone forms them. Governments must watch out that nothing trammels our diverse faculties, but must not permit themselves to take a hand therein. What would the inhabitants of a house say if the guards they had placed at the gates to stop any strangers from intruding and to calm down any domestic disturbance, gave themselves the right to control the actions of those inhabitants [384] and to prescribe them a way of life, under the pretext of preventing these intrusions and disturbances, or under the even more absurd one that their way of life would be sweeter following these changes? The governors are these guards, put in place by individuals who come together precisely so that nothing shall trouble their peace of mind or upset their doings. If the governors go further, they become themselves a source of trouble and upset.

The use of penal laws then becomes the most culpable abuse of the right to punish. Rather than extend this terrible right, we should strive to restrain it.

1. See Constant's Note A at the end of Book XV.

Instead of multiplying the number of crimes, we should reduce it. It is not a crime in man to mistake his own interest, always supposing he does so; it is not a crime in man to want to manage himself by his own lights, even when government finds them imperfect. It is a crime in government, however, to punish individuals because they do not adopt as their interest what seems so to other men or because they do not rank their own judgments of enlightenment beneath those of others, when, after all, each person is the judge in the last resort. To subordinate individual wishes to the general will, without absolute necessity, is gratuitously to set up obstacles to all our progress. Individual interest is always more enlightened on what concerns it than collective power, whose fault is the sacrificing to its purposes, without care or scruple, of everything which opposes it. It needs to be checked and not to be encouraged.

To increase the force of collective authority is never other than giving more power to some individuals. If the wickedness of men is an argument against freedom, it is an even stronger one against power. For despotism is only the freedom of one or a few against the rest. Burke says that freedom is power.[2] One can likewise say that power is freedom. [385]

CHAPTER TWO

On Three Pernicious Ideas

Three ideas are particularly dangerous when they take hold of the minds of the governing group; these are the ideas of uniformity, ideas of stability, and the ill-considered desire for premature improvement.

CHAPTER THREE

On Ideas of Uniformity

M. de Montesquieu, who in his admirable work grasped almost everything, in a short chapter condemns the ideas of uniformity, but in few words, without enlargement and more by way of drawing the reader's attention to the subject rather than himself analyzing and exploring it more deeply.

"There are," he says,[3] "certain ideas of uniformity which sometimes lay hold of great minds, witness their appeal to Charlemagne, but infallibly

2. Edmund Burke, *Réflexions sur la Révolution de France et sur les procédés de certaines sociétés à Londres relatifs à cet événement,* Paris, Laurent; London, Edward, s.d., p. 12: "But when men act in a body, freedom is *power.*"

3. See Constant's Note B at the end of Book XV.

enthuse small ones. These find in them a type of perfection they recognize, because it is impossible not to detect it in them: the same concentration on public order, the same measures in commerce, the same laws in the State, the same religion throughout. Is this always to the good, however, without exception? Is the evil of change always less than the evil of having to endure? Might not the greatness of genius consist in knowing in which cases uniformity is needed and in which cases differences?"

If the author of *The Spirit of the Laws* had appealed to history, he would easily have shown that absolute uniformity is in several circumstances contrary to the nature both of men and things.

It is clear that different portions of the same people, placed in circumstances, brought up in customs, living in places, which are all dissimilar, cannot be led to absolutely the same manners, usages, practices, and laws, without a coercion which would cost them more than it is worth. The small advantage of offering a smooth surface over which the lofty eye of government can freely stray, without encountering any inequality which offends it or obstructs its view, is only a puny compensation [386] for the sacrifice of a host of sentiments, memories, local tastes, out of which individual happiness, that is to say, the only real happiness, is composed. The chance which submits to the same government diverse local peoples does not in any way alter the inner mentality of each member of these. The series of ideas, from which their moral being has gradually been formed since their infancy, cannot be modified by a purely nominal, external arrangement, most of the time independent of their will, which has nothing in common with their ways, the private and real source of their griefs and pleasures.

It is by sacrificing everything to exaggerated ideas of uniformity that large States have become a scourge for humanity. To renounce that idealist perfection would be to retain for the large States many of the advantages of small ones and combine these with the advantages deriving from greater size.

For morality, justice, peace, a certain kind of happiness, and all natural affections, small States are preferable to large ones. For external security, which is the guarantee of private happiness, for national independence, without which a State is the plaything or victim of its neighbors, for the enlightenment which is the strongest barrier against oppression, large States have huge advantages over small ones. The mix of economic and political organization being much more varied in these adds greatly to everyday experience. Prejudice dies sooner. The kind of abuse which is reformed swiftly and almost spontaneously in a large State can be kept going forever in a country enclosed within narrow limits. It is because the Roman empire had conquered three-quarters of the world that slavery was destroyed. If that empire had been divided into a multitude of independent States, none would have given the lead with the abolition of slavery, since the immediate advantage to its own detriment this would have given its neighbors would have struck each one of them.[4] There are acts of justice capable of enactment only simultaneously and which therefore never happen, because if they happen partially, the most generous become temporarily victims of their generosity.

In recognizing the advantages of large States, however, one must not underestimate their multiple and terrible drawbacks. Their [387] size requires an activism and force at the heart of government which is difficult to contain and degenerates into despotism. The laws come from a point so far from those to whom they are supposed to apply that the inevitable effect of such distance is serious and frequent error. Local injustices never reach the heart of government. Placed in the capital, it takes the views of its surrounding area or at the very most of its place of residence for those of the whole State. A local or passing circumstance thus becomes the reason for a general law, and the inhabitants of the most distant provinces are suddenly surprised by unexpected innovations, unmerited severity, vexatious regulations, undermining the basis of all their calculations, and all the safeguards of their interests, because two hundred leagues away men who are total strangers to them had some inkling of agitation, divined certain needs, or perceived certain dangers.

I am not even sure whether in terms of prestige, that noble motive of human action, large countries are not fatal. Today small States are scorned as too restrictive a field of action. But a very populous society puts an almost insurmountable barrier in the way of personal distinction. To win the admiration of one's fellow citizens one must uplift the mass of the people. The larger the country, the heavier that mass. Therefore we see in overlarge countries a small State forming at the center. That small State is the capital. All ambitions go there to vent themselves. Everywhere else is immobile, inert, becalmed.

One could guard against most of these drawbacks by abjuring ideas of conformity or at least by restricting them to a very few objects. The government of a large country must always partake somewhat of the nature of federalism. The rules in this respect are very simple and all start from the

4. See Constant's Note C at the end of Book XV.

principle which is the basis of this book. The management of the affairs of everybody belongs to everybody, that is, to the government instituted by everybody. What touches only a minority should be decided by that minority. What relates only to the individual must be referred only to the individual. It cannot be said too often that the general will is no more worthy than the individual one, when it steps [388] outside its jurisdiction. Suppose a nation of twenty million souls, split between a number of communes. In each commune, each individual will have interests which concern only him and which should consequently not fall under the jurisdiction of the commune. Others will concern, as well as him, all the people in the commune, and his other interests will be within the communal jurisdiction. These communes, in their turn, will have interests which are their internal business only and other interests which concern the whole society. I appreciate that I am jumping the intermediary stages. The first will be within the competence of the communal legislation, the latter of the general. Uniformity is admissible only for the latter.

Notice that under the idea of interests I include habits. Nothing is more absurd than to claim one can violate men's habits on the pretext of better directing them in terms of their interests. Their prime interest is happiness, and habits form an essential part of their happiness.

If governments observed these rules, large States would be a better solution in several respects and would cease to be an evil in several others. The capital would cease to be a unique center, destructive of any other centers. It would become a link between diverse centers. Patriotism would be reborn, the patriotism which cannot exist save by attachment to local interests, mores, and customs. Just as man's nature struggles obstinately, though almost always unsuccessfully, against the no less obstinate errors of government, so one sees this kind of patriotism, the only real kind, reborn from its ashes, once the government stays its hand for an instant. The magistrates of the smallest communes will be delighted to embellish them; their inhabitants will find pleasure in everything which gives them even the deceptive sense of corporate identity and of being brought together by individual links. One feels that if they were not stopped in the development of this innocent inclination, there would soon form in them a kind of communal pride, so to speak, pride in the town and province; and this sentiment would be singularly [389] favorable to morality. It would also be singularly favorable to the love of the metropolis itself, which would seem the protector and tutelary deity of all the little fatherlands living in the shelter of its power, instead of what it is today, their implacable adversary and ever threatening enemy. How bizarre that those who called themselves ardent friends of freedom have worked relentlessly to destroy the natural basis of patriotism, to replace it with a false passion for an abstract being, for a general idea deprived of everything which strikes the imagination and speaks to memory! How bizarre that to build an edifice, they have begun by crushing and reducing to powder all the materials they needed to use. They almost designated by numbers the different parts of the empire they claimed to be regenerating, as they did so designate the legions intended to defend it, so greatly did they seem to fear that some moral idea might manage to link itself to what they were instituting and upset the uniformity which seemed to them so beautiful and desirable. This strangeness is explained, however, when we reflect that these men were drunk with power. Local interests and memories contain a principle of resistance which government allows only with regret and which it is keen to uproot. It makes even shorter work of individuals. It rolls its immense mass effortlessly over them, as over sand. These individuals furthermore, detached from their native soil, with no contact with the past, living only in a swift-moving present and thrown like atoms on a monotonous plain, take no interest in a fatherland they nowhere perceive and whose totality becomes indifferent to them, because their affection cannot rest on any of its parts. In these large countries where local interests, customs, and habits, treated with contempt, are constantly sacrificed to what are called general considerations, "patriotism," as M. de Pauw says, "would be a figment of the imagination even if these states were not governed in so despotic a way that no interest could be known there save that of the despot himself."[5] [390]

CHAPTER FOUR

Application of This Principle to the Composition of Representative Assemblies

The mania for leveling a country by uniform institutions, the hatred of local interests, the desire to make them disappear, have today led to a singular approach to the composition of representative assemblies. Montesquieu seems to have had a presentiment of this approach and to have wanted to refute it in advance. "One knows much better the needs of one's own town," he says, "than those of other towns. And one judges better as to the capacity of one's neighbors than that of one's other compatriots. Therefore the members of

5. See Constant's Note D at the end of Book XV.

the legislative body should not be drawn in general from the body of the nation. It is more fitting that in each principal place the inhabitants choose themselves a representative."[6] In recent years precisely the opposite has been said. When a large population, spread over a vast area, it was asserted, appoints its representatives, without any intermediary, this operation forces it to divide itself into sections. These are set at distances which do not allow communication or mutual agreement. The result is sectional choices. Unity in elections must be sought in the unity of the electoral body.[7] "The choices must not flow from below, where they will always necessarily be done badly, but from above, where they will always necessarily be done well." The electoral body should be placed "not at the base but at the summit of the political establishment."[8] Only a body thus placed can really know the object or the [391] general purpose of all legislation. This reasoning rests on a very exaggerated idea of the general interest, of the general purpose, of all the things to which this phrase applies; but what is this general interest save the dealings which operate between all individual interests? What is general representation but the representation of all the partial interests which must negotiate on matters common to them? The general interest is doubtless distinct from particular ones. But it is not contrary to them. The talk is always as if it gains from their losing. It is only the outcome of these combined interests. It differs from them only as a body differs from its parts. Individual interests are what most interest individuals. Sectional interests, to use the word devised to wither them, are what interest sections the most. Now, it is these individuals and sections which make up the body politic. It is therefore the interests of these individuals and these sections which must be protected. If one protects all of them, one will thereby remove from each whatever it contains which might harm the others. Only thus can the true public interest be reached. Public interest is only individual interests prevented from harming each other. The principle on which rests the need for the unity of the electoral body is therefore completely erroneous. A hundred

6. See Constant's Note E at the end of Book XV.

7. Constant is citing a part of the discourse by Jacques-Fortunat Savoye de Rollin, given to the Legislative Body on 13 ventôse an IX (4 March 1801), in favor of the *Projet de loi relatif à la formation des listes d'éligibilité.* This discourse appeared in the *Moniteur* of 15 ventôse an IX, No. 165, p. 687.

8. Pierre-Jean-Georges Cabanis, *Quelques considérations sur l'organisation social en général et particulièrement sur la nouvelle constitution,* Corps législatif, Commission du Conseil des Cinq-Cents, séance du 25 frimaire an VIII (16 December 1799), Paris, Impr. nat., frimaire an VIII (1799), pp. 25–26.

deputies elected by a hundred different parts of the country bring individual interests and the local preferences of their constituents inside the assembly. This base is useful to them. Forced to debate together, they soon notice respective sacrifices which are indispensable. They strive to keep these at a minimum, and this is one of the great advantages of this type of appointment. Necessity always ends by uniting them in common negotiation, and the more sectional the choices have been, the more the representation achieves its general purpose. If you reverse the natural progression, if you put the electoral body at the top of the structure, those it appoints find themselves called to pronounce on a public interest with whose elements they are unfamiliar. You charge them with negotiating for sections or regions they do not know or whose interests and reciprocal needs they scorn. I want [392] the representative of a section of the country to be its instrument, abandoning none of its real or imaginary rights, such that having defended them, he will be biased in favor of the section whose mandatory he is, because if each one supports his constituency, the bias of each will in union have all the advantages of the impartiality of all. Assemblies, however sectional their composition, tend all too often to contract an esprit de corps which isolates them from the nation. Placed in the capital, far from the section of the nation which elected them, representatives lose sight of the usages, needs, and way of life of their constituents. They lend themselves to general ideas of leveling, symmetry, uniformity, mass changes, and universal recasting, bringing upset, disorder, and confusion to distant regions. It is this disposition we must combat, because it is on particular memories, habits, and regional laws that the happiness and peace of a province rest. National assemblies are scornful and careless with these things. How would things fare if these instruments of the public will had no connection save with a body placed at the top of the social edifice? The larger a State is, the less admissible is a single electoral body. The stronger the central government, the more necessary is it that choices start from below rather than above. Otherwise you will have corporate bodies vacantly deliberating and inferring from their indifference to individual interests that they are devoted to the general interest.

CHAPTER FIVE

Further Thoughts on the Preceding Chapter

I have let myself get drawn into looking at a question which I confess interests me greatly, and although it breaks out of the precise limits of this work in some respects, I cannot refrain from adding a few further thoughts here on the drawbacks of the appointment of representative assemblies by a single body and on the advantages of the opposite system.

[393] Whatever discredit one heaps on intrigue, on efforts to captivate a fickle and emotional multitude, these things are a hundred times less corrupting than the circuitous endeavors one needs to win over a small number of men in power. Intrigue is dangerous in a senate, dangerous in an aristocratic parliament, but not in the context of the nation, whose nature it is to act from emotion. The misfortune of a republic is when there is no intrigue.[9] Nothing vile is pleasing to the people as a whole. But powerful individuals are only too prone to enjoying the humility of prayers and the baseness of adulation. What has to be done to carry a large meeting has to be done in broad daylight, and modesty moderates public actions. But when people cringe before a few men whom they are imploring individually, they grovel in the shadows, and servility knows no limits. If election by the people sometimes entails culpable seduction, most often it demands honorable and useful means, kindness, benevolence, justice, and protection. When the election depends upon an electoral college, another route is mapped out. It is certainly not toward the countryman's dwelling but toward the palace of the electoral college that the candidates direct their steps. They are dependent not on the people but on the government, and if dependence on inferiors makes citizens, dependence on superiors makes slaves. It is a sad education for the people's mandatories which imposes on them an apprenticeship in dissimulation and hypocrisy, condemning them to humiliating supplication, to obsequious salutation, to adroitness, genuflection, and flattery, doubtless to prepare them for the unbending courage which has to check despotism and plead the cause of the weak against the strong. There are eras when anything at all resembling energy is feared, when gentleness, flexibility, and hidden gifts and private virtues are vaunted. Then are dreamed up modes of election best suited to reward these precious gifts. These, however, are eras of degradation. Let sweetness and flexibility find favor with courts, and let hidden talents declare themselves; let private virtues [394] find their reward in domestic happiness. The choice of the people belongs to men who command attention, who attract respect, who have acquired the right to esteem, confidence, and popular recognition. And these more energetic men will also be more moderate. People always take mediocrity as peaceful. It is peaceful only when it is

9. See Constant's Note F at the end of Book XV.

locked up. When chance invests it with power, it is a thousand times more incalculable in its motion, more envious, more obstinate, more immoderate, and more convulsive than talent, even when emotions lead the latter astray. Education calms the emotions, softens egotism, and soothes vanity.

One of the greatest advantages of representative government is to establish frequent relations between the diverse classes of society. Sectional election requires on the part of the powerful classes sustained consideration for the lower classes. It forces wealth to conceal its arrogance, power to moderate its action by placing in the people's votes a reward for justice and kindness and punishment for oppression. This advantage disappears when you entrust elections to the choice of a great electoral college.

Perhaps it will be objected that in granting political rights only to property owners, I am lessening this advantage of the representative system. But under modern social conditions there is no line of demarcation between small owners and nonowners such that the rich can win over the former by oppressing the latter. Nonproprietors, artisans in the small towns and villages, day laborers in the hamlets are all relations of small owners. They would make common cause against the oppressor. So to get the votes of those who have the vote, you will have to treat them all considerately. [395] This everyday device for happiness and harmony must not be lightly renounced, nor should we disdain this motive for benevolence, which may start as a mere calculation but soon becomes a habitual virtue.

The complaint is that wealth is concentrated in the capital and the countryside drained by the continual taxation it bears, which never returns to it. Popular election pushes owners back to the properties from which they distance themselves. When they could not care less about popular suffrage, their reckoning is confined to getting out of their property the greatest possible revenue. Popular election suggests they adopt a nobler reckoning, much more useful to those who live under their domination. Without popular election they need only credit, and this need groups them together around the central government. Under election by the people they have to be popular. Bringing them back toward the source of their popularity, it roots their political existence in their possessions. The benefits of feudalism have sometimes been praised for keeping the lord in the midst of his vassels and sharing out the opulence equally between all the parts of the territory. Popular election has the same desirable effect without entailing the same abuses. People constantly talk of encouraging agriculture and honoring work. They try awarding prizes, capriciously doled out, and medals which public opinion wrangles over. It would be simpler to give the farming classes a degree of importance. But this importance cannot be created by decree or edict. Its basis must be grounded in the interests all hopes have in its being recognized and all ambitions in treating it carefully. In replacing artificial devices, which they try out and change, with respect for the principles of freedom, governments would attain more swiftly and surely the purpose they must have in mind. In letting men enjoy the rights which belong to them, you free them from having to have recourse to uncertain resources and complex improvisations with no durable effect, because their stability depends not on the nature of things but on the arrangements of a few individuals. In sum, only sectional election by the people can invest national representation with real force, and give it deep roots in public opinion. You will never surmount or render silent the feeling which cries out to us that the man we [396] have not elected is not our representative. And should calumny pursue him, or government menace him personally, against these attacks will he know to whom to run? To whom will he say: I have faithfully fulfilled the mission with which you entrusted me; I am persecuted for having protected you? Where will he find a voice which recognizes his own and which replies to him? What fraction of the people will believe itself bound up with him in his courage and danger? The whole nation? But the whole nation is nothing. Can a nation spread across an immense territory manifest a view or experience a spontaneous impulse? Only in always speaking of the entire nation, in destroying all fractions, in intercepting all communication between them and those who defend them, in recognizing their mandatories as mere representatives of an abstract being, who never has positive existence, only thus does despotism become impregnable in its lair. When assemblies which call themselves representative are not selected by the people, they are helpless before the executive power. If they put up some resistance to it, it demands to know by what right. What is your authority? How can you be the representatives of the people? Did they appoint you? If public opinion disapproves a law or protests against some arbitrary act, then the government cries: what are these seditious claims? Has not the national representative chamber discussed, deliberated, consented? Or perhaps, has its silence not sanctioned things? Only the legitimate institutions of the nation can express its sovereign will. The executive power is protected from all blame, since the people's delegates approve it. Thus by turns the unfortunate nation and its so-called mandatories are treated like a game. Thus the semblance of representation never constitutes any barriers, but serves as an apologia for all excesses. It would be an error, as M. Necker observes, to believe that the part given to the people in the election of lawmakers has no purpose save ensuring further the suitability of those chosen.[10] Six hundred fifty men drawn by lot from the rich and cultivated class which supplies the membership of the English House of Commons would form in my view a body as enlightened as the one which results today from the British elections. All the advantages we have just described, however, would vanish. There would be no more consideration for inferiors, [397] no more inviolable credentials for opposing the government, and no more of this salutary movement spreading life, strength, and health through all the parts of the body politic. Citizens are interested in their institutions only when they are called to participate in them with their votes. Now, this interest is indispensable in the formation of a public spirit, that power without which no freedom lasts, that guarantee against all the perils, always invoked in certain countries without its ever being created. Public spirit, based on popular election, has sustained Great Britain, in the midst of the most expensive and desperate war. It is through popular election that press freedom, under very easily offended ministers, has survived every crisis. Without popular election, a country's citizens never have this sense of their importance which makes them see the glory and freedom of their country as the most important part of their individual patrimony. I know that lately some among us have conceived many prejudices against popular elections. Nevertheless, until our times all experience testifies in their favor. The people of Athens, free in their choice, says Xenophon, whom one would never suspect of overfondness for democracy and its storms, have never asked for positions touching on their city's safety or honor to be given to men unworthy to fill them.[11] Livy shows us the outcomes of the Roman

10. Jacques Necker, *Dernières vues de politique et de finance, offerte à la nation française,* s.l., an X, 1802, p. 4: "It would be a mistake to reckon that by this political disposition one had had in view only to make more sure of the suitability of the chosen."

11. Constant is inspired directly by Montesquieu here: "It never happened," says Xenophon, "that the lower class ever demanded elected officers who might compromise their safety or glory." *De l'esprit des lois,* Livre II, Ch. 2, *éd. cit.,* p. 533. It is amusing to observe that Gaëtano Filangieri uses the same quotation, and without giving his source, in *La science de la législation,* Paris, Cuchet, 1786, t. I, pp. 191–192. Constant, who also knew this work, could just as easily have found this example from Xenophon in Filangieri. This shows once again how far Montesquieu was read and used. Thanks to a reference supplied by Montesquieu, one can go back to Xenophon, *La république des Athéniens* I, 3. Compare Xenophon, *Anabase, Banquet, Economique, De la chasse, République des Lacédémoniens, République des Athéniens,* new translation with observations and notes by Pierre Chambry, Paris, Garnier, 1954, p. 510.

Comitia, proving always that the spirit of the people was different depending on whether they were demanding the right to control the high positions in the Republic or whether, the combat over, the victory won, they were pronouncing calmly, according to conscience and reason. Despite the efforts of their tribunes and the interests of their class, their choices were constantly directed toward the most virtuous and the most [398] illustrious.[12] Since 1688 the elections in England have brought no one into the House of Commons save enlightened property owners. One could scarcely cite a man of distinguished political talent whom that election has not honored, when he has sought it. The profound peace of America, the firm moderation she has deployed in difficult circumstances, the speeches and acts of Jefferson, the choice of such a man by representatives elected by the people, constitute a justification of its franchise which nothing can weaken, because it cannot be attributed to inaccurate or exaggerated accounts. If, in the history of the ten years which have just passed by, certain facts seem unfavorable to popular election, special causes explain this. First of all, we have never really had popular election. From the introduction of representation in our political institutions, the intervention of the people has been feared. Electoral colleges have been created, and these have distorted the effects of the election. Popular governments would be the triumph of mediocrity, were it not for a sort of moral electricity with which nature has endowed men, as though to ensure the dominance of genius. The larger the assemblies are, the more powerful is this electricity, and since, when it is a question of election, it is useful that this electricity directs the choices, the assemblies charged with the appointment of the people's representatives must be as numerous as is compatible with good order. In England, the candidates harangue the electors who surround them from the height of a rostrum, in the middle of a public place or an open space full of people. In our electoral colleges, numbers were restricted and proceedings severe. A rigorous silence was prescribed, and no question was put such as might agitate minds or subjugate, for an instant, individual ambition or local egoism. Now, uneducated men are fair only when they are carried along. They are carried along only when, brought together in a crowd, they act and react on each other almost boisterously. You cannot attract the attention of several thousand citizens without great wealth or far-reaching reputation. In a gathering of two or three hundred, a few domestic

12. The Titus Livy example seems to come from Montesquieu too, *De l'esprit des lois,* Livre II, Ch. 2 (*éd. cit.,* p. 533).

connections can seize a majority. To be selected by the people, you need supporters beyond their purview and the positive advantages this brings. To be chosen [399] by a few electors, it is enough to have no enemies. The advantage lies entirely with negative qualities, and luck even favors the untalented. As regards many issues, the national representatives in France have been less advanced than public opinion. I am not speaking of party questions. During civil turmoil, education has no effect on these. I am speaking of matters of political economy. It is just that our electoral assemblies, with the obstacles they put in the way of all personal influence and their encouragement of calumny, made election a lottery with the dice often falling on mediocre or unknown men. In this first respect, we cannot judge popular election in France because it has simply not existed. Secondly, for election to be popular, it must be essentially free, which it never was at any point during the Revolution. Who is not aware that the first moves of an institution may be accompanied by troubles alien to it? The overthrow of what has been, the passions stirred in opposite directions, all these things are ordinarily contemporary with great political changes among peoples of advanced civilization, but derive in no way from the principles or nature of what one wishes to establish. To decide against popular election on the basis of the happenings of the French Revolution, is to judge national assemblies by comparison with Cromwell's Parliament or royalty by comparison with Charles VI's demented reign. Finally, during the ascendancy of our assemblies, no constitution placed real limits on legislative power. Now, when legislative power is quite limitless, when the nation's representatives think themselves invested with boundless sovereignty, when no counterweight exists to their decrees either in executive or judiciary power, the tyranny of those elected by the people is as disastrous as any other, whatever name it bears. The absolute, unlimited sovereignty of the people was transferred by the nation, or as is usual, at least in its name, by those who dominated it, to representative assemblies. These exercised an unparalleled despotism. This had to be, as we have sufficiently demonstrated earlier. [400] The constitution[13] which first put an end to this period of despotism and madness still did not sufficiently limit the legislative power. It established no counterweight to its excesses. It did not enshrine either the indispensable veto of the executive power or the equally indispensable possibility of the dissolution of the representative assemblies. It did

13. That of 5 fructidor an III (22 August 1795).

not even guarantee, as do some American constitutions, the most sacred rights of individuals against the encroachments of legislators.[14]

It is hardly surprising that the legislative power has continued to do harm. People have laid the blame on popular election. This was a profound mistake. It was absolutely not the mode of appointment of the legislators which needed blaming but the nature of their power. The fault was not in the choices made by those represented but in the unchecked powers of their representatives. The ill would not have been less had the mandatories of the nation appointed themselves or had they been appointed by a corporate body however constituted. There was no counterweight, no suppression, no check to their will, decorated though it was with the name of the law. That was the source of the ill. When legislative authority covers everything, it can do only ill, no matter how it is appointed. If you restrict it to things in its jurisdiction, if it is asked to pronounce only on punishments for crimes in the future, on what proportion of individual property must be assigned to public use, on the means of defense to be directed against foreign enemies; if, far from being able to conspire against freedom, its only power is to guarantee and defend it, do not fear to leave to the people the choice of holders of that tutelary power. It will do only good things. For it to do so, however, it must emanate from its true source. The representatives of the nation, proud of their national mission, must place their hope and find their reward only in the votes of those they represent. I will close this digression with two considerations all the more important in their touching on power as much as freedom. The appointment of representative assemblies by an electoral college creates an authority which is neither that of the government nor of the people. And if that authority develops a feeling of hatred for the government, it is in vain that the latter may be surrounded with public affection, [401] in vain that it deserves it. The people who do not have right of election can change nothing in the makeup of the assemblies which speak in their name. It would be in vain too if the government had the right to dissolve them. Dissolution is nothing without popular election, for there is no longer any recourse to the wishes of the people. If the electoral college agrees with the government, the nation will be faced, without being able to make itself heard, with the removal of its most faithful mandatories, the true representatives of its will. If the electoral college is hostile to the government, it will be in vain that the people surround the latter with their love and confidence. Government and nation will see

14. See Constant's Note G at the end of Book XV.

seditious representatives reelected, without any constitutionally legitimate opposition possible, whom the unanimous disavowal of their constituents will not be able to deprive of their position as their deputies. A remarkable era in the annals of the British Parliament brings out the importance of this consideration. In 1783 the English king dismissed his ministers. Almost the entire Parliament belonged to their party. The English people thought differently. The king having appealed to the people in this, via a dissolution of the House of Commons, an immense majority gave its support to the new government. Now, suppose popular election replaced by the authority of an electoral college, if the majority of that college had leaned toward a party which had neither the assent of the governors nor the governed, this party would have had control of affairs, despite the unanimous manifestation of the national will. So true is it that you do not increase the real and legitimate force of government by attacking the people's rights and that it is impossible to create a stable organization if you budge from the principles on which freedom rests. If it were claimed that with a bit of skill or lots of force the government will always dominate the electoral body, I would reply first of all that this hypothesis of a representative assembly which is only the instrument of one or a few men is a terrible one. It would be a thousand times better to have no assemblies at all. Oppression is never so terrible in the name of one man as when it borrows the appearances of freedom. One man would never dare to wish on his own what he orders his agents to will, when they call themselves [402] organs of an independent authority. Think of the Senate of Tiberius or Henry VIII's Parliament. But I would next say that a disorderly agency can react against the hand which employs it. A government which makes use of an assembly which it dominates always courts the risk of seeing it suddenly turn against it. The most enslaved corporate bodies are also the most violent when some unforeseen event occurs which breaks their fetters. They wish to break the opprobrium of their long servitude. The same senators who had voted public holidays to celebrate the death of Agrippina and to congratulate Nero for the murder of his mother condemned him to be beaten with rods and thrown in the Tiber.

I know that people want to frighten souls with exaggerated pictures of the tumults of popular elections. More than once a witness of the apparent disorders which accompany contested elections in England, I have seen how unreliable the descriptions made of them are. Unquestionably, I have seen elections accompanied by uproar, brawls, violent disputes, insults often of the grossest sort, everything which characterizes the class which physical labor deprives of any culture or elegance, any refined occupation. But election did not bear any less on men of notable talent or wealth. And once this operation was over, everything returned to the customary order. Artisans and workmen, recently obstinate and turbulent, became hardworking, docile, even respectful again. Satisfied with having exercised their rights, they complied all the more readily with social superiorities and conventions, in that they were aware, behaving thus, that they were obeying only the independent calculation of rational interest. The morning after an election there was never the least trace of last night's disturbances. The people resumed their work, but they had become convinced of their political importance, and public awareness had received the necessary shaking to bring it alive again. Elections are like almost everything else relating to public order. It is by dint of troublesome precautionary measures that people effect them and nurture them. In France our spectacles and fairs are ringed with guards and bayonets. You might well think three French citizens incapable of meeting without two soldiers to separate them. [403] In England twenty thousand men assemble. Not a single soldier appears among them. The security of each one is entrusted to the reason and interest of each. The crowd, feeling itself the depositary of public order and individual security, guards this duty scrupulously. I will go further. Everything which people invent about the English elections could be proved without my changing my opinion. I would tell myself that for the sense of freedom to penetrate the heart of the nation, it is perhaps necessary sometimes that freedom clothe itself in forms, popular, stormy, boisterous ones, within its understanding. I would rather see a few unforeseen accidents as a result of this, than see the nation becoming indifferent and discouraged because of the absence of these forms. When the nation takes no interest in its rights, power will break out of its confines. Then it undertakes insane wars and allows itself to engage in illegal vexation. And if your counter-argument concerns a few individual misfortunes, a few men dead through suffocation by the crowd or in unexpected brawls, I will ask you whether those who are deported to far, distant shores do not perish, or those whom a worthless whim send beyond the seas on murderous expeditions, or those who are locked up in prisons. If these things are prevented only by freely elected representation, anyone who reflects will willingly run the very improbable risk of some fatal mischance to obtain that unique safeguard against the suspicions of tyranny and the madness of ambition.

CHAPTER SIX

On Ideas of Stability

It is the same with ideas on stability as it is with those on uniformity. They are the source of the greatest and most troublesome mistakes.

There is no doubt that a certain degree of institutional stability may be desirable. There are advantages which develop only with time. Like freedom, habit is a natural need of man. Now, where all stability is lacking, habits cannot take birth. A man who lived fifty years in an inn, forever thinking he was due to leave next day, would learn [404] only the habit of having none. The idea of the future is an element in habit, no less necessary than the past. A nation which perpetually devoted all its strength to seeking political improvements would neglect all the improvements, individual, moral, and philosophical, which are obtained only through peace, and would sacrifice the end to the means. But for the very reason that institutions are means, they must naturally adapt to the times.

By a common enough misunderstanding, when an institution or a law no longer produces the good it once did, it is thought that to restore its former utility it must be established in what is called its old purity. But when an institution is useful, it is so because it chimes with contemporary ideas and enlightenment. When it degenerates or falls into disuse, it is because it chimes no longer. Its usefulness then ceases. The more you reestablish it in its original purity, the more you render it disproportionate with the rest of things.

The vagueness of words always misleads us. It has often been said that governments must conserve, but what they should conserve has not been said. People have not grasped that it should conserve only guarantees of freedom, of the independence of individual faculties and, to that end, of individual physical safety. The result is that governments have believed, or pretended to, that they must use the authority entrusted to them to conserve a certain body of opinions and practices, sometimes as they found them established, sometimes as people said they had once been. The trend of government has habitually in this sense been in the opposite direction to the nature and ends of the human race. The human race being progressive, everything opposing that progress is dangerous, whether or not the opposition is successful.

When opposition is effective, there is stagnation in human faculties, degradation, prejudice, ignorance, error, and consequently crime and suffering.

If on the contrary the static principle is not decidedly the stronger, there is struggle, violence, convulsions, and disasters.

Upheavals are rightly feared; but people go to the opposite extreme with exaggerated ideas of stability, and these ideas, opposing the progress of things, occasion a [405] reaction which produces upheavals. The best way of avoiding them is to fall in with the imperceptible changes inevitable in moral as in physical nature.

The exaggerated idea of stability comes from the desire to govern men by prejudices, to inspire in them just on one's say-so an admiration for ancient things. I much esteem ancient things. I have said so more than once in this book. I esteem them because all interests share in them. Whenever an institution has lasted a long time, unless it has always been maintained by violence, there has been transaction between this institution and the interests having to coexist with it. This transaction itself has, however, modified the institution. This modification is precisely what makes it useful and applicable. To oppose this modification on the grounds of keeping the institution more intact is to take from what is old its most useful character and most precious advantage. The thinking of some writers in this respect is incomprehensible. "When it is impossible for an ancient law to achieve its purpose," says one of them,[15] "this is a clear indication . . . that the moral order contradicts this law too blatantly and, in this case, it is not the law, but mores which must be changed." Who would not have believed that this author was going to say that the law should be changed? How, moreover, does one change mores?

The French Revolution filled many wise men and all peaceful ones with a great respect for and love of stability. The leaders of that Revolution had begun by declaring that everything must be destroyed, changed, re-created. Their successors had thought themselves no less mandated to proceed with arbitrary destructions and reconstructions. This constantly renewed operation must have led an unhappy, weary nation to want above all any kind of lasting State at all. Hence the admiration for certain peoples seemingly with no purpose save the imposition on the future of eternal institutions and the blocking of all change. This admiration has not always been thoughtful. Historians have sometimes been appreciative of these peoples for their intentions without examining whether they succeeded.

15. See Constant's Note H at the end of Book XV.

Nothing is more laughable in this respect than an article on China, [406] by a writer I have already cited.[16] Having recognized that there has scarcely been a century without that empire undergoing civil wars, invasions, dismemberments, and conquests, and having admitted that these terrible crises exterminated entire generations each time, "honor," he exclaims, "to the wise legislators and profound moralists" . . . who have kept all dangerous novelty away from China. And what would novelty have produced more unfortunate? It is true that he adds that these legislators had principles in mind more than people. This is just as Robespierre said: "let the colonies perish, rather than a principle."

Men are inclined to enthusiasm, or to get drunk on certain words. Provided they repeat these words, the reality matters little to them. Two years of horrible and bloody servitude did not stop the French from dating their acts from the fourth year of liberty. A revolution, a change of dynasty, and two hundred thousand men massacred every hundred years do not discourage the panegyrists of China from vaunting the stability of that empire. This stability does not exist for the governed, since they are periodically slaughtered in huge numbers each time a usurper founds a dynasty. It does not exist for the governing class, since the throne is rarely in the same family for several generations. It does exist for institutions, however, and that is what our political writers admire. It is as if institutional stability were the sole end in view, regardless of human happiness, and the human race here on earth only as a means to this.

CHAPTER SEVEN

On Premature Ameliorations

If government acts badly when it stops the natural progress [407] of the human race, and guided by false ideas of stability, opposes the imperceptible changes brought into institutions by the progress of ideas, it does no less harm when it encroaches on the proper dictates of the time and devotes itself to thoughtless projects of improvement or reform.

16. Antoine Ferrand, *op. cit.,* t. I, p. 456 (1803 edition): "There have been scarcely any centuries for four thousand years when that vast and beautiful empire has not been exposed to civil wars, invasions, conquests, and dismemberments. But it is just this which makes its moral stability most astonishing." And on p. 457: "Honor must therefore be rendered to the wise legislators and profound moralists, who, in so to speak amalgamating China with its most ancient laws and morals, made them inseparable, and made of this amalgam the most powerful preservative against all dangerous novelty."

We will have to deal in detail with this subject when we talk about revolutions, which are usually, in their intentions or at least in the language of their authors, only vast reforms or general improvements. Here we have to consider only the endeavors of proper and stable governments, less hazardous endeavors than popular revolutions, but which have nevertheless more than once been pernicious enough.

When government says to public opinion as Séide does to Mahomet, "I acted in advance of your order," public opinion replies, as did Mahomet to Séide, "It should have been waited for,"[17] and when government refuses to wait, public opinion invariably takes its revenge.

The eighteenth century was fertile in examples of this kind.

Chance brings a man of genius to the government of Portugal. He finds that country plunged into ignorance and bent under the yoke of priesthood. He fails to work out that to break this [408] yoke and dispel this deep night he needs a base of support in the national outlook. By a mistake common to those in power, he seeks this base in authority. He thinks by striking a rock he will make a spring flow from it.[18] But his imprudent haste turns against him the few independent minds fit to support him. They oppose a vexatious government whose unjust means render its purposes at least doubtful. The influence of the priests grows with the very persecution of which they are victims. The marquis de Pombal wishes in vain to turn against them the powerful weapons they hold. Censorship, aimed at condemning works favorable to the Jesuits, itself falls victim to condemnation. The nobles rise. The prisons fill. Frightful punishments bring consternation everywhere. The minister becomes an object of horror to all classes. After twenty years of tyrannical administration, he is robbed of his protector by the king's death. He barely escapes the scaffold, and the nation blesses the moment when an apathetic and superstitious government replaces the government claiming to be reformist.[19]

In Austria, Joseph II succeeds Maria Theresa. He observes sadly that the education of his subjects is inferior to that of all neighboring peoples.

Impatient to eliminate an inequality which offends him, he calls to his aid all the means with which his power provides him. He does not neglect

17. A quotation from *Fanatisme, ou Mahomet le prophète,* by Voltaire. Hofmann points out that Constant took the part of Zopire in this play at the beginning of 1806. Séide's exact words are: "I have anticipated your order."

18. Like Moses on Mount Horeb, *Exodus* 17, 1–7.

19. Constant summarizes here what Sebastien-Joseph de Carvalho e Melo (marquis de Pombal) says in his *Mémoires,* s.l, 1784, t. I, pp. 118–124.

even those promised by freedom. He establishes it for the press. He encourages writers to uncover all abuses and thinks he is helping them marvelously by lending them the support of power. What results from this unnatural alliance? That obscure monks and ignorant nobles struggle successfully against the projects of the philosopher, because the philosopher was emperor. His authority is drained in the redoubling of effort. Resistance makes him cruel. His administration becomes odious through excessive severity and iniquitous spoliation. The regrets which go with sterile good intentions, the sadness of being misunderstood, perhaps also the grief of wounded vanity, drive Joseph to his grave. His last words are a confession of his impotence and misfortune;[20] and since the end of his reign, every day [409] we see some of the abuses he thought he had destroyed breaking out and rising anew.

Of all monarchs who have arrogated to themselves the difficult function of speeding up their peoples' progress toward civilization, those of Russia are certainly the most excusable. One cannot deny that from the time of Peter I,[21] the monarchs of that vast empire have been much more enlightened than their subjects. With the exception of a few bizarre things inseparable from any plan spontaneously constructed in the minds of powerful men, the reforms planned and executed by the autocrats of Russia were incontestably real improvements. But the great adopted them only by calculation or imitation, without being able to convince themselves, on their own account, of their intrinsic merit, and regarding philosophy and education, just as luxury and the arts, as adornments necessary to a nation wishing to become European; the people submitted to these changes only by constraint, after numberless persecutions. None of these sound ideas, perceived by government, took root. None of the institutions it commanded became habitual. Morality suffered from the abolition of ancient usages which had always served as its base. Enlightenment made little progress, because such progress depends on a series of ideas powerless until the series is complete and which cannot be introduced by an absolutist government. Peter I's efforts to advance reason remained fruitless because they were in principle vicious. Reason is no longer itself when it lacks freedom. In Russia there is a show of things French at the court and among the nobles, of things Prussian in the army and English in the navy, but the mass of the people in its opinions, customs, and outlook, even down to its clothes, is still an Asiatic nation.

20. See Constant's Note I at the end of Book XV.

21. [Known in modern writings in English as Peter the Great. Translator's note]

It is only since the beginning of the reign of Alexander that Russia has some chance of enlightenment. This young prince seeks not at all to reform the people but to moderate the government. He does not direct thought; rather he restrains government.[22] Now, thought is strengthened when redundant activity is removed from government. For a people to progress, it suffices that government does not shackle them. Progress is in human nature. The government which leaves it alone favors it enough. [410] May Alexander persevere in this at once prudent and generous way and protect himself against the mistrust which seeks to interrupt and the impatience which wants to push ahead.

If we attributed the poor results of so many reforms and innovations attempted in vain by government to the nature of the administrations which presided over these attempts, and if we claimed that, resting on improper bases and always fearful of disturbing them, they were incapable of doing lasting good, because they could want such good only half-heartedly, if we thought that less mistaken governments, ones which had not forced themselves to tread carefully when remedying abuses, would have progressed more crisply, destroyed without difficulty everything in need of destruction, established painlessly everything desirable, experience would soon come and overturn that chimerical supposition.

Doubtless the governments we have cited as examples were in a particularly difficult situation. Pulled by the spirit of the age, they aimed at honoring philosophy, but they did not dare frankly to renounce the support of prejudice. They accepted a few of the most evident rights of the human race, but from their high rank they believed they could represent this acceptance as a gracious one. They thought they owed it to themselves to keep in reserve the right to do all the harm they did not do, not that, to do them justice, they made use of it, but in disclaiming for ordinary purposes the practice of despotism, they retained the theory as part of their beloved decorative pomp. They felt strongly, nevertheless, that security alone could merit gratitude, and they strove, by way of conditional sentences and preambles full of restrictions, to produce security without giving constitutional guarantee. This inherently self-destructive double task contributed greatly, I like to believe, to their faults and reverses. But have we not seen in our country, during the first years of the Revolution, a government free of all oppositional intent finding itself first of

22. See the letter from F. C. de La Harpe to Alexander I, in Jean-Charles Biaudet and Françoise Nicod, *Correspondance de Frédéric-César de La Harpe et Alexandre Ier,* t. I, 1785–1802, Neuchâtel, La Baconnière, 1978, pp. 316–330.

all forsaken, then attacked by public opinion, solely for having pushed forward and precipitately carried out improvements which that very opinion had long seemed to be demanding? The government had taken a few stray and as yet uncertain inclinations and still partial reflections for a general will.

[411] But, someone will ask, how can you know precisely what the state of public opinion is? You cannot count votes. It is only after some particular measure has been taken that opposition appears. Then it is often too late to withdraw. To say that we should not run ahead of public opinion is therefore to say nothing.

I reply first of all that if you allow opinion the right of expression, you will know it readily. Do not provoke it, nor excite hopes by indicating the direction in which you want it to pronounce, for then, to please government, flattery will assume the shape of opinion. Put an irreligious monarch at the head of a devout people and the most flexible of his courtiers will be precisely the most unbelieving. As soon as a government declares for some philosophy, a phalanx forms around it, all the more clamorous in the favored opinion in having none at all itself; and government readily takes the supine surrounding agreement for universal feeling. If government stays neutral, however, letting people debate, opinions join combat and enlightenment is born of their clash. A national outlook forms, and the truth brings together such agreement that it is no longer possible to fail to recognize it.

Secondly, thinking tends to modify gradually laws and institutions which clash with it. Let it do this work. It has the double advantage of softening the execution of defective laws which persist and preparing their abrogation.

When you want to destroy an institution which seems improper to you, let people break free of it, but do not require them to. Allowing this, you call to your aid all educated forces. Requiring it, you arm many interests against you. I will use an example to make myself clear. There are two ways to do away with monasteries. One is to open their doors, the other [412] to drive away their inhabitants. The former does good, without doing bad. It breaks chains but does not violate sanctuary. The latter overturns all the expectations based on public faith. It insults old age, which it drags, listless and defenseless, into an unknown world. It undermines an incontestable right of individuals, namely to choose their way of life, to hold their property in common, and to come together to profess the same doctrine, to attend the same rituals, to enjoy the same prosperity, and to savor the same relaxation. And this injustice turns against reform the very outlook which only recently seemed to uphold it.

In short, any improvement, any amelioration contrary to the habits of a large section of the nation, must as far as possible be adjourned till the time is right. This spares the present generation and prepares the one which must follow. Youth, innovation's collaborator, progresses. Old age has no interest in declaring hostilities, and the change anticipated in this way becomes almost a habit before it is affected.

Time, says Bacon, is the great reformer.[23] Do not refuse its help. Let it go before you, so it can smooth the way. If it has not prepared what you set up, your orders will be in vain. Your institution, however good in theory, is only a mechanism and not part of your administration. It will not be more difficult to rescind your laws than you found it to rescind other ones; and all that will be left of your rescinded ones will be the harm they have done.

CHAPTER EIGHT

On a False Way of Reasoning

An error slides constantly into the arguments used to support the indefinite latitude allowed to govenment action. [413] From negative facts positive theories are derived. When, for example, people rave about the power of the law, about the influence of the guidance government gives to the intellectual faculties of man, they cite the corruption of Italy, fruit of superstition, the apathy and degradation of the Turks, a product of political and religious despotism, French frivolity, the result of a despotic government resting on vanity. From government's ability to do great harm it is concluded that it can do much good. These two questions are very different.

If the English example is pleaded to us, far be it from us to lessen our praise for more than a century of public spirit and freedom. But again two things are being confused, the organization of government in the English constitution and the intervention of that government in individual relations. The latter is being seen as causing the effects of the former. England has political institutions which guarantee freedom. It has institutions of production which hinder it. It is because of the former and despite the latter that England flourishes.[24] We are far from denying freedom's benefits. We recognize them joyfully and desire them ardently; but freedom is precisely the opposite of what is being proposed to us.

23. Francis Bacon, *De augmentis scientiarum,* Book VI, *Exempla antithetorum* XL, *The works of Francis Bacon,* collected and edited by James Spedding, Robert Leslie Ellis, and Douglas Denon Heath, London, 1858, vol. 1, p. 704.

24. See Constant's Note J at the end of Book XV.

CONSTANT'S NOTES

A. [Refers to page 321.]
Prussian monarchy, Introduction.[25]

B. [Refers to page 322.]
Book XXIX, Ch. 18.

C. [Refers to page 324.]
De Pauw, Recherches sur les Grecs, I, 173.[26]

[414] D. [Refers to page 326.]
Recherches sur les Grecs, I, 81.

E. [Refers to page 327.]
Esprit des lois, XI, 8.[27]

F. [Refers to page 329.]
Montesquieu, Esprit des lois, II, 2.

G. [Refers to page 335.]
The members of the legislature of New Jersey make an oath not to vote against laws which assure periodic elections, trial by jury, freedom of conscience, and that of the press. Those of South Carolina take the same oath and moreover one promising not to enact any retroactive law nor to establish any noble titles.

H. [Refers to page 339.]
Ferrand, Esprit de l'histoire, II, 153.

25. Honoré-Gabriel Riqueti, comte de Mirabeau, *De la monarchie prussienne sous Frédéric le Grand,* London, 1788, t. I, pp. viii–ix.

26. Here is the exact text of Cornelius de Pauw at the point indicated by Constant: "The condition in which Greece was placed made the abolition of slavery there impossible; for it would have been necessary for all the republics in that part of the world to be in exact agreement. . . . And as long as they did not free the helots who were the basis of their power, the other states could not give liberty to the slaves who were equally the basis of theirs."

27. In Ch. 6 of Book XI, *éd cit.,* p. 587.

I. [Refers to page 342.]

Joseph II demanded that after his death it should be inscribed on his tomb that he had been unlucky in all his enterprises.

J. [Refers to page 345.]

See Smith, Richesse des nations, Livre IV.[28]

28. Adam Smith, *op. cit.*, Livre IV, Ch. 5, t. III, pp. 244–245: "This assurance which the laws of Great Britain give to each individual, to be able to count on the enjoyment of the fruits of his own labor, is on its own enough to make a country prosper, in spite of all these regulations and twenty other laws of commerce no less absurd. . . . The natural effort of each individual to improve his condition, when that effort is given the right to develop with freedom and confidence, is [415] a principle so powerful that, on its own and without help, not only is it capable of bringing society to prosperity and affluence, but it can even surmount a thousand absurd obstacles with which the folly of human laws comes to impede its march, although the effect of these obstacles is always more or less to undermine its freedom or attenuate its confidence."

BOOK XVI

On Political Authority in the Ancient World

Ch. 1. Why among the ancients political authority could be more extensive than in modern times. 351
Ch. 2. The first difference between the social State of the ancients and that of modern times. 352
Ch. 3. The second difference. 353
Ch. 4. The third difference. 355
Ch. 5. The fourth difference. 358
Ch. 6. The fifth difference. 359
Ch. 7. The result of these differences between the ancients and the moderns. 361
Ch. 8. Modern imitators of the republics of antiquity. 365

CHAPTER ONE

Why among the Ancients Political Authority Could Be More Extensive Than in Modern Times

Before finishing this work I believe I must resolve a difficulty which perhaps has already struck more than one of my readers. The principles I represent as the basis of all possible freedom today are directly opposed to the principles formerly adopted for political organization by most of the free nations of antiquity. If we except Athens, all the Greek republics submitted individuals to an almost boundless political jurisdiction. It was the same in the great centuries of the Roman Republic. The individual was entirely sacrificed to the collectivity. The ancients, as Condorcet remarks,[1] had no notion of individual rights. Men were so to speak just machines, their springs regulated and all their movements directed by the law. Yet it is the ancients who offer us the noblest examples of political freedom history brings down to us. We find among them the model of all the virtues which the enjoyment of that freedom produces and which it needs for its persistence.

One cannot reread, even today, the beautiful annals of antiquity, one cannot retrace the actions of its great men, without feeling some emotion or other of a profound and special type, which nothing modern makes one experience. The old elements of a nature so to speak earlier than ours seem to reawaken in us at these memories. It is hard not to regret these times, when human faculties were developing in a premapped direction, but on a vast scale, so strong in their own powers, and with such a sense of energy and dignity. When we give in to these regrets, it is impossible [420] not to tend to imitate what we regret. As a result, those who since the Renaissance have striven to draw the human race out of the degradation into which those two linked scourges of superstition and conquest had plunged it, have for the most part believed they had to draw from the ancients the maxims, the institutions, and the practices favorable to freedom. But they failed to recognize many of the differences which, in distinguishing us in essence from the ancients, make almost all their institutions inapplicable to our times. Since this misjudgment contributed more than people think to the misfortunes of the Revolution which signaled the end of the last century, I think I must devote several chapters to bringing out these differences.

1. See Constant's Note A at the end of Book XVI.

CHAPTER TWO

The First Difference between the Social State of the Ancients and That of Modern Times

It has often been observed that the ancient republics were confined within narrow limits. From this truth has been drawn a consequence which it is not within our brief to examine here, namely that a republic is impossible in a large State.[2] But another consequence which has not been drawn seems to me to flow much more naturally from it. This is that States much larger than the ancient republics had to modify in quite different ways the duties of citizens, and that the degree of individual freedom could not be the same in both cases.

Each citizen in the ancient republics, circumscribed by the smallness of their territory, had great personal importance politically. The exercise of political rights there was everybody's constant enjoyment and occupation. For example, in Athens the whole people took part in trials. Their share of sovereignty was not as in our time an abstract supposition. Their will was a real influence and [421] not susceptible to mendacious falsification and corrupted representation. If political power was oppressive, each citizen consoled himself with the hope of exercising it. Today the mass of citizens is called to exercise sovereignty only in illusory fashion. The people can only be slaves or free; but they are never in charge.

The happiness of the majority no longer rests in the enjoyment of power but in individual freedom. Among the ancients the extension of political power constituted the prerogative of each citizen. In modern times it consists in the sacrifices individuals make.

In the ancient republics, while the exercise of political authority was a right for all, at the same time submission to that fearsome power was also a necessity for all. The people engaged in sovereign debate in the public place. Every citizen was visible and de facto subject to that sovereignty. Today the great States have created a new guarantee, obscurity. This guarantee reduces the dependence of individuals on the nation. Now it is clear, absolutely clear, that a dependence which on the one hand gives less enjoyment and on the other can be avoided more easily is one which cannot last.

2. This was on the other hand the subject of a "grand treatise" on politics, from a work abandoned in 1806, entitled "On the Possibility of a Republican Constitution in a Large Country," of which only the *Fragments* remain.

CHAPTER THREE

The Second Difference

A second difference between the ancients and the moderns stems from the very different condition of the human race in these two periods. Formerly small peoples, almost without reciprocal relations, joined battle over a limited territory. These peoples pushed by necessity one against another, fought or threatened each other endlessly. Those who did not want to be conquerors could not put down the sword for fear of being conquered. They bought their security, independence, their lives at the price of war. Though history presents us alongside these small nations with some large trading or peaceful nations, such nations are much less well known than the warlike ones. We see Egypt only through the mendacious accounts of its priests, distorted further by the exaggerations of [422] Greek credulity. On the Phoenicians we possess only a few geographical data. We follow their sea journeys on the map. We speculate which shores they touched upon. We know almost nothing, however, about their institutions, mores, or internal life. The Athenians are the only people of antiquity who are not exclusively warlike and about whom history nevertheless bequeaths us some precise details. Moreover, Athens differed much less from today's societies than did other small peoples of the same period. By a remarkable singularity, however, those who offer us antiquity as a model choose by preference exclusively bellicose peoples like the Spartans and the Romans. This is because only these nations lend support to their theoretical viewpoint, only they brought together great political freedom and an almost total absence of individual freedom.[3]

Our world is precisely the opposite of the ancient one. Everything in antiquity related to war. Today everything is reckoned in terms of peace. In former times each people was an isolated family, born hostile to other families. Now a mass of people lives under different names and divers modes of social organization, but homogenous by nature. It is civilized enough to find war burdensome; it is strong enough not to need to fear invasion by still barbarian hordes, relegated to the very ends of its territory. Its tendency is uniformly toward peace. The warlike tradition, a legacy of remote times, plus crimes and mistakes by governments, born of violence, retarded the effects of this tendency. It makes more progress every day, however. People

3. See Constant's Note B at the end of Book XVI.

still fight today. Powerful men usually learn social enlightenment more slowly than those they govern. They twist their governance to favor their prejudices. Governments sometimes have a passion for war; the governed no longer do. Even governments seek justification for it. They no longer profess love of conquest, nor hope of personal glory by feats of arms. We made this point before.[4] No Alexander would dare to propose to his subjects, straightforwardly, the invasion of the world, and Pyrrhus's speech to Cyneas[5] [423] would seem to us the height of insolence and folly. Today a government which spoke of military glory as an end would be failing to recognize and scorning the spirit both of nations and our era. It would be wrong by a thousand years, and even if it were successful at first, it would be curious to see which would win this strange wager between our century and this government. War no longer exists as a purpose but only as a means. Peace and with peace affluence and to gain affluence production: such are the sole purposes to which the human race now aspires. Civilized peoples battle only because wrong views and false reckoning make them see rivals where they should see only emulators and also persuade them that to weaken their competitors is to strengthen themselves while to ruin them is to enrich themselves. This mistake changes nothing, however, deep down in their character. To the degree the character of the ancients was warlike, ours is pacific. For them a successful war was an infallible source of wealth for individuals. For us a successful war always costs more than it is worth. The outcomes of wars are no longer the same. There is no longer any question of invading entire countries in order to reduce their inhabitants to slavery and to divide up their lands.

In ordinary wars, the frontiers of large States or their distant colonies can fall to the power of the enemy. The center stays intact and apart from some pecuniary sacrifices it continues to enjoy the advantages of peace. Even when extraordinary circumstances and motives which stir up all the abysses of the human heart make hatred more inveterate and hostility more violent, as for example during the French Revolution, the fate of conquered countries is still in no way comparable [424] to what it was in antiquity.

4. In Book XIII, Ch.1.

5. A reference to the dialogue between King Pyrrhus and his minister Cyneas, related in Plutarch, *Vies*, t. VI, *Pyrrhos-Marius—Lysandre-Sylla*. Text edited and translated by Roger Flacelière and Emile Chambry, Paris, Les Belles Lettres, 1971, pp. 43–44. Cyneas asked the king what the latter would do after conquering the Romans. Pyrrhus replied that he envisaged new conquests forever until there were no more peoples to submit. The purpose of the apologue is to show the absurdity of the spirit of conquest.

Now the restrictions on political power are necessarily different in a habitual state of war.

War demands more extensive public force than peace does and force of a different order. The public force necessary for peace is entirely negative, namely public safeguards. War needs active force. The discipline it brings in informs all other institutions. To succeed war needs common action. In peace each man needs only his work, efforts, and individual resources. It is as a collective being that a people profits from the fruits of war. Each man enjoys separately those of peace and enjoys them in a way all the more complete in its being more independent. The purpose of war is fixed: victory, conquest. This purpose is always manifest to interested parties. It joins them, enchains them, makes of their efforts, plans, and wills an indivisible whole. Peace presents no precise purpose. It is a condition in which each person freely forms projects, meditates on his means, gives play to his personal plans. Warrior peoples must consequently bear the pressure of political power more readily than pacific peoples. The purpose of the free institutions of the former is to prevent usurpers from seizing political power, the property of the whole mass. The latter wish in addition to limit power in itself, so that it does not bother either their economic reckonings or their rights. The former say to governments, lead us to victory, and to assure it to us, subject us to severe disciplinary laws. The latter tell them, guarantee us against violence and do not interfere with us.

CHAPTER FOUR

The Third Difference

In the third place, none of the republics people have wanted us to imitate was commercial. The limits of this work prevent us from citing all the causes which constituted obstacles to the progress of commerce among the ancients. Ignorance of the compass forced them not to lose sight of the coast during their navigations more than was [425] absolutely necessary. To go beyond the columns of Hercules, that is, pass through the Strait of Gibraltar, was considered the most audacious venture. The Phoenicians and Carthaginians, the most skillful navigators among the ancients, did not dare to till very late and for long had no imitators. In Athens, which as we will say below was the most commercial republic of antiquity, the maritime rate of interest was about 60 percent, while the ordinary rate was only 12 percent, so much did the idea of long-distance navigation imply danger.

Religious prejudices were opposed to maritime trade among several peoples of antiquity. For example, there was the horror of the sea among the Egyptians, as still today among the Indians, whereby sacred rites forbade the lighting of fire on the ocean, thus preventing all long-range navigation, because food cannot be cooked. Independently of these factual proofs, simple reasoning suffices to show that war must have come before trade. The one and the other are only different means of reaching the same end, which must forever be man's end, that is, to assure oneself the possession of what seems desirable. Trade is only homage made to the power of him who has what we would like to seize. It is the desire to get by mutual agreement what we no longer hope to take away forcibly. A man who was always the strongest would never have the idea of trade. It is experience, which, proving to man that war, that is, the use of force against the force of other people, is exposed to divers opposing checks and failures, brings him to resort to trade, that is, to a gentler and surer way of engaging the interest of others so that they consent to what suits one's interest. War is therefore older than trade. The one is an impulsion, the other a calculation. The spirit of modern peoples is essentially commercial. Trade makes a large extension of political power at once more harassing and easier to evade: more harassing, since trade casts greater variety into men's economic dealings, and government has to multiply its activities to get at these dealings in all their manifestations; easier to elude because trade, [426] changing the nature of property, makes this part of human existence, a part which soon becomes its most important one, almost untouchable by government. Trade gives to property the new quality of mobility. Without mobility property is only a usufruct. Government can always exert an influence on a usufruct, since it can take away one's right of possession. Mobility, however, puts an invisible and invincible block on this boundless power of government. The effects of trade extend further still. Not only does it free individuals from the tyranny of communal government, but by creating credit it subjects communal government in some respects to individuals. It has very often been remarked that money is despotism's main weapon but also its most powerful brake. Credit subjected to public opinion makes those who govern dependent on the governed. Force is pointless. Money hides or flees. All the State's operations are suspended. In antiquity credit did not have the same influence.[6] A deficit of sixty

6. See Constant's Note C at the end of Book XVI.

million made the French Revolution. A deficit of six hundred million under Vespasian did not shake the empire in the least.[7]

Thus governments in antiquity were necessarily stronger than individuals. Individuals are today stronger than their governments.[8]

Trade has another effect. In antiquity each citizen saw not only his affections but his interests and his fate bound up in his country's lot. His patrimony was ravaged if the enemy won a battle. A public reversal removed him from the rank of free man, condemning him to slavery. No one had the means of moving his wealth. In [427] modern nations, thanks to trade, individuals shape their own futures, despite events. They move their assets far away; governments cannot penetrate their transactions; they take along with them all the comforts of private life. Moreover, in antiquity war isolated nations. Their mores were different, their dispositions savage, and expatriation almost impossible.[9] Trade has brought nations together, giving them almost the same mores and habits. Their leaders may be enemies, but the peoples are compatriots. Trade has modified even the nature of war. Trading nations were in the past always subjugated by warrior peoples. Now they resist the latter successfully.[10] Carthage struggling against Rome in antiquity was bound to fail; the weight of things was against her. If the struggle between Rome and Carthage happened today, however, Carthage would enjoy the best wishes of all the peoples. She would have for allies the outlook and the mores of the century. Just as war, as we have already shown, favors a vast extension of political power, so trade is favorable to individual freedom.[11]

This observation is borne out, even when applied to contemporary nations. People in Athens enjoyed an individual freedom much greater than in Sparta, because Athens was at once warlike and commercial[12] and Sparta was exclusively warlike. This difference makes itself felt under all forms of political organization. Under despotism, as under freedom, war gathers men around government, trade isolates them from it.

7. Charles Ganilh, *Essai politique sur le revenu public des peuples de l'antiquité, du moyen-age, des siècles modernes et spécialement de la France et de l'Angleterre, depuis le milieu du XVe siècle jusqu'au XIXe,* Paris, Giguet et Michaud, 1806, t. I, pp. 64–65. "When Vespasian mounted the throne, he declared that the state was unsustainable unless a way were found of raising 6,900,000,000." Hofmann points out that Constant omitted a zero.

8. See Constant's Note D at the end of Book XVI.

9. See Constant's Note E at the end of Book XVI.

10. See Constant's Note F at the end of Book XVI.

11. See Constant's Note G at the end of Book XVI.

12. See Constant's Note H at the end of Book XVI.

[428] If we could enter here into historical details, we would show how among the Athenians trade had made the most essential differences between the ancient and modern peoples disappear. The outlook of the Athenian traders was like the outlook of ours. During the Peloponnesian War they withdrew their holdings from the Athenian mainland and sent them to the islands of the archipelago.[13] Trade had created circulation between them. They understood the use of bills of exchange.[14] From this, because it is all connected, flowed a vast softening in manners, more indulgence toward women,[15] more hospitality to strangers,[16] and an exceeding love of individual freedom. In Sparta, says Xenophon,[17] citizens run when the magistrate calls them. In Athens a rich man would be in despair if anyone thought he was subservient to the magistrate. If the completely modern character of the Athenians has not been remarked on enough, this is because the general spirit of the age influenced philosophers, and they always wrote in an inverse direction from the national mores.

CHAPTER FIVE

The Fourth Difference

Fourthly, the universal practice of slavery among the ancients lent their mores something severe and cruel which made it easy for them to sacrifice the gentle affections to political interests. The existence of the slaves, that is, of a class of men who enjoy none of the rights of humanity, changes absolutely the character of the peoples among whom that class exists. The inevitable consequence of slavery is the weakening of pity, of sympathy for pain. The slave's pain is a resource for the owner. At equal levels of civilization, a nation which has slaves must be much less compassionate than one which does not. Antiquity, even among the most orderly peoples, and the individuals most distinguished by their [429] rank, elevation, and enlightenment, supplies us with numerous and almost incredible examples of inhumanity inspired in the master by his untrammeled power over the enslaved.[18] Reading the address by

13. See Constant's Note I at the end of Book XVI.
14. See Constant's Note J at the end of Book XVI.
15. See Constant's Note K at the end of Book XVI.
16. See Constant's Note L at the end of Book XVI.
17. See Constant's Note M at the end of Book XVI.
18. See Constant's Note N at the end of Book XVI.

Lysias,[19] we can scarcely conceive a social condition so ferocious that such an address could actually be articulated. Two men have bought a slave girl destined for their common pleasure, an initial outrage against decency and nature. She becomes fond of one to the other's disadvantage. The latter comes before the judges, demanding publicly from the court his share of the slave whom he has legitimately bought. To establish the facts he alleges, he demands that she be subjected to torture, waxing indignant that his opponent objects to this, and seeing nothing in his objections save the illegal refusal of a litigant of bad faith perfidiously repudiating the best way of bringing out the truth. The torments of the slave, the profanation of everything holy in humanity and love, the horrible mix of torture and pleasures, which would revolt any modern mind, count for nothing, either with him who makes this shameful demand, or the judges to whom he appeals, or the spectators who listen to him, or Lysias, who cold-bloodedly composes a harangue in support of this claim.

The absence of slavery joined to the progress of civilization has given us more human mores. Cruelty, even to further our interest, has become generally alien. Abstract reasoning and the public good have made it impossible for us.

CHAPTER SIX

The Fifth Difference

Lastly, mankind has not aged by more than twenty centuries without changes in character. The ancients were right in the youth [430] of moral life. The moderns are in its maturity or perhaps its old age. This observation can be proved, if need be, by simple examination of ancient writings. Their poetry is all of a kind and direct. Their poets' enthusiasm is true, natural, complete. Modern poets are always trailing some ulterior motive or other drawing on experience and destroying enthusiasm. We might say they fear to seem dupes and rather than lending themselves to an irresistible impulse, these are men who pore over the poetry with their readers. The first condition of enthusiasm is not to observe oneself too knowingly, but the moderns never stop observing themselves, even in the midst of their most sensitive or violent impulses.

19. Le quatrième discours *Au sujet d'une accusation pour blessures avec préméditation de meurtre*. Lysias, *Discours,* text edited and translated by Louis Gernet and Marcel Bizos, Paris, Les Belles Lettres, 1924, t. I, pp. 80–84.

The word "illusion" has no equivalent in any ancient language because the word comes into being only when the thing no longer exists. The philosophy of the ancients is exalted even when it claims to be abstract. Modern philosophy is always dry, even when it strives to be exalted. There is poetry in the philosophy of the ancients and philosophy in the poetry of the moderns. Ancient historians believe and affirm; modern historians analyze and doubt. The ancients had complete conviction about everything. We have almost none save about the hypocrisy of conviction. Now, nothing is isolated in nature. Literature always bears the impress of the general character. Less worn out by civilization, the ancients had more vivacious impressions of things. Their warlike habits inspired in them great activity, profound confidence in their strength, scorn for death, a standard indifference to pain, and therefore greater devotion, energy, and nobility. The moderns, wearied by experience, have a sadder and thereby more delicate sensibility, a more habitual openness to emotion. Egoism itself, which mingles in with this faculty of emotion, can corrupt but not destroy it. To resist the power which suffering has over us, we are forced to avoid the sight of it. The ancients faced it without fear and tolerated it without pity. A woman of very superior intelligence has very wisely remarked how much less refinement there was in the sensibility of the ancients than in ours, by comparing [431] Racine's *Andromache* with Virgil's, though the latter is incontestably the most sensitive of the ancient poets.[20] Writers who have come after her and copied her without acknowledgment,[21] have attributed the difference to religious causes. This is an inversion of the ideas. This difference makes itself felt in religion as elsewhere. Religion is not its cause, however. Its cause lies in the progress of civilization, which gentles the character by weakening it, and which, making domestic relations safer, less menaced, less interrupted, thereby makes of them a more constant and intimate part of human life. The ancients, like children, believed docilely, and listened with respect. They could accept without repugnance a whole ensemble of institutions made up of traditions, precepts, usages, and mysterious practices as much as from positive laws. The moderns have lost

20. Madame de Staël, *De la littérature considérée dans ses rapports avec les institutions sociales,* revised, corrected, and enlarged second edition, Paris, Maradan, an IX. *Préface de la seconde édition,* t. I, pp. 13–14.

21. A reference to François René de Chateaubriand, *Génie du christianisme ou beautés de la religion chrétienne,* Deuxième partie, Livre II, Ch. 10. In the Paris edition, by Migneret, 1802, t. II, pp. 96–98, Chateaubriand takes up the idea of a comparison, but does not, strictly speaking, plagiarize Mme de Staël.

the ability to believe for a long time and without analysis. Doubt is endlessly at their shoulder. It weakens the force even of what they do take on. The lawmaker cannot speak to them as a prophet. He makes positive laws for them to give their existence security. They cannot be dominated, however, except by habit. Every advance in life gives preeminence to a different faculty, among nations as among individuals. Imagination was dominant among the ancients as reason is with us. Now imagination runs to meet what one wishes to persuade it of. Reason waits and rejects, and even when it yields does so only reluctantly. From this results a truth whose consequences are as important as they are extensive. Nothing was easier than recasting ancient peoples by their institutions. Nothing would be more impossible than treating modern peoples this way. Among the ancients an institution was effective the moment it was set up. An institution among the moderns is effective only when it has become a habit. In the remote times of antiquity peoples had so few habits that they changed names almost as often as rulers. Dionysius of Halicarnassus[22] informs us that Italy was designated in succession [432] by six different appellations according to the names of those who seized that country one after another. Leaders of nations and earth's conquerors, try to designate a street by your name today. All your might will not make people forget their habit and substitute this new name for it.

CHAPTER SEVEN

The Result of These Differences between the Ancients and the Moderns

Because of all these differences, freedom cannot be the same among the moderns as it was among the ancients. The freedom of ancient times was everything which assured the citizens the biggest share in the exercise of political power. The freedom of modern times is everything which guarantees the citizens independence from the government. The character of the ancients gave them above all the need for action, and this need sits very well with a great extension of political power. Moderns need calm and various satisfactions.[23] Calm is found only in a small number of laws preventing its being disturbed, satisfactions in an expansive individual freedom. Any legislation demanding the sacrifice of these satisfactions is incompatible with

22. See Constant's Note O at the end of Book XVI.

23. [The French word "*jouissances*," which Constant uses, can mean both private pleasures and the enjoyment of property tenures and so on. Translator's note]

the present state of the human race. In this respect nothing is more curious to observe than the speeches of French demagogues. The wittiest of them, Saint-Just, delivered all his speeches in short sentences, proper to arouse tired souls. And while he seemed to suppose the nation capable of the most painful sacrifices, in his very style he recognized it as incapable even of attention. One must not demand of modern peoples the love and devotion the ancients had for political freedom; it is civil freedom which men in our era cherish above all. This is because not only has civil freedom gained in advantages, owing to the multiplication of private decision making, but political freedom has lost them, owing to the size of societies. The only group among the ancients to demand a sort of individual independence were the philosophers. Their independence, however, was in no sense like personal freedom, which [433] seems desirable to us. Their independence consisted in renouncing all the joys and affections of life. Ours on the contrary is precious to us only in guaranteeing us these joys and permitting us these affections. The progress of mankind resembles the individual's. The young man believes he loves his country more than his family and sometimes the world more than his country. But as he gets older, the scope of his feelings narrows, and as if warned by instinct of the weakening of his powers, he no longer tires himself loving faraway things. He keeps close to him what remains of his power to feel. Similarly, as the human race ages, home-based affections replace grand political interests. What needs to be done, therefore, is to purchase political freedom as cheaply as possible, that is, to leave as much personal freedom as possible,[24] in all its forms, and in every respect. The tolerance of the ancients would not suffice for us, being purely national. Each nation's religion was respected, but each member of a given State was forced to abide by his country's religion.[25] The religious freedom civilization demands today is of a different kind. It is an individual freedom each man wants to be able to practice privately. Laws on morals, celibacy, or idleness are intolerable. These laws assume a subjugation of the individual to the body politic of a kind we could no longer tolerate.[26] Even the laws against begging, however necessary they might be, are difficult and odious to operate, involving something against the grain of our practices.

For the same reason life must not be subject to many shocks. The social ramifications are much greater than before. Even groups which seem to be

24. See Constant's Note P at the end of Book XVI.

25. See Constant's Note Q at the end of Book XVI.

26. See Constant's Note R at the end of Book XVI.

enemies are joined by imperceptible but indissoluble links. Banishments, confiscations, spoliation by the state, unjust in all eras, have today become absurd and pointless as well. Property, having assumed a much more stable nature and having identified itself more intimately with human existence, demands [434] much more respect and much more freedom. Man having lost in imagination what he has gained in positive knowledge and for this very reason being less given to enthusiasm, legislators no longer have the same power over him. They must renounce any disruption of settled habits, any attempts to affect opinion powerfully. No more Lycurgus, no more Numa, no more Mahomet.[27] M. de Pauw's observations on music apply to legislation. "The most inferior of music," he says, "produces among barbarian peoples sensations incomparably stronger than the sweetest melody can excite among civilized peoples." He continues, "The more the Greeks wished to perfect music, the more they saw its marvels weakening."[28] This was precisely because they wished to perfect music, that is to say, were judging it. All their savage ancestors had done was listen to it.[29] I would not want to affirm that modern man is not given to enthusiasm for certain viewpoints, but he certainly no longer is for men. The French Revolution is very remarkable in this regard. Whatever one may have been able to say about the inconstancy of the peoples of the ancient republics, nothing compares with the volatility we have witnessed. Study carefully, even in the violence of the best-prepared unrest, the obscure ranks of the blind, submissive populace, and you will see them, just as they are following their leaders, fix their gaze in advance on the moment when the latter must fall. You will spot in their meretricious exaltation a bizarre mix of analysis and mockery. Though they strive to numb themselves by their acclamations, and recoup themselves by their raillery, at the same time they will seem to you to distrust their own conviction, to have a personal presentiment, so to speak, of the time when the prestige will be dissipated. People are astonished that the most marvelous enterprises, the most unexpected successes, prodigious actions of courage and skill, today cause almost no sensation. This is because the good sense of the human race warns it that all this is not done on its behalf. This is governmental display. Since governments alone find [435] pleasure in it, they alone can bear the costs. The activity of those in power has become much less necessary since contentment, for most men, is

27. See Constant's Note S at the end of Book XVI.

28. See Constant's Note T at the end of Book XVI.

29. See Constant's Note U at the end of Book XVI.

now based on private relationships. When conditions were essentially warlike, people admired courage particularly, because courage was the most indispensable quality in the leaders of the peoples. Today, conditions being essentially pacific, what those in government are asked for is moderation and justice. When they lavish countless great spectacles of heroism and creation and destruction on us, we are tempted to reply to them: the least grain of benevolence would be far more to our liking. All the moral institutions of the ancients have become inapplicable to us. The institutions I call moral, as opposed to purely political ones, are those which like censorship or ostracism attributed to society, or some number of men or other, a discretionary jurisdiction operating not according to legal and judicial principles but on the vaguely conceived idea of the moral character of certain individuals, of their intentions and of the danger they could pose to the State. I call the practice which made all the citizens of the ancient republics prosecutors a moral institution. This was an honorable function. People sought to distinguish themselves in the pursuit and denunciation of the guilty. In our times the function of the prosecutor is odious. A man would be dishonored if he exercised it without legal remit. All this results from the same cause. Formerly public interest went before safety and individual freedom. Today safety and individual freedom come before the public interest.

Peace, calm, and domestic contentment being the natural and invincible tendency of modern peoples, more sacrifices have to be made for that calm than the ancients made. Disorder is not always incompatible with political freedom, but it always is with civil and individual freedom.

Political freedom offering less satisfaction than formerly and the disorders it can entail being more unbearable, we must conserve only what is absolutely necessary in it. To claim today to console men with political freedom for the loss of their civil freedom is to go in the opposite direction from the present-day spirit of the human race. Far from opposing one of these freedoms to another, [436] we should present the former only as the guarantee of the latter. I would be misunderstood, nevertheless, if it were claimed that arguments against political freedom could be drawn from this conclusion. Many men today would like to draw this inference from it. Because the ancients were free, their inference is that we are destined to be slaves. They would like to constitute the new social State with a small number of elements they claim to be uniquely adapted to the situation of the modern world. These elements are: prejudices to frighten men, greed to corrupt them, frivolity to stupefy them, coarse pleasures to degrade them, despotism to rule them, and, of course, positive knowledge and exact science to serve the despotism more adroitly. It would be bizarre were such to be the end point of forty centuries during which the human race has mastered more moral and physical means. I cannot believe it. The inference I draw from the differences which mark us off from antiquity is absolutely not that we should abolish public safeguards but that we should extend satisfactions. It is not political freedom that I want to renounce, but civil freedom that I am demanding along with other forms of political freedom.

Governments have no more right than before to arrogate to themselves illegitimate power; but legitimate governments have less right than in former times to fetter individual freedom.[30] We still possess today the rights we owned at all times, the eternal rights to justice, equality, and safeguards, because these rights are the purpose of human societies. But governments, which are only the means of attaining this purpose, have new duties. The progress of civilization, the changes effected by the centuries in the predisposition of the human race, require of them more respect for the habits and affections, in a word for the independence of individuals. They must handle these sacred things more prudently and more gently every day. [437]

CHAPTER EIGHT

Modern Imitators of the Republics of Antiquity

The truths we have just developed are unrecognized today, as much by the speculative philosophers who during the eighteenth century, it must be added, with a courage worthy of praise, laid claim to the forgotten rights of the human race, as by more hotheaded and less enlightened men, who have wanted to put into practice the principles of these philosophers. From this have followed mistakes and absurdities which seem almost inexplicable to us, in the theorizing of some of our most famous writers. We will cite only one example of these, taken at random.

Ancient legislators had a deep hatred of wealth. Plato refused to give laws to Arcadia solely because of its opulence.[31] All the men of government of antiquity saw in poverty the source of all virtue and glory. Modern moralists have copied these maxims. They have not considered that if wealth was

30. See Constant's Note V at the end of Book XVI.

31. Hofmann was unable to find a specific passage on Plato's refusal to give laws to Arcadia, but notes that the philosopher's contempt for wealth is to be found in Book V of the *Laws*. The French text he cites is in *Oeuvres Complètes,* t. XI/2, text edited and translated by Edouard des Places, Paris, Les Belles Lettres, 1951, pp. 99–102.

corrupting among the warlike people of antiquity, this is because it was the fruit of conquest and pillage which, swiftly penetrating the lands of poor people unused to its possession, soon intoxicated them.

Wealth would become corrupting again, if owing to some violent upsets we fell back again in this respect into the condition of the ancient peoples, that is, if the poor and ignorant class, suddenly seizing the spoils of the educated class, had at their disposal riches they could use only deplorably and coarsely. When wealth is the gradual product of assiduous work and a busy life or when it is transmitted from generation to generation by peaceful possession, far from corrupting those who acquire it or enjoy its use, it offers them new means of leisure and enlightenment and consequently new motives for morality. Because they did not consider differences of period, our moralists have wanted to swim against the current. They have recommended privations to peoples schooled to the imperatives of power and riches and, by a singular contrast, while all the laws were calculated to encourage the acquisition [438] of wealth and discover new sources of it, all the moralizing aimed to present it as a scourge.[32]

The errors of our philosophers, innocent as long as they were merely theoretical, became terrible in application. During the French Revolution, when the flow of events put in charge of things men who had adopted philosophy in a preconceived way, these men thought they could make public power work as they saw it done in the free States of antiquity. They believed everything must still today yield to collective authority, that private morality must be silent before the public interest, that all the violations of civil liberty would be redressed by the enjoyment of political liberty in its widest sense. But collective authority did nothing but harm individual independence in every sense, without destroying the need for it. Private morality was silent; but since the public interest does not exert the same sway over us as over the ancients, it was to a hypocritical and ferocious egoism that private morality saw itself sacrificed. The great sacrifices, the acts of devotion, the victories won in Greece and Rome by patriotism over the natural affections, served among us as a pretext for letting loose the most unchecked individual passions, in a wretched parody of the most noble examples. Because inexorable but just fathers had once condemned their criminal children, their modern imitators had innocent enemies put to death.[33] Lastly, the institutions which

32. See Constant's Note W at the end of Book XVI.

33. For these sacrifices of children by their father, see Mme de Staël, *Des circonstances actuelles, éd. cit.*, p. 244.

in the ancient republics surrounded political freedom, the foundation of civil freedom, with a strong guarantee, resulted only in the violation of civil freedom, without establishing political freedom.

Among the writers of the eighteenth century, there is one above all who has pulled opinion along this mistaken and dangerous course, namely the Abbé de Mably.[34] Mably, whom people nicknamed the Spartan, was a pure-hearted man who cherished morality and thought he loved freedom, but was possessed assuredly of the falsest mind and the most despotic outlook ever to exist.[35] As soon as he happened [439] upon a vexatious measure, in any country, he thought he had made a discovery and proposed it as a model. He detested most of all individual freedom, and when he came upon a nation which was completely deprived of this, he could not stop himself admiring it, even when it had absolutely no political freedom. He raved over the Egyptians, because he said with them everything was fixed by law. Every moment in the day was filled by some duty. Everything bowed before the legislator's empire, even relaxation, even necessities. Love itself was subject to this honored intervention, law by turns opening and closing the nuptial bed.[36] For some time people have repeated the same absurdities about the Egyptians. We are recommended to imitate a people suffering from a double servitude, pushed back by their priests from the sanctuary of all knowledge, divided into castes of which the lowest was deprived of all the rights of society and of humanity itself, retained by a yoke of iron in an eternal infancy, an immobile mass, equally incapable of educating or defending itself and constantly the prey of the first conqueror who came to invade, I will not say their fatherland, but their territory. These new apologists of Egypt must be recognized as more consistent in their theorizing than the philosophers who have heaped the same eulogies on it. They set no value on freedom, on the dignity of our nature, on the activity of the mind, on the development of the intellectual faculties. They want only to serve despotism, for lack of the ability to possess it.[37] If enslaved Egypt seemed to Mably to merit an almost boundless admiration, solely because all individual independence was suppressed there, one can see that Sparta, which brought together the forms of republicanism with the

34. On Mably and his possible influence on the revolutionaries, see the clarifications by Ephraïm Harpaz, "Mably et la postérité," *Revues des sciences humaines,* 1954, pp. 25–40; "Mably et ses contemporains," *ibid.,* 1955, pp. 351–366; "Le social de Mably," *Revue d'histoire économique et sociale,* t. XXXIV, 1956, pp. 411–425.

35. See Constant's Note X at the end of Book XVI.

36. See Constant's Note Y at the end of Book XVI.

37. See Constant's Note Z at the end of Book XVI.

same bondage for individuals, must have excited his even more enthusiastic admiration. This vast monastery seemed to him the ideal of the free republic.[38] He had a profound contempt for Athens, and would readily have said of that first nation of Greece, what some grand seigneur or other of an academician said of the academy: What a frightful despotism; everybody does what he likes there! The regret [440] he expresses constantly in his works is that the law can get at actions only. He would have liked it to get at thoughts and the most fleeting impressions, and to pursue man without respite, leaving him no shelter where he could escape its power. He constantly took government for freedom, and all means for extending the action of government over the recalcitrant part of human existence, whose independence he deplored, seemed to him good. Mably is, after Rousseau, the writer who has had the most influence on our Revolution. His austerity, his intolerance, his hatred for all the human passions, his eagerness to enslave them, his excessive principles concerning the jurisdiction of the law, his relentlessness against individual freedom, which he treated as a personal enemy, the difference between what he recommended and what had existed, his ranting against wealth and even against property, all these were bound to please a group of men overheated by their recent victory, men who, conquerors of a power they called law, were very pleased to extend that power over everything. It was weighty authority for them, that a writer with no stake in the question, who always pronounced anathemas against royalty, had, buried away in his study, long before the Revolution, drafted in axiomatic form all the maxims necessary for organizing the most absolute despotism, under the name "republic." Mably had noticed in antiquity, independently of law proper, what he termed institutions. It would be difficult to define precisely what he understood by this word. It was an ensemble of laws, habits, traditions, and ceremonies, calculated to appeal to the imagination and to lend to established constitutions the support of this vague but irresistible power. Mably did not reflect that the very philosophers of antiquity, who so sang the praises of institutions to us, were mostly speaking of an earlier time, and it was the same with these things as with ghosts. No one has seen any; but everyone has in his family some tale which attests their existence.[39] Mably exalted therefore beyond measure the [441] institutions of antiquity and the need to establish ones like them, and our legislators began to establish institutions. But since institutions rest on habits, this was to want to create habits, that is to say,

38. See Constant's Note AA at the end of Book XVI.
39. See Constant's Note BB at the end of Book XVI.

to create a portion of the past. They instituted national holidays, ceremonies, periodic assemblies. Soon it was necessary to require the observance of these fairs, attendance at these assemblies, respect for these ceremonies, under threat of severe penalties. A duty was made of what should be voluntary. Celebration of freedom was surrounded with constraint.[40] Those in government were astonished that the decrees of a day did not immediately erase the memories of several centuries. They called habits ill will. The slow, gradual effects of childhood impressions, the direction imprinted on imagination by a long sequence of years, seemed to them acts of rebellion. The law being the expression of the general will, it seemed to them that it should make all other forces give way, even those of memory and time. All these efforts, all this harassment, gave way beneath the weight of their own extravagance. There is no saint so humble in the most obscure hamlet who has not battled successfully against the whole national government, ranged in arms against him. Supporters of all theoretical systems of this kind always mistake effect for cause. Because habits transform themselves into institutions, they think nothing easier than transforming institutions into habits. They want to support all the natural sentiments, honor, patriotism, paternal power, conjugal love, respect for old age, by means of institutions. This is to pursue a course opposite to nature. Institutions have to be created by the spontaneous motion of sentiments. For them to be powerful but not tyrannical, their origin must be lost in the night of time. For their head to reach toward heaven and cover us with its shade, their roots must be hidden in the earth's bosom. They are useful as a heritage; they are merely oppressive when drafted as laws. Government is in rightful place only when it is a curb. Then none of its actions is worthless. But when it wants to encourage, direct, arouse, and enthuse and comes forward with pretentious talk, always followed with coercive measures, it is ridiculous in failure and despotic in constraint.

[442] One can include under the heading of ill-conceived institutions what some political writers[41] have termed penalties for infamy and rewards of honor, isolated, spasmodic attempts, vicious in inspiration, liable to bias and contradiction and irrelevance, by means of which government wishes to put itself in the place of the most easily offended and delicate feelings, believing it can distribute honor and shame at will.

40. Constant himself, as President of the Commune of Luzarches, had scrupulously ensured that the observation of fairs and the revolutionary calendar be respected. See Hofmann's thesis, Première Partie, Ch. 2, pp. 92–93.

41. See Constant's Note CC at the end of Book XVI.

If the penalty for shameful behavior is accompanied by deprivation of certain rights, by exclusion from certain offices, then it becomes a positive punishment, not solely a case of disapprobation. If the honorific rewards the government bestows carry with them an entitlement to certain prerogatives, the rewards are no longer purely honorific. They come into the category of compensation which society can grant for services it has received. Then the vocabulary is inaccurate. But if both of these measures are separated from any drawback or any advantage of a different sort, then that is a nonsense. This is to require the government to play the part of public opinion. Shame diminishes and honor withers, when government arrogates to itself the right to apply them. Human intelligence must be perverted and the most delicate strands of inner feeling ruffled, to make men submit to government in questions pertaining to morality. Consider how under the monarchy itself, at a time when vanity was raised to its highest possible degree of susceptibility by all the artificial means it is in the nature of this government to employ, consider, I repeat, how many useless attempts and proclamations there were by government to stigmatize dueling.

People have often praised the moral effect of Roman censorship. But the censors had legal power and inflicted real punishments. They inflicted them arbitrarily in truth. This arbitrariness was counterbalanced, however, by the simplicity of ancient mores, and by the chance every citizen, as an almost immediate spectator of all the actions of his fellows, had to evaluate the justice of the censors. When these magistrates debarred the dictator Mamercus, who had reduced their terms of office to eighteen months, from entering the Senate, this vengeance excited the indignation of the Senate and the people, and Mamercus was amply compensated by public opinion.[42] [443] The fact is, however, that all the fellow citizens of this dictator were gathered together in the same town, and witnesses and judges of the injustice he was experiencing. In a State like France, the power of the censors would be an intolerable tyranny. If the government of a large nation dared to declare, by way of a public act, without trial, that an individual was dishonored, it would not be the individual but this entire nation that this government would be declaring incapable of all sense of honor, and the nation would protest against this decree by not endorsing the government's decisions.

42. Aemilius Mamercus, consul and dictator in 438, 437, 433, and 426 B.C., in 433 B.C. reduced the term of office of censors from five years to eighteen months. Constant probably got this from Machiavelli, *Discours sur la première décade de Tite-Live,* Ch. XLIX, in *Oeuvres complètes, op. cit.,* p. 485.

Censorship degenerated even in Rome, when the size of the Republic, the complexity of social relationships, and the refinements of civilization had taken away from the institution the thing which served it as both a base and a limit. It was not censorship which had created good mores, but the simplicity of the mores which constituted the power and efficacy of censorship.[43]

In the present state of society, individual relations are made up of fine nuances, changeable and elusive, which would be distorted in a thousand ways if one tried to give them clearer definition. Public opinion alone can affect them. It alone can judge them because its nature is the same. Times of civil upheaval, I must confess, are particularly unfavorable to the power of opinion, which is a kind of moral sense which develops only in tranquillity. It is the fruit of leisure, security, and intellectual independence.

Revolutionary shocks and reactionary excesses make it disappear. Scaffolds, deportations, and massacres leave purely moral nuances powerless. Public opinion can exist only where there remains neither anything despotic nor any political divide. Public opinion and arbitrary power are incompatible. The former must overcome the latter or be suffocated. Divisions on party lines, which make this or that belief the blackest of crimes or the highest of virtues, are destructive of public opinion because its basis is falsified and it follows a totally mistaken direction. In such cases one has to wait and leave things to happen. I would add that the law should be silent, if I did not think that in these circumstances those who make the laws are aiming precisely [444] to falsify public opinion. They prevent man from retiring into himself, from consulting his own heart, from thinking according to his own lights. And as if his self-interest was not enough for them to corrupt him, they also want to stupefy him by giving themselves the false appearance of appealing to his own judgment and reason.

43. See Constant's Note DD at the end of Book XVI.

A. [Refers to page 351.]
Mémoires sur l'instruction publique.

B. [Refers to page 353.]
"In Rome, as in all the Republics of Antiquity, the force of the constitution, that is to say, political freedom, was perpetually altered by individual freedom." Antoine Ferrand, Esprit de l'histoire, I, 242.[44] Gross ignorance; it is precisely the opposite.

C. [Refers to page 356.]
The public revenue of the ancients, says Ganilh,[45] was made up from the work of slaves, the plundering of the conquered, and tribute from subjugated peoples. There was nothing there which could give birth to credit such as we conceive it today, because there was nothing there which depended on the views and the individual confidence of members of the society. This claim is perhaps a bit too general, since the citizens of Athens and Rome, from the time of Servius Tullius, paid taxes on their wealth to the State. But these taxes were nothing compared to what was drawn from allied peoples and the provinces. And the author's basic outlook is no less true because of that.

[445] D. [Refers to page 357.]
See on this subject an excellent work which has just appeared. [See Constant's previous note and also footnote 45.] The differences between our era and antiquity in this regard are perfectly expounded, along with the results of these differences.

E. [Refers to page 357.]
In Latin the word *hostis* meant, equally, a stranger or an enemy. Cicero, De Officiis, Liber I.[46]

44. Antoine Ferrand, *L'Esprit de l'histoire ou lettres politiques et morales . . .*, Paris, Vve Nyon, 1802.

45. Charles Ganilh, *op. cit.,* t. I, pp. 66–67.

46. See Ganilh, *op. cit.,* t. I, p. 221, n. 1. Ganilh's note supported the following text: "The ancients were in a permanent state of hostility between themselves. Without mutual communication, they saw and treated each other as enemies." Cicero in *Les devoirs,* I, 37, says, "Among our ancestors in fact we called *hostis* him whom now we call *peregrinus,* foreigner." Text edited and translated by Maurice Testard, Paris, Les Belles Lettres, 1965, t. I, pp. 121–123.

F. [Refers to page 357.]
"In modern wars," observes Smith, " the huge expense of firearms gives a great advantage to the nation most in a position to meet this expense and therefore to a civilized and wealthy rather than a poor and barbarous one. In ancient times rich and civilized nations found it difficult to defend themselves against poor and barbarous ones. In modern times poor and barbarous nations find it difficult to defend themselves against civilized and opulent ones." Richesse des nations, Livre V, Ch. 1.[47]

G. [Refers to page 357.]
There are some ingenious ideas on the links between commerce and individual and political freedom, in Walckenaer's Essai sur l'histoire de l'espèce humaine, pp. 250 onward.[48]

H. [Refers to page 357.]
All commodities, says Isocrates, Panégyrique, p. 114, which [446] are dispersed only in small portions in the other markets of Greece, are found together in abundance in the Piraeus.[49]

I. [Refers to page 358.]
Xenophon, De la république des Athéniens.[50]

J. [Refers to page 358.]
Isocrates recounts in his Trapezeticus that a stranger who had brought corn to Athens presented a bill of exchange drawn on a town in the Euxine from a merchant named Stratocles.[51]

47. Adam Smith, *op. cit.*, t. IV, pp. 122–123.

48. C.-A. Walckenaer, *Essai sur l'histoire de l'espèce humaine*, Paris, Du Pont, 1798, Livre VI, pp. 251–368, *Des peuples cultivateurs, après l'introduction des manufactures et du commerce et la séparation des professions.*

49. This note is taken from Cornelius de Pauw, *op. cit.*, t. I, pp. 70–71. Hofmann does not know to which edition Constant's page reference (114) relates. The reference is to the *Panegyric* of Isocrates in his *Discours*, text edited and translated by Georges Mathieu and Emile Brémond, Paris, Les Belles Lettres, 1938, t. II, p. 24.

50. Xenophon, *La république des Athéniens*, II, 16: "But as they did not have the chance to build their city on an island, here is what they do. Confident in their maritime superiority, they deposit their wealth in the islands, leaving Attica to be ravaged, because they understand that if they have mercy on it they will lose other more important goods." Xenophon, *Anabase . . . , éd. cit.*, p. 518.

51. Isocrates, *Trapésitique*, 35–37. See the edition of the *Discours, éd. cit.*, t. I, pp. 81–82. Constant has taken the example and the reference from Cornelius de Pauw, *op. cit.*, t. I, p. 335.

K. [Refers to page 358.]

"Provided that peace and friendship continue to reign in the life of the household, there is great respect for the mothers of the family. There is even indulgence of the sins which nature makes them endure, and when they succumb to the irresistible tyranny of the passions, the first weakness is forgiven and the second forgotten." Xenophon, Dialogue between Hieron and Simonides.[52]

L. [Refers to page 358.]

Proofs of this hospitality to be found. Art, industry. The law of Solon. The émigrés who come to Athens with their whole family to establish a trade or a factory, can from that moment be raised to the dignity of citizens. Samuel Petit, [447] Compilation of the Laws of Athens, Livre II, titre III.[53] Plutarch, Solon.[54]

M. [Refers to page 358.]

Xenophon, Respublica Lacedaemoniorum.[55]

N. [Refers to page 358.]

"Cum omnibus horis aliquid atrociter fieri videmus aut audimus, etiam qui natura mitissimi sumus, assiduitate molestiarum sensum omnem humanitatis ex animis amittimus." Cicero, Pro Roscio.[56] Cicero speaks in this passage about the mores of Romans in general. One could apply it, however, to the slave in particular. Everyone knows how little men who have lived for a long time in the colonies are susceptible to pity. Xenophon, his treatise on the Republic of Athens, goes as far as maintaining that people treated the slaves with too much consideration.[57]

52. All this note and the reference are from Cornelius de Pauw, *ibid.*, p. 191.

53. It is again from Cornelius de Pauw (*op. cit.*, t. I, p. 69) that Constant has drawn this illustration with the references to Samuel Petit and Plutarch.

54. Plutarch, *Solon,* 24, 4: "He permitted citizenship to be granted only to people banished in perpetuity from their country or who come to set up in Athens with all their family with a view to establishing a trade." Plutarch, *Vies,* t. II, *Solon, Publicola, Themistocle, Camille,* text edited and translated by Robert Flacelière, Emile Chambry, and Marcel Juneaux, Paris, Les Belles Lettres, 1961, p. 39.

55. Xenophon, *La république des Lacédémoniens,* VIII, 2: "in the other States, the most powerful do not even want to have the appearance of fearing the magistrates and regard such fear as a mark of baseness. In Sparta, on the contrary, the most notable men are the most submissive to the authorities; they glory in their humility and pride themselves when they are called on, obeying not by walking but at the double." Xenophon, *Anabase . . . , éd. cit.,* p. 489.

56. "When all the time we see or notice some atrocity or other, for all our very sweet disposition, the repetition of these painful events drives any feeling of humanity away from our hearts." Cicero, *Pro Sex. Roscio Amerino,* in *Discours,* t. I, text edited and translated by H. de la Ville de Mirmont, Paris, Les Belles Lettres, 1921, p. 126.

57. This example and the reference come from Cornelius de Pauw, *op. cit.,* t. I, p. 168.

[448] O. [Refers to page 361.]
Livre I, Ch. 1.[58]

P. [Refers to page 362.]
Speaking of republics before and after their corruption, M. de Montesquieu says: "One was free with the laws, and wishes to be so against them." This could be said in another sense of the ancients and the moderns.

Q. [Refers to page 362.]
Plato in his tenth book of The Republic upheld as legitimate the accusations of impiety.[59] The first philosophers who adopted true principles of tolerance were the neo-Platonists.

R. [Refers to page 362.]
In Athens the law of Solon against idleness fell rapidly into disuse, as violating the rights of a free people. Freedom consists, Socrates said, in working or not as one wishes.[60]

S. [Refers to page 363.]
"Ancient legislators excelled in the formation of public spirit. But their political miracles must be attributed less to the wisdom of some people than to the weakness of others. They were speaking to humanity in its infancy. The modern legislator, [449] relying solely on the authority of reason, may well demand belief, but he cannot enforce it." Toulongeon, De l'esprit public.[61]

58. Dionysius of Halicarnassus, *Les antiquités romaines,* Paris, Ph.-N. Lottin, 1723, pp. 16–23.

59. Plato, *La république,* X, XIII, 615c, in *Oeuvres complètes,* t. VII, 2e partie, text edited and translated by Emile Chambry, Les Belles Lettres, 1934, p. 115. See also Plato's other great work on politics, *Les lois,* Livre X, in *ibid.,* t. XII/1, text edited and translated by A. Dies, Paris, Les Belles Lettres, 1956, pp. 141–148. The same example is found in Cornelius de Pauw, *op. cit.,* t. II, p. 46.

60. *Ibid.,* p. 62: "Solon had the advance and prosperity of Athenian manufactories so much at heart that he took it upon himself to make a law against idlers, one which soon fell into disuse . . . The true freedom, said Socrates, consists in working when one wishes and not working when one does not." There is another note by Constant on this law of Solon in Annexe I, Principes de politique (Hofmann's edition), p. 654.

61. François-Emmanuel d'Emskerque, vicomte de Toulongeon, *De l'esprit public. Mémoire désigné pour être lu à la dernière séance de l'Institut national,* Paris, Impr. de Du Pont, 1797, pp. 9–10: "We are astonished by the ease of domination the ancient legislators had: it is because they were talking to the human mind still in its infancy. People believed in apparitions, political miracles, and auguries. The strong, simple man listened and believed. The mature human mind no longer believes on trust. To give it laws you have to persuade it, which is more difficult than giving it to believe something."

T. [Refers to page 363.]
Recherches sur les Grecs. Partie III, 6.[62]

U. [Refers to page 363.]
The Athenians, who may be regarded in many respects as moderns in the bosom of antiquity, were of all the Greeks the ones who attached least importance to music. Xenophon tells us in his République d'Athènes[63] that they did not set great store by men committed solely to harmony. The fact is that the taste for music is a passion only among simple peoples, not far advanced in civilization. The Athenians, more advanced than any other ancient people, had this taste less than any other; but their philosophers, who, as we have said, wrote endlessly and in the opposite direction from the national mores and inclinations, did not on this account recommend or praise music any the less.[64]

V. [Refers to page 365.]
"In the present state of civilization and in the commercial system under which we live, all public power must be limited and an absolute power cannot subsist." Ganilh, Histoire du revenu public, I, 419.

[450] W. [Refers to page 366.]
"Greek politicians, who lived under popular government, did not recognize any force other than virtue which could sustain it. Those of today speak only of manufactures and commerce, finance, wealth, and even luxury." Montesquieu, Esprit des lois, III, 3. He attributes this difference to the republic and the monarchy. It should be attributed to the dissimilar conditions of ancient and modern times.

X. [Refers to page 367.]
The work of Mably, De la législation ou principes des lois, is the most complete code of despotism imaginable. Combine these three principles: 1. Property is an evil. If you cannot destroy it, weaken its influence in every way. 2. Individual freedom is a scourge. If you cannot annihilate it, restrain it at least as much as possible. 3. Legislative power is unlimited. It should be extended to everything and everything be made to bow before it. You will feel how difficult it is to escape from this terrible combination. So a constitution based on Mably would be the combined one of Constantinople and Robespierre. Here are some axioms transcribed with scrupulous

62. Cornelius de Pauw, *op. cit.*, t. II, pp. 121–122.

63. Xenophon, *La république des Athéniens*, I, 13, in Xenophon, *Anabase . . .*, *éd. cit.*, p. 512.

64. This remark on music among the Athenians, and the reference to Xenophon, come from Cornelius de Pauw, *op. cit.*, t. I, p. 225.

fidelity.[65] Control morality, p. 175.[66] Do not be frightened of poverty.[67] What does it matter if such and such an arrangement makes commerce flourish and doubles the State's revenues? 176.[68] The establishment of property casts you back into an abyss, p. 186.[69] [451] What does the population matter? It is more valuable for the human race to have a few virtues than many advantages and to count only a million happy men than a multitude of wretched ones, 187.[70] Diminish the State's finances, 193.[71] Forswear all public debt, 197.[72] Ban useless arts and impose on the necessary ones a certain coarseness. Extend your sumptuary laws to everything, 199.[73] Proscribe commerce. Render its agents vile, 200.[74] Prevent selling, the alienation of goods, and

65. Hofmann says that unless Constant found these axioms in a commentary by Mably, his claim of fidelity to Mably's text is not upheld. Hofmann could find them in none of the most cited editions. In the instances which follow he has collated the axioms with the text of *De la législation ou principes des lois,* published in t. IX of the *Oeuvres complètes de l'abbé de Mably* (Lyon, J.-B. Delamollière, 1792).

66. "For my part, I make do with demanding morality, and I am not at all scared of poverty" (p. 16).

67. See previous note.

68. An amalgam of two distinct passages in the original: "What does a superiority one owes to wealth matter?" (p. 17) and "Such and such an arrangement would make commerce flourish, some other would enrich the treasury and double the State's revenues" (pp. 19–20).

69. "You see with what wisdom nature had prepared everything to lead us to common ownership of assets, and prevent our falling into the abyss into which the establishment of property has thrown us" (p. 58).

70. "I could think it more worthwhile for the human race to have a few virtues than many advantages. What will happen to the population? people will say. I reply that it would be better to count only a million happy men on the whole earth than to see on it that numberless multitude of the poor and enslaved who live only a half-life in degradation and poverty" (p. 68).

71. "The laws will always put up only a useless resistance to the efforts of avarice and the vices which flow from it, if they do not start by diminishing the finances of the State" (p. 97).

72. This formulation perhaps summarizes what Mably says (pp. 107–108) on rampant greed allied to public debt.

73. "I hope that useless arts will never be reestablished among us; that they are forbidden. I hope they will let the necessary arts retain a certain coarseness, which suits them so well" (p. 122) and "I would not stop talking to you about the sumptuary laws, if I wished to have you know all their advantages. They must be extended to everything" (pp. 112–113).

74. Summary of a long diatribe against trade (pp. 113–115).

wills, 202.[75] Set up agrarian laws, ibid.[76] Do not allow citizens to go abroad to amass wealth, 203.[77] Establish state education and do not tolerate the arbitrary rules the paterfamilias devises for himself in this respect, 278.[78] Be in fear of atheists and deists, 286.[79] Life imprisonment for the former, 297.[80] Do not permit deviation from the official religion, [452] 299.[81] Lock up the deists. Instruct them in their prison and, if they are guilty twice of declaring their opinions, life sentence as for atheists, 302.[82] Do not allow new religions, nor citizens to profess the traditional one without making use of its official ministers, 310,[83] etc.

It will be agreed that it is strange that this should be the writer endlessly quoted in the national forum,[84] as a fitting guide for the establishment of freedom. I will add that his historical erudition is as inaccurate as his political principles are wrong and persecutory. He adopts with blind credulity everything the historians have passed on to us on Lycurgus, without stopping for an instant over the difficulties of every kind which surround everything to do with this legislator. He constantly exaggerates the political influence of Sparta on Greece, without taking into account that Athens possessed at least as much influence as Sparta and counting for nothing the disproportion between these two powers. Sparta had a bigger area and more fertile than Athens, Megara, Corinth, Argos, and Sicyon combined. But he did not wish to recognize this disproportion because he needed to cite a great example in favor of the moral institutions of the Spartans. I must say, however, that when Mably leaves his exaggerations to touch upon less vague subjects, he shows a much better wit. In the third book of his Principes des lois, when he is dealing specifically with positive laws,

75. Summary of pp. 116–120.

76. "You will never restrain these active and haughty feelings if you do not have recourse to agrarian laws" (p. 120).

77. "What care must not the laws take in order that the citizens do not go abroad in order to amass wealth they will repatriate?" (p. 125).

78. "The republic will never form excellent citizens, as long as education is not public and general. Will you let the paterfamilias make his own rules in this respect?" (p. 309).

79. Phrase summarizing pp. 324 and following.

80. On p. 354, Mably, contrary to Plato, who demands death for atheists, says he would believe "his law wiser, if it made do with sentencing an incorrigibly guilty man to lifetime incarceration."

81. Summary of Ch. 3 of the last book, *On the Need for a State Religion* (pp. 355 and following).

82. "When a deist is locked up for violating the law of silence imposed on him, let nothing be forgotten with regard to instructing him and making him understand his fault [. . .] If after a long correction a deist still has the same thirst for fame and martyrdom, it will finally be necessary to reconcile yourself to treating him like an atheist" (pp. 364–365).

83. Summary of pp. 388–389.

84. See the article by Ephraïm Harpaz, "Mably et ses contemporains," *op. cit.*, pp. 360–366, for numerous examples which uphold Constant's remark.

he develops several very just ideas and several very useful truths. His Observations sur l'histoire de France[85] are one of the best works on this matter. Even so, I think him one of our writers most full of false notions, ones most dangerous for freedom.

[453] Y. [Refers to page 367.]
Entretiens de Phocion.[86]

Z. [Refers to page 367.]
See the new Essais de morale et de politique[87] and L'Esprit de l'histoire by M. Ferrand. "The religious and political laws," says this latter, "were in perfect agreement with society's duties. Both took hold of the citizen from the moment of his birth and together educated the man for society. Both followed him through all the jobs and activities of his life, to correct his whims and repress his passions. They inspected and ruled his work and even his pleasures. The Egyptian seemed to be always under this double protection, and this severe social constraint was what assured his freedom. The law assigned each person his job which ran from father to son. This rule perhaps denied Egypt some superior men, but it gave her something more worthwhile, continuity in useful men. The law laid down a uniform direction for these restless minds, who might have proved a trouble to the State, taking only their imagination as a guide." (To choose his vocation and the sort of work he does, using only his imagination as a guide, is the distinctive quality of a restless mind!) "Read about the revolutions of all empires, always the work of a few men who wished to rise above their stations." (This is to say often the work of a few men who felt that society was imposing on them unjustifiable constraints. Now, the more you multiply constraints of this kind, the more you multiply reasons for revolutions and therefore attempts at them.) "Our modern philosophers have endlessly repeated that the best laws are those which leave greater latitude to man's will. Send them back, these scourges of humanity, [454] to the infancy of the human race."[88]

85. Honoré-Gabriel Bonnot de Mably, *Observations sur l'histoire de France.* The first edition had appeared in Geneva in 1765. In *Oeuvres complètes de l'abbé de Mably, éd. cit.,* t. I–II.

86. "All the moments of their day were filled with some duty [. . .] Everything was prescribed by law, even relaxation and human functions [. . .] Finally, love itself, that passion, Aristias, too often so imperious, so puerile, so fiery, so weak, was only a simple relaxation after work; it was the law which opened and closed the queen's apartment to the prince." Honoré-Gabriel Bonnot de Mably, *Entretiens de Phocion sur les rapports de la morale avec la politique,* in: *Oeuvres complètes de l'abbé de Mably, éd. cit.,* t. IX, pp. 71–72.

87. Louis-Mathieu Molé, *op. cit.,* pp. 211–214. If Constant calls Molé's *Essais* new, this is probably to distinguish them from those Francis Bacon brought out in 1597 under the same title.

88. Antoine Ferrand, *op. cit.,* lère éd. (1802), t. I, pp. 63–66; 2e éd. (1803), t. I, pp. 72, 75–78. The passages quoted by Constant (he has not mentioned the numerous excisions) are the same in both editions; however, in the second, Ferrand is even more eloquent on this subject and has added between p. 72 and p. 75 a long development.

(Actually one has to return to the infancy of the human race, that is, to the centuries of ignorance and barbarism, to believe that it might be useful or legitimate to constrain the will of man in cases which do not hurt other people.)

AA. [Refers to page 368.]
Isocrates and Plato testify that the Spartans were for the most part so little schooled that they knew neither how to read, nor sign their name, nor calculate beyond their fingers.[89]

BB. [Refers to page 368.]
Mably fails to recognize a difference between the ancients and the moderns we have already indicated elsewhere. All the modern peoples have been conquered by barbarians from the north. The ancient peoples seem not to have been conquered but only civilized by foreign colonies. Now, the goings-on of peoples who have been conquered and peoples who have not undergone this are very unlike. The latter [unreadable words in Constant's text] to give themselves institutions they do not have. The former seek to rid themselves of institutions they have had imposed on them. Hence they have a habit of resistance which lasts and is directed not only at institutions imposed by force but at all kinds of institutions. The modern nations have struggled against theirs in all sorts of ways, in barbarous times by force, in corrupted times by mockery. Now, this last weapon is terrible, in that it is destructive not only of the past but also of the future.

CC. [Refers to page 369.]
Filangieri.[90]

DD. [Refers to page 371.]
Esprit des lois, VII, 14; XXIII, 21.[91]

89. Hofmann was unable to determine to what passages by Isocrates or Plato this observation refers, nor in which author's work Constant found the reference.

90. Gaëtano Filangieri, *La science de la législation, éd. cit.*, t. IV, pp. 42–64, Ch. VII *Des peines d'infamie.*

91. In Livre XXIII, Ch. 21 notably, where Montesquieu declares: "The corruption of morals destroys censorship, itself established to destroy the corruption of morals; but when this corruption becomes general, censorship no longer has any force." *Ed. cit.*, p. 692.

BOOK XVII

On the True Principles of Freedom

Ch. 1. On the inviolability of the true principles of freedom. 383
Ch. 2. That the circumscription of political authority, within its precise limits, does not tend to weaken the necessary action of the government. 385
Ch. 3. Final thoughts on civil freedom and political freedom. 386
Ch. 4. Apologia for despotism by Louis XIV. 392

CHAPTER ONE

On the Inviolability of the True Principles of Freedom

This work has sought to determine the extent and jurisdiction of political authority on the various things which include all the interests of men. Let us now see what principles of freedom result from our analysis and whether these can be overdone or misused.

Individuals must enjoy complete freedom of action for all innocent or unimportant actions. When, in a given situation, an action unimportant in itself can threaten public safety, such as a certain way of dressing which can serve as a password, a society has a right to forbid it. When an action of the same kind is part of a guilty action, such as brigands agreeing to a rendezvous before effecting an assassination, society has the right to deal harshly with this unimportant action, in order to interrupt a crime already begun. In the two cases society's intervention is legitimate because its need is proven. But equally in the two cases it is legitimate only on this condition.[1]

Individuals must enjoy complete freedom of opinion either private or public, as long as that freedom does not produce harmful actions. When it does produce such, it becomes identified with them, and under this heading it must be repressed and punished. Opinion separated from action, however, must remain free. The only function [460] of the government is to confine it to its proper domain, speculation and theory.

Individuals must enjoy a boundless freedom in the use of their property and the exercise of their labor, as long as in disposing of their property or exercising their labor they do not harm others who have the same rights. If they do so harm them, society intervenes, not to invade anyone's rights but to guarantee the rights of all.

Now, what abuses can result from these principles which are the only true principles of freedom, and to what exaggeration are they susceptible?

A singular error which I indicated at the start of this book and of which one must accuse Rousseau and Mably above all, but from which almost no political writer has been exempt, has confused all ideas on this question.

The principles of political authority have not been distinguished from those of freedom.

1. Constant had already spoken of the jurisdiction of the government on the actions of individuals in Book V, Ch. 2.

Since in the theorizing of philosophers friendly to humanity, the principles of government tended to take away from oppressors of human societies the powers they had usurped and to return those powers to the whole society, it was not grasped that this last was only a preliminary operation which had merely destroyed that which should not exist, but by means of which one was deciding nothing as to what should be put in its place.

Thus the dogma of national sovereignty having been first proclaimed and then abused, it was thought that a principle of freedom was being abused, when it was only an abuse of a principle of government.

Because where citizens are nothing, usurpers are everything, it was believed that for the people to be everything it was necessary that individuals be nothing. This maxim is palpably false. It implies that freedom is nothing other than a new formula for despotism. Where the individual is nothing, the people are nothing. Can it be thought that the people get rich from the losses of each of their members, as a tyrant enriches himself from what he steals from each one of his subjects? Nothing is more absurd. The people are rich by way of what their members possess, free because they are free. The people gain nothing from members' sacrifices. Individual sacrifices are sometimes necessary, but they are never a positive gain, either for individuals or the nation.

Those who hold or usurp power may, to legitimate their encroachments, borrow the name of freedom, [461] because, unfortunately, the word is boundlessly obliging; but they can never borrow its principles or even any of its maxims.

When, for example, a mistaken majority oppresses the minority or, which happens far more often, when a ferocious and noisy minority seizes the name of the majority to tyrannize society, to what does it lay claim in justification of its outrages? The sovereignty of the people, the power of society over its members, the abnegation of individual rights in favor of the society, that is to say, always principles of government, never principles of freedom.

How indeed could the latter be invoked in favor of the opposition? What do they establish? That society has no right to be unjust toward a single one of its members, that the whole society minus one is not authorized to obstruct the latter in his opinions, nor in those actions which are not harmful, in the use of his property or the exercise of his labor, save in those cases where that use or that exercise would obstruct another individual possessing the same rights.

Now, what do oppressive majorities or minorities do? Precisely the opposite of what these principles establish. It is not therefore these principles they exaggerate or abuse. They act from directly opposite assertions.

When can opinions put out by the press become a means of tyranny? It is when a single man or group of men seize exclusive control of the press and make it the organ of their opinion, represent this opinion as national, and wish on this authority to make their view prevail over all others. But in that case, what principles can this man or men proclaim in support of their behavior? Not the principles of freedom, which forbid making any opinion dominate, even that of everyone against that of a single other soul, but the principles of political government, which, exaggerated and submitting individuals with all their rights and without reserve to the sovereign community, permit the restraining, obstructing, and proscribing of the opinions of individuals.

These examples could be multiplied infinitely. The result would always be the same. It was by derivation from this error that Burke said freedom is a power.[2] Freedom is a power only in the sense that a shield is a weapon. So when one speaks of possible abuses of the principles of freedom, [462] such an expression is inaccurate. The principles of freedom would have prevented anything under the heading of abuses of freedom. These abuses, whoever their author, taking place always at the expense of another's freedom, have never been the consequence of these principles, but rather their reversal.

CHAPTER TWO

That the Circumscription of Political Authority, within Its Precise Limits, Does Not Tend to Weaken the Necessary Action of the Government

The circumscription of political authority, within its precise limits, does not tend to weaken that necessary authority. On the contrary, it gives it the only real strength it can have. The jurisdiction of authority must be scrupulously limited; but once that jurisdiction is fixed, it must be so organized as always to be capable of attaining swiftly and completely all the purposes within its remit. Freedom gains everything from the government's being severely confined within the bounds of its legitimacy; but it gains nothing from government's being feeble within those bounds.

The weakness of any part of government whatsoever is always an evil. That weakness in no way diminishes the drawbacks to be feared, and it destroys the advantages to be hoped for. In loosening public safeguards it places absolutely no obstacles to usurpation, since usurpation results from powers the government encroaches upon and public safeguards from powers which belong to it legitimately. Now, in weakening government, you

2. See Book XV, Ch. 1, n. 2.

force it to encroach. Unable to attain its necessary purposes with the means which belong to it, in order to attain them it has recourse to means it usurps, and from that usurpation, so to speak forced, to spontaneous usurpation, boundless usurpation, there is but a single step. If you extend government to everything, however, lovers of freedom and all independent men, that is to say everything on earth which has some value, will not be able to submit to such an idea. They would readily have accepted that the government be all-powerful within [463] its jurisdiction; but constantly finding it transgressing that jurisdiction, they will want to diminish a power which they will not be able to limit. In that way, they will organize, as we have seen in a number of examples, governments which are too weak, and accordingly become usurpatory. It is quite unnecessary to sacrifice the least part of the principles of freedom for the organization of legitimate and sufficient government authority. The principles coexist with this authority, both protecting it and protected by it; for they stand against the possibility that factions may overthrow it, by laying claim to these rights of society, opposed to those of individuals, these axioms of unlimited sovereignty, this despotism of the so-called general will, in a word, this popular power without limits, dogmas which are the pretext for all our upheavals and which have been represented as principles of freedom, while they are precisely the opposite.

The principles of freedom, such as we have defined them, are useful and necessary to everybody, for they preserve the rights of all people as individuals, those of society and those of government. These principles are the sole lasting means of real happiness, of assured peace, of ordered activity, of improvement, of tranquillity and durability.

CHAPTER THREE

Final Thoughts on Civil Freedom and Political Freedom[3]

That this book has dealt exclusively with issues connected to civil freedom does not mean to insinuate that political freedom is something superfluous. Those who would sacrifice political freedom in order to enjoy civil freedom the more peacefully are no less absurd than those who would sacrifice civil freedom in the hope of further extending political freedom. The latter sacrifice the end to the means. The former renounce the means under the pretext of achieving the end. One could apply to taxation all the arguments used

3. [This heading is inconsistent with the title page on p. 458 of the French text. Translator's note]

against political liberty. One might say that in order to conserve what one has it is ridiculous [464] to begin by sacrificing a part of it. Provided that the people are happy, it is sometimes said, it matters little if they are free politically. But what is political freedom? It is the ability to be happy without any human power being able arbitrarily to trouble that happiness. If political freedom is not one of the individual possessions nature has given man, it is what guarantees them.[4] To declare it worthless is to declare the foundations of the building one lives in superfluous. Those in government, the argument continues, have nothing to gain from the unhappiness of the governed. Consequently, political freedom, that is, the safeguards of the governed against the government, is scarcely necessary. This assertion is not correct, however.

First, it is not at all true that the interests of the governors and the governed are the same. The governors, whatever the political organization, being always limited in number, are threatened with loss of power if others attain it. They therefore have an interest in the governed not getting into government, that is to say, they clearly have an interest distinct from that of the governed. I have said elsewhere[5] that property tended to circulate and spread, because owners remain owners when others become such. For the opposite reason power tends to concentrate. As a result, as soon as a man passes, by whatever means, from the class of the governed to the class of the governors, he adopts the interests of the latter. This is the spectacle offered in Rome for the most part by the defenders of the popular cause when success crowned that ambition; and we see the same thing among the ministers in England.

Representative government does not lift this difficulty. You choose a man to represent you because he has the same interests as you. By the very fact of your choosing him, however, your [465] choice placing him in a different situation from yours gives him a different interest from the one he is charged with representing.

This drawback can be prevented by the creation of various sorts of positions in government invested with different kinds of powers. Then the holders of these powers, mutually contained in such a way as to be unable to make their own interests prevail, draw close to those of the governed whose interests are the average ones of everybody. Such is the advantage of the division of powers. One should not delude oneself, however, as to the efficacy of these

4. Constant has earlier said, in Book I, Ch. 3, "Individual rights are freedom; social rights are the guarantee."

5. See notably Book X, Ch. 10 and Book XI, Ch. 4.

devices or flatter oneself that these two sets of interests ever get to be amalgamated completely.

An incontestable maxim is that it is always in the interests of the greater number that things go well, rather than badly. It is sometimes in the interests of the smaller number that things go badly rather than well.

In the second place, if we examine the different ways in which the governors can abuse their power, we will find that their interest is not at all not to abuse it, but to do so only to a certain point. For example, they have an interest in not dissipating the state's revenues, in such a way as to impoverish it and remove all its resources. But they like to appropriate the largest possible portion of these revenues, to give them to their creatures and to use them in pointless pomp and display. Between what is right and necessary and what would be obviously dangerous, the gap is vast, and assuming prudence and an ordinary degree of patriotism in the governors, we may properly suppose that if they are not contained they will get as close as possible to this latter line without passing it. It is the same with military ventures. They will not expose themselves to being overwhelmed by the numbers of their enemies. They will not draw neighboring nations on to the home ground by attacking them gratuitously. They can indulge at will, however, in warlike enterprises. They will take advantage of this ability by provoking or continuing wars which, without entailing the loss of the State, will add to their power, which always increases in times of danger. To this end they will sacrifice public peace and the well-being of many citizens. It is the same furthermore with despotic actions. The governors will avoid causing popular revolt by multiplying vexations beyond all measure. They will allow themselves smaller oppressions, though: these are in the nature of things. They are in the personal interest [466] of the individual governors. When they are not in their lasting or well-understood interest they are likely to be in their passing interest, their passions and their whims, which suffices for us to anticipate and fear them. The very supposition that they will bring to these abuses a certain restraint rests on the prudence and enlightenment we attribute to them. But they can be misled by false initiatives, carried away by hateful passions. Then all moderation will disappear and excesses will reach a peak.[6] To say that the interests of governments are always consistent with those of the governed is to understand the interests of governments abstractly. This commits with respect to government the same error

6. See Constant's Note A at the end of Book XVII.

Rousseau commits with regard to society. There is a note to add. Let us for a moment accept this principle. Let us agree that a monarch, separated by an immense distance from his subjects, has nothing to gain in happiness or even by way of caprice, from offending individuals. The government is not made up solely of the man who is at the head of the State. Power subdivides; it is shared among thousands of subalterns. So it is not true that the numerous members of the government have nothing to gain from the unhappiness of the governed. Every one of them has, on the contrary, very close to him, someone of equal or lower rank, whose losses would enrich him, whose fields would improve his fortune, whose humiliation would flatter his vanity, whose banishment would rid him of an enemy, a rival, an inconvenient monitor. If it is true in some respects that the interests of the government, considered at the top of the social edifice, always coincide with those of the people, it is no less incontestable that the interests of the lower ranks of government can often be opposed to them. A coming together impossible to hope for would be necessary were we to suppose despotism to be compatible with the happiness of the governed. At the summit of the political hierarchy a man without personal passions, closed to love, hatred, favoritism, anger, jealousy, a man active, vigilant, [467] tolerant of all opinions, attaching no amour propre to persistence in errors committed, consumed with the desire for good, and knowing, nevertheless, how to resist impatience and to respect the rights of the time. Further down the scale of powers, ministers endowed with the same virtues, in a position of dependence without being servile, in the midst of despotism without being tempted to fall in with it out of fear or to abuse it from self-interest, lastly, everywhere in the lowest positions, the same combination of rare qualities, the same security, the same love of justice, the same selflessness. If a single link of this chain of preternatural virtues happens to be broken, everything is in peril. The two halves thus separated would both remain beyond reproach, but the good would not be assured. The truth would no longer make its way accurately to the summit of power; justice would no longer descend, pure and whole, into the obscure ranks of the governed. A single wrong transmission is enough to mislead the government, to set it in arms against innocence. When it is claimed that political freedom is not necessary, it is always believed that relations are only with the head of the government, but in reality one has them with all the agents of lower rank, and the question is no longer one of attributing to a single man distinguished qualities and never-failing impartiality. One has to suppose the existence of a hundred or two hundred thousand angelic creatures above all the weaknesses and vices of humanity.[7] If we put the happiness of the governed in purely physical pleasures, it is possible to say with some reason that the interest of the governors, above all in the large modern societies, is almost never to trouble the governed in these pleasures. If we place the happiness of the governed higher, however, in the development of their intellectual faculties, the interest of most governments will be to stop this development. Now, since it is in the nature of the human race to resist when there is a wish to arrest the [468] development of its faculties, the government will have recourse to constraint to achieve this. The result is that by a detour it will press on the physical pleasures of the governed in order to dominate them in areas of their existence which seem to have only a very distant connection with these pleasures.

Lastly, it is said every day that the clear interest of each man is not to infringe the rules of justice, and yet laws are made and punishments set up for criminals. So often is it noted that men endlessly deviate from their clear interest! One could surely expect much the same of governments!

Political freedom is accused of throwing people into continual agitation. One could easily show that while the conquest of that freedom can inebriate slaves, the enjoyment of it forms men worthy of its possession. But were this assertion against freedom proven, nothing would result from it in favor of despotism. To hear the supporters of this shameful politics you would believe it a sure guarantee of peace. If we look at history, though, we will see that absolute power almost always crumbles at the moment when long efforts having delivered it from every obstacle seem to promise it the longest duration.

The kingdom of France, says M. Ferrand, III, 448, "brought together under the unique authority of Louis XIV all the means of force and prosperity. . . . Her greatness had long been retarded by all the vices with which

7. One finds something of an echo, still very clear, of this theme of subaltern power in *La France nouvelle* of Prévost-Paradol. Indeed he says in his preface: "Who can tell me, however, that in producing this book I have not labored above all for the advance of some subaltern agent, capable of thinking he has an interest in laying hands on this innocent treatise on politics and history, perhaps to prove his zeal, perhaps, even more innocently, because discovering nothing reprehensible in this writing, he is afraid just because of this of having understood it imperfectly, and is afraid of not seeming at all sufficiently scandalized," pp. ii–iv in the edition by M. Lévy, 1868. Later on he says again: "We are therefore reduced, when we pick up our pen, to reckoning with not only the calculated resolution of those who really have power, but with the foolish eagerness of those who have been the smallest fragment of it." *Ibid.*, p. v.

a moment of barbarism had overburdened her and whose rusty deposit it had needed almost seven centuries to remove entirely. But that rust had gone. All the springs had just received a last tempering. Their action had been made freer, their play swifter and more certain. They were no longer checked by a multitude of alien movements. Now only one movement gave motion to all the others.[8] Well, what is the result of all this, of this unique and powerful energy, of this precious unity? A brilliant reign, then a shameful one, then a weak one, and then a revolution. In the recently published *Memoirs* of Louis XIV, [469] one finds this prince complacently recounting the details of all the operations for the destruction of the power of the body of judges (Parlement), of the clergy, of all intermediary powers. He keeps congratulating himself on the reestablishment or growth of royal authority. He holds it as merit on his part in his successors' eyes. He was writing about 1666. A hundred twenty-three years later the French monarchy was overthrown.

In England absolute power was established under Henry VIII. Elizabeth consolidated it. People rave about the boundless power of this queen. But her successor was endlessly engaged in struggle against the nation people thought subjugated, and the son of this successor lost his head on the scaffold. The fourteen centuries of the French monarchy are constantly advanced as proof of the stability of absolute monarchy; but of these fourteen centuries, twelve were consumed by the struggle against feudalism, an oppressive system but as opposite as one could conceive to the despotism of a single man. There is no government, none, less monarchical than the government of the third race, especially in the last three centuries, says a writer who is moreover the most extreme supporter of absolute monarchy.[9] Apologists of despotism, the system you favor has three chances. Either it rouses the people to overthrow it; or it weakens the people, and then if foreigners attack they overthrow it; or if foreigners do not attack it, it wastes away more slowly, only in a way more shameful and just as certain. It has often been said that the prosperity of republics is fleeting. That of absolute power is much more so. No despotic state has lasted in full vigor as long as English freedom. The reason for this is simple. This political freedom, which serves as a barrier to government, is also a support for it, guiding it on its way, sustaining it in its efforts, moderating it in its onsets of madness,

8. The quotation from Ferrand is from p. 449, above all, and in the second edition of 1803.

9. See Constant's Note B at the end of Book XVII.

and encouraging it in its moments of apathy. Political freedom draws together around government the interests of all the various groups. Even when it struggles against government, [470] it imposes on it certain controls which render its deviations less ridiculous and its excesses less odious. When political freedom is totally destroyed, government, finding nothing which regulates it, nothing which directs or contains it, tends to go out of control. Its steps become uneven and erratic. Sometimes it rages and nothing calms it. At others it is dejected and nothing can rally it. Thinking it was shaking off its opponents, it has got rid of its allies. Everything confirms this maxim of Montesquieu, in proportion as a monarch's power becomes immense, his security diminishes.[10]

CHAPTER FOUR

Apologia for Despotism by Louis XIV

It is rather curious to hear Louis XIV on despotism. He makes an apologia for it and not without skill.

"We must remain in agreement," he says, "that nothing so securely establishes the happiness and peace of provinces, as the perfect coming together of all authority in the person of the sovereign. The least division made in it always produces very great misfortunes and, whether the parts detached from it end up in the hands of individuals or certain companies, they can never be other than in a violent condition. The prince who must keep them united in his person could not possibly permit their dismemberment without making himself responsible for all the misfortunes which flow from this. . . . Not counting the revolts and internal wars which the ambition of the powerful inevitably produces when it is not checked, a thousand other ills are born again from the sovereign's slackness. Those closest to him, the first to see his weakness, are also the first who want to gain advantage from it. Each one of them necessarily having people who act as ministers to their greed, they give these at the same time license to imitate them. Thus by degrees corruption spreads everywhere and becomes the same in all occupations. . . . of all these various crimes, the people alone are the victims. It is only at the expense of the weak and the poor that so many people [471] mean to accumulate their monstrous fortunes; instead of a single king whom the people ought to have, they have a thousand tyrants at once."[11]

10. See Constant's Note C at the end of Book XVII.
11. *Mémoires de Louis XIV, éd. cit.*, pp. 17–19.

All this reasoning is founded on the error this book seeks to refute. It is thought that despotism must be somewhere, either in the hands of one man or of several. Rather than despotism, however, we can establish in its place something called freedom. Then it does not at all follow from the fact that the head of the supreme power has only limited authority, that subaltern agents possess what would make his authority absolute. They too have only limited authority. Far from oppression spreading and descending from rung to rung, all are contained and checked. Louis XIV paints us a picture of a free government as if despotism were everywhere in it and freedom nowhere. The complete opposite is the case. Despotism is nowhere in it because freedom is everywhere. The weakness of an absolute government is the misfortune of peoples, because power drifts randomly and the strong seize hold of it. Wisely established limits are the good fortune of nations because they circumscribe power, in such a way that no one can abuse it.

CONSTANT'S NOTES

A. [Refers to page 388.]

It is insane to believe, says Spinoza, that only that person will not be carried away by his passions, whose situation is such that he is surrounded by the strongest temptations and who most easily and at least risk yields to them.[12] "The sovereign justice of God," says Ferrand, "derives from sovereign power." From which he concludes that sovereign power in the hands of a man must be sovereign justice; but he should have proven that this man would be a God. Esprit de l'histoire, I, 445.[13]

[472] B. [Refers to page 391.]

M. Ferrand, Esprit de l'histoire, III, 38.[14]

C. [Refers to page 392.]

Esprit des lois, Livre VIII, Ch. 7.

12. Hofmann failed to locate this passage in Spinoza. The idea, however, is found in Ch. 6 and 7 of the *Traité de l'autorité politique,* in the discussion on monarchy. Spinoza, *Oeuvres complètes,* text translated, revised, and presented by Roland Caillois, Madeleine Francès, and Robert Misrahi, Paris, Gallimard, 1954, pp. 1008–1046.

13. The reference is to the second edition of 1803. The exact sense of Ferrand's sentence is comprehensible only if we lay out the whole paragraph from which it is drawn. "In a word, the interest of the legitimate sovereign is to maintain [472] everything in order. Therefore the more legal force it has, the more order will be maintained. The sovereign justice of God comes from this sovereign power."

14. Antoine Ferrand, *op. cit.,* 2e éd, 1803, t. III, p. 38, n. 1: "Consequently there is no government less monarchical than that of the second race, during the last hundred years." Elsewhere (p. 148) in the same tome, Ferrand says: "to examine the character of all the kings of the third race is to be convinced that only one, Louis XI, was able to form and execute this venture" ["to take royal authority a greater step forward than all it had taken till then," *ibid.,* p. 147].

BOOK XVIII

On the Duties of Individuals to Political Authority

Ch. 1. Difficulties with regard to the question of resistance. 397

Ch. 2. On obedience to the law. 398

Ch. 3. On revolutions. 405

Ch. 4. On the duties of enlightened men during revolutions. 407

Ch. 5. Continuation of the same subject. 413

Ch. 6. On the duties of enlightened men after violent revolutions. 419

CHAPTER ONE

Difficulties with Regard to the Question of Resistance

Political authority not being limitless, it is clear that the duties of individuals toward it are not unlimited. These duties diminish in proportion to the government's encroachments on aspects of individual life outside its jurisdiction. When these encroachments are taken to the limit, it is impossible for resistance not to result.

Government is like taxation. Each person agrees to sacrifice a portion of his wealth in order to finance public expenditure, whose purpose is to assure him the peaceful enjoyment of what he retains; but if the state demanded from each person all his wealth, the guarantee it offered him would be illusory, since there would no longer be anything to which it could apply. Likewise each person agrees to sacrifice a part of his freedom in order to assure the remainder; but if the government invaded all his freedom, the sacrifice would be purposeless.

We know all the dangers of the only too well-known question of resistance. We know to what abuses and crimes it opens the way. No one today can utter the word revolution without an unease bordering on remorse. Nevertheless, whatever line one takes on this question of resistance, it will always present a lot of difficulties.

In countries where authority is divided, if the holders of that authority are in dispute, one has to choose between them, and resistance against one lot or the other is forced on us. The English constitution requires both chambers and the king to cooperate in the establishment of taxes and the making of laws. If the king wished [476] to raise taxes in opposition to one of the two chambers, to obey the king would be to resist the lawful authority of Parliament. If one or both chambers wanted to pass a law independently of the royal sanction, to obey them would be to resist the lawful authority of the crown.

Even in those countries where power is concentrated in a single person, however, the question of resistance is less simple than it appears. It certainly rests with each citizen not to resist the government. It does not rest with him, however, to prevent others from resisting and overthrowing it. Now, if this government is overthrown, should one immediately rally around the new government? This principle would sanction every violent outrage. It would become a fertile source of the very ills one is seemingly striving to avoid, since it would give audacity the continual attraction of recompense, by legitimating initial success. Movements which overthrow usurping governments are acts of resistance, just as much as those which overthrow established ones. The overthrow of the Committee of Public Safety was quite simply an act of resistance. Should we have stayed submissive forever to the Committee of Public Safety? If we say all power comes from God, then Cartouche was one such power and Robespierre another. But the problem would still not be resolved. Former government can, after its fall, still have resources, supporters, and hopes. At what time, by what indication, according to what calculation, moral or numerical, does the duty of individuals, founded on divine right or on such other basis as one may choose to give it, get transferred from their former to their new masters? Finally, could one seriously make out the case that resistance is always illegitimate? Can one condemn it under Nero, Vitellius, or Caracalla? One may think one is getting out of the difficulty by way of abstract, general maxims, which seem to oust personal judgment. But the complexities and nuances of circumstance render these maxims useless and sterile in application.

CHAPTER TWO

On Obedience to the Law

Resistance can be of two kinds, negative disobedience or disobedience to the law, positive resistance or active opposition to government.

Let us deal first with negative resistance, a less complicated question [477] and less dangerous to examine than that of positive resistance. It has nevertheless its own particular difficulty.

The authority of government can be limited in a precise way, because law can limit it. The limitation is external. It is easy to see if it is transgressed. It is not the same with the jurisdiction of the law, however. The law being the only written rule which can exist, it is much less easy to say what constitutes a transgression in it.

Pascal,[1] Chancellor Bacon,[2] and many others like them have cut short the discussion, by positing that in principle one must obey the law without

1. Constant is probably thinking of the *Pensées,* Fragment No. 60, where the author declares, for example: "Custom is the whole of equity, just because it is received. This is the mystical basis of its authority. Whoever seeks to reduce it to principles, destroys it. Nothing is so faulty as these laws which redress errors. Whoever obeys them because they are just, obeys what he imagines to be justice, but not the essence of the law. Law is all of a piece. It is the law and nothing more. He who seeks its reasons will find them feeble and slight. . . ." Blaise Pascal, *Oeuvres complètes,* editing and annotation by Louis Lafuma, Paris, Le Seuil, 1963, p. 507, (L'Intégrale).

2. See Constant's Note A at the end of Book XVIII.

questioning because it is the law. To refute this assertion, we need only identify its strict meaning.

Is the claim that the name "law" always suffices to enforce obedience? If a number of men or even one man with no official function call the expression of their individual wills the law, are the other individuals in society obliged to conform to this? An affirmative answer is absurd, but a negative one implies that the title "law" does not impose a duty to obey and that this duty supposes an anterior identification of the source from which that law derives.

Is the claim that questioning is permitted, when it is a matter of establishing that what is presented to us as law derives from a legitimate authority; [478] but that this last point being cleared up, examination has no further place regarding the actual content of the law?

In the first place, if we wish always to allow for the inevitable abuse of all the faculties man has been granted, the examination of the legitimacy of legislative authority will open the way to disturbances just as great as examination of the law itself.

Secondly, an authority is legitimate only in virtue of the function given to it. A municipality and a police court magistrate are legitimate authorities. They would cease to be such, nevertheless, if they assumed the right to make laws. In all systems, therefore, individuals must be granted the use of their intelligence, whatever the system, not only for the understanding of the characters of the authorities but for judging their actions. This means the content of law must be examined, along with its sources.

We see therefore that Pascal's proposition is illusory, once we do not want it to lead to absurdity.

Man has the right to use his learning, for it is the only instrument of understanding he has, to evaluate the source of a law. If you refuse him this, you lay yourself open to his stabbing you at the will of the first brigand calling himself a lawmaker.

Moreover, man possesses the right to examine the content of a law, since it is only in terms of the content that he can determine the legitimacy of its source. If you challenge his right here, you allow the most subaltern of authorities endless and disorderly encroachments on all existing authority.

Note that the very people who declare implicit obedience to the laws to be strictly binding always make an exception to the rule of what touches them. Pascal excepted religion. He absolutely did not bow to civil authority in religious matters; and he braved persecution for his disobedience in this respect.

[479] Driven by the determination not to recognize any natural law, Bentham necessarily had to maintain that law alone created offenses, that any action prohibited by law became a crime;[3] and in this way pigheadedness kept this writer, who, it must be added, stands out on every page against the mistakes and encroachments of government, back in the ranks of the apologists of the most absolute and servile obedience.

Fortunately, he refutes himself in his definition of offenses. "An offense," he says, "is an act from which ill results."[4] But does the law which forbids an action from which no ill results create an offense? Yes, he replies, for in attaching a penalty to that action, it ensures that an ill results.[5] On this reckoning, the law can attach a penalty to my saving my father's life, to my not killing him. Would this suffice to make filial devotion a crime, and parricide an obligation? And this example, horrible though it be, is not an empty speculation. Have we not seen the condemnation, in the name of the law, in a thousand political revolutions, of fathers for having saved their children, of children for having succored their father?

Bentham refutes himself much better, when he speaks of imaginary offenses.[6] If the law created offenses, no offense created by the law would be imaginary. Anything the law had declared criminal would be such.

The English author makes use of a comparison very apt for clarifying the question. Certain actions innocent in themselves, he says, are ranked among the offenses, just as among certain peoples healthy foods are treated as poisons or unclean things.[7] Does it not follow that, just as the mistake of these peoples does not turn into poison the healthy food they envisage as such, the law's mistake does not convert into offenses the innocent

3. See Constant's Note B at the end of Book XVIII.

4. Jeremy Bentham, *op. cit.,* t. I, p. 158.

5. Constant, it seems, basing himself on what Bentham says, *ibid.,* t. II, pp. 382–383, imagines what the latter's response would be on "the ill which a penal law produces."

6. See Constant's Note C at the end of Book XVIII.

7. Jeremy Bentham, *op. cit.,* t. II, pp. 380–381. Here is the passage to which Constant refers: "If one has grasped the idea of a true offense, it will easily be distinguished from offenses of imaginary ill, those acts innocent in themselves, ranked among offenses by prejudice, antipathies, administrative errors, and ascetic principles, almost as healthy foods are regarded among certain peoples as poisons and unclean eating. Heresy and sorcery are offenses of this class."

actions [480] it declares guilty? It endlessly happens that when we are talking abstractly about law, we assume it is what it ought to be. When we are practically concerned with what it is, we find it to be quite other. Hence the endless contradictions in theories and terms.

The word "law" is as vague as the word "nature." To abuse the latter is to overthrow society. To abuse the former is to tyrannize individuals. If we have to choose between the two, at least the word "nature" evokes an idea virtually the same for all men. The word "law" can be applied to entirely opposite ideas.

When our orders have included murder, informing, and spying, these orders have not been in the name of nature. Everyone would feel that there was contradiction in the terms; these have been demanded of us in the name of the law, so there was no longer a contradiction.

To wish to leave nature entirely out of account in a legislative system is to take away from the laws simultaneously their sanction, their basis, and their limit. Bentham even goes so far as to say that any action, however neutral, being liable to prohibition by law, then we must owe to the law the freedom to sit down or stand upright, to enter or leave, to eat or not eat, because the law could forbid us these.[8] We owe this freedom to the law, just as the vizier who gave thanks every day to his highness that his head was still on his shoulders was indebted to the sultan for not having been beheaded.[9] But any law which pronounced on these unimportant actions would have pronounced illegitimately; it would not have been a law.

[481] Obedience to the law is without doubt a duty; but this duty is not absolute, but relative. It rests on the supposition that the law flows from its natural source and is confined within legitimate limits. This duty does not cease absolutely when the law deviates from this rule only in a few respects. Public peace is worthy of many sacrifices. We would be morally blameworthy if through too inflexible an attachment to our rights, we resisted all the laws which seemed to us to threaten them. No duty, however, binds us to

8. *Ibid.*, t. I, p. 157: "I can remain standing or sit down, enter or leave, eat or not eat, etc. The law says nothing about that. The right that I exercise in this respect, however, I get from the law, because it is the law which criminalizes all violence by which people might try to prevent me doing as I please."

9. This anecdote appeared earlier in the *Journal intime,* dated 21 December 1804: "In the midst of this reverie the idea which dominates me is of this Turk who said: I give thanks every day to His Highness for having my head on my shoulders."

these so-called laws, whose corrupting influence menaces what is noblest in our being, to these laws which not only restrain our legitimate freedoms and stand in the way of actions they have no right to forbid, but require from us ones contrary to the eternal principles of justice and pity, ones man cannot adhere to without being false to his nature.

The political theorist we have refuted above himself agrees with this truth.[10] If the law, he says, is not what it ought to be, should it be obeyed or violated? Should we stay neutral between the law which requires evil and morality which forbids it? We have to see whether the probable ills of obedience are less than the probable ills of disobedience. He recognizes in this passage the rights of individual judgment he denies elsewhere.

The doctrine of boundless obedience to the law has perhaps been the cause of more evil than all the other errors which have led men astray. The most execrable passions have dug in behind this convention, on the surface impassive and impartial, and indulged in every excess. Do you want to bring together under a single viewpoint the consequences of your doctrine of blind and implicit obedience to the law? Remember that the Roman emperors made laws, that Louis XI made laws, that Richard III made laws, that the Committee of Public Safety made laws! There exists no natural sentiment that a law has not forbidden, no duty whose fulfillment a law has not prohibited, no virtue a law has not proscribed, no affection a law has not punished, no treason a law has not remunerated, no heinous crime a law has not ordered. It is therefore necessary to put [482] limits on this alleged duty of obedience. It is necessary to identify those characteristics which mean that a law is not a law.

Retrospective operation is the first of these. Men have consented to the fetters of law only in order to attach to their actions definite consequences, according to which they might direct and choose the line of behavior they wished to follow. Retroactivity robs them of this benefit. It violates the terms of social agreement. It conceals the price of the sacrifice it has imposed. Governments, having neglected the safeguards they should have taken, often think they can make good their fault by extending the influence of laws which experience has shown them to be necessary over the past itself. The atrocious aspect of a crime, the indignation it incites, the fear that a guilty person's going unpunished, as he takes advantage of the law's silence, may encourage other guilty people, even after the law has pronounced, these sometimes lead wise men to justify this extension of government. This is the

10. See Constant's Note D at the end of Book XVIII.

annihilation of all justice, making the governed pay the penalty for the lack of foresight of their governors. Better to let a man guilty of the most odious crime escape than to punish an action not prohibited by an existing law.

A second feature of illegality in the laws is the prescription of immoral actions. Any law demanding informing or denunciation is not a law. Any law which interferes with the propensity of man to give refuge to anyone asking for shelter is not a law. Government is instituted to oversee things. It has the means of accusation, pursuit, exposure, handing over, and punishment. It does not have the right to make these duties, necessary but painful, fall on the individual, who occupies no official position. It must respect that sensibility in citizens, the most precious part of our being, which leads us to unquestioning pity and help for the weak oppressed by the strong.

It is to make individual pity inviolable that we have made the authority of government commanding. We wanted to conserve in ourselves feelings of sympathy, by charging government with the severe duties which might have wounded or withered these feelings. I make an exception, nevertheless, of crimes against which even sympathy itself rises up. There are actions so atrocious that all men are disposed to agree on their punishment. [483] Then the prosecution of guilty people is not repugnant to their affections, nor does it dull their sensibilities, nor diminish their moral sense. But these actions are very few. We can positively rank in this category only criminal assaults against human life. Attacks on property, although very criminal, do not at all rouse in us sufficient indignation to stifle all pity. As for misdemeanors which we might call artificial, in the sense that they are misdemeanors only because they infringe certain positive laws, to force individuals to support prosecution of these is to harass and degrade them. I have sometimes wondered what I would do if I were trapped in a town where it was forbidden under pain of death to give shelter to citizens accused of political crimes. My answer to myself was that if I wanted to make my life secure, I would give myself up to imprisonment as long as that measure was in force.

Any law which divides the citizens into groups, which punishes them for what is not within their control, which makes them responsible for other actions than their own, any such law is not a law.

It is not, let us repeat, that the resort to resistance, always dangerous, is to be recommended. It puts society in peril. Let it be forbidden, not out of deference to a usurping government, but out of consideration for the citizens who are deprived of the benefits of living in society by continual struggle. As long as a law, although bad, does not tend to deprave us, as long as the encroachments of government demand only sacrifices which render us neither base nor savage, we can acquiesce in them. We compromise only on our own behalf. If the law demands, however, that we trample on our affections or duties, if, on the absurd pretext of a gigantic and false devotion to what it by turns calls monarchy or republic, or prince, or nation, it forbids us fidelity to friends in need, if it demands from us treachery to our allies, or even the persecution of vanquished foes, then anathema and disobedience to this corrupting government and to the drafting of injustices and crimes which it decorates with the name of law.

[484] A positive duty, general and unreserved, whenever a law seems unjust, is not to become its executor. This passive resistance entails neither upheavals, nor revolutions, nor disorders. It would be a fine spectacle to see a criminal government in vain drafting sanguinary laws, mass banishments, and deportations and finding in the vast and silent nation trembling under its power no executor of its injustices, no accomplice of its heinous crimes.

Nothing excuses the man who lends assistance to a law he believes wicked, the judge who sits in a court he believes illegal or pronounces a sentence of which he disapproves, the minister who gets a decree carried out against his conscience, the satellite who arrests a man he knows to be innocent to hand him over to his executioners. Under one of the most oppressive governments which has ruled France, a man seeking a post exonerated himself from this move by saying that his only alternative was between obtaining a position or stealing on the public highway. But if the government refuses your requests, someone replied to him, will you take to stealing then?

Terror is no more valid an excuse than all the other base passions. Woe betide those eternally compromised men, on their own say-so, tireless agents of all the present tyrannies, and posthumous denunciators of all those overthrown ones.

We have innumerable proofs of this. These men never get over the dishonor they have accepted. Their broken spirit never regains an independent outlook. We pretend in vain, whether out of calculation, or kindness, or pity to listen to their wretched, faltering excuses. In vain we seem to be convinced that by some inexplicable marvel they have suddenly regained their long since vanished courage. They themselves do not believe it. They no longer have the ability to hope on their own behalf. [485] They drag after them the profound memory of their inexpiable opprobrium, and their heads, bent under the yoke they have carried, stoop by habit, and helplessly so, to receive another yoke.

They tell us that they serve as executors to unjust laws only to lessen their severity, that the government whose depositories they agree to become would do worse ill still if it were remitted to less pure hands. Mendacious dealings which open the way to a boundless career for all crimes. Each man trades with his conscience and for each level of injustice the tyrants find worthy executors. I do not see why, on such arguments as these, one should not become the executioner of innocence, on the grounds that one would strangle it more gently. It is a thousand times better that atrocious laws should be carried out only by obviously criminal men.

These dubious though as yet untainted men lessen the odium of the most horrible institutions in the eyes of the people, who thus become accustomed to putting up with them. Without them, without the prestige of their over-vaunted names, the institutions would be overthrown from the start by public indignation. Then, when the evil gets to a pitch, these worthy souls withdraw, leaving the field free to scoundrels. In this fashion, the service they do us is to cover assassins who are still weak with a shield, to give them time to become the strongest kind.

CHAPTER THREE
On Revolutions

It would be a childish endeavor to seek to present individuals with fixed rules relative to revolution. Revolutions share in the nature of physical upheavals. Hidden causes prepare them. Chance decides them just as chance can retard them. The lightest circumstance, or an event less important than a thousand others which had produced no effect, sometimes suddenly gives the unexpected signal for the subversive movement. The contagious fury spreads. Spirits are raised. Citizens feel themselves pushed as though involuntarily [486] to the overthrow of existing order. Chiefs are far outdistanced by the crowd, and revolutions operate without anyone really knowing as yet what people want to destroy and what they want to build.

It would also be impossible to judge revolutions in a general way by their consequences. These have not all been dire. The expulsion of the Tarquins established Roman freedom. The Swiss insurrection has given close to five valuable centuries of peace and good fortune to Switzerland. The banishment of the Stuarts has given England a hundred twenty years of prosperity. The Dutch are indebted to the rebellion of their ancestors for a long enjoyment of peace and civil freedom. The American uprising has been followed by political arrangements which permit man the freest development of all his faculties. Other revolutions have had different results: that of Poland, for example, that of Brabant under Joseph II, several in Italy, and yet others.

It is only to governments that one can give useful advice for the avoidance of revolutions. The most absolute resignation on the part of individuals is a powerless guarantee against these terrible crises, because that resignation cannot exceed certain limits. Long-lasting injustice, repeated and growing, insolence, more difficult to endure even than injustice, the intoxication of power, the shocks of government which offend all interests in succession, or its negligence which refuses to listen to complaints and lets grievances accumulate: these things produce, sooner or later, such fatigue, such discontent, that all the counsels of prudence cannot stop that mood. It penetrates all minds with the air that is breathed. It becomes habitual feeling, everyone's idée fixe. People do not get together to conspire; but all those who do get together do conspire.

It is in vain then that the government aspires to maintain itself by force. It is a matter of appearances. The reality does not exist. Governments are like those bodies struck by a thunderbolt. Their outer contours are still the same, but the least wind, the slightest shock, are enough to reduce them to dust.

Whatever physical means surround those in power, it is always public opinion which creates, gathers together, keeps available, and directs these means. These soldiers who seem to us, and indeed are at such and such a given moment, blind machines, [487] these soldiers who shoot their fellow citizens indiscriminately, as though without pity, these soldiers are men, with moral faculties, with sympathy, sensibility, and a conscience which can suddenly awake. Public opinion has the same sway over them as over us, and no order can affect that sway. Watch it running through the ranks of the French soldiery in 1789, transforming into citizens men brought together from all parts, not just of France, but of the world, reanimating spirits crushed by discipline, enervated by debauchery, driving the ideas of freedom into these ignorant minds like a prejudice, a new prejudice breaking the bonds which so many ancient prejudices and entrenched habits had woven. Later on look at the changeable and swift opinion, sometimes detaching our soldiers from their leaders, sometimes rallying them around the latter, rendering them by turns rebellious or devoted, defiant or enthusiastic. In England, after the death of Cromwell, watch the republicans, concentrating all power in their hands, having at their disposal armies, treasure, civil authorities, Parliament, and the courts. Only dumb opinion was against them; suddenly all their resources are dissolved, everything is shaken and crumbles.

Choke malcontent opinion in blood is the favorite maxim of certain statesmen. But you cannot choke opinion. Blood flows, but opinion survives, takes up the charge again, and triumphs. The more repressed it is, the more terrible is it.[11] When it cannot speak it acts. "In London," one Englishman says, "the people express themselves through petitions; in Constantinople by means of fires." He might have added that in London the monarch's measures are criticized. In Constantinople he is not censured, merely strangled.

CHAPTER FOUR

On the Duties of Enlightened Men during Revolutions

Shall we conclude from the fact that individual wills have little influence on the causes of revolutions that in the midst of these social convulsions, each person battered by the storm can surrender himself without resistance to the ungovernable waves, live from day to day, submitting to the [488] events whose rapid succession drags him along, taking counsel from chance? I do not think so. In the stormiest of circumstances there is always a direction pointed out by morality. Therefore there is always a duty to fulfill.

Two movements are natural to any nation overthrowing institutions it finds oppressive or vicious. The first is to wish to see everything destroyed and constructed anew, the second to display implacable severity to those who profited from the vices of the former institutions. These two movements are precisely what makes revolutions dire, what takes them beyond the people's needs, prolongs their duration, and jeopardizes their success. Enlightened men must strive to stop or suspend them.

People say we should take advantage of periods when everything is shaken up in order to reshape it all. The Constituent Assembly is party to this indeed very specious sophism. He who would have qualms about overthrowing an edifice still in existence, and offering a tolerable shelter, finds it legitimate to bring about the ruin of a half-destroyed edifice, in order to raise in its place one more regular in its parts and overall. Yet from this there result all the greatest evils of revolutions. Not only are all the abuses

11. See Constant's Note E at the end of Book XVIII.

related, but they result from all the ideas. The agitation is communicated from one end to the other of the immense chain. One abuse destroyed, a second of them is attacked, and a third, and people get excited during the struggle. Soon they see everything as an abuse. On this basis they appeal from the present majority to the future majority which they flatter themselves they will either dominate or convince. They run through the whole circle of human ideas. They run ahead of opinion, always hoping to drag it behind them.

Ordinarily there are two stages in revolutions, a first when unanimous feeling overthrows what everybody finds intolerable, a second when by means of an artificial prolongation of a movement no longer nationwide, there is an attempt to destroy everything contrary to the viewpoint of a few. If the enlightened men can stop the revolution at the first stage, the chances of success are good. The revolutions where this principle has been observed have been the shortest, happiest, and least bloody. The Tarquins oppressed Roman freedom. They were driven out. Otherwise, however, the whole organization of Rome stayed intact. The agitation stopped, calm was reestablished, the Republic rose and steadied itself. Doubtless in conserving constitutionally everything which was not royalty, Rome conserved very numerous abuses. These abuses, however, were proportionate [489] to the state of opinion. If the kings, the priesthood, and the patricians of Rome had all been overthrown simultaneously, the revolution would never have finished, and Rome would have been annihilated.

In England in 1688 the Stuarts were driven out, but nothing new was built. The Commons remained, the Peers remained, the Magna Carta and the constitutional monarchy remained. All the elements of the established order were reassembled and brought together and combined. The result was a constitution which has already given England more than a century of good fortune.

It is the same with the Americans. They have retained almost all the institutions which thrived among them before their independence. By contrast, in the case of nations which reject all their memories and think everything must be changed, reformed, and built from scratch, revolutions never end. Interminable divisions tear these peoples apart. With everyone judging according to his own lights the best that is possible, or practical, or ideal, there are as many revolutions, at least attempted, as there are diverse opinions on this inexhaustible subject. Each hidden interest adopts one approach as its standard, and the nation succumbs sooner or later to lassitude, its resources depleted.

An improvement, a reform, the abolition of an abusive practice, all these things are useful only when they follow what the nation wants. They become fatal when they precede it, because then they are no longer improvements but tyrannical acts of force. The important thing is not that they take effect quickly but that the public outlook moves in this direction and that the institutions are at one with the ideas.

Individuals have the same duties to society as society to individuals. It has no right to stop the development of their intellectual faculties nor to put limits on their progress. They, however, have no right to stand in judgment on the progress society should make and drag it violently toward a purpose going beyond its present wishes. By what right might a minority meditate on changes of which the majority disapproved? Might this be in terms of a greater enlightenment or wisdom than the rest of the citizens have, or a greater capacity for sound judgment as to what is useful? But by what signs will you recognize these quite exceptional qualities in a minority? Who will be judge of these characteristic signs? The minority themselves probably, since the majority cannot be consulted. Thus it is from its private eminence that this minority derives its mission; I am about as fond of kings who derive their power from God or their swords.

[490] All these rushed reforms have as devices for freedom, improvement, and enlightenment all the drawbacks with which we have reproached government; they put force in place of reason. Would it not be absurd to forgive the supporters of revolution for what we detest in the agents of government?

Men who get ahead of opinion fall without knowing it into a very bizarre contradiction. In order to justify their dire initiatives, they say that they absolutely must not steal from the present generation the benefits of the system they are claiming to be establishing; then, to excuse the sacrifice of the present generation, they exclaim that only by narrow calculation is it not sacrificed without hesitation to the immense weight of future generations.

These men complain constantly of ill will: a new contradiction in terms. Are they not acting in the name of the people? Do they not rest everything they are doing on the general will? So what can ill will be? Can there be a mass will to which all individuals are opposed? To listen to them, you would think ill will is a magic power which by some miracle or other forces the people constantly to do the opposite of what they wish. They attribute the misfortunes their premature policies occasion to the opposition such policies encounter. This is no excuse at all; one should not make changes which provoke such opposition. The very difficulties these changes encounter are a condemnation of their authors.

There is a point of view from which the legitimacy of violent measures in the pursuit of improvement has not yet, to my knowledge, been envisaged. If there were a system of government perfect in all its parts, after the consolidation of which the human race had merely to relax, one might be excused for dashing, in sudden and violent effort, toward this system, at the risk of offending individual people or even whole generations. The sacrifices would be compensated for by the eternity of happiness assured to the long line of future generations. But no government is perfect. Improvement is gradual and indefinite. When you have once improved some of your institutions, many other desirable improvements will remain. The very improvement you have established and achieved will need further refinements. Thus you are not as you imagine doing uncertain and temporary harm to achieve positive and lasting good; you are doing certain and positive harm in exchange for uncertain, relative, and temporary advantage.

[491] "The National Assembly," said Chamfort, "in 1789 gave the French people a constitution stronger than itself. It must hurry to lift the nation up to this height. . . . [12] Legislators must act like those skillful doctors who, treating an exhausted sick person, help the digestion of revigorating food by means of stomachic medicine." [13] The unfortunate thing in this comparison is that legislators are most of the time patients who call themselves doctors.

A nation cannot be sustained at a level to which its own disposition does not lift it. To sustain it there one would have to treat it violently, and the very fact that it was being treated violently would bring it back down and it would collapse.

For tyranny, Machiavelli says, everything must change;[14] one could likewise say that to change everything one must resort to tyranny. That is what people do.

12. Chamfort specifically states at this point, "by means of good public education."

13. Nicholas-Sébastien Roch, known as Chamfort, *Maxims and Thoughts,* Ch. 8 *On Slavery and Freedom: France before and after the Revolution;* in *Oeuvres de Chamfort,* collated and published by one of his friends, Paris, an III, t. IV, p. 206.

14. We come across this quote from Machiavelli again in Mme. de Staël's notes, *Des circonstances actuelles, éd. cit.,* p. 382. The exact text runs: "But he who wants merely to establish that absolute power the ancients called tyranny must on the contrary leave in existence nothing of the established order." Machiavelli, *Discours sur la première décade de Tite-Live,* Ch. XXV, in *Oeuvres complètes, éd. cit.,* p. 441.

When a nation is shallow and imitative, it finds nothing more powerful than editorial slogans. They are short, they seem clear, they are inscribed easily in the memory. Cunning men throw them to fools who seize them, because they are thus spared the trouble of thinking. They repeat them, because this gives them the appearance of understanding. Hence it arises that propositions whose absurdity astonishes us when they are analyzed, slip into a thousand heads and are repeated by a thousand tongues, such that one is endlessly reduced to proving what is obvious. Among these dire slogans, there is one we have heard repeated a thousand times during our Revolution, one whose repetition all violent revolutions invite; [492] it is that despotism is necessary to establish freedom. This axiom justifies all oppressions along with their indefinite prolongation, since the duration of this despotism to which it is claimed that freedom will owe its birth cannot be specified.

Freedom is priceless, however, only because it gives our mind precision, our character strength, and our souls elevation. All these benefits of freedom depend on its existing in reality. If you use despotism to bring in freedom, you get only its worthless forms; the essence will always escape you. The victory you win is opposed in its very essence to the proper spirit of the institution. And just as its successes will not persuade the conquered, so they will not reassure the conquerors.

What must we say to the people in fact, so that they will get the advantages of freedom into their minds? You were subject to privileged castes; most people lived for the ambition of the few. Unequal laws protected the strong against the weak. You had only precarious enjoyments, that is, rights, of which despotism threatened to rob you at every moment. You took part neither in the making of your laws nor in the election of your public officials. All these abuses are going to disappear. All your rights will be rendered to you. The men who want to form between despotism and freedom some kind of insane alliance, however, what can they say? No privilege will separate the citizens, but at all times men who seem to us enemies will be smashed with no right to a hearing. Virtue will be the only distinction among men; but those most given to persecution and violence will create for themselves by means of tyranny a patriciate guaranteed by terror. The laws made by the will of the people will protect property; but at every moment the fate of individuals or groups under suspicion will be confiscation. The people will elect their magistrates, but if they do not do it according to requirements prescribed in advance, their choice will be nullified. Opinion will be free, but any opinion contrary not only to the general policy [493] but also to its slightest day-to-day enactments will be punished like a violation. So, following a revolution against despotism, against the enslavement of opinion, despotism is found reinforced a thousandfold, and opinions are a thousand times more enslaved. To each word, each gesture, each outpouring of friendship, each cry of unhappiness, a fearful influence is attributed. Discussion of the victorious opinion is banned. The outrages committed by the fallen government are recalled in exaggerated form in order to stifle thought. Thought control is the distinctive mark of the new government. That men be made free, they are hounded with the fear of torture. Tyrannical government being denounced, the most tyrannical of governments is constructed.

To sustain what is thought to be freedom by despotic means requires the invention of far more persecution and deception than straightforward governmental control does. It is not enough to destroy an innocent man; he must be calumniated in the eyes of all. It is not enough to give power to those the people reject; the people must be forced to choose them. Forbidding press freedom is not enough; newspapers must parody it. It is not enough to impose silence on representative assemblies; a worthless simulation of opposition must be set up, tolerated as long as it is puerile, and dissolved when it gives offense. It is not enough to dispense with the nation's will; the addresses of a minority calling itself the majority must be put forward. All the time things are dragged far off course by increasing difficulties. There is absolutely no end to a tyranny seeking to extract from people by force the appearances of consent.

The war against public attitudes is less evil when the despotism is blatant, since it is not of the essence of despotism to depend on them. Usually despotism secures at least domestic calm, because it can rule more easily in silence. Institutions claiming to be free ones, however, when they employ despotic means, bring together all the ills of a monarchy under an oppressive tyrant with all those of a republic rent by factions. Quiet men are persecuted for being apathetic, ardent men because they are dangerous. [494] Servitude guarantees no rest; human activity lacks all purpose and joy. Freedom is adjourned until factions are destroyed. As long as freedom is postponed, however, factions are never destroyed. Despotism weighs on all the factions in turn; in the gaps between, there is nothing free. The coercive measures adopted by dictatorship, pending public approval, militate against this approval being realized. Such dictatorship flails around in a vicious circle, signaling an historic era it is destined never to achieve, since the means adopted on the pretext of achieving it prevent its ever happening. Force makes itself more and more necessary, growing anger feeds on itself, laws are hammered out like weapons, certain branches of law become declarations of war,[15] and the blind friends of freedom, who thought they could impose it by way of despotism, turn all free spirits against them, their only support the vilest toadies of power.

More: unjust laws directed against freedom's enemies inevitably fall on its true friends. To invest governments with arbitrary power is to given them an interest distinct from that of the governed. This interest becomes then their sole concern, and it is only to make it prevail that they employ the wider means with which they were entrusted for the public good. It should not be thought that one can take the side of wickedness in one branch of the law, and stay true to justice in the rest. One single barbarous law will set the character of all legislation. Heated feelings or calculation produce the first law and fear or necessity the second. No just law can coexist with a single despotic measure. One cannot deny freedom to some people and accord it to others. Let us imagine a single harsh measure against people not legally convicted. You can no longer tolerate freedom of the press. It will be used to stir up the people in favor of victims who may be innocent. You can no longer respect individual freedom. Those you wanted to deprive of their rights will take advantage of this and merge with the rest of the citizens. You can no longer leave industry to itself. It will supply those proscribed with resources. Your friends will suffer the consequences of your actions against your enemies. Your enemies will benefit from what you do for your friends. Men would like compromises with freedom, to leave its circle for a day, because of some obstacle or person or given purpose, before returning [495] to its order. They would like to have the security of the rules with the advantages of exceptions to them. Nature runs contrary to this. Freedom is a complete and ordered system. A single deviation destroys it, just as in arithmetical calculation a mistake of one digit or a thousand falsifies the result equally.

CHAPTER FIVE

Continuation of the Same Subject

The second duty of enlightened men is more important still, since it is a function not only of prudence but of morality.

When an improper constitution or long-established custom confers on those in the governing group or on some class or other vexatious privileges

15. The comparison of laws with weapons and of certain branches of law with declarations of war comes from Mme. de Staël, *op. cit.*, p. 37.

or despotic usages, the fault lies not with the governing group nor with this class but with the nation which has tolerated what should not exist. No one is guilty if he profits from a faculty he found ready-established and which society had peacefully granted him. The people can reclaim their rights because these are imprescriptible. They can take away from government an unjust prerogative. They can deprive a class of an oppressive privilege. They cannot, however, punish either one of them. They have lost all right to demand compensation or to exercise vengeance for damage to which they had seemed to resign themselves.

In the absence of this principle, revolutions no longer have any term. An abominable, retroactive course is entered, where each step, on the pretext of a past injustice, leads to a present one. People fall into the same absurdity with which they reproach the supporters of the most defective institutions. Men are punished for what they were and could not not be. A revolution gets turned into an era of new inequality whose newness renders it only the more revolting. There are sown for the future the seeds of iniquity, regret, suffering, and resentment. The generations allegedly to be freed are bequeathed the seeds of discord, hatred, and misfortune.

The groups you proscribe, those grown rich on abuses, are at the same time the most cultivated. If you go so far as destroying even [496] the individuals who compose them, you diminish proportionately the body of national enlightenment. The education of a nation is not the work of a day. It is not enough to strive to instruct that lively majority formerly kept in ignorance by an imperfect social order. The task is long. Pressing events will perhaps not wait until this task is achieved. Enlightened men have to be spread out between all the parties to preserve them from despotism. The Greeks pardoned captives who recited the verses of Euripides.[16] The least bit of enlightenment, the least germ of thought, the least refined sentiment, the least mark of elegance must be carefully protected. These are so many elements indispensable to social happiness. They must be saved from the storm. This is necessary both for the sake of justice and for the sake of freedom itself. For all these things, by more or less direct pathways, end in freedom.

16. This phrase picks up one by Mme., de Staël, from *Des circonstances actuelles*, Livre II, Ch. 4 (*ed. cit.*, p. 298): "Jadis, des Grecs prisonniers en Sicile obtinrent leur liberté de leurs ennemis en leur récitant quelques vers d'Euripide." [In times past, Greek prisoners in Sicily obtained their freedom from their enemies by reciting to them some verses of Euripides.] It seems, however, that Mme. de Staël found it in Plutarch, *Vies parallèles, Vie de Nicias*, paragraph 29.

Doubtless this duty is hard to fulfill. Revolutions scarcely begin before the friends of freedom find themselves split into two sections. On one side are ranged the moderate men, on the other the violent. Only these latter, however, remain united a long time, because the spur they have been given prevents their separating, and they are exclusively absorbed in an idea common to them. Moderate men, not being drawn by a dominant preoccupation, lend their ears readily to individual considerations. Pride awakens in them, courage is shaken, their steadfastness wearies, personal calculation, repulsed for a moment, takes up the charge again. Cowardice takes a thousand forms and disguises itself in a thousand ways to hide itself from its own gaze. It does not call itself only prudence, reason, wisdom, and knowing what is valuable; it sometimes assumes the title of independence. How many men have I seen leaving the most just and the weakest party, because they were, so they said, too independent to be associated with any party. This language heralded the fact that they were going to move to the stronger side, and their proclamation of independence was only a prouder wording of cowardice.

[497] A terrible ally, fanaticism, very active in political questions, as in religious ones, is committed to the violent side. Fanaticism is nothing save the rule of a single idea which wishes to triumph at any price. It is probably more absurd still when the question is freedom than it is when the question is religion. Fanaticism and freedom are incompatible. One is based on examination; the other forbids research and punishes doubt. The one thinks through and evaluates all views; the other sees the most timid objection as an assault. The one seeks to persuade, the other issues orders. The one, in a word, considers the need for victory a misfortune and treats the vanquished as equals whose rights it is keen to recognize, the other hurls itself on all questions as if on enemy redoubts and sees in its adversaries only still-dangerous captives it must immolate, so as no longer to have to fear them.

Whatever the natural incompatibility between love of freedom and fanaticism may be, however, these two things combine easily in the minds of men who, not having contracted the habit of reflection, can receive ideas only on the word of others, more in the form of a mysterious revelation than as a sequence of principles and consequences. It is in the shape of a dogma that the notion of freedom dawns in unenlightened minds, and its effect then is as with any other dogma, a kind of exaltation, of fury, impatience with contradiction, the inability to tolerate the slightest reservation, the slightest change in the creed. This rule of faith, brought thus to bear on questions which touch all interests, on opinions which, subject to the law of circumstances, become criminal today when yesterday they were a duty, is much more to be feared than when it is enclosed in an abstract circle of theological subtleties. These subtleties leave in peace, in the bosom of their families, many men indifferent to shadowy discussions. What obscure life, however, what immobile existence, what unknown name could succeed in disarming fanaticism in the political field? This obscure life, this unknown name, this immobile existence, are in its eyes treasons. Inactivity seems punishable to it, domestic affections a forgetting of patriotism, happiness a suspect purpose. Those who desire or regret it, it will call conspirators. Armed for freedom, it bows joyfully before the harshest slavery, provided that it is exercised in the name of its cherished doctrine. It battles for the cause and renounces its effect. Severity, injustice, and slights of all kinds on the part of its leaders seem to it meritorious acts, as it were gauges of sincerity. It finds the educated bothersome because they find it hard [498] to embrace an opinion without certain restrictions and nuances. It is suspicious of the person of proud spirit, because proud spirits experience some kind of antipathy to the strongest people and serve the powerful only with distaste. The only qualities it demands are belief and will. It sees in morality obstacles, weakness, and chicanery. All is well if the end is good. It violates laws because they are made only for the friends, not the enemies of the fatherland. It betrays friendship because there cannot be friendship between the people's defenders and oppressors. It neglects its most solemn commitments because fulfilling them might supply dangerous men with means they could direct against public safety. It effaces even the very last vestiges of pity. It is moved not at all by the sight of grief, nor does it fade at all with age. We have seen old men, overcome with sufferings which told them that the end was near, strike their victims with a failing hand, showing themselves unyielding at the edge of the tomb and remaining pitiless in the presence of eternity.

Fanaticism has the fatal property that its very sincerity freezes the courage of those who wish to fight it. It is easy to stand up to the injustice of the wicked, because it is known that in the bottom of their hearts they render homage to those they persecute. It is nothing to attack frontally enemies recognized as such. We resign ourselves willingly to the hatred of these adversaries. We are separated from them by fixed barriers. We fight them in the name of everything which raises the spirit, everything dear to the heart. But to bring down on one's head the distrust of men one wishes to serve, to lose that popularity which is so vast a recompense for danger, such a means of consoling and saving innocence, to repel the repeated applause of an excited crowd listening to you, responding to you, saluting you, and following you like some tutelary God, to give up the support of one's party without gaining the good will of the opposing party, to be disowned by those very people who share your opinions most keenly and who are devoted enthusiastically to the cause you cherish, that is real discouragement, the deepest misery. When disinterested men, brave, ardent for freedom, free from all egoism or low passion, in their suspicions come to pursue the friends of humanity and morality, they are animated, in the midst of their mistakes, by a conviction so firm that it takes away from those they suspect part of the sense and the strength of innocence.

[499] This is still not the whole story. Fanaticism, contained initially in a few energetic minds, seems to communicate itself by rapid contagion to timid and weak characters. They learn its language out of self-interest. They speak its language in order to please it. Soon, however, its ascendancy subjugates them. They become intoxicated by what they say. Each word they utter is a commitment into which they enter. They are driven forward in this course by the very feelings which might induce them to flee. Sometimes they dread their victims, more often their own side. If mutual recognition were possible, their terror would be less; but they all react on each other. Thus in our country men made ferocious by fear got drunk on their own terror. Thus there spread over France this inexplicable vertigo which people called the Reign of Terror.

Fanaticism then loses even the qualities which ennoble it. It furnishes pretexts for all forms of vice. The ungrateful friend, the faithless debtor, the obscure informer, the prevaricating judge, find their apologia written in advance in the agreed language; and this banal justification, prepared for all crimes, succeeds in corrupting that host of equivocal souls, who have neither the audacity of crime nor the courage of virtue.

Once they reach this stage, revolutions destroy all morality. They break the regular sequence of causes and effects. They separate actions from their natural consequences. They break all equilibrium between obligations and sacrifices. There are no longer easy duties nor safe virtues. Everything becomes devotion or heroism; and charisma takes over all the vulgar souls incapable of these great efforts.

Each person in the sinking vessel seizes a plank and repels the companion in misfortune who would like to attach himself to him.[17] Each man

17. An almost identical image occurs in Mme. de Staël's *Des circonstances actuelles, op. cit.,* Livre II, Ch. 2, p. 236.

abjures the links of his past life, isolating himself in order to defend himself and seeing in the friendship or misfortune which implore him only an obstacle to his safety.

[500] One thing only keeps its price. It is not public opinion. There no longer exists any glory for the powerful nor respect for victims. It is not justice. Its laws are unrecognized and its forms profaned. It is wealth. Wealth can disarm tyranny and seduce some of its agents. It can appease proscription, making flight from it easier. In sum, it can spread a few material joys across a life which is always under threat. Thus shameful leanings form an alliance with the most unbridled manias. People amass wealth to enjoy possessions. They possess to forget inevitable dangers. The response to others' misfortune is hardness, to one's own, insouciance. There is bloodletting alongside festivities. In their fierce stoicism people reject sympathy; they throw themselves into pleasure in sybaritic voluptuousness.

Lost in this chaos, enlightened men no longer find any voice to respond to them. All reasoning seems perverted, and no one feels above reproach. Rectitude is a prosecuting voice to be got rid of, to be distorted for the sake of a peaceful life. Each man is haunted by the memory of some troubling fact, on which all his logic focuses. You may believe he is expounding a whole theory to you; he is really trying to justify an hour of his life.

One reflects, sorrowfully, on oneself, on morality, on the principles one has adopted from childhood. To remember some ideas of moderation or prudence is to be regarded as a traitor. One is regarded as culpable when one takes up with any zeal the cause of some unfortunate soul. Faced with all the evidence of disapproval one meets, one is tempted to reproach oneself with a crime, whereas in fact one is fulfilling a duty. Shame upon him, however, who, charged with preserving his country from the perils which the blind furies are preparing for it, him whose duty is to protect weak, oppressed, and defenseless beings, shame I say, if he loses heart. Woe to freedom's friends if they compromise with that spirit of persecution whose nature is to scorn all compromise. Their cause is henceforth dishonored. Sooner or later, this spirit, not finding them zealous enough, will turn its weapons against them, snatch their banners from them, thrust them into the ranks of the enemy, and proscribe them as turncoats. Then they will have the courage to die, a sterile courage, for which the future will pay them little regard. For want of courage earlier, for not having struggled against injustice from its very first moves, they will die without glory, at once the victims and the authors of the crimes they have suffered. [501]

CHAPTER SIX

On the Duties of Enlightened Men after Violent Revolutions

One might believe that when revolutions calm down, a time of compensation or at least of rest begins for humanity's friends. Sometimes, however, fate reserves for them one last and painful ordeal.

The people, weary of an oppression operating in the name of freedom, seem to ask, in order to resign themselves almost joyfully to a new oppression, only for a different name for this oppression. It is enough to tell the people straightforwardly that it is not in the name of freedom that they are being trampled underfoot. What a strange reversal of ideas. All the laws have been violated by an unlimited government, and it is not the laws that are invoked but a government of the same unlimited character. A boundless despotism has weighed hard on everyone, and the cry is not for freedom but for another despotism. All the rages which during the violence of revolutions proved so fatal are reproduced under other forms. Fear and vanity formerly travestied the party spirit in its implacable furies; their insane manifestations now surpass the most abject servility. The pride which survives everything scores another success in the baseness in which fear seeks refuge. Cupidity seems openly to sacrifice its opprobrium as a guarantee to tyranny. The new power is fortified by everything remembered. It inherits all the criminal theories. It thinks itself justified by everything which has happened before it. It parades its contempt for men and its scorn for reason. It fortifies itself on all the attacks and all the mistakes by the very people it has just repressed or punished. It is no longer subject to the brake of public opinion, which sometimes contains established despotism. It is absolutely without the purity of intention, the disinterestedness, the good faith which characterize the [502] blind masses in the midst of their fury. Around it there gather every ignoble desire, every deft calculation, and every refined degradation. To its feet there hastens false argument, to astonish it with its zeal and surpass it in its cries, obscuring all ideas and calling the voice which would contradict it sedition. Intelligence comes to offer its services, intelligence which, separated from conscience, is the vilest of instruments. The apostates of all opinions gather swiftly, conserving from their former opinions only the habit of culpable methods. Crafty turncoats, famous in the annals of vice, slip into place; their quick dexterity carries them from yesterday's to today's prosperity, so that at all times they blight everything good, belittle everything elevated, and insult everything noble.

Mediocre talents, joined with subaltern natures, set themselves up in the name of power as guardians of thought. They declare what questions the human mind may ponder. They allow it to frolic, subordinately, however, in the narrow enclosure they have conceded it. Anathema on its head, though, if it should ever break out of that enclosure, or scorn puerile subjects, or not abjure its celestial origin. Religion is no more than a vile instrument of government and reasoning only a cowardly commentary of power. The weirdest doctrines are arrogantly advanced. The prejudices of all the ages and the injustices of all countries are brought together as materials of the new social order. People go back to distant centuries and traverse faraway countries to put together from a thousand scattered parts a truly complete servitude which can be laid down as a model. The dishonored word flies from one mouth to another, never leaving from any real source, never carrying conviction anywhere, a tiresome sound, lazy and ridiculous, which leaves neither truth nor justice with any expression which is not soiled. Such was the reign of Charles II, the result of thirty years of civil wars, a forever shameful one, where we saw all the excesses of madness succeeded by all those of degradation.

Such a state is more disastrous than the most stormy revolution. One can at times detest the seditious Roman tribunes, but one is dejected by the contempt one experiences for the Senate under the Caesars. [503] One may find Charles I's enemies hard and guilty, but a profound disgust seizes us for Cromwell's creatures. When the ignorant parts of society commit crimes, the enlightened classes stay blameless; and since the natural thrust of things sooner or later puts power back in their hands, they can easily restore a public opinion which is misled rather than corrupted. When these classes themselves, however, disavowing their ancient principles, shed their habitual decency and permit themselves execrable examples, what hope remains? Where can one find in the nation a germ of honor, an element of virtue? Everything is only mire and blood and dust. A cruel destiny, in all eras, for the friends of freedom. Unrecognized, suspected, surrounded by men incapable of believing in impartiality, courage, disinterested conviction, distressed in turn by the feeling of indignation when these oppressors are at their strongest and by that of pity when they have become victims, they have always wandered the earth, the butt of all parties, isolated in the midst of generations sometimes raging and sometimes depraved.

It is on them, however, that the hope of the human race rests. We owe to them that great correspondence across the centuries, which gives evidence in ineffaceable letters against the sophisms which all the tyrants renew. Owing to this correspondence Socrates has survived the persecutions of a blind populace. Brutus and Cicero are not entirely dead under the proscriptions of the infamous Octavian. Lucan and Seneca were able to defy Nero's henchman, Boethius the prisons and the sword under Theodoric. Their example has done good long after their deaths. Let their successors not lose courage. The same rewards await them in a distant future, but one brilliant in glory. When they are no more, the truths they have repeated in vain will be listened to. No effort is wasted on that road where the nature of things necessarily leads men. It is a matter only of knowing how to struggle long-term, perhaps all one's life.

Let them therefore raise their voices anew. Let them not abjure their principles. They have nothing to reproach themselves with. They have need neither of expiation nor disavowal. They possess intact the treasure of a pure reputation. Let them dare to avow the love of generous ideas. These do not cast on them an accusatory light.

[504] To no avail do the weariness of nations, the anxiety of leaders, the servility of political instruments form an artificial assent which people call public opinion. It is absolutely not this. Men never cut themselves off from freedom. To say that they do is to say that they love humiliation, suffering, destitution, and poverty. To represent them as absorbed in their domestic feelings and individual economic decisions is to paint them, by a crude contradiction, as both putting an excessive price on their possessions and none at all on the lasting nature of these. For security is nothing else but the lasting of things. To say that men can cut themselves off from freedom is to claim that they resign themselves painlessly to being oppressed, incarcerated, separated from what they love, interrupted in their work, deprived of their goods, harassed in their opinions and their most secret thoughts, and dragged into prisons and to the scaffold. Since security is instituted against these things, it is to be preserved from these scourges that we invoke freedom. It is these scourges the people fear, curse, and detest. Wherever and under whatever name they encounter them, they take fright and recoil. What they abhorred in what their oppressors called freedom was not freedom, but slavery; but if slavery were presented under its true names, its true forms, is it credible that they would detest it less?

However active the inquisition may be, with whatever care its precautions multiply, enlightened men always retain a thousand ways of making themselves heard. Despotism is to be feared only when it has choked reason in its infancy. Then the former can stop the progress of the latter and keep the human race in a long imbecility. When reason gets on the march, however, it is invincible. Its supporters may perish, but it survives and triumphs. There exists only a moment to proscribe it with advantage. Once this has passed, all efforts are in vain. The intellectual struggle is engaged, thought is separated from power, truth dawns in every mind.

After the inestimable advantage of being the citizen of a free country, no situation is perhaps sweeter than being the courageous commentator of a subjugated yet enlightened nation. Times when despotism, disdaining a hypocrisy it deems pointless, decks itself in its true colours and insolently deploys banners known for ages are not without compensations. [505] How much better it is to suffer from the oppression of one's enemies than to blush from the excesses of one's allies. The defenders of freedom encounter then the agreement of the best part of the human race. They plead a noble cause openly to people and are seconded by the wishes of all men of good will. Persecution followed by glory is largely recompensed. He who succumbs confidently bequeaths to his contemporaries the care of defending his memory and completing his work.

Missionaries of truth, if the road is cut off, redouble in zeal and effort. Let light penetrate everywhere; if it is obscured, let it reappear; if it is repelled, let it come back. Let it reproduce, multiply, and transform itself. Let it be as indefatigable as persecution. Let some march bravely while others slip adroitly into place. Let the truth spread, sometimes resounding and sometimes repeated very low. Let all rational endeavors combine, let all hopes revive, let everybody work, serve, and wait. "There is no prescription for useful ideas," said a famous man.[18] Courage can come back after despondency, light after ignorance, ardor for the public good after the sleep of indifference.

Despotism, immorality, and injustice are things so against nature that all it takes is an incident, an effort, a brave voice to pull man back out of that abyss. He comes back to morality by way of the misfortune which results from a general forgetting of morality. He comes back to freedom because of the oppression made to weigh on him by all power he has neglected to limit. No nation's cause is hopeless. What could be more savage than England during the civil wars of Charles I and his Parliament?[19] What could be more degraded than that same England during the reign of Charles II? And yet, forty years after having offered the world horrible examples of savagery, twenty years after having given it shameful examples of license and [506] baseness, England regained its place among the wise, virtuous, and free peoples, and has kept it.

18. See Constant's Note F at the end of Book XVIII.
19. See Constant's Note G at the end of Book XVIII.

A. [Refers to page 398.]
It is enfeebling to the power of the law to look for its motives, he says.

B. [Refers to page 400.]
Corps complet de la législation, Ch. 2, p. 70.[20]

C. [Refers to page 400.]
Code Pénal, Partie 3, Ch. 1.[21] The legislator's lack of skill, he adds, often itself creates an opposition between the natural sanction and the political one. He therefore recognizes a natural sanction.

D. [Refers to page 402.]
Bentham, Principes de législation, Ch. 12.[22]

E. [Refers to page 407.]
Bentham, III, 189.

[507] F. [Refers to page 422.]
Administration des finances, II, 76.[23]

G. [Refers to page 422.]
It was proposed in the Long Parliament to deport and have sold in Algiers the nobles with their families, not excluding pregnant women, on whose behalf some members protested. Parliamentary Register.[24]

20. Jeremy Bentham, *op. cit.*, t. I, p. 154: "Thus to declare by law that such and such an act is prohibited is to establish that act as an offense."
21. *Ibid.*, t. II, pp. 380–384.
22. Hofmann failed to find the passage quoted by Constant.
23. Jacques Necker, *op. cit.*, t. I, p. 77 (error in Constant's numbering).
24. Hofmann could not establish this reference.

Additions to the Work Entitled *Principles of Politics Applicable to All Governments*

Book I: Exposition of the Subject

Chapter 1: The Purpose of the Work[1]

This work, started long ago, has continued under several successive governments in France. Measures are recalled and censured in it which no longer apply. So are others, however, which still obtain, and consequently I do not think people will believe that I have sought to please today's government by attacking yesterday's. I have followed the principles,[2] independently of circumstances, and I have not deliberately turned aside either for praise or blame. So many errors which seemed to have become dead letters, so many sophisms one might have thought discredited, so many iniquitous practices apparently dead and gone, have reappeared, sometimes under the same names, sometimes with new ones, that I have come to think that I must speak out against these things, whether past or present, equally strongly. So many truths one might have considered universally recognized have been called into question or even put aside, without our being deigned a word of explanation or excuse, that I thought I must not enunciate a single truth, however obvious it might appear, without bringing to mind the evidence for it. My purpose has been to compose an elementary work. A work of this kind, on the fundamental principles of politics, has seemed to me to be lacking in all the literatures I know.

[512] This work originally contained two parts, constitutional institutions and the rights of individuals, in other words, the means of public security and the principles of freedom. Since the first are contestable and the second incontestable, I thought I should present the latter separately.

I have therefore removed from my work everything on the forms of government. I had treated the full extent of this subject. The division of citizens into governors

1. M. Patrice Thompson has published this addition to Book I, Ch. 1 in his book *La religion de Benjamin Constant: Les pouvoirs de l'image,* Pisa, Paccini, 1978, Annexe II, pp. 552–557. Hofmann admits that the whole passage reads like an introduction to *Principles of Politics,* but he has preferred to keep it as an addition in the way that Constant presented it.

2. ["Principles," as in the title of the work. Translator's note]

and governed, political powers, executive power and its exclusiveness, whether temporary or for the lifetime of the person in whom it is vested, the dangers of this exclusiveness in the election of the Head of State, the mode of election established in France, the tendency to military government of elective exclusiveness, the complexity of executive power, the objections which the history of so many ancient republics as well as modern revolutions furnishes against that complexity, the abuses natural to executive power, however it is composed, the guarantees against these abuses, the limitation of controls on the law of peace and of war, the right to resist taxes, the independence of the judiciary, accountability, the organization of the armed forces, the legislative power, abuses thereof, safeguards instituted or to be instituted against these abuses, the unlimited power which gives the executive exclusive initiative, the division into two chambers, the veto, the dissolution of legislative assemblies, popular election, in other words, and the advantages found only therein, the two systems substituted successively in France for popular elections, the formal description of a constitution in which all powers would be elective and all the rights of citizens recognized, the weak aspects of this constitution and the means of remedying these, such have been my research preoccupations. A generation must feel young and think forcefully, however, to involve itself with such discussions. In the amphitheater in Constantinople, amid the factions of the blues and the greens,[3] they would have been out of place. They would have brought out the suspicions of the former and wearied the frivolity of the latter.

[513] When political questions have caused long agitation and numerous misfortunes, there is established in many minds a conviction that on everything connected with government reasoning is valueless. The errors of theorizing seem much more tiresome than abuses of practice. Since they are indeed more unlimited and incalculable in their results, the attempts of faulty theorizing have a disadvantage from which such abuses are free. A man bends to institutions he finds established, as to the rules of physical nature. He arranges, according to their very faults, his interests, his economic reckoning, and the planning of his life. All his relationships, hopes, means of employment, and happiness are organized around

3. The blues and greens were originally the respective colors of the charioteers who competed for the prize in the races in the hippodromes of Constantinople and the Byzantine Empire, above all in the sixth and seventh centuries; the two rival factions which disturbed the Empire at that period were also designated by the same device, the aristocrats standing up for the blues and the people for the greens. This historical allusion was common in Constant's time, when it evoked the profound and irremediable antagonism between those who supported the Revolution and those who supported monarchical reaction. Bentham, without referring to the history of his own time, speaks of it in order to denounce the futility of political hates: "Have we not seen the citizens of Rome and Constantinople divide themselves into implacable factions on behalf of actors, charioteers, and gladiators? And to give importance to these shameful quarrels, did they not pretend that the success of the Greens or the Blues presaged plenty or famine, the victories or reverses of the Empire?" *Op. cit.*, t. I, p. 15.

that which exists. During revolutions, however, since everything changes at every instant, men no longer know where they stand. They are forced by their own needs, and often also by the way they are threatened by government, to behave as if that which has just appeared must always subsist; and predicting nevertheless the next changes, they possess neither the individual independence which ought to result from the absence of security, nor security, the only compensation for the sacrifice of freedom.

It is therefore not surprising that after repeated revolutions, any idea of improvement, even abstract and separated from any particular application, is odious and inconvenient and that the aversion it inspires extends to everything which seems to indicate the possibility of a change, even in the most indirect way. It is quite understandable, moreover, that those with the reins of government favor this natural disposition. Even if we attribute to the governors the purest of intentions, they are bound to reserve for themselves the privilege of meditating on the good they want to do; or if they entrust this delicate task to some of the subordinate collaborators surrounding them, this can only be in part. They are happy to see that submissive and flexible minds are undertaking to indicate to them some of the detail needed for achieving their purpose or, better still, to make available to them by minor innovations the means government thinks it has discovered. The independent thinker, however, who claims to grasp at a glance the overall picture, which the governing group allow people to concern themselves with at the very most only in bits, and then functionally and without passing judgment, the philosopher who goes back to the first principles of power and of social organization, even when he isolates himself from present things, and fixing on his memories or his hopes, wishes only to speak with regard to the future or pronounce only on [514] the past, seems to them nevertheless a presumptuous rhetorician, a tiresome observer, a dangerous sophist.

In this way the fatigue of the people combines with the anxiety of its leaders to circumscribe the domain of thought on all sides. It has been said that under the monarchy there was an intermediary class, the nobility, who conserved some independence but only insofar as this decorated and consolidated submission. Similarly, in the state of things we are describing, there forms an intermediary class which demands from reason only what is necessary to limit its sway. Educated men, but without power, elegant subalterns, who take style as the purpose and some restrained and secondary ideas as the means, set themselves up as organs of opinion, the supervisors of thought. They raise an altar to literature, in contravention of philosophy. They declare on which questions human intelligence may exercise itself. They allow it to frolic but subordinately and with circumspection, in the space they have granted it. Anathema on it, however, if it transgresses that space, if, not abjuring its celestial origin, it gives itself over to forbidden speculations, if it dares to think that its noblest destiny is not in the ingenious decoration of frivolous subjects, adroit adulatory praise, and sonorous declamation on unimportant subjects, but that heaven and its own nature have made of it an eternal tribunal, where everything is examined, weighed, and in the last resort judged.

When an inopportune mind wishes to launch itself thoughtlessly from abstract theory to violent practice and, trusting to its own perhaps incomplete and defective speculations, destroy and change everything, madness is probably present and crime even more so. Only perfidiously, however, could immobile, solitary thought be compared with solitary action or reckless advice. Action is for the moment; thought's judgments are for centuries. It bequeaths future generations both the truths it has been able to uncover and the mistakes which seemed to it truths. Time, in its eternal progression, gathers and separates them.

In Athens, a citizen who deposited on the altar an olive branch surrounded with sacred little bands could freely explain himself on matters political.

I might be accused rather of dealing with obvious things and establishing inapplicable principles. Men who have renounced reason and morality find all one says in this direction so many paradoxes or commonplaces; and since truths are disagreeable to them, above all in their consequences, what constantly happens is that they disdain any initial assertion as not needing demonstration and protest against the second and the third as unsustainable and paradoxical, [515] although the latter may obviously be the necessary and immediate conclusions of the former.

Stupidity is singularly fond of repeating axioms which give it the appearance of profundity, while tyranny is highly adroit in seizing upon stupidity's axioms. Hence it arises that propositions whose absurdity astonishes us when they are analyzed slip into a thousand minds, are repeated by a thousand tongues, while men who want to agree are continually reduced to demonstrating the obvious.

I have quoted a lot in my book and mainly from living authors, or those recently dead, or from men whose very name is authoritative, such as Adam Smith, Montesquieu, and Filangieri. I have made a point of affirming that often I was only reproducing, with softened expression, opinions to be found in the most moderate of writers.

One habitual ruse of the enemies of freedom and enlightenment is to affirm that their ignoble doctrine is universally adopted, that principles on which rest the dignity of the human race are abandoned by unanimous agreement, and that it is unfashionable and almost in bad taste to profess them, thinking taken very seriously in France. I have tried to prove to them that this so-called unanimity is a lie.

An example more imposing still than the theories of even the most estimable writers has, it is true, come to the rescue of my principles, precisely while I was laboring to expound them. It is the conduct of the American government, such as it was pronounced by the President of the United States on his installation and such as it has been for the last ten years.[4]

"Although the will of the majority," said Mr. Jefferson, on 4 March 1801, "must prevail in all cases, that will, to be legitimate, must be reasonable. The minority possess equal rights which equal law must protect. To violate these rights would be

4. This brief introduction to the quotation from Jefferson which follows makes it apparent that the drafting took place in 1810.

an oppression. It is sometimes said that man must not be entrusted with his own self-government. But then how could one entrust to him the government of others? Or have angels perhaps been found, in the form of kings, to govern us? To prevent men from doing each other mutual harm and to leave them otherwise full freedom to manage themselves in the efforts of their work and in their progress toward improvement, that is the sole purpose of a good government. Equal and right justice for all men, whatever [516] their condition or their belief, religious or political, peace, trade, straightforwardness with other nations, without insidious alliances with any, the maintenance of the governments of the individual States in all their rights, as the most convenient administration for our domestic interests and the most certain bulwark against antirepublican tendencies, the conservation of the federal government, in its full constitutional vigor, as the guarantee of our peace within and our security without, scrupulous attention to the right of election by the people, a sweet and sure correction of abuses, which otherwise the sword or revolutions destroy, when no peaceful remedy has been prepared, an unreserved acceptance of the decisions of the majority, a well-disciplined militia, our best safeguard in time of peace and during the first moments of a war, until regular troops can back it up, the supremacy of the civil over the military authority, economy in public expenditure, in order that the working class be taxed only lightly, faithful settlement of our debts and an inviolable respect for public confidence, the dissemination of education and an appeal to public rationality, against all abuses of whatever sort, religious freedom, press freedom, freedom of persons under the protection of habeus corpus and trial by juries impartially chosen, such are the essential principles of our government. The watches of the night of our wise men and the blood of our heroes have been consecrated to their triumph. This is the profession of our political faith, the educational text of the citizens, the touchstone by which we can appreciate the services of those in whom we put our confidence; and if we deviated from these principles in moments of error and alarm, we would have to hasten to retrace our steps and regain the path which alone leads to peace, freedom, and security."[5]

These principles, put into practice with so much success in a huge, flourishing republic, are those which I have tried to establish in this book, and I have devoted myself to this task with all the more zeal and confidence in that having some time carried out legislative functions in the State which they named the French Republic, [517] I find myself free again[6] without having done a thing or expressed an opinion, which forces me to alter in the slightest detail the intellectual system which I believe to be the only true or useful one, and the only one worthy of good men.

5. *Jefferson's First Inaugural Address,* 4 March 1801, the whole text of which can be found in the complete edition by Henry Steele Commager, *Documents of American History,* New York, F. S. Crofts, 1947, pp. 186–187. In the Lausanne manuscript of the *Additions,* Jefferson's text is in English.

6. Constant was a Tribune from January 1800 to January 1802.

Notes Referring to the Original Chapter

1. *Extremes do not only touch but also follow each other.* "Everything which tends to restrain kings," said M. de Clermont-Tonnerre, "is received with delight, because people remember the abuses of royalty. Perhaps there will come a time when everything which tends to restrain the rights of the people will be received in the same fanatical spirit, because the dangers of anarchy will be no loss strongly felt." II, 232.[7]

2. *the first conquest of our century.* Order of the day of His Majesty the Emperor in the Moniteur of 22 January 1806: "There is no censorship at all in France. Every citizen in France can publish such books as he judges suitable, provided he accepts accountability. No work may be suppressed, no author may be prosecuted save by the courts or following a decree by His Majesty where the text would threaten the first prerogatives of public security and interest. We would be falling again into a strange situation, if a simple clerk could arrogate to himself the right to prevent the publication of a book or force an author to retract from or add anything to it. Freedom of thought is the first conquest of the century. The Emperor wishes it conserved," etc.[8]

Chapter 2: Rousseau's First Principle on the Origin of Political Authority

Notes

1. *the world knows only two kinds of power.* [518] *There is force, the illegitimate kind.* "A town," said Louis XIV, speaking of Genoa, "formerly subject to my ancestors and which had no other rights of sovereignty than those it drew from its rebellion." Mémoires I, 24. If republics, formerly subject to monarchies, have no other rights of sovereignty than their rebellion, then kings could well have no other rights than their usurpation.

Chapter 3: Rousseau's Second Principle on the Scope of Political Authority

Notes

1. *the general will must exercise unlimited authority over individual existence.* "The voice of the greatest number," (says Rousseau), "always obliges everyone else. This is a

7. Stanislas-Marie de Clermont-Tonnerre, *Opinion sur une motion de M. Mirabeau, combattue par M. Barnave,* in: *Recueil des opinions . . . , op. cit.,* t. II, p. 232.

8. On the direct causes of this curious proclamation, which must have surprised Constant greatly, see Gustave Le Poittevin, *La liberté de la presse depuis la Révolution, 1789–1815,* Geneva, Slatkine-Mégariotis Reprints, 1975, pp. 159–161 (Reprint de l'éd. Paris, 1901).

consequence of the contract itself. One may ask how a man can be free and forced to comply with wills which are not his own. How can those opposing be free and subject to laws to which they did not consent? The question is badly put. The citizen consents to all the laws, even to those passed in spite of him and even those which punish him if he dares to break one of them. The constant will of all the members of the State is the general will. When a law is proposed in the people's assembly, what is asked of them is not precisely whether they approve of the proposition or reject it, but whether or not it conforms to the general will which is their own. Each one giving his vote gives his opinion thereon, and from the counting of votes the declaration of the general will is derived. Therefore when the contrary opinion to mine is carried, this means only that I was in error and that what I had estimated to be the general will was not such. If my minority opinion had carried, I would have done something other than I had wished. It is then that I would not have been free."[9] Rousseau merely pushes the theory back here and expresses it in other words. How does it arise that the declaration of the majority makes the general will clear to the eyes of the minority? It makes clear only that that will is of the majority. What should have been said is that the society has agreed that when a determination is necessary, the will of the majority constitutes law. Then, although it may not be true that when a minority obeys an opinion contrary to its own, [519] it is all the freer for it, although it may be still less true that an individual, whose individual opinion had prevailed, would not be free and would be doing something other than his will, in the very act of doing it, it is conceivable that each person submits to the sacrifice, because others agree to submit to it. This, however, can be only when a resolution is needed. Otherwise the sacrifice has no purpose.

Chapter 4: Rousseau's Arguments for Boundless Political Authority

Notes

1. *He* (Rousseau) *forgets that all the preserving qualities which he confers on the abstract being he calls sovereignty are born in the fact that this being is made up of all the separate individuals without exception.* Jean-Jacques's system and all the reasoning it rests on are forgetful of reality, a terrible, vicious flaw. Man is counted in it as some numerical value. When the words *all or everyone* are spoken, we are led to believe that the discussion is of units or collections of units, which differ not at all among themselves and cannot change their nature. It is taken as shown that none of these figures can encroach on another. These figures being moral beings, however, the result of the bringing together of ten of these figures is not directly proportional to their numerical value, but proportional to the moral value of each one of them. This means that just adding them together one does not get the modified sum of their respective strengths, but only the tenfold multiplication of the individual force of one of them.

9. Jean-Jacques Rousseau, *Du contract social,* Livre IV, Ch. 2, *éd. cit.,* pp. 440–441.

Chapter 6: The Consequences of Rousseau's Theory

Notes

1. *They ask it from the owner of political authority, the people.* "The people's name is a forged signature to justify its leaders." Bentham.

[520] *Chapter 8:* Hobbes's Opinion Reproduced

Notes

1. *This was no longer a man, this was a people.* One sees how easily Rousseau's system leads to the most absolute despotism. Furthermore, we have remarked already that the supporters of this kind of government had avidly seized on it. Men, by uniting, says M. Ferrand, have surrendered, at a word from the general will, all the forces of individual will. Préface de l'esprit de l'histoire.[10] Does not this sentence seem to be from Rousseau?

Note that M. Ferrand and others never stop reproaching freedom's friends for losing themselves in abstractions. When, however, they speak to us of the general will personified and of the sovereign who is no longer a man but a people, can we say they avoid them?

Chapter 9: On the Inconsistency with Which Rousseau Has Been Reproached

Notes

1. *He* (Rousseau) *has declared that sovereignty cannot be alienated, nor represented, nor delegated.* "Sovereignty," he says, "cannot be represented politically, for the same reason it cannot be alienated. It consists in the general will, and the will is not amenable to representation. It is the same or it is different. There is no in between."[11] This idea of Rousseau arises because he has never defined either the nature or above all the limits of the general will. If we call the will of the members of a society on all things the general will, doubtless it cannot be represented; but if we call the general will only the will of the members of society on those things which society makes common to them, it can be represented, that is to say that a smaller association can be made with the same purpose and can make its decisions according to the same interests as the larger. [521] "The people's deputies," he continues, "are not and cannot be its representatives; they are only its commissioners; they cannot conclude anything definitively."[12] It would be just as right to say, however, that the majority

10. "[Men] have not been able to join up and enjoy the benefit of civil liberty, without renouncing the fatal prerogatives of savage freedom, without submitting, at a word from the general will, all the forces of each individual will." Antoine Ferrand, *op. cit.*, 1803 edition, Préface, pp. xxi–xxii.

11. Jean-Jacques Rousseau, *Du contrat social,* Livre III, Ch. 15, *éd. cit.*, p. 429.

12. *Ibid.*, pp. 429–430.

cannot conclude anything definitively; since the majority is only the representative of the whole and one is aware of the absurdities this system leads to. "Any law," he says, finally, "which the people personally have not ratified is null; it is not a law."[13] Rousseau does not explain, however, how the ratification of the majority binds the minority. The power of the majority is explained only by considering it as representing everybody.

13. *Ibid.*, p. 430.

Book II: On the Principles to Replace Received Ideas on the Extent of Political Authority

Chapter 1: On the Limitation of Political Authority

Notes

1. *When this government is extended to purposes outside its competence, it becomes illegitimate.* Under Pericles the sale of five thousand citizens, because they had been born to foreign mothers, was tyrannical. The institutions under Lycurgus concerned with the private lives of citizens were tyrannical. Our laws on the mercantile system are tyrannical. See Smith IV, chapters 1–8.[14] Peter I's law that his subjects should cut off their beards was tyrannical. Finally, any law which prescribes to someone what he must do for his own utility is tyrannical. The law can decide between one man and another and between a man and society. Any law, however, which regulates the conduct of a man in relation to himself, and only himself, is tyrannical. All these tyrannical laws are nonetheless justified in Rousseau's theory.[15] [522]

2. *Even if it were the whole nation, except for the man it is harassing, it would be no more legitimate for that.* "Pellitur a populo victus Cato; tristior ille est qui vicit, fascesque pudet rapuisse Catoni. Namque hoc dedecus est populi, morumque ruina. Non homo pulsus erat: sed in uno victa potestas, romanumque decus." Petronius.[16] (Cato, defeated, is driven out by the people. Less fortunate is that man who defeated him, and is ashamed to have seized the symbols of authority from Cato. For this is the dishonor of the people and the ruin of morals. It was not a man who was driven out, but in one man was the power and honor of Rome defeated.)

Chapter 2: On the Rights of the Majority

Notes

1. *than that of the smallest of minorities.* Law has been defined as the expression of the majority will.[17] This definition is very faulty and very dangerous, in that it appears

14. Adam Smith, *op. cit.*, t. III, pp. 1–503.

15. The examples supplied in this note 1 of Ch. 1 come from Jean-Charles-Léonard Sismondi, *Recherches sur les constitutions . . .*, *op. cit.*, p. 112.

16. Petronius, *Satiricon*, CXIX, vers. 45–49. In place of *hoc dedecus est populi* the text has *hoc dedocoris populo.* The French text, translated from the Latin by Alfred Ernout, Paris, Les Belles Lettres, 1922, p. 137, runs in English: "Cato was beaten and repulsed by the people. His conqueror, more humiliated than he, blushed to have carried off the fasces [rods of authority] of a Cato, for, and this is what shows the infamy of the citizens and the ruin of manners, this is not a man excluded from power, rather in him it is the power and honor of Rome which fall."

17. This in any case is the formulation of Article 6 of the Declaration of the Rights of Man and the Citizen, of 26 August 1789.

to give the general will unlimited power. It should be added: on those things where the general will has a right to will.

2. *fixed principles from which the majority never deviates.* With the system of unlimited rights of the numerical majority, one would be poised to make the whole world one people. For how would a notional territorial line change that right? If thirty thousand neighbors do not want the same thing as a nation of thirty million, by what right do they resist? And if we granted them the right to resist, how would a city already an enclave not have the right to become a neighbor again? [523]

3. *They represented it* [the majority] *as a real person.* It is never fundamentally the majority who oppress. People steal its name and then use the arms it has supplied. The interest of the majority is never to oppress. The sum of misfortunes which exists in a society extends more or less to all members and increases when there is injustice. To harm an individual or class is to harm the whole.

Chapter 3: On the Insignificance of the Way Government is Organized When Political Power Is Not Limited.

NOTE

1. *there are things about which the legislature has no right to make laws.* There are unalterable principles, of which the whole nation is guardian, that the nation itself cannot infringe, and which are not numbered in the mass of opinions which it submits to those it charges with exerting its will. The reason is simple, namely that the nation itself has no right to a will contrary to these principles.

Chapter 7: On the Principle of Utility Substituted for the Idea of Individual Rights

Bentham says that if the supporter of utility found an action in the catalogue of virtues which resulted in more pain than pleasure, he would expunge it from this catalogue. I, 5.[18] This is remarkable, in that he says elsewhere[19] that it is bad to speak of natural rights, because each man wants to judge them according to his individual judgment. But is this not what he makes the supporter of utility do? In all systems one has to come back to individual judgment.

If one wants to judge according to conscience, says Bentham, I, 31, one will not be able to distinguish between an enlightened conscience and a [524] blind

18. Jeremy Bentham, *op. cit.* The exact text is: "If the supporter of the principle of utility should find, in the banal catalogue of the virtues, an action which led to more pain than pleasure, he would not hesitate to regard that alleged virtue as a vice."

19. See, for example, *ibid.,* t. I, p. 11. "Since each man having the same right as another to lay down his feeling as a rule for all feelings, there would no longer be a common measure nor universal court to which one could appeal over it." See also *ibid.,* p. 133.

one.[20] If, however, one wishes to judge according to the principle of utility, neither will one distinguish good and bad calculations on this basis. "In the immense variety of ideas on natural laws," says Bentham, Principles of Legislation, Ch. 13, "won't every person find reasons to resist human laws?"[21] He will find the same, however, in the principle of utility, applied in his way.

20. The exact text says: "For if one judges everything by feeling, there is no longer any way of distinguishing between the injunctions of an enlightened conscience and those of a blind one."

21. *Ibid.*, p. 137.

Book III: On Arguments and Hypotheses in Favor of the Extension of Political Authority

Chapter 1: On the Extension of Political Authority beyond Its Necessary Minimum, on the Grounds of Utility

Notes

1. *writers of all persuasions.* "All government is instituted for men's happiness. Therefore everything which can assure their happiness must be a part of government." Ferrand, Esprit de l'histoire, I, 107.[22]

2. *In some respects Montesquieu.* Bentham in his Principles of legislation, Ch. 12, entitled On the limits which separate morality from legislation, begins with a false proposition. "Morality," he says, "is the art of directing men's actions in such a way as to produce the greatest possible sum of happiness. Legislation has precisely the same end."[23] It is through confounding thus the purpose of legislation and that of morality that we have given legislation the growth which has become so disastrous. Bentham feels it himself, for he says a little further on that the means of legislation are very different, and its jurisdiction much more extensive than that of morality, that there are acts useful to the community which the law must not require and harmful acts [525] that it must not forbid.[24] He concludes with this obvious maxim: "Do not make the power of the laws intervene except to stop men hurting each other."[25] The definition he begins with, however, is equally inexact. The purpose of legislation is far more to safeguard men against the evil they might do themselves than to procure for them the greatest sum of possible happiness. The definition of morality and legislation seems to me to be that the first indicates to men how they might be happy, in rendering their fellows happy, and that the second preserves them from what might, on the part of their fellows, prevent them from making

22. Antoine Ferrand, *op. cit.,* 2e éd. (1803). The correct citation is: "All government must be instituted for the happiness of the men who are subject to it. . . ."

23. Jeremy Bentham, *op. cit.,* t. I, p. 98.

24. It is worth citing the whole paragraph to which Constant refers: "But although these two arts (morality and legislation), or two sciences, may have the same purpose, they differ greatly as to their extent. All actions, be they public or private, belong to morality. This is a guide which can lead the individual, as if by the hand, in all the details of his life, in all his relations with his fellows. Legislation cannot, and if it could it ought not to, exercise a continual and direct intervention on men's conduct. Morality prescribes to every individual the doing of all that is advantageous to the community, his personal advantage included. But there are many acts useful to the community which law must not command. There are likewise many harmful acts which it should not forbid, although morality does. Legislation, in a word, has just the same core as morality, but not the same circumference." *Ibid.,* pp. 98–99.

25. *Ibid.,* p. 103.

themselves happy, without hurting others. The singular thing here is that Bentham joins two definitions which contradict each other and which I oppose equally. For he says elsewhere that any law is a necessary evil.[26]

3. *in this theoretical system political authority has absolutely no limits nor can have.* Why is judicial power the least dangerous of all the powers? Because its nature is perfectly understood. People know it is essentially rigorous, that it is indispensable, but that the good it produces is only the absence of ill. Furthermore, it is not easily extended beyond its limits and when people have wanted to abuse it, they have had to distort it and turn it into a political power instead of a judicial one. Those holding other powers have not wished to be confined to such narrow limits. Consequently they have tried to deceive people over the nature of their duties. Instead of presenting themselves as guardians of public order, that is to say, as a sort of political constabulary, they have posed as the fathers of the people. They have benefited from being surrounded by affection, or telling themselves this, rather than mistrust, and have been able to abuse their powers much more easily.

[526] 4. *Nothing simpler than the questions on which these functions call governments to pronounce.*[27] "In the system of natural freedom," says Smith, IV, 9, V, 1, "the sovereign has only three duties to fulfill, three duties in truth of great importance, but clear, simple, and within the grasp of an ordinary mind. The first is the duty to defend the society from any act of violence or invasion on the part of other independent societies; the second is the duty to protect, as far as possible, each member of the society against the injustice and oppression of any other member, that is to say, the duty to establish a proper administration of justice; and the third of setting up and maintaining certain public works and institutions which the private interest of an individual or group of individuals would never get around to setting up or maintaining because the profit would never reimburse the expenditure of an individual or group of individuals, although with regard to a whole society this profit more than reimburses the expense."[28]

Chapter 3: Are Governors Necessarily Less Liable to Error Than the Governed?

Notes

1. *less impartial than the governed.* It is a mistake to take it that there is a huge gulf between those who lay down and those who accept the law. Their respective educations are always in a certain ratio and do not shift much. Nature grants no privilege to any individual. No one runs ahead of his country and era by much, and those who do so most are perhaps the least proper to dominate them.

26. Hofmann was unable to find this definition by Bentham.

27. [N.B.: This commentary should have been included under Additions, Book III, Ch. 3. In Hofmann's text it appears as point 4, Ch. 1. It is not clear whether the error is from Constant or Hofmann or both. Translator's note]

28. Adam Smith, *op. cit.,* t. III, p. 557.

2. *It is not the same with the numberless functions,* etc. The marquis de Mirabeau, [527] in the first book of his L'ami des hommes,[29] establishes a very accurate distinction between positive and speculative laws. According to him, positive laws limit themselves to maintenance; speculative ones extend to guidance. He does not draw extensive consequences from this distinction. His purpose was not to fix the limits of government functions, and although in the rest of his book he may constantly be led by the force of things to restrain these functions de facto, he nevertheless admits their legitimacy in law and strives only to indicate how they may be at their most useful and advantageous. We whose purpose is different will adopt the same distinction, but in order to follow up all it results in. When the government punishes a harmful action, when it penalizes the violation of a contractual undertaking, when it builds or repairs roads or canals, it fulfills a positive function. When it comes down hard on an action which is not harmful on the grounds that it could lead indirectly to one that is, when it imposes on individuals certain rules of conduct which are not a necessary part of the work to which they are contracted, when it harasses the management of property or the carrying out of work, when it seeks to dominate public opinion, either by punishments or rewards, or by seizing control of education, it arrogates to itself a speculative function, since it is basing itself on calculations, on suppositions, on hypothetical cases, in short, on speculations. Government in its positive functions does not act in a spontaneous way. It reacts in response to facts, to antecedent actions, which have taken place independently of its will. In its speculative function it does not have to react against facts or acts already performed, but to foresee future actions. It acts spontaneously therefore. Its action is the product of its own will.

The positive functions of government are of an extremely simple nature, and in their exercise its action is neither equivocal nor complicated. Its speculative functions are of a different nature. They have no factual base, not being exercises over factual things. They start from a supposition, a presumption. They can vary, extend, and become infinitely complicated. Positive functions often let government stay motionless. Speculative functions never let it do so. Its hand, which at times prevents, at times controls, at times creates, at times repairs, can [528] sometimes be invisible, but never stay inactive. Its action taking its source from its will, it must necessarily reason, suppose, guess. This indicates clearly how difficult it is in so many respects to draw the limits of speculative functions. Sometimes government places barriers of its own choosing just short of criminal activity, with a view to then establishing penalties against the overturning of these barriers. Sometimes it has recourse to prohibitive measures, against actions which, neutral in themselves, seem to it nevertheless dangerous in their indirect consequences. Sometimes it builds up coercive laws to compel men to do what seems useful to it. At other times it extends its scope to what people believe. On yet further occasions it modifies or limits the tenure of property, arbitrarily regulating its forms and deciding on, ordering, or prohibiting its transmission. It subjects the work of production to numerous impediments, encouraging it on

29. Hofmann could not find the distinction in the place indicated by Constant.

one side, restraining it on another. Actions, conversations, writings, mistakes, truths, religious ideas, philosophical systems, moral attachments, inner feelings, uses, habits, customs and manners, institutions, all that is vaguest in man's imagination, most independent in his nature, everything there belongs to the government domain. It enfolds our existence on all sides, takes hold of our first years, surveys and restrains our least movements, sanctifies or combats the most uncertain of our conjectures, modifies or directs our most fugitive impressions.

The difference, then, between speculative and positive functions is that the latter have fixed boundaries, rather than the unlimited ones the former have, once they are accepted.

The law or governmental action, according to which the government might send citizens to the frontiers to defend these when they are attacked, would be a law or positive government action, since obviously its purpose would be to repel an aggression committed and prevent the native territory being invaded. The law or government action according to which the government might oblige citizens to carry the war into the country of another nation, which it suspected of considering an attack, would be a law or action of a speculating government, since that government would not be acting on a factual basis, against some committed action, but following a speculation, against a presumed one. So, in the first case, government authority would be limited, since the government could not take action against a fact, if there were no such fact. In the second, on the contrary, government authority would be limitless, speculation always being at the government's discretion.

Another difference between positive and speculative functions is that when the government limits itself to the former, [529] it cannot make mistakes; but when it arrogates the latter to itself, it exposes itself to error of every kind.

When government passes a law against assassination or theft, since its severity is directed only against determinate actions, it cannot go astray. If, however, government makes laws against the decay of trade or the stagnation of industry, it runs the risk of taking for means of encouragement things which are not such. A law against theft or assassination can be more or less perfect and therefore more or less attain its purpose. It is impossible, however, that it will work completely against this purpose. A law to encourage trade can destroy it. A law to favor production can run counter to it.

There is therefore in the speculative functions of government a double drawback. Not being susceptible to limitation, they lay themselves open to arbitrariness. Obliging government to act on suppositions, they multiply the chances of mistakes.

Chapter 4: Are Governmental Mistakes Less Dangerous Than Those of Individuals?

Notes

1. *freely set himself straight.* Nature has given our errors two great correctives, personal interest and experience. If personal interest makes mistakes, the very losses incurred will enlighten it. What our interests have undergone will put them on a far

more secure track than prohibitions could. The man with a vested interest will not have seen proof that prohibitions are necessary. For him their value exists only in the foreboding of governments. Individual interest will never see them as safeguards, only as obstacles.

2. *it is better to run the natural risk of individual mistakes.* "Everything man does for himself," says Godwin, Political Justice, VI, Ch. 8,[30] "is a good. Everything his fellow citizens or country do for him, against his consent, is an ill." Godwin is right, and it is an ill in several respects. First, there is a violation of each person's rights. Justice prefers that every man be judge of what constitutes his own happiness. When you strike a blow against this individual prerogative, even if you are right a thousand times over [530] in the individual case, you are spurning a general principle, which cannot be upturned without the widest and most serious consequences. Secondly, however, it is very doubtful whether, even in the individual circumstance, you are likely to be right. You are subject to error every bit as much as the man whose interest you claim to know better than he himself. On this matter you are much more liable to error than he, for he is very much better acquainted with the overall details of his existence than you who perceive only one side of it, you to whom that one-sided and incomplete awareness can suggest very wrong notions. Thirdly and finally, nothing is beneficial save by consequence, persistence, and agreement and unless it lasts. Now, what you do for a man, against his will, he will undo. Whatever work you have built up at the expense of part of his freedom, with the remainder of that freedom, he will try to destroy it. There will therefore be no cohesion, no continuity, no persistence: instead there will be struggle. If you are right and the violence you are doing the man really is in his interest, do you know what the result will be? It is that you will separate him from his interests and he will not be wrong to separate himself from them. For the interest of his independence is much more important to his happiness than the individual interest in whose name you are claiming to subjugate him. If he gave in to you in this case, in which you are right, you would demand the same submission in another case in which perhaps you would be wrong. It is therefore in his lasting interest to resist you, even when you are acting in his interest of the moment.

Chapter 5: On the Nature of the Means Political Authority Can Use on the Grounds of Utility

NOTES

1. *calmly set out again to make what they called laws.* We have seen better still. We have seen our legislative assemblies forget the laws they have passed and pass them a second time.

30. Benjamin Constant, *De la justice politique, op. cit.,* p. 270.

Book IV: On the Proliferation of the Laws

Chapter 1: Natural Causes of the Proliferation of the Laws

The laws have been defined as the expression of the general will. This is [531] a very false definition. The laws are the declaration of men's relations between themselves. From the moment society exists, it establishes certain relations between men. These relations are true to their nature, for if they were not true to their nature, they would not become established. These laws are nothing other than these relationships observed and voiced. They are not the cause of these relationships, which on the contrary are anterior to them; on the contrary, they declare that these relationships exist. They are the declaration of a fact. They create, determine, and institute nothing, except forms and procedures such as to guarantee that which existed before their institution. It follows that no man, no fraction of society, nor even the whole society can, properly speaking and in an absolute sense, attribute to itself the right to make laws. The laws being only the expression of relations which exist between men and these relations being determined by their nature, to make a new law is only a new declaration of what existed previously.

The law is not in the gift of the legislator. It is not his spontaneous work. The legislator is to social order what the physician is to nature. Newton himself was able only to observe it and tell us the laws he recognized or thought he recognized. He did not to all appearances delude himself that he was the creator of these laws.

One thing excuses governments for the proliferation of the laws. This, that everybody solicits them to this end. Does a man think up a new project? Soon he is asking the government for it. Men who most favor freedom are not free from this error. The economists, etc.

Chapter 2: The Idea Which Usually Develops about the Effects Which the Proliferation of the Laws Has and the Falsity of That Idea

The complicated institutions of government and legislation have created such a number of artificial relations between men that there is no longer room for their true nature. Their moral existence, their will, their judgment find themselves choking under their civil, political, and legal existence, an existence if not opposite to the former, at least totally modified. There has been done for the entire life of man what constitutions did for [532] primary assemblies.[31] Reports have been drafted in advance, in which only the name and the date have been left blank and on the basis of which the human race resigns itself docilely to modeling all its actions. Men today have nothing in their own right. In the case of the inner life, there are positive religious dogmas. For external activity there is the law; with the result that when law or

31. [Assemblies of citizens, voted in, and acting as an electoral college. Translator's note]

religion collapse, men no longer have any guidance and no longer know what they must do.

I read in the Declaration of Rights that no man is a good person if he does not strictly and rigorously observe the laws.[32] Does this mean that if I am a good son, a good husband, a good father, a good friend,[33] but I forget or I break one of the thirty-two thousand laws which compose our code, I will not be a good man? I perceive in this doctrine a morality every bit as artificial as that of the fakirs of India, who attach virtue or crime to the observance or nonobservance of practices with no value or danger.

Chapter 3: That the Principal Benefit Which Supporters of Democratic Government Are Looking for in the Proliferation of the Laws Does Not Exist

The more a government measure is contrary to justice and reason, the more it entails disorder and violence, and then the need for the measure is justified in terms of this disorder and violence. If, on the grounds that most crimes are committed on the highways and that by forcing citizens to stay at home in their houses we would prevent these crimes, the law told them not to leave their homes and put guards everywhere to arrest the lawbreakers, the citizens, condemned either to neglect the looking after of their interests and to interrupt their reciprocal dealings or to disobey the law, would probably take the second course. The guards would come forward to arrest them and they would put up some resistance. Brawls, threats, fighting on the [533] highways would multiply more than ever and the legislator would conclude from this the necessity of the law which was the initial cause of all these calamities. He would take the effect for the cause: this is the history of many laws.

Often, when the execution of a law meets a thousand obstacles, people imagine these obstacles could be lifted by a new law. This new law is eluded in turn. This is remedied by a third law. You go on like this to infinity. If after you are worn out with fruitless attempts you go back to the first law, fertile source of so many secondary laws, and try to repeal it, you will for the most part see that everything would go better for it, and you would succeed by this repeal, not only in freeing yourself from a bad law, but from a whole series of laws necessary to assure, even imperfectly, the carrying out of your first law.

"You have never in your life," says the Abbé Galiani, p. 250, "bound anything, whether with string or with thread, without giving it one twist too many or making one extra knot. It is in our instinct, whether we are small or great, always to go

32. "Nobody is a man of goodwill if he is not a frank and religious observer of the laws." Article 5 of the *Duties* enumerated in the *Déclaration des droits et des devoirs de l'homme et du citoyen,* put at the head of the Constitution, 5 fructidor an III (22 August 1795).

33. A reference to Article 4 of the same *Déclaration:* "Nobody is a good citizen if he is not a good son, a good father, a good brother, a good friend, and a good husband."

beyond the natural measure, following the force of our intention."[34] I conclude from this that one should bind things as lightly as possible.

After the earthquake at Lisbon,[35] the marquis de Pombal, in order to prevent the people leaving en masse, set up a cordon of cavalry on the banks of the Tagus and had the roads leading out into the country guarded by large detachments of infantry. No quake occurred, and so these precautions had no inconvenient consequences. If it had been repeated, however, it is clear that the obstacles put in the way of the people's flight would have increased the despair and unhappiness, since one would have had to battle against the soldiers as well as the elements.

Chapter 4: On the Corruption Which the Proliferation of the Laws Causes among the Agents of the Government

Even when the government stays strictly within the limits prescribed by its purposes, it always more or less corrupts the instruments it uses. To corrupt is to substitute for moral considerations, which would decide for us if they were the only ones to make themselves heard, considerations of another kind. [534] Any addition to, any change in, the motives which must determine men's conduct, any threat, any promise, be it of pecuniary recompense, or of power, is a form of corruption. Now, this form of corruption is inseparable from government, within whatever narrow limits you enclose it. It needs agents who, sometimes, function without thought and obey without conviction. These agents are necessarily corrupted. If, along with the natural functions with which it is invested, the government adds functions which do not belong to it, such as, for example, influencing the opinions and outlook of the governed, the corruption of its agents will increase indefinitely. When the government is only an instrument of repression, punishing crimes people have been able to commit, its agents have only little latitude. They are in the inevitably wrong and unhappy situation of obeying without being convinced, and for motives of a quite different nature from conviction. Nothing is left to their arbitrary decision, however. In everything which is not purely repression, though, the solitary barrier having once been breached, despotism no longer finds anything to slow down its march. There results from this a much wider terrain for the corruption of agents. This corruption is aggravated further by the contempt it arouses. The natural feeling that the government should leave citizens free in the occupational, wealth-seeking, and moral part of their lives is so strong that the very men who have not adopted this political view look on the agents of the other approach with nothing but aversion and disdain. Now, this contempt tends to corrupt them more and more. In this way, through its wrong measures, the government, in order to achieve a good which it does not attain, and which it is not in its capacity to attain, creates a real ill. Its true purpose is not to do good but to prevent ill and to do so by way of penal laws. It corrupts in this case only a very small

34. Ferdinando Galiani, *Dialogues . . . , op. cit.,* pp. 249–250.
35. Which ravaged the city in 1755.

number of those who carry out these laws, and the dealings of these men with society being neither frequent nor complicated and always hostile, the corruption penetrates the social body less. Whereas when the government wants to do positive good, since it corrupts its agents in the same way and since there are more of them, and their dealings with society are more frequent, more various, and less hostile, the harm is much greater.

Coercive laws, intended to force the governed to such and such an action, have one further drawback than prohibitive laws, intended only to forbid such and such an action to the governed. The absence of action is more difficult to determine than the action itself. Against this negative crime a more constant, positive, and inquisitorial surveillance is called for.

[535] In cases where coercive laws were absolutely necessary, rewards should be attached to obedience rather than punishments attached to transgression. Since the State cannot be lavish with rewards, however, there should at the same time be as few as possible laws of this kind.

Chapter 5: Another Drawback of the Proliferation of the Laws

There were excesses in our old institutions. There are still more in our present ones. Most of the time it is a matter not of adding to them, but reducing them. I deliver you from a ferocious animal, said Voltaire, and you ask me what I am putting in its place.[36] This witticism could be applied to many laws. Let us guard against concluding, from the host of laws which have been established, that a host of laws is necessary to public order. Let us consider which laws would seem indispensable to us if the idea of the laws came up for the first time.

36. Hofmann could not find this quotation, which might come, as so often with the "words" of Voltaire, from an oral source.

Book V: On Arbitrary Measures

Chapter 1: On Arbitrary Measures and Why People Have Always Protested Less about Them Than about Attacks on Property

It is in Ch. 15 of Livre XXVI of The Spirit of the Laws that Montesquieu establishes principles much more favorable to property than to freedom. Examining his arguments carefully, however, we see that they apply with as much force to freedom as to property. "It is," he says, "a paralogism to say that the individual good must yield to the public good. That holds only in the cases where it is a question of the authority of the city, that is to say, the freedom of the citizen. This does not hold in cases where the ownership of goods is at stake, because the public good is always that each person invariably keeps the property which the civil laws bestow on him." How is it, however, that Montesquieu has not felt that the public good was always also that each person keeps his legitimate freedom? Why is it untoward that, on the grounds of the public good, blows should be struck at property? It is because a single attack of this kind takes away from all [536] property all guarantee and because the whole system of property is destroyed. It is the same, however, with freedom. "Let us take it as a maxim," he continues, "that when it is a question of the public good, the public good is never that one should deprive an individual of his goods nor even that one should take away the least portion of them."[37] We can say as much for freedom, and experience shows it.

Chapter 2: On the Grounds for Arbitrary Measures and the Prerogative of Preventing Crimes

Notes

1. *government suspicions.* The need to prevent crimes is sometimes only a pretext for government idleness, its members sometimes preferring to enchain us than to survey us. They must learn, however, that government is painstaking work and that it is to us, the governed, that peace and freedom belong, while the portion of the governors is enthrallment, anxiety, and work. Governments too often mistake public security and individual safety. Legislators and magistrates in all countries, the peace of the State depends on the sacrifice of your peace. If you must be spared all alarm, freed from all solicitude, released from every care, your work has lost its whole point, and what will you have left then? Prestige and power. No, this is not what your portion is. The society which raises you to the post you occupy commits you thereby to an indefatigable watchfulness. It is to you to watch the sky and the winds, to avoid rocks, to steer the ship and hold the rudder unremittingly. It is not right to leave the passengers to their anxieties, in order to give the pilot a chance to sleep.

37. Montesquieu, *De l'esprit des lois,* Livre XXVI, Ch. 15.

2. *Of being nuanced infinitely.* [Constant's whole sentence is: "The exemplary nuances here are infinite."] At a time of trouble, it may be legitimate and wise to order the citizens to carry some means of identification or to provide themselves with some such from the public authorities. If this requirement bore on one individual class only, however, it would be supremely unjust.

Additions

Sometimes the legislators, to palliate the injustices they commit, under the pretext of preventing crime or providing for public safety, resort to a subterfuge as odious [537] as it is illusory. They seem to pity those they hurt, to groan themselves under their harassment, and seek to make amends for this by tokens of esteem and interest. This, however, is to deprive the oppressed of their last remaining support. When a citizen is pursued by a powerful man, if it is a matter of taking his life, his reputation, or his property, it is to be hoped that hearts will be moved and that he will find defenders. When the victim is adorned with flowers, however, when he is seemingly honored, when it is claimed that injustice adds to his glory, the path of the crime is made smooth. This is not a punishment, those who want the ruin of an innocent tell you, this is a precaution, which becomes almost a triumph for the person who is its object. Ostracism transported to modern times.

As prohibitive laws are much more favorable to the encroachments of authority than are the penal laws, government is pleased to exaggerate the small influence of the latter in order to have wider recourse to the former.

Chapter 4: On the Effect of Arbitrary Measures in Terms of Moral Life, Industry, and the Duration of Governments

Notes

1. *When there is no security, there is no moral life.* Despotism is hurtful in that it prevents any long-term reckoning of the world. Now, moral life especially needs this kind of reckoning. The moment perhaps favors vice; time alone favors virtue.

2. *of production.* The large-scale enterprises of merchants are always necessarily intertwined with public affairs. In monarchies, however, public affairs are most of the time as suspect to merchants as they seem to them secure in republican States.

Additions

Despotism in favor of virtue is infinitely more dangerous than despotism in favor of crime. When scoundrels violate due process at the expense of honest men, one knows that this is one crime more. The very violation of due process makes you pay particular attention to it. You learn uncomplainingly and through misfortune to regard such process as sacred, as protecting and conserving the social order. When good men violate due process at the expense of scoundrels, however, the people no longer know where they stand. Due process and the law appear to them like obstacles in the way of justice. They somehow get used to these things and put together some sort of theory of an equitable [538] despotism, which is the overthrow of any kind of thinking, because in the body politic, only due process is stable and resistant to men. The foundations themselves, that is, justice and virtue, can be disfigured. Their names are at the mercy of whoever wants to use them. A feature of all political parties is that they do not hate despotism as such, the first thing in need of hate in a free society, but only this or that despotic act, which seems contrary to their purposes and interests. Once talk of circumstances is allowed, circumstances can always be invoked against principles. Factions march from one circumstance to another, constantly outside the law, sometimes with pure intentions, sometimes with perfidious projects, eternally asking for large-scale measures, in the name of the people, of freedom, of justice. In everything public well-being demands, there are two ways of proceeding, the one legal and the other arbitrary. The first is the only one permissible and always in the long run the one the government finds itself the better for. As long as arbitrary government is considered only as something simply to be snatched from one's enemy so one can put it to use, that enemy will strive in his turn to seize it, and the struggle will be forever, because arbitrary measures are inexhaustible.

In republics, all arbitrary measures, all formulae intended to serve as a pretext for oppression, rebound on their authors. I find a striking example of this in the Acts of the Constituent Assembly and I will use to recount it the words of one of its members: Clermont-Tonnerre, IV, 90: The National Assembly wanted to declare absolute freedom of religious opinion. The Catholic priests, the supporters of the dominant religion, forced the Assembly to modify this principle by adding this sentence: provided that the manifestation of religious opinion does not threaten public order. Soon this same dominant religion was cruelly abused by this obscure and vague sentence, whose adoption its influence had secured. The overardent friends of the Revolution took advantage of the redraft they had opposed to crush, against all reason, those who had wrung it out of them.[38]

[539] The ancients believed that places soiled by crimes had to undergo an expiation; and my belief is that land sullied by an act of despotism needs, for purification, a resounding punishment of the guilty person. Every time in any country I see a citizen arbitrarily incarcerated without seeing shortly afterward the hireling who arrested him and the jailer who received him, and the politician, whoever it was, who violated due process, dragged into the same prisons, I will say: this nation does not know how to be free, nor wish to be so, nor merit it, having not yet learned the first notions of freedom.

If it were given to man to invert, just once, the order of the seasons, whatever advantage he might derive from this privilege in a particular circumstance, he would nonetheless experience as a result an incalculable disadvantage, in that

38. Stanislas-Marie de Clermont-Tonnerre, *Réflexions sur le fanatisme*, in: *Recueil des opinions, op. cit.*, t. IV, p. 90.

subsequently he would no longer be able to rely on the unvarying regularity and uniform sequence which serve as a base for his working activities.

Chapter 5: On the Influence of Arbitrary Rule on the Governors Themselves

By giving themselves the prerogative of prevention, governments so multiply their duties that their responsibility becomes endless. Their respect for the most solemn treaties, their consideration for individual freedom, can be considered criminal.

Book VI: On Coups d'Etat

Chapter 1: On the Admiration for Coups d'Etat

Notes

1. *cannot legitimate in individuals.* Men in coming together merely put in common what each of them before possessed in isolation. A thousand individuals who link up, in that linking up give a guarantee and some force to the previous rights they had, but do not create for themselves any new rights. The rights of the majority are only the aggregation of the rights of each one. Nations are only aggregations of individuals. Their rights are only the joining up of individual rights. So what could this public morality be which some wish to oppose to private morality? Public morality consists only in the aggregation of individual duties and rights. Now, injustice, not being anyone's right, cannot be the right of all. How could individuals acquire by coming together rights which they did not have in isolation?

2. *which you wish to seize.* The Triumvirs, says M. Ferrand, I, 392,[39] "agreed to withdraw from a republic whose loss had become inevitable those who insisted on wishing to defend it." Approval of banishments.

39. *L'esprit de l'histoire,* 2e éd, t. I, p. 392.

Book VII: On Freedom of Thought

Chapter 2: On Freedom of Thought

Notes

1. *praiseworthy tolerance.* Each man, says M. Ferrand, must have the freedom to think what he pleases, but not to propagate his opinions if they are dangerous, just as he is permitted to have some poison in his closet but not to distribute it nor to make use of it.[40] Among the sentences which prove the extent to which men are the dupes of words, this one, which has been repeated by many a writer, is one of the most remarkable. We find it anew in the preambles of edicts, in all the sweet-talking discussions of tolerance [541] which were employed to try to slow its development. It is a fact that enlightened men believed for some time that they should be obliged to those in government for this alleged indulgence. The government made it meritorious on their part that they allowed us to think what seemed reasonable to us! But how could they stop us doing so? By what means did they penetrate the secret of our thoughts, that we had been forbidden to express? They claimed our gratitude and imposed a shameful silence on us and did us all the harm they could. They said they respected our independence of thought. Yes, just as long as they did not know what it was, just as long as it stayed silent and sterile, locked up inside us, deprived of all expression, bereft of all social communication, of that fertile source of accuracy and perfecting. Man has a need, however, to express his thought. Thought itself is something real only when it is expressed. What could government do against thought it knew nothing of? It is insolent scorn on tyranny's part that it should claim to grant as a favor something it cannot refuse.

Chapter 3: On the Expression of Thought

Notes

1. *speech and writing.* Independently of speech and the press, individuals have another way of expressing their opinions, that is to say, coming together to discuss them. All our memories rebel against the exercise of that faculty, one so dangerous when it is abused. I will most assuredly not excuse those wild and monstrous gatherings which flung the nation into excesses of all kinds. I know only one circumstance which justifies meetings of opinion between unsophisticated individuals: this is the need to speak up for oppressed individuals. A sort of contagious courage forces the weak to appear strong. An assembly, in moments of danger, is normally directed by the bravest. Esprit de corps makes up for the lack of a sense of justice, and usurpation by a minority cannot take place. In all other circumstances, however, the groups which citizens arrange between themselves to discuss their

40. Hofmann could not find this sentence in *L'esprit de l'histoire.*

opinions are more harmful than useful. They are mostly controlled by so-called reformers who substitute themselves for current thinking and the public will. They are a small minority who want control in the name of everybody. These men surround their theories with a force quite other than truth. They set up within the associations they dominate a sort of government, which has all the [542] weight of proper government, without any of its advantages. Government by clubs is the most degrading tyranny, the most inhuman and the coarsest. Should we conclude that the government has the right to ban these associations, to limit the number of members, to forbid the discussion of certain dangerous questions? All laws of this kind are evaded or arbitrary. They require moreover the resources of corruption, since one section of society has to be degraded in order to spy on and denounce the other. Now, any time when, in the case of any objective whatsoever, it is impossible to make a law which is at once precise and feasible and does not need corrupt agents, this objective neither demands nor admits of law. Another remedy must be looked for, and this remedy is freedom. Let government not forbid associations; let it maintain, however, true freedom. Let it defend the freedom of individuals against associations seeking to stifle it. These associations, in losing all means of doing harm, would soon lose all their importance. If the individuals who get together harm the safety of those not forming part of their association, let the government come down hard on these disturbers of peace and order, not as members of a society or sect, but as disturbers. It would be easy to prove that during the French Revolution, the clubs acquired their monstrous power only because right from the start, in order to group citizens under their banners against their will, they used forceful means which the government should have punished. A penal law carried out, for there would have been no need to make any, penal laws existed already, would have been of more value than any number of prohibitive laws. It would have been more certain in effect and more easy of execution. Since, however, prohibitory laws are more favorable to encroachments by government and to its idleness than penal laws are, it likes to overstress how little influence the former have, and to make wide use of the latter. People suppose that political questions are more likely to stir up human passions than are questions of any other sort. This is an error. The intrinsic importance of a question has less impact on the ardor with which men become agitated than that which they attach to themselves. Party bias has less to do with understanding the thing in dispute than with the commitments pride has assumed, the sacrifices people have made, the dangers they run, the allies who surround them, and the enemies they are fighting. In the amphitheater of Constantinople, there was murder over the chariot races and the colors blue and green, just as bitter as murder on the crossroads of Paris in the name of religion and liberty.[41] People sought [543] lettres de cachet against gluckistes and piccinistes,[42] as they did against Jansenists and Atheists. So regard associations like individuals. Ignore them if they

41. See Constant's Note A at the end of the Additions.

42. The rival supporters of the operas by Gluck and Piccini in the late eighteenth century.

are peaceful. Be harsh with them if they trouble the peace. Punish acts. Leave the rest to freedom. But know how to ensure and guarantee it. You will find it, essentially and infallibly, a healing force.

2. *from unthinking enthusiasm.* I admit for an instant that certain books may corrupt manners or shake the principles of morality. Men should be taught to preserve themselves from these dangers by their own efforts and reason and through defending themselves. If all you do is force to one side corrupting ideas and dangerous sophisms, men will find themselves unprepared when they meet them and will let themselves be disarmed or perverted much more quickly. Children, whose head we have always wrapped for fear they might fall over and hurt it, fall one day when their head is not wrapped, and they crack it. If it is in the interests of one individual to spread bad maxims, it will be in the interests of a thousand others to refute them.

3. *the instruction servitude gives.* The sudden achievement of freedom intoxicates slaves. The enjoyment of freedom forms men worthy of possessing it.

It is absurd to wish to conceal truths contrary to the established constitution. The established order being reversible, the less men have reflected on the errors it contains and the less they are prepared for the order which must replace it, the more disorder and misfortune will there be in its overthrow and the sequences thereof.

"A people assured of its rights enjoys them in calm and peace. If it misuses them, it is because it mistrusts them. Its haste is the effect of its fear." Bentham, III, 190.

4. *the exaggeration which defies its laws.* "Under the Ancien Régime in France, it was enough that a book on moral science was published in Paris to inspire an unfavorable prejudice." Bentham, III, 178. The true censorship is that of an enlightened public, which withers dangerous opinions and encourages useful discoveries. The audacity of a lampoon, in a free society, will not save it from general contempt. By a contradiction easy to explain, however, the public's indulgence in this respect is always proportionate to the severity of the government. Bentham, III, 20. [544]

Chapter 4: Continuation of the Same Subject

Notes

1. *about China.* The press in China is as free ostensibly as in England, that is to say that each person may be by occupation a printer. The expeditious way, however, in which in this country any type of fraud is punished, without the formality of any juridical institution, is enough to stop the freedom of the press. The printer, seller, reader of any written thing which offends the government are equally liable to be punished by a caning. The publication of a work containing reflections on the conduct of the government or its principal agents would be followed by the certain death of the author and publisher. So nothing appears on government and politics except in the Peking Gazette. M. de Pauw observes in his Recherches that China is

governed entirely by the birch whip and the bamboo cane.[43] To these two things he should have added the annual calendar and the imperial gazette. For these are two instruments of constant use in the government's hands. This gazette serves to spread to all corners of the empire praise of the virtues and fatherly affection of the sovereign, who occupies the throne. It takes the form of a small pamphlet. It is published every two days. The missionaries claimed that the punishment for a lie inserted in this gazette would be immediate execution. It is famous, however, for descriptions of battles which have never been joined and for announcing victories which have never been won. The missionaries explained themselves badly. They meant only that the editor of the gazette would be punished if he took it upon himself to insert some article which had not been sent to him by the government. [545]

Chapter 5: Continuation of the Same Subject

NOTES

1. *All man's faculties go together.* "As for the evil which can result from censorship, it is impossible to evaluate, since it is impossible to say where it stops. It is nothing less than the danger of stopping all human intellectual progress in all occupations. If that had been true just of men in official positions, what would the result have been today? Religion, law, medicine, morality, all would still be in darkness." Bentham, III, 22–23.

2. *must perish and fall.* Governments would like men to be pliant so that they will obey them and brave so that they will defend them, ignorant so they will never hold any opinion of their own, and enlightened so they will be skillful instruments. This combination of opposed and incompatible things can never last long however.

3. *changes of scene.* The observation that when a government, putting obstacles in the way of thought, prevents its subjects from being busy on their own account, it must itself keep them busy and therefore it must do extraordinary things, is circumstantial. Governments which obstruct individual activity also have the option of doing nothing and remaining inactive, by forcing the nation to remain thus. This is what they often do. Then they and the nation become stupefied.

Caesar, once he had taken away the Romans' freedom and thereby their one and only pastime, had to announce to them the war against the Parthians. Louis XIV, having succeeded in making the yoke of government heavier, threw France into a series of wars, caused the devastation of the Palatinate, and turned Europe upside down, just to give sustenance to the anxiety of a newly enslaved nation. Nothing is more natural. Under this kind of administration, the government puts itself in the place of the nation. The talk is no longer of the nation, as in free States, but of the government. Now, in such circumstances, the government must constantly prepare what to have discussed. Members of the government find themselves vis-à-vis the

43. Cornelius de Pauw, *Recherches philosophiques sur les Egyptiens et les Chinois,* Berlin, G.-J. Decker, 1773, t. II, p. 332: "This government resorts mainly to the birch and the baton."

governed, in some degree in the situation of favorites vis-à-vis the king, though their connections may otherwise be very different. Louvois pushed Louis XIV into a disastrous undertaking, so as to take away from him any time to think about the behavior of his ministers. Governments which [546] take away from the governed the legitimate exercise of their various talents must use gigantic undertakings to keep them in a state of continual stupefaction.

4. *silent wastes.* There are, I know, men so fixated on the need for power, so devoured by a bitter, somber egotism, that even this picture will not shock them. Thought must die, so that they can dominate,[44] and were arts, science, and letters to die with thought, they would happily strip the human race of all the dignity of its nature, to perpetuate their hold over that wretched, mutilated species. One might think some genie of evil had cast them onto earth from some unknown planet, when it gave them a man's face, for the ruin of humanity.

Addition

Thought is a human need like all the others. It is impossible to bid this need be silent by asking men to settle for a different one. All man's needs want to be satisfied.

44. See Constant's Note B at the end of the Additions.

Book VIII: On Religious Freedom

Chapter 1: Why Religion Was So Often Attacked by the Men of the Enlightenment

Notes

1. *revolt against its commands.* Need of freedom of conscience, making the most delicate of women emigrate to an uncivilized land, where they perished, for lack of food. Recherches sur les Etats-Unis, I, 34.[45]

Chapter 2: On Civil Intolerance

Notes

1. *without government permission.* The Lutherans and the Calvinists got together in Strasbourg. "This gathering required government approval, [547] without which Protestant communities are not allowed to change their teachings." Journal des Débats, 6 thermidor an X [25 July 1802].

Chapter 3: On the Proliferation of Sects

M. Hume gives rather ingenious reasons for religions being salaried, but then they should all be so. Smith, V, 1.[46]

Chapter 7: On the Utilitarian Case for Religion

Bentham, following his single principle, that of utility, wishes to submit religion to the calculus. Does he not feel, though, that he is undermining it at its very core, by presenting it as useful, rather than presenting it as divine? I would add that he is degrading it. I would add further that he is presupposing one lot of men judging religion and imposing it on another lot. For the rest his principles are good, such as nonintervention by government in religious matters. Bentham, III, 134.[47]

Chapter 8: Another Effect of the Axiom That the People Must Have a Religion

Those who defend religion today defend it as a prop of despotism.

45. Hofmann was unable to find this reference in the work of Cornelius de Pauw.

46. Adam Smith, *op. cit.,* t. IV, pp. 199–202, in which he cites a passage in Hume's *History of England.*

47. Constant is criticizing here the whole of Ch. 18 of the fourth part of the *Principes du code pénal:* pp. 134–137, entitled *Emploie du mobile de la religion.*

Chapter 9: On Tolerance when Government Gets Involved

The Interim [Edict] of Charles V[48] is one of the most agreeable [548] examples, notwithstanding the consequences, of all those which history offers us of tolerance on the part of government.

Government is in error, furthermore, when, dazzled by the chimera of a pointless and impossible harmony, it wishes to reconcile different beliefs. The least dissimilarities, unnoticed as long as government does not interfere, become germs of discord if it does. Frederick William, the father of Frederick the Great, astonished at not seeing the same discipline rule the religion of his subjects as ruled his barracks, wished one day to reconcile the Lutherans and the Reformed church. He extracted from their respective doctrines what caused their disagreements and ordered them to be in agreement. Until then these two sects had lived separately but in a perfect understanding. Condemned to union, they immediately began a bitter war, attacking each other and resisting the government. On the death of Frederick William, Frederick II ascended the throne. He set all opinion free. The two sects battled, without drawing his attention; they talked without being heard. Soon they lost hope of success and the vexation of fear. They fell silent. The differences subsisted and the dissensions were pacified.

On the question of belief there is only one principle: complete freedom. Any time people want to depart from this, they fall into more or less shocking absurdities, but always equally dangerous ones, because all of them stand together and one necessarily harks back to the others. The idea of granting tolerance to already existing opinions and refusing it to those which might come to birth starts from the presupposition that believing or not believing is an effect of the will. According to this principle, one thinks oneself singularly human in lending oneself to the weaknesses which habit has made necessary and justified in prohibiting any novel deviation. It is forgotten that the essence of the human spirit is to go forward, to follow the chain of its ideas, to draw the consequences of these principles, and that these consequences being as proven for that human spirit as the principles from which it draws them, it is an absurdity to accept the latter while outlawing the former. This is to claim to tolerate the cause provided it does not produce an effect. This outlook, however, so absurd when it is spelled out, has been followed by several philosophers, so difficult is it to disengage oneself from prejudices and so strongly do the very prejudices one has conquered leave a false orientation in the mind which has shaken them off. [549] Complete intolerance is less inconsistent than this type of softened intolerance. If government has rights over public opinion, why should it not exercise its rights over ancient error as much as on the novel kind? If government has no such rights, why should it claim to have them over the future and not the past? Is it because it would seem to it easier to exercise its rights over the future? Vain hope. The need to draw consequences is no less imperative than that of

48. The Interim of Augsburg was an edict proclaimed on 15 May 1548, provisionally regulating conflicts between Protestants and Catholics.

believing what seems to us proven. The mind cannot condemn the premises it has agreed to sterility, and the tyranny which wishes to prevent it going from ideas to ideas is every bit as vexatious and against nature as that which orders it to abjure the ideas it has adopted. Governments founded on prejudices and yet hugely ambitious in recent years for philosophical glory have avidly adopted the approach I am fighting against here. It was indeed particularly convenient for them. To give to the people a little piece of the truth while detaching from truth the quality which makes it victorious, that is, extension and conquest, this would have been at once to the advantage of error and the honor of enlightenment. Truth, however, does not admit of such mutilation. However it is divided and fragmented, its smallest fraction carries within itself an aptitude for conquest. It enlarges, it develops, it brings its consequences on, forms its army, and you will see it ranged in battle, when you still think its sparse elements are in the isolation to which you are pleased to condemn it.

Book IX: On Legal Safeguards

Chapter 1: On the Independence of the Courts

Notes

1. *its immovable members.* From the fact that in Athens the people as a whole pronounced judgments, M. de Montesquieu concludes that in republics the power to judge must be revocable at pleasure.[49] One might note, however, that then it is the whole people who do the judging and, given that, also note that each republic is in a single town and has no more than twenty thousand citizens. When this writer appears not to [550] wish that the power of judges be permanent, Esprit des lois, XI, 6, he speaks less of judges than of juries. This is made clear by this sentence: "judges ought to belong to the same circle as the accused and his peers."[50] Elsewhere he recognizes that judicial power submitted to the people is so dangerous that the Roman legislators permitted the accused to go into exile before the trial, I, 59.[51] Judges could be temporary among the ancients but cannot be so now, our more complicated social relationships being such as to permit a thousand late but sure acts of vengeance against an independent judge who has reverted to ordinary citizenship. It is good that legislative power depends on the people. It is good that judicial power does not.

2. *the sale of offices.*[52] Under a despotic monarchy, the sale of offices, as a further guarantee of fixed tenure, was good. The choices of the monarch would surely not have been better. A distinction must be made among the functions of French courts, between those functions connected with legislation, courts always being challenged over these, and those connected with the administration of justice. The first would have been better discharged by an assembly appointed by the nation. It is a good thing, however, that the latter were removed from government remit. This was a shelter against despotism.

3. *l'esprit de corps in the judiciary.* Esprit de corps is one of the best barriers against servility toward government or factions, in a nation in which everybody lets himself get dragged along by the dominant opinion. Nobody dares to hold an opin-

49. Montesquieu, *De l'esprit des lois,* Livre XI, Ch. 6, where in particular this passage occurs: "The power to judge must not be lodged in a permanent Senate, but exercised by persons drawn from the body of the people."

50. The exact sentence is: "The judges should be of the same social condition as the accused and his peers."

51. In Livre XII he evokes "an Athenian and Roman law which permitted the accused to retire before the judgment." The reference to t. I, p. 59, probably means that Constant is referring to the 1749 Amsterdam edition of *L'esprit des lois.*

52. [Under the ancien regime, not only were many administrative positions in the government apparatus hereditary, but as a complement to this, their holders could also sell them. Translator's note]

ion against everybody else's. Esprit de corps, on the contrary, acts as a shield, and individuals who want to resist the dominant opinion, reassured by that ally, link up with it. An irremovable body of judges is necessary so that a judge, when he judges according to his conscience, is not afraid of offending the government under which he may soon find himself an ordinary citizen again. In a nation which on the one hand is used to despotism and finds it rather convenient for its natural impatience and on the other carries to extremes all the views it has seized upon, the independence of the courts is the sole thing which can make that nation lose the habit [551] of despotism and endow it with principles it cannot abuse. The claims laid against despotism by courts, being always founded on facts, carry with them a conviction and a weight of which theories separated from facts are not capable.

4. *that no judgment is without appeal.* "The maxim which says that the criminal shall have no appeal is the most absurd ever to enter the mind of man. He who has lost his case, in the first instance, by some trivial law, may appeal to a higher court, while he who has been unjustly condemned to be burned alive by nine municipal magistrates cannot appeal. Now if imbecility itself came to dictate our laws, it would not say anything worse or more horrible than that. For the result of it is that a trivial law is a more important object than the honor and life of a man consigned to the most cruel torments." De Pauw, Recherches sur les Grecs, II, 6.

5. *the institution of the jury system.* The main arguments of one author who has attacked the jury system (Gach, president of a court of first instance in the Department of the Lot)[53] rest on the lack of zeal, and the carelessness, ignorance, and frivolity in France. He does not indict the jury system but the nation. It must be remembered, however, that if his arguments are sound, we would have to renounce the jury system in France. We surely know, however, that an institution may at first seem little suited to a nation, because of lack of familiarity, and yet become suitable, if the institution is intrinsically good, because the nation gets used to it and acquires the capacity it was lacking.[54] It would be repugnant to me to think a nation careless of the first of its interests, the administration of justice and the protection afforded to innocence accused. The French, says Gach, will never be well-informed nor determined enough [552] to fulfill the purposes for which juries were instituted. Such is our indifference to everything connected with public administration, such is the power of egotism and individual interest, the tepidness, the absence of public spirit, that the law establishing trial by jury cannot be carried

53. The man named Gach, first name unknown, wrote a brochure entitled *Des vices de l'institution du jury en France,* Paris, Petit, an XIII (1804). Perhaps it is this work Constant invokes in his letter of 19 April 1806 to Prosper de Barante (published in the *Revue de deux mondes,* t. XXXIV, 1906, p. 242). He would not have been able to read it in this case until after redrafting his Book IX of *Principes de politique,* and that would explain why he speaks of Gach only in the Additions and not in the text.

54. See Constant's Note C at the end of the Additions.

out.[55] But who does not feel that what we need is a public spirit to overcome this tepidness and this egotism? This public spirit would be created by the habit of justice and freedom. Is it to be thought it would exist among the English without the overall pattern of their political institutions? Where the institution of the jury is constantly suspended, however, the freedom of the courts violated, the accused arraigned before commissions, this spirit cannot come to birth. People indict the setting up of juries. It is the way they are undermined which should be indicted. Gach invokes twelve years' experience.[56] Twelve years of revolutions! The jury, he says, will not be able, as the spirit of the institution requires, to separate its inner conviction from documentary evidence, the evidence of witnesses and other evidence, things which are not necessary when conviction exists and insufficient when it does not.[57] But this is chicanery. There is no principle for separating these things. On the contrary, these are the elements of conviction. The spirit of the institution is solely to the effect that the jury not be bound according to a numerical or legal calculation, but by the impression which the overall mix of objects produced in documentary evidence, witnesses' evidence, and other evidence has given it. Now, the enlightenment of simple good sense is enough for a jury to know and be able to declare whether, after having heard the witnesses, read through the details of objects, and compared the evidence, it is convinced or not.

If juries, he continues, find a law too severe, they will absolve the accused and declare the circumstance not in keeping with their conscience. He considers the case of a man accused of giving shelter to his brother and thereby incurring the death penalty.[58] This example, for me, far from militating against the jury as an institution, constitutes its greatest praise. It shows that this institution puts [553] obstacles in the way of laws contrary to humanity, justice, and morality. We are men before we are jurors. So, far from blaming the juror who, in this case, pronounced contrary to his conscience and thus failed in his duty as a juror, I would praise him for fulfilling his duty as a man and running in a way within his power, to the help of a man ready to be condemned to death for an action which is not a crime. The example given by Gach does not prove that there should not be juries. It proves that there should not be laws which pronounce a death penalty against a man for giving shelter to his brother. With this type of reasoning, the

55. Hofmann holds that Constant has been imprecise. The proper text is: "Juries will never be well-informed enough nor determined enough to fulfill the intentions, the principal object of the jury system [. . .] Such is our indifference to everything connected with public administration; such among us is the power of egotism and individual interest, the tepidness, or rather the absence of public spirit, that the new law which will establish trial by jury will not be carried out in its most essential particulars." Gach, *op. cit.*, pp. 10–11.

56. "I have for my part the strongest of all authorities, that of the facts, of the experience of twelve years." *Ibid.*, p. 12.

57. Constant is not quoting but summarizing Gach's book, pp. 38–39.

58. Constant is not quoting but summarizing. *Ibid.*, pp. 40–41.

objection militates against any judicial organization, since one could invent laws so atrocious that no judge, with a jury or not, replaceable or permanent, would wish to apply them.

There is a good definition of the jury: "It is," says Lauze de Péret (De la garantie individuelle), "the reason of the guilty party, in his normal state of innocence, who stands in judge of that same reason, led astray for the moment by the crime."[59]

The jury judges morally, the judge materially. The jury judges in the way the good sense of every individual would judge, as the good sense of the accused himself would judge, if he were not partial because his own case is involved. The judge pronounces according to the laws dictated by the common interest of the society.

When punishments are excessive, says Gach, or seem so to juries, they will absolve the guilty person, although they will be totally convinced as to his crime. I reply that this is the fault of the punishments and not of the juries.[60] Punishments must not be excessive, and if they seem excessive to juries, this is because they are so, since jurors have no interest in finding them such. It will be said that this is to submit punishments to constant revision by juries. I reply, however, that only in extreme cases will juries resolve to stray from their functions. For, I repeat once more, they are as citizens interested for the sake of public safety in not so straying. Now, in extreme cases, that is to say, when they find themselves between the sense of justice and humanity and the letter of the law, it is not an evil if they so deviate. There should not be a law which so repels the humanity of the common man that juries, selected from within a nation, cannot make up their minds to agree to the application of that law; and the establishment [554] of permanent judges, whom habituation would reconcile to so barbarous a law, far from an advantage, would be an evil.

People say that juries will fail in their duty, at some time out of fear, at another out of mercy. If it is out of fear, the fault belongs to civil administration's being too negligent. If it is a matter of pity, it is too harsh a law which is at fault.

Several objections against the institution of juries, drawn from their irresolution, from their susceptibility to seduction, could, apart from a few things, apply to judges. If we consider a country in which judges were sometimes harassed and slighted by the government and sometimes abandoned by that same government to the vengeance of the families or accomplices of accused persons, as juries were during the French Revolution, is it to be believed that judges would be much firmer and less shakeable than juries?

The drawbacks of the jury system are all on the side of indulgence. Those of the judges are on the side of severity.

"If there is no country," says Gach, "where the arts and sciences are cultivated with more success than they are in France by a small number of privileged intelligences, no more is there anywhere the mass of the nation wallows in a more

59. P.-J. Lauze de Péret, *Traité de la garantie individuelle et des diverses preuves en matière criminelle,* Paris, Impr. de Caillot, 1805, p. iv.

60. Constant does not quote but summarizes Gach's book, *op. cit.,* p. 42.

profound ignorance of everything connected with the laws and public administration."[61] Why is this so? It is because there has always been in the sanctuary of the laws and in public administration a great deal of arbitrariness, and the nature of government distanced French people from these things, and because, to draw closer more precisely to the subject we are dealing with, the formal understanding of criminal trials in France was restricted, and this raised a barrier between justice and the citizens. Change all these things and you will see the national character lose that frivolity and break out of that ignorance, which are only the result of all the bad institutions and which some people cite as a reason for perpetuating them. A people does not remain indifferent to what touches its freedom, its security, its honor, and its life, when it is allowed to get involved in it. When it is indifferent to these great things, it is because it has been forcibly kept from them. The jury system is in this respect all the more necessary to the French people in that the nation seems temporarily not fit for it. It would find in it not only the general advantages inherent in this institution, but also the particular advantage of rebuilding its moral education. [555]

Chapter 3: On Punishments

Notes

1. *do not lose all their rights.* When individuals disrupt the security of society through criminal activity, they lose some of their rights, which this society has the authority to restrain, in order to stop them hurting it. Normally, however, this principle is pushed much too far. The guilty man, separated from his fellow citizens, handed over to the jailers, then to the executioners, seems a being apart, whom nature spurns, whom public pity forsakes, and whom humanity repudiates. I am talking here only of a convicted felon, for it is obvious that short of an overthrow of all justice, the accused, not yet tried, retains all the rights compatible with the measures necessary for his not escaping his trial. The criminal, however, even when convicted, is not stripped of all his rights. One he has is to demand that his trial be public, because human actions are made up of a host of nuances which law cannot grasp. Even when the guilty person is given a punishment, if his action is attenuated by some of these nuances which legal justice could not take into account, public opinion ought to compensate him for this. In the second place, he has the right that the punishment he undergoes is not revolting to human nature and is not open to arbitrary aggravation by the whim of those carrying it out.

2. *all experimentation with torture.* People believe too much in frightful tortures. In Athens the death of condemned people was very sweet, since each chose the manner of his own death. There was no more crime there than elsewhere.

3. *life sentences.* I am always fearful that once life sentences are accepted, one or other of the numerous prisons whose establishment would be necessary might not sooner or later turn itself into a State prison, a metamorphosis all the easier in that almost everywhere, for plausible reasons of public safety, only government permission can open the

61. Gach, *op. cit.*, p. 90.

entrance to these lugubrious habitations. I do not like citizens getting used to passing coldly by a prison without asking who it is who is locked up in it, without finding out whether anyone there is a languishing victim of some illegal act, without being able to get in so as to convince himself with his own eyes that the wretchedness of the detainees is not at all aggravated by the harshness or greed of their guards. [556]

4. *happiness in debasement.* Indelible branding has the same drawback as public works. It prevents any return to virtue and it points to criminals happy in their shame. Bentham allows it for counterfeiters, because in branding the latter it does not remove from them their means of subsistence. "Despised as knaves," he says, "they will still be employed as people of talent."[62] But will this not be a very immoral thing, to show people known knaves, employed as people of talent? And if, as is probable, they get used to their shame, what spectacle is more corrupting than satisfaction in opprobrium?

5. *the establishment of colonies.* Bentham makes a rather strong objection to the establishment of colonies. Deportation is a good thing, he says, for those without resources in their own country. For it is nothing else than a free passage to the place of deportation for him who has committed a crime. II, 426.[63] There is a means of preventing this drawback. This would be to have the deportation preceded by some positive punishment, such as a more or less long imprisonment. This precaution would deter someone tempted to commit a crime in order to get to a new country. The punishment must be separated from the new abode, however. The guilty party must begin his new career without being pursued by society. The good fortune of which the guilty partake in their new refuge would not have a demoralizing effect, like that sometimes experienced by those condemned to public works. The people would not witness this, and they would have proof of the punishment previously undergone by the criminal.

Additions

Say in this chapter that punishments must be varied and refer to Bentham's work.[64]

Speak in this chapter of the right which those who have been unjustly detained, or condemned, in a word, have suffered from the errors of the law, to be compensated at public expense.

62. Jeremy Bentham, *op. cit.*, t. II, p. 421.

63. Constant does not quote, as one might think, but rather interprets Bentham's thought in this place.

64. This is above all the Third Part of the *Principes du code pénal,* entitled *Des peines, op. cit.*, t. II, pp. 380–434.

Book X: On the Action of Government with Regard to Property

Chapter 4: On the Status Property Should Occupy in Political Institutions

Notes

1. *by treating it with disfavor.* What I say of property, that once it exists, it has to be given power, I say of all institutions; in countries where there is a nobility, that nobility must be given strong legal authority. If we do not want to give it such, all aristocratic distinctions must be abolished. In a word, one must will what one wants. The nobility, in the condition it was in in France, immediately before the Revolution, was an absurd and dangerous institution, precisely because it offended without having powers of containment.

2. *or annihilated.* "Woe," says Ganilh, II, 251, "to governments which separate power from wealth!" He adds: "and wealth from freedom!" Indeed, what is needed is that everybody be in a position to acquire some wealth and that those who possess it be entrusted with conserving it.

3. *should comprise proprietors.* Can nonproprietors, people will say, be represented by proprietors? In the same way as the represented by the representatives. For representatives, by becoming such, cease in many respects to be in the same situation as the represented.

Chapter 5: On Examples Drawn from Antiquity

Notes

1. *Examples drawn from antiquity.* Cicero, De officiis, Livre II, ch. 21, edition d'Olivet, III, 359, quotes this sentence from the Tribune Philippe; non esse in civitate duo millia hominum qui rem haberent.[65] And he reproaches him with a criminal action in having held such a discussion with the people, because he was inclined to the sharing of wealth. But if in the year 649 B.C., the era of the Tribunate of Lucius Marcus Philippus, there were in the immensity of the Roman realm [558] only two thousand citizen proprietors, had not property, rather than being a blessing granted by society, become an intolerable abuse, and out of respect for the people, should not a pointless respect for property be abjured? No; but the organization of property needed correcting, being very defective in Rome. Palliatives had been tried. Laws against deeds of trust and entailments and those which gave an equal part to all the sons and daughters tended to divide landed properties. The aristocracy, however, tended to bring them together. This was not the vice of property but of aristocracy.

65. "There are not in the city two thousand people who have any property." Cicero, *Les devoirs,* II.21.73. Text edited and translated by Maurice Testard, Paris, Les Belles Lettres, 1970, t. II, p. 55.

Among the ancients, where property was not familiar and mobile, political rights could not attach to proprietors alone without injustice. In modern times the opposite obtains.

Among the ancients, the poor were always indebted to the rich. In modern times it is usually the rich who are indebted to the poor. It is important to examine the outcomes of this difference. One of the most striking is that relations between proprietors and nonproprietors are utterly different in the two cases. Among the ancients, the rich demanded from the poor what the latter did not have, money, and that demand requiring for its satisfaction violence, and usually not being satisfied despite this violence, there resulted continual hatred and opposition between these two classes. In modern times the rich demand from the poor what the poor can always supply, labor, and the result is a much greater mutual accord. This could be identified as a reason property could not serve as the basis of political rights in antiquity and can in modern times.

Chapter 7: That Territorial Property Alone Brings Together All the Advantages of Property

Notes

1. *business property.* Agriculture has a further advantage over business which I have not mentioned. [559] It demands much more intelligence and makes much more use of it than jobs in industry do. Smith, I, 10, 264. See Mirabeau, Ami des hommes, on the difference between the farming groups and the artisans, I, 54 and following.

Chapter 8: On Property in Public Funds

Additions

A certain disadvantage of the use of public debt is that it facilitates the undertaking of war, because instead of providing for the expenditure it demands, by taxes which will always be more or less difficult to control and a heavy burden, we defray it by borrowings which are easy to get hold of, on account of the inducements which go with them and the burden of which weighs only in a partial and remote way on the people. Smith, V, 3.[66]

"It has been said that a public debt attached to the government's fate all the creditors of the State, and that these creditors, linked with its good fortune and bad alike, became its natural supports. This is very true; but this means of self-preservation, applying to a bad order of things as to a good, is in every respect as dangerous to a nation as it can be useful." Say, V.[67]

"The growth of public debt distorts the public spirit by multiplying in some nations the number of people who have an interest contrary to the common interest.

66. Adam Smith, *op. cit.*, t. IV, pp. 490–491.
67. Jean-Baptiste Say, *op. cit.*, t. II, p. 523.

The rentiers want, above everything, all the wealth of the royal treasury, and since the weight of taxes is the easiest source of this, taxpayers and the people above all who make up the biggest part of these and have no money to lend, find today in the very bosom of the State an opposing faction whose influence grows every day. The growth of public debt increases the power of government by accustoming a large part of the nation to fear above everything the slightest shaking in the works of government or the slightest change in its practices. Administration of Finances, II, 378–379.

[560] This is a remarkable effect of complexity in the political organization of the government machinery. The natural interest of any nation is to pay the fewest contributions possible. The creation of a public debt means that the interest of a large part of the nation is in the growth of taxation.

The contradiction is apparent. The credit which on the one hand weakens government power on the other hand fortifies it.

Chapter 9: On the Amount of Landed Property Which Society Has the Right to Insist upon for the Exercise of Political Rights

Note

1. *is to swallow small ones.* If the rich alone can be powerful, the powerful will become richer every day.

Chapter 10: That Owners Have No Interest in Abusing Power vis-à-vis Nonowners

Notes

1. *no longer form a distinct class.* It is because the different classes of society are mingling that all political power can be put in the hands of the property owners. If they formed an exclusive class they would pass unjust laws because they would become exclusive in outlook. This is what has happened in Europe across several centuries. Owners have for a long time, for example, wanted to limit the duration of leases the better to conserve the properties in their possession. They fancied that a lease agreed by their predecessors ought not to prevent them, year after long year, from enjoying the full value of their lands. Greed, however, always perceives things badly. The proprietors did not foresee how such a rule would erect obstacles to all improvement and thereby harm their true interests in the long run.

2. *their most faithful supports.* What, however, if owners formed an interest for rendering landed property inalienable? It would be as governors, not as owners, that they would perform this tyrannical act; and let it not be said that this is to evade the objection by verbal trickery. It is so true that this would be in their governmental capacity, that if you supposed government to be in the hands [561] of nonowners, these governors would be just as able to form an interest to make the functions of government inalienable. Secondly, if the countries in which owners adopted such a resolution contained rich nonlandowners, the latter would leave the country and

the disadvantages of the resolution would fall back on landowners. If this country contained only poor nonlandowners, even when landowners did not adopt such a resolution, the acquisition of landed property would be closed to nonproprietors, who would have no means of acquiring it.

Chapter 15: On Laws Which Favor the Accumulation of Property in the Same Hands

Notes

1. *of entailments.* Entailments, says Smith, III, 2,[68] were invented to perpetuate a state of affairs which was in itself a great calamity, I mean the distribution among a very small number of conquerors of an enormous area of lands, and which as a result were inevitably for the most part uncultivated. Given this state of affairs, entailments were reasonable. There was no public justice. Force was the only guarantee against spoliation. Force was located only in sizeable property which provided a certain number of vassals sufficient for the holder's self-defense. To make properties smaller was to lay them open to invasion by neighbors. Entailments therefore had a reasonable purpose in the given situation, although the situation itself was a vicious one. Entailments, however, as is the way with most human institutions, have outlasted this purpose.

Entailments, insofar as they favor the perpetuation of immense indivisible properties, are unfavorable to farming. A very considerable landowner necessarily neglects a large part of his property. One has only to compare, says Smith, III, 2, the large estates which have remained in the same families without interruption since the times of feudal anarchy, with the possessions of small owners nearby, to judge without any other argument how unfavorable to cultivation overlarge properties are. Properties are like States. Properties which are too small are disadvantageous because the owner is too poor to cultivate them well. Those which are too large, however, [562] are just as disastrous because the owner has neither the interest nor the time to survey all the parts of them equally. Entailments tie down individuals and generations without taking into consideration the changes which may arise in the condition of either.

Chapter 16: On Laws Which Enforce the Wider Spreading of Property

Notes

1. *to strengthen paternal power.* Some have wanted paternal power fortified in institutional ways, and they have sought to underpin it, as with all impracticable ideas, by ancient example. Among the ancients the scope of paternal power, against which other philosophers have widely inveighed, was not a disadvantage. Nor is the legal diminution of that power, one which so many moralists eloquently deplore

68. Adam Smith, *op. cit.,* Livre III, Ch. 2, t. II, pp. 413–421.

today, a very great evil. The reconciliation of these two apparently contradictory claims lies in the differences between the ancients and us. See Book XVI.

It is not to be doubted nevertheless that the revolutionary shake-up took the diminution of paternal power too far. To remedy this abuse, however, we do not need to establish institutions but to destroy some. Do away with your laws forbidding wills, greater freedom granted to fathers will reestablish their power. Remove the obstacles and the drawbacks will disappear. It is by interfering with everything that you pile these up, and then you complain about them and think you can remedy by even more laws the inconveniences which occur only because there are too many laws already. All the good things about paternal power derive from its being purely natural and moral. If you incorporated it into law, you would destroy its nature. It is not necessary for laws to combat it, but it is necessary that they do not interfere with it. It exists independently of law and must continue thus. To undermine it is unjust. To wish to add to it is pointless, and everything which is pointless becomes disastrous when legislated. Otherwise do not intrude the crudities of government into the delicacy and independence of nature. What you think you are sanctioning, you are corrupting. You are spoiling what you are trying to improve. [563] Paternal power is necessarily arbitrary. Such power is good when it is in the nature of things. It would be disastrous if it existed by law. Paternal power offers us an example of what I constantly say, that usually the abolition of a law would produce a number of advantages which seem mutually quite alien, and for each one of which separately, a host of laws are made which again have their particular drawbacks. The abolition of all entailments on the one hand, and perfect freedom to make wills on the other, that is to say two legal excisions, would produce at once the reestablishment of paternal power and a more equal distribution of wealth. These are advantages which it is believed one can get to by positive laws, but such outcomes one arrives at only imperfectly and pays for in multiple inconveniences, while the absence of two positive laws would produce them much more securely at the same time as it would, by delivering individual freedom and therefore taking away from men certain reasons for violating the law, be just for that reason a very great good.

Chapter 17: The Consequences of Attacks on Property by the Government[69]

Materials[70]

We are not speaking here of confiscations and other political attacks on property. One cannot consider such violence as routine practice for ordered government. These acts are of the nature of coups d'Etat and all arbitrary measures whose

69. [This is new material. There is no Ch. 17 in the original Book X. Translator's note.]

70. A large part of this "material" comes from Constant's discourse before the Tribunat on 28 ventôse an IX (19 March 1801) on the public debt, published in *Archives parlementaires . . . , op. cit.*, t. II, pp. 652–660.

consequences we have examined above. It is therefore against coups d'Etat and against arbitrary measures that we need to take a stand. Confiscations are only one part of these and an inseparable part. When men's life and freedom are not respected, how could their property be so?

The spoliation which occupies us in this chapter is that which governments allow themselves, to reduce their debts or increase their resources sometimes on the pretext of necessity, sometimes of justice, but always claiming the interest of the State. For just as the zealous apostles of the people's sovereignty think that public freedom gains from the constraints put [564] on individual freedom, our financiers today believe that the State enriches itself by the ruin of individuals.

These attacks on property are divided into two classes.

In the first, I put part or total bankruptcies, reductions in national debt, either in capital or interest, the payment of these debts in instruments of a lower value than their nominal value, the debasement of money, fiscal retainers, delayed payments, etc.

I put in the second category the acts of government against men who have dealt with government departments in order to supply them with the wherewithal for their military and civil activity, retrospective laws or measures against the newly rich, *chambres ardentes*,[71] the cancellation of contracts, concessions and sales made by the State to individuals.

There has been recourse to a great variety of names to designate these things. "The obscurities of language," remarks an English author (Bentham, I, 348), "have served financiers in deceiving the simple. They have said, for example, a retainer and not a theft."

It is rather curious to note that the same artifice has served legislators who have made manifestly unjust laws. The émigrés during the French Revolution were punished by death and the confiscation of their goods. When the wish was to treat deported people the same way, that is to say, men who had been forced to leave their country, while others were being punished for having left it, it was said bluntly that they belonged among the émigrés, which drove the word out of use and extended the thing.[72] Just as all injustices have a deep similarity between themselves, so there is also analogy in the language of all injustices.

[565] Once a national debt exists, there is only one way to soften its harmful effects, and that is to respect it scrupulously. One gives it in this way a stability which assimilates it, as far as its nature permits, to the other forms of property.

One cannot accept as a means of diminishing the bad effects of public debts that of not paying them. This would be to want to fight an inevitable evil by a pointless

71. [The name given to the extraordinary commissions under the ancien régime, authorized to punish the condemned by burning. Translator's note]

72. Constant is referring to the laws which followed the coup d'Etat of 18 fructidor an V, and which reactivated those of the Terror. See on this subject the extensive treatment by Georges Lefebvre, *Le Directoire*, Paris, A. Colin, 1971, Ch. 8, pp. 87–96. See also Jacques Godechot, *Les institutions . . .*, *op. cit.*, pp. 454–456.

and even larger one. Bad faith can never be a remedy for anything. Far from attaining the desired purpose, one would add to the immoral consequences of a property which gives its possessors different interests from the nation of which they are a part, the even more disastrous consequences of uncertainty and arbitrariness. Arbitrary government and uncertainty are the prime causes of what has been called *agiotage* [gambling]. It never develops more forcibly and actively than when the State is in violation of its agreements. All the citizens are in such circumstances forced to seek in the risks of speculation some compensation for the losses which the government has made them undergo.

Any distinction between creditors, between credits, any enquiry into the transactions of individuals, any research of the route public bills of exchange have followed, of the hands they have passed through till their maturity date, is criminal mismanagement. A government contracts debts and in payment gives government paper to those to whom it owes money. These are forced to sell the instruments it has given them. On what pretext would it proceed from this sale to query the value of these instruments? The more it questions the value, the more they will lose. It will rely on this new depreciation in order that they cash in at a price even lower. This double progression reacting on itself will soon reduce credit to zero and individuals to ruin.

The original creditor has been able to make of his claim what he wanted. If he sold his credit, the fault is not in him, whose need has forced him to this, but in the State which paid him only in promissory notes which he has found himself forced to sell. If he has sold his credit at a giveaway price, the fault is not in the purchaser who has bought it with unfavorable prospects; the fault is again with the State which has created these unfavorable prospects, since the credit sold would not have fallen to a giveaway price if the State had not inspired mistrust.

Setting it so that a note loses value as it passes to a second hand in any circumstances the government is not in a position to know, since these circumstances are free and independent variables, you cause circulation, which has always been regarded [566] as a means of wealth, into a cause of impoverishment. How can one justify this policy which refuses creditors what they are owed and discredits what it has given them? On what basis can the courts condemn the debtor, a creditor himself of a bankrupt government? Well then! Dragged off to a prison stripped of what belonged to me because I have been unable to clear the debts I have contracted on public trust, I will pass in front of the palace whence emanated these thieving laws. On the one side sits the government which robbed me, on the other the judges who punish me for having been robbed.

Any nominal payment is criminal mismanagement. Any issuing of paper which cannot be at will converted into specie, any alteration in the value of money, are false acts. The governments which have recourse to these guilty expedients are nothing but forgers armed with public power.[73] The government which pays a

73. See Constant's note D at the end of the Additions.

citizen in false values forces him into payments of like nature. In order not to enervate economic exchanges and render them impossible, it is obliged to legitimate all such operations. By creating the need for some people to behave in this way, it furnishes everybody with the excuse. Egotism, far more subtle, more adroit, more prompt, and more diversified than government, rushes forward at the given signal. It confounds all precautionary measures by the speed and complexity of its frauds. When corruption has the justification of necessity, it knows no more limits. If the government wants to establish a difference between its transactions and those of individuals, the injustice of it is only the more scandalous.

A nation's creditors are only a part of that nation. When taxes are imposed to pay the interest on the national debt, the matter weighs on the whole nation. After all, the State's creditors, as taxpayers, pay their share of these taxes. By a State bankruptcy, on the contrary, the debt is thrown on the creditors alone. This is therefore to conclude that since a burden is too heavy for a whole nation, it will be carried more easily by a quarter or an eighth of it.

Any enforced reduction in repayment is government default. You have dealt with individuals according to conditions you have freely offered. They have fulfilled these conditions. They have lent you their funds, which they have withdrawn from branches of production which offered them positive returns. You owe them everything you have promised them. The fulfillment of your promises is the legitimate indemnity of the sacrifices they have made and the risks they have run. If you regret having suggested onerous conditions, the [567] fault is yours and in no way theirs, since all they have done is accept them. The fault for this is doubly yours, since it is your earlier breaches of trust above all which have made your conditions onerous. If you had inspired full confidence, you would have obtained better conditions.

If you reduce the debt by a quarter, who will prevent you reducing it by a third, by nine-tenths, by the whole lot? What guarantees will you be able to give to your creditors or to yourself? Whatever one does, the first step makes the second one easier. If strict principles had held you to the fulfillment of your promises, you could have cast about for funds in an ordered and economic way. You, however, have sought yours in fraud. You have regarded it as acceptable that they are at your disposal, they absolve you from all work, privation, and effort. You come back to them constantly, since you no longer have any sense of integrity to hold you back.

Such is the blindness of governments when they abandon the paths of justice, as it is of those who have deluded themselves that by reducing their debt through an act of government, they would rally credit which seemed to be flagging. They have set off from a badly understood principle which they have badly applied. They have thought that the less they owed, the more confidence they would inspire, because they would be better placed to pay their debts. They have confused, however, the effect of a legitimate release and the effect of a default. It is not enough that a debtor can fulfill his commitments; he must further want to, and there must be means to hold him to it. Now, government which takes advantage of its authority to annul part of its debt proves that it lacks the will to pay. Its creditors cannot constrain it thereto. What do its resources matter therefore?

A public debt is not like commodities of basic necessity and ongoing need. The fewer there are of these commodities, the more valuable they are. They have intrinsic value, and their relative value grows with their scarcity. The value of a debt, on the contrary, depends only on the reliability of the debtor. Once this reliability is shaken, value is destroyed. You can reduce the debt in vain, to half, a quarter, or an eighth. What is left of it is only all the more discredited. Nobody needs nor wants a debt which does not get paid. When it comes to individuals, the power to fulfill their commitments is the main condition, because the law is stronger than they. When it is a question of governments, however, the principal condition is will.

There is another kind of default in relation to which governments seem to conduct themselves with even less scruple. Involved in useless ventures, maybe through ambition, or imprudence, or indiscreet activity, they contract with merchants [568] for the supplies necessary for these enterprises. The terms they get are disadvantageous. This has to be. The interests of a government can never be defended with as much zeal as private interests. This fate is common to all transactions where the parties cannot look after themselves, and it is an inevitable one. In this situation the government takes a dislike to certain men who have merely taken advantage of the profit inherent in their situation. It encourages harangues and calumnies against them. It exaggerates its own losses, this is to say its own ineptitude, and because it has been ignorant and inept, it believes it has the right to be violent and unjust. It cancels its deals, it delays or refuses the payments it has promised. It takes general measures which, to reach a few suspects, without proper investigation, surround a whole class. To palliate this iniquity, it needs to represent these measures as hitting only those at the head of the enterprises from which their incomes are being removed. The hostility of the people is worked up against certain odious or tarnished names. The men who are plundered, however, are not isolated. They have not done everything on their own. They have used artisans and manufacturers who have given them real value and service. It is on the latter that the plundering, which seems to be being carried out only against the former, comes to fall. These same people, who, always credulous, applaud the destruction of a few fortunes, allegedly immense ones, which therefore irritate them, do not work out that all this wealth, based on works whose instrument they had been, tended to reflect back even on them, while the destruction of this wealth took away from them themselves the payment for their own work.

Governments always have a more or less great need for the men who deal with them. A government cannot buy with cash transactions as an individual can. It must either pay in advance, which is impracticable; or what it needs must be supplied to it on credit. If it ill-treats the suppliers, what happens? Honest men withdraw, not wishing to work in a business enfeebled from the start. Only rogues come forward and, foreseeing that they will not be paid properly, they take the question of payment into their own hands. A government is too slow, too encumbered, too lumbering in its movements, to follow the nimble decision making and rapid maneuvers of individual interest. We have seen governments wanting to vie with individuals in corruption, but the corruption of the latter was always more skillful. The only effective course for government is loyalty.

The first effect of disfavor cast on a branch of trade is to drive away from it all the traders whom greed does not seduce. The first effect of a despotic system is to inspire in all good men the desire not to encounter this despotism [569] and to avoid transactions which could connect them with this terrible power.

In all countries, economies founded on the violation of public trust have unfailingly met their punishment in the transactions which have followed. The returns to wickedness, despite its arbitrary withholdings and its violent laws, are always paid a hundredfold more than the returns to honesty would be.

Governments lose all credit by enforced reductions of public debt. They unsettle the value of their credit by evaluating it according to the loss it experiences. In this case their own negotiations become ruinous. By changing the value of money, they lose as creditors of the taxpayer and in their purchases what they gain as debtors.[74] By treating suppliers unjustly, they make honest people withdraw, and they find only rogues with whom to deal.[75] Lastly, by destroying credit, they range against them all the creditors of the State, and from this come revolutions.

In England the State's undertakings have always been sacred since 1688. So the State's creditors are one of the classes most interested in preserving the government. In France under the monarchy, violations of public trust having been frequent, the creditors of the State, at the first announcement of a deficit, showed themselves eager for a revolution. "Each man believed he saw his safety in taking away from the sovereign the administration of finance and locating it in a national council." Bentham, Principes du Code civil.[76]

Despotism with regard to property is soon followed by despotism with regard to persons. This is first because despotism is contagious and secondly because the violation of property naturally provokes resistance. In this case the government deals severely with the oppressed person who resists, and because it wanted to seize his property from him, it is led to aim a blow at his freedom.

Add that by throwing men into uncertainty about what they own, you provoke them to encroach upon what they do not own. Without security, the economy becomes a matter of trickery, and moderation, imprudence. When everything can be taken away, one must grab as much as possible, because that gives one more chance of retaining something [570] from the spoliation.[77] When everything can be taken away, as much as possible must be spent, because everything spent is so much snatched away from despotism.[78]

74. See Constant's note E at the end of the Additions.
75. See Constant's note F at the end of the Additions.
76. Jeremy Bentham, *op. cit.*, t. II, p. 79.
77. See Constant's note G at the end of the Additions.
78. See Constant's note H at the end of the Additions.

"Kings," says Louis XIV in his Memoirs, "are absolute lords and have naturally the full and free disposition of all their subjects' goods."[79] When kings regard themselves as absolute lords of all their subjects possess, however, the subjects hide what they possess or dissipate it. If they hide it, this is how much is lost to agriculture, trade, industry, and to prosperity of all kinds. If they lavish it on frivolous, coarse, or unproductive pleasures, this again is so much deflected from worthwhile uses and efficacious economic decisions. Louis XIV believed he was saying something favorable to the wealth of kings. He was really saying something which would be bound to ruin kings by ruining nations.

Chapter 18: To Be Done. Conclusions from the Above Considerations

Materials

In order to sum up the principles which must guide the action of government on property, I will say that government must constrain property when there is an obvious need for public safety.[80] This prerogative distinguishes its jurisdiction over property from its jurisdiction over persons, for it would not have the right to make an attempt on the life of a single innocent, even if this were for the safety of a whole nation. In all the cases, however, in which public safety is not threatened, government must guarantee property and leave it free.

79. *Mémoires de Louis XIV, op. cit.*, t. I, p. 156. The original text says: "All the goods possessed, as much by the people of the church as by laymen, to be used at any time as by wise stewards, this is to say, according to the general need of the State."

80. See Constant's note I at the end of the Additions.

Book XI: On Taxation

Chapter 4: On Various Types of Taxes

Notes

1. *the price cannot rise.* Commodities or merchandise do not rise in price solely because they cost more on account of their scarcity. Ordinarily, when an output costs more to produce than its market value, or at least when it costs such a lot and has so feeble a market price that profit is nil or very little, producers turn away from this production and concentrate on another more profitable one. If, however, they could not turn aside from this production, they would have to continue to concentrate on it even at a loss, and the output remaining at the same level, the price would not increase. Little by little, doubtless, the number of producers would diminish, and output being smaller, its price would rise because of its scarcity. If this production, however, were of a fundamental necessity, this would be a new misfortune. Argument against the land tax. First of all, it ruins the farmers, who, being able to produce only the same output and being able to ruin themselves only the more swiftly if they do not produce it, cannot like manufacturers make production scarcer in order to make it dearer. Next, it ruins agriculture, and before equilibrium between the costs and the value of commodities can be established, the people suffer from dearth.

On all occasions when the producer cannot diminish his workforce nor his output, the tax weighs heavily on him. The case here is that of an owner of land.

2. *revoltingly iniquitous.* For the financial drawbacks of the tax on patents, see Sismondi, Législation de commerce, II, 89 and following.

3. *as to the third.* "Fraud is the defect of the tax on consumption (indirect tax). Injustice is the defect of the tax on rent (direct tax)."Canard, Principes d'économie politique.[81] [572]

Chapter 5: How Taxation Becomes Contrary to Individual Rights

Notes

1. *as the lottery.* What governments believe they gain in money by the lottery tax, they lose and more, even in money, by the harm this tax does to production and by the crimes which it makes the working class commit, crimes which, leaving aside moral considerations and envisaging them only in fiscal terms, are an expense for the State.

81. Nicolas-François Canard, *Principes d'économie politique,* Paris, F. Buisson, 1801, p. 175.

Chapter 6: That Taxes Bearing on Capital Are Contrary to Individual Rights

Notes

1. *encroach upon capital.* See on the effect of consumption of capital by nations, Sismondi, I, 4.[82] "If the expenditures of the three productive classes exceed their incomes, the nation must inevitably impoverish itself." Sismondi, I, 94 and following.[83]

2. *The State which taxes capital.* Government economy is what most favors a country's prosperity, because it leaves more capital at the working disposal of individuals.

Chapter 7: That the Interest of the State in Matters of Taxation Is Consistent with Individual Rights

Notes

1. *Several of the mines in Peru.* From 1736 the tax on mines in Peru had been reduced from a fifth to a tenth. Smith, I, 11.[84]

[573] *Chapter 8:* An Incontestable Axiom

Notes

1. *Levying always produces an ill.* The first general effect of a tax is to diminish the seller's profit by reducing consumption in the areas of production taxed. What follows is that those who cultivated these areas abandon them to take up more lucrative ones. They increase the competition in these and consequently reduce the profits. Therefore the tax has an influence on all the sources of rent. Before the tax is spread over all of them, however, and the burden of the taxed branch is shared between all the others, in such a way as to produce equilibrium, there operates a more or less lasting friction, which makes the tax disastrous. "Any old tax is good, any new tax pernicious." Canard, Principes d'économie poltitique.[85]

2. *the most deplorable.* "Republics die from luxury," says Montesquieu, "monarchies from poverty."[86] He concludes from this that economy is suitable for republics and luxury for monarchies. A singular conclusion: for what does the observation

82. [Hofmann says the reference is almost certainly wrong. Translator's note]

83. This time the figures do refer to the tome and pages of Sismondi.

84. Adam Smith, *op. cit.*, t. I, pp. 354–355.

85. Nicolas-François Canard, *op. cit.*, p. 197.

86. *De l'esprit des lois,* Livre XII, Ch. 4. Jean-Baptiste Say, *op. cit.*, t. II. p. 380, criticizes this same quotation from Montesquieu by saying: "A constant truth which proves that frugality enriches States and prodigality ruins them. If prodigality ruins monarchies, however, it could not be suitable for them, since it is not suitable for any State to become dependent and poor."

itself, on which he bases this conclusion, mean? That republics enrich themselves by prudent economy and monarchies ruin themselves by luxury.

Chapter 9: The Drawback of Excessive Taxation

NOTES

1. *any pointless tax is a theft.* "What the well-being of the State demands, obviously enough, is decisiveness and a characteristic touch of inspiration. The taxes appropriate to this public well-being, of which a sovereign is judge and guardian, are proof of justice. What exceeds this measured proportion ceases to be legitimate. There is therefore no other difference between individual excesses and those of the sovereign, if only because the injustice of the former comes from simple ideas which each person can easily distinguish, while the latter, being linked to government complexities, whose extent is as vast as it is involved, no one can judge [574] other than by conjecture. . . .[87] It is a violation of the most sacred trust to use the sacrifices of the people on careless largesse, on pointless expenditures and undertakings foreign to the good of the State. . . .[88] The unreasonable extent of taxation is moreover a constant source of ills and vexations." Administration des finances, I, Ch. 2.[89]

Chapter 10: A Further Drawback of Excessive Taxation

ADDITION

Excessive taxation is often excused by the alleged necessity of encircling governments with an aura of magnificence. The claim is that to inspire men with respect for their institutions we must bedazzle them with the brilliance of those who hold power. This axiom is equally false in republics and monarchies. In the latter, the unassuming stance of the monarch, being voluntary and thereby meritorious, produces a much deeper impression than the display of a wealth extorted from the governed. Frederick II [the Great] and Charles XII inspired more real respect in this regard than Louis XIV. Ostentation is even less necessary in republics. It is possible that an aristocracy requires that the opulence of the governing class impress the people. This opulence, however, must belong by heredity to this class and must not be raised from daily taxation, a source at once ignoble and odious. As to elected governments, ostentation there produces none of the effects attributed to it. What is done with the avowed purpose of striking, dazzling, or seducing inevitably fails in this purpose. No personal veneration results from trappings which themselves have nothing personal about them. This borrowed magnificence is like our actors' makeup. Pomp has influence on the nation as spectator, when it is brought into the government by the individual and not when it is

87. Jacques Necker, *op. cit.*, t. I, p. 43.

88. *Ibid.*, p. 47.

89. *Ibid.*, p. 48; the fuller text reads: "Until now I have looked at the unreasonable extent of taxation only in terms of justice; one can also identify in this extent a constant source of ills and vexations."

so to speak conferred on him, in his governmental capacity. The advantageous effects we expect from ostentation are made up of memories, habits, [575] and traditional reverence. Governments which do not have these supports must renounce these means. If pomp is pointless, however, there is an elegance of form proper to governments; this elegance chimes with the greatest simplicity, just as the most brutal vulgarity goes with display and ostentation. This formal elegance commands true respect. It is the slow and sure effect of education and of life's whole experience. It is the guarantee of justice, its consequences far more important than one might think. Vulgar men can be moved; but for each occasion when they will be, how many occasions will there be when they remain insensitive and brutal? We should not forget, moreover, that to move vulgar spirits will require an intensification of the sounds and symptoms of grief. Now, as to silent but profound grief, they will not even notice it. How many timid or delicate impressions will recoil before their loathsome and wild persons? How many innocents will there be whose offended pride will freeze the tongue and strangle speech?

Vulgarity and violence are the two greatest scourges in men with power. They put an insurmountable barrier between them and everything noble, enlightened, delicate, and profound in human nature. Vulgar men, irascible men, even when their intentions are pure, are responsible for all the good that they are not asked to do and all the ill which is done without people daring to complain.

An author famous for his writings on how to relieve the burdens of the downtrodden poor, M. de Rumford, says in his memoirs on poorhouses and workhouse prisons, that care of physical needs contributes much to the moral improvement of men, and that he has often observed the most rapid change in criminals themselves, when purer air, better clothes, and healthier food had lifted them, so to speak, into another world. The absence of physical care, he says, creates a sorrow, a malaise which puts the soul into an irritable frame and throws something convulsive and wildly disordered into feelings and actions.[90]

Here I am speaking as much of the coarseness of appearance and of that irascibility which powerful men wish to use as a resource so that they will not have to apologize for it as a vice. These things throw our being into a kind of convulsive agitation, which chokes all the [576] sweeter feelings. Man has an influence on himself by his voice, his gestures, his discourse, and just as his inner sensations act on the behavior he adopts, so these adoptions react on his inner life. At some stages of our Revolution, people fell into the most ridiculous contradictions. They had wanted to clothe the government with magnificence and sanctify the vulgarity of its membership. It had not been grasped that what was good in popular institutions was simplicity, the absence of pointless pomp and of an ostentation humiliating to the poor man, and what was good in aristocratic institutions was the elegance of the mores, the loftiness of spirit, and the delicacy of feeling, results all of an education whose provision wealth had permitted. There had been brought together the drawbacks of two systems, stupid ostentation combined with ferocious brutality.

90. Hofmann believes this reference is to Benjamin, comte de Rumford, *Essais politiques, économiques et philosophiques,* t. I, Geneva, G.-J. Manget, 1799, pp. 44–45 and 97–99.

Book XII: On Government Jurisdiction over Economic Activity and Population

Chapter 1: Preliminary Observation

Additions

It is proven that the economy flourishes only under freedom; but if the contrary were demonstrated, the restrictions put on freedom on the pretext of special support for production have consequences so disastrous for general contentment and for morality that it would be better to let the economy languish than attack freedom.

Chapter 4: On Privileges and Prohibitions

Notes

1. *Thus we have three real losses.* Here is a fourth one of them. Manufactures which, by keeping going thanks to privileges, diverting funds from those which do not need privileges to sustain themselves, cause the latter to deteriorate owing to shortage of sufficient funds. Sismondi, Législation de commerce, II, 53.

2. *combinations which make up for this.* Of two things one must occur, either a commerce cannot take place without a state-supported company, and then the company has nothing to fear from the competition [577] of individual firms, or if the company has something to fear from this, then the trade can be conducted without a privileged company, in which case a company of this kind is an injustice.

3. *will enlighten all the citizens.* It is obvious that each individual in his particular position is far better placed to judge the type of activity his capital can most advantageously set to work than any politico or legislator will be able to do for him. Smith, IV, 2.[91]

4. *it ruins itself.* Commercial companies have this disadvantage, that their directors are like governments. Governments soon develop an interest different from that of the governed. The directors of these companies soon have an interest different from that of the company.

5. *bankruptcy.* A very remarkable example of the unfortunate effects of state-supported companies is the history of French trade with the Indies, from 1664 to 1719. The company, created in 1664, had an exclusive monopoly. By 1708 it had lost close to twenty million. During this time, merchants from St. Malo engaged in interloping, beset with all the difficulties and dangers of smuggling. They profited by it. In 1708 these traders had the idea of buying the privileges of the company which impeded them and became themselves a privileged company. Their profits

91. Adam Smith, *op. cit.*, t. III, pp. 52–60. Constant does not give an exact reference.

ended immediately and within eleven years they took the losses of the Company of the Indies, whose monopoly they had acquired, to thirty million. Savary, Dictionnaire de Commerce, IV, p. 1075.[92]

6. *wardenships.* Apprenticeships prevent individuals from following this or that trade. Guild masters and wardenships are organizations which determine their own numbers and the conditions of admission.

7. *the most iniquitous.* When one of the conditions of apprenticeship is paying to be accepted into the trade, this is the height of injustice. For it is to keep from work those who have most need for work.

8. *the most absurd.* The result of fixing the number of people [578] working in each trade is that it is more likely than not that this number will not be proportionate to the needs of consumers. This is because there can be too many or too few. If there are too many, the men in this trade, being unable to take up another since the guild masters in any other would drive them away, work at a loss or do not work and fall into poverty. If there are too few, the price of the labor rises, agreeably to the greed of these workers.

9. *the surest spur to such perfecting.* A singular pretension of government, which, as Sismondi says, II, 285, wants to teach manufacturers their craft and consumers to know their taste![93]

10. *to appraise their merits.* I exempt from full freedom of trade professions which touch on public safety, architects, because an unsound house affects all citizens, pharmacists, doctors, lawyers.

11. *the price of the goods.* Apprenticeships are oppressive from the consumers' viewpoint because by diminishing the numbers of workers, they increase the labor costs. Therefore they harass the poor man and cost the rich one a surcharge.

12. *the English towns.* England, despite its system of prohibitions, has always tended to liberalize production. Apprenticeships have been restricted to existing trades since the statute of Elizabeth which established them, and the courts have welcomed the most subtle distinctions tending to remove from these statutes as many trades as possible. For example, you have to have had an apprenticeship to make carts but not to make carriages. Blackstone.[94]

92. Jacques Savary des Bruslons, *Dictionnaire universel de commerce,* Geneva, Cramer et Cl. Philibert, 1750, t. IV, col. 1075–1097, s.v. Compagnie des Indes. Constant found this information in Sismondi, *De la richesse commerciale . . . , op. cit.,* t. II, pp. 309–310 and n. 2.

93. This is not a quotation, but an interpretation of the following text: "This first law on corporations was backed up by a host of regulations on how artisans must work, on the qualities their work must have, and on the visits of the judges to whom it is fitting to subject them. As if the consumers for whom the work is intended, and who buy only what suits them, were not the best of all judges for the inspection of the goods." Jean-Charles-Léonard Sismondi, *op. cit.,* t. II, pp. 284–285.

94. Hofmann was unable to find anything on carts and carriages in the six-volume French version of Blackstone's commentaries, Paris, Bossange, 1822–1823, though it has a detailed index.

[579] 13. *no corporation.* Notice how freedom, as the simple absence of law, brings order to everything. Combinations of individuals practicing the same trade are mostly a conspiracy against the public. Shall we conclude from this that these combinations should be forbidden by prohibitive laws? Not at all. By forbidding them the government condemns itself to much bother, to surveillance, to punishments which would entail grave drawbacks. Just let government refuse to sanction these combinations. Let it not recognize any right to restrict the number of men in this or that job. Just doing this will deprive combinations of any purpose. If twenty persons in a particular trade wish to combine to push up the price of their work to too high a level, others will come forward to do the job at a lower price.

14. *the rigging of daily wages.* See on the efforts of guild masters to lower and workmen to raise the daily wages and of the impotence of government intervention in this regard, Smith, I, 132–159, Garnier's translation.[95] The rigging of the daily wage is the sacrifice of the larger party to the smaller.

15. *the national wealth.* It is to be remarked that at the same time that French manufacturers demand [import] prohibitions to support their manufactures, they all complain of the lack of capital. (See the Statistics from the *départements* published by the government.)[96] This proves that there is not enough capital for the existing businesses. Now, if they abandoned prohibitions and if free admission of foreign products were to cause the abandonment of part of the industry, the capital would relocate in the direction of the remaining parts. It would no longer be consumed feeding failing manufactures, and truly viable manufactures would gain thereby, as well as the whole body of consumers.

16. *and perfect itself.* The prohibitions on products of foreign manufacture tend to extinguish emulation by indigenous products. "What is the point," says Sismondi, II, 163, "of seeking [580] to do better when the government has undertaken to find buyers for the very persons who do the worst?"

17. *this greater value.* One would think, to see the precautions which governments take against the exportation of specie, that people export it at a loss, simply to play tricks on them.

18. *must remain free.* "All the times when we chide a nation about the means for fulfilling its obligations, it is as if, in order to increase the credit of a merchant, we forbade him to pay his debts." Sismondi, I, 200.

19. *It will not be exported unprofitably.* To justify the precautions taken against the exportation of specie, people greatly exaggerate the fantasies, foolish expenses, and prodigality of individuals. These things, however, make up only an infinitely small part of the total expenditure; and to prevent this very small ill, a much worse one is done, and there is even incurred, by way of payment for spies and legal proceedings, a much greater expense.

95. Contrary to his usual practice, Constant refers here to the tome and the pages of the work by Adam Smith cited. In his normal referencing this would be Livre I, Ch. 8.

96. The reference and the example very probably come from Jean-Charles-Léonard Sismondi, *op. cit.*, Livre III, Ch. 2, t. II, pp. 156–220.

The fantasies which lead to the unproductive flight of specie are expenses particular to the rich. Now, the rich man will always have ways of getting his specie out, since he will always be able to pay the smuggling premium.

The supporters of bans on the export of specie say quite correctly that specie, in facilitating exchange and accelerating circulation, creates commerce. Are they not forgetting, however, that commerce creates money, that is to say, brings back specie? They write always as if the purpose of those who demand freedom for the exportation of specie were to drive out everything which is in the country, and they expound very well the benefits of specie and the drawbacks of its disappearance. See Ferrier, Du gouvernement, pp. 13–18.[97] Permitted exportation, however, is not forced exportation. The logic of the defenders of prohibitions is to suppose that all dangerous and injurious things would be done as soon as they were not forbidden. They assert this very complacently, and then they fully demonstrate the evil which will result from it, for example, in the case of specie. They do not examine whether even when its leaving is not prohibited, specie would, indeed, leave. They give themselves over to a pathetic picture of the evils [581] a country would experience if it were deprived of all its specie. This is a logical ruse which deceives much of the world. You affirm one thing; you demonstrate from it a second thing, which is incontestable; and you conclude from the obviousness of the second assertion the truth of the first, although there is no connection between the two. "If France," says Ferrier, "saw herself losing every year just twenty million, at the end of fifty years, her specie would be reduced by half." Manufactures would fall, etc. The second assertion is true, doubtless, once one has admitted the first. The difficulty is that the first is not true and can never be true. This is a thing which happens frequently in all disputes. One of the combatants wittingly changes the question, and the other one, not noticing that the question has changed, lets himself be drawn into following his adversary and battling on a false terrain. The opponents of free exportation, instead of proving that exportation set free would cause all the specie to leave, have assumed the thing proven and then demonstrated the bad effects of its leaving. Then their antagonists, instead of proving that free exportation drives out only the superfluous specie, have been pushed by the heat of the discussion to combat everything their opponents said and begun to maintain that all the specie's leaving would not be a bad thing. See Smith.[98] Thus sophisms by one group set the logic of the opposing group.

To judge this question sanely, one must set off from two principles. First, on all the occasions a people have too little specie, it will not exit, even if exportation is allowed. Secondly, all the times there is too much specie, it will be impossible to prevent its exit, even if exportation is forbidden.

97. François-Louis-Auguste Ferrier, *Du gouvernement considéré dans ses rapports avec le commerce,* Paris, A. Egron, an XIII (1805). The pages indicated by Constant correspond to Ch. 2 *De l'argent, considéré comme moyen d'échange—En quel sens il est richesse pour le pays.*

98. Adam Smith, *op. cit.,* Livre IV, Ch. 1 *Du exportation du numéraire,* t. III, pp. 3–52.

20. *piled up law after law.* Contradictory measures by governments. They strictly forbid exportation of specie, and they create paper money whose natural and inevitable effect is to expel the specie from their country. See Smith,[99] Sismondi,[100] and Say.[101]

21. *of a middleman class.* A law which everywhere and always has been judged extremely useful is that which forbids any hand to intervene between the farmer and the urban consumer. Is it not obvious, however, that the manufacturer [582] is always distracted from his work by the sale of output, that he can produce more and better output if some capitalist takes care of sales? Why make an exception in this respect of agriculture? If the peasant has to take his commodities to town, he necessarily loses considerable time. He spends what he gets for his products on luxurious town living. The men get drunk and the women corrupted. This way of things depraves and ruins the country people. Mirabeau, Monarchie prussienne, I, 169.[102]

22. *competition.* "As soon as a branch of commerce or any specialized work is of use to the public, this will be all the more true when competition is more freely and generally established in it." Smith, II, Ch. 2.[103] The principle of competition applies to everything. "The establishment of several banks issuing promissory notes is better," observes Say, II, Ch. 15,[104] "than the establishment of one. Then each establishment of this kind seeks to merit the favor of the public by offering it the best conditions and the soundest security."

23. *that the minimum is missing.* Whoever carefully examines the dearths and famines which have afflicted some part of Europe, during the course of this century and the two preceding ones, on a number of which we have very precise data, will find that no dearth has ever arisen through any coming together of domestic sellers of wheat nor of any other cause than a real scarcity of wheat, perhaps caused sometimes and in a particular place by the ravages of war, but in by far the largest number of cases, by bad years, while a famine has never derived from any other cause than by violent measures of government and by improper means used by government to try to remedy the difficulties of high prices. The trade in wheat, without restrictions, harassment, or limits, which is the most efficacious safeguard against the misfortunes of a famine, is also the best palliative for the dire consequences of scarcity. "For there are no remedies against the consequences of real starvation. They can be alleviated only." Smith, IV, Ch. 5.[105] He shows very clearly in the same [583] chapter that the more you put discredit on the wheat trade and

99. *Ibid.*

100. Jean-Charles-Léonard Sismondi, *op. cit.,* Livre I, Ch. 5 *Du numéraire,* t. I, pp. 136–137.

101. Jean-Baptiste Say, *op. cit.,* Livre II, Ch. 17 *Du papier monnaie,* t. II, pp. 42–52.

102. Honoré-Gabriel Riqueti, comte de Mirabeau, *De la monarchie prussienne sous Frédéric le Grand,* London, 1788, t. I, pp. 167–168.

103. Adam Smith, *op. cit.,* t. II, p. 310.

104. Jean-Baptiste Say, *op. cit.,* t. II, p. 21.

105. Adam Smith, *op. cit.,* t. III, p. 215.

the more you surround it with dangers, by causing those who devote themselves to this trade to be looked on as monopolists, the more you cause those who devote themselves to this trade, despite the discredit and the dangers, to want to be compensated for this by large profits. The people then find themselves in years of scarcity in the hands of unscrupulous men, who get revenge for the people's disdain by taking advantage of their distress.

24. *to forbid producing.* The Maremma of Tuscany produced four times more wheat than was necessary for feeding its inhabitants, before exportation was forbidden. The grand dukes of the House of Medici prohibited it, and the lands remained uncultivated. Sismondi, II, 128.[106] The exportation of wool is severely forbidden in England. What has the result been? That the number of rams has diminished and that wool has become more rare and of lower quality. The first fact was established by a Parliamentary inquiry in 1802. The second all English people recognize. Sismondi, II, 35.[107]

25. *a habitual calamity.* See some excellent ideas in Bentham, Principes du Code civil, Ch. 4,[108] on the intervention of laws regarding subsistence.

26. *when it comes to the means of carrying it out.* On grain legislation, in the Bibliothèque de l'homme publique, XII, pp. 110 and following.[109] "Any commodity, without exception, must be traded freely if one wants it in abundance. It is enough to harass and restrict its sale to cause its cultivation to be neglected and to make it rare."[110] Permission to certain individuals to export does more harm than good, since without bestowing more freedom it adds uncertainty to irritation. Thus it is false reasoning to conclude from the harm permission to individuals causes that general freedom would be harmful too. When exportation is forbidden, what happens? Wheat becomes dirt cheap; during that year it is squandered, and [584] in the following years very little and poor quality is grown and there is famine. If people do not want a general system and rely on the prudence of the government, the government's committing the least error results in the greatest inconvenience, and not only that, but individual interest, which is the best and only guarantee of supplies, knowing it can be thwarted at each second by the arbitrariness, the whim, or the mistakes of the government, loses its assurance and thereby its dynamism. It puts its cunning in the service of fraud rather than in useful economic calculation. First, because its calculation can be unexpectedly hampered. Secondly, because on all the occasions when fraud is possible, there is more to gain by it than from any

106. Constant does not quote but summarizes the argument of these pages, pp. 128–129.

107. Constant should have said pp. 133–135.

108. Jeremy Bentham, *op. cit.*, t. II, pp. 13–14.

109. Marquis de Condorcet, *De la législation des grains depuis 1692. Analyse historique à laquelle on a donné la forme d'un rapport à l'Assemblée nationale,* in *Bibliothèque de l'homme public,* Paris, Buisson, 1790, t. XII, pp. 105–243.

110. *Ibid.*, p. 20. Only this sentence is a quotation. What follows it is a summary of pp. 110–111.

other financial operation, p. 111. The disadvantages of warehouses, pp. 119–120, 178. Laws against monopolies. Sequence of measures which harass people and are always useless, pp. 148–164. The excellent edict of 1774, p. 192. The need to take precautions on account of the people's prejudices, pp. 205–211. Excellent report presented to the Assembly of Notables on the commerce in grain. Prohibitions encourage sudden exportation at rock-bottom prices, because they get lifted precisely when grain is cheap, p. 222. To the price of wheat maintained at a modest level by the government there must be added the expenses of the measures necessary to keep it at that level. For nothing is as dear as vexations. Now, these expenses fall back on taxpayers, p. 228. The prohibition on exporting is an indication of shortage, which has the infallible effect of raising prices, p. 234.[111]

27. *and the most convenient.* See Smith on the effects of prohibitions with regard to exportation of and cornering in grains, III, 2.[112]

28. *the question of the rate of interest.* The law must not guarantee usurious rates. At the same time, however, it must grant an assured guarantee to legal rates. For if it does not protect legal rates against all risk, the difficulty of getting oneself paid these rates would cause a resurgence of usury. By firmly guaranteeing legal rates and not usurious ones, the law reconciles everybody. Lenders will prefer legitimate profit, if it is safe, to a larger profit which is precarious. If, on the contrary, no profit is assured, lenders will seek, risks being equal, the largest [585] profit. N.B.: I do not know if all this is fair and does not contradict my principles. Perhaps the best and the simplest is for the law to guarantee all rates of interest however high they may be. Then the security will generate competition and this by itself will bring rates down.

29. *failed against it.* Frederick William, father of Frederick the Great, was violently prejudiced against the Jews. He harassed them in a thousand ways. He also had to give them privileges, to compensate them for his harassments. He allowed them, for example, exclusive right to lend at usurious rates, because they did not enjoy as much security for the funds they lent as Christians did. A singular arrangement, according to which he authorized the villainy of the former because he had left them defenseless before the villainy of the latter.

30. *must not be fixed.* Rising interest rates are not always the sign of a bad financial situation. Rates can rise when the scale of capital employed becomes greater, through a more extensive market or a new commerce opening up to a nation. The lowering of interest rates is therefore like falling profits. Such a fall is a sign, sometimes of prosperity, sometimes of the opposite, Sismondi, I, 78. The rate of interest has not fallen in America, despite the rapid growth of public wealth, because the need for capital grows, through the progress of industry, at the same time and even faster than the stock of capital. The rise and fall of interest rates and the rise and fall

111. Constant's three last references do not correspond perfectly to Condorcet's text, although one cannot be sure to which passages they would relate better.

112. This second chapter of Livre III is called *Comment l'agriculture fut découragée en Europe après la chute de l'empire romain, op. cit.*, t. II, pp. 413–439.

of profit levels, being sometimes a sign of prosperity and sometimes of the opposite, cannot serve as a rule for steering government measures. N.B.: This is contrary to note 28 above.

31. *It causes the flight.* In Italy, many rich people have scruples about lending at interest. What is the result? That they hide their specie. This fact is proved by the extreme credulity with which the public adopts all the stories of the discovery of treasure. Sismondi, I, 144. Thus the fruit of the religious teaching which forbids lending at interest is only the vanishing of a supply of funds which would have stimulated industry. We ask who gains from this religious teaching.

[586] 32. *in Athens.* Freedom of trade was always full and complete in Athens. There was no monopoly or exclusive privilege. Neither was there any law against usury. Those, however, who demanded excessively high interest rates were scorned by public opinion. De Pauw, I, 372.

33. *Public scrutiny will moderate them.* "Usury has constantly been awoken when the wish was to limit the rate of interest or abolish it entirely. The fiercer the measures were and the more severely were they carried out, the more the price of money rose. This was the result of the natural process of things. The more risks the lender ran, the more he needed to be compensated by a high insurance premium. In Rome, during all the time of the Republic, the rate of interest was enormous. The debtors, who were the plebeians, constantly menaced their creditors, the patricians. Mahomet forbade the rate of interest." What happens? In Muslim countries money is lent usuriously. The lender indemnifies himself for the use of the capital he parts with and again for the danger of the contravention. The same thing happened in Christian countries, above all in relation to the Jews. Say, Livre IV, Ch. 14.[113]

ADDITIONS

1. "The production encouraged mostly by a system of prohibitions is that which serves to benefit rich and powerful people. That which brings advantages to the poor and needy is almost always neglected or crushed." See Smith, IV, 8.[114]

2. Governments formerly had the policy of blocking the invention or the establishment of machines which economize on labor. Montesquieu approves of them.[115] This was on the pretext [587] that these machines reduced a number of workers to inactivity and poverty. Following the invention of the machine-made stockings frame, the intendants of several provinces inveighed against a discovery

113. Jean-Baptiste Say, *op. cit.*, Livre IV, Ch. 14, t. II, pp. 279–280. [Hofmann points out that Constant's quote is accurate at the beginning but later drops into paraphrase. Translator's note]

114. Adam Smith, *op. cit.*, t. III, p. 465.

115. Montesquieu, *De l'esprit des lois,* Livre XXIII, Ch: 15, where he says, for example: "These machines, whose purpose is to compress skill, are not always a good thing. If a product is at a middling price, which suits the buyer and the workman who made it equally well, machines which would simplify production, that is to say diminish the number of workers, would be pernicious."

which they said would reduce fifty thousand individuals to beggary. The inventor was forbidden to profit from his secret or to communicate it. They even made sure he was put in the Bastille. What happened? On his release he took refuge in England, the English turned his discovery to profit, and ten years afterward France was obliged to procure it with much more expense and difficulty. Since that time, industry of that type has multiplied its products. The poor have benefited, because they are now better clothed, and beggary, far from increasing, has diminished. Say.[116]

Chapter 5: On the General Effect of Prohibitions

NOTES

1. *men preparing for every kind of crime.* "There are always many inconveniences from the unnecessary imposing of laws contrary to individual interest and easy to infringe in secret, since this is a way of enticing men to free themselves by degrees from the burden of their conscience. To forbid what one cannot prevent and to expose citizens to continual inquisition, to attach grave punishments to crimes which one can never recognize and yet can always suspect, is to weaken the respect due to the law." Administration des finances, III, 55–56. "All the times we forbid a thing naturally permitted or necessary, we simply make dishonest people out of those who do it." Esprit des lois, XXI, 20.

[588] 2. *artificial crimes.* Can a country whose law forbids alike theft, murder, the sale or purchase of such and such a material and such and such a commodity, have any just ideas on moral good or evil?

3. *to consider criminal.* "Such a smuggler," says Smith, V, 2,[117] "doubtless guilty of breaking the laws of his country, nevertheless often finds he is incapable of violating those of natural justice. He was born to be in every way an excellent citizen, if the laws of his country had not taken it upon themselves to make criminal actions which in no way at all receive this character from nature."

116. Jean-Baptiste Say, *op. cit.*, Livre I, Ch. 7, t. I, p. 36. There is a total confusion as to the invention of the machine-made stockings. It was an Englishman, William Lee, who invented machine-made stockings, at the end of the sixteenth century. The circumstances surrounding this discovery have remained obscure, and the legend has somewhat modified the facts. What is certain, however, is that William Lee, faced with his compatriots' lack of interest in his machine, emigrated to France, perhaps invited by Henry IV, who had promised to bestow certain privileges upon him. The assassination of the king in 1610 called everything into question. We do not know whether William Lee died wretched in France or returned to England. In any case, his frame was repatriated and the stocking industry flourished in that country in the middle of the seventeenth century. Finally, in 1656, Louis XIV decided to establish a stocking industry in his castle in Madrid. He entrusted this duty to Jean Andret, who brought back the secret from England. For more details, see *L'histoire générale des techniques,* published under the direction of Maurice Dumas, t. II *Les premières étapes du machinisme,* Paris, PUF, 1965, pp. 236–249.

117. Adam Smith, *op. cit.*, t. IV, pp. 440–441.

4. *in North America.* The bad effect of government action on production is seen in the influence of commercial regulations in Georgia. Pictet, Tableau des Etats-Unis, II, 308.[118]

Additions

1. The Tartars, on their arrival in China, noticed that there were many disadvantages for agriculture in the irregularity of Cantons which were overpopulated, those underpopulated, and those totally unpopulated. They thought seaborne commerce was the source of the trouble, since it drew to the coast families from landlocked provinces where the fields were left fallow. They had the idea of forbidding seaborne commerce and in six provinces of demolishing houses less than three leagues from the sea, and forcing the inhabitants to withdraw deeper into the country. What happened? These people built no houses at all and waited in holes dug in the earth till the Tartar prohibitions fell into disuse. For the least enlightened men have a singular instinct, a prescience which warns them that everything excessive passes away. Indeed, the Tartars relaxed the ban on fishing and seaborne commerce. These families, persecuted so that they would cultivate the soil and who, instead of cultivating it, dug holes in it so they could live in them, left their holes and set themselves up again on the coasts. De Pauw. Egyptians and Chinese.[119] [589]

2. Regulations were passed in France to keep watch on the conservation of woods belonging to individuals, so they could not cut them down without permission. The result of these regulations was that individuals feared to plant trees which they had no right to cut down. Steuart, Political Economy, I, 146.[120]

Chapter 6: On Things Which Push Governments in This Mistaken Direction

Notes

1. *about the business outlook.* Men in public administration who are guided by the business outlook think the measures which enrich merchants or manufacturers, and quickly to boot, also increase the national wealth. They do not reflect that the wealth of these merchants or manufacturers is formed only at the expense of other individuals in the nation. People do not believe the nation is likely to be enriched when a man who has a gaming house makes a large fortune at the expense of many individuals. The nation is no more enriched when a manufacturer, by virtue of a monopoly, acquires an immense fortune at the expense of

118. Charles Pictet de Rochemont, *Tableau de la situation actuelle des Etats-Unis d'Amérique,* Paris, Du Pont, 1795. Constant's reference is not faithful.

119. Cornelius de Pauw, *Recherches philosophiques sur les Egyptiens . . . , op. cit.,* t. I, pp. 81–82.

120. James Steuart, *An inquiry into the principles of political economy, being an essay on the science of domestic policy in free societies,* J. Williams and R. Moncrieffe, 1770, t. I, p. 146.

many individuals. See Sismondi, Législation du commerce, II, 115 and following.[121] The interest of merchants and leading manufacturers is always opposed to that of the public. Consequently, any proposals coming from this group as to law or the regulation of commerce must be received only with extreme suspicion. Smith, I, 11.[122] Transplantation of the economic decision making of a particular interest group to the administration of public affairs. An individual would gain a lot from being able to make counterfeit money with impunity. Governments have believed they would gain comparably from so doing.

2. *large roads.* Smith points out on this occasion, I, 11,[123] that the roads were opened and that from [590] this time these petitioners, despite their fears, saw their rents increase and their cultivation improve.

Chapter 7: On the Supports Offered by Government

Notes

1. *A regime of subsidies:* See for the absurdity of subsidies the example of the one granted by the English government for the transport of grain in Ireland. Tableau de la Grande Bretagne, I, 305, 333, 338, 351–352.[124]

2. *of constraint and harshness.* A provincial intendant in France, with a view to encouraging the production of honey and the work of the bees, demanded statements of the number of hives kept in his province. In a few days all the hives were destroyed. Administration des finances, tome not given, p. 238.[125]

3. *from their natural usage.* "Any system which seeks, either by special subsidies to attract to a particular type of industry a larger amount of society's capital than would naturally make its way there, or by special obstacles forcibly to deflect an amount of capital from a particular industry, in which it would otherwise seek employment, is a system truly subversive of the purpose it espouses as its first and last objective. Very far from accelerating society's progress toward opulence and real growth, it retards it. Very far from increasing, it diminishes the real value of the annual output of land and of the work of society." Smith, IV, 9.[126]

4. *will not bring the same zeal.* One could regard as a subsidy the practice whereby workers in Persia are paid by the court, even when they are not working or are ill. Since people are always disposed to praise the government, Chardin bestows eulogies on this practice, Voyages de Perse, II, p. 19.[127] One can consider [591] from the same point of

121. Jean-Charles-Léonard Sismondi, *op. cit.*, t. II, pp. 115–118.

122. Adam Smith, *op. cit.*, t. II, pp. 163–165.

123. *Ibid.*, t. I, pp. 307–308.

124. The author of the *Tableau de la Grande Bretagne,* quoted earlier, Alexandre-Balthazar de Paule, baron de Baert-Duholant.

125. Hofmann did not manage to locate this anecdote in Necker's work.

126. Adam Smith, *op. cit.*, t. III, p. 556.

127. *Voyages de M. le chevalier [Jean] Chardin en Perse et autres lieux de l'Orient,* Amsterdam, J.-L. de Lorme, 1711. Hofmann could not find the reference. Constant got it from Cornelius de Pauw, *Recherches philosophiques sur les Egyptiens . . . , op. cit.*, t. I, p. 277.

view the practice in Siam whereby those who excel at their work are employed for six years by the court. La Loubère, Relation de Siam, Tome I, Partie II.[128]

Chapter 8: On the Equilibrium of Production

Notes

1. *A people's first need is to subsist.* The Chinese missionaries attribute the famines so frequent in China to the distillation of rice. Who does not feel, however, that in a country where grain is short, it would be more useful to sell it than to distill it, since there would be more need for bread to eat than for spirit to drink. De Pauw, Egyptians and Chinese, I, 80.

2. *the marquis de Mirabeau.* See the Ami des hommes for supports for agriculture, I, pp. 44–54.

Chapter 9: Final Example(s) of the Adverse Effects of Government Intervention

Notes

1. *Only by not acting.* In his Mémoires, Livre XIX,[129] Sully regards the proliferation of edicts and regulations in relation to commerce and industry, as a direct obstacle to the prosperity of the State. See Garnier's observations in his [592] Preface to Smith, on the nonintervention of the government in industry, xxii–xxiii.[130] It is the same with men as it is with flocks of sheep. It has been remarked that flocks of sheep prospered particularly in enclosed meadows because they were allowed to pasture freely there and they were troubled by neither the shepherd nor his dog. "Such is the misfortune of France," says Sismondi, I, 166, "that she always borrows from each theory of political economy whatever is most ruinous in it. Following the political economists she crushed the countryside with the land tax. Following the mercantilists she shackled commerce with her customs houses and impoverished consumers. Following the disciples of Law, she dissipated public wealth twice over along with that of the capitalists, first by the creation of banknotes and then by promissory notes."[131]

128. Simon de la Loubère, *Du royaume de Siam,* Amsterdam, A. Wolfgang, 1691, t. I, Deuxième Partie, pp. 212–213. The example and the reference are supplied by de Pauw, *ibid.,* and Hofmann notes that Constant repeats the latter's error. The Siamese had to serve six months a year at court and not six years.

129. *Mémoires de Maximilien de Béthune, duc de Sully,* Liège, F.-J. Desoer, 1788, t. V, pp. 219–220. The sentence which Constant presents is word for word from Jean-Baptiste Say, *op. cit.,* t. I, pp. 321–322.

130. The Roman numerals refer to Garnier's Preface to Adam Smith, *op. cit.,* t. I.

131. [Assignats or promissory notes were issued by the Revolutionary governments. Translator's Note]

Chapter 10: Conclusions from the Above Reflections

Addition

"The regulations of commerce," says Smith, IV, 7,[132] "have this double drawback, that not only do they cause the birth of very dangerous ills in the state of the body politic, but furthermore these ills are such that it is often difficult to cure them without occasioning, at least for a while, even greater ills." "When we consider closely," says Say, I, 35,[133] "the harm which the regulatory system causes when it is set up, and the evils to which one can be exposed in abolishing it, we are naturally led to this reflection: if it is so difficult to give freedom to industry, how much more reserved ought we to be when it is a matter of taking it away?"

Chapter 11: On Government Measures in Relation to Population

Notes

1. *see Mirabeau,* l'Ami des hommes, I, p. 33, on the monastic institutions. Ibid., p. 38, why the condition of Protestant States is better than that of Catholic States.

[593] 2. *All detailed legislation.* See Mirabeau, Ami des hommes, I, 39.

132. Adam Smith, *op. cit.,* t. III, p. 384.

133. Jean-Baptiste Say, *op. cit.,* Livre I, Ch. 35, t. I, p. 292.

Book XIII: On War

Chapter 1: From What Point of View War Can Be Considered As Having Advantages

Notes

1. *now only a scourge.* The new way of making war, the development of arms and artillery, have lessened the good effects of war. Modern courage has the character of indifference. Gone is that élan, that will, that pleasure in the development of the physical and moral faculties which hand-to-hand combat produced. See Mirabeau, l'Ami des hommes, on necessary wars and wars undertaken through the fantasy of governments, I, 27–29.[134]

2. *limitless power.* The prompt establishment of boundless power is the remedy which can, in these cases (those of extremely large States), prevent breakup: a new misfortune on top of enlargement. Esprit des lois, VIII, 17.

Addition

Let government not get this wrong. It would search in vain to the ends of the earth after glory, tribute money, empire, and the world's wealth. All it would earn is astonishment. Without morality and freedom, success is only a meteor, which gives life to nothing in its path. People scarcely raise their heads to contemplate it for an instant, before each person continues on his way, silent and cheerless, striving to flee from despotism, misfortune, and death. [594]

Chapter 5: On the Mode of Forming and Maintaining Armies

Addition

One of the functions of government being to repel foreign invasions, it follows that governments have a right to demand of individuals that they contribute to the national defense. It is impossible to restrict this right within precise limits. Its extent depends entirely on the attacks to which the society finds itself exposed. Governments can set themselves certain statutory limitations in this respect for the convenience of the citizens and the greatest possible facility in the organization of the armed forces. For example, they can fix the age before and after which no military service can be demanded, decide on the necessary exemptions from such service, and establish due processes to ensure that their laws in this regard will not be disobeyed. None of these rules, however, can be regarded as absolute. For a rule of this nature to be absolute, one would need the enemy's consent, since the

134. Victor Riqueti, marquis de Mirabeau, *L'ami des hommes . . . , op. cit.;* in the places indicated by Constant, one finds the idea that wars do not particularly cut down populations, but are especially fatal on account of the physical damage they entail.

robustness of the defense must always be proportionate to the violence of the aggression. One can never therefore affirm that any citizen or class whatsoever will not be obliged to contribute to that defense, since one can never affirm that the contribution of everyone will not be required. What has brought into people's minds the idea of absolute and irrevocable dispensation or exemptions is that governments have often taken their defensive measures hugely beyond what was necessary, because they had the ulterior motive of turning them into means of attack. So individuals, unable to put limits on the warlike disposition of their governors, have sought at least to protect themselves from some of the consequences of this mania, by supposing that there could be between them and the government certain undertakings in virtue of which it would forgo using them in war. Governments for their part have encouraged this idea, seeing in this never more than very limited renunciation the authorization for them to deploy, as their fancy took them, all those not covered by it. In reality, however, an absolute dispensation is an absurd thing. It is to promise a man that he will be exempt from defending his country, that is, from defending himself, if an enemy comes to attack it. Governments have very clearly sensed this absurdity. They have taken advantage of it in order to say to those without absolute dispensation that they could not refuse to participate in any venture, however faraway or pointless. When the danger came close to their borders, however, they knew very well to tell these bearers of so-called irrevocable dispensations that it was part of their duty as well as in their interest to fight. Doubtless the application of this principle varies according to the extent and circumstances of a country. [595] In a very large realm, it is almost impossible that all the citizens should ever be reduced to taking up arms. The principle exists notwithstanding that, however. In this way the state of the modern world restrains or modifies this principle. The need to fight scarcely bears on any save the group particularly dedicated for more or less of the time to military service. The dwellers in towns, the artisans, the bourgeois, the farmers in the countryside, in a word, all those not formally enrolled, are not held to any resistance toward the enemy.

Book XIV: On Government Action on Enlightenment

Chapter 3: On Government in Support of Truth

Notes

1. *for finding it.* The claim governments make for the control of public intellectual life becomes supremely ridiculous under representative institutions, where opinions, being publicly discussed, come deprived of all mystique. No opinion in this case can be imposed with that fearsome solemnity, born of the union of force and mystery, which accompanied the promulgation of the Zend-Avesta[135] and the Koran. "It is far from being the case," says Bentham,[136] "that as much intellect, careful reckoning, and prudence have been employed to defend society as to attack it or to prevent crimes rather than commit them." What Bentham says springs from the fact that individuals are always more reflective and adroit than governments. It is an error to assume a huge gulf between those who dictate the laws and those who receive them. Their respective degrees of enlightenment are always in a certain ratio, and they do not diverge. Nature grants no privileges to any individual. No one gets far ahead of his time and place, and those who do are perhaps the least proper to dominate them.

2. *of any government whatever.* Political despotism, whether it follows or violates the rules of justice, is, [596] says Aristotle, the overthrow of all law.[137] I will likewise say that the influence of government on thought, whether in the particular circumstances it is exercised in a manner consistent with truth and reason, or contrary to them, is nevertheless in principle the overthrow of all reason and truth. One cannot put the truth to use if one does not know whence it comes, and how and by what chain of reasoning it derives. Dialogues sur le commerce des blés, 162.[138]

3. *belittled our own judgment.* He who, to uphold the authority of an opinion, uses force rather than reasoning may have pure intentions but really causes the greatest of evils. "To summon up in defense of the truth any help other than the facts is

135. [The Zend-Avesta are the sacred writings of the Parsees, usually attributed to Zoroaster. Translator's note]

136. Hofmann has not been able to locate this remark by Bentham.

137. Perhaps Constant is referring to *Politics,* I. III. 4: "Certain people think there is a science, that of the power of the master, and that it is the same for the head of the family, the master, the statesman and the king, as we said at the beginning. For others the denomination of master is against nature: it is only in virtue of the law that one is a slave and the other free; in nature there is no difference; consequently such authority is not just, since it is violence." Aristotle, *Politique,* translated by Jean Aubonnet, Paris, Les Belles Lettres, 1960, t. I, pp. 16–17.

138. Ferdinando Galiani, *op. cit.,* p. 162: "A truth that pure chance brings to birth like a mushroom in a meadow is no good for anything. We do not know how to use it if we do not know where it comes from, how and by what chain of reasoning it derives. A truth outside its intellectual ancestry is as harmful as error."

the most foolish of errors. He who accepts the truest proposition under the influence of government is not accepting a truth but a lie. He does not understand the proposition, for to understand it would be to grasp the force of the argument which accompanies it, the meaning of all its terms, and their respective compatibility. What he is accepting is what is convenient for submission to usurpation and injustice." Godwin, Political Justice.[139]

Additions

The history of the introduction of Greek philosophy in Rome is a remarkable example of the impotence of government [597] either against truth or error. There was much truth but also error in the philosophy brought to the Romans by the Athenian embassy.[140] On the one hand, the progress of enlightenment had driven the Greek philosophers into rejecting absurd fables, to lifting themselves up to more refined religious notions, to separating morality from vulgar polytheism and placing its principles and its security in the heart and reasoning of man. On the other hand, in the schools of several philosophers, the abuse of a subtle dialectic had unsettled the natural and incontestable principles of justice, submitted everything to interest groups, and in this way sapped the dynamic of all action and stripped virtue itself of what is most noble and pure in it. First of all, the Senate took up Greek philosophy en bloc, an initial mistake which the government could not avoid committing, since it is part neither of its business nor its power to devote itself to the in-depth analysis of any viewpoint whose surface features are all it can ever grasp. The Senate, having taken philosophy en bloc, suffered more for ill than good. This was bound to be so. The sophistry of Carneades, which, glorifying a contemptible flair for impartially attacking directly opposite opinions, spoke in public, sometimes for, sometimes against, justice, should have inspired very critical safeguards against this hitherto unknown intellection. As a result, the Senate banned all Greek philosophy, a second and doubly unfortunate mistake. For in the first place, the Senate was banning, on appearances it had misunderstood, the thing which alone, at a time of moral corruption, could call Romans back to the love of freedom, truth, and virtue. Cato, who decided on the ban on Greek philosophy, did not know that a century after him, this same philosophy, better studied and understood, would be the sole refuge of his grandson against the treasons of fortune and the haughty clemency of Caesar. In the second place, the stern measures taken by the Senate against Greek philosophy served only to prepare for it a triumph whose very delaying made it all the more complete. The representatives from Athens were sent back precipitately to their country. Stern edicts against all foreign doctrines were frequently

139. William Godwin, *Enquiry Concerning Political Justice . . . , op. cit.* (1793 edition), t. II, pp. 551–552.

140. [This was a temporary and not a permanent embassy, a three-man visit in 153 B.C., including Carneades, the head of the Academy founded in Athens by Plato. Carneades outraged Roman opinion by delivering two speeches on successive days, for and against justice. Translator's note]

renewed. Pointless efforts! The impetus had been triggered. It could not be stopped by government means.

Now let us suppose that the Senate of Rome had intervened neither for nor against Greek philosophy. The enlightened men of this capital of the world would have examined the new [598] doctrine impartially. They would have separated the truths it contained from the sophisms which had been introduced by means of these truths. It was, to be sure, not difficult to show that the arguments of Carneades against justice were only wretched quibbles. It was not difficult to reawaken in the heart of Roman youth the indelible feelings which are in the heart of all men, and to raise the indignation of these still youthful minds against an exposition which, consisting entirely in equivocation and chicanery, ought by the simplest analysis soon to find itself covered with ridicule and scorn. This analysis, however, could not be the work of government, which ought only to render it possible by leaving discussion free. For discussion, when it is banned, takes place nonetheless, but imperfectly, with confusion, intense emotion, resentment, and violence. Some would like to replace this discussion by edicts and soldiers. These means are convenient and seem sure. They have the air of bringing everything together, ease, brevity, dignity. They have only one fault: they never work. The young Romans kept all the more obstinately in their memory the discourses of the Sophists, whose persons it seemed to them had been unjustly driven out. They regarded the dialectic of Carneades, less as an opinion needing examination than as a good in need of defense, since they were threatened with having it snatched from them. The study of Greek philosophy was no longer a matter of simple speculation, but of what seemed far more precious still, at a stage of life when the mind is endowed with all the forces of resistance, a matter of triumph over government. The enlightened men of riper age, reduced to choosing between the abandonment of all philosophical study or disobedience to the government, were forced to the latter course by the enjoyment of letters, a passion which grows every day because its enjoyment is of itself. The former followed philosophy into its Athenian exile; the latter sent their children there. And philosophy, returning later from its banishment, had all the more influence, in that it arrived from afar and had been acquired with more difficulty.

The Aristotelian metaphysics was anathematized by this fearsome power, which made passions and thoughts and sovereigns and subjects bend under its yoke. It was against the ashes of a philosopher dead for twenty centuries that the Council of Paris, under Philip the Fair, directed its thunderbolts, and this dumb dust emerged victorious from the combat. The metaphysics of the preceptor of Alexander was more than ever adopted in the schools; it became the object of a religious veneration. It had its apostles, its martyrs, its missionaries, and the theologians themselves bent the dogmas of Christianity, in order to reconcile them with the maxims [599] of the peripatetics, so irresistible is public opinion in its progressive advance, and so far is power, civil, religious, and political, forced in spite of itself to follow that advance, happy in order to save appearances, to sanction what it wanted to forbid, and to put itself at the head of the movement it had initially claimed to be stopping.

The Interim of Charles V is a memorable example of the ideas governments contrive for themselves as regards their authority on public opinion. The Interim, as we know, was an order to believe provisionally such and such dogmas, until it was decided which dogmas one should believe. It is an idea which can be conceived by governments only in a state of drunkenness, that of telling man to believe as true for a while that which one announces can be declared false later.

Chapter 4: On Government Protection of Enlightenment

Notes

1. *in the widest sense of that expression.* Human faculties can be divided into two classes, those whose purpose is to satisfy needs or to procure present enjoyment, and those which lead to future improvement. Agriculture, commerce, the exact and natural sciences must be placed in the first class; the second takes in morality, the knowledge of earlier opinions and facts, everything which tends to establish relations between us and the past generations or to prepare such relations between us and the generations to follow. We can call the first faculties work faculties, the second intellectual faculties.

2. *almost all encourage them.* We have seen men who cultivated the sciences, indifferent to the situation of their fellow citizens and their country, continuing their studies with the same composure in the midst of the most bloody proscriptions and under the most degrading despotism, and indiscriminately permitting diverse tyrannies to make use of their discoveries or to take pride in their success. Considered from this point of view, the arts and sciences are truly only a kind of work of a more difficult nature, of a more extensive use than that of the manufacturer and artisan, but nevertheless separated from the great purpose of, [600] and no less foreign to, what good minds understand particularly by philosophy. Doubtless, even then scientists serve philosophy by their results, but we cannot attribute to those who devote themselves in this way any merit. It occurs in spite of them or without their knowing. Insofar as there is any within them, they make science into a vulgar trade, which provides only nourishment for curiosity and an instrument for government, of whatever kind it may be. Once it gets involved in protecting them, power tends to give them their direction.

3. *the agreed sphere.* The hope of favors from government leads men committed to science to choose compliantly the subject of their research according to the fantasy of the powers of the moment. They deny themselves the leisure they need. They no longer believe themselves accountable for their own time, to themselves, to the public, to posterity, but to their patrons and protectors. They hasten to publish conjectures which are still uncertain, as though they were definitive findings; they put forward as discovery that which is not such, or which is worse still, they recoil before the truths to which the sequence of reasoning and experiment leads them, if these truths get too close to certain opinions which are in disfavor. All their faculties are vitiated by the intrusion of motives foreign to the nature of their study and to the love of what is true and to freedom of thought.

4. *persecution is the more valuable.* How much brilliance persecution promotes. Socrates, before falling victim to the anger of the Athenians, was so obscure that when Aristophanes cast him in the open-air theater in The Clouds, delegates of the allied towns, who were at the opening performance, went home very disgruntled that they had been occupied for such a long time with the spectacle of a man called Socrates, in whom they took no interest. Elien, Histoires Diverses, II, 13.[141]

Additions

Governments which claim to favor enlightenment fasten haphazardly on the viewpoints which they protect. Sometimes, by charlatanry or gracious condescension, they submit themselves to a vain show of discussion; but to them reasoning is just superfluous politesse. Their mulishness guarantees them the obedience of all who surround them. Look at Frederick the Great disputing with the philosophers, Frederick the Great, of all men the most fit to relinquish power. Intellection constitutes his avant-garde; but you are aware, behind it, of the force, almost shameful, of his complacency, and of the despotism which sees itself as infallibly right.

[601] No one wants the influence of enlightenment more than I; but it is precisely because I want it, because I prefer it to any other sort of approach, that I do not want a distorted version. It is in order to conserve in all its vigor the domination of the whole of the educated class that I reject, with revulsion, its subordination to a small section of itself, often the less enlightened part. I would hope to prevent the free, gradual, and peaceful activity of all from being slowed down, and even halted, by privileges granted to the few.

To listen to the writers on government policy for education, one would think that we have only to tear open a veil, to make a long-concealed light shine.

The Athenians had a tribunal for assessing plays. Never did any tribunal pronounce more absurd judgments. This was the tribunal which crowned the tragedies of Dionysius the Elder, who had been accused of letting himself be suborned. De Pauw, Recherches sur les Grecs, I, 145, 184–187.[142] Elien, Histoires Diverses, II, 8.[143] Diodore de Sicile, XVII. Quintilian.[144]

There are two parts to the existence of man in society, the one he holds in common, which he makes dependent on other people, and the other, which he keeps private and independent. I call the first social existence, the second, individual existence. Man has obviously more means for perfecting his individual existence than his social existence. For he is obliged to adjust the latter to the faculties of the majority of his fellows, and cannot thus go beyond the common ground, whereas

141. *Histoires diverses d'Elien,* translated from the Greek with commentary, Paris, Moutard, 1772, p. 60.

142. Hofmann says that the first page (p. 145) of Cornelius de Pauw cited carries no reference to the judgment of theatrical pieces.

143. *Histoires diverses d'Elien, op. cit.,* p. 49.

144. Hofmann was unable to locate the references to theatrical judgments in Diodorus Siculus or Quintilian.

he is free to take his individual existence to whatever degree of improvement his faculties allow him. The result is what we have said more than once, that when it is necessary to submit the individual to society, society's way of thinking, that is to say, the common way of thinking, however imperfect it may be, must prevail sovereignly. In all other cases, however, individual ways of thinking must stay free. It is not that individual abilities cannot come together to act with more force or perseverance. It is necessary, though, that they come together freely, that they are not forced to mingle and place themselves by contract on a common basis. Any time [602] they come together, there is on both sides some curtailment of faculties. Any transaction between individual minds to form a collective one takes place at the expense of the more perfect ones.

Chapter 5: On the Upholding of Morality

Notes

1. *attributed to it.* The government by its wrong measures or its so-called promotion of morality does as much harm to morality as to freedom. It substitutes for subtle motives and the instinct for good, which drive our decent actions, motives which deprive these actions of any morality or merit, just as in the case of opinions, it substitutes for the chain of reasoning which should lead us to the truth by way of conviction, reasons which, not belonging to rational argument or to evidence, lead us to believe that the truth has all the disadvantages of error. For the perfection of the species it perverts individuals, just as for the happiness of the species it oppresses them.

Additions

See Mirabeau, *The Friend of Men.* On the prerogative of the sovereign on the affections, I, 9. On the efforts of governments to lead men to frugality by honor and by example, p. 22.

In China the law has sought to regulate everything. In the event, however, it has regulated only manners. It has not regulated moral behavior. The people there are overwhelmed with constraints and lost in corruption.

Morality, like sentiment, like affection, belongs uniquely to individual human resilience. The individual pronounces according to a thousand nuances, a thousand ramifications, a thousand subtleties which it is impossible to determine precisely and therefore to submit to collective authority. The true judge of morality is the heart of man, and the executor of its judgments is opinion, free and hence individual opinion, separated from government and in no way distorted by its association with power. There is an important distinction which must not be misunderstood. Since most actions opposed to morality also upset public order, society must repress these actions. This is not, however, because of their intrinsic merit or demerit. It is because they are contrary to the purpose of the public security for which political government was instituted. We must be wary of confusing two absolutely different things, the aversion which an action invokes in the individual being insofar as it is immoral, and the severity which the political body [603] exercises against that action insofar as it is perturbative. When an immoral action is at the same time contrary to social order, it should be envisaged in two ways: as immoral such that public opinion stigmatizes it; as contrary to order such that government represses it. These are two different tribunals whose competences are, and must forever remain, distinct. They do so remain; for we see every day force being exercised and public opinion refusing to ratify its judgments. The edict on duels, says M. Ferrand, gave new life to the viewpoint it was intended to destroy, IV, 333.[145] This distinction, however, must still be recognized in theory, so that it can never be obscured in practice. If we confused these two things, we would give to the collective body a necessarily boundless jurisdiction over moral life, since for all the issues on which the collective body pronounces, there exists no higher body which can quash its decisions. Because we have not sanctified this distinction in a sufficiently formal way, there has come about some kind of notion of a liaison between morality and the collective authority, a liaison which, being purely artificial and arbitrary, is not amenable to definition and renders morality, which is at once the holiest of individual properties and the most unchangeable rule of this universe, a protean thing, modifiable by government, at the mercy of institutions, and able to vary in each country, in each century, under each government.

Coercive laws, which under various penalties would enforce actions commanded by morality, such as gratitude, would have this bad effect, that they would substitute motives of fear for natural ones.

When government interferes only to maintain justice, dangerous feelings moderate and sociable ones are developed. From the single principle of equality flow all the forms of improvement. Once the rights of all are guaranteed, that is to say, once individuals are prevented from using violence against each other, the result is that the sole means of happiness is the exercise of virtue. If governments would content themselves with guaranteeing the rights of everybody, riches would no longer be anything save means of physical enjoyment and not of oppression, privilege, or superiority over other men. Now, physical pleasures being necessarily very limited, the rich would soon wish to draw from their opulence another advantage. They would use it to gain the affection of their fellows, since this opulence would no longer [604] enable them to dominate the latter. This use of wealth would have led to all the social virtues without the intervention of government. It is the same with all those questions over which governments arrogate to themselves a moral influence.

Bentham, I, 101, gives a very good example of the bad effects of intervention by government, aimed at repressing certain vices.[146]

145. Antoine Ferrand, *op. cit.*, (2e éd. of 1803) t. I, p. 333.

146. The example Bentham chose is drunkenness and fornication. He concludes by saying: "Instead of having suppressed a vice, the law will have sown some new and more dangerous ones."

Chapter 6: On the Contribution of Government to Education

Notes

1. *a body of doctrine.* From the fact that an idea is useful as an individual one, one should not always conclude that it would be equally so were it to be established as a dominant or collective one. Mirabeau said: there exist no national truths.[147] I say: there exist no governmental truths. Thought in its nature is one and individual. It is impossible to make a collective being of it. It can be tortured, choked, or killed. But its nature does not change.

2. *active and independent.* It is necessary to arrange as far as possible that the teachers need a lot of pupils, that is to say, to distinguish themselves by their work and their knowledge. The only way of attaining this purpose is not to give them a salary sufficient for their ease, but only such that an accident, or illness, or some circumstance which took away their pupils from them for a while, would not reduce them to poverty. To wish to replace this dependence, which teachers must have on the public, by making them dependent on an alien authority, such as that of the government or some of its agents, is a bad measure in several respects. First, there are other ways of pleasing that authority than by zeal, activity, and knowledge. Secondly, that authority does not have the necessary enlightenment. It can be exercised capriciously and insolently, and it is in the nature of power that it often is exercised thus. . . . "Everything which obliges or commits a number of students to remain in a college or a university independently of the merit [605] or reputation of the masters," such as on the one hand the necessity of taking certain degrees, which can be conferred only in certain places, and on the other scholarships and aid granted to poor students, have the effect of lessening the zeal and reducing the need for knowledge on the part of the masters privileged thus under any arrangement whatever. . . .[148] What has happened in relation to government has happened rather generally in relation to education. Most public establishments have the appearance of having been set up not for the benefit of the scholars but for the convenience of the masters. Smith, V, I.[149]

3. *human knowledge.* All the fine establishments in America are private, the great hospital in Philadelphia, the reform school, the libraries, the canals, the bridges, the schools known as academies, the charitable pharmacies, the marine societies, the locks on the waterways, the high roads. Pictet, Tableau des Etats-Unis.[150]

147. Constant quotes (accurately) the comte rather than the marquis de Mirabeau; Hofmann could not find the sentence in question in the sizeable work of the famous orator.

148. Adam Smith, *op. cit.,* Livre V, Ch. 1, t. IV, p. 146.

149. Adam Smith, *op. cit.,* t. IV, p. 149, "The discipline of colleges and universities in general is not instituted for the advantage of the scholars, but for the interest, or to put it better, for the convenience, of the masters."

150. Charles Pictet de Rochemont, *op. cit.,* t. II, pp. 90–100.

Additions

"Morality must be learned everywhere and taught nowhere." Say, V, 8.[151]

Is a candidate required to prove himself? The proper thing to do is not to consult the professors, who are judges and partial, who must find everything which comes from their school good, and everything which does not come from it bad. . . . We have to determine the candidate's merit and not the place where he studied nor the time he studied there; since the demand that a certain course be taken in a designated place is to displace another course which could be a better one. To prescribe a certain course of study is to proscribe any other more expeditious possibility.[152]

It is impossible, people will say, for the government not to control educational establishments which it funds or where it pays the salaries. It is impossible [606] to separate instruction entirely from education. Instruction itself would suffer, since lacunae would necessarily result. Yes, but then the government must allow individuals the right to set up private schools and all parents the right to choose between government-managed education and education managed by private individuals.

Garnier, in his Notes on Smith,[153] shows very clearly that the government when it offers free education, other than of the elementary sort, deflects the manual workers of society in a detrimental and worthless way from their natural occupations. See also Smith's observations on the drawbacks of scholarships, I, 10.[154]

You can teach facts by rote, but reasoning never.

"The natural arrangement of education, leaving the choice, the manner, and the burden of education to the parents, can be compared to a series of experiences, whose purpose is the perfecting of the general intellect. Everything advances and develops through this emulation of individuals, through this difference between ideas and between minds, in a word, through the variety of individual stimuli. But if everything were thrown into a single mold, if teaching were to assume everywhere the character of legal government, errors would perpetuate themselves, and there would be no more progress." Bentham, II, 200–201.

151. Jean-Baptiste Say, *op. cit.,* t. II, p. 438.

152. Adam Smith, *op. cit.,* Livre V, Ch. 1, Art. 2, *De la dépense qu'exigent les institutions pour l'éducation de la jeunesse.* Constant does not cite or summarize, but refers to the whole body of this Article 2, t. IV, pp. 146 and following, especially.

153. Germain Garnier, *Notes du traducteur,* in: Adam Smith, *op. cit.,* t. V, pp. 1–10, Note I, entitled: *How far should government get involved in education?*

154. Adam Smith, *op. cit.,* t. I, p. 271.

Book XV: The Outcome of Preceding Discussion Relative to the Action of Government

Chapter 1: The Outcome of the Preceding Discussion

Notes

1. *less bad and more good.* Everything in nature has its disadvantages, but the institutions consistent with nature have the advantage that since nature is essentially conservative, it has ensured that these disadvantages will not be without remedy, whereas in institutions contrary to nature, [607] since the conserving force is not there, the disadvantages which they entail are often irreparable. Thus by requiring that each man be charged with looking after his own interests, nature has without doubt exposed the human race to two very great evils. Strong feeling and false reckoning are such that individuals often acquit themselves very badly in the task entrusted to them. If, however, fearful of the danger attaching to this natural arrangement, we have the idea of charging one man to watch over the interests of another, or of several others, what is the result of this artificial institution? First of all, the same disadvantages arise as from the natural institution, since the same passions, the same erroneous reckonings, can be found in the person who has been entrusted with interests which are not his own. The natural institution, however, carried its own remedy. Every man suffers from the errors he commits in his own affairs and does not delay in putting things right. The artificial institution, by contrast, is without remedy. The man who, against nature's wish, decides for another, does not suffer in the least from the errors he commits. They bear upon other people. They do not enlighten him at all; he does not put them right therefore. Moreover, what would be implied if he gained from it? A further risk. He whom you have deprived of the right of looking after his interests will perhaps resist the man you have put in his place, and both will find themselves the worse for it. On all occasions when that which is natural, that is to say just, that is to say conforming with equality (equality, justice, nature: it is the same thing), seems to you to entail disadvantages and you do not know their remedy, trust in experience, which will straightaway show them to you, unless you have brought, which happens almost always, something artificial to the natural institution, and then it is usually this addition which is creating the disadvantages or blocking the restorative power of action. Whenever an institution which is against nature is suggested to you and you do not see its disadvantageous side, it is only experience which you are lacking. The disadvantage exists and will soon develop.

2. *in the name of rendering it happy.* "It is absurd to reason on men's happiness other than in terms of their own desires and sensations. It is absurd to wish to demonstrate in a set of calculations that a man is fortunate, when he thinks himself unfortunate."[155]

155. Jeremy Bentham, *op. cit.,* t. II, p. 181.

Bentham's argument against slavery, but which applies to everything. Government has been defined as the institution aimed at creating the happiness of men. There is a great difference between guaranteeing the happiness individuals create for themselves, or create between themselves, and taking over their role in the construction of their happiness. It is almost always [608] by claiming to do it that governments cease to do so.

ADDITION

The ordinary goings-on of governments: they begin by doing harm. They notice this. Instead of stopping the harm they have done, by warding off the cause, and returning to a salutary inaction, they build up various types of counteractivities and produce, inadequately and painfully, through two opposing pressures, what would have existed naturally, but more completely and less painfully, from freedom alone.

Chapter 5: Further Thoughts on the Preceding Chapter

NOTES

1. *frequent relations between the diverse classes.* It is a disadvantage for any mode of election if the electors and the elected are separated. See Smith on the advantageous influence of popular election in giving rise to some consideration for the lower class of farmers.[156]

Chapter 6: On Ideas of Stability

NOTES

1. *disproportionate with the rest of things.* We find fault with innovators for making laws of opposite outlook to existing public opinion, and we are right. They prefer the future, or what they call the future, to the present, and they have no right to do this. The law, however, which perpetuates itself when it is no longer the [609] expression of national sentiment, makes a mistake of the same kind, with the sole difference that it is before the past which it wants the present to bow. Now, time plays no part in it. Past public opinion no longer exists; it cannot motivate laws. No more does future public opinion exist; perhaps it never will. It too cannot motivate laws. Present public opinion is the only one which really exists.

2. *And what would novelty have produced more unfortunate?* China is a precise example of a nation where everything has been rendered static. So our new political writers

156. Constant refers to the following passage: "One encouragement, however, which is far more important than all the rest, is that in England the peasant class enjoys all the security, independence, and regard which the law can procure for it." Adam Smith, *op. cit.*, Livre III, Ch. 4, t. II, p. 485. Nowhere else did Hofmann find any reference to the regard which comes with popular election. Elsewhere Smith has suggested that voting by shepherds is associated with social unrest. Livre V, Ch. 1, t. IV, pp. 239–240.

go into ecstasies about or on Chinese institutions, institutions which have had the result, however, of China having been constantly conquered by foreigners less numerous than the Chinese. To make the Chinese static it has been necessary to destroy in them the energy which would have served to defend them.

Addition

At the moment when certain institutions were established, since they were proportionate to the condition of morals and received opinions, or rather that they were the actual effect of these opinions and morals, they had a relative utility and goodness. These advantages have lessened to the extent that the human spirit and institutions have become modified. Governments often think they do great good by reestablishing institutions in what they call their purity. This purity, however, turns out to be precisely the thing most contrary to contemporary ideas and the most liable in consequence to do harm. From this difference between institutions which are static and ideas which are progressive, there results the bulk of the contradictions and false arguments of governments and writers. They see that in a certain period a certain institution was useful, and they imagine that if now it is harmful, this is because it has degenerated. It is precisely the opposite. The institution has stayed the same, but the ideas have changed and the cause of the evil to which you want to bring a solution or remedy is not in the degeneration of the former but in the imbalance between the two. Government connections with the law are a matter on which it is very important to come to some agreement. Two types of imperfections must be distinguished in the laws, one their opposition to morality, the other their imbalance with regard to current ideas. A law can be at variance with morality through the effect of ignorance and universal barbarism. This, then, is the misfortune of the age. A law can be at variance with morality through the effect of error or of the specific corruption of a government. Then it is the crime of the lawmaker. [610] Antiquity offers us an example of the first kind of imperfection, in the tolerance of ancient philosophers for slavery. Modern times supply us with examples of the second, in the unjust decrees which were enacted during our Revolution. In this latter case the evil is much more incalculable than in the former. The legislator puts himself not only in opposition to morality, but to public opinion. Not only does he outrage the former, but he oppresses the latter. He fights simultaneously against what ought to be the case and against what is. From this there follows an important truth. It is that no anterior example can legitimate an injustice. This injustice was excusable when the human spirit had not recognized it as such, only as an inevitable misfortune. With the enlightening of the human spirit, the excuse ceases and the government which prolongs or renews the injustice renders itself guilty of a double outrage.

The laws which bear the impress of general intellectual imperfection are in balance with the period for which they exist. More perfect laws would clash with ideas. According to this reckoning, the needs of the people not being the origin of their laws, and their authors acting spontaneously and fallibly, the people find themselves exposed to all the drawbacks attached to the imbalance of laws with ideas and to all those whose provenance may be in the mistakes of lawmakers.

Chapter 7: On Premature Ameliorations

Additions

At all times when improvements are the natural and real product of the general will, this is to say, of what are felt to be the needs of everybody, expressed through the freedom of the press, the sole faithful and independent interpreter of public opinion, these improvements have at least a relative worth. When, however, the government makes itself judge, it looks for that relative worth in its own ponderings, its own opinions, in its own enlightenment, and the improvements, which are supposed to be acquiring the highest degree of perfection possible, are sometimes contrary to the general wishes and not in line with current ideas, and sometimes contrary to the eternal and universal principles of morality. Governments which arrogate to themselves the right to improvement are, when they are corrupt, hypocrites, and even when they are well-intentioned, wholesale gamblers with the system, to whose multiform errors the people find themselves [611] constantly sacrificed. The laws which bear the impress of general intellectual imperfection are in harmony with the time for which they exist. More perfect laws would clash with the ideas.

There are improvements which, taken abstractly, are incontestable. As long as the nation does not want them, however, this is because it does not need them, and time alone, and free expression of individual opinion, through the press, can make it want them. Government must not even be accorded the right to promote these improvements. This would be to attribute to it a function which belongs only to enlightened individuals. Now, government cannot be composed of such individuals, and enlightened individuals, moreover, have useful power by way of public opinion, only because they do not possess formal power.

"Oh hammer-blow reformers, you are the most unfortunate of gardeners." Mirabeau, The Friend of Men, I, 78.

I often say we should respect the habits of peoples, yet at the same time I propose many things which seem contrary to these habits. It must be observed, however, that I propose only negative things. This is to say that I counsel governments not to exert their authority in favor of such and such a set of restrictions, which they believe in their interest to maintain. By no longer exerting their authority in this direction, they do not hurt existing practices at all. They permit each person to continue to do freely what formerly they commanded him to do. It can happen that for a long while the acquired habit may be the stronger. Bit by bit, however, if it is contrary to the real interest of individuals, they will free themselves from it, one after the other, and the good will be accomplished without any great shock. Imagine a herd whose owner had, for a long time and by misjudgment, kept it on arid, sterile soil, surrounding it with a fence. If to have it transported to a better pasture you have it taken out by force, by exciting the dogs against it and frightening it with shouts, you may well find that several of the beasts will be wounded hurling themselves outside and even that the fright may be so great that many scatter and get lost. Just take down the fence, however, and leave the flock in peace. It will stay some time on the land where it is used to pasturing; but bit by bit, it will spread out all around, and after some time and imperceptible movement it will arrive in the fertile meadow where you want to transport it.

People always give great praise to statesmen who work for the future. Is it truly necessary, however, is it really natural, that in the matter of government men work for the future, that is to say, for generations who do not exist yet [612] and of whose condition, ideas, dispositions, and circumstances one is in ignorance?

Charlemagne is always praised to us as a great legislator, and to prove it they tell us that his monarchy fell only when his laws fell. The talent of a legislator, however, would have lain in making laws which did not fall. The praises given to all these legislative talents are like those accorded to constitutions, by its being said that they would work perfectly if everyone were willing to obey them, as if the art of constitutions were not by definition to get oneself obeyed by everybody.

Greece owes the brilliance of her annals more to the progressive way in which she civilized herself than to any circumstances unique to her. Greeks were left by happy chance to the sure and slow movement of domestic civilization. The foreign colonies which came there carrying the seeds of some arts were not strong enough to conquer, nor refined enough to corrupt, nor informed enough to enlighten. The leaders of these colonies were ordinarily either criminals fleeing the punishment menacing them in their own country, or ambitious people driven out by enemy factions. Wandering at random, they were blown by the winds onto some unknown shore. They found there inhabitants who, constantly exposed to incursions by neighboring nations, and to seeing themselves carried off along with their beasts and wives, had conceived an invincible hatred against all foreigners. The newcomers were bound to add to this hatred by the violence necessary for their subsistence and for their safety. Thus the early days were spent in continual stress on both sides and reciprocal massacres. Established finally on a small territory, the new colonists found that all that surrounded them were numerous and untamed hordes, whom they could conquer but not subdue and to whose incursions they were frequently exposed. As to their original homeland, the emigrants could not, given the reasons which had forced them to abandon it, keep up any relationship with it. On the contrary, it often happened that their compatriots were their most mortal enemies. Thus it is easy to see that the civilization of Greece must not be attributed to the colonies which established themselves there. It was time alone which civilized the Greeks, and this slower way is also the best of all ways.

One can reduce the other ways to three, civilization by conquerors, civilization by the conquered, and last, civilization by tyrants. The Americans furnish us with an example of the first, the barbarians of the north and the Chinese with one of the second, and the Russians with a case of the third.

[613] When it is the conquerors who take on the education of the conquered, they begin by degrading their pupils. Their interest of the moment does not

demand that they make men of them, but slaves. It is therefore to form humble and hardworking slaves, deft and docile machines, that these teachers, with power to hand, strive successfully. It is only after eight or ten generations that the sad remains of the indigenous peoples, their community reduced to a hundredth part of the numbers of their ancestors, begin to mingle with their oppressors, and to civilize themselves imperfectly, through the imitation of their corrupted mores and through the adoption of their erroneous opinions.

When, on the contrary, subjugated peoples civilize their masters, they enervate them without softening them, and they degrade them without policing them. The vices of luxury come to join with the ferocity of barbarism, and from this mixture are born the most dire effects. In the history of these peoples, the rapine, the violence, the devastation which characterize the uncivilized man, are accompanied by the cowardice, the weakness, the shameful pleasures of man, corrupted by a long abuse of civilization.

Lastly, when a despot wants to police his slaves, he thinks he need only wish this. Accustomed to seeing them tremble and grovel at the least sign, he thinks they will enlighten themselves similarly. To hasten their progress, he conceives of no other expedients than those of tyranny. He believes that, in this way, he is preparing his peoples for enlightenment, freedom's very daughter. He wants his subjects to learn, think, and see only as he does, and he gets irritated equally by nostalgia for the old mores and by the censure of new institutions. What are the results of these mad efforts? Let us cast a glance on that vast empire whose rapid progress people often vaunt. We will see there the great, prizing above everything else servile imitation in the practices of their neighbors; the sciences in the hands of foreigners who, obscure in their own country, come to seek wealth and renown in a nation they despise; and the people reduced to a condition of slavery, with no inkling that they are supposed to be undergoing enlightenment.

Those who make law by means of the lash seem to me like chickens which, bored with sitting, break their eggs in order to make them hatch.

When you set up an institution without the popular consciousness being ready for it, this institution, however good it may be in principle, is not an organization, but a mechanism.

[614] "We do nothing better than what we do freely and by following our natural talents." The Spirit of the Laws, XIX, 5.

What we say about speculative functions, etc., in the Additions to Ch. 1, Book III, must be placed in this chapter.

Chapter 8: On a False Way of Reasoning

Additions

Diverse and almost constant causes of error. First, confusion of ideas. Secondly, the effect taken for the cause. Thirdly, negative effects advanced as proofs of positive assertions. Fourthly, interest placed on the commitment to the purpose, without examination of the means. Fifthly, *because of* instead of *despite.*

Book XVI: On Political Authority in the Ancient World

Chapter 2: The First Difference between the Social State of the Ancients and That of Modern Times

Notes

1. *within very narrow limits.* "The citizens," says Sismondi, IV, 370, "find consolation for the loss of their liberty in the acquisition or sharing of a large power. This compensation exists only in a State where the citizens are few in number and where consequently the chance of coming to supreme power is large enough or close enough to mitigate the daily sacrifice which each citizen makes of his rights to this power. Thus in the republics of Antiquity there was no civil liberty. The citizen had seen himself as a slave of the nation of which he was a part. He gave himself over entirely to the decisions of the sovereign, without challenging the legislator's right to control all his actions, to constrain his will in everything. On the other hand, however, he was himself in turn this sovereign and this legislator. He knew the value of his suffrage in a nation small enough that each citizen could be a power, and he felt that it was to himself as sovereign that as a subject he sacrificed his civil freedom.[157] One senses [615] how illusory such a compensation would be" in a country which counted millions of active citizens.[158]

Chapter 4: The Third Difference between the Ancients and the Moderns

Notes

1. *Ignorance of the compass.* "Men, not knowing the use of the compass, were scared of losing sight of the coast, and given the state of imperfection in the art of shipbuilding, they did not dare to abandon themselves to the impetuous waves of the ocean. To traverse the Pillars of Hercules, that is to say, to navigate beyond the Straits of Gibraltar, was for long regarded in Antiquity as the most daring and astonishing enterprise. The Phoenicians and the Carthaginians, the most skillful navigators and the most knowledgeable shipbuilders in these ancient times, did not even attempt this passage until very late, and they were for a long time the only people who dared do it." Smith, Wealth of Nations, I, 3.[159]

2. *his interests and his fate bound up.* "Modern nations which are complete and able to exist by themselves remain almost in the same condition when their governments are overthrown." Say, IV, Ch. 12.[160]

157. Jean-Charles-Léonard Sismondi, *Histoire des républiques italiennes du moyen-âge,* Paris, H. Nicolle, 1809, t. IV, p. 369.

158. *Ibid.,* p. 370.

159. Adam Smith, *op. cit.,* t. I, p. 42.

160. Jean-Baptiste Say, *op. cit.,* p. 264.

3. *They move their assets far away.* When a citizen found only savages outside his country, and thus only death or deprivation of all human society were the consequences of expatriation, the fatherland to which one owed life and all the goods which make it precious could demand many more sacrifices than today, when a citizen, leaving his country, finds everywhere almost the same mores, the same physical commodities, and in many respects the same moral ideas. When Cicero said: "Pro qua patria mori, et cui nos totos dedere et in qua nostra omnia ponere et quasi consecrare debemus,"[161] [616] it was the case that the fatherland contained then everything a man held dear, and that to lose his fatherland was to lose his wife, his children, his friends, all his affections, all his possessions. The time of patriotism has passed. To be able to demand sacrifices from us, the fatherland must be dear to us, and to be dear to us, it must not strip us of all that we love. Now, what do we love in our fatherland? Freedom, security, public safety, the ownership of our goods, the possibility of rest, activity, glory, and a host of rights of all kinds. The word "fatherland" brings into our imagination much more the coming together of all these enjoyments than the topographical idea of a particular country. If it is suggested to us that we sacrifice all these enjoyments to the fatherland, this is to suggest that we sacrifice to the fatherland, the fatherland itself. This is to want to make us dupes of words. This applies equally to society. There are only individuals in society. Society means all individuals. Now, to sacrifice the happiness of all individuals to society, that is to say, to all individuals, is that not a contradiction in terms?

4. *a stranger or an enemy.* Hatred of strangers among the ancients, in the midst of the greatest civilization. Nations, says the jurist Pomponius, Leg V O de captivis, with whom we have no friendship, no hospitality, no alliance, are not our enemies. However, if one thing which belongs to us falls into their power, they are its proprietors. Free men become their slaves, and they are in the same situation with respect to us.[162]

Additions

Among the ancients, individuals were often fed or drew their resources from the wealth of the public. Among the moderns, the wealth of the public is made up of the wealth of individuals.

The spoils of the vanquished and the ransoms of prisoners were the sole funds allocated by the Spartans to public needs.

161. Cicero, *De legibus*, II, 2, 5. [It is for the fatherland that we must die, to it we must wholly devote ourselves, in it we must place and consecrate, so to speak, everything which is ours. Translator's note]

162. Sextus Pomponius, *Ad Q. Mucium*, Liber XXXVII, *De captivis et de pos liminio.* The title means, "Concerning prisoners of war and the right to reclaim their former status." The text runs: "For if we have neither friendship nor mutual hospitality nor a treaty made for the purpose of friendship with some nation, the latter are, to be sure, not at war with us, but that which comes to them from our property becomes theirs, and a free man of ours, taken prisoner by them, becomes their slave too; and it is the same if something comes to us from them." Otto Lenel, *Palingenesis iuris civilis*, Leipzig, 1889, t. II, col. 77.

[617] "It is in following absurd ideas drawn from the mores of the Romans, that Valerius Maximus and Juvenal spoke of Demosthenes as if he had been the son of a blacksmith, who lived only by the labor of his hands. On the contrary, this was a most illustrious citizen and most distinguished by his wealth."[163] His father had possessed two manufacturing plants, where he worked fifty-two slaves. Demosthenes in his first address against his tutor Aphobes. The noblest families of Attica had factories themselves. Pauw, Philosophical Dissertations on the Greeks, I, 68.[164]

Montesquieu remarks in The Spirit of the Laws, XX, 2, that commerce unites nations but does not similarly unite individuals,[165] from which it results that nations being united, they mingle, that is to say that there is no patriotism, and the individuals not being united, they are no longer anything but traders, that is to say, they are no longer citizens.

The spirit of the ancients was so uncommercial that Aristotle numbered brigandage among the means of acquisition.

"Today lands are discovered by sea voyages. In former times, seas were discovered by land voyages." Montesquieu, The Spirit of the Laws, XXI, 9.

Chapter 7: The Result of These Differences between the Ancients and the Moderns

Notes

1. *are intolerable.* Even when the spirit of the age did not incline toward civil liberty, the size of societies would make that freedom necessary. Laws on mores, celibacy, and idleness are impossible in a large state, and it would be vexing beyond measure to carry them out, if they were tried.

[618] 2. *as the guarantee of the latter.* It would be less absurd today to want to turn slaves into Spartans than to create Spartans by means of freedom. In former times, where there was freedom, people bore privation; today, everywhere there are privations, one would need slavery to get people to resign themselves to these. The people who most value the good things life has to offer, including its physical pleasures, are at the same time the only free people in Europe. Among the ancients, the enlightened class placed more importance on mores than on political freedom and the common people more importance on political freedom than on individual freedom. With us it is only, on the one hand, thinkers and, on the other, the common folk who place importance on political freedom. Say why.

163. Cornelius de Pauw, *op. cit.,* t. I, p. 68.

164. *Ibid.,* pp. 67–68. Constant is summarizing, rather than citing.

165. Here is what Montesquieu says in the indicated place: "But if the spirit of commerce unites the nations, it does not unite individuals in the same way. We see that in the countries which are driven only by the spirit of commerce, there is traffic in all human actions and all the moral virtues: the littlest things, those that humanity demands, are made and exchanged there for money."

Additions

Among the ancients the function of the citizen prosecutor was honorable. All citizens took this function upon themselves and sought to distinguish themselves in the accusation and pursuit of guilty people. With us the function of the prosecutor is odious. A man would be dishonored if he took on the function today without an official appointment. That is to say that among the ancients, public interest went before individual safety and freedom, while with us, individual safety and freedom go before the public interest.

Chapter 8: Modern Imitators of the Republics of Antiquity

Notes

1. *After Rousseau.* In his treatise on the government of Poland, J.-J. Rousseau brings out very shrewdly the obstacles which confront the introduction of new mores and habits in a nation and even the danger of starting up a struggle against these mores and habits.[166] Unfortunately, [619] only his absolute principles have been taken up, his Spartan fanaticism, everything which was unworkable and tyrannical in his theories, and in this way, his most enthusiastic supporters and admirers, fixing on only what was defective about him, have managed to make him of all our writers the most fertile in false notions, in vague principles, and the one most dangerous for freedom.

2. *institutions into habits.* In enlightened times, observes Mr. Gibbon in his Miscellaneous Works,[167] men rarely run the risk of establishing customs recommendable only by their purpose and usefulness. The people who respectfully follow the wisdom of their ancestors, will despise that of their contemporaries and consider such institutions only from the point of view which would give rise to ridicule. For an institution to be efficacious, its author must be God or time. It could well be with institutions as with ghosts. No one has seen one, but everybody has among his ancestors someone who has seen one.

166. Jean-Jacques Rousseau, *Considérations sur le gouvernement de Pologne et sur sa réformation projetée,* published for the first time in the *Collection complète des oeuvres de Jean-Jacques Rousseau, citoyen de Genève,* Geneva, 1782, t. I, pp. 418–539. Constant is probably referring to this passage called *Application:* "But a great nation which has never mingled with its neighbors must because of this have many mores which are singular to it and which perhaps are degraded day by day by the general momentum in Europe for adopting the tastes and mores of the French. The ancient usages should be maintained and reestablished and suitable ones be introduced, which are proper to the Poles. These usages, if they were neutral or even bad in certain respects, provided they were not essentially so, will always have the advantage of enhancing the affection of the Poles for their country and of giving them a natural repugnance for mingling with strangers. I regard as good fortune their having the appearance of individuality. Guard this advantage with care." In Jean-Jacques Rousseau, *Oeuvres complètes, éd. cit.,* t. III, p. 962.

167. Hofmann could not find this passage in Gibbon's *Miscellaneous Works.*

3. *shame diminishes and honor withers.* Bentham has included in his penal code[168] offenses against honor and reparations for these offenses. He has brought to this enumeration his characteristic penetration. His actual chapter on this subject, however, is a proof of the impossibility of doing anything by law which belongs solely to the domain of public opinion. He wants the man who thinks himself insulted to be able to force the alleged offender to declare that he had no intention of being scornful of him. The question, however, cannot be resolved before a court because the very supposition is humiliating. The response would not be, as Bentham supposes, a simple disclaimer, even in the case in which the intention to insult had not existed in the first place, because the disclaimer, being open to the charge of duress, is such that any man of honor would refuse it. Finally, the reparation laid down by the court could well be shameful for the defendant, but it would in no sense be honorable for the plaintiff. Public opinion must be left to itself with its drawbacks and advantages.

[620] ADDITIONS

The ancients, having less need of individual freedom than we, attached the highest importance to laws about social mores. We give a comparable importance to constitutional mechanisms.

Among the Greeks and the Romans, the poor and the rich really formed two classes, of which one was composed of creditors, the other of debtors, and the inadequacy of the means of trade and production prevented these two classes from mixing. This meant that among the ancients insurrections were much more genuine than in our case. Now, that which is true is in all cases less violent than that which is artificial. An artificial insurrection, independently of the violence of an insurrection, has the further violence necessary to produce it; and moreover, calculation is much more immoral than nature. I have seen during the Revolution men who had organized artificial insurrections, suggesting massacres, to give the insurrection, they said, a popular or national air. When I see the blind confidence which many moderns have accorded the assertions of the ancients on the power of institutions and the series of conclusions they draw from some fact often reported as a vague rumor or contained without explanation in a single line, I am reminded of the traveler who, having seen an Arab prince who, having nothing better to do, whittled a stick with his knife, concluded from this that the thing was a fundamental and very wise institution of this State, namely that all men, including princes, learned a trade.

The ancients accepted their institutions as improvements. We struggle against ours as if they were imposed by conquest.

168. Jeremy Bentham, *op. cit.*, t. II, pp. 335–351, in Ch. 14 *De la satisfaction honoraire,* and pp. 352–358, in Ch. 15 *Remèdes aux délits contre l'honneur.*

Book XVII: On the True Principles of Freedom

Chapter 1: On the Inviolability of the True Principles of Freedom

Notes

1. *a singular error.* "There has been a confusion," says Montesquieu, XI, 2, "between the power of the people and the freedom of the people." By an error of the same kind, Bentham regards as indirect means of government many things which are only the absence of all government intervention. He observes, for [621] example, III, 7, that the rivalry between the Catholic and Protestant churches has contributed a lot to the reform of papal abuses; that free competition is the best way of lowering either the prices of goods or the rate of interest. It is, however, a complete abuse of vocabulary to call these things indirect means of government.

Chapter 3: Final Thoughts on Civil Freedom and Political Freedom

Notes

1. *is something superfluous.* In everything relating to man, we have to distinguish two things, the purpose and the means. In human societies, happiness is the purpose and security the means. Security is therefore not a good in itself. On the contrary, it has a number of drawbacks; but since it is the necessary means for achieving the purpose, we have to resign ourselves to its drawbacks. In private affairs, where the formalities we observe entail costs, delays, discussions, as well as in public affairs, where the authorization accorded to government restrains individual freedom, it would assuredly be more convenient to put our trust in the good faith and wisdom of each person. Public security is necessary, however, because the adverse results even of the perversity of a small number would be greater for all than that which results from formal prescriptions and agreed restrictions. Public security, though it is not an absolute good, is therefore a relative good, since it is of greater value than the evil it prevents. Two consequences flow from this. First, the security having to be complete and certain, in order to render it such we have to make all the indispensable sacrifices, but things must not go beyond that; since if it is right to endure necessary inconveniences, it is folly to add to them anything superfluous. Secondly, any system in which the disadvantages of security exceed the strict minimum is essentially vicious. Let us apply these principles to the political institution. We recognize its necessity, so we must accord it everything needed to make it secure. Everything it needs, I stress, but nothing that it does not need, such as what is demanded under various pretexts by the holders of various powers, ambitious delegates who never think their prerogatives sufficient either in intensity or extent.

2. *are scarcely necessary.* "In surrounding the sovereign with the necessity of being just, it will impose on the subject the obligation [622] to submit." Ferrand, I, 146.

3. *excesses will reach their peak.* The interest of a despot is never the same as that of his subjects. One single man clothed with despotic power has no means of governing according to his fantasy other than by brutalizing all those he governs. As long as we are not reduced to the level of simple machines, the possessor of power is threatened. Instruments reason. Agents have scruples. Those who have none pretend in order to raise their political price. Moreover, you cannot buy everybody. The despot is rich only from what he takes from his subjects. Now, those he buys want him to give them more than they had. Therefore to enrich some he must plunder others, either directly by taking their goods or indirectly by taxing them. The result of this is that, short of the brutalizing of everybody, there are always two classes under despotism who are not devoted to the government, the one which has been stripped of everything and is disgruntled, and that which without being plundered is not enriched. This one keeps its independence, and independence is as troublesome for despotism as disgruntlement.

4. *a brilliant reign,* during which France drained itself in continual wars, toward the end of which three million French people were persecuted, banished, treated with the most revolting barbarism, and after this reign, a long reign in which the most excessive corruption developed in which France lost her foreign reputation, in which the finances fell into irreparable disorder, in which all the elements of trouble, discontent, and overthrow accumulated to the point when the best-intentioned prince could not put them right, and then the most bloody of revolutions. Truly a fine outcome for the cruelties of Louis XI and Richelieu.

5. *the French monarchy was overthrown.* The following passage is curious to reread in the Mémoires of Louis XIV, when we reproach him with what happened seventy-four years after his death to his grandson. After having painted what he calls the wretchedness of kings who are not absolute,[169] he continues thus: "But I have spent too long on a reflection which will seem to you pointless or which can at most help you to recognize the wretchedness of our neighbors, since it applies all the time in the State where you are to reign after me. [623] You will find no authority which is not honored to hold its origin and character from you, no administrative body whose opinions dare to deviate from terms of respect, no company which does not believe itself obliged to put its principal greatness in the good of serving you, and its sole security in its humble submission." Mémoires, I, 62–63.[170] How difficult absolute monarchy is to maintain in a large State. Clovis established an absolute monarchy. Under his successors it divided and fragmented. The great lords became sovereign and Clovis's line ended by being deprived of a royal authority, already virtually nullified. Charlemagne reestablished it. It disappeared again under Louis the Debonair, and the feudal system, one of the most opposed to monarchy as we understand it, rose on its ruins. A new revolution put Hugues Capet on the throne, but royal authority did not revive. It did not reestablish itself positively until the reign of Louis XIII, and a hundred fifty years later the monarchy fell.

169. See Constant's Note J at the end of the Additions.

170. *Mémoires de Louis XIV, op. cit.,* t. I, pp. 62–63.

6. *Apologists for despotism.* Do you want to judge despotism in relation to the different classes? For educated men think of the death of Traseus[171] and Seneca, for the common folk think of the burning of Rome and the devastation of the provinces, for the emperors themselves, of the death of Nero and that of Vitellius.

ADDITIONS

It is not true that despotism protects us against anarchy. We think it does only because for a long time our Europe has not seen a real despotism. But let us turn our gaze on the Roman empire after Constantine. We find that the legions were constantly in revolt, with generals proclaiming themselves emperors and nineteen pretenders to the crown simultaneously raising the flag of rebellion. Without going back to ancient history, let us look at the sort of spectacle presented by the territories ruled by the sultan.

When a violent revolution overthrows a despotic government, moderate men and men of peace judge despotism more favorably, first, because present ills make us forget past ones; secondly, because in centralized states revolutions are sometimes caused by government weakness, and that weakness, although fatal in its consequences, nevertheless gives to the governed temporary rights which they come to regard [624] as the inherent advantages of absolute power while they are only the effects of its weakness and steps to its destruction.

If human wickedness is an argument against individual freedom, it is an even stronger one against despotism. The fact is, despotism is simply the freedom of the few against everybody else. Those governing have all the temptations and therefore all the vices of private men and power to boot.

A man can write good tragedies without being acquainted with the rules of dramatic art. If his tragedies are good, however, this is because he will have observed the rules without being aware of them. Similarly, a prince may make his people happy although in the constitution of the State there are no guarantees thereof. If this prince makes his people happy, however, it is because he conducts himself as if there were political guarantees in the constitution of the State. These examples prove the worthlessness neither of rules of art nor of political guarantees. They prove that one may act sometimes by instinct in ways consistent with these. From the very fact, however, that in acting thus one does well, it can be inferred that it would be better were these things known and established in advance. Political freedom is an art like all the others. Now, an art, as Laharpe puts it very well, Course in Literature, II, 252, is only the outcome of experience reduced to method. The purpose of this art is to spare those who follow us the whole road those who have preceded us followed, and which would have to be retrodden if we did not have guides.[172]

171. [Constant probably means Thrasea Paetus, stoic philosopher and senator, who was condemned by Nero in A.D. 66 and took his own life. Translator's note]

172. Jean-François Laharpe, *Lycée ou cours de littérature ancienne et moderne,* Paris, H. Agasse, an VII (1799), t. II, p. 252.

Chapter 4: Apologia for Despotism by Louis XIV

Additions

"If we wanted," says Louis XIV, I, 271, "to deprive ourselves of all things as soon as they might bring us any ill, we would soon be deprived, not only of everything which makes our greatness and our convenience, but also of everything which is most necessary to our subsistence. The foods which nature chooses for the nourishment of man serve sometimes to choke him. The most salutary remedies [625] are infinitely harmful when they are badly managed. The most prudent laws often bring to birth new abuses, and religion, which ought to be only the object of our profoundest reverence, is itself liable to suffer the most terrible profanities from the world, and yet there is no one who would dare to conclude from all this that it would be better to go without meat, cures, laws, and religion." Do not these arguments apply to freedom with as much force as to all these things?

Book XVIII: On the Duties of Individuals to Political Authority

Chapter 1: Difficulties with Regard to the Question of Resistance

Additions

Governments which have their origin in the national will, or what they name such, find themselves in an embarrassing situation with regard to resistance. If they declare that resistance is always a crime, they recognize that they have participated in this crime and have inherited its outcomes. If they affirm the legitimacy of resistance, they authorize it against their own acts, once they are unjust or illegal.

Chapter 2: On Obedience to the Law

Notes

1. *If the law created offenses.* Those who claim that it is the law alone that creates offenses enter a vicious circle on this question: why is it an offense to disobey the law?

2. *which he denies elsewhere.* When we find, says Bentham, I, 5,[173] in the list of offenses some neutral action, some neutral action, some innocent pleasure, we must not hesitate to transfer this alleged offense to the class of legitimate acts, to grant our pity to alleged criminals and reserve our indignation for the so-called virtuous who persecute them.

[626] 3. *retroactivity.* Most bad laws are made only to serve a purpose demanding a retroactive effect. Almost all the laws which passionate feelings and factions produce would be void if they were not retroactive.

4. *decorates with the name of law.* Laws like those which wanted to force the French to leave their parents and children, separated from their country by political opinions, to perish of poverty and hunger in distant climes, raised against themselves all honest and generous sentiment. These impious laws are always evaded while they are extant, and repudiated with horror at the first moment of calm and freedom.

5. *to a law he believes wicked.* Ambitious or greedy men who want to be executors of bad laws say that in accepting power their aim is only to do as much good as possible; this means that they are ready to do all the wickedness they are commanded to do.

Additions

The Law of Solon: each citizen will be allowed to cut off the life not only of a tyrant and his accomplices but even of a magistrate who maintains his office after

173. Jeremy Bentham, *op. cit.*, t. I, p. 5.

the destruction of democracy. Andocides, On Mysteries,[174] Travels of Anacharsis, Introduction, p. 120: a good law against instruments.[175]

"To say that there is nothing just nor unjust save what positive laws ordain or forbid is to say that before any circle was drawn the radii were not all equal." The Spirit of the Laws, I, 1.

Chapter 3: On Revolutions

Notes

1. *and directs these means.* "Nothing appears more surprising to those who consider human affairs with a philosophical eye than the ease with which the great number is governed by the small and the implicit submission with which men [627] subordinate their feelings and their passions to those of their leaders. When we seek out, however, by what means this miracle is effected, we find that, since strength is always on the side of the governed, the governors never have any support save public opinion. It is therefore on public opinion alone that all government rests, and this maxim extends to the most despotic and to the most military as well as to the most popular and the freest. The sultans of Egypt and the Roman emperors might well have been able to drive their unarmed subjects before them like brute beasts; but when it came to their Praetorians or their Mamelukes, they had to act according to their views and interests." Hume, Essays, IV, 27.[176] "Opinion is of two kinds, interested opinion, and opinion as to justice. The latter has always had much more influence than vested interest. This can easily be shown by the attachments all nations have to their ancient governments and even to the names which have received the sanction of Antiquity. Whatever unfavorable judgment we come to on the human race, it has always been profligate of its blood and its treasure, for what it thought was the maintenance of public justice. Probably at a first glance no proposition could seem more vitiated by the facts. Men, having joined a faction, violate shamelessly and remorselessly all the virtues of morality and justice in order to serve that faction; and yet, when a faction is securely grounded, people rest on the principles of law. It is then that men show the greatest perseverance and the greatest devotion to these principles." Ibid.[177]

Additions

When arbitrary governments oppress citizens, friends of freedom sometimes confuse the right of resistance with the right to mount a revolution. There is never-

174. Andocides, *Sur les mystères,* I, 96–98, in *Discours,* text edited and translated by Georges Dalmeyda, Paris, Les Belles Lettres, 1930, pp. 47–48.

175. Jean-Jacques Barthélémy, *Voyage du jeune Anacharsis en Grèce,* Paris, Venice, J. Storti, 1790, t. I, p. 120. [Presumably Constant means "instruments of justice." Translator's note]

176. David Hume, *Essays and Treatises on Several Subjects,* Basil, J.-J. Tourneisen, new ed. 1793, t. I., pp. 27–28. Constant's translation is very close to the original text.

177. *Ibid.,* pp. 28–29, *passim.*

theless a great difference, and this difference is very important. Resistance, properly called, tends simply to repulse oppression,[178] while the purpose of revolutions is to organize government under new forms. These two things are absolutely distinct. Resistance is a positive, individual, imprescriptible right which is subordinate only to considerations arising from utility, the chance of success, the danger of upset, and the comparison of the ill which it can entail with the one it wishes to prevent. To make a revolution, however, is never a right; it is a power with which one is accidentally cloaked. [628] The evils of revolutions establish nothing against the legitimacy of resistance; the legitimacy of resistance establishes nothing in favor of revolutions. It has to be said, though, that since resistance often leads to revolutions, this danger must form part of the reckoning of the oppressed and encourage them either to tolerate the evil they suffer or to do what they can so that the resistance they put up does not entail excessively violent shocks and fatal upheavals. Revolutions and resistance, by nature distinct, are subject to totally different rules. An isolated man, a minority, has the right to resist. At all times when individuals are oppressed, it matters not whether they are a majority or a minority in society. In their respect the guarantee has been violated. If we rejected this opinion as disruptive, we would fall first of all into all the pitfalls of giving the majority endless power, since if majority acceptance could legitimate the oppression of the minority, there is all the more reason the positive will of the majority could have this result. Secondly, to permit resistance only when most people are repressed would be, regardless of the injustice of these arrangements, in fact to forbid resistance in all cases. The trick of governments which oppress citizens is to keep them separated from each other and to make communications difficult and coming together dangerous. Then oppression by the majority can never be identified. In sum, the nature of political guarantee is such that it cannot be violated in the case even of one person without its being destroyed for everybody. In matters of despotism, one single victim represents the whole collectivity. I do not speak here only of right. When it comes to its execution, it is clear that we have to bring circumstances into account. The exercise of our most obvious prerogatives must be subordinated to considerations of utility. Ill-considered recourse to force, even against the most outrageous encroachment, is fatal and must therefore be condemned. The man who, threatened with an arbitrary arrest, stirred up his village, would be guilty not for resisting but for his wild enterprise and the ills it could entail. If a minority or even a single man, however, has the right to resist, no minority of any sort ever has the right to stage a revolution.

From the absence of this distinction a great confusion of ideas has resulted. When today some unfortunate persecuted person uses the means still available to him to protest against despotism or evade it, he is not seen as a man under attack defending himself, but as aggressively ambitious; and oppressed people who invoke the help of the law are regarded as factions which infringe it. As happens commonly,

178. See Constant's note K at the end of the Additions.

the two opposing groups [629] have seized on this confusion to take advantage of it. Oppressive governments have asked for nothing better than the depiction, as future usurpers, of those who resisted present usurpation; and those aspiring to tyranny have been quick to call themselves victims in order to legitimate their rebellions.

Resistance is legitimate anytime it is founded on justice, because justice is the same for everybody, for one person as for thirty million. A revolution is legitimate, however, just as it is useful, only when it is consistent with universal sentiment. This is because new institutions can be salutary and stable, in a word, free, only when they are desired by the whole society in which they are being introduced. The surest way for a government to gain the goodwill of public opinion is to leave it free. It is only ever tyranny which alienates the opinion of the majority; for the majority has nothing to gain from opposition to government. Therefore the less tyranny we have, the less risk will there be of the alienation of public opinion.

Chapter 4: The Duties of Enlightened Men during Revolutions

Notes

1. *Therefore there is always a duty to fulfill.* It is in persuading ourselves that it is useless to struggle against the violence of extraordinary situations, that we make them, indeed, irresistible. Each person says to himself: even if I fulfilled my duty, others would not fulfill theirs, and I would sacrifice myself fruitlessly. This reasoning results indeed in no one's doing what he should. If on the contrary each man said to himself: even if other people did not fulfill their duty, I wish to fulfill mine, it would turn out that everybody would do as he ought. We create the impossibility of the good by resigning ourselves to this impossibility.

2. *would bring it back down and it would collapse.* The public spirit is the fruit of time. It forms through a long sequence of acquired ideas, sensations experienced, successive modifications, which are independent of men and are transmitted and modified again from one generation to another. The public spirit of 1789 was the result, not only of the writings of the eighteenth century, but of what our fathers had suffered under Louis XIV, our ancestors under Louis XIII. The public spirit is the heritage of the experiences of the nation, which adds to this heritage, its experiences of every day. To say that the public spirit must be re-created is to say that we must take the place of time, and this [630] usurpation at least is beyond the usurpers' power. The assemblies and political clubs have exactly that pretension, wishing to replace with superficialities what they are lacking in depth. They put themselves in the place of the people to make them say what they do not say. They take upon themselves the question, the answer, and even the praise which it seems to them their own opinion merits. There is always a public spirit, that is to say, a public will. Men can never be indifferent to their own fate nor lose interest in their futures. When governments do the opposite of what the people want, however, the latter grow weary of expressing it, and since a nation cannot, even through terror, be forced to

tell itself lies, they say that the public spirit is asleep, holding themselves the while ready to choke it, if ever it should allow the suspicion that it is awake.

Additions

Enlightenment gets men to perceive a way forward from existing institutions; the disturbance revolutions cause either puts out the light or overreaches it.

The first device of the United Provinces after their uprising: a vessel without mast or sails, in the midst of the waves, with these words: *incertum quo fata ferant.*[179]

The French revolutionaries have wanted, like Medea, to rejuvenate the old man in a bath of blood and the old man got out of the bath, as that had to be so, a thousand times older than before.

A revolution interrupts all inquiry and abstract reflection, all those patient works of the mind to which the human race owes its progress. Such works require security; their needs embrace the future. How shall one commit oneself to them when nothing guarantees a peaceful philosopher a day of life, an hour of tranquillity? Enlightenment requires impartiality and detachment. How does one stay impartial amid stirred-up passions, disinterested when all interests are compromised?

Against what abuses are revolutions directed? Against the subservience of public opinion. Are not opinions a thousand times more subservient, however, during and long after a revolution? Is not every word, every gesture, every outpouring of friendship, every cry of unhappiness attributed with a fearful influence? Has there ever been a revolution in which the discussion of the prevailing viewpoint has been allowed? You complain about attempts by the government to dominate thought, and is not such domination the very stuff of revolutions? You intend to make men free, and your method is to influence [631] by fear! You inveigh against usurping governments, and you organize a government a thousand times more usurping in its principles and more terrible in its measures! Is slavery then a means of leading men to freedom? Is terror an education calculated to make them brave, independent, and magnanimous?

Revolutions make the power of the majority terrible; whereas in ordinary times the majority and the minority are day-to-day variable things, revolutions turn them, in a lasting way, into different parties of slaves and masters, oppressed and oppressors.

Popular factions treat public opinion with all the more contempt in that the leaders of these factions call themselves the people and therefore public opinion.

The wider the realm of education is, the less violent revolutions are. The more prejudices and vague notions subsist, the bitterer the struggle and the more doubtful success. A year of delay is a year gained. During this year, new truths can be

179. ["Unsure whither the fates are carrying us." Constant gives no attribution for the Latin, but it is in Virgil, *Aeneid,* III, 7. Virgil has described how Aeneas and his companions after the siege of Troy wander about and land on the coast of Africa, where Dido, the queen of Carthage, invites them all to dinner. Aeneas then narrates the earlier events to her, and in this passage a large band of survivors gather under his leadership, build ships, and set sail without knowing where they are going. Translator's note]

discovered or truths formerly known but still locked up in a small number of heads can be more completely clarified or more universally spread. A few more of the facts can win over a thousand opponents.

When truths which are still within the grasp of only a few people are introduced violently and excessively into political institutions which must rest on general agreement, many men who rightly find fault with this dangerous haste are inclined to carry over their disapproval onto the truths which are its purpose. This disposition is natural; but it is out of place and can become disastrous. It is always by a false reckoning that one devotes oneself to a bad cause, whatever the reason for this effort. We must start from the proclaimed truth even if it is inconvenient. When this truth is cast unprepared into a working politics which should comprise only recognized truths, we ought, rather than striving in vain to restrain it, since it does not compromise, to surround it instead as quickly as possible with the factual backing it has not yet acquired. The impatient and impetuous men who have arrived at this truth only by instinct do not know how to give it this factual backup. By condemning oneself to defending error, one discredits reason and moderation itself. These two very precious things feel the effect of being used to support principles which are not perfectly and rigorously true, and the element of false reasoning to which they are linked reflects on them and weakens them. Anyway, some enlightened men do not take this approach. There are some who cleave to the principles right through the turbulence and dangers. The elite [632] of the nation is divided. This very small minority finds itself split again. Equally respected names provide patronage to the two extreme parties, to the one which wants to retain the mistake as much as to the one which carries truth beyond limits. Disorder increases and is prolonged by the very fact that conscientious men are disunited on the means of repressing it.

There are times when all the harshnesses of freedom are of use to despotism.

Chapter 5: Continuation of the Same Subject

Notes

1. *in sybaritic voluptuousness.* Revolutions destroy the equilibrium between obligations and sacrifices. What is in settled times only a simple straightforward duty becomes a courageous effort, a heroic act of devotion. In a storm, which threatens with death anyone who does not grasp hold of a plank, a raging egotism seizes each person. Each unfortunate soul struggling against the waves is afraid that one of his fellow unfortunates, attaching himself to him, may drag him to the depths of the sea. Likewise, in the imminent dangers of political convulsions, men untie themselves from everything which formerly united them. They are frightened that a friendly hand may slow them down as it rests on them. They separate themselves off in order to defend themselves the more easily. Wealth becomes the sole means of independence, the cardinal happiness, the unique hope of safety. People flatter themselves that their wealth is appeasing tyranny or that they are disarming its agents. Prestige is no longer sought. There exists neither glory for the powerful nor interest for the victim. Wealth is precious when it comes to leaving a country or

when one fears a public crisis every day or a personal banishment. It is more sensible to ransom your life than to prove your innocence, to come to terms with the greed of your judges rather than convincing them at the level of justice. It is no longer a question of arguments but of motives, nor of truth, but of calculation. The absence of security detaches one at once from all sympathy for the sorrows of others and from all confidence in one's own existence. Tenderness is stoically repudiated; people hurl themselves into sybaritic voluptuousness.

Additions

The oath sworn by the inhabitants of one of the Philippines: this is true, as it is true that one man never kills another.

[633] Those who spoke of religious freedom were called fanatics. Those who spoke of persecutions were called philosophers. Lacretelle.

Political fanaticism struggles more over the cause than over the effect.

Let the friends of freedom never forget that if crime or persecution penetrate their army, it is freedom which will bear the judgment and, sooner or later, the innocent will bear the punishment of the guilty whom they thought were their allies.

Unhappiness consists less in the actual suffering which injustice causes its victims than in the contagious passions which it excites: vengeance, terror, foul lying, culpable expectation, shameful calculation. Injustice invokes these passions which hasten to her voice. They draft their cries of fury as legal decisions. They clothe their rage with abstract forms. Persecutors and persecuted, all of them thrash around hating each other, and suffering. He whom chance preserves from personal grief is diminished by the sight of the crime or consumed with indignation; and such is the condition of this nation whose general happiness was the sole concern of your vast conceits, and legitimated your outrages.

To have an opinion triumph, it is not enough to have it adopted blindly; it must be adopted in such a way that its very adoption turns upon itself. This is the case with fanaticism for freedom.

Suffering no longer figures in the reckoning of our discussion nor in our laws. At the time of the project for the deportation of the nobility,[180] no one pleaded the case as to the physical and moral pain with which this measure would strike down the proscribed caste. In the execution of the laws on conscription,[181] the unhappiness of old men losing at a stroke the last objects of their affections and the last resource of their wretched old age was treated with utter disdain; and even those who argued against the atrocious law of hostages[182] did not cite the suffering of the victims

180. This proposition was first made by Boulay de la Meurthe, 3 vendémiaire an VI (24 September 1797), after the coup d'Etat of 18 fructidor. See Georges Lefebvre, *La France sous le Directoire (1795–1799)*, Paris, Editions sociales, 1977, p. 453.

181. References to the mass levy proposed by Jourdan on 9 messidor an VII (27 June 1799). Compare *ibid.*, p. 673.

182. The law of hostages was adopted 22–24 messidor an VII (10–12 July 1799); see *ibid.*, p. 676.

except as a secondary consideration. Any interest in the adversaries seemed to the party men a treason. Pity seemed seditious and sympathy conspiratorial.

The blood which revolutions spill is not the worst evil they cause. An earthquake which engulfs a hundred thousand individuals at a stroke is appalling only because of the sorrow [634] of those who survive. When man perishes by the hand of man, however, death has very different and far more terrible effects. The depravity of murderers, the anguish of victims, the regret, the indignation, the rage of those who are robbed of the dearest objects of their affections, the resentments which pile up, the mistrust which spreads, the vengeance-seeking which erupts, the breaking of bonds, the punishments which call forth further punishments, such are the real misfortunes.

When it is an enraged people who are threatening the property and persons of the citizens, the latter can have recourse to the law, but when the law itself becomes the instrument of proscription, all is lost.

If you drag the people far from the moral order in order to achieve a purpose, how will you restore morality to the people, when the purpose is achieved?

Chapter 6: On the Duties of Enlightened Men after Violent Revolutions

Notes

1. *mediocre talents.* Thus Swift paints the Lilliputians for us, as they come running from all sides, surrounding Gulliver in their thousands as he sleeps on the ground, and taking advantage of his sleep to tie him up.

2. *all the excesses of degradation.* Certain men who reason soundly on a thousand questions do so badly on one particular and sometimes very important one. This disparity in their faculties and the way their logic suddenly abandons them thus are quite astonishing. The key to this unfortunate enigma is not in their intelligence but in their character. Their sophisms do not derive from errors but from a fact. Some circumstance has distorted their judgment, damaging some vital sensibility. On that day they were weak, cowardly maybe, and cowardice made them cruel. This memory haunts them, and their whole stance is only a generalized excuse, which we cannot understand as long as we do not know the circumstance.

Addition

A maxim of certain men: a revolution is a town taken by assault. Fools kill, wise men plunder.

Note

3. *never cut themselves off from freedom.* It is never right to claim that the people's wish is for despotism. They can be dropping with fatigue and want to rest [635] awhile, just as the exhausted traveler can fall asleep in a wood although it is infested with brigands. This temporary stupor, however, cannot be taken for a stable condition.

Addition

"Most of the nations of Europe are still governed by moral rules. If, however, through long abuse of power or large-scale conquest, despotism established itself to a certain degree, there would be no moral rules nor moral climate left intact; and in that beautiful part of the world, human nature would suffer for a while the insults it already gets in the other three parts." The Spirit of the Laws, Livre VIII, Ch. 8.

In some countries some people do not begin to pity the oppressed until they see that the latter have a chance of becoming oppressors.

If the soldier's mission is perilous, who would dare say that the friend of freedom's mission is without danger? The soldier fights in the open fields. He is filled with warlike audacity. He gives and receives honorable wounds. He dies covered with laurels. Who will tally the number of peaceful and selfless men, however, who, from the depth of their retirement, want to enlighten the world, and who, seized by tyrannies of all kinds, have died slowly in dungeons or at the stake? Only intellectual activity is always independent whatever the circumstances. Its nature is to survey the objects it is evaluating and to generalize on what it observes. Individuals count for nothing to intellectual activity, which is neither seduced by nor fears them. It takes up again across the centuries, despite revolutions and over the tombs of generations swallowed up by time, the great task of the search for truth. The courage of generals and the suppleness of ministers can serve tyranny and freedom alike. Thinking alone is unyielding. Never can despotism make it into an instrument, and hence arises the hatred which all tyrants bestow on it.

So redouble your efforts, eloquent, brave writers. Study the old elements of which human nature is composed. You will find everywhere morality and freedom in everything which at all times produced true emotions, in the characters which have served as the model for heroes, in the feelings which have served as an inspiration for eloquence, in everything which since the beginning of the world bound nations to their leaders and the esteem of posterity to the memories of past centuries. You will find these principles everywhere, serving some people with an ideal model, marking out for others the road to glory, and always gaining universal assent. And say all this well to government lest it gets it wrong. See page 493, above, Book XIII, Chapter 1, Addition.

[636] What do perfidious interpretations and absurd objections matter to us? Do we not know that the men who attack us are of a different kind, speaking a different language from us? Of these, some were born just the way we see them. The others got that way by relentless work. They have broken with their own hands, by what they have striven successfully to do to themselves, everything in them that was noble and sensitive. They have acquired a degradation far better calculated and far more complete than those which nature alone had the responsibility for degrading. Between them and us there is nothing in common. We must pass through that ignoble rabble just as Captain Cook's little troop crossed, amid the screams of the savages, the newly discovered islands. These courageous navigators have perished. Civilization, however, benefits from their conquests, and a grateful Europe deplores their loss.

No, never does a whole people become unworthy of freedom, never does a whole people give up on it. Amid times of the most profound degradation, when the impossibility of success forces even the bravest to inaction, there remain spirits which suffer and seethe in silence. Joy of a friend of liberty in Rome, during the election of the emperor. Tacitus.

Your sycophants can bring you in homage their cold irony against courage and virtue. You can ban courage and virtue from your presence. You will not banish them from the earth nor even from your empire. The hatred of oppression has been transmitted from age to age, under Dionysius of Syracuse, under Augustus, Domitian, under Louis XI and Charles IX.

There are beings to whom the spirit of evil seems to have said: I need you to frustrate everything which is good, to bring low everything which is high, to wither everything which is noble, and I endow you with a cold smile, an impassive look, skillful silence, and bitter irony.

The moral, philosophical, and literary system of the nineteenth century. A great revolution has taken place. It has had its effects, but it has also had its causes. To conserve the effects, that is to say, the power and the wealth that have been gained, to destroy the causes, that is to say, the principles. To seduce weak heads by the appearance of rational arguments, frivolous minds by elegance and luxury.

FIN

A Few Additional Points

[637] There is nothing more revolting than the laws of England relating to the settlement of the poor in the parishes. These laws, by obliging each parish to look after its poor, have at first the appearance of benevolence. Their effect, however, is that no poor person, or more precisely, poor man, having only his work for subsistence, can leave one parish to set up in another without the consent of the latter, a consent which he never obtains, an initial blow to individual freedom and a very serious blow, since such a man as cannot earn his living by the type of work he has adopted in the parish where he is domiciled is prevented from going to another where he would earn it more easily. The second result is that the poor rate in each parish, falling on all the individuals of that parish, leads everybody to be interested in opposing the moving in of a poor man or even one who, having only his work to support him, would be impoverished by illness or lack of employment. Hence there is persecution and harassment against the poor working man who tries to change his residence, a persecution demoralizing for those who carry it out, and cruel for him on whom it falls. Smith, I, 10.[183] As harassment always rebounds on its authors, the result of these contraints is often that one parish has a surplus of labor while another is in deficit. In this case the price of a day's labor rises to an excessive level, and this increase is a burden to the same proprietors who, for fear of seeing the costs of maintaining the poor fall on them, are opposed to the setting up of individual workmen in their parish. Thus from society's having intervened to ensure the subsistence of the poor, work has become difficult for them and they have been subjected to a number of vexations.

A bad decision by governments: when a town is poor, they believe that by setting up some establishment there, not on the basis of commerce or of industry but of luxury, they will enrich it. It is thus when it comes to reviving the poor towns of France or Holland, and the talk is of setting up bishoprics and law courts there, that is to say, men who consume without producing. See on this error and on the effect of these measures, Smith, II, Ch. 3.[184]

Great nations are never impoverished through the prodigality and bad conduct of individuals, but sometimes very much so by [638] those of their government. Smith III, 3,[185] and the reflections which follow on the system of luxuries and prices.

A State enriching itself only by productive consumption, the question is decided against luxury. See, on the disadvantages of unproductive consumption, Sismondi, I, 4. "The more the propertied classes maintain unproductive workers, the less they can maintain productive ones," Sismondi, I, 4, 117.[186]

183. Adam Smith, *op. cit.*, t. I, pp. 283–285.

184. *Ibid.*, t. II, pp. 336–351.

185. Constant draws the moral lesson from Ch. 3 *Comment les villes se formèrent et s'agrandierent après la chute de l'Empire romain. Ibid.*, t. II, pp. 439–462.

186. This is the tome, chapter, and page of Sismondi's book.

If regulations are suppressed, said an apologist for prohibitions in the middle of the last century, sovereigns are no more than great men distinguished by a certain glamour, but marked by no utility. I understand. Rules are not made for the benefit of the governed, but so that those in government will not seem useless!

A government which wishes to seize hold of public opinion in order to control it is like Salmoneus who wanted to hurl a thunderbolt.[187] He made a great noise with his brass chariot and scared the passers-by with his flaming torches. One fine day the thunderbolt came out of the clouds and consumed him.

Et cum singulorum error publicum fecerit, singulorum errorem facit publicus. Seneca, Epistulae, 81.[188] With this difference, that in the first case there is less force.

"The need to study the countries of modern Europe in all respects, and the possibility of achieving a deep knowledge of their affairs, has always seemed to me to derive from one of the greatest ills of humanity. Indeed, if the ambition and greed of all governments just on their own force them to inform themselves carefully of their respective strengths, the motive which leads them at least in general to strive to know down to the most minute details that which concerns their own domains is neither more reasonable nor of a different nature; and if to avoid ruffling too vigorously men and their doings, I concede that there are a number of administrators in whom [639] the mania for surveying everything in their country springs from a purer source, from the sincere desire the better to fulfill their duties, would I have any less the right to conclude from all this that their inquisitive activity is a great evil which derives from that other murderous sickness of wanting to overgovern? When those who rule empires hold to good principles, there are two concerns only: maintaining external peace by a good system of defense, and conserving domestic order through the exact, impartial, and unvarying administration of justice. Everything else will be left to individual effort, whose irresistible influence, bringing about a greater sum of access to various rights for each citizen, will unfailingly produce a larger quantity of public happiness. No sovereign, no minister, no committee, can on his own know the business of a thousand men, and each individual sees his own very well in general." Mirabeau, Prussian Monarchy, Introduction.[189]

187. [Salmoneus, King of Elis, in the Peloponnese. Translator's note]

188. Seneca, *Lettres à Lucilius,* 81, 29. The exact text is "et cum singulorum error publicum fecerit. . . . " (The error of individuals has made the general mistake; today the general mistake makes that of individuals.) [Seneca is talking about the things which Stoic philosophers used to despise—wealth, honor, power, etc., and he writes more fully as follows: "For they are not praised because they are desirable, but they are desired because they have been praised, and when the mistaken belief of individuals has caused a general one, the general one causes the mistaken belief of individuals." The French text is from the translation by Henri Noblot, Paris, Les Belles Lettres, 1965, p. 100: "L'erreur des particuliers a fait l'erreur generale; aujourd'hui l'erreur generale fait celle des particuliers." Translator's note]

189. Honoré-Gabriel Riqueti, comte de Mirabeau, *op. cit.,* t. I, p. aIV.

Mistakes in legislation are a thousand times more disastrous than all other calamities. The implication is that we must reduce as far as possible the chance of these mistakes. Now, if the only purposes of the government are preservation and public safety, the chance of mistakes will be considerably reduced. There are just a few simple means for achieving public security and preservation. For the improvement of happiness, there are complicated and countless ones. If the government gets the former wrong, its error is only negative, as also are the consequences of this error. It does not do all it should, it does not attain in everything the purpose it ought to, but the bad that faults of this nature entail is reparable. This is an ill whose effect ceases with its cause. If, on the contrary, the government gets its attempts at improvement wrong (and as I said, there are a thousand times more chances of making mistakes following this course), its errors are prolonged, men adapt to them, habits form, interests gather around this corrupt nexus, and when the mistake is recognized, it is almost as dangerous to destroy it as to let it continue. In this way mistakes of this second kind produce ills whose intensity and duration are incalculable. Not only do they entail ills *qua* authorized mistakes, they entail even more of them when they are recognized. Government often hesitates to destroy them. In that case, vacillating and indecisive, it acts very uncertainly, making despotism bear down on all the citizens. Finally, new problems appear even when the government has made [640] its mind up. Decisions are reversed, the agreed links are torn apart, customary behavior is offended, and public trust is shaken.

"Compare the effects in governments which obstruct the publication of thought and those which give it free rein. You have on one side Spain, Portugal, Italy. You have on the other England, Holland, and North America. Where is there more decency and happiness? In which of these is more crime committed? In which is society more gentle?" Bentham, III, 20.

"What is a censor? It is an interested judge, an unrivalled judge, an arbitrary one who conducts clandestine proceedings, condemns without hearing, and decides without appeal." Bentham, III, 22.

Between the lawmaker and the member of government, when one or the other exceeds his prerogative, there is this difference, that the legislator has a ferocious pride and the minister a puerile vanity. The one wants to be obeyed rather than flattered, because flattery coming from many people will convince him less of his merit than obedience would. The other likes to be flattered more than he wishes to be obeyed, because to dispense with obedience after having demanded it would seem to him a second proof of power.

The lawmaker's clumsiness, says Bentham, often itself creates an opposition between the natural and the political sanction, III, 24.[190] He therefore admits that there are natural sanctions.

190. Here is the text by Bentham: "The means we are going to present are such as will end in several cases this internal discord, diminish this tension between motives, which often exist only through the clumsiness of the lawmaker, by the clash he has created himself between the natural and the political sanction, between the moral sanction and the religious one."

One can say in general of all banks, as much of deposit banks as of those which issue bills, for whose value they are supposed to have the cash, what Say says, Livre II, Ch. 14,[191] of deposit banks only. "It has been called into question whether such a thing could survive in a State whose government was without responsibility or limits. Only public opinion can decide on a question of that sort. Everyone may have an opinion, but no one is obliged to disclose it."

Ganilh shows manifestly, in his digression on public credit, II, 224–251,[192] that this essential and so to speak unique agent [641] is incompatible with absolute power.

Banks, said Montesquieu, are incompatible with pure monarchy. This is to say, in other words, that credit is incompatible with arbitrary power.

The same men who, touchy zealots of independence, when they struggle against the government, believe they cannot check its powers sufficiently, exhaust themselves in multiplying and enlarging them, when from being opponents of governments they become its inheritors. It is in the writings of the most austere reformers, the most implacable enemies of existing institutions, that one finds the most absolute principles on the jurisdiction of political authority.

191. Jean-Baptiste Say, *op. cit.*, t. I, pp. 16–17.

192. Charles Ganilh, *op. cit.*, t. II, pp. 224–251.

CONSTANT'S NOTES

A. [Refers to page 452.]

What can one imagine more frivolous than the differences between colors on racehorses? This difference, however, created the bitterest factions in the Greek empire, the Prasini and the Veneti, who did not suspend their animosity until after they had caused the downfall of that unfortunate government. Hume, Essays, VIII, p. 54.[193]

B. [Refers to page 455.]

"In a free nation, it is often an unimportant matter whether individuals reason well or badly. It is enough that they reason. . . . Likewise, under a despotic government, it is equally pernicious whether one reasons well or badly. It is enough that such thinking is taking place at all for the very basis of government to be scandalized." Esprit des lois, Livre XIX, 27.

[642] C. [Refers to page 460.]

I say this only of fixed and legal institutions, not of mores and practices which law cannot change.

D. [Refers to page 471.]

Say, II, 5.[194]

E. [Refers to page 474.]

There are arguments by Montesquieu such as one can hardly conceive he has allowed himself: this is above all when he deals with production, trade, or money. "The Roman Republic," he says, "was not in a position to settle its debts. It made some copper money. It gained on its creditors by 50 percent. This operation gave a great shock to a State which needed as little upset as possible. The purpose was to free the Republic from its creditors. The purpose was not to free up the citizens among themselves. That required a second operation. It was ordered that the penny [denarius], which had till then been worth only six as,[195] should now be worth sixteen. The result was that while the republic's creditors lost a half, the

193. David Hume, *Essays and Treatises on Several Subjects*, Basil, J.-J. Tourneisen, 1793, t. I, p. 54.

194. Jean-Baptiste Say, *op. cit.*, t. I, pp. 449–465.

195. [This was a Roman copper coin, originally twelve ounces, reduced by successive deliberate government devaluations to only half an ounce by the early second century B.C. Translator's note]

creditors of individuals lost only a fifth." Esprit des lois, Livre XXII, Ch. 11. But with what did the creditors of the Republic pay their own creditors?

F. [Refers to page 474.]
On the injustice of revocations, annulments of treaties, etc., see Ganilh, I, 303.

G. [Refers to page 474.]
Men get used to regaining quickly that which can be taken from them quickly. They strive to regain by cunning what has been taken from them by violence.

H. [Refers to page 474.]
"In such an order of things," says Bentham, Principes du Code Civil, Ch. 11, "there would be only one wise course for the governed, that of prodigality. There would be only one mad course, that of economy."[196] See Ch. 9 and 10 of the same work.

[643] I. [Refers to page 475.]
The valley of Chamonix is protected from avalanches only by woods belonging to a host of individuals. If these woods were cut down, the valley of Chamonix would be covered with snow as another valley called "white path" [*sic*] was for the same reason. The ownership of these woods, however, being spread between a crowd of poor individuals, each one of these individuals must be all the more tempted to cut down his section of the wood in that the cutting down of this section would do no harm in isolation. It is clear that in such a case the government must intervene to counterbalance this individual tendency and that it has the right to restrain the free disposal of individual property. I do not know, however, whether it would be the duty of society to compensate the owners. Whatever the case, however, it is clear that this right derives from a local circumstance. It is the same with diverse restrictions of several kinds which it would take too long to talk about.

J. [Refers to page 516.]
"This subjugation which forces the sovereign to take the law from his people is the last calamity which may befall a person of our rank."[197]

K. [Refers to page 521.]
Hence it follows that the best constitutions are those in which the powers are combined in such a way that one can resist the branch of government which is oppressive, without resisting the whole government.

196. Jeremy Bentham, *op. cit.*, t. II, p. 49.
197. *Mémoires de Louis XIV, op. cit.*, t. I, p. 60.

INDEX

absolute authority. *See* despotism; unlimited/absolute authority
abuse: freedom/liberty (*liberté*), 383–85; government financial abuses, 470; old laws, 67–68, 445; proprietorial government, 184; revolutions, 407–8
Académie Française, xviii
action, freedom of, 383
Additions, xiii
Adolphe (Constant), xviii
Aemilius Mamercus, 370
Aeneid (Virgil), 523 n. 179
agricultural property. *See* landed proprietors; property and property rights
Agrippina, death of, 336
Ahriman, 138
d'Alembert, Jean le Rond, 222 n. 26, 304
Alexander I, 194, 342
Alexander the Great, 63, 354, 497
America: civilization by conquerors, 508; economic activity, government jurisdiction over, 248; education, 502; governmental principles as outlined by Jefferson, 428–29; popular election *vs.* electoral college, 333, 335; public debt, 180; reelection rules, 192; religious freedom, 138; revolution of, 405–6, 408; thought, freedom of, 531
anarchy: despotism as protection against, 517; illegitimacy of, 7–8
the Ancients (*see also under specific ancient states*): commerce and industry amongst, 355–58, 510–12; crimes, purification of places soiled by, 448; education, 309–10, 313; extensive reach of political authority compared to modern world, 351; freedom/liberty (*liberté*), 361–65, 512–13; governors *vs.* governed, 48; Greek philosophy banished from Rome, 496–97; hereditary privileges, 187–88; individual liberty, 351, 358, 365, 512, 514; judicial independence, 459; "The Liberty of the Ancients Compared with That of the Moderns" (Constant), xviii; modern imitation of, 365–71, 513–14; morality and virtue, 359–61, 512, 514; popular election *vs.* electoral college, 332–33; progress over time, differences wrought by, 359–61; property and property rights, 171–73, 183, 187–88, 190, 201, 362, 465–66; prosecutors, 513; public debt, 356–57; religion, 260–62, 356; slavery, tolerance of, 172, 358–59, 506; small *vs.* large States, 172, 352, 510; truth, influence of, 37; warlike nature of, 353–55, 360, 364, 366
Andocides, 520
anticompetitive activities, 230, 249
Antiquity. *See* the Ancients
Apollo Belvedere, 132
appeal, right of, 153, 460
apprenticeships, 231–32, 258–59
Arabs, 50
arbitrary measures, 73–74; crime control, 74–77, 446–47; despotism, xiii; economic activity, government jurisdiction over, 250–51; governors affected by, 80, 449; individual liberty *vs.* property concerns, 73–74, 446; innocence as specious argument for,

arbitrary measures (*cont.*)
77–78; interests of governors *vs.* governed, 413; judicial power and, 151; life sentences, 158; morality and virtue, 77–80, 447–49; privileges and proscriptions, 186
Arcadia, 365
aristocracy (*see also* hereditary privileges and property): privileges: deportation of nobility and law of hostages, 519, 525–26; Hobbes on, 21, 22
Aristophanes, 200, 499
Aristotle: acceptance of metaphysics of, 497; brigandage as means of acquisition, 519; coups d'Etat, 100; despotism as overthrow of all law, 495; hereditary privileges, 188; limitation of political authority, 37; property and citizenship, 177, 188, 190
armies. *See* military; war and peace
assembly, freedom of, 337, 451–53
assets: the Ancients, 357, 377 n. 69, 511; economic activity, government jurisdiction over, 236; property and property rights, 176, 180; taxation, 214–18
association, freedom of, 451–53
Athens and Athenians: arbitrary measures, 78 n. 8; commerce and industry, 355, 357–58; daily wages, 232; education, 309, 313; extension of political authority, 50; Greek philosophy banished from Rome, 496–97; interest rates, 247, 487; judicial independence, 459; Mably's contempt for, 368; music, 376; people's direct share in sovereignty, 352; plays, tribunal for assessing, 499; popular election *vs.* electoral college, 332; property and property rights, 172; scope of political authority, 428; slavery, 374; torture, 463; trade freedoms, 487; war and peace, 353
athletics, 310
aubaine, law of, 236
Augustus, 265, 528
Austria, 115, 126–27, 158, 205
authority/power, 530–32; absolute (*see* despotism; unlimited/absolute authority); ancient world, political authority in (*see* the Ancients); concentration, tendency toward, 387; Constant's lack of distinction between authority and power, xiii; division of powers, 36, 387–88, 397; executive power, 153, 162; extension beyond necessary minimum (*see* extension of political authority); freedom as power, power as freedom, 322, 385; the general will, Rousseau's theory of (*see* the general will); government credit, compared to, 34; Hobbes on, 21–24; human penchant for, 63; individual duties to (*see* duties of individuals to political authority); judicial (*see* judicial power); legislative (*see* legislative bodies and powers); limitation of (*see* limitation of political authority); means used to wield, good *vs.* harm of, 57–59, 441; mercy, prerogative of, 162; origin of, 6–8; principles of freedom distinguished from principles of, 383–85; property and property rights, 173–74, 183–85, 467–68; resistance to, 397–98, 519; scope of, 8–16, 34, 321–22; subaltern power, 389–90; unlimited (*see* despotism; unlimited/absolute authority)

Bacon, Francis, 345, 398
Bacon, Roger, 306
Baert-Duholant, Alexandre-Balthazar de Paule, baron de, 266, 271, 490 n. 124
banks, 532
Barante, Prosper de, 460 n. 53
barbarians and barbarism: the Ancients, 353, 363, 373, 508; economic activity, government jurisdiction over, 231; enlightenment, 299; extension of political authority, 50; inviolability of freedom, 380; music, 363; taxation, 221; thought, freedom of, 118, 120–22; war and peace, 277
Barrow, John, 127
Barthélémy, Jean-Jacques, 520 n. 175
Bastiat, Frédéric, xi
Beccaria, Cesare, 11, 157 n. 10

Beeke, 201

the "Benjamine" (*Acte additional aux constitutions de l'empire*), xviii–xix

Bentham, Jeremy: coups d'Etat, 92; daily wages, governments setting, 267; education, 503; enlightenment, government action as to, 495; futility of political hates, 426n. 3; government financial abuses, 470; grain exports, 485; indirect means of government, absence of government intervention regarded as, 515; legislative errors, disastrousness of, 531; morality and legislation, 437–38; morality enforced by government, 501; obedience/disobedience to the law, 400–402, 423, 519; origins and scope of political authority, 432; press, freedom of, 117, 453, 454; property and property rights, 534; public opinion, expression/repression of, 407; punishments, 464, 514; religious freedom, 456; slavery and happiness, 504–5; thought, freedom of, 531; truth and error, 298–301; utilitarianism, 39–43, 435–36, 456

Bernadotte, Jean Baptiste Jules, xvii

Bëthune, Maximilien de, duc de Sully, 272, 491

Biot, Jean-Baptiste, 304

Blackstone, William, xvi, 481

Blanc, Louis, xviii

blues and greens (chariot-racing teams, Constantinople), 426, 452

Boethius, 421

Bohemia, 144

Bonald, Louis Amboise de, 6n. 9, 108n. 10

Bonaparte, Napoleon, xvii–xviii, xix, 76n. 5, 108n. 10

Bossuet, Jacques-Bénigne, 143, 147, 167n. 2

Botany Bay, 160

Boulay de la Meurthe, Antoine Jacques Claude Joseph, comte, 525n. 180

Brabant, 144, 406

branding as punishment, 464

Brillat-Savarin, Jean-Anthelme, 157n. 10

Britain. *See* England/Great Britain

Brune (General), 76n. 5

Brunot, Ferdinand, 7n. 10

Brunswick, duke of, xvi

Brutus, 421

Buffon, George Louis LeClerc, comte de, 264–65

Burke, Edmund, xvi, xx, 107n. 8, 322, 385

Burnet, Gilbert, 125

business. *See* commerce and industry

Byzantine Empire/Constantinople, 87, 121–22, 407, 426, 452

Cabanis, Pierre-Jean-Georges, 304, 327n. 8

Le Cahier rouge (Constant), xvi

Calas, Jean, 152

Caligula, 31

Calvinism and Calvinists, xvi, 100, 113, 456

the Camilli, 284

Canard, Nicolas-François, 476, 477

Capet, Hugues, 516

capital, taxes on, 214–15, 217, 223, 477

capital punishment, 125–26n. 25, 157–58, 240, 248, 461

capitalism and capitalists. *See* commerce and industry; economic activity, government jurisdiction over

Caracalla, 92, 398

Carneades, 496–97

Carthage and Carthaginians, 20, 190, 355, 357, 510

Cartouche, 398

Carvalho e Melo, Sebastien-Joseph de, marquis de Pombal, 270, 341, 444

Cassation, Court of, 161

Catherine II (the Great), 158, 255

Catholic reform stimulated by Protestantism, 138

Catilina, 85, 98, 99

Cato (Publius Valerius), 434, 496

Cato the Elder (Marcus Porcius Cato), 200

Cécile (Constant), xvi, xvii

Cecrops, 50

celibacy, 260, 261–62, 265

censorship, Roman, 370–71

censorship of the press. *See* press, freedom of
Cévennes insurrection, 100
Chamfort (Nicholas-Sébastien Roch), 410
Chamonix, valley of, 534
Chandieu, Henriette de, xvi
Chardin, Jean, 490
chariot-racing teams, Constantinople, 426, 452
Charlemagne, 48, 322, 508, 516
Charles I (England), 155, 420, 422
Charles II (England), 103, 125, 271, 420, 422
Charles V (Hapsburg), 127 n. 27, 457, 498
Charles VI (France), 334
Charles IX, 528
Charles XII (Sweden), 279, 280, 478
Chateaubriand, François-René de, 147, 360 n. 21
China: civilization by conquered peoples, 508; farming in, 265, 489, 491; morality enforced by government, 500; nail-growing by scholars and mandarins, 265; press freedom, 117, 127, 453–54; rice distillation, 491; stability/stagnation, 340, 505–6
Cicero: duties of enlightened men after violent revolutions, 421; political authority in the ancient world, 372, 374, 511; religious freedom, 465; thought, freedom of, 85, 98, 99
Cincinnatus, 173, 284
circumscription of political authority. *See* limitation of political authority
citizen soldiers, 282–86
citizenship and property (*see also* property and property rights): 165–67, 169–71, 465
civil *vs.* political freedom, 386–92, 515–17
civilization, development of, 359–61, 508–9
classes of society: citizenship rights, 165–67; despotism judged by, 517; educated classes (*see* educated classes); education of lower classes, 313; representative government establishing relations between, 330, 505; truth, government interpretation of, 303–4; uneducated classes, 50, 143, 303, 313
Classical world. *See* the Ancients
Clermont-Tonnerre, Stanislas-Marie de, 145–46, 430, 448
The Clouds (Aristophanes), 499
Clovis, 120–21, 516
clubs, government by, 452
coercive laws. *See* prohibitive or coercive laws
Collatinus, 110–11
collection of taxes, 207, 213–14
colonies, penal, 159–60, 464
colors, racing, 426, 452, 533
combinations, 230, 480
commerce and industry: the Ancients, 355–58, 510–12; arbitrary measures destructive of, 79; business property, 174–77, 466; combinations, 230, 480; companies, 230–31, 480; competition and anticompetitive activities, 230; gold and silver specie, exportation of, 236–37, 482–84; government contracts, 473–74; government jurisdiction (*see* economic activity, government jurisdiction over); grain exports, 238–44, 258, 267–68, 484–86; imports and exports, 233–44; *laissez faire,* 116; mobility of property, 356; monopolies, 229–30; peace, importance of, 169; poor towns, government revival of, 529; press, freedom of, 119–20; property accumulated in same hands, 193; proprietorial government, abuses of, 184; taxation of patents, 210–11; war and peace, 278–79, 281
common interest: legislation in name of, 92; public interest confused with interests of all, 34–35
Common Sense (Paine), 12, 17 n. 31
companies, 230, 480
Company of Wines, Portugal, 248
compensation for unjust conviction or detention, 464
competition and anticompetitive activities, 230, 249

Condillac, Etienne Bonnot de, 20, 118, 202
Condorcet, Marie-Jean-Antoine-Nicolas de Caritat, marquis de: the Ancients' notion of individual rights, 351; economic activity, government jurisdiction over, 485 n. 109; education, 308, 316–17; enlightenment, government actions as to, 304, 308, 316–17; extension of political authority, 53; limitations on political authority, 27, 32 n. 1; scope of political authority, 11
conquest (*see also* war and peace): ancient spirit of, 353–55; civilization via, 508–9; wars of, 280, 281–82
conscription *vs.* voluntary recruitment, 289–93, 493–94
conspiracy, 76, 86, 406
Constant de Rebecque, (Henri-) Benjamin: biographical details, xvi–xviii; translation of, xi–xiv; works of, xii–xiii, xvi–xix
Constant de Rebecque, Juste, xvi
Constantine, 517
Constantinople / Byzantine Empire, 87, 121–22, 407, 426, 452
constitutional issues: the "Benjamine" (*Acte additional aux constitutions de l'empire*), xviii–xix; coups d'Etat, 89–97; modern importance attached to, 514; popular election *vs.* electoral college, 334–35; popular sovereignty and, 11; role in *Principles,* xiv, xx, 3–5; violations of constitution, halting, 93–97
consumption, taxes on, 207, 211–13, 217–18
Du contrat social (The Social Contract). See Rousseau, Jean-Jacques
Cook, James (Captain), 527
cordon bleu and *cordon noir,* 257
corruption: arbitrary measures leading to, 78, 106; constitutions, 96; despotism, 309, 392; economic activity, government jurisdiction over, 228, 229, 252; fanaticism, 417; government agents corrupted by proliferation of laws, 65–67, 444–45; intrigue, 329; judiciary, 151; Louis XV, 108; mass petitions, 93; morals and censorship, 380 n. 91; property and property rights, 170, 173–74, 181, 185, 190–93, 195; punishment leading to, 158, 160; religious freedom, 133, 139, 141; taxation, 211, 213, 216, 221; thought, freedom of, 105, 106, 108; wealth, 368
cotton manufacturers' reaction to silk textiles, 250–51
Council of Paris, 497
coups d'Etat: arguments for and against, 85–89, 450; constitutional issues, 89–97; extension of political authority, 57, 58
Cours de politique constitutionelle (Constant), xix
courts. *See* judicial power
Couthon, Georges, 5 n. 6
Cramm, Wilhelmine von, xvi
credit and creditors: ancient *vs.* modern world, 356–57, 514; arbitrary measures, moral consequences of, 79, 81; authority/power compared to government credit, 34; banks, 532; interest rates set by government, 244–47; public debt, 179–82, 200–201, 356–57, 466–67, 470–74
Crete, 309
crime and penal laws: arbitrary measures as means of crime prevention, 74–77, 446–47; compensation for unjust conviction or detention, 464; death penalty, 125–26 n. 25, 157–58, 240, 248, 461; due process, importance of, 154–55; economic activities, government restriction of, 247, 488; extension of authority, 321–22; extension of political authority, 48–49; innocent persons treated as potentially criminal, 74, 447; minimal extent of political authority, 38; privileges, punishment for use of, 413–18, 525–26; proliferation of laws, effect of, 64, 443–44; punishments, 157–62, 321–22, 463–64; rights of guilty persons, 157, 463; sources of crime, 400–401
Croce, Benedetto, xxi

Cromwell, Oliver, 155, 284, 334, 406, 420
cruelty, 157, 359
currency, exportation of, 236–37, 482–84
Cyneas, Pyrrhus's speech to, 354

dearth and famine: grain exports, 238–44, 258, 267–68, 484–86; rice distillation in China, 491; taxation, 213, 476
death penalty, 125–26n. 25, 157–58, 240, 248, 461
Declaration of the Rights of Man, 12, 434n. 17, 443
decorations of merit, 257, 370
defensive wars, 287
demand and prices. *See* prices, scarcity, and demand
democracy. *See* representative government; republican governments
Demosthenes, 270, 512
denunciation, laws requiring, 403
depopulation: government actions to control, 260–65, 492; rural depopulation, 256–57
despotism (*see also* unlimited/absolute authority): anarchy, as protection against, 517; Aristotle's definition of, 495; civilization imposed by, 509; consequences of, 390–92, 516–17; Constant's concern with, xiii, xxi; economic activity, government jurisdiction over, 237–38; education, 310–13; enlightenment, 509; examples of tyrannical laws, 434; extension of political authority leading to, 322; freedom opposed to, 392–93, 411, 518, 523–24; Hobbes and, 21; illegitimacy of, 7–8; individual liberty, importance of, 384; intellectual activity under, 306, 498–99; interests of governors *vs.* governed, 516; Louis XIV, reign of, 113, 391–92, 392–93, 516, 518; morality and virtue, 77–80, 447–49, 527; press freedom, 110, 121–24, 385; proliferation of laws no protection from, 65–66, 67, 443–44; public debt, 180, 474; public opinion not compatible with, 370–71; religion as prop of, 456; thought, repression of freedom of, 103; war and peace, 277, 279–80
Diodore de Sicile (Diodorus Siculus), 499
Diogenes Laertius, 317
Dionysius of Halicarnassus, 361
Dionysius of Syracuse, 528
Dionysius the Elder, 499
Discours sur Tite-Live (Machiavelli), 52, 60
dissolution of representative assemblies, 335–36
division of labor, 234, 258–59, 492
division of powers, 36, 387–88, 397
Domat, 167 n. 2
Domitian, 528
doubt as condition of modern world, 360–61
due process, xxi, 58, 90, 153–57
duels, edict on, 501
Dumont, 43
the Dutch, xvi, 209, 220, 222, 405, 529, 531
duties of individuals to political authority, 397; obedience to the law, duty of, 398–405, 519–20; resistance, 397–98, 519–22; revolutions, 405–22, 520–28 (*see also* revolutions)

East India Company, 248
economic activity, government jurisdiction over, 227–28, 259, 480, 492; business interests, pressure of, 248–51, 489–90; daily wages, setting, 232–33, 267, 482; despotism, 237–38; division of labor and, 234, 258–59, 492; equilibrium of production and individual interests, 255–57, 491; foreign products, importation of, 233–36, 482; gold and silver specie, exportation of, 236–37, 482–84; grain and food, commerce in, 238–44, 258, 267–68, 484–86; guilds, apprenticeships, and corporations, 231–32, 258–59, 481–82; imports and exports,

233–44; interest, rate of, 244–47, 269, 486–87; legitimate forms of, 228; machines economizing on labor, blockades of, 487–88; monopolies, 229–31, 239; morality and virtue, 227, 231, 238, 247, 252, 254; patents, 266; price controls (*see* prices, scarcity, and demand); privileges, 228–47; prohibitions, 228–51, 480–90; property and property rights, 228; rights and freedoms, 227–28, 480; supply and demand (*see* prices, scarcity, and demand); supports, 228, 251–55, 490–91; types of, 228
economics: commercial economics (*see* commerce and industry); physiocrats, 273 n. 109; politics, connection to, xxi; war's economic effects, 278–79
Edict of Nantes, Revocation of, 126
educated classes: extension of political authority, 50, 53, 54; intellectual property of professionals, 177–79; preservation of, 414; truth, government interpretation of, 303–4
education: government role in, 308–14, 502–3; salutary effects of, 330
Egypt, 123, 309, 353, 357, 367, 520
elected governments. *See* representative government
Elien, 499
Elizabeth I (England), 271, 391
emotion and religious feeling, 131–32
emphasis, Constant's use of, xiii
d'Emskerque, François-Emmanuel, vicomte de Toulongeon, 375
energy: ancient *vs.* modern world, 360; governors, importance in, 329–30
England/Great Britain (*see also* Scotland): citizen soldiers, 284; Constant as exponent of British classical liberalism, xvi, xvii, xviii; division of powers and resistance to political authority, 397; economic activity, government jurisdiction over, 229, 232, 248–51, 254, 271, 481, 485, 490; education, 313, 314; feudal estates, 195 n. 38; government's ability to do harm or good, 345, 505, 509; hereditary privileges, 187; interests of governors *vs.* governed, 387; nonproprietors, restrictions on movement of, 201–2; paid and unpaid political positions, 190; poor laws, 529; popular election *vs.* electoral college, 332–34, 336–37; press, freedom of, 107, 117; public debt, 180, 181, 200, 474; reelection rules, 192; republicans after death of Cromwell, 406–7; revolution, recovery from, 422; the Stuarts, 104, 405, 408; taxation, 209, 220, 222, 223; wool exports, 485
enlightenment: despotism, 509; education, government role in, 308–14, 502–3; errors, usefulness of, 298–301; freedom/liberty (*liberté*) required for, 307; government action on, 297–98, 304–7, 315, 498–500; interests of government and, 304–7; leisure as indispensible condition of, 170; morality, government upholding, 307–8, 500–501; preservation of enlightened/educated persons, 414; property and property rights, 170, 174; religious freedom, opposition to, 131–35; revolution and, 407–22, 522–28; sciences, 304–5; Scottish Enlightenment's influence on Constant, xvi; theory of cycles of enlightenment and barbarism, 118; truth, government support of, 301–4, 493–94
enoblement of farming or labor, 257
Enquiry Concerning Political Justice (Godwin), xviii
entailment, 193, 468
enterprise, 230, 246, 248, 257, 447, 473
enthusiasm, ancient *vs.* modern, 359, 363
equal rights: citizenship and property, 166, 182; limitation of political authority, 31; property and property rights, 166, 182, 185–86
error, mistake, and inconsistency: governors *vs.* governed, errors of, 47–48, 50–56, 438–41; legislative errors, disastrousness of, 531; original text of *Principles,* errors in, xii; Rousseau, inconsistency of thought of, 24–26,

error, mistake, and inconsistency (*cont.*) 432–33; supposed usefulness of errors, 298–301; thought, freedom of, 297–98; truth, government support for, 301

"esprit de corps" in the judiciary, 151–52, 459–60

Esprit des lois (*The Spirit of the Laws*). *See* Montesquieu, Charles-Louis de Secondat, baron de la Brède et de

Euripides, 414

excessive taxation, 205, 220–21, 478–79

executive power, 153, 162

exports and imports, 233–44

extension of political authority, 47–49, 321–22; governors *vs.* governed, errors of, 47–48, 50–56, 438–41; harm heaped on harm, 505; legitimacy of government and, 49–50; means used by political authority, good *vs.* harm of, 57–59, 441; proliferation of laws, 58–59; utility, on grounds of, 47–49, 54–55, 437–38

extradition, 160

factions and factionalism: arbitrary measures, 74, 75, 448; coups d'Etat, 85–86; due process, 155; education controlled by government, 310; extension of political authority, 59; freedom, principles of, 386, 520, 521, 523; judicial independence, 151, 459; limitation of political authority, 33; property and property rights, 170, 176, 467; revolutions, 412, 533; scope of political authority, 10, 13, 426; thought, freedom of, 110

family: armies, forming and maintaining, 289–90; despotism destructive of, 79; education, parental rights regarding, 313; marriage, 260, 261–63, 265; population, government actions to control, 260–65, 492; property and property rights, 175, 193–95, 196–99, 468–69

famine and dearth: grain exports, 238–44, 258, 267–68, 484–86; rice distillation in China, 491; taxation, 213, 476

fanaticism and violent revolution, 415–18, 524–26

Fanatisme, ou Mahomet le prophète (Voltaire), 341 n. 17

Fauriel, Claude-Charles, 132, 286n. 8

fear as political passion, 173

federalism and Federalists, xx, xxi, 324

Federalist Papers, xxi

Fénelon, François de Salignac de la Mothe-, 47, 147

Ferguson, Adam, xvi

Ferrand, Antoine: absolute monarchy, 390–91, 394; the Ancients' scope of political authority, 372; coups d'Etat, 98, 99, 450; duels, edict on, 501; Egypt, ancient, 379; extension of political authority, 437; interests of governors *vs.* governed, 394, 515; scope of political authority, 9–10, 27, 432; stability/stagnation, 340, 346; thought, freedom of, 451

Ferrier, François-Louis-Auguste, 483

feudal system, 193–95, 468

Fiévée, Joseph, 108n. 10

Filangieri, Gaëtano: modern imitation of ancient republics, 380; popular election *vs.* electoral college, 332n. 11; population measures, 265n. 70, 273; press freedom, 120; scope of political authority, 428

Florence: grain export prohibitions by House of Medici, 485; hereditary privileges, 188–89, 202; wool exports, 485

foodstuffs, commerce in, 238–44, 258, 267–68, 484–86

force: governments formed by, 6, 7, 51, 54, 99; military spirit amenable to, 283; revolutions, 406, 409–13, 523–24

foreign influence as pretext for war, 280

foreign invasion. *See* war and peace

foreign products, importation of, 233–36, 482

foreigners, political rights of, 166, 169, 177

France. *See* French Revolution; *more specific entries*

Francis, Sir Philip, 107n. 8

Franklin, Benjamin, 12 n. 25
Franks, 120 n. 19, 189
fraud: economic activity, government restriction of, 245, 247; interest rates and usury, 245; taxes inviting, 212, 216, 476
Frederick II (the Great): due process, 155; economic activity, government control of, 255; French *vs.* German literature under, 306; intellectual activities of, 306, 499; religious freedom, 457; taxation, 478; thought, freedom of, 107, 115, 120
Frederick William of Prussia, 107–8, 115–16, 457, 486
freedom / liberty (*liberté*), 383–85 (*see also* individual liberty; *specific freedoms*): abuses of, 383–85; the Ancients, 361–65, 512–13; centrality of concept to Constant's thought, xx; citizen soldiers as threat to, 283–85; constitutional security confused with, 10–11; definition of, 10–11; despotism opposed to, 392–93, 411, 518, 523–24; economic activity, 227–28; enlightenment requiring, 307; excessive taxation, 220–21; fanaticism incompatible with, 415–18; French Revolution, Constant's explication of, xviii; government not weakened by, 385–86; harm or good, government's ability to do, 345; inviolability/inalienability, 383–85, 421–22, 527–28; political *vs.* civil freedom, 386–92, 515–17; power as freedom, freedom as power, 322, 385; principles of government/political authority distinguished from, 383–85; proliferation of laws, effects of, 63; security *vs.*, 515; translation of concept, xii; truth, government support for, 301–4, 493–94; war and, 277–79, 281–82, 287–88
French Revolution, xiv, xvii–xviii, xix, 5; the Ancients, imitation of, 351, 366–71; arbitrary measures, use of, 74, 75, 77; citizen soldiers, 282–83; citizenship and property, 171; clubs, government by, 452; Committee of Public Safety, overthrow of, 398; constitutions of, 96; coups d'Etat and constitutional issues, 89, 91; deportation of nobility and law of hostages, 519, 525–26; due process, 155–56; education, 310–11, 313; freedom by despotic means, 411, 523; governmental ostentation, 479; governors *vs.* governed, views as to, 48; hatred and hostility fostered by, 354; hereditary privileges, 187, 188–89; individual rights, 12; judicial power, independence of, 151; legitimacy of forms of government, 7–8; popular election *vs.* electoral college, 334; population of France and, 264–65; premature innovation, 343–44; press, freedom of, 108–9, 113–14, 123; property and property rights, 171, 187, 188–89, 196, 470; public debt, 5, 357; public opinion, 58, 406–7; Reign of Terror, xviii, 74, 75, 417, 470; stability, desire for, 339, 506; thought, freedom of, 103; truth, government support for, 303–4; truth, influence of, 37; unlimited nature of political authority, effect of concept of, 13, 19–20; volatility *vs.* peaceful existence, 363; war, liberation as pretext for, 281–82
Fronde, war of, 113
Furet, François, xviii

Gach (first name unknown) on jury system, 460–63
Galiani, Ferdinando (Abbé), 268, 443–44, 495 n. 138
Galileo, 306
Ganilh, Charles: the Ancients, 357 n. 7, 372, 376; banks, 532; property and property rights, 534; taxation, 218, 222 n. 25, 222 n. 28, 223 n. 30, 223 n. 31, 224 n. 38; war and peace, 294
Garnier, Germain: economic activity, government jurisdiction over, 264, 269, 270, 272, 491; education, 503; property and property rights, 202
Gauls, conquest of, 120–21
the general will, xviii, xx; consequences of theory of, 19–21, 24–26; laws

the general will (*cont.*)
defined as expression of, 442; legitimacy of government and, 7, 31; majority/minority opinion, 430–33; origin of political authority in, 608; prerogatives of society from government, distinguishing, 17–19; scope of political authority and, 8–16
Genoa, 430
Geoffroy, 108 n. 10
German romanticism, xvii
Germany (*see also* Prussia): French *vs.* German literature under Frederick II (the Great), 306; peasant war of 1524–1525, 173; press freedom, 115; taxation, 205; work as form of punishment, 158–59
Gibbon, Edward, xvi, 107 n. 8, 513
Girondists, xvii
Gluck, Christoph Willibald, 452
Godwin, William: Constant influenced by, xvi; Constant's translation of *Enquiry Concerning Political Justice,* xviii; extension of political authority, 441; property and property rights, 161 n. 13, 167 n. 3; truth, government support of, 316, 496
Goethe, Johann Wolfgang von, xvii
gold and silver specie, exportation of, 236–37, 482–84
Goths, 14, 189
Gournet (physiocrat), 273 n. 109
government, 530–32 (*see also* specific types): Antiquity, people's direct share in sovereignty during, 352; arbitrary measures, effect on government of, 80, 449; definition of, 7; different forms of, xiv, 5, 20; economic activity, control of (*see* economic activity, government jurisdiction over); education, role in, 308–14, 502–3; enlightenment, action on, 297–98, 304–7, 315, 498–500; force, formed by, 6, 7, 51, 54; harm or good, ability to effect, 345, 505, 509; indirect means of government, absence of government intervention regarded as, 515; limitation of political authority not weakening, 385–86; morality, upholding, 307–8, 362, 500–501; population, actions regarding, 260–65, 492; prerogatives of society from government, distinguishing, 17–19; principles of freedom distinguished from principles of, 383–85; property controls, 192–93, 469–75; religion maintained or reestablished by, 139–44, 303, 457–58; taxation, compatibility of individual rights with interests of state in, 215–19, 477; taxation, government opulence fed by, 219–21, 478–79; taxation, right of, 205; truth, support of, 301–4, 493–94; war resulting from ambition of, 277, 286–88, 493
government agents: proliferation of laws, corruption by, 65–67, 444–45; subaltern power, 389–90
governors *vs.* governed: errors, liability to, 47–48, 50–56, 438–41; interests of, 387–92, 413, 515–17
The Gracchi, 85, 98
grain exports, 238–44, 258, 267–68, 484–86
Great Britain. *See* England/Great Britain
Greece, ancient (*see also specific city-states*): development of civilization in, 508; extent of political authority in, 351; music, 363
greens and blues (chariot-racing teams, Constantinople), 426, 452
guilds, 231–32, 258–59, 481–82
the Guises, 85
Guizot, François, xxi
gymnastics, 310

habits of peoples, respect for, 325, 368–69, 507
happiness: extension of government under pretext of, 321, 504–5; habits as essential part of, 325; political freedom and, 387; purpose of society, viewed as, 515; small *vs.* large States, 323
Hapsburgs. *See* Austria; *specific rulers*
Hardenburg, Charlotte von, xvi
harm or good, government's ability to effect, 345, 505, 509

Hegel, xxi
helots, 172–73
Helvétius, Claude-Adrien, 22, 316
Henry III (France), 85, 98, 257 n. 38
Henry IV (France), 85, 250
Henry VIII (England), 336, 391
hereditary privileges and property: accumulation of property in same hands, 193–95, 468; citizenship and property rights, 182, 185–89; transfer, disposal, and transmission of property, 196–99, 468–69
historians, ancient *vs.* modern, 360
hoarding, 239
Hobbes, Thomas, 21–24
Hochet, Claude, 51 n. 6
Holbach, Paul Henri Dietrich, baron d', xxi, 9n. 13, 9n. 15, 134n. 2
Holland, xvi, 209, 220, 222, 405, 529, 531
honor and independence, national, 279
honorary awards, 257, 370
hostages, law of, 525
Hume, David, xvi, 125, 221, 456, 520, 533
Hungary, 115

identification documents, 447
illegal/immoral/unjust laws, 402–5
illegitimate governments. *See* legitimacy of government
illusion, concept of, 360
imagination in ancient *vs.* modern world, 361
imports and exports, 233–44
improvement. *See* innovation and progress
inalienability/inviolability of freedom, 383–85, 421–22, 527–28
inalienability of goods, 193–95
inconsistency. *See* error, mistake, and inconsistency
independence and honor, national, 279
India: the Ancients' opposition to maritime trade, 356; trade with, 229, 248, 266
Indies, French trade with, 480–81
individual liberty, xx, xxi, 384; the Ancients, 351, 358, 365, 512, 514; arbitrary measures infringing, 73–74, 446; duties to political authority (*see* duties of individuals to political authority); economic activity, 227–28; education, 313; legitimate forms of government and, 31, 365; limitation of political authority, 31, 39; proliferation of laws, effects of, 63; public *vs.* individual morality, 450; scope of political authority and, 10–12, 15–16; taxation, 214–19, 223, 476–77; truth, government support for, 301–4, 493–94; utility *vs.*, 39–43, 435–36
industry. *See* commerce and industry
informers, 403
innocence and innocent persons: action, freedom of, 383; the Ancients, modern imitation of, 366; arbitrary measures, innocence as specious argument for, 77–78; compensation for unjust conviction or detention, 464; dangerous results of innocent actions, right of government to intervene in, 76; due process, importance of, 154–57; treatment of innocent persons as potentially criminal, 74, 447
innovation and progress: ancient *vs.* modern world, 359–61; premature improvements, 340–45, 409–13, 507–9, 522–23; stability/stagnation, 338–40, 505
the Inquisition, 114
institutions (*see also* mores): ancient *vs.* modern acceptance of, 361; establishment of, 368–69, 460; establishment *vs.* formation by habit, 321, 368–69; modern imitation of antiquity, 368–69; premature improvements, 509
intellectual property, 177–79
intellectual thought: despotism and repression, under, 306, 498–99; effects of contempt for, 13–15; press freedom and, 112, 118–20, 124; religions, proliferation of, 137–38; sciences and enlightenment, 304–5; truth, government support for, 301–4, 493–94
interest rates, government setting of, 244–47, 269, 486–87

Interim of Charles V, 498
internal disorder. *See* crime and penal laws
intrigue, 329
inviolability/inalienability of freedom, 383–85, 421–22, 527–28
Ireland, 229, 490
Islam, 50, 246, 341, 363, 487, 495
Isocrates, 373, 380
italics/underlining, Constant's use of, xiii
Italy and Italian states (*see also specific city-states*): appellation by conquerors, 361; arbitrary measures, 74–75, 77; corruption of Italian government, 345; economic activity, government jurisdiction over, 480; Hapsburg loss of territories, 127; interest and usury, 487; property and property rights, 188; religious freedom, 137; revolutions in Italy, 406; thought, freedom of, 531
d'Ivernois, Sir Francis, 264

Jacquerie, 14
James II (England), 155
Jefferies (Jeffreys), George, first baron Jeffreys of Wem, 155
Jefferson, Thomas, 333, 428–29
Jesuits, 341
Jews, civil intolerance of, 147
Joseph II, 144, 158, 341–42, 347, 406
jouissances, 361 n. 23
Jourdan, Jean-Baptiste, comte, 525 n. 181
Journal intime (Constant), xvi, 285 n. 7, 401 n. 9
judicial power, xix, xxi; appeals, 153, 460; due process, xxi, 58, 90, 153–57; independence of courts, importance of, 151–53, 459–63; jury system, 153, 459–63; least dangerous of all governmental powers, 438; mercy, prerogative of exercising, 160–62; punishments, 157–62, 463–64
Julius Caesar, 85, 120–21, 454, 496
July Revolution, xviii
Junius, letters of, 107
jurisdiction: economic controls (*see* economic activity, government jurisdiction over); governmental (*see* government); judicial (*see* judicial power)
jury system, 153, 459–63
justice and the laws, 10, 86, 236, 522
Juvenal, 512

Kant, Immanuel, xx, 147
Koran, 495

La Barre, Jean-François Lefebvre, knight of, 152
Lacedaemonia. *See* Sparta
Laconia, 172–73
Lacrites, 270
Laharpe, Jean-François, 517
laissez faire, principle of, 116
land as reason for war, 280, 281–82
land tax, 207–10, 214–15, 476
landed proprietors (*see also* property and property rights): citizenship requirements, 174–79, 466; economic activities, government jurisdiction over, 250; representative government, 330–33
language, discovery of, 106–7
lansquenets, 165
large *vs.* small States. *See* small *vs.* large States
Larousse, Pierre, 167 n. 2
Lauze de Péret, J.-P., 462
law, xiii, xxi, 47–48, 80; absence of laws, 59; definition of laws, 442; freedom/liberty (*liberté*) and, 10–11; general will, defined as expression of, 442; illegal/immoral/unjust laws, 402–5; justice and the laws, 10, 86, 236, 522; morality and virtue, promoting, 47–48, 437–38; multiplicity of laws (*see* proliferation of laws); obedience to the law, duty of, 398–405, 519–20; old laws, abuse of, 67–68, 445; positive *vs.* speculative laws, 439–40; prohibitive or coercive laws (*see* prohibitive or coercive laws); proliferation of laws (*see* proliferation of laws); property ownership, laws encouraging, 196–99, 468–69; retroactive laws, 402–3, 519; rule of law, xiii, xxi, 80, 257; source and content of law, right to evaluate, 399; tyrannical laws,

examples of, 434; war and weapons, laws as, 413
Lee, William, 488n. 116
Lefebvre, Jean-François, knight of La Barre, 152
legislative bodies and powers, xix, xx–xxi; errors in legislation, disastrousness of, 531; popular election *vs.* electoral college, 335; proliferation of laws, 65–66, 442
legitimacy of government: coups d'Etat in countries with written constitutions, 91; extension of political authority, 49–50; the general will and, 7, 31; illegitimate forms, 7; importance to Constant of, xiii; individual liberty and, 31, 365; justice and the laws, importance of acting within boundaries of, 86; obedience/disobedience to the law, 399
Leuctra, battle of, 310
Levelers, 14
liberty (*liberté*). *See* freedom / liberty
"The Liberty of the Ancients Compared with That of the Moderns" (Constant), xviii
life sentences, 158, 463–64
limitation of political authority, 31, 321–22, 434; extension beyond necessary minimum (*see* extension of political authority); individual liberty, 39; majority/minority opinion, 31–35, 434–35; minimum extent of political authority, 38; necessary action of government not weakened by, 385–86; possibility of, 36–38
Linguet, Simon Nicholas Henri, 167n. 3, 240
Lisbon earthquake, 444
Livy (Titus Livy), 88n. 5, 111n. 12, 202, 281, 332–33
local interests and customs, 325–27
Locke, John, xx, 10n. 19, 307
lotteries, 213, 216–17, 476
Loubère, Simon de la, 491
Louis XI, 257n. 39, 394n. 14, 402, 516, 528
Louis XIII, 516, 522
Louis XIV: apologia for despotism by, 392–93, 518; effects of reign of, 390–91, 516, 522; excessive taxation and ostentatious display, 478; extension of political authority, 51; Genoese sovereignty, 430; press, freedom of, 103, 108, 113–14, 454–55; property and property rights, 475; religious freedom, 139–40; war and ambition of, 280
Louis XV, 108
Louis XVI, 28, 104, 109
Louis XVIII, xviii
Louis-Philippe, xviii
Lucan, 421
Lucian (Lucain), 294n. 12
Lucius Flaccus, 99
Lucretia, rape of, 110–11
Luddism, 487–88
Lutherans, 456, 457
Lycurgus, 48, 363, 434
Lyon, siege of, 283
Lysias, 270, 359

Mably, Honoré-Gabriel Bonnot de (Abbé): the Ancients revered by moderns, 367–68, 376–80; extension of political authority, 47; principles of freedom distinguished from principles of government/political authority, 383; property and property rights, 167n. 3, 169, 202; scope of political authority, 9
Machiavelli: change and tyranny, 410; Constant influenced by, xiii, xiv; extension of political authority, 52, 60; hypocritical conquests, 281; property and property rights, 171, 188, 202n. 48
Machiavellianism, 301
machines economizing on labor, blockades of, 487–88
magistracy, 190
Magna Carta, 408
Mahomet, 50, 341, 363
Maintenon, Mme. de, 140
Maistre, Joseph de, 6n. 9
Le Maistre Pierre Patelin, 89n. 6

majority/minority opinion: enlightened persons' duties in time of revolution, 409; the general will, 430–33; limitation of political authority, 31–35, 434–35; oppression, leading to, 384
Mamercus, 370
Marcus Aurelius, 92
Maremma of Tuscany, 485
Maria Theresa, 341
Marius, 85
marriage, 260, 261–63, 265
mass petitions, 91–93
materialists, 297
Le médecin malgré lui (Molière), 233
Medici, House of, 485
mediocrity, 329–30
Ménard (General), 76n. 5
merchants. *See* commerce and industry
Mercier de la Rivière, Pierre Paul Le, 273n. 109
mercy, prerogative of exercising, 160–62
merit, orders of, 257, 370
Messenia (Mycenae), 172–73
middlemen, 238–39, 484
military (*see also* war and peace): citizen soldiers, 282–86; conscription *vs.* voluntary recruitment, 289–93, 493–94; due process, 156; forming and maintaining armies, 289–93, 493–94; press freedom, 120–21; public opinion affecting, 406; spirit of, 283–85
Mill, John Stuart, xix, xxi
ministers, status and responsibilities of, xix
minority opinion. *See* majority/minority opinion
Mirabeau, Honoré-Gabriel Riqueti, comte de, 58n. 12, 321, 466, 483, 502, 530
Mirabeau, Victor Riqueti, marquis de: economic activity, government jurisdiction over, 257, 260, 261–62, 491, 492; extension of political authority, 58n. 12, 439; morality, government upholding of, 500; premature innovation, 507; war, 493n. 134
mistakes. *See* error, mistake, and inconsistency
mobility of property, 356
modern world: ancient and modern worlds contrasted and compared, 351–66; constitutional issues, importance attached to, 514; credit and creditors, 356–57, 514; doubt as condition of, 360–61; energy of, 360; enthusiasm, 359, 363; extension of political authority, 351; historians, 360; imagination, 361; imitation of the Ancients, 365–71, 513–14; innovation and progress, 359–61; "The Liberty of the Ancients Compared with That of the Moderns" (Constant), xviii; morality and virtue, 359–61, 512, 514; philosophy, 360; poetry, 359; refinement of sensibilities, 360; religious freedom, 362, 375; war and peace, 277, 353, 361–65
Mohammed (Mahomet), 50, 341, 363
Molé, Louis-Matthieu, 5n. 7, 9n. 13, 12n. 28, 23n. 40, 24n. 42, 379n. 87
Molière, 233
monarchy, xiv, xvii, xix–xxi, 5; absolute power/despotism, effects of, 390–92, 516; governors *vs.* governed, liability to error of, 51; Hobbes on, 21, 22; means of political authority, 58; personal independence *vs.* personal security, 59
money, exportation of, 236–37, 482–84
Mongol peoples, 137–38
monopolies, 229–31, 239
Montesquieu, Charles-Louis de Secondat, baron de la Brède et de, xvi, xvii; ancient *vs.* modern world, 375, 376, 380n. 91, 512; banks, 532; Constant and Mme. de Staël influenced by, xvi, xvii; death penalty, 157n. 10; due process, 154n. 3; economic activity, government jurisdiction over, 251, 270, 271–72, 487; extension of political authority, 47, 52; government economy *vs.* luxury, 477; gymnastics, 310; indirect means of government, absence of government intervention regarded as, 515; interest rates, 270; intrigue, role of, 346; judges and juries, 459; local representation, 326–27; monarchy, power of, 392; moral

consequences of arbitrary measures, 81; morality and despotism, 527; obedience/disobedience to laws, 520; popular election *vs.* electoral college, 332 n. 11, 333 n. 12; population growth, 263–64, 265 n. 70; premature innovation, 509; privileges, 186, 202; proliferation of laws, 67, 69; property and property rights, 73, 167 n. 2, 200, 201 n. 43, 202, 446; public debt, 201 n. 43, 533–34; reason, 533; scope of political authority, 5, 10–11, 428; thought, freedom of, 103; truth, government support for, 302, 316 n. 26; uniformity, 322–23; war, 285
morality and virtue: ancient *vs.* modern world, 359–61, 512, 514; arbitrary measures, 77–80, 447–49; despotism, 77–80, 447–49, 527; economic activity, government jurisdiction over, 227, 231, 238, 247, 252, 254; educational principles, 314; error, supposed usefulness of, 298–301; fanaticism and abusive revolution, 418, 524–25; government upholding of, 307–8, 362, 500–501; justice and the laws, importance of acting within boundaries of, 86; law prescribing immoral actions, 403; legislation promoting, 47–48, 437–38; linked sequence of causes and effects, defined as, 302; lotteries, 213, 216–17; press, freedom of, 106, 112–13, 453; proliferation of laws, effects of, 63–64, 443–44; public *vs.* individual morality, 450; religion, 307; religions, proliferation of, 138; religious belief and, 133, 141–42; revolutions, 418, 422, 524–25, 527; Roman censorship, 370–71; sciences, 305; superstition, 186; tolerance, 144, 375, 457–58
Morellet, André (Abbé), 230, 268
Morelly, 167 n. 3
mores: the Ancients, 353, 357–59, 370, 371, 374, 376, 511–14; coups d'Etat, 86; habits of peoples, respect for, 325, 368–69, 507; premature improvements, 509; stability, 339; taxation, 479; uniformity, 325
Moslem religion, 50, 246, 341, 363, 487, 495
multiplicity of laws. *See* proliferation of laws
Muslim religion, 50, 246, 341, 363, 487, 495
Musset, Alfred de, 4
Mycenae (Messenia), 172–73

Nantes, Revocation of Edict of, 126
Napoleon, xvii–xviii, xix, 76 n. 5, 108 n. 10
national sovereignty, 279, 384
natural freedom, duties of sovereign in system of, 438
nature: institutions consistent with, 504; vagueness of concept of, 401
necessities and necessary expenditures, taxation of, 213, 217
Necker, Jacques: economic activity, government jurisdiction over, 246, 268 n. 86, 270, 490 n. 125; enlightenment and reason, power of, 423; extension of political authority, 47; father of Mme. de Staël, xvi; interest rates, 246; militiamen, 294; popular election *vs.* electoral college, 331–32; religious freedom and persecution, 142 n. 8, 147; taxation, 201 n. 44, 217, 224 n. 37, 478
negative resistance to political authority, 398
neo-Platonism, 375
Nero, 336, 398, 421, 517
the Netherlands, xvi, 209, 220, 222, 405, 529, 531
new ideas, Constant's views on, 285 n. 7
New Jersey, 346
Newton, Isaac, 442
nobility (*see also* hereditary privileges and property; privileges): deportation of nobility and law of hostages, 519, 525–26; Hobbes on, 21, 22
Numa, 48, 50, 363

obedience to the law, duty of, 398–405, 519–20
Octavian, 421

opinion: freedom of (*see* thought, freedom of); majority/minority (*see* majority/minority opinion); public (*see* public opinion)
order, public. *See* public order and security
orders of merit, 257, 370
Ormuzd, 138
Ossian, 133

Paine, Thomas, 12, 17 n. 31, 107 n. 8
Papia Poppaea, 265
parents. *See* family
Pascal, Blaise, 167 n. 2, 398, 399
patents: economic activity, government jurisdiction over, 266; taxation, 210–11, 216
patriotism, 325–26, 511
Paule, Alexandre-Balthazar de, baron de Baert-Duholant, 266, 271, 490n. 124
Pauw, Cornelius de: the Ancients, 363, 373n. 49, 373n. 51, 374n. 52, 374n. 53, 374n. 57, 512; arbitrary measures, 78n. 8; economic activity, government control of, 270n. 92, 489, 490n. 127; enlightenment, government action as to, 310n. 19, 317 n. 35, 499; patriotism, 326; religious freedom, 456n. 45; scope of political authority, 25 n. 44; thought, freedom of, 453–54; uniformity, 324, 346
pay. *See* salaries and wages
penal colonies, 159–60, 464
penal laws. *See* crime and penal laws
penalties and punishments, 157–62, 321–22, 463–64
Péret, J.-P. Lauze de, 462
Pericles, 78n. 8, 434
persecution of religion. *See* religious persecution
Persia, 138, 309, 490
Peruvian mines, 216, 477
Peter I (the Great), 341, 434
Petit, Samuel, 374
Petronius, 434
Philip the Fair, 497
philosophy, ancient *vs.* modern, 360
Phoenicians, 353, 355, 510
physiocrats, 273n. 109
Piccini (composer), 452
Pictet de Rochemont, Charles, 271 n. 97, 489, 502
pity, 403
Plato, 37, 365, 375, 378, 380, 496n. 140
Plutarch, 374, 414n. 16
poetry, ancient *vs.* modern, 359
Poland, 32, 33 n. 2, 406, 513
political power and authority. *See* authority/power
political *vs.* civil freedom, 386–92, 515–17
Pombal, Sebastien-Joseph de Carvalho e Melo, marquis de, 270, 341, 444
Pomponius, 511
popular sovereignty: Athenian people's direct share in sovereignty, 352; constitutional issues, 11; dangers of, xix; Hobbes's views, 22; Rousseau's theories, 11, 15–16, 18; Siéyès on, 27
population: government actions to control, 260–65, 492; rural depopulation, 256–57
Portugal, 248, 270, 341, 444, 531
positive resistance to political authority, 398
positive *vs.* speculative laws, 439–40
possessions. *See* property and property rights
poverty and the poor: economic activity, government jurisdiction over, 247–48; education, 313; English poor laws, 529; government revival of poor towns, 529; population growth, 263–64; taxation leading to, 206, 213, 214–18, 220–21, 478
power. *See* authority/power
Prasini, 533
prayer wheels, 137–38
premature improvements, 340–45, 409–13, 507–9, 522–23
prerogatives: governing class prerogatives extended by creation of duties, 321; mercy, exercising, 160–62; societal prerogatives distinguished from government prerogatives, 17–19
press, freedom of, xviii, xix–xxi, 5, 105–

12, 451–53; censorship, 1806 order against, 430; current and historical situations, 107–9, 113–17, 453–54; despotism, 110, 121–24, 385; expression of thought, 105–12, 451–53; intellectual thought and, 112, 118–20, 124; judiciary, independence of, 152; morality and virtue, 106, 112–13, 453; negative effects of denial of, 117–23, 454–55; nonrepresentative governments, replacing rights in, 112–13, 123–24; premature innovation, 341, 342, 507; public opinion, 92, 112–13; safeguard of rights by, 110–11
Prèvost-Paradol, Lucien-Anatole, 390 n. 7
prices, scarcity, and demand: business interests, 249, 250; daily wages set by government, 233; equilibrium of production, 256; grain exports, 238–43, 250, 267–68, 484–86; interest rates, 247, 486–87; political freedom and, 515, 529; privileges, trade guilds, and competition, 230–32, 481, 482; progressive prosperity, theory of, 249; taxation, 208, 211, 213, 476
primogeniture, 193, 197
Principles of Politics Applicable to All Representative Governments (Constant): completion and publication of, xviii; format and content of, xix–xxi; microcosm of Constant's political thought, viewed as, xviii–xix; purpose of work, 3–5, 425–30; translation of, xi–xiv
private education *vs.* public education, 312–13
private (individual) morality *vs.* public morality, 450
private opinion, freedom of. *See* thought, freedom of
privileges, 185–86 (*see also* hereditary privileges and property): economic activity, government jurisdiction over, 228–47, 480–88; education controlled by government, 312–13; punishment for use of, 413–18, 525–26
production, equilibrium of, 255–57, 491 (*see also* commerce and industry; economic activity, government jurisdiction over)
professionals, intellectual property of, 177–79
progress. *See* innovation and progress
prohibitive or coercive laws: arbitrary measures, 447; economic activity, government jurisdiction over, 228–51, 480–90; extension of political authority, 57, 58; morality, government enforcement of, 501; proliferation of laws, 67, 445; taxes disguised as prohibitions, 211–12; thought, freedom of, 452
proliferation of laws: arbitrary measures *vs.*, 73; corruption of government agents by, 65–67, 444–45; crime and violence, 64, 443–44; despotism, no protection from, 65–66, 67, 443–44; extension of political authority, 58–59; individual morality falsified by, 63–64, 442–43; natural causes of, 63, 442; old laws, abuse of, 67–68, 445
proliferation of religions, fear of, 137–39, 144, 456
propaganda, 57–58
property and property rights, xxi, 165, 383; abolition of property, 167–69; accumulation of property in same hands, 193–95, 196, 468; agricultural property owners (*see* landed proprietors); amount of landed property required for exercise of political rights, 182, 190, 467; the Ancients, 171–73, 183, 187–88, 190, 363, 465–66; arbitrary measures *vs.* individual liberty, 73–74, 446; business property, 174–77, 466; citizenship rights and, 165–67, 169–71, 465; economic activity, government jurisdiction over, 228; entailment, 193, 468; equal rights, 166, 182, 185–86; family and paternal power, 175, 193–95, 196–99, 468–69; freedom to enjoy property, 383; government actions, 192–93, 469–75; hereditary (*see* hereditary privileges and property); inalienability of goods, 193–95; intellectual property, 177–79;

property and property rights (*cont.*)
landed property owners (*see* landed proprietors); mobility of property, 356; nonpropertieds' first concern to become propertied, 170; paid and unpaid political positions, 190–91; power and oppression, 173–74, 183–85, 467–68; primogeniture, 193, 197; public funds, property in, 179–82, 466–67; reelection rules, 191–92; salary/wealth *vs.* property, 174; social convention, property as, 167, 192; splitting up of property, natural tendency toward, 196; status of property in political institutions, 168–71, 465; territorial property owners (*see* landed proprietors); transfer, disposal, and transmission, 196–99, 468–69; widest spread of ownership, laws encouraging, 196–99, 468–69; wills, 197–98, 468–69
prosecutors, 513
protection of government: economic activity (*see* economic activity, government jurisdiction over); education, 308–14, 502–3; enlightenment, 297–98, 304–7, 315, 498–500; morality and virtue, 307–8, 362, 500–501; premature improvements, 340–45, 409–13, 507–9, 522–23; religion, 139–44, 303, 457–58; stability, 338–40, 361–65, 505–7
Protestantism: Calvinism and Calvinists, xvi, 100, 113, 456; Catholic reform stimulated by, 138; celibacy and depopulation, 262; Lutherans, 456, 457; suppression of (*see* religious persecution)
Prussia: Frederick II (*see* Frederick II); Frederick William, 107–8, 115–16, 457, 486; freedom of the press, 107, 115–16
public funds and public debt, 179–82, 200–201, 356–57, 466–67, 470–74
public interest: confused with interests of all, 34–35; legislation in name of, 92
public morality *vs.* individual morality, 450
public opinion: despotism not compatible with, 370–71; expression/repression of, 407; government influence over, 57–58, 108, 530; government support *vs.* revolution, 406–7; honorary awards, 370; intellectual property residing in, 178; legislation based on, 91–92; premature innovation, 344, 371, 409–13, 522–23; press freedom and, 92, 112–13; revolutions, 406–13, 522–24; stability *vs.* stagnation, 505; war, pretexts for, 279–80
public order and security: arbitrary measures, 74, 445, 448; assembly, freedom of, 337; enlightenment and error, 300, 500; excessive taxation, 221; extension of political authority, 57–59, 438; freedom and, 515; judicial independence, 152 n. 2; property and property rights, 176; punishments, 158; religious freedom, 148 n. 16; uniformity, 323
public *vs.* private education, 312–13
publicity, 39, 109, 110, 112, 253
punishments, 157–62, 321–22, 463–64
pure spirit, doctrine of, 297
pyramids, Egypt, 123
Pyrrhus's speech to Cyneas, 354

Quesnay, François, 273 n. 109
Quintilian (Quintilien), 499

Racine, Jean, 360
racing colors, 426, 452, 533
Raphael, 132
reason, power of, 421–22
Récamier, Jeanne-Françoise Julie-Adélaïde, Mme. de, xvii
reciprocity of foreign trade, 235–36
reductions in public debt, 470–74
refinement of sensibilities, ancient *vs.* modern world, 360
reform. *See* innovation and progress; revolutions
Reign of Terror, xviii, 74, 75, 417, 470
religion: the Ancients, 260–361, 356; Aristotelian metaphysics, 497; Calvinist heritage of Constant, xvi; Catholic

reform stimulated by Protestantism, 138; celibacy, 262; classical liberalism, spiritual dimension of, xviii, xxi; common interest confused with interests of all, 34–35; Constant's writings on, xvii; defining, 133; despotism, as prop of, 456; destruction by government maintenance, 143; error, supposed usefulness of, 298–301; importance to Constant of, 131–35; interest and usury, 245, 246, 486–87; Lutherans, 456, 457; morality and virtue, 133, 138, 141–42, 307; Protestants (*see* Protestantism); thought dominated by, 297

On Religion Considered in Its Sources, Its Forms, and Its Developments (Constant), xvii, xviii

religious freedom, 131–35, 456; ancient *vs.* modern concept of, 362, 375; civil intolerance, 135–37, 456; Constant's espousal of, xxi; Enlightenment opposition to, 131–35; government maintenance or reestablishment of religion, 139–44, 303, 457–58; harm caused by religious persecution, 144–46; necessity of people to have a religion, 141–43, 456; proliferation of sects, fear of, 137–39, 144, 456; tolerance, principle of, 144, 457–58; utilitarianism, 142, 147, 456

religious persecution: Cévennes insurrection, 100; harm caused by, 144–46; judiciary, independence of, 152; Louis XIV, 103, 113; Louis XVI, 103; sacraments, refusal to take, 126

representative government, xviii, xix, xx; classes of society, establishing relations between, 330, 505; dissolution of representative assemblies, 335–36; governors *vs.* governed, liability to error of, 51–55; Hobbes on democracy, 21, 22; interests of governors *vs.* governed, 387; judicial power, independence of, 151; landed proprietors, 330–33; local *vs.* general representation, 326–28; paid and unpaid political positions, 190–91; popular election *vs.* electoral college, 327–37, 505; property and citizenship, 171, 190–92, 465; reelection rules, 191–92; war and peace, 281–82, 287–88

republican governments, xiv, xvii, 5; arbitrary measures taken by, 448; intrigue, role of, 329; personal independence *vs.* personal security, 59; property and citizenship, 171

resistance to political authority, 397–98, 519–22

retroactive laws, 402–3, 519

revolutions, 405–7, 520–21 (*see also* French Revolution) abuses and evils of, 407–8; avoidance of, 406; duties of individuals to political authority, 405–22, 520–28; enlightened men, duties of, 407–22, 522–28; fanaticism and violence, 415–18, 524–26; force, 406, 409–13, 523–24; freedom obtained by despotism, 411–13; morality and virtue, 418, 422, 524–25, 527; obedience to the law, 398–405, 519–20; period following violent revolution, duties during, 419–22, 526–28; political thought, consequences for, 427; premature improvements, 406–13, 522–23; privileges, punishment for use of, 413–18, 525–26; public opinion, 406–13, 522–24; resistance differentiated from, 520–22; stages of, 408; wealth, 418, 524–25

Richard III, 402

Richelieu, 113, 516

rights (*see also* individual liberty): appeal of judicial sentences, 153, 460; citizenship rights, 165–67; economic activity, 227–28; equality of (*see* equal rights); guilty persons, 157, 463; press freedom as safeguard of, 110–11; press freedom replacing in nonrepresentative governments, 112–13, 123–24; private property (*see* property and property rights); taxation, 205–7, 214–19, 223, 476–77; utility *vs.*, 39–43

Riqueti, Honoré-Gabriel, comte de Mirabeau, 58n. 12, 321, 466, 483, 502, 530

Riqueti, Victor. *See* Mirabeau, Victor Riqueti, marquis de
Robespierre, Maximilien-François-Marie-Isidore de: Committee of Public Safety, overthrow of, 398; death penalty, 157 n. 10; due process, 155; the general will, xviii; limitation of political authority, 31; Mably's views, 376; property rights, 167 n. 2; stability/stagnation, 340
Roch, Nicholas-Sébastien (Chamfort), 410
Rochemont, Charles Pictet de, 271 n. 97, 489, 502
Rollin, Jacques-Fortunat Savoye de, 327 n. 7
Romans: anarchy *vs.* despotism, 517; Carthaginian wars, 357; censorship, 370–71; citizen soldiers, 283–85; coups d'Etat, 85, 92, 98; extension of political authority, 50, 55; extent of political authority in, 351; Greek philosophy banished by, 496–97; hereditary privileges, 188; interests of governors *vs.* governed, 387; judicial independence, 459; obedience/disobedience to the law, 402; popular election *vs.* electoral college, 332; population laws, 265; property and property rights, 183, 188; public debt, 533–34; public opinion, 520; Tarquins expelled by, 405, 408; taxation, 221; tribunes *vs.* Senate under the Caesars, 420; war, pretexts for, 277–78; warlike nature of, 353
romanticism, German, xvii
Rose, George, 201 n. 45
Roubaud, Pierre-Joseph-André, 268 n. 89
Rousseau, Jean-Jacques: consequences of theories of, 19–21, 23–26, 432–33; Constant and Mme. de Staël influenced by, xvii, xviii, xx; defense of, 25–26; extension of political authority, endorsing, 47; First Principle on origin of political authority, 6–8, 430; the general will, concept of (*see* the general will); inconsistency of thought of, 24–26, 432–33; influence on Revolution of, 368, 513; interests of governors *vs.* governed, 389; prerogatives of society from government, distinguishing, 17–19; principles of freedom distinguished from principles of government/political authority, 383; proliferation of laws, 67; religion, civil intolerance of, 135–36, 147; scope of political authority, 3, 5; Second Principle on scope of political authority, 8–16, 430–32; slavery, 194 n. 36; taxation, 219
rule of law, xiii, xxi, 80, 257 (*see also* law)
Rulhière, Claude Carloman de, 100, 125, 126 n. 26
Rumford, Benjamin, comte de, 479
Russia, 342–43, 508

safeguards: due process, xxi, 58, 90, 153–57; judicial independence, 151–53, 459–63; mercy, prerogative of exercising, 160–62; punishments, 157–62, 321–22, 463–64
Saint-Just, Louis, 362
salaries and wages: government setting of, 232–33, 267, 482; paid and unpaid political positions, 190–91; property and citizenship, 174; teachers, 311–12, 502
Salmoneus (king of Elis), 530
sanctions and punishments, 157–62, 321–22, 463–64
Savary des Bruslons, Jacques, 481
Savoye de Rollin, Jacques-Fortunat, 327 n. 7
Say, Jean-Baptiste: banks, 532; Constant influenced by, xvii; economic activity, government jurisdiction over, 491 n. 129, 492; foreign imports, 267 n. 77; interest rates, 269 n. 89, 487 n. 113; Montesquieu critiqued by, 272 n. 107; morality and education, 503; particular *vs.* general facts, 266; politics and economics, connection between, xxi; population controls, 266; property and property rights, 533; public debt, 466; silk and cotton manufacturers, 272; Smith on imports quoted by, 234 n. 13;

specie, exportation of, 484; stability of nations, 510; stocking industry, Luddism of, 488; supply and demand, 273 n. 111; taxation, 222 n. 24, 224 n. 34, 224 n. 36, 477 n. 86; war and peace, 294
scarcity. *See* famine and dearth; prices, scarcity, and demand
Schauenbourg (General), 76 n. 5
Schiller, Johann Christoph Friedrich von, xvii
Schlegel, August Wilhelm and Friedrich von, xvii
sciences and enlightenment, 304–5, 498
Scotland (*see also* England/Great Britain): Constant's studies in Edinburgh, xvi; feudal estates, 195 n. 38; foreign products, importation of, 234; press, freedom of, 104, 125; religious freedom, 138; Smith on wine imports, 234; the Stuarts, 104, 405, 408
Scruton, Roger, xi
security. *See* public order and security
Ségur, Louis-Philippe, 108 n. 9
Selim II, 8
Seneca, 421, 517, 530
separation (division) of powers, 36, 387–88, 397
serfdom, 193–95, 468 (*see also* slavery)
Seven Years' War, 116
Sextus Pomponius, 511
Siam, 491
Siéyès, Emmanuel, 12, 27, 202 n. 50
silk textiles, cotton manufacturers' reaction to, 250–51
silver and gold specie, exportation of, 236–37, 482–84
Sirven, Pierre-Paul, 152
Sismondi, Jean-Charles-Léonard: ancient *vs.* modern world, 510; arbitrary measures, 75 n. 3; economic activity, government jurisdiction over, 267, 481–86, 490, 491; extension of political authority, 32 n. 1; productive and unproductive consumption, 529; property and property rights, 202 n. 51; scope of political authority, 3 n. 1; taxation, 223, 476, 477
slavery: Antiquity's tolerance of, 172, 358–59, 374, 506; Constant's opposition to, xviii; happiness and, 504–5; limitation of political authority, 37; property and property rights, 172, 193–94; punishments for crime, 158–59; Rousseau on, 194 n. 36; size of government and abolition or continuance of, 324
small government, concept of, 12, 38, 321–22, 340–45, 507–9 (*see also* limitation of political authority)
small *vs.* large States, 323–25; the Ancients, 172, 352, 510; armies, forming and maintaining, 291–92; representative government, 328
Smith, Adam: commerce and trade in ancient world, 510; Constant influenced by, xvi, xviii, xxi; economic activity, government jurisdiction over, 229, 234, 248, 266–73, 480–92; education, 317, 502, 503; entailment, 468; extension of political authority, 438; government's ability to do harm or good, 345; interest rates, 246, 269, 270; limitations of political authority, 434; politics and economics, connection between, xxi; popular election *vs.* electoral college, 505; poverty, alleviating, 529; poverty and population growth, 263; property and property rights, 195, 200–202, 466, 468; proprietorial government, abuses of, 184; religious freedom, 137 n. 5, 456; scope of political authority, 428; taxation, 222, 224, 477; war in ancient and modern times, 373
smuggling, 211–12, 270, 488
The Social Contract (Du contrat social). See Rousseau, Jean-Jacques
societal prerogatives distinguished from government prerogatives, 17–19
Socrates, 375, 421, 499
Solon, 48, 247, 374, 375, 519–20
Sophists, 497
Sophocles, 313
South Carolina, 346

sovereignty (*see also* authority/power): national, 279, 384; popular (*see* popular sovereignty)
Spain: Alcavala tax, 212, 216, 218; depopulation of, 261; press freedom, 114, 120, 531
Sparta: commerce and industry, lack of, 357–58; education, 309–10; Mably's affinity for, 367–68, 378; property and property rights, 172–73; public need, funds for, 511; warlike nature of, 353
specie, exportation of, 236–37, 482–84
speculative *vs.* positive laws, 439–40
speculators, 238
speech, freedom of, 105–6 (*see also* press, freedom of): thought, freedom of; assembly for expression of opinion, 337, 451–53
Spinoza, Benedict (Baruch), 394
The Spirit of Conquest and Usurpation and Their Relation to European Civilization (Constant), xvii
The Spirit of the Laws (Esprit des lois). *See* Montesquieu, Charles-Louis de Secondat, baron de la Brède et de
sports, 310
stability, 338–40, 361–65, 505–7
Staël, Mme. Germaine de: ancient *vs.* modern world, 360, 366; arbitrary measures, 76n. 5; Constant's relationship with, xvi–xviii; fanaticism, 417n. 17; laws compared to weapons and war, 413n. 15; life and works, xvi–xviii; limitations on political authority, 37n. 4, 43n. 12; Machiavelli's comments on tyranny and change, 410n. 14; pardon via recitation of Euripides, 414n. 16; privileges, 186; reelection rules, 191n. 34
Steuart, James, 489
Stewart, Dugald, xvi
stocking industry, Luddism of, 487–88, 488
Stoic philosophers, 530n. 188
the Stuarts, 104, 405, 408
study of governments and countries, 530
subaltern power, 389–90
subsidies, 251, 490
Suffetes, 20
Sulla, 99
Sully, Maximilien de Bëthune, duc de, 272, 491
superstition and morality, 186
supply and demand. *See* prices, scarcity, and demand
Swabia, 173
Sweden (Charles XII), 279, 280, 478
Swift, Jonathan, 526
Switzerland: Constant and, xvi; economic activity, government jurisdiction over, 229; insurrection in, 405; war of 1789 against, 76
System of Nature (Holbach), xxi, 134

Tacitus, 309, 528
Talleyrand-Périgord, Charles-Maurice de, 96
Tarquins, expulsion of, 405, 408
taxation, 205; armies, forming and maintaining, 290; capital, taxes on, 214–15, 217, 223, 477; collection of, 207, 213–14; consumption, taxes on, 207, 211–13, 217–18; contrary to individual rights, 212–14, 476; enforcement costs, 216; excessive, 205, 220–21, 478–79; fraud, leading to, 212, 216, 476; freedom/liberty (*liberté*) affected by excessiveness of, 220–21; government's interests compatible with individual rights, 215–19, 476; government's opulence, excessive taxation feeding, 219–21, 478–79; government's right to tax, 205; individual rights, 214–19, 223, 476–77; inevitable ills produced by, 219–20, 477–78; interest of state compatible with individual rights, 215–19, 477; land tax, 207–10, 214–15, 476; lotteries, 213, 216–17, 476; minimal extent of political authority, 38; necessary and reasonable amount of tax, 205; necessities and necessary expenditures, 213, 217; new taxes, perturbation caused by, 207; patents, 210–11, 216; poverty caused by, 206, 213, 214–18, 220–21, 478; productive expenditures,

217–18; prohibitions disguised as, 211–12; rejection or acceptance of, 205–6; rights regarding, 205–7; smuggling, 211–12; theft, excessive taxation as, 220, 478; types of, 207–12, 476; wealth, 206, 220–21, 478–79
teachers, independence of, 311–12, 502
tenure, 312
terminology. *See* vocabulary
Terray, Joseph-Marie (Abbé), 268, 269
territorial pretexts for war, 280, 281–82
territorial proprietors. *See* landed proprietors
testamentary transfer of property, 197–98, 468–69
Thebans, 310
theft, excessive taxation as, 220, 478
Theodoric, 421
Theomnestes, 270
thought, freedom of, 103–4, 297, 383, 451; comparison of obstructive and free governments, 531; error, mistake, and inconsistency, 297–98; expression of thought, 105–12, 451–53 (*see also* press, freedom of); talent and ambition, persons of, 124; truth, government support for, 301–4, 493–94
thought, intellectual. *See* intellectual thought
Thrasea Paetus (Traseus), 517
Tiberius (Tiberias), 67, 75, 92, 336
Titus Livy, 88 n. 5, 111 n. 12, 202, 281, 332–33
Tocqueville, Alexis de, xvi, xix, xxi
tolerance, 144, 375, 457–58
torture, 157, 463
Toulongeon, François-Emmanuel d'Emskerque, vicomte de, 375
trade. *See* commerce and industry
tradition and stability, 338–40, 505–7
translation of Constant, xi–xiv
Traseus (Thrasea Paetus), 517
Treilhard, Jean-Baptiste, 236 n. 16
Tronchet, 167 n. 2
truth: government support of, 301–4, 493–94; influence of, 37; supposed usefulness of error to cause of, 298–301
Turgot, Anne-Robert-Jacques, 268, 269
Turkish sultanate, 8, 517, 520
tyranny. *See* despotism

Ulloa, Antonio de, 223
underlining/italics, Constant's use of, xiii
uneducated classes, 50, 143, 303, 313
uniformity, 322–26
unimportant actions, laws aimed at controlling, 383, 401
United Kingdom. *See* England/Great Britain
United States. *See* America
unity of electoral body, 326–28
unlimited/absolute authority (*see also* despotism): consequences of, 390–92, 516; Hobbes on, 21–24; organization of government in cases of, 35–36, 435; Rousseau's theory of, 3–21; Siéyès on, 12, 27
Ustariz, Don Geronimo de, 216, 223 n. 31
usurpation: ancient *vs.* modern world, 355; coups d'Etat, 90, 91; enlightenment, 496; freedom, principles of, 384–86, 522–23; premature ameliorations, 340; property and property rights, 185; resistance and obedience, 397, 403; scope of political authority, 31, 42 n. 9, 430; *The Spirit of Conquest and Usurpation and Their Relation to European Civilization* (Constant), xvii; thought, freedom of, 451
usury and interest rates, 244–47, 269, 486–87
utility and utilitarianism: arbitrary measures justified by, 74; Bentham's theory of, 39–43, 435–36; extension of political authority on grounds of, 47–49, 54–55, 321–22, 437–38; means used by political authority on grounds of, 57–59, 441; religious freedom, 142, 147, 456

Valerius Maximus, 512
Valerius Publicola, 88
the Valois, 85
Vauban, Sébastian Le Prestre de, 219

Veneti, 533
Venetian nobles, 171
Vespasian, 357
Villers, Charles de, 132
Virgil, 360, 523 n. 179
virtue. *See* morality and virtue
Vitellius, 398, 517
vocabulary: "all" and "everyone," 431; governors *vs.* governed, liability to error of, 55; political meaning of Constant's terminology, xi–xii, xiii; power of words, Constant's concept of, 3–4
Voltaire, 4, 152 n. 1, 279 n. 2, 306, 341 n. 17, 445 n. 36

wages. *See* salaries and wages
Walckenaer, C.-A., 373
war and peace, xx–xxi (*see also* military; *specific wars*): advantages of war, 277–79, 493; the Ancients, warlike nature of, 353–55, 360, 364, 366; arbitrary measures, based on, 75–76; armies, forming and maintaining, 289–93, 493–94; citizen soldiers, 282–86; civil/domestic life affected by politics of war, 277–78, 282–86; civilization via conquest, 508–9; commercial interests, importance of peace to, 169; defensive wars, 287; denunciations of war, 277; despotism, 277, 279–80; economic effects of, 278–79; freedom/liberty (*liberté*), 277–79, 281–82, 287–88; governmental ambition, war resulting from, 277, 286–88, 493; minimal extent of political authority, 38, 321; modern penchant for peace, 277, 353, 361–65; press freedom, 120–21, 454–55; pretexts for war, 279–82; rule of law compared to war, 413; safeguards against government war mania, 286–88; taxation, 206; technological advances in military machinery, 278, 493
wardenships, 231–32, 481–82
wealth: the Ancients' distrust of, 365–66; fanaticism and abusive revolution, 418, 524–25; landed property *vs.*, 174; paid and unpaid political positions, 190–91; taxation, 206, 220–21, 478–79; war, economic effects of, 278–79
Wealth of Nations (Smith), xviii (*see also* Smith, Adam)
Webbe, John, 12 n. 25
Weber, Max, xiii
whaling, Montesquieu on, 272–73
wheat exports, 238–44, 258, 267–68, 484–86
wills, transfer of property by, 197–98, 468–69
words. *See* vocabulary
work as a form of punishment, 158–59
working class and citizenship rights, 166–67
wrestling, 310

Xenophon, 200, 332, 358, 373, 374, 376

Zend-Avesta, 495
Zoroastrianism, 138, 495

The typeface used for this book is Monotype Baskerville, which is based on the types of the English type founder and printer John Baskerville (1706–75). Baskerville is the quintessential transitional face: it retains the bracketed and oblique serifs of old style faces such as Caslon and Garamond, but in its increased lowercase height, lighter color, and enhanced contrast between thick and thin strokes, it presages modern faces.

Printed on paper that is acid free and meets the requirements of the American National Standard for Permanence of Paper for Printed Library Materials, Z39.48-1992. ♾

Book design by Barbara Williams, Durham, North Carolina
Typography by G&S Typesetters, Austin, Texas
Printed and bound by Worzalla Publishing Company, Stevens Point, Wisconsin